国际税收基础

（第五版·中英双语）

［美］布莱恩·J. 阿诺德（Brian J.Arnold） 著

《国际税收基础》翻译组 译

CTP 中国税务出版社

图书在版编目（CIP）数据

国际税收基础：第五版：汉文、英文 /（美）布莱恩·J. 阿诺德著；《国际税收基础》翻译组译．— 北京：中国税务出版社，2024.1
ISBN 978-7-5678-1403-5

Ⅰ.①国… Ⅱ.①布… ②国… Ⅲ.①国际税收－基本知识－汉、英 Ⅳ.① F810.42

中国国家版本馆 CIP 数据核字（2023）第 198345 号

著作权合同登记号
图字：01-2023-5566

书　　名：国际税收基础（第五版·中英双语）
GUOJI SHUISHOU JICHU (DI-WU BAN · ZHONGYING SHUANGYU)
作　　者：［美］布莱恩·J. 阿诺德（Brian J. Arnold）　著
《国际税收基础》翻译组　译
责任编辑：范竹青
责任校对：姚浩晴
技术设计：林立志
出版发行：中国税务出版社
北京市丰台区广安路 9 号国投财富广场 1 号楼 11 层
邮政编码：100055
网址：https: // www.taxation.cn
投稿：https: // www.taxation.cn/qt/zztg
发行中心电话：（010）83362083/85/86
传真：（010）83362047/49
经　　销：各地新华书店
印　　刷：北京天宇星印刷厂
规　　格：787 毫米 ×1092 毫米　1/16
印　　张：39
字　　数：567000 字
版　　次：2024 年 1 月第 1 版　2024 年 1 月第 1 次印刷
书　　号：ISBN 978-7-5678-1403-5
定　　价：148.00 元

翻译组成员

张志勇　　陈　新　　姚　宁

梁若莲　　王立利　　韩凌宇

陈格格　　韩永品

译者序

自2019年威科出版《国际税收基础》第四版至今，四年已经过去了。这期间，国际税收领域又经历了诸多变化和发展。为及时反映国际税收的新面貌，本书作者布莱恩·J. 阿诺德先生，通过威科于2023年初出版了《国际税收基础》第五版。

《国际税收基础》第五版在原有基础上做了大幅度的修订和扩充，涉及2018年以来，国际税收领域取得的最新进展，尤其是OECD包容性框架提出的“双支柱”解决方案所带来的诸多理论和实务问题。

《国际税收基础》中英双语版自首次出版以来，一直受到国内众多读者的普遍好评。在获悉《国际税收基础》第五版出版的消息后，中国税务出版社及时与威科联系新版引进事宜，并组织开展翻译出版相关工作。

参加《国际税收基础（第五版·中英双语）》翻译工作的人员包括韩凌宇（第1章、第2章）、姚宁（第3章）、陈格格（第4章）、

Translator's Words

Four years have elapsed since Wolters Kluwer released the fourth edition of *the International Tax Primer* in 2019. During this period, the field of international taxation has experienced many changes and advancements. In order to timely reflect the new landscape of international taxation, Mr. Brian J. Arnold, the author of *the International Tax Primer*, with the help of Wolters Kluwer, published the fifth edition of *the International Tax Primer* in early 2023.

The fifth edition of *the International Tax Primer* has undergone significant revisions and expansions, covering the latest developments in the international taxation since 2018, especially the numerous theoretical and practical issues brought about by OECD Inclusive Framework's two-pillar approach for dealing with the digitalization of the economy.

The bilingual Chinese-English version of *the International Tax Primer* has received widespread acclaim from numerous readers in China since its first publication. Therefore, upon learning the publication of the fifth edition, China Taxation Publishing House promptly contacted Wolters Kluwer regarding the introduction of the new bilingual version and simultaneously initiated its translation.

Participating in the efforts of translation of this new version are Han Lingyu (Chapters 1 and 2), Yao Ning (Chapter 3), Chen Gege (Chapter 4), Han Yongpin

韩永品（第5章）、陈新（前言、第6章、第7章和国际税收术语表）、王立利（第8章）和梁若莲（第9章）。陈新和我本人审校了全书各章节。

张志勇

2023年9月

(Chapter 5), Chen Xin (Preface, Chapters 6 and 7 and Glossary of International Tax Terms), Wang Lili (Chapter 8) and Liang Ruolian (Chapter 9). Chen Xin and myself have proofread, with necessary revisions, each chapter of the Chinese translation.

Zhang Zhiyong

September 2023

译者序（第四版）[①]

2005年，我和我的几位同事翻译了布莱恩·J. 阿诺德和迈克·J. 麦金太尔撰写的《国际税收基础》（第二版）。一晃十五年过去了，国际税收领域发生了巨大的变化。其中最重要的变化无疑是2008年全球金融危机后，由二十国集团（G20）倡导或背书、经济合作与发展组织（OECD）推动的税基侵蚀和利润转移（BEPS）项目、多边税收征管互助公约、金融账户涉税信息自动交换。我们欣慰地看到，这些事件及其推动的国际税收理论和实务的发展，都在本书第四版中得到了充分的阐释。在当前这个重要的变革时期，将第四版中译文连同原文呈现给国内读者，是十分有意义的。

令人遗憾的是，本书第一版及第二版的作者之一迈克·J. 麦金太尔已于2013年谢世。悲痛之余，我们对布莱恩·J. 阿诺德先生能继续推动这项国际税收知识普及工作表示钦佩。这也鞭策我们付出更大的努力将新版的内容忠实地呈现给读者。不过，尽管付出了大量努力，我们依然感到将本书中的一些英文术语和表述译为贴切的中文，存在

① 考虑翻译的延续性及译者的贡献，本书特别收录第二版、第四版译者序。——编者注

Translator's Words (the 4th Edition)[①]

In 2005, my colleagues and I translated *International Tax Primer* (the 2nd Edition) co-authored by Mr. Brian J. Arnold and Mr. Michael J. McIntyre. The 15 years elapsed since then have witnessed enormous changes in international taxation, with the most influential reflected in Base Erosion and Profit Shifting (BEPS) project, the Multilateral Convention on Mutual Administrative Assistance in Tax Matters and Common Reporting Standards, initiated or endorsed by G20 and driven by OECD in the aftermath of the global financial crisis in 2008. It is delightful to see that these events and the development of international taxation theory and practices that they have boosted are all covered and elaborated on in the 4th Edition of the Primer. At this critical juncture of changes, it is of great significance to introduce the new edition and the translated version thereof to Chinese readers.

To our grief, Mr. Michael J. McIntyre, one of the authors for the 1st and 2nd Editions of the *Primer*, passed away in 2013. Admiring Mr. Brian J. Arnold all the more for his sole efforts to renew this international tax literature, we took it as our obligation to exert ourselves to present the latest edition faithfully to our readers. Despite considerable efforts, to render exactly the English terms and meanings

① Editor's Note: Considering the continuity of translation and the contribution of the translators, the Translator's Words of the second and fourth editions are specifically included.

许多困难。因此，译文中的不当之处，敬请读者批评指正。

参加第四版翻译工作的都是税收实务工作者，其中韩凌宇翻译第1章、第2章；姚宁翻译第3章；陈格格翻译第4章；韩永品翻译第5章；王晓悦、李然翻译第6章；陈新翻译前言、第7章和术语表；王立利翻译第8章；梁若莲翻译第9章。陈新及我本人审校了全书各章节。孔向荣为本书的出版做了大量的协调和组织工作，在此一并致谢。

张志勇

2020年5月

into their Chinese equivalents has proved quite a challenge. Any suggestions and comments offering better translation will, therefore, be cordially appreciated.

Participating in the effort of translation are experts from the tax practice field: Ms. Han Lingyu for Chapters 1 and 2; Ms. Yao Ning for Chapter 3; Ms. Chen Gege for Chapter 4; Ms. Han Yongpin for Chapter 5; Ms. Wang Xiaoyue and Ms. Li Ran for Chapter 6; Mr. Chen Xin for the Preface, Chapter 7 and the Glossary; Ms. Wang Lili for Chapter 8; and Ms. Liang Ruolian for Chapter 9. Mr. Chen Xin and myself have proofread, with necessary revisions, each chapter of the Chinese translation. Thanks must also go to Mr. Kong Xiangrong for his coordination and arrangements related to the publishing of the book.

Zhang Zhiyong

May 2020

译者序（第二版）

多年来，我和我的同事一直在为学习英语的税务工作者和税务研究人员寻找一本关于国际税收的原版基础读物。当我们得到布莱恩·J.阿诺德和迈克·J.麦金太尔合著的新版《国际税收基础》一书时，顿觉如愿以偿。为了帮助更多的人了解税收，特别是国际税收，我们决定将这本书作中英对照读物出版。

当我们向两位教授提出把他们的著作介绍给中国读者时，他们欣然同意授权我们在华出版此书。感激之余，我们也深感自己的英语理解力和中文表达能力不足以忠实展示原著的韵味。此外，文中的许多概念罕见于国内的税收读物，将其译成贴切的中文实属不易，虽经多次集体推敲，仍有译不达意之感。希望我们的努力能起到抛砖引玉之效，这不仅是为了语言的贴切，更是为了准确把握国际税收理论与实务的迅速发展。

参加本书翻译工作的是国际税务司的几位同事，其中苑善武翻译前言以及第 1 章、第 2 章；王晓悦翻译第 3 章；侣海林翻译第 4 章；毛晓红翻译第 5 章；冯立增翻译第 6 章；我本人翻译第 7 章。王裕康

Translator's Words (the 2nd Edition)

For years my colleagues and I have been looking for a textbook which can quench the thirst of Chinese readers for learning international taxation in good and easy English. When the latest release of *International Tax Primer* was presented before us, we knew we had got it.

Speaking to Professor Michael J. McIntyre, the co-author of the book, for his permission to translate the book into Chinese was a pleasant experience. We got a clean "OK" from him without any preconditions attached. Although to obtain the English copyright from the Kluwer Law International took a rather lengthy process, we finally made it and now we possess the exclusive right to publish the book in a Chinese-English comparative version format.

While we are most grateful to Professor McIntyre, we are not really sure that our understanding of the English terminology and our expressions in Chinese have allowed us to match the beauty of the original version. Since many of the concepts in international taxation are new to us, we acknowledge the difficulty in putting them into exact Chinese equivalents. Any suggestions and comments offering better translations will, therefore, be cordually appreciated.

Participating in the effort of translation are my colleagues from the International Taxation Department: Mr. Yuan Shanwu for Chapters 1 and 2; Ms. Wang Xiaoyue for

不但承担了词汇表的译定工作，还负责通校了全书各章节。苑善武为本书的编排工作、王晓悦与出版社联系版权事宜均付出了大量精力，在此一并致谢。

张志勇

2004 年 11 月

Chapter 3; Ms. Lu Hailin for Chapter 4; Ms. Mao Xiaohong for Chapter 5; Mr. Feng Lizeng for Chapter 6 and myself for Chapter 7. Mr. Wang Yukang made his special contribution by hashing out the as-good-as possibel translation to each item of the glossary and provereading the full text. Thanks must also go to Mr. Yuan Shanwu and Ms. Wang Xiaoyue, the former for his editing chore and the latter for her liaison work with the publisher.

Enjoy the book.

Zhang Zhiyong

November 2004

前言

《国际税收基础》第一版源于经济合作与发展组织（OECD）20世纪90年代的一个培训教材编写项目。该教材原系OECD在苏联解体后，用于向欧洲新兴经济体开展的培训活动。我邀请了韦恩州立大学的迈克·麦金太尔和我一起准备这些教材。遗憾的是，OECD未能接受我们编写的教材。至少在我们看来，其主要原因是这些材料没有充分体现OECD在若干国际税收问题上的立场。然而，OECD慷慨地允许我们以这些材料为基础，编写了《国际税收基础》这本书。

令我惊喜的是，本书前四个版本受到了来自世界各地的国际税收学者的欢迎。我希望新一代的学者发现，本书第五版将有助于他们完成掌握国际税收这项越来越具有挑战性的任务。

迈克·麦金太尔和我共同撰写了本书的前两个版本。他抱病多年，于2013年去世。迈克关于国际税收的真知灼见仍然体现在本书的后续版本之中。

《国际税收基础》第五版做了大幅度的修订和扩充，涉及2018年以来国际税收领域取得的进展，尤其是OECD包容性框架为解决经济

Preface

The first edition of the *International Tax Primer* began in the 1990s as a project to develop materials for the Organisation for Economic Co-operation and Development (OECD) for use in its outreach activities with emerging economies in Europe after the breakup of the Soviet Union. I recruited Mike McIntyre of Wayne State University to work with me in preparing those materials. Unfortunately, the materials we prepared proved to be unacceptable to the OECD largely because, in our view, at least, they did not adhere sufficiently to the OECD positions on several international tax issues. However, the OECD generously permitted us to use the materials as the foundation for what became the *International Tax Primer*.

Much to my surprise and delight, the first four editions of the Primer were well received by students of international tax from all over the world. I hope that a new generation of students will find this fifth edition to be helpful in the increasingly challenging task of understanding international tax.

Mike McIntyre, my co-author on the first two editions, passed away in 2013 after a long illness. Mike's insight and knowledge about international tax can still be seen in the subsequent editions of the Primer.

The fifth edition of the *International Tax Primer* has been revised and expanded substantially to deal with the developments in international tax that have occurred since 2018, especially the OECD Inclusive Framework's proposed two-pillar

数字化对国际税收体系带来的问题所提出的“双支柱”方案。2018年本书第四版出版后不久，包容性框架就着手优先开展“双支柱”相关工作。我自然而然地想到，一旦能够了解到“双支柱”提案的具体情况，而且相对确定这些提案将会得到落实，编写本书的新版就是必要的且时机恰当的。2020年10月，支柱一和支柱二的详细蓝图发布了，但反响不佳，整个项目似乎陷入了困境。因此，我搁置了出新版的计划。然而，在2022年期间，“双支柱”提案经过修订，并随后获得欧盟、G20和美国的赞同。我觉得是时候推进第五版了。

如同本书之前的各个版本，此版不包含脚注或相关的参考书目。鉴于本书的基础性和目的，我依然认为脚注并无必要，而且脚注会降低正文的可读性，此外，我认为任何有必要的或有助益的参考内容在正文中都已提及。同样，相关书目没有必要列出，主要是因为涉及国际税收的文献汗牛充栋，而且借助于互联网，也相对容易查找文献来源。

我要感谢我亲爱的朋友——波士顿学院法学院名誉教授休·奥尔特的协助，他阅读了第五版若干章节的初稿，并指出了若干有待修改以使其更易于理解之处。我还要感谢我的助手卡罗尔·哈格里夫斯，她经验老到、幽默风趣，本书前后五个版本手稿的编辑和校对都由她完成。

本版手稿的更新截至2022年11月30日。

布莱恩·J. 阿诺德
加拿大安大略省艾尔萨克雷格
2022年11月

approach for dealing with the problems for the international tax system posed by the digitaliza-tion of the economy. Shortly after the publication of the fourth edition in 2018, the Inclusive Framework began its work on the two pillars on a priority basis. Quite naturally, I thought that a new edition of the Primer would be necessary and appropriate once the details of the two-pillar proposals became available, and it was relatively certain that the proposals would be implemented. Detailed Blueprints for Pillar One and Pillar Two were issued in October 2020 but were not well received, and the entire project appeared to be in jeopardy. As a result, I put my plans for a new edition on hold. However, over the course of 2022, after the two-pillar proposals were revised and later endorsed by the European Union, the G20 and the United States, I decided that it was appropriate to proceed with a fifth edition.

As with previous editions, the Primer does not contain any footnotes or a selected bibliography. Given the basic nature and purpose of the Primer, I continue to believe that footnotes are unnecessary and would make the text less readable; any references that I considered to be necessary or helpful are provided in the text. Similarly, I believe that a selected bibliography is unnecessary, largely because there is an extensive literature dealing with international tax, and, with the Internet, it is relatively easy to find relevant sources.

I want to acknowledge with thanks the assistance of my dear friend, Hugh Ault, Professor Emeritus, Boston College Law School, who read several draft chapters of this fifth edition and pointed out several places where the text could be revised to make it easier to understand. I also wish to thank my assistant, Carol Hargreaves, who has edited and proofread the manuscripts for all five editions of the Primer with her customary skill and good humor.

The manuscript is up-to-date as of November 30, 2022.

Brian J. Arnold
Ailsa Craig, Ontario, Canada
November 2022

目录

Table of Contents

CHAPTER 7

CHAPTER 8

An Introduction to Tax Treaties

1 引言

1.1 本书撰写目的

一国在设计其国际税收规则，并使之与其贸易伙伴的税制体系相协调时，会面对一系列重要问题。本书将在这方面为读者提供基础性分析。国际税收问题曾经仅为一小部分税务专家关注的重要课题，这些专家主要是大型跨国企业的税务顾问，及其在发达国家税务部门的同行。随着世界各国在经济上日益一体化，国际税收问题的重要性越加凸显。现在，许多中小企业以及个人都在从事**跨境交易**，因此企业和他们的税务顾问经常遇到跨境税收问题。而且，大多数国家的政府也必须关心国际税收，这既是为外国投资营造友好环境，也是为了保护本国税基。

尽管本书的主要对象是初次接触国际税收的学生、政府官员和税务从业人员，但我还是热切地希望在国际税收领域有丰富经验的人也能从中获益。在我的工作中，当分析复杂的国际税收问题时，很多时候都不得不回头查阅基本原则，而实际上本书的目的就是阐明这些基本原则。

国际税收筹划即便不能说是深陷于特定国家税收规则的技术细节之中，也可以说是完全以这些细节作为基础的。因此，在本书中，有必要就某些问题提供一些细节，以便对这些问题的讨论具有实际意义。但是，如果不聚焦于国际税收的一般原则和基本架构，本书就会迷失其方向。我试图通过既阐述一般规则，又时常列举不同发达国家和发展中国家的实际做法，来平衡对具体性和一

CHAPTER 1
Introduction

1.1 OBJECTIVES OF THIS PRIMER

This Primer on international taxation provides the reader with an introductory analysis of the major issues that a country must confront in designing its international tax rules and coordinating those rules with the tax systems of its trading partners. At one time, international tax issues were important only to a small circle of tax specialists, primarily the tax advisers of large multinational corporations and their counterparts in the tax departments of developed countries. As the countries of the world have become increasingly integrated economically, the importance of these issues has mushroomed. Many small- and medium-sized firms, as well as individuals, now engage in **cross-border transactions** that cause them and their tax advisers to confront international tax issues on a regular basis, and most national governments must care about international tax, both to present a hospitable environment for foreign investment and to protect their revenue base.

Although this Primer is intended mainly for students, government officials, and tax practitioners who are confronting international tax for the first time, I fondly hope that those with considerable experience in international tax may also find it useful. Many times in my work, I have been forced to return to fundamental principles in analyzing complicated international tax issues. In essence, the objective of this Primer is to articulate those fundamental principles.

International tax planning is firmly grounded, if not mired, in the technical minutiae of a particular country's tax rules. As a result, in this Primer, it has been necessary to provide a certain amount of detail on some issues in order for the discussion of these issues to have any practical significance. However, the objectives of a primer would be lost if it did not focus on the general principles and fundamental structure of international tax. I have tried to balance the need for both the specific and the general by illustrating general principles with frequent

般性的需求。

本书中的许多示例仅为了说明问题，而并非对特定国家法律的权威阐述。本书没有试图审视所有国家的做法。我避免从任何特定国家（包括我最为熟悉的那些国家）的角度出发撰写本书。相反，我尝试识别并讨论对多数国家而言，具有相关性和重要性的国际税收问题。

引言第 1.2 节介绍了“国际税收”一词的含义；第 1.3 节列举了引领各国设计其国际所得税规则的最重要目标；第 1.4 节介绍了税务顾问在筹划国际交易中的作用，并列举了一些典型的国际税收筹划技巧的示例；第 1.5 节介绍在国际税收方面发挥重要作用的主要国际组织；第 1.6 节介绍了国际税收的简史。

第 2 章介绍了各国定义其管辖权范围的规则。依据定义的管辖权，一国得以对其居民和非居民的所得征税。第 3 章探讨了对一国居民全球所得课税所涉及的问题。如果一国对其居民的全球所得征税，而另一个国家因为该所得发生、取自或来源于该国，而对同一所得征税，这一所得将不可避免地被双重征税。第 4 章讨论了缓解纳税人上述以及其他形式国际双重征税风险（如双重居民身份的情形）的机制。

与第 3 章对应，第 5 章探讨了一国对非居民取得或来源于该国的所得征税的问题。第 6 章探讨为防止跨国公司避税而调整公司间转让定价，所涉及的**转让定价规则**这一备受争议的问题。第 7 章讨论了涉及国际交易的各种反避税规则，例如**受控外国公司（CFC）规则**和**资本弱化规则**或**收益剥离规则，以及对抗混合实体与混合金融工具使用的规则**。第 8 章概述和分析了双边税收协定，其通常所依据的**经济合作与发展组织（OECD）协定范本**和**联合国（UN）协定范本，以及统御所有协定的《维也纳条约法公约》的有关条款**。

第 9 章讨论一些重要的新兴问题，这些问题贯穿之前章节讨论的诸多议题。这些新兴问题包括 OECD 针对**税基侵蚀和利润转移（BEPS）**发起的倡议，OECD

references to the actual practices of a variety of developed and developing countries.

The many examples provided throughout this Primer are given for illustrative purposes only and are not meant to be definitive statements about the laws of particular countries. No attempt is made to survey the practices of all countries. I have avoided writing from the perspective of any particular country, including those countries with which I am most familiar. Instead, I have tried to identify and discuss issues of international tax that are relevant and important to most countries.

Section 1.2 of this introductory chapter describes the meaning of the term "international tax." Section 1.3 identifies the most important goals that should guide countries in designing their international income tax rules. Section 1.4 describes the role of the tax adviser in planning international transactions and offers a few examples of typical international tax planning techniques. Section 1.5 describes the major international organizations that play an important role with respect to international tax, and section 1.6 provides a brief history of international tax.

Chapter 2 describes the rules that countries have adopted for defining the scope of their jurisdiction to tax residents and nonresidents on their income. Chapter 3 examines the issues involved in taxing residents of a country on their worldwide income. If one country taxes its residents on its worldwide income and another country taxes the same income because it arises, is earned, or has its source in that country, the income will inevitably be subject to double taxation. The mechanisms used to mitigate the risks to taxpayers of this and other forms of **international double taxation** (such as dual-resident situations) are addressed in Chapter 4.

As a counterpart to Chapter 3, Chapter 5 examines the issues involved in a country's taxing nonresidents on their income earned in or sourced in the country. Chapter 6 examines the controversial issue of **transfer pricing rules** for adjusting intercompany transfer prices to prevent the avoidance of tax by multinational corporations. Chapter 7 discusses a variety of anti-avoidance rules dealing with international transactions, such as **controlled foreign company (CFC) rules**, **thin capitalization** or **earnings-stripping rules**, and rules to counter the use of **hybrid entities** and **hybrid financial instruments**. Chapter 8 provides an overview and analysis of the provisions of bilateral tax treaties and the **Organisation for Economic Co-operation and Development (OECD)** and **United Nations (UN) Model Treaties** on which they are generally based, as well as the relevant provisions of the *Vienna Convention on the Law of Treaties*, which governs all treaties.

Several important emerging issues that cut across the issues addressed in the earlier chapters are addressed in Chapter 9. Those issues include the OECD's initiative against **Base Erosion and Profit Shifting (BEPS)**, the OECD's **Pillar One** and **Pillar Two proposals**, the

支柱一与支柱二提案，联合国协定范本下技术服务费的征税，适用仲裁解决国际税收争议，以及给数字经济所得征税带来的挑战。

第 9 章后是一个全面的国际税收术语表。表中术语第一次在本书中使用时，以黑体字显示。词汇表中术语的含义反映其在国际语境内的含义；一些术语在国内语境下的含义可能略有不同。

1.2 国际税收是什么?

为方便起见，本书使用了“国际税收”一词，因为国际税法更确切的表述应为特定国家所得税法的国际方面。除了少数例外，税法不是“国际”的，而是主权国家的产物。至少可以认为，无论是主权国家的惯例，还是联合国或 OECD 等国际组织的作为，都无法创设凌驾各国的国际税收法律。

税收协定可能是一国所得税制度中最明显的“国际”方面。大多数发达国家都已与其主要贸易伙伴，并且通常也和其次要贸易伙伴签订了税收协定。许多发展中国家也有广泛的协定网络。在过去的 25 年中，税收协定的数量呈指数级增长——如今已有超过 3500 个双边税收协定。这些协定对其签署国（通常称为**缔约国**）的征税权施加了重大限制。但是，税收协定通常不开征税收；在大多数国家，协定本质上完全在于其缓解作用。尽管税收协定是主权国家之间具有约束力的协议，但在许多国家，除非将税收协定明确纳入国内税法，否则它们对纳税人没有任何效力。

本书所称的国际税收的范围极为广泛。它涵盖一国所得税法涉及境外因素的所有税收问题，例如，商品与服务的跨境贸易，跨国企业的跨境制造、生产和资源开发，个人或投资基金的跨境投资，以及作为雇员或独立承包人习惯性在居住国以外工作的个人。这些活动通常会在至少两个国家的税法下产生国际税收问题，即取得所得的人为其居民的国家，以及产生所得所在的国家。

taxation of fees for technical services under the UN Model Treaty, the use of arbitration to resolve international tax disputes, and the challenges posed by taxation of income derived from the digital economy.

There is an extensive glossary of international tax terms following Chapter 9. The first time a term included in the glossary is used in the text, it is shown in boldface type. The meanings of the terms in the glossary reflect their meanings in an international context; some of the terms may have slightly different meanings in a domestic context.

1.2 WHAT IS INTERNATIONAL TAX?

The term "international tax" is used in this Primer for convenience because international tax law is more correctly referred to as the international aspects of the income tax laws of particular countries. With minor exceptions, tax laws are not "international"—they are creations of sovereign states. Arguably at least, there is no overriding international law of taxation arising either from the customary practice of sovereign states or from the actions of some international body such as the UN or the OECD.

Tax treaties are perhaps the most obvious "international" aspect of a country's income tax system. Most developed countries have entered into tax treaties with their major trading partners and often with their minor trading partners as well. Many developing countries also have extensive treaty networks. The growth in the number of tax treaties over the past twenty-five years has been exponential—there are now over 3,500 bilateral tax treaties in existence. These treaties impose significant limitations on the taxing powers of the signatories to the treaty (often referred to as the **contracting states**). However, tax treaties do not generally impose tax; in most countries, they are exclusively relieving in nature. Although tax treaties are binding agreements between sovereign states, in many countries, they do not have any effect on taxpayers unless they are specifically incorporated into a country's tax law.

The scope of what is called international tax in this Primer is extremely broad. It encompasses all tax issues arising under a country's income tax laws that include some foreign elements: for example, cross-border trade in goods and services; cross-border manufacturing, production, and resource development by a multinational enterprise; cross-border investment by individuals or investment funds, and individuals working outside the country where they usually reside as employees or independent contractors. These activities usually present international tax issues under the tax laws of at least two countries: the country in which the person earning the income is resident and the country in which the income is earned.

一些国际税收问题源于极其复杂的情况。在多个国家设有外国**子公司**的跨国公司的重组，就是一个例子。其他情况可能很简单，例如，**居民**个人从外国公司取得股息，或就抚养在外国居住的配偶或子女的费用申请扣除或抵免，都有可能在某些国家的税法下产生国际税收问题。

一国的国际税法包括两大方面：

（1）对居民个人和法律实体从境外取得的所得课税；

（2）对**非居民**从境内取得的所得（即在一国发生或来源于一国的，但由另一国居民取得的所得）课税。

本书中，第一个方面被称为“对居民来源于境外的所得征税”，第二个方面被称为“对非居民来源于境内的所得征税”。显然，一个国家（通常称为**居民国**）对居民来源于境外的所得征税，对应着另一个国家（通常称为**来源国**）对非居民来源于境内的所得征税。

涉及一国的资本或其他资源输出的交易，通常被税务分析者称为**向外**或“对外”交易。相反，**向内**或“对内”交易通常指从境外输入资本或其他资源的交易。被一国视为向外交易，通常涉及对居民纳税人境外来源所得征税的规则。相反，向内交易通常涉及一国对非居民境内来源所得征税的规则。某些情况下，某一项交易可能会同时受到这两类规则的影响。例如，**境外子公司**清算后并入境内**母公司**的情形。

国际税收不仅限于所得税。它可能包括遗产税、赠与税、继承税、一般财富税、增值税、关税，以及各种特定税种，包括**数字服务税**。遗产税、赠与税和增值税的国际方面尤为重要。例如，当居民收到来自非居民或在境内无住所的个人的遗产或赠与时，或者在境外拥有财产的个人去世时，与财富转让有关的税种就会产生国际方面的重要影响。类似地，其他国家就商品与服务，包括数字化的商品与服务的输出，对本国企业和消费者开征增值税，将引发重要的税收和竞争

Some international tax issues arise out of extremely complex situations. The reorganization of a multinational corporation with foreign **subsidiaries** in several countries is an example. Other situations may be quite simple. For example, an international tax issue may arise under some countries' tax laws if a **resident** individual receives a dividend from a foreign corporation or attempts to claim a deduction or credit for the support of a dependent spouse or child residing in a foreign country.

The international tax law of a country has two broad dimensions:

(1) the taxation of resident individuals and legal entities on income arising in foreign countries; and

(2) the taxation of **nonresidents** on domestic income (i.e., income arising or sourced in one country but derived or earned by a resident of another country).

The first dimension is referred to in this Primer as the "taxation of residents on **foreign source income**," and the second dimension as the "taxation of nonresidents on domestic source income." Obviously, what is the taxation of residents on foreign source income for one country (generally referred to as the **residence country**) is the taxation of nonresidents on domestic source income for another country (generally referred to as the **source country**).

A transaction that involves the export of capital or other resources from a country is often referred to by tax analysts as an **outward-bound** or "outbound" transaction. Conversely, the term **inward-bound** or "inbound" transaction is commonly used to refer to a transaction involving the import of capital or other resources from a foreign country. A transaction that a country considers to be an outward-bound transaction typically involves its rules for taxing the foreign source income of resident taxpayers. In contrast, inward-bound transactions typically involve a country's rules for taxing nonresidents on domestic source income. In some circumstances, a single transaction may have consequences under both sets of rules. An example is the liquidation of a **foreign affiliate** into a domestic **parent corporation**.

International tax extends beyond income tax. It may include estate taxes, gift taxes, inheritance taxes, general wealth taxes, value-added taxes, customs duties, and a variety of special levies, including **Digital Services Taxes** (DSTs). The international aspects of estate and gift taxes and value-added taxes are particularly important. For example, wealth-transfer taxes have important international implications when a resident receives a bequest or gift from a nonresident or non-domiciled individual or when a person dies owning property in a foreign country. Similarly, the imposition of value-added taxes on supplies of goods and

力问题。这些重要的问题不在本书讨论的范围内。本书仅讨论所得税法的国际性问题。

1.3 国际税收规则的目标

一个国家在设计其国际税收规则时，通常应力求推进以下四项主要的所得税目标。这些目标经常互相冲突，因此一国必须设法在其间达成平衡。国际税收的一些政策目标可以通过单边行动有效实现。然而，其他目标只能通过与其他国家的合作才能实现。

收入考量。各国政府筹集税收收入，以便为公共产品和服务提供资金。从纯粹的国家角度来看，每个国家都希望最大化其税收收入。但是，这一目标与其他目标相冲突，如吸引外国投资的需求，也与其他国家的收入增长目标相矛盾。从国际角度来看，每一个国家都应从跨国活动产生的所得中，获取其应有的税收收入份额。为了实现**国际公平**这一目标，一国必须保护其本国税基，也就是说，必须建立良好的本国税制和有效的税收征管体系来实施这些税收规则，并且必须避免缔结不当限制自身对居民和非居民境内来源所得征税的税收协定。

公平。与可能存在的其他税种相比，所得税的主要优势是公平。一般来说，公平的实现系通过对取得相同所得的个人施以相同的税负，而不考虑所得的来源或类型（所谓的横向公平），并使税负与个人的支付能力相称（所谓的纵向公平，即收入越多，以累进的方式纳税越多）。涉及对公司和其他法律实体的税收时，公平的讨论没有意义，因为这些实体是被法律创造出来的虚拟概念；它们与自然人不同，在现实世界中没有任何有形存在。虽然公司和其他法律实体可能要缴税，但是，这些税收必然最终由自然人——公司的股东、雇员或客户承担。目前尚不清楚，公司所得税在多大程度上被分别转嫁给其股东、雇员或客户。由于公司所得税终极负担者可靠信息的缺失，常使各国难以针对居民公司来源于境外

services, including digital goods and services, by foreign countries on domestic businesses and consumers raises important revenue and competitiveness issues. These issues are beyond the scope of this Primer, which is restricted to international aspects of income tax law.

1.3 GOALS OF INTERNATIONAL TAX RULES

In designing its international tax rules, a country should generally seek to advance the four major goals of income tax described below. Often these goals conflict, so a country must try to achieve a balance among them. Some of the policy goals of international tax can be pursued effectively through unilateral action; however, other goals can be achieved only through cooperation with other countries.

Revenue considerations. Governments raise tax revenues to fund public goods and services. From a purely national perspective, every country wants to maximize its tax revenues. However, this goal conflicts with other goals, such as the need to attract foreign investment and other countries' revenue-raising goals. From an international perspective, each country should obtain its fair share of the tax revenues from income generated by transnational activities. To achieve this goal of **internation equity**, a country must protect its domestic tax base—that is, it must develop a good domestic tax system and an effective tax administration to enforce its tax rules, and it must avoid entering into tax treaties that inappropriately limit its right to tax the domestic source income of residents and nonresidents.

Fairness. The primary advantage of an income tax over other potential taxes is fairness. In general, fairness is achieved by imposing equal tax burdens on individuals with equal income, without reference to the source or type of the income (so-called horizontal equity), and by making those burdens commensurate with individuals' ability to pay (so-called vertical equity—the more you make, the more you pay progressively). Fairness is not a relevant consideration with respect to taxes imposed on corporations and other legal entities because such entities are legal fictions created by the law that, unlike natural persons, do not have any tangible existence in the real world. Although corporations and other legal entities may pay tax, that tax must ultimately be borne by natural persons—the shareholders, employees, or customers of a corporation. It is unclear to what extent the corporate tax is passed on to its shareholders, employees, or customers; this lack of solid information as to the incidence of the corporate tax often makes it difficult for countries to implement good tax policies for taxing resident corporations on their foreign source income and nonresident corporations on their domestic source income. When

的所得以及非居民公司来源于境内的所得，实行恰当的税收政策。在讨论涉及公司的公平时，实际上是指对经济效率和中性的考量（随后另作论述）。

对于居民个人而言，公平要求对境内和境外来源的所得足额征税。此外，必须对境外来源所得予以征税，无论该所得是直接取得的还是通过某些外国实体取得。但是，没有国家有能力对在本国取得所得的非居民实施公平标准，因为没有国家能对非居民发生于其境外的全部所得征税。例如，A 国的居民个人可以从 A 国、B 国和 C 国取得所得。通常，B 国仅对该个人从 B 国取得的所得拥有税收管辖权。B 国不了解也不能对该个人在 A 国和 C 国取得的所得征税。但是，各国可以通过努力制定公平且适当的国际税收标准、课征与这些标准相符的税收，同时与其他国就双方居民的税收征管开展合作来提升公平。

竞争力考量。尽管每个国家都应该关心非居民的福利，但其首要职责是促进本国公民和居民的经济利益。为此，一国应避免采取削弱本国竞争力及其居民企业在全球经济中竞争地位的税收措施。

在国际背景下，各国相互竞争是常态。税收竞争是各国争夺就业和投资的一种方式——通过普遍地或对某些活动的所得减少或取消税收。但是，特定国家的竞争力取决于众多其他因素，包括受教育劳动力、现代化基础设施、政治稳定性、保护投资者法律制度的完备，以及自然资源。各国可以通过取消其税法中鼓励资本和就业机会外流，或抑制资本和就业机会流入的规定来提升竞争力。从中长期来看，**税收优惠**并不能提高一个国家的竞争力。这些和其他以邻为壑的政策会招致外国政府的报复性反应，并导致“逐底竞争”，最终损害所有国家的利益。这样的政策削弱了所有国家政府对流动性资本所得实行公平有效课税的能力。

资本输出中性和资本输入中性。**资本输出中性**原则或**资本输入中性**原则通常在国际税收政策的讨论中占显著地位。尽管其重要性值得怀疑，但读者应当清楚

commentators talk about fairness with respect to corporations, they are really referring to considerations of economic efficiency and neutrality, which are discussed below.

For resident individuals, fairness requires the full taxation of both domestic and foreign source income; moreover, foreign source income must be taxed whether the income is earned directly or through some foreign entity. However, no country has the power to impose a fairness standard on nonresidents earning domestic source income because no country can tax all the income of nonresidents that arises outside its borders. For example, an individual resident in Country A may earn income in Country A, Country B, and Country C. In general, Country B has jurisdiction to tax only the individual's income arising in Country B. It will not have any information about, and cannot take into account, the individual's income earned in countries A and C. Countries can promote fairness, however, by contributing to the development of fair and appropriate international tax standards, by imposing tax burdens that are consistent with these standards, and by otherwise cooperating with other countries in the assessment and collection of tax on their residents.

Competitiveness considerations. Although every country should care about the welfare of nonresidents, its primary duty is to advance the economic interests of its own citizens and residents. To this end, a country should avoid tax measures that undermine its competitive position and the competitive position of its resident enterprises in the global economy.

In the international context, countries compete. Tax competition is one way in which countries compete for jobs and investment—by reducing or eliminating taxes generally or on income from certain activities. However, a particular country's competitiveness depends on a wide variety of other factors, including an educated labor force, modern infrastructure, political stability, and an established legal system with protection for investors and natural resources. Countries can enhance their competitiveness by removing provisions of their tax law that tend to encourage the movement of investment and jobs out of the country or that discourage the importation of capital and jobs. In the medium and long run, a country's competitiveness is not enhanced by **tax incentives**; these and other beggar-thy-neighbor policies invite a retaliatory response by foreign governments and a "race to the bottom" to the detriment of all countries. Such policies erode the ability of all governments to impose fair and effective taxes on income from movable capital.

Capital-export and capital-import neutrality. The principles of **capital-export neutrality** or **capital-import neutrality** usually figure prominently in discussions of international tax policy. Readers should be aware of these concepts, although their importance is doubtful.

这些概念。

资本输出中性原则，是指一国的国际税收规则既不应鼓励也不应阻止资本外流。如果一国对其居民（包括居民企业）的全球所得（包括其外国子公司取得的所得）征税，即可实现资本输出中性。实践中，政策制定者通常至多将资本输出中性作为涉及公司的次要目标。几乎每个国家都欢迎资本流入，并通过税收和其他经济政策加以鼓励。相比之下，一般认为资本外流会减少一国的国民财富，许多国家已经采取措施，阻止资本外流（尽管其税法也许包含有意或无意鼓励外流的规定）。审慎的政策制定者在阻止资本外流时会小心从事，因为对资本外流的限制也可能阻止资本流入。例如，一个国家如果对支付给非居民的股息、利息、特许权使用费征收过高的**预提所得税**，很可能会遏制非居民在该国投资。

根据资本输入中性原则，在一个国家开展经营活动的纳税人无论是哪个国家的税收居民，都应承担相同的税负。资本输入中性一般通过一国对其居民（包括居民企业）来源于境外的所得（包括其外国子公司的所得）免税来实现。因此，如果 A 国不对 A 国居民企业从其外国子公司取得的所得征税，那么，子公司将仅在其居民国且取得所得的国家，以和该国其他居民企业一样的方式被征税。

大多数国家所采用的国际税收规则都包含一些与资本输出中性和资本输入中性相符的特征，有的与资本收入中性相符。例如，大多数国家对居民个人的全球所得征税，这反映了资本输出中性。但大多数国家不对居民控制的外国公司获得的境外来源所得征税（特殊情况除外），这反映了资本输入中性。当涉及公司取得的境外经营所得时，资本输入中性被广泛接受，从而此类所得仅在其取得所得的国家征税。具体地说，公司居民国或者对此类所得免税，或者居民国税收可以递延到汇回该所（通常以股息的方式）之时。

税收分析者也会提及另外一个中性概念——**资本所有权中性**。资本输出中性和资本输入中性侧重于资本所在的位置，但资本所有权中性侧重于资本的所

The principle of capital-export neutrality is that a country's international tax rules should neither encourage nor discourage outflows of capital. Capital-export neutrality would be achieved if a country taxes its residents, including its resident corporations, on their worldwide income, including income earned by their foreign subsidiaries. In practice, policymakers typically treat capital-export neutrality as, at best, a secondary goal with respect to corporations. In virtually every country, capital inflows are generally considered to be desirable and are encouraged through tax and other economic policies. In contrast, capital outflows are generally thought to diminish a country's national wealth, and many countries have adopted measures designed to discourage capital outflows (although their tax laws may also contain provisions that have the intended or unintended effect of encouraging outflows). Prudent policymakers exercise caution in discouraging outflows because limitations on capital outflows may discourage capital inflows. For example, a country that imposes excessively high **withholding taxes** on dividends, interest, and royalties paid to nonresidents is likely to discourage nonresidents from investing in that country.

According to the principle of capital-import neutrality, taxpayers doing business in a country should be subject to the same tax burden irrespective of where they are resident. Capital-import neutrality is generally achieved to the extent that a country exempts its residents, including its resident corporations, from tax on their foreign source income, including income earned by their foreign subsidiaries. Thus, if Country A does not tax corporations resident in Country A on the income earned by their foreign subsidiaries, the subsidiaries will be subject to tax only by the countries in which they are resident and earn income, in the same way as other corporations resident in those countries.

Most countries have adopted international tax rules that contain some features that are consistent with both capital-export neutrality and capital-import neutrality. For example, most countries tax resident individuals on their worldwide income, which reflects capital-export neutrality. In contrast, most countries do not tax foreign source income earned by foreign corporations that are controlled by residents (except in special circumstances), which reflects capital-import neutrality. Capital-import neutrality is widely accepted with respect to foreign business income earned by corporations so that such income is taxable only by the country in which it is earned. Further, such income either is exempt from tax by the country in which the corporation is resident, or that country's tax is deferred until the income is repatriated, usually in the form of dividends.

Tax analysts also refer to another concept of neutrality—**capital-ownership neutrality**. Whereas capital-export neutrality and capital-import neutrality focus on the location of

有权。在基于资本所有权中性的理想税收制度下，税收不会扭曲纳税人对资产的所有权。如果所有国家都实行全球课税或属地课税，则可以实现资本所有权中性。

所得税的公平和效率最终不仅取决于任何一个国家的所得税法，而且还取决于所有国家所得税法的累积效应。通过将其所得税制度与其贸易伙伴的税收制度进行协调，各国几乎不会蒙受损失，反而获益颇多。税收协定是实现这种协调的主要手段。

所得税协定有两个主要操作性目标——降低从事跨境交易纳税人的双重征税风险，以及确保跨境交易产生的所得不会完全规避税收（有时称为**双重不征税**或**无国籍所得**）。通过遵循相同模式的所得税协定促进国际税收规则的协调，可以推进实现这两个目标。税收协定的其他辅助性目的包括防止歧视非居民和外国人，以及在信息交换、税收征收和争议解决等方面开展征管合作。几乎所有现代所得税协定都在实质性内容方面，基于 OECD 协定范本和联合国协定范本。尽管联合国协定范本包含一些选择性附加条款，相较于 OECD 协定范本所允许的而言，允许来源国对更多的所得征税，但是，联合国协定范本在很大程度上以 OECD 协定范本为基础。税收协定将在第 8 章中进行讨论。

1.4 税务顾问在国际交易筹划中的作用

税务顾问在国际交易方面的作用与其在国内交易方面的作用类似。税务顾问最重要的责任也许是确保客户不会落入任何陷阱或遭遇异常情况，从而导致税收超过可以合理预期的水平。这种防御性的税收筹划通常不应将税务顾问置于与一国税务官员对抗的境地，后者也在寻求保证纳税人的税收负担恰当合理。国内和国际税务顾问也通常熟悉可用于最大限度地减少纳税的国际税收策略。这些策略往往涉及利用低税或无税（无论是普遍如此，抑或只是针对某些特定类型所得）

capital, capital-ownership neutrality focuses on the ownership of capital. Under an ideal tax system based on capital-ownership neutrality, tax would not distort the ownership of assets by taxpayers. Capital-ownership neutrality is achieved if all countries tax on either a worldwide or a territorial basis.

The fairness and efficiency of income taxation ultimately depend not just on the income tax laws of any one country but on the cumulative effects of the income tax laws of all countries. Countries have little to lose and much to gain by coordinating their income tax systems with the tax systems of their trading partners. Tax treaties are the primary means for achieving such coordination.

Income tax treaties have two primary operational goals—to reduce the risk of double taxation of taxpayers engaged in cross-border transactions and to ensure that income from cross-border transactions does not escape tax entirely (sometimes referred to as **double nontaxation** or **stateless income**). Both of these goals are advanced by measures that promote the harmonization of international tax rules through the adoption of income tax treaties that follow the same general pattern. Other ancillary objectives of tax treaties include the prevention of discrimination against nonresidents and foreign nationals and administrative cooperation in exchanging information, collecting tax, and resolving disputes. Virtually all modern income tax treaties are based in substantial part on the OECD and UN Model Treaties. The UN Model Treaty is based heavily on the OECD Model Treaty, although it contains some alternative and additional provisions that allow source countries to tax more income than is permitted under the OECD Model Treaty. Tax treaties are discussed in Chapter 8.

1.4 THE ROLE OF THE TAX ADVISER IN PLANNING INTERNATIONAL TRANSACTIONS

The tax adviser's role with respect to international transactions is similar to his or her role with respect to domestic transactions. Probably the tax adviser's most important obligation is to ensure that clients do not fall into any traps or anomalies that result in levels of taxation beyond what might reasonably be expected. Such defensive tax planning should not ordinarily put the tax adviser in an adversarial role with a country's tax officials, who should also be seeking to impose appropriate tax burdens on taxpayers. Domestic and international tax advisers are also expected to be acquainted with international tax strategies that might be used to minimize taxes. These schemes often involve the use of countries with low or no taxes, either in general or on

的国家，这些国家通常被称为**避税地**。

由于从事国际交易的纳税人经常面对缴纳过多税收的高风险，因此，国际税务顾问可能会比其国内同行花更多时间，从事防御性的税收筹划。这些过多纳税的风险通常产生于两个或多个国家对相同项目的所得，都主张征税权的情况。许多重要的国际税收规则旨在缓解或消除这种双重征税。第 4 章讨论通常用于双重征税救济的措施。

激进的税收筹划活动虽然引人注目，具有新闻价值，但在大多数国际税务顾问的业务中所占比例相对较小。但是，这些活动可能构成某些大型法律事务所和会计事务所的主要业务，并已导致各国政府以日益复杂的反避税立法作出回应。在第 6 章、第 7 章和第 8 章中，讨论了旨在打击国际**避税**的最重要的规则。这些规则并未迫使避税地破产消失，个人投资者和跨国企业仍有广泛的国际避税机会。

税务顾问的作用取决于所涉及的交易或投资是对内的还是对外的。对于居民纳税人的对外投资，税务顾问通常与客户保持持续的关系，并且熟悉客户的全部事务。因此，客户通常主要向国内税务顾问寻求有关交易的国内外税收后果的建议。虽然国内税务顾问通常没有资格提供有关国外税法的咨询意见，但是，客户常常希望其能够对外国税法咨询意见起到过滤器的作用，而且外国税务顾问通常与国内税务顾问打交道，而不是直接与客户打交道。相反，当税务顾问为非居民的对内投资提供咨询建议时，其作用通常会受到更多的限制。通常，此类建议仅限于税务顾问所在的特定国家的税收后果，且该顾问可能不会持续参与非居民的总体税收筹划。同样，如前所述，在这种情况下，税务顾问可能直接和外国税务顾问打交道，而不是直接与客户打交道。

无论涉及对内投资还是对外投资，国内税务顾问在对国际交易提供咨询时，总是会与外国律师、会计师或者商业顾问打交道。由于在基本法律概念、税法和会计惯例上存在差异，税务顾问在这方面发挥作用会遇到困难。同时，语言和文化的差异也可能会加大这些困难。

certain types of income; these countries are commonly referred to as **tax havens**.

International tax advisers are likely to spend more of their time engaging in defensive tax planning than their domestic counterparts since taxpayers engaged in international transactions frequently confront serious risks of paying excessive levels of tax. These risks typically arise when two or more countries claim the right to impose tax on the same items of income. Many important international tax rules are designed to mitigate or eliminate such double taxation. The measures commonly used to relieve double taxation are discussed in Chapter 4.

Although visible and newsworthy, aggressive tax planning activities occupy a relatively modest part of the practice of most international tax advisers. However, these activities may constitute a major part of the practice of some large law and accounting firms and have caused governments to respond with increasingly complex antiavoidance legislation. The most important of the rules designed to combat international **tax avoidance** are discussed in Chapters 6, 7, and 8. These rules have not driven tax havens out of business—opportunities for international tax avoidance are still widely available to individual investors and multinational enterprises.

The role of the tax adviser depends on whether the transaction involved is an outward-bound or inward-bound transaction or investment. In the case of an outward- bound investment by a resident taxpayer, the tax adviser often has an ongoing relationship with the client and is familiar with the client's total affairs. Consequently, the client usually looks primarily to the domestic tax adviser for advice concerning both the domestic and foreign tax consequences of a transaction. Although the domestic tax adviser is not generally qualified to provide advice concerning foreign tax law, the client often expects the tax adviser to act as a filter with respect to foreign tax advice, and it is not unusual for foreign tax advisers to deal with the domestic tax adviser rather than with the client directly. In contrast, when the tax adviser is providing advice concerning an inward-bound investment by a nonresident, the role is often more restricted. Usually, the advice is limited to the tax consequences in the tax adviser's particular country, and the adviser may not be involved in the overall tax planning for the nonresident on an ongoing basis. Also, as indicated earlier, in this situation, the tax adviser may deal with the foreign tax advisers rather than directly with the client.

Whether an inward-bound or an outward-bound investment is involved, domestic tax advisers consulting on an international transaction invariably deal with foreign lawyers, accountants, or business advisers. The role of tax advisers in this regard may often be difficult because of differences in basic legal concepts, tax laws, and accounting practices. These differences may be exacerbated by language and cultural differences.

尽管税务顾问可能没有法律资格提供有关外国税法的建议，但了解外国税制大有裨益。这些知识使税务顾问更有效地与外国税务顾问打交道，并根据两国法律就交易结构提供可供选择的方案，以达到理想的税收结果。国际税收执业的另一个重要方面是提高向客户和外国税务顾问提出正确问题的能力，从而取得有关客户现状和拟议交易的准确信息。

从纳税人的角度来看，任何投资或交易的外国税收后果通常与国内税收后果同等重要，甚至更为重要。例如，T 为一个国家居民，并计划在另一个国家进行**证券投资**。显然，T 会关注其居民国如何对境外来源所得征税，以及用于消除双重征税的规定。但是，T 也会关注外国税收的水平。如果其居民国通过对境外来源所得免税来消除重复征税，那么，她就只需要关注外国税收。

但是，如果 T 的居民国提供**外国税收抵免**，情况会更加复杂，原因将在第 4 章中详细说明。简言之，对外国的税收提供抵免的国家通常会将抵免额限制在对境外所得课征的国内税收的金额范围内，即针对该境外所得，外国的税收超过本国税收的部分不允许退税，尽管超额部分可能允许向以后年度结转。如果 T 有权享受其境外所得所缴税收的抵免，她需要关注外国的税收是否超过本国税收。在这种情况下，T 的实际税率等于外国税率。

举一个更复杂的例子，以说明外国税法对税务顾问的重要性。假设一家跨国企业出于商业原因，意欲重组其跨国企业集团。在没有特殊处理规定的情况下，根据跨国企业开展业务或子公司所在国家的税法，这种重组可能会导致重大不利的税收后果。但是，许多国家允许某些类型的企业重组可以在免税的基础上进行（或更准确地说，在递延纳税基础上进行，因为转让资产所应计的任何收益和损失，都将在最终处置资产时被征税）。因此，跨国企业在决定是否进行重组时，将向税务顾问寻求根据其母公司为其居民的国家的税法，以及该母公司的外国子公司所在国或开展业务所在国的税法，有关重组相应税收后果的建议。提供此建

Although a tax adviser may not be legally qualified to provide advice concerning foreign tax law, knowledge of foreign tax systems is an important asset. This knowledge enables an adviser to deal more effectively with foreign tax advisers and to suggest alternative methods for structuring transactions to provide desirable tax results under the laws of both countries. Another important aspect of international tax practice is developing the ability to ask clients and foreign tax advisers the right questions in order to obtain accurate information about the client's current situation and the proposed transactions.

From the taxpayer's viewpoint, the foreign tax consequences of any investment or transaction are often as important as, or even more important than, the domestic tax consequences. Consider, for example, an individual, T, who is resident in one country and plans to make a **portfolio investment** in another country. Obviously, T is concerned about how her country of residence will tax the foreign source income and the provisions available for relieving double taxation. T is also concerned, however, about the level of foreign tax. If her residence country relieves double taxation by exempting foreign source income, the foreign tax is the only tax she needs to be concerned about.

However, if T's country of residence provides a **foreign tax credit**, the situation is more complex, for reasons explained in detail in Chapter 4. In brief, countries that grant a credit for foreign taxes typically limit the credit to the amount of the domestic tax imposed on the foreign income—they do not allow a refund for any foreign tax in excess of their domestic tax on the foreign income, although a carryforward of excess credits may be allowed. If T is entitled to a credit for foreign taxes imposed on her foreign income, she needs to be concerned about whether the foreign tax exceeds the domestic tax, in which case, T will be subject to an effective rate of tax equal to the foreign tax rate.

To take a more complicated example of the importance of foreign tax law to the tax adviser, suppose that a multinational corporation wants to reorganize its multinational group of corporations for business reasons. In the absence of special relief provisions, such a reorganization might result in significant adverse tax consequences under the tax laws of the countries in which the multinational corporation carries on business or owns subsidiary corporations. Many countries, however, allow certain corporate reorganizations to occur on a tax-free basis (or, more accurately, a tax- deferred basis since any accrued gain or loss inherent in the transferred assets will be subject to tax when the assets are ultimately disposed of). In deciding whether to undertake the reorganization, therefore, the multinational corporation will look to its tax advisers for advice on the tax consequences of the reorganization under the tax laws of the country in which the parent corporation is resident and also under the tax laws of the

议绝非易事，因为处理企业重组的税收规则差异很大，而且通常存在着复杂的相互关联。

国内税法与国外税法的交叉，是国际税收研究和实践最具挑战性的特征之一。尽管税务顾问通常有资格仅就国内税法提供建议，但他们必须充分熟悉外国税法，以便能够识别潜在问题，并有效地与外国税务顾问打交道。此外，国外与国内法律的交叉不仅限于税收。交易的税收后果通常取决于交易背后的法律定性。例如，个人、信托、合伙企业、公司，或其他法律实体取得所得的税收处理可能不同。同样，如果一个纳税人被认定为转让财产或专有技术，或向他人提供服务，税收后果也可能各不相同。

根据涉及的法律权利和义务来确定所拟议交易的税收后果，在涉外背景下问题可能更加复杂，因为往往需要基于外国法律概念来确定本国税收后果。例如，如果一个国家的税收居民持有在另一个国家成立的有限责任公司（本质上是其投资者承担有限责任的实体，并在所得税上按穿透体处理）的权益，该所有者权益应该界定为合伙权益、公司股权，还是其他？并且，这种界定在两国间是否相同？如果该实体在两个国家的定性不同，则称为混合实体。混合实体所导致的问题将在第 7 章第 7.7 节中讨论。

税收往往并非企业作出直接对外投资初始决定的主要因素。就初始投资而言，其他因素，例如，投资回报率、政治稳定性、劳动力成本，以及进入外国市场更为重要。税收这一结果性因素，不应决定商业经营这一大局。但是，一旦作出投资决定，税收便是决定投资架构和融资方式，以及决定将投资利润再投资还是汇回的重要因素。客户希望税务顾问就外国企业利润汇回国内公司的各种方式提出建议，以及就向外国企业增资开展业务所涉及的税收后果提出建议。

一般来说，有关税收筹划要牢记的一个重点是，客户的组织体系必须能够承

foreign countries in which the foreign subsidiaries of the parent corporation are located or carry on business. Providing this advice is no easy matter because the tax rules governing corporate reorganizations vary widely and often interact in complex ways.

This intersection of domestic tax law and foreign tax law is one of the most challenging features of the study and practice of international tax. Although tax advisers are usually qualified to give advice only on their domestic tax law, they must be sufficiently familiar with foreign tax laws to be able to recognize potential problems and deal efficiently with foreign tax advisers. Further, the intersection of foreign and domestic law extends beyond tax. Tax consequences of transactions often depend on the underlying legal results of the transactions. For example, the tax consequences may differ where income is earned by an individual, a **trust**, a partnership, a corporation, or some other legal entity. Similarly, the tax consequences may differ if a taxpayer is considered to have transferred property or know-how or to have rendered services to another person.

The problem of determining the tax consequences of a proposed transaction on the basis of the underlying legal rights and obligations is exacerbated in the foreign context because domestic tax consequences often must be determined on the basis of foreign legal concepts. For example, if a resident of one country holds an interest in a limitada or limited liability company (which is, in essence, an entity that provides limited liability for its investors and flow-through treatment for income tax purposes) organized in another country, are the ownership rights characterized as an interest in a partnership, as shares in a corporation, or as something else? And is the characterization the same in both countries? If the entity is characterized differently by the two countries, it is known as a hybrid entity. The issues raised by hybrid entities are addressed in Chapter 7, section 7.7.

Often, tax is not a major factor in the initial decision of an enterprise to make a **direct investment** abroad. Other factors, such as the return on investment, political stability, labor costs, and access to foreign markets, are much more important as far as the original investment is concerned. The tax "tail" should not wag the commercial "dog." Once the decision to invest has been made, however, tax is an important factor in determining the way in which the investment is structured and financed and in determining whether to reinvest or repatriate the profits from the investment. Tax advisers are expected to provide advice on the tax consequences of the various ways in which the profits of a foreign enterprise might be repatriated to the domestic corporation and to provide advice on the tax consequences of providing the foreign enterprise with additional capital to finance its activities.

One important point about tax planning in general that must be kept in mind is that

受税收筹划带来的经营上的影响。如果从操作角度看，税收筹划过于复杂，那么节省的税收可能被增加的管理成本所抵消。此外，如果企业实际上无法根据税收筹划方案来经营，该方案在税收方面的有效性将受阻。例如，一个税收筹划方案可能涉及在避税地设立外国子公司，从国内母公司购买商品再销售给国外客户。这样的税收筹划可能以将货物交付给避税地子公司为条件。因此，如果从母公司直接将货物运到最终客户，从商业角度来看更为合理，但税收筹划方案的成功实施可能得不到保障，实际上，还可能会对纳税人造成重大惩罚。

对于外国投资结构的安排，存在着许多种不同的方法。例如，制造企业可能会通过以下一种或多种方式在外国销售其商品：

—— 通过例如邮购、互联网销售或流动销售代理，将其制造的商品直接出售给外国顾客；
—— 将其商品出售给非关联的外国分销商，再销售给顾客；
—— 在外国设立由仓库和销售人员或代理组成的**分支机构**，以销售商品；
—— 在外国设立外国销售子公司，以销售商品；
—— 建立外国控股公司，该公司在该国设立外国销售子公司，以销售商品；或者
—— 许可非关联的外国公司在该国制造和销售其商品。

根据特定国家（以及不同国家）的税法，这些选择的税收后果可能会有很大差异。

一国的居民企业在安排对另一国的对外投资结构时，要面对的基本选择之一，是设立外国分支机构，还是外国子公司。分支机构与子公司之间的本质区别在于，子公司是独立的法律和应税实体，而分支机构是居民企业的一部分或其中的一个部门。因此，当居民企业通过外国分支机构开展业务时，由于分支机构不

the client's organization must be able to live with the operational implications of the tax plan. If the tax plan is too complex from an operating viewpoint, any tax savings may be offset by additional administrative costs. Moreover, if the business is unable to operate, in fact, in accordance with the tax plan, the effectiveness of the plan for tax purposes may be jeopardized. For example, a tax plan might involve the establishment of a foreign subsidiary in a tax haven to purchase goods from the domestic parent corporation and resell them to customers abroad. Such a tax plan might be conditional on the delivery of the goods to the tax haven subsidiary. Therefore, if the goods are shipped by the parent corporation directly to the ultimate customers because that is the sensible thing to do from a commercial perspective, the success of the tax plan may be jeopardized, and indeed, significant penalties may be imposed on the taxpayer.

There are many different ways of structuring foreign investments. For example, a manufacturing enterprise might sell its goods in a foreign country in one or more of the following ways:

- sell its manufactured goods directly to customers in the foreign country through, for example, mail-order sales, sales over the Internet, or sales by itinerant sales agents;
- sell its goods to an unrelated foreign distributor for resale to customers;
- establish a **branch** in the foreign country consisting of a warehouse and sales employees or agents to sell its goods there;
- establish a foreign sales subsidiary in the foreign country to sell the goods;
- establish a foreign holding company, which establishes a foreign sales subsidiary in the country to sell the goods; or
- license an unrelated foreign corporation to manufacture and sell its goods in the foreign country.

The tax consequences of these alternatives may vary considerably under the tax laws of a particular country (and from country to country).

One of the fundamental choices that a corporation resident in one country faces in structuring a foreign investment in another country is the choice between a foreign branch and a foreign subsidiary. The essential difference between a branch and a subsidiary is that a subsidiary is a separate legal and taxable entity, whereas a branch is a part or division of the resident corporation. As a result, where a resident corporation carries on its business through a foreign branch, the resident corporation may be taxed on the profits of the branch because the branch is not a legal entity separate from the corporation. Further, for general law purposes,

是与居民企业分离的法律实体，居民企业要就分支机构的利润缴税。此外，在一般法律意义上，居民企业应对其外国业务活动引起的任何法律义务（如涉及产品缺陷）承担责任。相反，如果是由外国子公司开展国外业务活动，该公司作为独立的法律实体，应就其利润缴税，并对其自身的法律义务负责。当然，该一般规则也有例外。

总而言之，税务顾问需要在国际交易的税收筹划方面执行两项职能。首先，税务顾问必须在合理的范围内量化实施交易的税收成本和收益，并评估这些成本和收益的税收风险。其次，需要提出建议，以便最大限度地减少应纳税额。通常，在国际税收筹划的税收最小化方面，涉及确定交易结构的各种方法，并根据税收后果以及与企业总体运营计划的兼容性，推荐一种方法。

尽管必须针对每个客户的具体情况，制订国际交易的税收筹划方案，但是可以列举出某些常见类型的税收筹划。下面介绍两种类型的国际税收筹划，以使读者了解这一行为的本质。以下示例已做了较大简化。

避税地实体。国际税收筹划十分重视对低税或无税国家的利用。这种避税地能够以多种方式减少高税收国家居民的税收。一种常见的方法是在避税地设立受控外国企业。

例如，假设 A 国居民 A 公司在该国生产商品，该国以 30% 的税率征收公司税。A 公司产品不仅在 A 国销售，还销往其他国家。A 公司在 A 国就全球利润缴税。A 公司在 TH 国成立了全资子公司 TH 公司，该国不征收任何所得税。TH 公司按**独立交易价格**从 A 公司购买商品，并再销售给 A 国以外的客户。因此，归属于 A 国以外销售的利润将由 TH 公司而非 A 公司取得。因为 TH 公司是一个独立的法律和应税实体，并且税务顾问会确保它不是 A 国的税收居民，TH 公司取得的利润通常不会被 A 国或 TH 国征税。因此，假设 TH 公司的利润为 200 万元，则此项交易将使应付给 A 国的税额减少 60 万元（200 万元 ×30%）。

如果 TH 公司没有任何员工，并且从不将从 A 公司采购的商品交付给客户，则 A 国可能将 TH 公司视为虚假安排而忽略，并将其利润视为由 A 公司取得。即

the resident corporation is responsible for any legal obligations (e.g., with respect to product defects) arising out of its foreign business activities. In contrast, if the foreign activities are carried out by a foreign subsidiary corporation, that corporation, as a separate legal entity, is taxable on its profits and is responsible for its own legal obligations. There are, of course, exceptions to this general rule.

In summary, a tax adviser is expected to perform two functions with respect to tax planning for international transactions. First, tax advisers must, within a reasonable range, quantify the tax costs and benefits of carrying out transactions and assess the tax risks of those tax costs and benefits. Second, they are expected to provide advice for minimizing the amount of tax payable. Often, this tax-minimization aspect of international tax planning involves identifying various methods of structuring a transaction and recommending one method over others in light of the tax consequences and the compatibility of the proposed structure with the overall operating plan of the enterprise.

Although tax planning for international transactions must be tailored to each client's particular situation, certain common types of tax planning can be identified. Two types of international tax planning are described below to give some flavor of the nature of the exercise. The following examples have been simplified drastically.

Tax haven entities. International tax planning focuses heavily on the use of countries that levy little or no tax. Such tax havens can be used in a wide variety of ways to reduce taxes on residents of high-tax countries. One common way is to establish a CFC in a tax haven.

For example, assume that ACo is resident in and manufactures goods in Country A, which levies corporate tax at a rate of 30%. ACo sells its manufactured goods not only in Country A but also in several other countries. ACo is taxable in Country A on its worldwide profits. ACo incorporates a wholly owned subsidiary, THCo, in Country TH, which does not impose any income taxes. THCo purchases manufactured goods from ACo at their **arm's-length price** and resells them to clients outside Country A. As a result, the profits attributable to sales outside Country A will be earned by THCo, not by ACo. Because THCo is a separate legal and taxable entity and because the tax advisers will ensure that it is not resident in Country A, the profits derived by THCo are not usually taxable by either Country A or Country TH. Thus, assuming that THCo's profits are 2 million, this transaction will reduce the taxes payable to Country A by 600,000 (30% of 2 million).

If THCo does not have any employees and never takes delivery of the goods acquired from ACo, Country A may disregard THCo as a sham and consider its profits to be derived by ACo. Even if THCo actually performs selling and marketing functions, some countries have rules

使 TH 公司实际履行销售和营销功能，一些国家仍有规则，将 TH 公司的所得归于 A 公司。这些“受控外国企业”（CFC）规则将在有关国际避税的第 7 章第 7.3 节中讨论。

传统上，大多数自我定位为避税地的国家都提供广泛的保护，防止向外国政府披露涉及其境内居民企业和金融机构交易的详细信息。这些保密制度使高税收国家的税务机关难以发现其居民避税或逃税的企图。由于位于列支敦士登和瑞士等避税地的大银行促成了一系列引人注目的大规模逃税案件，这种情况在 21 世纪初期发生了巨大变化。这些事件导致银行保密制度的消除，以及各国税务机关实施通用国际标准，在相互之间应要求和自动地开展信息交换。为防止避税和逃税而在信息交换方面取得的重要进展，将在第 8 章第 8.8.4 节中讨论。

择协避税。另外一类国际税收筹划涉及使用税收协定减少税收。常见的例子是一国居民在另一国设立“导管”公司，以利用该另一国的税收协定网络。

假设 A 国居民 A 公司开发了有价值的无形资产，并打算将其许可给其他国家的制造商使用。A 国与一些潜在被许可人为其居民的国家没有税收协定，A 国与其他国家的税收协定规定特许权使用费的预提税率为 15%。A 国对其居民公司从有重要参股的外国公司取得的股息免税。A 公司将其无形资产转让给在 B 国成立的全资子公司 B 公司。B 国与潜在被许可人为其居民的所有国家都有税收协定，并且这些协定免征特许权使用费的预提税。

上述安排的结果是，特许权使用费所发生的国家，通常也是被许可人为其居民的国家，不对该特许权使用费征税。B 国也可能不就 B 公司取得的特许权使用费征税（或以低税率征税），或者因为它是传统的避税地，或者因为它对有关无形资产的特许权使用费采取特别的低税制度。当 B 公司向 A 公司分配股息时，A 国由于对外国公司的股息采取**参股免税制**，不对股息征税。即使 A 国将 A 公司向 B 公司转让无形资产的交易视为应税交易，但由于在转让时很难准确确定无形

to attribute the income derived by THCo to ACo. These "controlled foreign company" (CFC) rules are discussed in Chapter 7, section 7.3 dealing with international tax avoidance.

Most countries that market themselves as tax havens have traditionally provided broad protection against disclosure to foreign governments of the particulars of transactions involving resident corporations and financial intermediaries located within their borders. These secrecy regimes made it difficult for the tax authorities of high-tax countries to discover attempts at tax avoidance and evasion by their residents. This situation changed drastically in the early 2000s as a result of a series of high-profile cases of widespread tax evasion facilitated by large banks in tax havens such as Liechtenstein and Switzerland. These incidents led to the elimination of bank secrecy and the adoption of a common international standard for the exchange of information between tax authorities, on request and automatically. The significant improvements in exchange of information to prevent tax avoidance and evasion are discussed in Chapter 8, section 8.8.4.

Treaty shopping. Another type of international tax planning involves the use of tax treaties to reduce tax. One common example involves the establishment by a resident of one country of a "conduit" company in another country in order to take advantage of that country's tax treaty network.

Assume that ACo, resident in Country A, has developed valuable intangible property and intends to license the property for use by manufacturers in several other countries. Country A does not have treaties with some of the countries where the potential licensees are resident, and the treaties that Country A has with the other countries provide for withholding taxes on royalties of 15%. Country A provides an exemption for dividends received by a corporation resident in Country A from foreign corporations in which the resident corporation has a substantial participation. ACo transfers its intangible property to a wholly owned subsidiary, BCo, established in Country B. Country B has tax treaties with all the countries where potential licensees are resident, and those treaties provide an exemption from any withholding tax on royalties.

The result of the above arrangement is that no tax will be imposed on the royalties by the countries where the royalties arise, which is usually where the licensees are resident. Country B may not tax the royalties derived by BCo (or may tax them at a low rate), either because it is a traditional tax haven or because it provides a special low-tax regime for royalties in respect of intangible property. When BCo distributes dividends to ACo, Country A will not tax the dividends because of its **participation exemption** for dividends from foreign corporations. Even if Country A treats the transfer of the intangible property by ACo to BCo as a taxable

资产的公允市场价值，因此对恰当数额的转让收益课税可能非常困难。

该示例说明了**择协避税**的问题。实际上，A 公司通过简单的权宜之计，即设立 B 国居民子公司而利用了 B 国的协定网络。B 公司发挥导管公司的作用，将被许可人支付的特许权使用费转变为支付给 A 公司的免税股息；B 公司在 B 国可能没有雇员和经营场地。这一安排的整体效果，是避免了特许权使用费来源国的预提税。择协避税将在第 8 章第 8.8.2.2 节中讨论。

1.5 参与国际税收的国际组织

尽管主权国家主要负责通过国内立法和税收协定建立国际税收体系规则，其他国际组织在国际税收方面也发挥着重要作用。本节简要介绍参与国际税收的四个主要国际组织——经济合作与发展组织（OECD）、国际货币基金组织（IMF）、联合国（UN）和世界银行集团。

OECD 无疑是最有影响力的国际税收组织。欧洲经济合作组织（OEEC）是第二次世界大战后成立的，是重建欧洲的马歇尔计划的一部分。1961 年，加拿大和美国加入了原仅包括欧洲成员国的 OEEC，OEEC 成为 OECD。截至 2022 年 11 月，OECD 由 38 个成员国组成，其中大多数是富裕的发达资本输出国。

OECD 的工作是通过以协商一致方式运作的各个委员会进行的。与税收问题相关的委员会是财政事务委员会，该委员会由成员国的高级税务官员组成。该委员会的工作由行政秘书处——税收政策与管理中心支撑，该中心拥有庞大的工作团队（目前有来自 40 个国家的约 200 人），在税收各领域均具有专业知识。OECD 一项核心税收工作是《OECD 关于所得和财产的税收协定范本》，该范本于 1977 年首次发布，并于 2017 年进行了最近一次修订。

财政事务委员会的日常工作通过若干工作组进行，这些工作组由成员国的高

transaction, it may have significant difficulty in taxing the appropriate amount of gain on the transfer because of the problem of accurately establishing the fair market value of the intangible property at the time of the transfer.

This example illustrates the problem of *treaty shopping*. In effect, ACo has taken advantage of Country B's treaty network by the simple expedient of establishing a subsidiary as a resident of Country B. BCo functions as a conduit to convert the royalties from the licensees into tax-exempt dividends paid to ACo; it may have no employees and no place of business in Country B. The overall effect of the arrangement is that the withholding taxes of the countries in which the royalties arise are avoided. Treaty shopping is dealt with in Chapter 8, section 8.8.2.2.

1.5 INTERNATIONAL ORGANIZATIONS INVOLVED IN INTERNATIONAL TAX

Although sovereign nation-states are primarily responsible for establishing the rules of the international tax system through domestic legislation and tax treaties, other international organizations play an important role with respect to international tax. The four major international organizations involved in international tax—the OECD, the International Monetary Fund (IMF), the United Nations (UN), and the World Bank Group—are described briefly in this section.

The OECD is unquestionably the most influential international tax organization. The Organisation for European Economic Co-operation (OEEC) was formed after World War II as part of the Marshall Plan for the reconstruction of Europe. It became the OECD in 1961 when Canada and the United States (U.S.) joined the European nations in the OEEC. As of November 2022, the OECD consists of thirty-eight member countries, most of which are wealthy developed capital-exporting countries.

The work of the OECD is conducted through various committees that operate by consensus. The relevant committee for tax issues is the Committee on Fiscal Affairs, which is composed of senior tax officials from member countries. The Committee's work is supported by an administrative secretariat—the Centre for Tax Policy and Administration—which has a large staff (currently over 200 people from 40 countries) with expertise in various aspects of tax. A centerpiece of the OECD's tax work is the OECD Model Tax Convention on Income and on Capital, first issued in 1977 and revised most recently in 2017.

The regular work of the Committee on Fiscal Affairs is conducted through several working parties composed of senior tax officials from member countries. The current working parties

级税务官员组成。目前的工作组及其职责范围如下：

—— 第 1 工作组：OECD 协定范本和协定相关问题。

—— 第 2 工作组：税收政策与统计。

—— 第 6 工作组：跨国企业和转让定价。

—— 第 9 工作组：消费税。

—— 第 10 工作组：信息交换与税收遵从。

—— 第 11 工作组：激进的国际税收筹划

若干非成员具有观察员地位，并以此身份参加 OECD 工作组的工作。

OECD 税收政策和管理中心在其他国际税收活动中也发挥着引领作用，这些活动远远超出了 OECD 成员国的范围。这些活动包括解决特定国际税收问题的论坛，所有准备致力于论坛目标的国家都可以参加这些论坛。全球税收透明度和信息交换论坛有 160 多个成员国，其工作包括通过对成员国的国内法和征管实践进行同行审议，确保成员国有效地执行信息交换的国际标准。

2012 年，二十国集团（G20）成员与 OECD（共计 46 个国家）启动了一项旨在防止税基侵蚀和利润转移（BEPS）的联合项目。2013 年，OECD 发布了《税基侵蚀和利润转移行动计划》，制定了雄心勃勃的工作安排，共包括 15 个具体的行动项目。各项工作的最终报告已于 2015 年 10 月完成（可在 www.oecd.org 上获得）。有害税收实践论坛通过对参与国实施同行审议，确保 OECD 成员国和非成员国根据 2015 年 BEPS 第 5 项行动计划最终报告《考虑透明度和实质性因素，更有效地打击有害税收实践》，消除各国的有害税收实践。税收征管论坛成立于 2002 年，旨在处理涉及税收征管的所有问题，目的是改善税收遵从；目前有 52 个成员。

OECD/G20 **包容性框架**建立于 2016 年 2 月，是实施 BEPS 一揽子最低标准的制度性安排，包括用于落实与 BEPS 相关修订税收协定的多边公约。包容性框

and their areas of responsibility are as follows:

– Working Party No. 1—the OECD Model Treaty and related treaty issues.
– Working Party No. 2—tax policy and statistics.
– Working Party No. 6—multinational enterprises and transfer pricing.
– Working Party No. 9—consumption taxes.
– Working Party No. 10—exchange of information and tax compliance.
– Working Party No. 11—aggressive international tax planning.

Several nonmember countries have observer status and participate in the work of the OECD working parties on that basis.

OECD Centre for Tax Policy and Administration also plays a leading role in other international tax initiatives that extend well beyond OECD member countries. These initiatives include forums to deal with specific international tax issues; participation in these forums is available to all countries that are prepared to commit to the objectives of the forum. The Global Forum on Transparency and Exchange of Information for Tax Purposes has over 160 member countries; its work involves ensuring that member countries effectively implement international standards for exchange of information through peer reviews of the domestic laws and administrative practices of member countries.

In 2012, the Group of Twenty (**G20**) nations and the OECD (forty-six countries in all) began a joint project aimed at preventing Base Erosion and Profit Shifting (BEPS). In 2013, the OECD released its *Action Plan on Base Erosion and Profit Shifting*, which set out an ambitious agenda with fifteen specific action items; the final reports were completed in October 2015 (available at www.oecd.org). The Forum on Harmful Tax Practices is responsible for ensuring that OECD member and nonmember countries eliminate their harmful tax practices in accordance with BEPS Action 5: 2015 Final Report (*Countering Harmful Tax Practices More Effectively, Taking into Account Transparency and Substance*) through peer reviews of participating countries. The Forum on Tax Administration was established in 2002 to deal with all issues involving tax administration, with the goal of improving tax compliance; it currently has fifty-two members.

The **OECD/G20 Inclusive Framework** was established in February 2016 as the institutional arrangement for implementing the BEPS package of minimum standards, including a multilateral convention to implement the BEPS tax treaty changes. The Inclusive Framework operates through a monitoring process and peer reviews and is open to all countries that agree

架通过监控过程和同行审议来运行，并且向所有同意实施 BEPS 最低标准的国家开放。截至 2022 年，它有 141 多个成员。包容性框架还负责支持一系列实用工具包的拟制，以帮助发展中国家应对 BEPS。

世界银行集团成立于 1944 年，由 5 个机构和 189 个成员国组成。它向发展中国家提供财政政策咨询和技术援助，其主要目标是消除贫困和促进可持续的经济繁荣。世界银行集团通过其全球税务团队，为各个国家提供有关税收政策和管理各个方面的咨询服务。

国际货币基金组织（IMF）成立于 1945 年，有 189 个成员国，其基本目标是确保国际货币体系的稳定，职责范围广泛涉及经济和金融问题。IMF 有条件地向其成员国提供贷款，使各国能够改善其财务状况。它还在经济、货币和税收问题上，向各个国家提供技术援助，包括税收政策建议、培训和立法的起草。

最后，联合国从 20 世纪 70 年代开始涉足国际税收问题。当时，联合国开始为发达国家和发展中国家之间的税收协定制定协定范本。第一个联合国协定范本——《联合国关于发达国家与发展中国家间避免双重征税的协定范本》（联合国协定范本）于 1980 年发布，并于 2001 年、2011 年，2017 年和最近的 2021 年进行了修订。联合国国际税务合作专家委员会（联合国专家委员会）负责制定联合国协定范本。联合国专家委员会接替原联合国专家组，该专家组于 1980 年制定了最初的联合国协定范本。专家委员会由 25 名成员组成，这些成员由其国家政府提名，由联合国秘书长任命，其中大多数来自发展中国家。各成员以个人身份任职 4 年，并不代表其国家政府，但是实际上许多成员都坚持其政府的立场。该委员会每年举行两次会议，一次在纽约，一次在日内瓦，为期 4 天。委员会的会议不仅对组成人员开放，而且对公众开放，在讨论过程中公众可以参加（但不能投票）。联合国成员国（在委员会没有成员的国家）政府的代表、其他国际组织（OECD 和 IMF）、民间团体、商业组织和学术界的代表时常出席这些会议。

此外，自 2012 年以来，联合国可持续发展筹资办公室能力建设部门与联合国专家委员会一道，积极向亚洲、南美洲和非洲的发展中国家提供税收技术援

to implement the BEPS minimum standards; as of 2022, it has 141 member countries. The Inclusive Framework is also responsible for supporting the preparation of a series of practical toolkits to assist developing countries in countering BEPS.

The **World Bank Group** was founded in 1944 and consists of 5 institutions and 189 member countries. It provides finance policy advice and technical assistance to developing countries, with the primary goals of eliminating poverty and promoting sustainable economic prosperity. The World Bank Group provides advisory services to individual countries on all aspects of tax policy and administration through its Global Tax Team.

The **IMF** was founded in 1945 and has 189 member countries. Its basic goal is to ensure the stability of the international monetary system, and its mandate extends broadly to economic and financial issues. The IMF provides loans to member countries, subject to conditions, to enable them to improve their financial positions. It also provides technical assistance to individual countries on economic, monetary, and tax issues, including tax policy advice, training, and legislative drafting.

Finally, the **UN** has been involved in international tax issues since the 1970s when it started work on developing a model tax convention for tax treaties between developed and developing countries. The first UN Model Convention—UN Model Double Taxation Convention Between Developed and Developing Countries (UN Model Convention)—was published in 1980 and revised in 2001, 2011, 2017, and, most recently, in 2021. The UN Model Convention is the responsibility of the UN Committee of Experts on International Cooperation in Tax Matters (the UN Committee of Experts), which is the successor to the UN Group of Experts that produced the original UN Model Convention in 1980. The Committee of Experts consists of twenty-five members nominated by their governments and appointed by the Secretary-General of the UN, with a majority from developing countries. The members serve for four-year terms in their personal capacity and not as representatives of their governments; however, in practice, many of the members adhere closely to their governments' positions. The Committee meets twice annually for four days, once in New York and once in Geneva. The meetings of the Committee are open not only to the attendees but also to the public, who can participate in the discussions (but not vote). The meetings are regularly attended by representatives of UN member governments (other than governments with members of the Committee), other international organizations (the OECD and IMF), civil society, business organizations, and academics.

In addition, since 2012, the Capacity Development Unit of the UN Financing for Development Office, in conjunction with the UN Committee of Experts, has been active in providing technical tax assistance to developing countries in Asia, South America, and Africa

助，并开发实用资讯，以帮助在国际税收方面经验不足的发展中国家。这项工作集中在4个主要领域：转让定价、税收协定、税收征管和防止税基侵蚀。关于税基侵蚀，能力建设部门发布了3个实用文件（工具包），为发展中国家提供了详细的实践指导，可用于开展税制分析，以确定税基侵蚀风险，并设计适当对策。这些文件涉及服务、利息、租金和特许权使用费所得，以及一般反避税规则，都可以在联合国网站上查阅。联合国还提供有关国际税收问题的以下出版物：

——《发展中国家转让定价实务手册》（2021年第三版）。

——《税收协定管理手册》（2013年）。

——《发展中国家税收协定谈判专题报告》（2014年）。

——《关于保护发展中国家税基若干问题的手册》（2017年第二版）。

2016年4月，IMF、OECD、联合国和世界银行创建了税收合作平台，作为这4个组织合作向发展中国家提供援助，以加强其税制体系的制度机制。该平台的主要初始目标是完成8个工具包，包含针对发展中国家应对税基侵蚀和相关问题的实用指南。尽管平台的工作由每个组织分别开展，但是他们都必须就平台标识下发表的任何报告达成一致。迄今为止，已经开发了有关税收优惠、转让定价可比性分析，被称为间接转让（处置拥有资产的居民公司股份获得的收益，此类资产如不动产、矿产或电信许可证），转让定价文档以及税收协定谈判的工具包。该平台还将参与能力建设活动，包括提供技术援助和培训者培训计划、建立有效的信息交换系统、为应对地下经济提供指引，以及就各种税收课题（尤其是税收征管、自然资源税收和收入统计）分享知识。

and in developing practical materials to assist developing countries that have little experience in international tax. This work has focused on four main areas: transfer pricing, tax treaties, tax administration, and protection against tax base erosion. With respect to base erosion, the Capacity Development Unit has published three Practical Portfolios (toolkits) with detailed practical guidance for developing countries to use in analyzing their tax systems to identify the risks of base erosion and designing appropriate countermeasures. These Portfolios deal with income from services, interest, rent and royalties, and general anti-avoidance rules; they are all available on the UN website. The following UN publications dealing with international tax issues are also available from the UN:

– Practical Manual on Transfer Pricing for Developing Countries (third edition 2021).
– Handbook on the Administration of Tax Treaties (2013).
– Papers on Selected Topics in Negotiation of Tax Treaties for Developing Countries (2014).
– Handbook on Selected Issues in Protecting the Tax Base of Developing Countries (second edition 2017).

In April 2016, the IMF, OECD, UN, and World Bank created the Platform for Collaboration on Tax as the institutional structure for the four organizations to cooperate in providing assistance to developing countries in strengthening their tax systems. The primary initial objective of the Platform is to prepare eight toolkits containing practical guidance for developing countries in dealing with base erosion and related issues. Although the work of the Platform is done separately by each of the organizations, they must all agree on any papers published under the Platform's banner. To date, toolkits have been developed on tax incentives, comparability analysis for transfer pricing, so-called indirect transfers (gains from the disposition of shares of resident corporations that own assets, such as immovable property and mining or telecommunications licenses), transfer pricing documentation, and tax treaty negotiations. The Platform will also engage in capacity-development activities, including providing technical assistance and train-the-trainers programs, building effective exchange of information systems, providing guidance on dealing with the underground economy, and sharing knowledge on various tax topics, especially tax administration, the taxation of natural resources, and revenue statistics.

1.6 国际税收简史

与当今的各种所得税不同，欧洲国家在 20 世纪初征收的所得税税率很低，而且仅对非常富有的个人征收。虽然有些国家对这些个人的总收入或全球收入征税，但国际税收并不是一个严重的问题，原因是很少有国家征收所得税，而那些征税的国家税率也很低。这种情况在第一次世界大战期间发生了巨大的变化，当时参与战争的国家相继开征所得税，以满足增长的收入需求，从而为其军事行动提供资金。此外，所得税的适用范围也扩大到中产阶级个人和法律实体。所得税广泛实施不可避免地导致纳税人的居民国和所得的来源国征税权的重叠。

作为结束第一次世界大战和平进程的组成部分，国际联盟成立于 1920 年，最初有 42 个成员国，其崇高目标是确保世界和平。1921 年，为回应国际商会的呼吁，国际联盟任命了一个由四名著名经济学家组成的特别委员会，要求其针对双重征税问题以及消除双重征税国际条约适用的通用原则，撰写一份报告。该报告由布鲁因（Bruins）教授（荷兰）、伊诺迪（Einaudi）教授（意大利）、塞利格曼（Seligman）教授（美国）和斯坦普（Stamp）教授（英国）于 1923 年完成。该报告所背书的国际税收解决方案至今沿用于 OECD 和联合国协定范本之中，即对不同类型的所得进行分类，并按照这些所得类型，把征税权分配给居民国或来源国。

1923 年的报告还赞同制定一个消除双重征税的协定范本。这促使国际联盟于 1925 年成立了一个技术专家委员会，起草有关所得税、遗产税和征管合作的协定范本。这项工作功成于 1928 年，产生了三个版本的所得税协定范本草案，其中反映出多处妥协，以满足居民国和来源国的利益（主要反映了债权国的利益，如荷兰、美国和英国，以及债务国的利益，如战后形成的其他欧洲国家）和他们不同的国内所得税制度。

第二次世界大战以后，欧洲经济合作组织（OEEC）及其继任者 OECD 主要

1.6 A BRIEF HISTORY OF INTERNATIONAL TAX

Unlike the income taxes of today, the original income taxes of European countries in the early twentieth century were imposed at very low rates and only on very wealthy individuals. Although those individuals were taxable by some countries on their total or worldwide income, international taxation was not a serious matter because few countries imposed income taxes and those that did imposed tax at low rates. This situation changed dramatically during World War I when countries involved in the war started to adopt income taxes in response to increased revenue needs to fund their military efforts. In addition, the scope of application of these income taxes was extended to middle-class individuals and to legal entities. The spread of income taxes inevitably led to overlapping tax claims of the countries in which taxpayers were resident and the countries in which income was earned.

The League of Nations was formed in 1920, initially with forty-two members, as part of the peace process ending World War I, with the lofty goal of ensuring world peace. In 1921, in response to a call from the International Chamber of Commerce, it appointed a special committee of four prominent economists to prepare a report on double taxation and the general principles for an international convention to eliminate double taxation. The report, by Professors Bruins (Netherlands), Einaudi (Italy), Seligman (United States), and Stamp (United Kingdom), was completed in 1923. It endorsed an approach to international taxation, still used in the current OECD and UN Model Treaties, requiring the classification of different types of income and the assignment of taxing rights with respect to those categories to residence or source countries.

The 1923 report also endorsed the adoption of a model treaty to eliminate double taxation, which led the League of Nations to establish a Committee of Technical Experts in 1925 to draft model treaties dealing with income tax, succession duties, and administrative cooperation. This work culminated in 1928 with three draft versions of an income tax model treaty, which reflected many compromises in order to satisfy the interests of residence and source countries (largely reflecting the interests of creditor nations such as the Netherlands, the U.S., and the United Kingdom (U.K.), and debtor nations, such as the other European countries emerging from the war) and their different domestic income tax systems.

After World War II, the Organisation for European Economic Co-operation (OEEC) and its successor, the OECD, continued the work on the development of a model income tax treaty, largely through the refinement of the early draft of the League of Nations. No attempt was

通过改进国际联盟早期草案的方式，持续致力于提交一份所得税协定范本，而并未试图采用另一种完全不同的多边公约的方式。后者则为世界贸易组织所采纳。OECD 于 1963 年制定了一份协定范本草案，随后于 1977 年制定了第一份正式的 OECD 协定范本；这些范本构成了目前 OECD 协定范本的基础。第一份联合国协定范本于 1980 年发布，该范本通过扩大来源国的征税权，更好地反映了发展中国家的利益。

总而言之，相关国际组织的工作从一开始就几乎完全集中于制定和完善所得税协定范本以消除双重征税，最近则扩展至通过广泛的双边税收协定网络防止避税。这些协定范本的异常成功，可以从基于 OECD 或联合国协定范本的双边税收协定数量的不断增加得到证明。但是，国际税收的一些问题并不能通过双边税收协定轻易得以解决，而需要多边合作，无论是通过协调一致的单边行动还是通过多边条约。最近，OECD 扩大了其处理国际税收问题的方式，通过多边条约和协调一致的单边行动（例如，针对支柱二全球最低税实施所拟议的同行审议程序），建议和促进对国内法的修改。这些动态将在第 9 章第 9.5.5.3 节中讨论。

本节的国际税收简史主要反映税收协定的发展。但税收协定的历史只是故事的一部分。有影响力国家的所得税制度跨境部分的单边进展也在国际税收史上发挥了重要作用。特别是美国的跨境税收规则对国际税收的架构，产生了实质性的影响。例如，美国在 1962 年通过了受控外国企业（CFC）规则，从那时起，50 多个国家制定了类似的规则。同样，美国率先在一般的独立交易原则下创新采用的转让定价方法，为 OECD 略加修改后吸纳，也为许多国家所采用。最近，美国于 2017 年引入了全球无形资产低税所得（GILTI）规则，即对美国跨国公司取得的境外低税所得征收最低税，也已成为 OECD 包容性框架支柱二全球最低税提案的基础。

made to take a fundamentally different approach by developing a multinational convention, as was done by the World Trade Organisation. The OECD produced a draft model treaty in 1963, followed by the first official OECD Model Treaty in 1977; these models form the basis for the current OECD Model Treaty. The first UN Model Convention was issued in 1980 to better reflect the interests of developing countries by providing expanded taxing rights for source countries.

In summary, the work of international organizations focused from the beginning almost exclusively on developing and maintaining model income tax treaties to eliminate double taxation and, more recently, to prevent tax avoidance through a widespread network of bilateral tax treaties. Those model treaties have been very successful, as evidenced by the ever-increasing number of bilateral tax treaties based on the OECD or UN Model Treaties. However, several problems of international taxation are not easily dealt with through bilateral tax treaties; these problems require multilateral cooperation, whether through harmonized unilateral action or multilateral treaties. Recently, the OECD has expanded its efforts to deal with international tax issues by recommending and facilitating changes to domestic law through multilateral agreements and through coordinated unilateral action (e.g., the proposed peer review process to implement the Pillar Two global minimum tax), which is discussed in Chapter 9, section 9.5.5.3.

This brief history of international tax has focused primarily on the development of tax treaties. But the history of tax treaties is only part of the story. Unilateral developments in the international aspects of influential countries' income tax systems have also played a significant role in the history of international tax. In particular, the international tax rules of the U.S. have had substantial influence on the shape of international taxation generally. For example, the U.S. adopted CFC rules in 1962, and since then, over fifty countries have enacted similar rules. Similarly, the U.S. has taken the lead in adopting innovative approaches to transfer pricing under the general arm's-length standard, which has been picked up by the OECD with some modifications and used by many countries. More recently, the adoption by the U.S. in 2017 of the Global Intangible Low-taxed Income (GILTI) rules, a minimum tax on the low- taxed foreign source income of U.S. multinationals, has become the basis for the OECD Inclusive Framework's proposed Pillar Two global minimum tax.

2 税收管辖权

2.1 引言

因为一国与某项所得或产生该项所得的活动之间存在联结度，所以，根据该国税法，可对该项所得予以征税。根据国际惯例，基于这种联结度的管辖主张被称为“**来源地管辖权**”。所有征收所得税的国家都行使来源地管辖权，也就是说，它们对发生或来源于本国的所得征税。

因为一国与取得某项所得的人之间存在联结，该国也可能对该项所得征税。这种针对人的所得的管辖主张被称为“**居民管辖权**”。一国居民管辖权适用的人通常应就其全球所得缴税，而无须考虑所得来源，也就是说，该人通常应就其境内来源所得和境外来源所得缴税。

人们常说，多数国家对居民的全球所得征税，对非居民来源于本国的所得征税。尽管这一说法在一定程度上属实，但远未说明多数国家的税制适用范围的详情。所谓对其居民全球所得征税的国家，并不对所有居民的所有全球所得征税。其实，这些国家通常对居民（特别是居民企业）在外国开展积极经营活动取得的所得，以及居民在其中拥有股份的外国公司取得的所得免予征税。同样，所谓按属地征税的国家（即仅对来源于本国的所得征税），通常也会对某些来源于境外的所得征税，例如，居民向非居民为其在境外实施技术服务所支付的费用。

除了少数例外，实施居民管辖权的国家，仅就其认为是居民的个人和法律实体的所得行使该管辖权，这也是“居民管辖权”这一用语的由来。一些国家（美

CHAPTER 2
Jurisdiction to Tax

2.1 INTRODUCTION

Income may be taxable under the tax laws of a country because a nexus exists between that country and the income or activities that generated the income. According to international usage, a jurisdictional claim based on such a nexus is called "**source jurisdiction.**" All countries that impose an income tax exercise source jurisdiction: that is, they tax income arising or having its source in their country.

A country may also impose tax on income because a nexus exists between the country and the person earning the income. Such a jurisdictional claim over a person's income is called "**residence jurisdiction.**" Persons subject to the residence jurisdiction of a country are generally taxable on their worldwide income without reference to the source of the income—that is, the person is typically taxable on both domestic source income and foreign source income.

It is frequently said that most countries tax residents on their worldwide income and nonresidents on their domestic source income. Although this statement contains a grain of truth, it is a gross oversimplification of the scope of the tax systems of most countries. Countries that are said to tax their residents on their worldwide income never tax all their residents on all their worldwide income. Instead, these countries usually exempt their residents (especially resident corporations) from tax on their income from active business carried on in foreign countries and on income earned by foreign corporations in which their residents own shares. Similarly, countries that are said to tax on a **territorial basis**—that is, they tax only income derived from a source in their country—often impose tax on certain items of foreign source income, such as fees paid by residents to nonresidents for technical services performed outside the country.

With few exceptions, countries that exercise residence jurisdiction do so only with respect to the income of individuals and legal entities that they consider to be residents: thus, the

国是其中突出的例子）既对其居民，也对其公民行使税收管辖权。这些国家主张不仅有权对其居民的全球所得征税，而且有权对其公民的全球所得征税，无论他们是哪个国家的居民。

如果一国居民从该国以外取得所得（境外来源所得），则该国根据其居民管辖权对该项所得的征税主张，可能与产生所得的国家基于来源地管辖权对同一所得的征税主张相重叠。各国基于居民管辖权的征税主张，也可能与其他国家基于公民身份的征税主张相重叠，或者在所谓的**双重居民身份纳税人**的情况下，与其他基于居民身份的征税主张相重叠。此外，所得来源地规则有冲突的两个国家，可能对同一所得都要求征税。除非得到令人满意的解决，基于居民和来源地的征税主张的相互冲突将导致双重征税，并阻碍国际贸易和投资。此外，双重征税对从跨境交易中取得所得的个人带来不公平的税收负担，有悖传统的税收公平观念。第 4 章将讨论各国在国内法和税收协定中，为纾解国际双重征税而采取的措施。

尽管从事跨国活动的人面临双重征税的风险，但是，他们也有可能实现国际避税（有时称为双重不征税）。这些机会是由于多数国家的居民管辖权和来源地管辖权之间不衔接，以及这些国家的税收规则不一致而导致的。对跨境交易的所得征税不足，既丧失了税收的效率，又显失公平。之所以说征税不足丧失了税收的效率，是因为它扭曲了经济行为，诱使纳税人从事税负较低的活动，而放弃可能产生较高税前收益率的应税活动。之所以称其显失公平，是因为取得相同数额所得的个人纳税人，没有缴纳相同数额的税收。

避税地国家加剧了对跨国所得征税不足的风险。尽管避税地可以从外国纳税人获得一些税收收入，但与因其行为而使其他税收管辖区损失的税收收入相比则相形见绌。许多国家的税法充满着复杂的规定，旨在保护其合法的税收主张免遭避税地国家以邻为壑的政策和优惠制度的侵害。第 7 章将介绍最重要的反规避规则。

各国为阻止滥用避税地而采取的单边行动通常是无效的，部分原因是来源

term "residence jurisdiction." A few countries—the U.S. is the primary example—exercise jurisdiction to tax their citizens as well as their residents. They assert the right to impose income tax not only on the worldwide income of their residents but also on the worldwide income of their citizens wherever they might be resident.

Where a resident of a country earns income derived outside the country (foreign source income), the claim of that country to tax the income based on its residence jurisdiction may overlap with the claim of the country where the income is earned to tax the same income based on its source jurisdiction. The claims of countries for tax revenue based on residence jurisdiction may also overlap with the claims of other countries based on citizenship or, in the case of so-called **dual-resident taxpayers**, on residence. In addition, countries with conflicting source-of-income rules may both claim to tax the same income. Unless resolved satisfactorily, the competing claims for tax revenue based on residence and source would result in double taxation and discourage international commerce and investment. In addition, the tax burdens imposed on individuals earning income from cross-border transactions would be unfair under traditional concepts of tax equity. The measures that countries have adopted in their domestic legislation and tax treaties to mitigate international double taxation are addressed in Chapter 4.

Although persons engaging in transnational activities face risks of double taxation, they also have possibilities for international tax avoidance (sometimes referred to as double nontaxation). These opportunities result from certain gaps in the residence and source jurisdictions of most countries and inconsistencies between the tax rules of those countries. The under-taxation of income from cross-border transactions is both inefficient and unfair. Under-taxation is inefficient because it distorts economic behavior; it induces taxpayers to engage in under-taxed activities instead of taxable activities that may produce higher before-tax rates of return. It is unfair because individual taxpayers earning equal amounts of income do not pay the same amounts of tax.

Tax haven countries increase the risks of under-taxation of transnational income. Although tax havens may obtain some revenue from foreign taxpayers, the amount is small in comparison with the amount of tax revenue that other taxing jurisdictions lose on account of their conduct. The tax laws of many countries are replete with complex provisions designed to protect their legitimate tax claims against the beggar-thy- neighbor policies and preferential regimes of tax haven countries. The most important anti-avoidance rules are addressed in Chapter 7.

Unilateral action by countries to block tax haven abuses has often been ineffective, in part due to the inability of source and residence countries to obtain information about transactions

国和居民国无法获取有关通过避税地实施交易的信息。时至今日，避税地仍存在着严格的银行保密规定和类似的不披露规定，从而助推了身为其他国家居民的跨国企业和富裕个人的避税和逃税行为。然而，在过去 20 年左右的时间里，通过 OECD 发起和领导的一项不懈行动——银行保密规定得以消除，同时各国之间为防止避税和逃税而进行的信息交换也得到了极大的改善。第 8 章第 8.8.4 节中讨论了近期为促进税收信息交换而做出的努力。

2.2 居民身份的定义

为了对居民（和非居民）征税，一国必须制定将个人和法律实体判定为居民或非居民的规则。下文第 2.2.1 节和 2.2.2 节分别介绍了确定个人和法律实体居民身份的规则。下文第 2.2.3 节讨论了涉及确定居民身份的一些税收协定问题。为了对居民来源于境内和境外的所得征税，显然需要确定居民身份（以及由此确定非居民身份）的规则。为了对非居民来源于本国的所得征税，这一规则也是必要的，因为一些类型的本国来源所得，比如股息和利息，其来源地的确定往往基于支付者的居民身份。

2.2.1 个人的居民身份

理想的居民身份标准，是个人和税务人员能够通过运用该标准，得到清晰、确定且公平的结果。确定性非常有必要，由于居民和非居民的纳税义务不同，因此个人需要知道他们是居民还是非居民，才能遵守一国的税法。然而，简单而确定的居民身份判定标准，可能是武断且不公平的，可能导致许多从事跨国活动的个人最终成为一个以上国家的居民。因此，对于绝大多数纳税人来说，最值得期待的是简单、确定和公平的标准，但还要辅之以更为精细的规则，以应对特殊情况。

在许多国家，个人的居民身份是以广泛的事实和情况标准确定的。个人拥戴

routed through tax havens. Until recently, tax havens had strict bank secrecy rules and similar nondisclosure rules that facilitated tax avoidance and evasion by multinational enterprises and wealthy individuals resident in other countries. In the last two decades, however, through a sustained project initiated and led by the OECD, bank secrecy has been eliminated, and the exchange of information between countries to prevent tax avoidance and evasion has been improved significantly. The recent efforts to facilitate exchange of information for tax purposes are discussed in Chapter 8, section 8.8.4.

2.2 DEFINING RESIDENCE

For taxing residents (and nonresidents), a country must provide rules that classify individuals and legal entities either as residents or nonresidents. The rules for determining the residence of individuals and legal entities are discussed below in sections 2.2.1 and 2.2.2, respectively. Certain tax treaty issues involving the determination of residence are addressed in section 2.2.3 below. The rules for determining residence (and, as a consequence, nonresidence) are clearly necessary for taxing residents on their domestic and foreign source income and for taxing nonresidents on their domestic source income since the source of some types of domestic source income, such as dividends and interest, is usually based on the residence of the payer.

2.2.1 Residence of Individuals

An ideal test of residence is one that individuals and tax officials can apply to obtain a clear, certain, and fair result. Certainty is highly desirable because the tax consequences for residents and nonresidents are different, and individuals need to know whether they are resident or nonresident in order to comply with a country's tax law. Nevertheless, a simple and certain test for residence may be arbitrary and unfair and may result in many individuals who engage in cross-border activities ending up as residents of more than one country. Therefore, the most that can be expected is a test that is simple, certain, and fair for the overwhelming majority of taxpayers but that is supplemented by more refined rules to deal with special circumstances.

In many countries, the residence of individuals is determined under a broad facts-and-circumstances test. The most significant manifestation of an individual's allegiance to a country is probably the maintenance in the country of a dwelling that is available for the use of the

某个国家的最重要表现，可能是在该国保有可供自己及其家庭使用的住处。以下因素通常也是相关的：

——个人产生所得的活动的地点；
——个人的家庭所在地；
——个人与国家的社会联系（例如，银行账户，俱乐部会员资格和驾驶执照）；
——个人的签证和移民身份；以及
——个人在该国实际停留的程度。

以此为标准，一国的税务机关主要根据客观事实，来判断某个人与该国的经济和社会联系，是否构成将该个人作为居民予以征税的正当理由。

除非得到一些简单推定的支持，否则，这种事实和情况标准由于既不确定，又难以实施，故而并不令人满意。事实和情况标准使用某些客观的检验，来建立推定的话，可以在确定性和公平性之间取得良好的平衡。这种标准的应用，在纳税人试图放弃一国居民身份的情况下，应该比纳税人取得一国的居民身份情况下更加严格。以下推定可以单独或组合使用，以形成对居民身份的初步判断：

——在一个纳税年度中，在一个国家停留183天或以上的个人在该年度为居民，除非他们证明自己在该国没有住处，且不是该国公民。
——在该国有住处的个人为居民，除非他们在另一个国家也有住处。
——一个国家的公民是居民，除非他们已在境外有住处，并且通常每年有183天以上在境外停留。
——在一个国家有住所的个人可以被视为该国居民。
——暂时离开某个国家但打算返回，并在该国继续居住的个人，尽管存在临时离境，仍然可以推定其依旧是该国居民。不过对于这种推定可能存在不同意见。
——在一个国家确立了居民身份的个人不能放弃居民身份，直至其在另一

individual and his or her family. The following factors are also usually relevant:

– the location of the individual's income-producing activities;
– the location of the individual's family;
– the social ties of the individual to the country (e.g., bank accounts, club memberships, and driver's license);
– the individual's visa and immigration status; and
– the extent of the individual's actual physical presence in the country.

Under this test, the tax authorities of a country decide, based largely on objective facts, whether an individual's economic and social connections with the country justify taxing the individual as a resident.

Unless buttressed by some simple presumptions, a facts-and-circumstances test is unsatisfactory because it is uncertain and difficult to apply. A facts-and-circumstances test that uses certain objective tests to establish presumptions may provide a good balance between certainty and fairness. It may be appropriate for such a test to apply more rigorously in situations in which a taxpayer is attempting to give up residence in a country than in situations in which a taxpayer is acquiring residence in a country. The following presumptions might be used, separately or in combination, to establish a prima facie case for residence:

– Individuals present in a country for 183 days or more in a taxable year are residents for that year unless perhaps they establish that they do not have a dwelling in the country and are not citizens of the country.
– Individuals that have a dwelling in the country are residents unless they also have a dwelling in another country.
– Citizens of a country are residents unless they have established a dwelling abroad and are regularly outside the country for more than 183 days per year.
– Individuals who are domiciled in a country may be considered to be residents of that country.
– Individuals who are temporarily absent from a country but intend to return and resume residence in the country may be presumed to remain residents of the country despite their temporary absence, subject to the rebuttal of that presumption.
– Individuals who have established residence in a country cannot relinquish residence status until they have clearly established residence status in another country.

个国家清晰地确立了居民身份。

—— 出于签证或移民目的而具有居民身份或非居民身份的个人，可能为所得税目的被推定具有相同的身份，尽管该推定可能会被推翻。

针对某些个人，可能需要特殊的规则。例如，应当将外交官、军事人员和其他政府雇员视为雇用这些人员的国家的居民，尽管按照事实和情况标准，这些个人因为大多数时间都在国外，未被判定为居民。

一些国家使用相当随意的规则来确定居民身份，该规则通常与在该国停留的天数有关。此类规则可以作为上述事实和情况规则的补充。常见但有缺陷的规则或推定是，将当年在一个国家中停留至少 183 天的个人在该年度视为居民。183 **天规则**可能在对边界实行严格控制的国家能够得以执行；但是，当许多个人频繁进入和离开该国而无须边境检查时，例如在欧盟成员国所发生的情况，特别是对于通常适用特殊规则的跨境工作人士，一国的税务机关就很难执行此项规则。在大多数国家，除非个人承担举证责任，证明其没有停留 183 天，否则，该规则可能无法有效执行。许多与一国存在实质性经济联系的个人，通过在 183 天期满之前离开该国家，可以轻易避免根据 183 天规则成为居民。结果，使用该规则的国家很可能关注的主要是不老练或无专业帮手的个人，而其中有些人可能实际上与该国并没有实质性的联系。

一些国家将在该国拥有住所的个人视为居民。根据某些国家的法律，“住所”是一个法律概念，通过这一概念可以建立个人与一个国家的永久联系。一般而言，住所所涉及的与一国的联系比居住更为永久。一个人的住所可以是在该人出生所在的国家，也可以是其父母的住所。OECD 协定范本和联合国协定范本第 4 条第 1 款提到住所，并以此作为界定居民身份的依据。

– Individuals who have either resident or nonresident status for visa or immigration purposes might be presumed to have the same status for income tax purposes, although that presumption might be rebuttable.

Special rules may be necessary for certain individuals. For example, it may be appropriate to deem diplomats, military personnel, and other government employees to be residents of the country that employs them despite the fact that these individuals might not be residents on the basis of a facts-and-circumstances test because they spend most of their time outside the country.

Some countries use an arbitrary test, often tied to the number of days of presence in the country, for determining residence. Such a test may be used as a supplement to the facts-and-circumstances test discussed above. A common, but defective, rule or presumption is that an individual who is present in a country for at least 183 days during the year is deemed to be a resident for that year. The **183-day test** is probably enforceable in countries that exercise tight control over their borders; however, it is extremely difficult for the tax authorities of a country to enforce when many individuals are frequently entering and leaving the country without border checks, as occurs in the countries of the European Union (EU), especially with respect to cross-border workers who are often subject to special rules. In most countries, the test probably cannot operate effectively unless the burden of proof is put on the individual to prove that he or she is not present for the 183-day period. Many individuals with substantial economic ties to a country can easily avoid becoming resident under the 183-day test by leaving the country before the 183-day threshold is passed. As a result, a country using that test is likely to catch mainly unsophisticated or ill-advised individuals, some of whom may not, in fact, have substantial ties to that country.

Some countries consider individuals who have their domicile in the country to be resident there. Domicile is a legal concept under the law of some countries by which an individual's permanent connection with a country is established. In general, domicile involves a more permanent connection with a country than a residence. A person's domicile may be the country in which the person is born or in which the person's mother or father is domiciled. Domicile is mentioned in Article 4(1) of the OECD and UN Model Treaties as a ground for defining residence.

2.2.2 法律实体的居民身份

公司的居民身份通常通过参照其注册地或管理机构所在地，或两者兼而有之来确定。**公司注册地标准**不仅为税务机关和公司提供了简便性和确定性，而且还允许公司自由选择其最初的居民身份归属地。那些将自己作为避税地的国家，通常会提供方便和廉价的安排，以便根据其法律进行公司注册。

一般而言，公司不能在不就其财产累积的收益（包括可能具有较高市场价值的无形财产）缴税的情况下，自由地更改其注册地。因此，注册地标准对公司为避税而转移居民身份的能力设置了一些限制。许多国家使用注册地标准，但通常与其他标准结合使用。但是，美国是完全依赖于注册地标准的国家之一。

对于从事国际业务的许多公司而言，在任何特定纳税年度内，可能在多个国家进行管理活动。因此，至少在理论上，**管理机构所在地标准**在其应用中，比注册地标准的确定性差。实际上，大多数使用该标准的国家都依据更实用的检测，例如，公司总部所在地，或公司董事会（或对公司事务负有最终责任和控制权的类似机构）举行会议的地点，来确定管理机构所在地。英国以及许多其前殖民地使用管理机构所在地标准。一些国家，例如，澳大利亚、加拿大和英国，同时使用注册地标准和管理机构所在地标准。

管理机构所在地标准很容易被用于避税目的，因为纳税人可以在不触发任何税收的情况下，完成管理机构所在地的变更。假定 A 公司是 A 国的居民公司，该国使用管理机构所在地标准。A 公司已开发了有价值的无形财产，打算将其许可给位于 B 国的纳税人。为了避免在 A 国就预期的特许权使用费缴税，A 公司将其管理机构所在地转移到 H 国（低税率国家）。A 公司无形资产累积的巨额收益在 A 国不必纳税，因为该资产没有发生转移。（但是，如第 3 章第 3.4.1 节中所述，一些国家已经采用了**退出税或离境税**，以防止纳税人通过更改居民身份避税。）A 公司接下来将该技术许可给 B 国的用户。由于 A 公司不再是 A 国居民，

2.2.2 Residence of Legal Entities

The residence of a corporation is generally determined by reference either to its place of incorporation or to its place of management, or both. The **place-of-incorporation test** provides simplicity and certainty to the tax authorities and corporations and also allows corporations to freely choose their initial place of residence. Countries that market themselves as tax havens typically offer convenient and inexpensive arrangements for incorporating under their laws.

In general, a corporation cannot freely change its place of incorporation without triggering a tax on gains that may have accrued in respect of its property, including intangible property that may have a high market value. Consequently, the place-of-incorporation test places some limits on the ability of corporations to shift their country of residence for tax avoidance purposes. Many countries use the place-of-incorporation test, although it is often combined with another test. However, the U.S. is a country that relies exclusively on a place-of-incorporation test.

For many corporations engaged in international operations, management activities may be conducted in several countries during any particular taxable year; as a result, the **place-of-management test** is less certain in its application than a place-of-incorporation test, at least in theory. In practice, most countries using that test employ practical tests, such as the location of the company's head office or the place where the board of directors of the company (or the equivalent body with ultimate responsibility for and control of the affairs of a company) meets, to determine the place of management. The place-of-management test is used by the U.K. and many of its former colonies. Some countries, such as Australia, Canada, and the U.K., use both the place-of-incorporation test and the place-of-management test.

A place-of-management test is easily exploited for tax avoidance purposes where a change in the place of management can be accomplished without triggering any tax. Assume, for example, that ACo is a corporation resident in Country A, which uses a place-of-management test. ACo has developed valuable intangible property that it intends to license to taxpayers located in Country B. To avoid tax in Country A on the expected royalties, ACo shifts its place of management to Country H, a low-tax country. The large accrued gain on ACo's intangible property is not taxable in Country A because no transfer of that property occurred. (However, as discussed in Chapter 3, section 3.4.1, several countries have adopted **exit or departure taxes** to prevent taxpayers from avoiding tax by changing their residence.) ACo then licenses the

因此 A 公司收取的特许权使用费规避了 A 国税收。

如果上例中的 A 国使用注册地标准，则 A 公司不能在不进行公司重组的情况下将其居民身份转移到 H 国，这可能会导致将其资产转让给在 H 国成立的公司。这样的转让将触发无形资产应计收益的实现，从而限制甚至消除 A 公司的避税机会。

仅使用公司注册地标准的国家（如美国）遇到了被称为公司倒置的避税筹划。通过这种筹划，跨国居民企业通过重组避免居民国税收，或利用其税收制度带来的某些好处。尽管倒置可以采用多种形式，并且总是相当复杂，但下面的简化示例说明了其总体思路。

假设 US 公司是一家总部位于美国的跨国公司，其股份的持有相当分散。该公司希望避免受到（在第 7 章第 7.3 节中讨论的）美国 CFC 规则的影响。为此，它在没有 CFC 规则的国家设立子公司（Forco），然后，安排其股东将其持有的 US 公司股份换成 Forco 的股份，并将所有 US 公司的外国子公司的股份转让给 Forco。最终结果是，就其任何美国股东而言，Forco 都不是受控外国企业，并且美国 CFC 规则不再适用于 US 公司，因为其外国子公司已成为 Forco 的子公司。

许多评论人士认为，公司所得税的恰当目的是通过公司对个人股东施加税收负担。根据这种观点，公司所得税是让公司代表个人股东预先缴纳，以防止其通过投资于公司而递延纳税。因为如果没有公司所得税，在取得股息或出售股份之前，个人股东不会就通过公司获得的所得缴税。因此，至少在理论上，可以参照公司股东的居民身份，作为确定公司居民身份的标准。但是，当一个以上国家的居民在公司中持有大量股份时，或者当公司的股票公开交易且股东的身份难以确定时，使用股东居民身份标准将产生严重的问题。从这种观点出发按逻辑得出的结论是，实际上，必须像对合伙企业一样对公司征税，每个国家都要对公司所得中居民股东应得的份额征税。

对于公司以外的法人实体，各国通常根据组织机构所在地标准，或管理机构所在地标准，确定居民身份。由于建立合伙企业的非规范性，有时候很难确定合

technology to users in Country B. The royalties received by ACo escape taxation in Country A because ACo is no longer resident in Country A.

If Country A, in the above example, used the place-of-incorporation test, ACo could not transfer its residence to Country H without undergoing a corporate reorganization that would probably result in the transfer of its assets to a corporation organized in Country H. Such a transfer would trigger a realization of the accrued gain on the intangible property, thereby limiting or even eliminating ACo's opportunity for tax avoidance.

Countries that use a place-of-incorporation test exclusively (such as the U.S.) have encountered avoidance schemes called corporate inversions, whereby resident multinationals reorganize to avoid or take advantage of certain aspects of the residence country's tax system. Although inversions take many forms and are invariably quite complex, the following simplified example illustrates the general idea.

Assume that USCo, a widely held U.S.-based multinational, wants to avoid the effects of the U.S. CFC rules (discussed in Chapter 7, section 7.3). To do so, it establishes a subsidiary (Forco) in a country without CFC rules and then arranges for its shareholders to exchange their shares of USCo for shares of Forco and for the shares of all USCo's foreign subsidiaries to be transferred to Forco. The end result is that Forco is not a CFC in respect of any of its U.S. shareholders, and the U.S. CFC rules are no longer applicable to USCo because its foreign subsidiaries have become subsidiaries of Forco.

Many commentators argue that the proper purpose of the corporate tax is to impose tax burdens on a corporation's individual shareholders. According to this view, the corporate tax is paid in advance on behalf of the individual shareholders of the corporation to prevent them from deferring tax by investing in corporations; otherwise, the individual shareholders would not pay tax on the income earned through the corporation until they received dividends or sold their shares. Therefore, the test of residence of a corporation might be determined, at least in theory, by reference to the residence of its shareholders. However, the application of a residence-of-the-shareholders test would present serious problems when residents of more than one country hold large blocks of stock in a company or when the stock of the company is publicly traded, and the identity of the shareholders is difficult to determine. Taking this view to its logical conclusion, in effect, corporations would have to be taxed like partnerships, with each country taxing the share of the corporate income attributable to its resident shareholders.

For legal entities other than corporations, residence is generally determined under either a place-of-organization test or a place-of-management test. Determining the residence of a

伙企业的居民身份。例如，在一些国家，可以根据相关方的行为建立合伙关系，而无须任何正式的法律文件。在许多国家，合伙企业在税收上被视为透明或穿透实体；换言之，由合伙人就其在合伙企业所得中的份额纳税，而合伙企业本身无须纳税。对于这些国家，合伙企业的居民身份通常是无关紧要的，因为合伙企业不是应税实体。

在根据一些国家的法律确定信托机构的居民身份时，也可能会遇到棘手的问题。当信托的注册国家、各受托人为其居民的国家、授予人或委托人所在的国家，以及受益人所在的国家均不相同时，问题尤为棘手。根据其国内法不承认信托概念的大陆法系国家也遭遇了难题。

2.2.3 与居民身份有关的协定问题

根据OECD协定范本第4条第1款，协定中一国的“居民”是指“由于住所、居所、管理机构所在地或任何其他类似标准”，在该国负有纳税义务的人。联合国协定范本第4条第1款将“注册地”列入“相关因素”清单。为避免个人在两个国家均被视为居民的情况，两个协定范本的第4条第2款都规定了一系列**加比规则**，以使协定中的个人仅在一个国家构成居民。第一项加比规则是一个人拥有永久住所的地方；第二项是个人重要利益中心所在的国家；第三项是个人习惯性居住的地方；第四项是国籍所在的国家。如果这些加比规则不能在协定目的下，有效地使个人仅成为一个国家的居民，则两个缔约国的“**主管当局**”有权根据OECD协定范本和联合国协定范本第25条**相互协商程序**（MAP）确定居民身份。大多数现代税收协定都严格遵守OECD协定范本和联合国协定范本中针对个人的加比规则。

对于在两个国家均构成居民的法律实体，在2017年前，OECD协定范本和联合国协定范本的第4条第3款的加比规则都规定该实体是其实际管理机构所在国家的居民。根据先前关于第4条的**注释**，实体的实际管理机构所在地就是关键

partnership is sometimes difficult because of the informality with which a partnership can be established; for example, in some countries, a partnership may be created by virtue of the course of conduct of the relevant parties without the necessity for any formal legal documentation. In many countries, partnerships are treated as transparent or flow-through entities for tax purposes; in other words, the partners are taxed on their share of the income of a partnership, but the partnership itself is not taxed. For these countries, the residence of a partnership is usually irrelevant because the partnership is not a taxable entity.

Difficult problems also can arise under the laws of some countries in determining the residence of trusts. These problems are especially difficult when the country of organization, the country where the trustee or trustees are resident, the country where the grantor or settlor is located, and the countries where the beneficiaries are located are all different. Difficulties also arise for civil law countries that do not recognize the trust concept under their domestic law.

2.2.3 Treaty Issues Relating to Residence

Under Article 4(1) of the OECD Model Treaty, a "resident" of a country for purposes of the treaty is a person who is liable to tax in that country "by reason of his domicile, residence, place of management or any other criterion of a similar nature." Article 4(1) of the UN Model Treaty adds "place of incorporation" to the list of connecting factors. To avoid situations in which an individual is considered to be resident in both countries, Article 4(2) of both Models provides a series of **tie-breaker rules** to make the individual resident in only one country for purposes of the treaty. The first tie-breaker is the place where an individual has a permanent home; the second is the country in which the center of the individual's vital interests is located; the third is the place of the individual's habitual dwelling; and the fourth is the country of citizenship. If these tie-breaker rules are ineffective in making an individual a resident of only one country for treaty purposes, the "**competent authorities**" of the two contracting states are mandated to determine residence pursuant to the **Mutual Agreement Procedure (MAP)** in Article 25 of the OECD and UN Model Treaties. Most modern tax treaties follow the tie-breaker rules for individuals in the OECD and UN Model Treaties closely.

For legal entities resident in both contracting states, until 2017, the tie-breaker rule in Article 4(3) of the OECD and UN Model Treaties provided that the entity was a resident of the country where its place of effective management was located. According to the prior **Commentary** on Article 4, the place of effective management of an entity was the place where

管理活动和商业决策实际作出的地方，即最高管理层就最重要的管理问题进行决策的地方。此外，根据注释，一个实体只能有一个实际管理机构所在地，尽管它可以有多个管理机构所在地。

实际管理机构所在地的加比规则常常难以应用，在许多国家中并不受欢迎，在许多双边协定中也没有使用。大多数双重居民实体都是出于避税目的而设立的。例如，一家具有双重居民身份的亏损公司可能有权在其为居民的两个国家都享受亏损的扣除。因此，许多协定规定，在多数协定条款下，双重居民实体不被视为任何一个国家的居民；其结果是，这样的实体无权享受协定的任何待遇。

2017 年，OECD 协定范本和联合国协定范本均对第 4 条第 3 款进行了修订，规定主管当局“应尽力”通过考量实际管理机构所在地、注册地或创立地，以及其他相关因素，以确立双重居民法律实体的居民身份。如果主管当局不能取得一致意见，则该实体除非主管当局另商同意，无权享受任何协定待遇。

美国坚持在其税收协定中包含通常所称的“保留条款”（有时被错误地称为“救助条款”）。典型的保留条款规定，除了某些例外，美国保留对居民和公民征税的权利，如同该协定未曾生效。例如，美国公民是某协定国居民的，无权享受协定中针对从美国取得股息所规定的减低预提税率。

2017 年，对 OECD 协定范本和联合国协定范本进行了修正，在第 1 条第 3 款中加入了类似的保留条款，规定除了某些例外，“本协定不得影响缔约国对其居民的征税。”

2.3 来源地管辖权

2.3.1 引言

按照国际惯例，一国对从本国发生、来源于本国，或从本国取得的所得，拥有首要征税权。如第 3 章所述，根据国际惯例，如果一国的居民管辖权与另一

key management and commercial decisions are in substance made—the place where decision-making at the highest level on the most important issues of management takes place. Moreover, according to the Commentary, an entity could have only one place of effective management, although it could have multiple places of management.

The place-of-effective-management tie-breaker rule was often difficult to apply, was not viewed favorably by many countries, and was not used in many bilateral treaties. Most dual-resident entities are established for tax avoidance purposes; for example, a dual-resident company with losses might be entitled to relief for such losses in both countries in which it is resident. Therefore, many treaties provide that a dual-resident entity is not considered to be a resident of either country for most treaty purposes; as a result, such an entity is not entitled to any of the benefits of the treaty.

In 2017, Article 4(3) of both the OECD and UN Model Treaties was amended to provide that the competent authorities "shall endeavor" to establish the residence of a dual-resident legal entity, taking into account its place of effective management, place of incorporation or creation, and other relevant factors. If the competent authorities cannot agree, the entity is not entitled to any treaty benefits except to the extent agreed by the competent authorities.

The U.S. insists on the inclusion in its tax treaties of what is commonly referred to as a "saving clause" (and sometimes mistakenly referred to as a "savings clause"). The typical saving clause provides, with some exceptions, that the U.S. reserves the right to tax its residents and its citizens as if the treaty had not come into effect. For example, a U.S. citizen resident in a treaty country is not entitled to the reduced rate of withholding provided in the treaty on dividends received from the U.S.

In 2017, the OECD and UN Model Treaties were amended to include a similar saving clause in Article 1(3), providing that, subject to certain exceptions, "[T]his Convention shall not affect the taxation, by a Contracting State, of its residents."

2.3 SOURCE JURISDICTION

2.3.1 Introduction

By international custom, a country has the primary right to tax income that arises in, has its source in, or is derived from that country. As discussed in Chapter 3, under international custom, the country of residence is generally expected to provide relief from double taxation

国的来源地管辖权相重叠，则居民国通常应该对双重征税给予纾解。换句话说，纳税人为其居民的国家仅拥有对纳税人从另一个国家取得或来源于另一个国家的所得的次要征税权。大多数税收协定都规定，所得的来源国有权首先对该所得征税，而居民国有义务消除对该所得的双重征税。尽管税收协定赋予了一国对来源于该国的所得征税的首要权利，但是协定通常规定，该来源国必须限制其对某些类别的投资所得课税的税率，并且还禁止来源国对某些类别的所得征税，即使这些所得发生于来源国。

尽管将优先权赋予来源地管辖区，但是，在国内税收立法和税收协定中，来源地的概念并未得到清晰的表述。与用语“居民身份”不同，国内法或税收协定未明确使用或定义“来源地”一词。因此，来源地规则通常隐含在其他规则中。例如，对居民支付给非居民的款项，如股息、利息和特许权使用费，征收预提税有一个隐含的来源地规则，即如果这些款项是由某一国家居民支付的，则该款项即来源于这个国家。

大多数国家对确定所得来源地只有粗略的规则，特别是对来自经营活动的所得。例如，在英国和前英国殖民地的国家中，从经营活动中取得所得的来源地被认为是实际经营活动的发生地。这样的规则太含糊，无法为纳税人或税务人员提供任何有意义的指导。

OECD 协定范本和联合国协定范本将隐含的来源地规则和能有效充当来源地规则的规则相结合。例如，根据第 11 条第 4 款，利息所得应由支付方为其居民的国家征税。又如，根据第 6 条，不动产产生的所得，包括矿山、石油或天然气井运营产生的所得，由不动产所在的国家征税。但是，OECD 协定范本和联合国协定范本没有包含针对营业利润的任何明确的来源地规则。根据第 7 条，缔约国一方居民取得的营业利润，仅在该居民通过位于缔约国另一方的常设机构进行营业的情况下，才应被缔约国另一方征税（第 7 条），并且仅限于归属于常设机构的利润。这项规则在功能上等同于来源地规则。

一般而言，根据 OECD 协定范本和联合国协定范本第 5 条，常设机构被定

where its residence jurisdiction overlaps the source jurisdiction of another country. In other words, the country in which a taxpayer is resident has only a secondary right to tax the taxpayer's income that is derived from or sourced in another country. Most tax treaties provide that the country in which income is sourced has the first right to tax that income and that the country of residence has an obligation to eliminate double taxation of that income. Although tax treaties give a country the first right to tax income sourced in the country, they usually provide that the source country must limit its rate of tax on certain categories of investment income and also preclude the source country from taxing certain categories of income, even where the income arises in the source country.

Despite the priority given to source jurisdiction, the concept of source is rather poorly developed in domestic tax legislation and tax treaties. Unlike the term "residence," the term "source" is not used or defined explicitly in domestic law or tax treaties. As a result, source rules are usually implicit in other rules. For example, withholding tax imposed on amounts paid by residents to nonresidents, such as dividends, interest, and royalties, has an implicit source rule that such amounts are sourced in a country if they are paid by a resident of the country.

Most countries have only sketchy rules for determining the source of income, especially income derived from business activities. For example, in the U.K. and countries that were former U.K. colonies, income from business activities is considered to have its source where the real business is carried on. Such a rule is too vague to provide any meaningful guidance to taxpayers or tax officials.

The OECD and UN Model Treaties provide a mixture of implicit source rules and rules that function effectively as source rules. For example, under Article 11(4), interest income is taxable by the country in which the payer is resident, and under Article 6, income derived from immovable property, including income arising from the operation of a mine or oil or gas well, is taxable by the country where the immovable property is located. However, the OECD and UN Model Treaties do not contain any explicit source rules for business profits. Under Article 7, business profits derived by a resident of one contracting state are taxable by the other contracting state only where the resident carries on business through a **Permanent Establishment ("PE")** located in that other state (Article 7) and only to the extent that the profits are attributable to the PE. This rule is the functional equivalent of a source rule.

In general, under Article 5 of the OECD and UN Model Treaties, a PE is defined to be a fixed place of business, such as an office, branch, factory, or mine, and also

义为固定的经营场所，例如，办公室、分支机构、工厂或矿山，并且还包括在某些情况下代表他人行事的人（所谓的非独立代理人常设机构）。但是，这些规则有几个例外和特殊规定。有关税收协定中对常设机构的定义进行的其他讨论，参见第 8 章第 8.7.3.2 节。OECD 协定范本和联合国协定范本的某些条款，例如，第 21 条（其他所得）措辞笼统，仅指在缔约国一方发生的所得，并没有进一步的阐述。在这种情况下，似乎不可避免地必须根据适用该协定的国家的国内法来确定这一具体所得的来源。

好的来源地规则应具有以下特征：

—— 应为许多国家广泛接受，以确保消除双重征税且不助长双重不征税。

—— 应在大多数国家普遍接受的合理基础上，划分所得和税收。

—— 对于纳税人和税务人员来说，执行起来应该相对清晰简单。

—— 应在对等的基础上适用（即一国不应单方面采用某项来源地规则，却反对另一个国家采用该来源地规则）。

—— 应将所得划分到与该所得有重要经济联系的国家（用 OECD BEPS 项目的语言来说，所得应在增加或创造价值所在的国家征税）。

—— 不应受到纳税人的操纵。

—— 不应将所得划分给不征税的国家。

下面的讨论通常适用于受雇所得、个人劳务所得、经营所得和投资所得的来源地规则，同时一并讨论 OECD 协定范本和联合国协定范本中包含的这些类型所得的来源地规则。

2.3.2 受雇所得和个人劳务所得

许多国家的一般规则是，由员工、独立承包商或专业人士提供个人劳务取得的所得的来源地是其提供劳务的所在国。如果纳税人因在多个国家提供劳务而获

includes a person acting on behalf of another person (a so-called dependent-agent PE) in some circumstances. However, these rules are subject to several exceptions and special provisions. For additional discussion of the definition of a PE for purposes of tax treaties, *see* Chapter 8, section 8.7.3.2.

Some provisions of the OECD and UN Model Treaties, such as Article 21 (Other Income), contain general wording that refers to income arising in a contracting state without any further elaboration. In these circumstances, it seems inevitable that the source of income for that particular purpose must be determined under the domestic law of the country applying the treaty.

Good source rules should have the following characteristics:

- They should be broadly acceptable to many countries in order to ensure that double taxation is eliminated and double nontaxation is not facilitated.
- They should allocate income and tax on a reasonable basis that is broadly acceptable to most countries.
- They should be relatively clear and simple for taxpayers and tax officials to apply.
- They should be applicable on a reciprocal basis (i.e., a country should not unilaterally adopt a source rule that it would object to another country adopting).
- They should allocate income to a country where the income has a substantial economic connection (in the language of the OECD's BEPS project, income should be taxable in the country where value is added or created).
- They should not be subject to manipulation by taxpayers.
- They should not allocate income to countries that do not impose tax.

The source rules that are generally applicable to employment and personal services income, business income, and investment income are discussed below. The source rules for these types of income contained in the OECD and UN Model Treaties are also discussed.

2.3.2 Employment and Personal Services Income

The general rule in many countries is that income derived from personal services performed by employees, independent contractors, or professionals has its source in the country where the services are performed. Difficult allocation issues may arise where a taxpayer is paid for services performed in more than one country. Allocation among the countries where an

得付款，可能会产生分配难题。在个人提供劳务的多个国家之间分配所得通常至少部分地基于个人在每个国家提供劳务所花费的时间。一些国家（包括一些南美和拉美国家）认为，如果劳务是（由顾客或客户）在本国消费或使用，即使该劳务是在境外提供的，该劳务所得也应视为来源于本国。

根据联合国协定范本第 14 条，只有服务提供者在来源国具有可以定期使用的**固定基地**（相当于常设机构），或在任意 12 个月内在来源国停留时间至少达到 183 天的情况下，由专业人士和其他独立承包商提供服务取得的所得，才应在提供服务的国家征税。OECD 协定范本在 2000 年取消第 14 条之前，规定了类似的除外情形。在遵循 OECD 协定范本的税收协定中，来自专业性服务和其他独立劳务的所得，应根据第 7 条，作为营业利润征税，并且可以免除在一国纳税，除非劳务提供者在该国拥有常设机构（而不是固定基地）。根据联合国协定范本第 5 条第 3 款（2）项，缔约国一方的居民纳税人如果在开始或结束于当年的任意 12 个月期间内，通过雇员或其他人员在另一国提供劳务的时间超过 183 天，则视为在另一国拥有常设机构。关于 OECD 协定范本第 5 条的注释也规定了类似的视同服务型 PE 的规则，可供各国选择采用。

从 OECD 协定范本中删除第 14 条的作用之一，是澄清第 5 条第 4 款中，准备性和辅助性活动对于常设机构的各种除外情况，以及第 5 条第 5 款和第 6 款中的代理型常设机构规则也同等适用于来自专业性和独立性劳务及其他经营活动的所得。在联合国协定范本下，这两个问题仍未解决，因为第 14 条没有任何关于准备性或辅助性活动的例外，也没有针对代理人的任何特殊规则。

联合国协定范本在 2017 年被修订，增加了第 12A 条，涉及技术服务费的征税。根据第 12A 条第 2 款，如果技术服务费发生于缔约国一方，则该国有权按缔约国双方同意的税率，对付款总额征税。如果费用由一国居民支付或由在该国拥有常设机构的非居民支付，且该费用在计算归属于常设机构的利润时得以扣除，则技术服务费被认为来源于该国。技术服务费，是指咨询、技术和管理费，但不包括支付给员工的费用，为个人劳务支付的费用，以及为在教育机构内进行教学

individual performs services is typically based, at least in part, on the amount of time spent by the individual performing the services in each country. Some countries, including several South American and Latin American countries, consider income from services to be derived in their countries if the services are consumed or used (by customers or clients) in their countries, even if the services are performed outside their countries.

Under Article 14 of the UN Model Treaty, income from services derived by professionals and other independent contractors is taxable by the country in which the services are performed only if the service provider has a **fixed base** (which is equivalent to a PE) regularly available in the source country or spends at least 183 days in any 12 month period in the source country. The OECD Model Treaty provided a similar exemption until the elimination of Article 14 in 2000. In tax treaties following the OECD Model Treaty, income from professional and other independent services is taxable as business profits under Article 7 and is exempt from tax by a country unless the service provider has a PE (rather than a fixed base) in that country. Under Article 5(3)(b) of the UN Model Treaty, a taxpayer resident in one contracting state is deemed to have a PE in the other state if the taxpayer furnishes services in the other state through employees or other personnel for a period of more than 183 days in any 12 month period beginning or ending in the year. The Commentary on Article 5 of the OECD Model Treaty provides a similar deemed services PE rule as an alternative provision that countries may adopt.

One effect of eliminating Article 14 from the OECD Model Treaty has been to clarify that the various exceptions to PE status for preparatory and auxiliary activities in Article 5(4) and the agency PE rules in Article 5(5) and (6) are equally applicable to income from professional and independent services, as well as other business activities. Both of these issues remain unresolved under the UN Model Treaty because Article 14 does not contain any exception for preparatory or auxiliary activities or any special rules for agents.

In 2017, the UN Model Treaty was amended to add Article 12A to deal with the taxation of fees for technical services. Under Article 12A(2), where fees for technical services arise in a contracting state, that state is entitled to impose tax on the gross amount of the payment at a rate to be agreed on by the contracting states. Fees for technical services are considered to arise in a state where the fees are paid by a resident or a nonresident with a PE in that state, and the fees are deductible in computing the profits attributable to the PE. Fees for technical services are defined to mean consulting, technical, and management fees but do not include amounts paid to employees, amounts paid for personal services, and amounts paid for teaching in or by educational institutions. (*See* Chapter 9, section 9.3.3 for a more detailed

或由教育机构支付的费用。（关于根据联合国协定范本第 12A 条，对技术服务费处理更加详细的讨论，参见第 9 章第 9.3.3 节。）

OECD 协定范本和联合国协定范本第 15 条均规定，除在来源国从事受雇活动以外，受雇所得仅应由雇员为其居民的国家征税。在来源国从事受雇活动时，只有在以下情况下，该国才有权对在该国从事受雇活动产生的所得征税：

（1）该雇员在来源国停留了 183 天或更长时间；或者

（2）该雇员的报酬是由来源国的居民雇主支付或代表该雇主支付；或者

（3）在计算可归属于非居民雇主在来源国的常设机构的利润时，该雇员的报酬可以扣除。

换句话说，缔约国一方的居民雇员为缔约国另一方的居民雇主（或在该国拥有常设机构的非居民雇主）提供受雇服务取得的所得，如果雇员的报酬由常设机构负担，那么，就可以在该另一方征税。否则，缔约国一方的居民雇员在缔约国另一方从事受雇活动取得的所得，只有该雇员在开始或结束于相关年度的任意 12 个月的期间内，在另一方停留 183 天或以上，该另一方才可以征税。（参见第 8 章第 8.7.3.3 节）。如果雇员是一个国家的税收居民，需要就其在另一个国家取得的受雇所得交税，则该所得将被双重征税，如第 4 章所述，居民国通常会就其从境外取得的受雇所得缴纳的境外税款给予抵免，抵减该境外受雇所得对应的税额。

2.3.3 经营所得

来源国对经营所得征税的差异很大。但是，有两种一般模式应予以关注。与 OECD 协定范本和联合国协定范本第 7 条相一致的最普遍的模式是，只有当纳税人通过位于一国的常设机构开展经营活动，并且所得可归属于该常设机构时，经营所得才会被该国征税。在这些制度中，常设机构规则不仅充当来源国征税的门槛，而且还是用来确定应税所得（即“可归属于”常设机构的所得）的手段。大

discussion of the treatment of fees for technical services under Article 12A of the UN Model Treaty.)

Article 15 of both the OECD Model Treaty and the UN Model Treaty provides that income from employment is taxable exclusively by the country in which an employee is resident unless the employment is exercised in the source country. Where the employment is exercised in the source country, that country is entitled to tax the income from employment exercised in that country only if:

(1) the employee is present in the source country for 183 days or more; or
(2) the employee is paid by or on behalf of an employer resident in the source country; or
(3) the employee's remuneration is deductible in computing the profits attributable to a PE in the source country of a nonresident employer.

In other words, an employee resident in one contracting state will be taxable by the other state on any income from employment duties performed in the other state for an employer resident in that state (or a nonresident employer with a PE in that state if the employee's remuneration is borne by the PE). Otherwise, income of an employee resident in one contracting state from employment exercised in the other contracting state is taxable by that other state only if the employee is present in the other state for 183 days or more in any twelve-month period beginning or ending in the relevant year (*see* Chapter 8, section 8.7.3.3). Where an employee resident in one country is subject to tax on employment income earned in another country, the income will be subject to double taxation, which will usually be relieved by the residence country giving a credit against its tax on the foreign employment income for the foreign tax on that income, as discussed in Chapter 4.

2.3.3 Business Income

The taxation of business income by source countries varies considerably. However, two general patterns can be noted. The most common pattern, consistent with Article 7 of the OECD and UN Model Treaties, is that business income is generally taxable by a country only if the taxpayer carries on business through a PE in the country and the income is attributable to that PE. In these systems, the PE rules serve not only as a threshold for source country taxation but also as the means for identifying the income subject to tax, namely, income "attributable" to the PE. Most European countries follow this general pattern; however, the definition of a PE

多数欧洲国家都遵循这种一般模式。但是，常设机构的定义在国内法下通常比税收协定中的定义宽泛。

在许多拉丁美洲和南美洲国家，常设机构的概念用于区分对非居民取得的服务所得是以净额还是以总额为基础征税。非居民通过在一国设立的常设机构提供服务取得的所得，在该国以净额为基础缴税（即允许非居民从取得的所得中扣除费用）。非居民在一国没有常设机构，而在该国提供或消费服务取得所得的，以总额（不允许任何扣除）为基础缴纳预提税。

根据 OECD 协定范本和联合国协定范本第 7 条的规定，归属于常设机构的所得数额是通过假定常设机构是独立的法人实体，并且与其所属企业的其他部门（包括总部），按照独立交易原则开展交易来确定的。常设机构与总部之间的**交易**（名义上等同于独立实体之间的交易）受各项独立交易转让定价规则约束。第 6 章将讨论各项转让定价规则。在实践中，大多数国家在很大程度上依赖于常设机构的会计账册来确定常设机构的所得，仅在认为存在滥用时，对这些账册进行调整。这样做的结果是使纳税人有足够的权力，自行决定可归属于常设机构的营业利润。向常设机构归属利润将在第 8 章第 8.8.5 节中讨论。

对营业利润征税的另一种通用模式是，将常设机构概念（或某种在功能方面相当的概念）作为对非居民征税的门槛要求，但使用明确的来源地规则，确定应税所得的范围。美国法律是这种方法最突出的代表。根据美国法律，大多数类别的毛所得都被分别认定一个来源，然后通常根据会计惯例，将各种扣除与各项毛所得相关联。一些经营所得项目要么分配给美国，要么分配给外国。例如，从动产的买卖中取得的所得被认为是来源自销售国。其他类别的所得通常通过公式在外国和美国之间分配。例如，在 2017 年美国税制改革之前，通常通过两因素（销售量和资产数量）公式在制造国和销售国之间等额分配从制造和销售存货中取得的所得。该来源地规则在 2017 年的税制改革中被废止，取而代之的规则是将全部所得分配给生产存货的国家。电信所得通常会在电信信号的产生国和接收国之间等额分配。

under domestic law is often broader than the definition in tax treaties.

In many Latin American and South American countries, the PE concept is used to differentiate between the taxation of income from services derived by nonresidents on a net or gross basis. Nonresidents who earn income from services through a PE situated in a country are taxable by that country on a net basis (i.e., the nonresidents are allowed to deduct expenses incurred in earning the income). Nonresidents who earn income from services performed or consumed in the country but who do not have a PE in the country are taxable on a gross basis (without the allowance of any deductions) through a withholding tax.

According to Article 7 of the OECD and UN Model Treaties, the amount of income attributable to a PE is determined by assuming that the PE is a separate legal entity and that it deals at arm's length with other parts of the enterprise, including the head office, of which it is a part. **Dealings** between a PE and the head office (notionally equivalent to transactions between separate entities) are subject to the arm's-length transfer pricing rules. Transfer pricing rules are discussed in Chapter 6. In practice, most countries determine the income of a PE by relying heavily on the books of account of the PE, with adjustments made to those books only in cases of perceived abuse. The effect is to give substantial discretion to taxpayers to determine the business profits attributable to a PE. The rules for the attribution of profits to PEs are discussed in Chapter 8, section 8.8.5.

The other general pattern for taxing business profits is that the concept of a PE (or some functional equivalent) is used as a threshold requirement for the taxation of nonresidents, but explicit source rules are used to determine the extent of the income subject to tax. U.S. law is the most prominent example of this approach. Under U.S. law, most categories of gross income are assigned a source. Deductions are then associated with items of gross income, generally in accordance with accounting conventions. Some items of business income are assigned exclusively either to the U.S. or to foreign countries. For example, income derived from the purchase and sale of personal property is considered to have its source in the country of sale. Other categories of income are apportioned between foreign countries and the U.S., often by formula. For example, before the 2017 U.S. tax reform, income from the manufacture and sale of inventory was apportioned equally between the country of manufacture and the country of sale, typically by a two-factor formula (sales and property). This source rule was eliminated in the 2017 tax reform and replaced by a rule that allocates all the income to the country in which the inventory is produced. Telecommunications income generally is apportioned equally between the country of origin of the telecommunication signals and the country of reception.

美国来源地规则的主要特征体现在对扣除的处理。许多扣除项目与毛所得的相互关联，是在与存货会计规则类似的会计规则下进行的，即根据存货会计规则，分摊折旧和其他固定成本等扣除项目，以确定销货成本。但是，利息支付、研发费用，以及某些其他费用适用特殊的分摊规则，因为这些费用难以与具体某业务的毛所得联系起来。

在各种所得和扣除方面，大多数国家缺乏细致的来源地规则。因此，所得和扣除在本国和外国之间划分，是按一般规则进行的，这给予纳税人很大的自行决定权。

2.3.4 投资所得

除了某些例外，多数国家都对非居民取得的投资所得，例如，股息、利息和特许权使用费，按照单一税率对支付款项的总额征收预提税。资本收益通常无须缴纳预提税，尽管一些国家采用了特殊的征管措施，如第 5 章第 5.8.5 节所述。投资所得的来源地通常由隐性来源地规则或与其功能相当的规则来确定。除了某些技术例外，多数国家都采用了 OECD 协定范本和联合国协定范本认可的以下规则：

—— 利息、股息和特许权使用费被认为发生或来源于支付方为其居民的国家（参见 OECD 协定范本和联合国协定范本第 11 条第 4 款和第 10 条第 4 款，以及联合国协定范本第 12 条第 4 款）。值得注意的是，投资所得的来源地规则取决于利息、股息或特许权使用费的支付方的居民身份。因此，即使仅根据所得来源地（属地课税）征税的国家，也需要规则来确定纳税人的居民身份，以便对利息、股息和特许权使用费征收预提税。根据第 11 条第 4 款，如果在计算归属于常设机构的利润时可以扣除利息，则该利息被视为来源于常设机构所在的国家。

—— 针对无形资产支付的特许权使用费，被视为发生于使用该资产并提供无形资产法律保护的国家，并由该国征税。根据一些国家的法律，

A key feature of U.S. source rules is the treatment of deductions. Many deductions are linked with gross income under accounting rules comparable to inventory accounting rules, under which deductions such as depreciation and other fixed costs are allocated for purposes of determining the cost of goods sold. However, special apportionment rules apply to interest payments, research and development expenses, and certain other expenses that are difficult to link with specific items of gross income.

Most countries lack sophisticated source rules with respect to income and deductions. Accordingly, income and deductions are allocated between domestic and foreign income in accordance with general rules that give considerable discretion to taxpayers.

2.3.4 Investment Income

With some exceptions, most countries tax investment income derived by nonresidents, such as dividends, interest, and royalties, through withholding taxes imposed on the gross amount of the payment at a flat rate. Capital gains are not usually subject to withholding tax, although special enforcement measures are used by some countries, as discussed in Chapter 5, section 5.8.5. The source of investment income is usually determined by implicit source rules or their functional equivalents. With some technical exceptions, the following rules have been adopted by most countries and are endorsed in the OECD and UN Model Treaties:

- Interest, dividends, and royalties are considered to arise or be sourced in the country of residence of the payer (see Articles 11(4) and 10(4) of the OECD and UN Model Treaties and Article 12(4) of the UN Model Treaty). It is notable that the source rule for investment income relies on the residence of the payer of the interest, dividends, or royalties. Therefore, even countries that tax exclusively on the basis of the source of income (territorial taxation) require rules to determine the residence of persons for purposes of their withholding taxes on interest, dividends, and royalties. Under Article 11(4), where interest is deductible in computing the profits attributable to a PE, the interest is considered to arise in the country where the PE is located.
- Royalties paid with respect to intangible property are considered to arise in and are taxable by the country where the property is used, and legal protection for the intangible property is provided. Some types of royalty income, such as royalties paid for the showing of motion pictures and royalties on computer software, may be

某些类型的特许权使用费所得，例如，为放映影片支付的特许权使用费，以及计算机软件的特许权使用费，可能被归类为经营所得。对OECD协定范本来说，并不需要特许权使用费的来源地规则，因为已将特许权使用费的税收管辖权完全赋予居民国。而根据联合国协定范本第12条，来源国有权对特许权使用费征税，适用的最高预提税率由协定双方协商确定。根据第12条第4款，特许权使用费被视为来源于支付方为其居民的国家，或者在计算常设机构所得时，可以扣除特许权使用费的情况下，常设机构所在的国家为来源国。

—— 来自企业运营的租金所得，通常根据上述第2.3.3节适用于经营所得的规则征税。不动产的租金所得应由不动产所在国征税；从中也可以看出，不动产租金所得即来源于不动产所在国。使用动产产生的租金所得，通常应由使用该财产的所在国征税，隐含之义为此项所得来源地是支付方为其居民的国家。动产产生的租金所得，根据OECD协定范本第7条，应作为营业利润征税。而根据联合国协定范本第12条，则应作为特许权使用费征税（针对属于工业、科学或商业设备的动产）。

—— 处置财产取得的收益来源地差异很大，并取决于财产的性质。处置不动产的收益几乎总是由不动产所在国征税。这是OECD协定范本和联合国协定范本第13条第1款的规定。处置在一国开展经营活动所使用的资产取得的收益，通常应由开展经营活动的所在国征税。根据OECD协定范本和联合国协定范本第13条第2款，处置用于通过常设机构在一国开展经营活动的财产所产生的收益，应由该国征税。OECD协定范本和联合国协定范本均允许同一国家对处置构成常设机构的不动产和资产的所得和资本收益征税。因此，将一项收益定性为所得或资本收益，主要由国内法决定，与税收协定无关。

—— 处置公司股份或在合伙企业或信托中的权益所产生的收益，通常仅由纳税人为其居民的国家征税。但是，如果非居民纳税人在居民实体中

classified as business income under the laws of some countries. No source rule for royalties is necessary under the OECD Model Treaty because exclusive jurisdiction to tax royalties is given to the residence country. However, under Article 12 of the UN Model Treaty, the source country is entitled to tax royalties, subject to a maximum withholding rate left to negotiations between the treaty partners. Under Article 12(4), royalties are considered to arise in the country where the payer is resident or, in the case of royalties deducted in computing the income of a PE, in the country where the PE is located.

- Rental income derived from the operation of a business is typically taxable under the rules applicable to business income discussed above in section 2.3.3. Rental income from immovable property is taxable by the country in which the property is located; therefore, implicitly, the source of the rent is that country. Rental income from the use of movable property is generally taxable by the country where the property is used; therefore, implicitly, the source of the income is the country in which the payer is resident. Rental income derived from movable property is taxable as business profits under Article 7 of the OECD Model Treaty and as royalties under Article 12 of the UN Model Treaty (for movable property that is industrial, scientific, or commercial equipment).
- The source of gains from the disposal of property varies considerably and depends on the nature of the property. Gains from the disposal of immovable property are almost invariably taxable by the country in which the property is located. This is the rule in Article 13(1) of the OECD and UN Model Treaties. Gains from the disposal of assets used in carrying on a business in a country are often taxable by the country in which the business is carried on. Under Article 13(2) of the OECD and UN Model Treaties, gains from the disposal of property used in carrying on a business through a PE in a country are taxable by that country. The structure of the OECD and UN Model Treaties allows the same country to tax both income and capital gains from the disposal of immovable property and assets forming part of a PE. Thus, the characterization of a gain as income or capital gain is determined under domestic law and is not relevant for purposes of the treaty.
- Gains from the disposal of shares of companies or interests in a partnership or trust are generally subject to tax exclusively by the country in which the taxpayer is resident. However, if a nonresident taxpayer owns a substantial interest in a resident entity, some countries impose tax on the gains. Article 13(4) of the UN

> 拥有重大权益，则某些国家会对此种收益征税。联合国协定范本第13条第4款允许缔约国对此类收益征税，OECD协定范本则不允许。同样，如果股份或权益的价值主要来源于位于一些国家不动产的价值，且不动产为某个公司、合伙企业或信托所有，则这些国家会对处置这种公司股份或在合伙企业或信托中的权益所产生的收益征税。OECD协定范本和联合国协定范本均允许缔约国对此类收益征税。实际上，该条款是一项反避税规则，旨在防止纳税人通过将财产由公司或其他法律实体持有，并转让公司的股份或在实体中的权益，以规避不动产所在国对不动产收益的征税。

如上所述，签订税收协定的大多数国家都同意，对根据国内法适用于利息、股息和特许权使用费的预提税率，进行一定程度的限制。限制的目的是确保来源国不对投资所得征收过多的税收，并在来源国和居民国之间分享税收收入。有关预提税的讨论，参见第5章第5.9.3节和第8章第8.7.3.5节。

一些税收协定规定了预提税零税率，从而完全取消来源国对某些类型投资所得的征税。几乎所有这类协定都存在于发达国家之间。零税率以两个假设为前提：协定国家之间的零税率类投资资金流量大致相当，并且来源国放弃的税收管辖权将由居民国行使。如第8章第8.2.1节所述，在许多情况下，这些假设并不反映实际情况。

在对投资所得征税方面，一些评论人士倾向于由居民国征税，而不主张由来源国征税。其理由是，在某些情况下，来源国预提税的作用可能与对支付方征收消费税类似，而居民国征税通常是对收款人征收所得税。作为预提税具有消费税效应的例子，假设一家外国银行要求借款人支付利息时不含来源国征收的任何预提税。在这种情况下，借款人可能会将预提税视为借款的额外成本。

从理论上讲，零预提税率可以简化管理，并且使公司间的转让可以不产生税收后果，从而促进经营效率。在实践中，零税率可能会助长避税筹划，并且

Model Treaty allows a contracting state to tax such gains, but the OECD Model Treaty does not. Similarly, some countries tax gains from the disposal of shares in a corporation or interests in a partnership or trust if the value of the shares or interests is derived principally from immovable property located in those countries and owned by the entity. Both the OECD and UN Model Treaties allow the contracting states to tax such gains. In effect, this provision is an anti-avoidance rule designed to prevent taxpayers from avoiding a country's tax on gains in respect of immovable property located in the country by holding the property in a corporation or other legal entity and then disposing of the shares of the corporation or interests in the entity.

As noted above, most countries entering into tax treaties agree to some limitations on the withholding tax rates applicable to interest, dividends, and royalties under their domestic law. The intent of these limitations is to ensure that the source country does not impose excessive taxes on investment income and that tax revenue is shared between the source country and the residence country. For a discussion of withholding taxes, *see* Chapter 5, section 5.9.3 and Chapter 8, section 8.7.3.5.

Some tax treaties eliminate source country taxation entirely for some types of investment income by mandating a zero rate of withholding; almost all of these treaties are between developed countries. The zero rate is premised on two assumptions: that the flow of investment funds between the treaty countries in the zero-rate categories is approximately equal and that the tax jurisdiction relinquished by the source country will be exercised by the residence country. As discussed in Chapter 8, section 8.2.1, in many circumstances, these assumptions do not reflect reality.

Some commentators favor residence taxation over source taxation of investment income on the ground that, in some circumstances, a withholding tax at source may operate as an excise tax on the payer, whereas a residence tax generally operates as an income tax on the recipient of the income. As an example of this excise-tax effect of withholding taxes, consider a foreign bank that requires a borrower to make interest payments net of any withholding tax imposed by the source country. In such circumstances, the borrower is likely to view the withholding tax as an additional cost of borrowing.

In theory, zero rates of withholding simplify administration and promote business efficiency by allowing intercompany transfers to be made without tax consequences. In practice, zero rates may promote tax avoidance schemes and, in the absence of complex anti-avoidance

在缺乏复杂的反避税规则的情况下，纳税人可能通过择协避税获得非协定本意的待遇。例如，某公司名义上是某协定国的税收居民，实为非居民受益持有，后者得以享受协定待遇，则为择协避税。有关择协定避税的讨论，参见第 8 章第 8.8.2.2 节。

rules, may provide unintended benefits through treaty shopping. Treaty shopping occurs, for example, when treaty benefits are obtained by corporations that are nominally resident in a treaty country but are owned beneficially by nonresidents. For a discussion of treaty shopping, *see* Chapter 8, section 8.8.2.2.

3 居民税收

3.1 引言

正如第 2 章所述，许多国家对作为居民的人（个人和法人实体）的全球所得征税，而对于作为非居民的人，则仅对其来源于境内的所得征税。因此，居民与非居民税收的本质区别在于，对于非居民，仅就其从一国范围内取得的所得（本国来源的所得）征税；而对于居民，需对其本国来源的所得及其从该国境外取得的所得（即境外来源所得）征税。虽然一些国家仅对无论是居民还是非居民的本国来源的所得征税（所谓的属地税制），但是，大多数国家至少对居民部分境外来源所得征税。因此，国际税收的典型模式可以表述为，对居民本国来源所得以及至少一部分境外来源所得征税的制度。非居民税收将在第 5 章讨论。

作为居民的人与作为非居民的人，其间的区别是一个基本问题并有重要影响。正如第 2 章所讨论的，虽然各国的具体规定差异较大，但是判定人的居民身份，通常基于该人与一个国家之间的个人和经济方面的联系，其与该国之间的联系越紧密越广泛，就越可能出于该国税收制度的目的，被认定为该国的居民。

本章考察涉及对居民就其全球所得进行征税的主要问题，而不是居民身份的认定，后者已经在第 2 章中讨论。在此引言之后，第 3.2 节考量对居民就其全球所得征税的税收政策原因、居民身份的税收影响和双重征税。接着讨论与境外来

CHAPTER 3
Taxation of Residents

3.1 INTRODUCTION

As discussed in Chapter 2, many countries tax persons—individuals and legal entities—who are residents on their worldwide income and nonresident persons only on their domestic source income. Thus, the essential difference between the taxation of residents and nonresidents is that nonresidents are taxed only on income derived from a country (domestic source income), while residents of a country are taxed on both their domestic source income and their income derived from outside the country (foreign source income). Although a few countries tax only domestic source income of both residents and nonresidents (so-called territorial taxation), most countries tax resident persons on at least some of their foreign source income. Therefore, the typical pattern of taxation internationally can be described as the taxation of residents on both their domestic source income and at least some items of their foreign source income. The taxation of nonresidents is dealt with in Chapter 5.

The distinction between resident persons and nonresident persons is a fundamental one and has important consequences. As discussed in Chapter 2, the determination of the residence of a person is usually based on the person's personal and economic connections to a country, although the specific rules vary considerably from country to country. The closer and more extensive a person's connections are with a country, the more likely it is that the person will be considered to be a resident of that country for purposes of its tax system.

This chapter examines the major issues involved in taxing residents on their worldwide income other than the determination of residence itself, which is dealt with in Chapter 2. Following this introduction, section 3.2 considers the tax policy reasons for taxing residents on their worldwide income, the tax consequences of residence status, and double taxation; it then discusses several practical issues with respect to the computation of foreign source income, including the treatment of foreign source losses. Section 3.3 discusses two important exceptions

源所得计算相关的若干实操问题，包括境外来源的亏损的处理。第 3.3 节讨论对居民就其全球所得征税的两个重要例外情况：通过非居民公司和其他法律实体取得的境外来源所得，以及仅临时成为一国居民的处理。第 3.4 节涉及几个特殊的问题，包括出境税或**离境税**、延续税、年度内居民和外汇损益的处理。

3.2 居民全球所得的税收

3.2.1 税收政策考量

乍看之下，对居民全球所得征税的国家，似乎超越了其税收主权，因其对从其领土之外取得的所得征税（**治外法权**）。但是，没有国际法限制一国对与本国有紧密联系的人征税的法定权力。虽然对于一国的征税能力，可能存在实际的限制（一国开征不能实现有效征收的税收，几乎没有意义），但是，一国居民显然是与该国有重大联系的人，因此，针对居民全球所得的税收，通常都是可以实现有效征收的。而且，随着国家之间信息交换有效性的提升，税务机关对于其居民境外来源所得信息的获取，近年来得到显著改善。

对居民个人全球所得征税的税收政策理由是公平和中性。如果两个居民取得同等数额的所得，则其应当承担相同的税负，即使一个居民的所得全部来源于本国，而另一个居民的所得全部来自本国以外。这一公平方面的理由基于以下假设：一国所有居民以公共商品和服务的形式从本国获得显著个人利益，故而无须考虑其所得的来源，都有理由对其征税。因此，生活于一国的个人可能从该国的基础设施（道路和公共安全）、法律体系、社会福利体系和教育体系中获益，即使该个人的全部所得都是从该国以外取得。中性方面的理由基于以下假设：一国不应为其居民在该国以外工作或者投资提供税收激励。如果居民境外来源的所得不受制于居民国税收，与本国来源的所得相比，居民会更乐于取得低税负的境外

to the taxation of residents on their worldwide income: foreign source income earned through nonresident companies and other legal entities and the treatment of persons who are resident in a country only temporarily. Section 3.4 deals with special issues, including exit or departure taxes, **trailing taxes**, the treatment of part-time residents, and foreign exchange gains and losses.

3.2 TAXATION OF RESIDENTS ON THEIR WORLDWIDE INCOME

3.2.1 Tax Policy Considerations

It may at first appear that countries that impose tax on the worldwide income of their residents are exceeding their sovereign authority to tax because they are taxing income that arises outside their territories (**extraterritoriality**). However, there are no international law constraints on a country's legal authority to tax persons who have close connections to the country. Although there may be practical constraints on a country's ability to tax (it makes little sense for a country to impose taxes that cannot be effectively collected), tax on the worldwide income of residents can usually be effectively collected because, by definition, residents of a country are persons with significant ties to the country. In addition, the access for tax authorities to information about their residents' foreign source income has been significantly improved in recent years through the increased effectiveness of exchanges of information between countries.

The tax policy justifications for taxing resident individuals on their worldwide income are equity and neutrality. If two residents have equal amounts of income, they should be subject to the same tax burden, even if one resident's income is derived totally from domestic sources while the other's income is derived exclusively from outside the country. This equity justification is based on the assumption that all residents of a country derive significant personal benefits from the country, in the form of public goods and services, that justify taxing them irrespective of the source of their income. Thus, an individual who lives in a country may derive benefits from its infrastructure (roads and public safety), legal system, social welfare system, and education system, even where all the individual's income is earned outside that country. The neutrality justification is based on the assumption that a country should not create a tax incentive for its residents to work or invest outside the country. If the foreign source income of residents is not subject to residence country tax, residents have an incentive to earn low-taxed

来源的所得，这种激励作用不利于本国经济。

公平的考量对公司和其他法人实体而言意义不大，因为这些实体不是其所得的最终受益所有人。相应的，对法人实体全球所得征税的理由主要在于中性方面的论证。这种中性是指资本输出中性，即纳税人将向税前回报最大化的地方投资。一国为实现这种类型的中性，必须对居民法人就其境外和本国投资产生的所得征税。如果对来自境外的所得不征税，或者与本国所得相比，按照较低的税率征税，一国的法人实体居民将倾向于在实行较低税率的国家投资，特别是无税或者低税的避税地。

然而，关于经营所得的中性论证的另一方面，即资本输入中性或者国际竞争，会考虑一国的实体居民需要在各个不同的国家，与这些国家或第三国的实体居民竞争。如果 A 国实体居民就其全球所得向 A 国纳税，其将不能有效地在 B 国与仅在 B 国纳税的 B 国的或者第三国的实体居民竞争（当然，假设 B 国税率低于 A 国）。虽然有关国际竞争的论证对学界来说复杂且有争议，但对政府来说是不能回避的。因此可以说，作为国际惯例，对法人实体取得的积极经营所得，一般都按照属地原则征税。换言之，居民公司取得的境外来源的经营所得，通常不再受制于居民国税收。

可以认为，一国对居民境外来源所得征税的原因之一在于由此会产生更多的税收收入。但是，正如第 2 章所述，如果这类所得在取得该所得所在的国家（来源国）应予征税，则来源国首先有权对其征税。居民国通常被认为负有消除双重征税的义务（尽管这不是法律义务，除非两国之间存在生效的协定），或者对境外来源的所得免于征收居民国税收，或者允许境外来源所得的来源国税收抵免居民国税收。因此，仅在居民国通过外国税收抵免消除双重征税，且来源国税收低于居民国税收时，才会产生更多的税收收入。消除双重征税的方法将在第 4 章讨论。

foreign source income in preference to domestic source income, and this incentive is detrimental to the domestic economy.

With respect to corporations and other legal entities, considerations of equity are of little significance because such entities are not the ultimate beneficial owners of their income. Accordingly, the justification for taxing legal entities on their worldwide income must rest primarily on the neutrality argument. This form of neutrality is referred to as capital-export neutrality—a taxpayer should invest where the pretax return is maximized. To achieve this type of neutrality, a country must tax its resident entities on income from both foreign and domestic investments. If income from foreign countries is not taxed or is taxed at a lower rate than domestic income, legal entities resident in a country will prefer to invest in foreign countries with lower tax rates, especially in tax havens with no or low taxes.

There is, however, another side to the neutrality argument with respect to business income—capital-import neutrality or international competitiveness—which suggests that entities resident in one country must compete in various countries with entities resident in those countries and in third countries. If the entities resident in Country A are subject to tax by Country A on their worldwide income, they will not be able to compete as effectively in Country B against entities resident in Country B or resident in third countries that are subject to tax only in Country B (assuming, of course, that the tax rate in Country B is lower than the tax rate in Country A). The arguments concerning international competitiveness, although complex and controversial to academics, have proved irresistible to governments. As a result, it is fair to say that the international norm is that active business income derived by legal entities is generally taxed on a territorial basis; in other words, the foreign source business income derived by a resident corporation is not usually subject to residence country tax.

It might be thought that one of the reasons for a country to tax its residents on their foreign source income is the additional tax revenue that will be generated. However, as explained in Chapter 2, to the extent that such income is subject to tax in the country in which it is derived (the source country), that country has the first right to tax the income. The residence country is generally considered to be under an obligation (although not a legal obligation unless there is a treaty in effect between the two countries) to eliminate double taxation, either by exempting the foreign source income from residence country tax or providing a credit against residence country tax for the source country tax on the foreign source income. Thus, additional tax revenue will be generated only if the residence country eliminates double tax through a foreign tax credit and only to the extent that the source country tax is less than the residence country tax. The methods for the elimination of double taxation are explored in Chapter 4.

3.2.2 居民身份的税收影响

在全球征税制度中，纳税人所得既包括从纳税人为其居民的国家取得的所得，也包括从该国以外取得的所得。对于法人实体，通常对其全球所得，以比例税率征税。与此不同的是，对于个人，通常对其全球所得，以累进税率征税，尽管税率的累进程度可能有限。例如，纳税人所得可能仅在超过起征额时应税。在一些国家，尽管对境外来源的所得不征税，但在确定纳税人其他所得的适用税率时，会将其计算在内（**累进免税**）。一些国家对某些类型的境外来源所得（特别是经营所得）予以免税，而其他类型所得需缴纳居民国税收。结果如上所述，仅因一国被称为对全球所得征税，并不意味着该国对居民取得的全部境外来源所得征税。

案例

X女士是X国居民，从X国取得100000元受雇所得，还从Y国居民公司取得10000元股息，从Z国银行账户取得3000元利息。股息需在Y国缴纳15%的预提税（即1500元），利息需在Z国缴纳10%的预提税（即300）。X女士的所得和在X国的应缴税款如下：

来源于X国所得	100000
境外来源所得：	
来源于Y国的股息	10000
来源于Z国的利息	3000
全球所得	113000
减：个人免税额	10000
应税所得	103000
应纳税额（40%）	41200
减：单身父母抵减	1200
外国税收抵免	1800
净应纳税额	38200

3.2.2 The Tax Consequences of Residence

In a worldwide tax system, a taxpayer's income includes both income from inside the country in which the taxpayer is resident and income from outside that country. Legal entities are usually taxable on their worldwide income at a flat rate; in contrast, individuals are usually taxable on that worldwide income at progressive rates, although the extent of the progression in the rates may be limited; for example, an amount may be taxable only if the taxpayer's income exceeds a threshold amount. In some countries, although foreign source income is not taxable, it is taken into account in determining the rate of tax on the taxpayer's other income (**exemption with progression**). In some countries, certain types of foreign source income (typically business income) may be exempt, while other types are subject to residence country tax. As a result, as noted above, just because a country is described as taxing on a worldwide basis does not mean that it taxes all foreign source income derived by residents.

Example

Ms. X is a resident of Country X. She has income from employment in Country X of 100,000. She also receives dividends of 10,000 from corporations resident in Country Y and interest of 3,000 from a bank account in Country Z. The dividends are subject to withholding tax in Country Y of 15%, or 1,500, and the interest is subject to withholding tax in Country Z of 10%, or 300. Ms. X's income and tax payable to Country X might look as follows:

Income from Country X	100,000
Foreign source income:	
Dividends from Country Y	10,000
Interest from Country Z	3,000
Worldwide income	113,000
Less: personal allowance	10,000
Taxable income	103,000
Tax payable (40%)	41,200
Less: single parent credit	1,200
Foreign tax credit	1,800
Net tax payable	38,200

3.2.3 双重征税

如果一国对其居民的全球所得征税，而另一国因前述所得中部分来源于本国，而对这部分所得征税，则该所得面临双重征税。由于多数国家坚持对从本国取得的或者来源于本国的所得征税，因此对居民的全球税收将不可避免地导致双重征税。公认的国际惯例是，来源国，即发生所得的国家、取得所得所在的国家，或者所得来源于其中的国家（这些术语通常用于表述来源国），对所得拥有首要征税权，居民国对所得拥有次要征税权。但是，居民国如果对前述所得征税，则必须对来源国税收进行抵减，以消除双重征税。居民国用于消除其居民取得的境外来源所得的双重征税的方法将在第 4 章讨论。

3.2.4 居民境外来源所得的计算

3.2.4.1 综述

由于居民就其全球所得纳税，因此有必要制定计算其本国来源所得和境外来源所得的规则。一般情况下，计算两种所得适用相同的规则。计入所得的收入项目相同，允许扣除的费用项目相同，适用相同的实现时间规则。然而，税收激励可能仅限于本国来源的所得。例如，一国可能为投资国内特定产业或区域的机器和设备提供加速折旧，或者为在该国范围内开展的研发活动提供加计扣除。

来源地规则与确定居民的全球所得无关，因为来源于本国和境外的所得，在计算其所得时，均应计入并予以征税。但是，如果对境外来源所得中的某些项目（如归属于外国分支机构或常设机构的所得）免于征税，则需要来源地规则。此外，在确定外国税收抵免限额时，也需要来源地规则。正如第 4 章详细讨论的，根据协定的要求（或者出于国际惯例和公平的考虑），对其居民的境外来源所得征税的国家应承担义务，允许境外来源的所得缴纳的外国税收抵免

3.2.3 Double Taxation

If one country taxes its residents on their worldwide income and another country taxes part of that income because it is derived from sources in that country, the income is subject to double tax. Worldwide taxation of residents inevitably results in double tax because most countries insist on taxing income that is derived or has its source in their countries. The well-established international norm is that the source country—the country in which the income arises, is derived, or has its source (all these terms are commonly used to describe a source county)—has the first right to tax the income and the residence country has a secondary right to tax the income; however, if the residence country does so, it must provide relief for the source country's tax in order to eliminate double taxation. The methods that residence countries use to eliminate double taxation of foreign source income earned by their residents are discussed in Chapter 4.

3.2.4 Computation of the Foreign Source Income of Residents

3.2.4.1 In General

Since residents are taxable on their worldwide income, rules are necessary to compute both their domestic source income and foreign source income. Typically, the same rules apply for the purpose of computing both types of income. The same amounts are included in income, the same deductions are allowed, and the same timing rules apply. However, tax incentives may be restricted to domestic source income. For example, a country may provide accelerated depreciation for investment in machinery and equipment used in certain domestic industries or areas of the country, or it may provide enhanced write-offs for domestic research and development activities carried out in the country.

Source rules are irrelevant for purposes of determining the worldwide income of residents since all income, domestic and foreign, is included in computing their income and is taxable. However, source rules are required if any items of foreign source income (e.g., income attributable to a foreign branch or PE) are exempt from tax. In addition, source rules are necessary for purposes of determining the limitation on the foreign tax credit. As discussed in detail in Chapter 4, a country that taxes the foreign source income of its residents is obligated by its treaties (and also by considerations of international practice and fairness) to allow a credit against

国内税收。但是，此项外国税收抵免通常不得超过对境外来源所得征收的本国税收的数额。

如果对境外来源所得予以征税，则为获取这些境外来源所得而产生的支出一般允许扣除。有时，所得确认时间与费用扣除时间可能严重不匹配。例如，纳税人可能为了获取境外来源所得而借款。利息将在当期扣除，但是股息等所得项目可能延至以后年度收到所得时才计入所得。同类时间错配还常出现在研发支出方面。

如果对境外来源所得免于征收居民国税收，原则上为取得该所得所产生的任何支出将不允许扣除。但是，许多国家允许扣除用于取得外国公司股权的借款利息支出，即使对从这些公司取得的股息已免于征收居民国税收。随着越来越多的国家对从外国公司取得的股息实行参股免税，这一问题变得越来越重要。OECD BEPS 第 4 项行动计划的最终报告《利息扣除和其他财务支出》涉及这一问题，第 7 章第 7.2 节将详细讨论。尽管为取得应当缴纳居民国税收的境外来源所得而产生的支出，在计算纳税人全球所得时允许扣除，但这类支出在计算境外来源所得的外国税收抵免限额时也应作为可扣除支出。第 4 章第 4.4 节将深入讨论这一问题。

3.2.4.2 外汇损益

境外来源所得通常为取得该所得所在国家的货币。同样，为取得这些境外来源所得而产生的支出也以外国货币发生。在全球税制下，居民所得一般必须以居民国货币申报。因此，以外币计量的收入和支出必须折算为本国货币，由此可能产生外币变动损益。理论上，每笔收入和支出应按照取得或发生时的汇率进行折算。一些国家出于实际考虑，允许按照平均汇率（按月、季或年），将外币结算的数额折算为本国货币。外币损益将在第 3.4.4 节进一步讨论。

its domestic tax for the foreign tax paid on the foreign source income. However, this credit for foreign taxes is typically limited to the amount of domestic tax on foreign source income.

Expenses incurred to earn foreign source income are usually deductible if the foreign source income is subject to tax. Sometimes there may be a serious mismatch between the timing of the recognition of the income and the timing of the deduction of expenses. For example, a taxpayer may borrow funds to finance the earning of foreign source income. The interest will be deductible currently but with respect to some items of income, such as dividends, the inclusion of the income may be postponed to subsequent years when the income is received. The same type of timing mismatch often occurs with respect to research and development expenses.

If foreign source income is exempt from residence country tax, in principle, any expenses incurred to earn such income should not be deductible. Many countries, however, allow the deduction of interest expense on borrowed funds used to acquire shares of foreign corporations even where dividends received from such corporations are exempt from residence country tax. This issue has become increasingly important as more countries have adopted participation exemptions for dividends from foreign corporations. The OECD's BEPS Action 4 Final Report: *Interest Deductions and Other Financial Payments* deals with this issue and is discussed in more detail in Chapter 7, section 7.2. Although expenses incurred to earn foreign source income that is subject to residence country tax are deductible in computing a taxpayer's world-wide income, these expenses should also be deducted in computing foreign source income for purposes of the limitation on the foreign tax credit. This issue is discussed further in Chapter 4, section 4.4.

3.2.4.2 Foreign Exchange Gains and Losses

Foreign source income is often earned in the currency of the foreign country in which it is earned. Similarly, expenses incurred to earn foreign source income are often incurred in foreign currency. In a worldwide tax system, a resident's income must generally be reported in the currency of the country of residence. As a result, amounts of revenue and expense expressed in foreign currency must be translated into the domestic currency, and gains and losses from movements in foreign currency may be realized. In theory, each revenue and expense item should be translated at the exchange rate applicable at the time that the amount is earned or incurred. For practical reasons, some countries allow amounts denominated in foreign currency to be translated into domestic currency using average exchange rates (monthly, quarterly, or annually). Foreign currency gains and losses are discussed further in section 3.4.4 below.

3.2.4.3 损失的处理

根据全球征税制度，居民的境外来源所得需要纳税。这意味着原则上应允许其扣除来源于境外的任何损失。虽然从理论视角来看，损失的处理应与境外来源所得的处理一致，但这也会产生问题，因为纳税人可能人为不恰当地利用营业损失扣除。例如，纳税人可能通过外国分支机构而不是境外子公司在外国开展业务，这样就可以在其居民国的全球所得中扣除开办阶段的损失。一旦企业获利，纳税人则可以将该运营资产转让给外国子公司（通常以可免税的方式），以使将来由外国子公司获取的利润免于被纳税人的居民国征税，如第 3.3.1 节所述。

如果居民国对部分境外来源的经营所得（如归属于外国常设机构的营业利润）免税，那么，归属于外国常设机构的来源境外的损失，也不得在计算纳税人全球所得时扣除。

一些国家试图保护其税基免受不恰当扣除境外损失的影响。基于此目的，这些国家制定了各种规定。例如：

——境外来源的损失扣除不得超过纳税人境外来源的利润；

——如果境外业务被出售或者转移给外国子公司，该项境外来源的损失扣除将被收回。

3.2.5 税收征管问题

对居民境外来源的所得征税，对居民国税务机关提出了特殊的管理和执法问题。税务机关要求纳税人提供境外来源所得的信息，以确保全部所得已申报，并核实所得计算是否准确。一般情况下，税务机关会首先试图从纳税人处获取这些信息。纳税人可能被要求通过涉税信息报告申报表定期提供，或者根据税务机关

3.2.4.3 *The Treatment of Losses*

Under a worldwide tax system, residents are taxable on their foreign source income. It follows that, in principle, they should be allowed to deduct any losses from foreign sources. Although this treatment of losses is consistent with the treatment of foreign source income from a theoretical perspective, it gives rise to problems since taxpayers can manipulate the deductibility of business losses inappropriately. For example, a taxpayer may commence business operations in a foreign country through a branch rather than a foreign subsidiary so that the start-up losses are deductible against the taxpayer's worldwide income in its country of residence. Once the business becomes profitable, the taxpayer can transfer the assets of the business to a foreign subsidiary—often on a tax-free basis—so that future profits derived by the foreign subsidiary are not subject to tax by the taxpayer's country of residence, as explained in section 3.3.1 below.

If the residence country exempts some foreign source business income (e.g., business profits attributable to a foreign PE), then any foreign source losses attributable to a foreign PE should not be deductible in computing the taxpayer's worldwide income.

Some countries try to protect their tax base against the inappropriate deduction of foreign losses. Various rules are used for this purpose. For example:

- deductions of foreign source losses may be limited to a taxpayer's foreign source profits; and
- deductions for foreign source losses may be recouped if the foreign business is sold or transferred to a foreign subsidiary.

3.2.5 Tax Administration Issues

Taxing the foreign source income of residents presents special problems of administration and enforcement for the tax authorities of the residence country. The tax authorities require information concerning the taxpayer's foreign source income, both to ensure that all the income is reported and to verify that the income is properly computed. Typically, in the first instance, the tax authorities will attempt to obtain this information from the taxpayer. Taxpayers may also be required to provide information about their foreign income-earning activities on a regular basis in their tax returns, through information-reporting returns, or pursuant to a

的特定要求，提供有关其境外收入活动的信息。根据两国税收协定的信息交换条款或者多边征管互助公约，居民国税务机关也可能从取得所得所在国家的税务机关获取信息。基于税收协定的信息交换将在第 8 章第 8.8.4 节中讨论。

当然，纳税人有时不愿向税务机关全面披露其境外来源的所得，因为与获得本国信息相比，税务机关获取本国以外的信息更为困难。纳税人也可能企图仅提供有利于自身的信息。因此，一些国家制定了抑制这种行为的规定。根据这些规定，如果纳税人没有披露全部信息，在日后涉及境外来源所得的法律诉讼中，将不允许纳税人增补信息。

通常一国的税务机关不能到另一国审计纳税人申报的境外来源的所得，除非收到纳税人和外国政府双方的邀请，这导致税务机关核实纳税人提供的涉及其境外活动的信息更加困难。一些国家通过签订在特定情形下实施联合审计的协议，以解决这个问题。

3.3 全球税收的例外

3.3.1 非居民公司和其他法人实体

虽然各国被称为按照全球法征税，但实际情况差异较大。理论上，如果实行全球征税国家的居民从另一国取得所得，则将就境外来源所得缴纳居民国税收。但是，如果居民设立一家外国公司或者其他外国实体，以获取境外来源所得，在缺乏受控外国企业（CFC）规则或**外国投资基金（FIF）规则**等特殊规定时，该所得将不予征税。外国实体通常被认为是独立于其居民持有者的纳税实体，而且在多数情况下，外国实体被认为是居民股东或所有者为其居民的国家的非居民。因此纳税人，尤其是特定国家的居民公司，可以通过设立外国公司或者诸如信托

specific request from the tax authorities. The tax authorities of the residence country may also obtain information from the tax authorities of the country where the income is earned under the exchange-of-information article of the tax treaty between the two countries or the Multilateral Convention on Mutual Assistance. Exchange of information under tax treaties is discussed in Chapter 8, section 8.8.4.

Not surprisingly, taxpayers are sometimes tempted not to provide full disclosure to the tax authorities concerning their foreign source income because it is much more difficult for the tax authorities to obtain information that is located outside the country than to obtain domestic information. Taxpayers may also be tempted to provide only favorable information. As a result, some countries have adopted rules to discourage this practice. Under these rules, if a taxpayer does not make full disclosure, the taxpayer is precluded from introducing any further information in any subsequent legal proceedings involving the foreign source income.

The tax authorities of one country are not generally allowed to visit another country for the purpose of auditing a taxpayer's reported foreign source income unless invited to do so by both the taxpayer and the foreign government, making it more difficult for the tax authorities to verify information provided by a taxpayer concerning its foreign activities. Some countries have addressed this issue by entering into arrangements providing for joint audits in certain circumstances.

3.3 EXCEPTIONS TO WORLDWIDE TAXATION

3.3.1 Nonresident Companies and Other Legal Entities

Although countries are said to tax on a worldwide basis, the reality is quite different. In theory, if a resident of a country that taxes on a worldwide basis earns income from another country, that foreign source income will be subject to residence country tax. If, however, the resident establishes a foreign corporation or other foreign entity to earn foreign source income, that income will not be subject to tax by the residence country in the absence of special rules such as CFC rules or **Foreign Investment Fund (FIF)** rules. The foreign entity is generally considered to be a separate taxable entity from the resident who owns it, and, in most cases, the foreign entity will be considered to be a nonresident of the country in which the resident shareholder or owner resides. As a result, it is relatively easy, especially for corporations resident in a particular country, to avoid paying tax to that country on foreign source income through the

等其他法人实体，较为容易地规避该国针对境外来源所得的税收。

案例

A 公司是 A 国居民，从 B 国营业活动中取得 1000000 元所得。由于 B 国税率（20%）低于 A 国税率（30%），故而假设 A 公司在 B 国设立一家常设机构，A 公司就其从 B 国取得的 1000000 元所得，向 B 国缴纳 200000 元的税款。假设 A 国实行全球课税，A 公司将就其从 B 国取得的 1000000 元所得，向 A 国缴纳 100000 元的税款（300000 元减除 200000 元 B 国税收抵免）。如果 A 公司在 B 国设立全资子公司，由其从 B 国取得本应由 A 公司直接取得的 1000000 元所得，则该子公司将向 B 国缴纳 200000 元税款。但是，A 公司在从子公司取得股息或者出售子公司股份之前，无须向 B 国或 A 国额外纳税。

如果 A 国对其居民公司从拥有实质性权益的外国公司取得的股息免税（许多国家如此规定），A 公司就可以使转移到 B 国的所得完全规避 A 国税收征收。即使 A 国对来自外国公司的股息征税，该项税收征收也会推迟到取得此股息之时，在外国子公司的情况下，这属于居民母公司的控制范围之内。

A 公司易于以较低成本实现当期节税 100000 元，只需要设立一家外国公司，并向其转移获取所得的资产。因此，毫不意外的是，受控外国企业和诸如信托等其他外国实体作为税收筹划工具被广泛运用。同样不意外的是，一些国家会出台针对性规定，防止利用这类境外实体规避或者延迟缴纳本国税收。第 7 章第 7.3 节和第 7.4 节将讨论这些规定。

3.3.2 临时居民

一些国家出台了针对临时居民的特殊规定，免除其承担居民税收中过于繁重的部分。临时居民（如公司高级管理人员）可能因住房、家庭和雇佣关系位于一国，而明显属于该国居民，但是他们仅打算在一段有限的时间内成为该国居民，

use of foreign corporations or other legal entities such as trusts.

Example

Corporation A, resident in Country A, derives income of 1 million from business activities in Country B. The tax rate in Country B (20%) is lower than the rate in Country A (30%). As a result, assuming that Corporation A has a PE in Country B, it will pay tax to Country B of 200,000 on the income of 1 million derived from Country B. Assuming that Country A taxes on a worldwide basis, Corporation A will also pay Country A tax of 100,000 on the income of 1 million earned in Country B (300,000 less a credit for 200,000 of Country B tax). If Corporation A establishes a wholly owned subsidiary corporation in Country B and that subsidiary earns the income of 1 million from Country B that would have been earned directly by Corporation A, the subsidiary will pay 200,000 of Country B tax; however, Corporation A will pay no additional tax to Country B or Country A until it receives dividends from the subsidiary or sells its shares of the subsidiary.

Where Country A exempts dividends from foreign corporations in which companies resident in Country A have a substantial interest (as many countries do), Corporation A can completely avoid Country A's tax on the income shifted to Country B. Even where Country A taxes dividends from foreign corporations, that tax is deferred until such dividends are received, which, in the case of foreign subsidiaries, is within the control of the resident parent corporation.

The immediate tax saving by Corporation A of 100,000 is easy and inexpensive to achieve; it simply requires the incorporation of a foreign corporation and the transfer of the income-earning assets to it. As a result, it is not surprising that the use of CFCs and other foreign entities, such as trusts, as tax-planning devices, is widespread. Nor is it surprising that several countries have responded to such planning with rules to prevent the avoidance or deferral of domestic tax by the use of such foreign entities. These rules are discussed in Chapter 7, sections 7.3 and 7.4.

3.3.2 Temporary Residents

Some countries have special rules for temporary residents to relieve them of some of the more onerous aspects of residence taxation. Temporary residents are persons, such as corporate executives, who may be clearly resident in a country because their homes, families, and employment are located in the country but who intend to be, and are, resident only for a limited period of time, usually less than five years. As residents of the country, they become subject to

通常不超过 5 年，而且实际情况也确实如此。作为一国居民，他们需要遵守所有涉及境外来源所得的税收规定，但因其只是临时离开母国，通常仍在母国保留重要经济利益。针对临时居民，全面适用居民国税收规定，可能导致严重问题，会阻碍专业人士在其他国家从事短期活动。

两个具体案例可用于说明这方面的问题。假设作为 A 国居民的某高级管理人员是其公司养老计划的成员。根据 A 国税法，该高级管理人员可以扣除向该计划的缴款，也不需要就雇主对该计划的缴款纳税。而且，在该计划中赚取和累积的所得免税，但从该计划分得的所得需要全额纳税。再假设该高级管理人员在 B 国获得临时职位，B 国不允许其扣除向养老计划的缴款，并将该项计划的雇主缴款部分视同雇佣的额外福利征税。B 国仅对养老计划分配中超出雇主和雇员缴款的部分征税。该高级管理人员计划在 A 国退休。对其作为 B 国居民期间向该计划所做的缴款，该高级管理人员将面临双重征税：一次是在 B 国，因为 B 国将对该高级管理人员就雇主向该计划的缴款征税，并且不允许扣除该高级管理人员自己的缴款；另一次是在 A 国，当该高级管理人员从该计划中取得分配之时。这种双重征税显然不公平，应予以消除。

第二个案例，假设 A 国居民 A，为其子女的利益，按照 A 国法律设立了一个信托。A 国对信托的累积所得征税，但依照适用于子女的税率。A 迁往 B 国暂时任职几年，从而受 B 国针对居民设立外国信托的特殊规定的约束。很可能 A 不是为了规避 B 国税收而设立上述信托，因为设立该信托时，其并不知晓未来将迁往 B 国。根据 B 国法律，A 的外国信托所得须在 B 国纳税，即使该信托所得在 A 国也应纳税。为消除这种双重征税，一些国家在规定的限期内，对临时居民免于适用外国信托和外国投资基金（FIF）规则。

all of that country's rules concerning the taxation of foreign source income, but because they are only temporarily absent from their home countries, these temporary residents often retain substantial economic interests there. The application of the full range of residence country rules to temporary residents can cause serious problems that may discourage talented persons from taking short-term postings in other countries.

Two specific examples may serve to illustrate the difficulties. Assume that an executive resident in Country A is a member of the company's pension plan. Under the tax law of Country A, the executive is entitled to deduct contributions to the plan and is not taxable on the employer's contributions to the plan. Moreover, the income earned and accumulated in the plan is not taxable. However, distributions from the plan are taxable in full. Assume further that the executive takes a temporary posting in Country B, which does not allow any deduction for the executive's contributions to the pension plan and taxes the executive on the employer's contributions to the plan as a fringe benefit from employment. Country B taxes distributions from the pension plan only to the extent that they exceed the employee's and employer's contributions to the plan. The executive plans to retire in Country A. To the extent of the contributions to the plan, while the executive is resident in Country B, the executive will be subject to double taxation: once in Country B because Country B will impose tax on the executive with respect to the employer's contributions to the plan and will not allow any deduction for the executive's own contributions, and again in Country A when the executive receives distributions from the plan. This double taxation is clearly unfair and should be eliminated.

As a second example, assume that A, a resident of Country A, establishes a trust under the laws of Country A for the benefit of his or her children. Country A taxes the income accumulating in the trust but at the tax rates applicable to the children. A moves to Country B to take a temporary position for a few years and becomes subject to special rules in Country B for residents who have established foreign trusts. Most likely, A did not establish the trust to avoid Country B tax because, at the time the trust was established, A might not have known about the future move to Country B. Under Country B's rules, A is taxable on the income of the foreign trust even though the trust is taxable on its income in Country A. To eliminate this double taxation, some countries exempt temporary residents from their foreign trust and FIF rules for a limited period of time.

3.4 特殊问题

3.4.1 出境或离境税

当一个人终止其对居民全球所得征税国家的居民身份时，其将不再就全球所得在该国负有纳税义务。但是，终止居民身份带来的问题并非如此简单。例如，如果该人持有居民公司的股权，其价值明显高于取得时的价值，应该如何处理？根据大多数税收协定，一国居民纳税人处置另一国居民公司股权取得的资本收益，仅在纳税人为其居民的国家纳税（除非股权价值主要归属于位于另一国的不动产）。因此，如果一个人迁往与其原居民国签有协定的另一个国家，则可以出售该股权，而原居民国无法予以征税。如果新的居民国是经过纳税人慎重选择的，该国将对出售上述股权实现的所得不征税或者征收很少的税。显然，原居民国难以接受此结果。

部分国家采用通常被称为出境税或离境税的特殊规定，防止离境居民规避本国税收。对全部财产征收出境税的国家包括澳大利亚、加拿大和挪威。法国、德国和荷兰等其他国家实施较为有限的出境税，仅适用于居民公司的特定股权。美国实施更为有限的出境税，仅适用于放弃美国公民身份的美国公民和放弃美国永久居民身份的美国永久居民（绿卡持有者）将有形资产转让到美国以外的情形。

通常，这些税种的征收要求离境居民不仅就直至纳税人终止居民身份之日已实现的所得和收益缴纳税款，还包括应计但未实现的所得或收益。例如，假设X是X国居民，于2022年9月30日终止居民身份。当时，X于2022年1月1日至9月30日期间的全球所得为70000元；X还拥有其数年前创办、目前经营非常成功的一家公司的股权。该股权现值为30000000元，股权的成本可忽略不计。X还拥有一家X国居民公司发行的计息债券，每年12月31日付息。如果X国不对离境居民征收任何税收，X将不就应计股息或者至9月30日的应计债券利

3.4 SPECIAL ISSUES

3.4.1 Exit or Departure Taxes

When a person ceases to be resident in a country that taxes residents on their worldwide income, the person will no longer be subject to tax on worldwide income in that country. However, the consequences of ceasing to be resident are not quite so simple. For example, what if the person owns shares of a resident corporation that are worth significantly more than when they were acquired? Under most tax treaties, capital gains derived by a taxpayer resident in one country from the disposal of shares of a company resident in the other country are taxable only by the country in which the taxpayer is resident (unless the value of the shares is attributable primarily to immovable property located in the country). Therefore, if the person moves to another country that has a treaty with his or her former country of residence, the shares can be sold without any tax imposed by the former residence country. If the new country of residence has been chosen carefully, it may impose no tax, or little tax, on the gain realized on the sale of the shares. Not surprisingly, the former country of residence is unlikely to find this result acceptable.

Several countries have adopted special rules, often called exit or departure taxes, to prevent the avoidance of domestic tax by departing residents. Countries that have adopted exit taxes applicable to all property include Australia, Canada, and Norway. Other countries, such as France, Germany, and the Netherlands, have more limited exit taxes that apply only to certain shares in resident companies. The U.S. has an even more limited exit tax that applies only to transfers of tangible property out of the U.S. by U.S. citizens who give up U.S. citizenship and U.S. permanent residents (green card holders) who give up that status.

Typically, these taxes operate by requiring the departing resident to pay tax not only on the income and gains realized up to the date that the taxpayer ceases to be resident but also on any accrued but unrealized income or gains. For example, assume that X, a resident of Country X, ceases to be resident on September 30, 2022. At that time, X's worldwide income from January 1, 2022, to September 30, 2022, is 70,000. X also owns shares in a company that was established several years ago and which is now very successful. The shares currently have a value of 30 million. The cost of the shares to X is nominal. X also owns an interest-bearing bond issued by a company resident in Country X. The interest on the bond is payable annually on December 31. If Country X does not impose any tax on departing residents, X will not pay tax

息纳税。当 X 于 2022 年 9 月 30 日之后，出售股权或者收到债券利息时，X 将不再是 X 国居民。即使 X 国对从 X 国取得利息和从 X 国居民公司的股权实现资本收益的非居民征税，X 国与 X 的新居民国之间也可能存在税收协定，阻止 X 国征税。

如上所述，基于 OECD 协定范本或联合国协定范本的税收协定通常不允许一国对其他国家居民处置因本国居民公司股权而产生的财产收益征税，除非该公司资产主要由位于该国的不动产组成。通常协定也将一国对支付给其他国家居民的利息征税限定在 10% 或 15%，可能明显低于居民取得利息适用的税率。

为避免上述结果，X 国可能决定对终止居民身份的人征收出境或离境税。根据这类规定，X 将被视为在离境时以公允市场价值处置股权，以及在终止居民身份前即取得应计债券利息。这些数额将被包括在截至 2022 年 9 月 30 日 X 的全球所得中，并在 X 国纳税。只要 X 国对 X 仍为 X 国居民期间取得或视同取得的所得征税，就不适用与 X 新居民国的协定，因而将不会妨碍 X 国对 X 这些所得征税。

离境税面临若干具体问题。最突出的是，纳税人通常可能因为没有实际收到所得或者出售财产，而没有资金纳税。因此，一些国家允许离境居民在提供最终纳税有效担保的前提下延迟纳税（需付息）。离境税也可能引发双重征税的严重问题。没有离境税的大部分国家，根据财产的销售收入与原始成本的差额，来计算处置财产的收益数额。如果纳税人终止征收离境税国家的居民身份，其将就离境时拥有的资本财产的应计收益纳税，即离境前资产价值（假设 1000 元）超过资产历史成本（假设 200 元）的部分（800 元）。如果纳税人在将来某个日期出售资产，其新居民国通常将对所有收益（假设 1800 元，即销售收入 2000 元减历史成本 200 元）征税，而不仅对原居民国未予征税的部分收益（1000 元）征税。因此，收益中的一部分（在本例中是 800 元）将受到双重征税。这种情况下，根

on the accrued gain on the shares or on the interest accrued to September 30 on the bond. When X sells the shares or receives the bond interest after September 30, 2022, X will no longer be resident in Country X. Even if Country X imposes tax on nonresidents deriving interest from Country X and realizing capital gains on shares in companies resident in Country X, there may be a tax treaty between Country X and X's new country of residence that prevents Country X from taxing.

As noted above, tax treaties based on the OECD or UN Model Treaties preclude a country from taxing residents of the other country on capital gains from disposals of shares of resident companies unless the assets of the companies consist primarily of immovable property located in the country. Treaties also typically limit the tax imposed by a country on interest paid to a resident of the other country to 10% or 15%, which may be significantly less than the rate of tax applicable to interest derived by residents.

To avoid these results, Country X may decide to impose an exit or departure tax on persons ceasing to be resident. Under these rules, X will be deemed to have disposed of the shares for their fair market value at the time of departure and to have received the interest accrued on the bond immediately before ceasing to be resident. These amounts would be included in X's worldwide income for the period ending on September 30, 2022, and would be subject to tax in Country X. The treaty with X's new country of residence would not apply to preclude Country X from taxing X on these amounts as long as Country X's tax is imposed on income derived or deemed to be derived at a time when X was still a resident of Country X.

Special problems are encountered with departure taxes. Most important, the taxpayer often may not have the funds to pay the tax because the income has not actually been received or the property has not actually been sold. Accordingly, some countries allow the departing resident to defer the payment of the tax (with interest) if appropriate security for the ultimate payment of the tax is provided. A departure tax may also cause serious problems of double taxation. Most countries without departure taxes measure the amount of a gain on the disposal of property as the difference between the sale proceeds and the historical cost of the property. If a taxpayer ceases to be resident in a country that levies a departure tax, the taxpayer will be subject to tax on the accrued gain in respect of capital property owned at the time of departure. The accrued gain is the amount of the value of the property immediately before departure (e.g., 1,000) in excess of the historical cost of the property (e.g., 200), so the accrued gain is 800. When the taxpayer sells the property at a future date, the taxpayer's new country of residence will usually tax the entire gain (e.g., 1,800, computed as proceeds of sale (2,000) less historical cost (200)) and not just the portion of the gain (1,000) that was not taxed by the former country of

据通行税收协定的规定，由于两国均基于纳税人居民身份征税（但各在不同年度，以致双重居民加比规则不适用），因此，任一国家都没有义务为另一国的税收提供抵免。

征收离境税的国家通常认为，成为其居民的纳税人系以公允市场价值取得其在当时拥有的资产。实际上对于纳税人来说，从税收角度看，纳税人的资产成本有所增加，即从其历史成本调整至纳税人成为居民时的价值。成本更新和离境税的总体结果是，一国仅对纳税人为该国居民期间的应计收益和损失征税；而对于纳税人成为居民前，或者纳税人终止成为居民后的应计收益和损失，该国不予征税。

3.4.2 延续税

部分国家采用所谓的延续税作为出境税的替代或者补充。根据延续税，即使居民根据一国判定居民身份的普通规则终止居民身份，该国仍对其全部或者特定所得项目征税。延续税形式多样，适用范围或宽或窄。例如，德国等一些国家对迁往特定避税地的原居民采用特殊规定，即仍将其视同为居民，继续对全部所得征税。美国对其公民放弃美国公民身份以规避美国税收的亦有类似规定。这些原美国公民在放弃美国公民身份后的 10 年内，继续负有美国纳税义务。

一类常见的延续税适用于资本收益。与上述 3.4.1 节讨论出境税的情形相同，高税负国家的居民在转变为对资本收益不征税或者低税国家的居民后处置资产，即可对应计资本收益规避征税。对离境居民征收的出境税仅对截至纳税人终止居民身份之日的应计收益征税。根据延续税的规定，如果纳税人终止居民身份时拥有的资产，在终止居民身份后一段期间内（通常 5 ~ 10 年）被处置，需就全部收益纳税。对一国原居民的资本收益征收延续税的基本操作，以及延续税与出境税的关系，如下例所示。

residence. Thus, a portion of the gain (800 in this example) would be subject to double taxation. In this situation, under the provisions of a typical tax treaty, neither country is obligated to provide relief for the other country's tax because both countries impose tax on the basis of the taxpayer's residence (but for different years, so that the tie-breaker rules for dual residents do not apply).

Countries that impose departure taxes often deem taxpayers becoming resident to have acquired property owned at that time for its fair market value. In effect, the taxpayer is given a step-up in the cost of the property for tax purposes from its historical cost to its value at the time the taxpayer becomes resident. The overall result of this step-up in cost and the departure tax is that the country taxes only gains and losses accrued while a taxpayer is a resident of the country; gains and losses accruing before a taxpayer becomes resident or after a taxpayer ceases to be resident are not taxable by that country.

3.4.2 Trailing Taxes

Some countries have adopted a so-called trailing tax as an alternative or supplement to an exit tax. Under a trailing tax, a country imposes tax on all or certain items of income of a resident, even if the resident ceases to be a resident under the country's ordinary rules for determining residence. These trailing taxes take a wide variety of forms and may be broad or narrow in scope. For example, some countries, such as Germany, have special rules under which former residents who move to designated tax havens continue to be subject to tax on their entire income as deemed residents. The U.S. has a similar rule for U.S. citizens who give up their U.S. citizenship to avoid U.S. tax. Such former U.S. citizens continue to be subject to U.S. tax for ten years after they renounce their U.S. citizenship.

One common type of trailing tax applies to capital gains. As noted above in section 3.4.1, dealing with exit taxes, residents of high-tax countries may avoid tax on accrued capital gains by shifting their residence to a country that does not tax capital gains or taxes them at a low rate and then disposing of the property. An exit tax on departing residents captures only the gain accrued to the date that the taxpayer ceases to be resident. Under a trailing tax, the taxpayer would be subject to tax on the entire gain if property owned at the time the taxpayer ceased to be resident is disposed of within a certain period after the taxpayer ceases to be a resident (typically five to ten years). The basic operation of a trailing tax on capital gains of former residents of a country and the relationship between a trailing tax and an exit tax are shown in the following example.

案例

A 国对资本收益征收 15% 的税收，但不对非居民处置居民公司股权而实现的资本收益征税（处置价值主要来自位于 A 国不动产的股权所实现的收益除外）。A 国居民 A 拥有一家 A 国居民公司的股权，原始成本 1000000 元，现值 10000000 元。如果 A 从 A 国迁往不对财产收益征税的 B 国，可能规避针对 9000000 元应计收益的 A 国财产收益税。为防范这种避税，A 国可能采用延续税。如果原居民在终止居民身份 5 年内处置财产，延续税将适用于涉及原居民在终止居民身份时拥有财产的财产收益。因此，根据延续税，如果 A 在终止 A 国居民身份 5 年内，以 13000000 元出让股权，其全部收益 12000000 元将向 A 国纳税。

如果 A 国征收出境税，A 终止 A 国居民身份时，9000000 元应计资本收益将在终止时被 A 国征税。当 A 4 年后以 13000000 元出售股权时，根据 A 国延续税，另外的 3000000 元资本收益（销售收入 13000000 元减去 10000000 元的认定成本）将被 A 国征税。但如果 A 等到终止 A 国居民身份 5 年后出售股权，延续税将不适用。

除非协定包含允许征收此类延续税的特殊规定，一国签订的任何税收协定将阻止该国实施延续税。OECD 协定范本和联合国协定范本第 13 条不允许对原居民取得的财产收益征收此项税收。因此，基于前例事实，如果股权出售时，A 国与 B 国的税收协定包含与 OECD 协定范本或联合国协定范本第 13 条相近的处理财产收益的条款，A 作为 B 国居民将有权获得该协定待遇，A 国将不会对 A 出售股权的财产收益征税，除非该股权价值主要由位于 A 国的不动产构成，或者所出售股权构成公司的实质性权益（仅联合国协定范本）。部分国家在税收协定中设置特殊规定，允许对特定财产收益征收延续税。

英国等一些国家对在相对较短期间内（英国是 5 年）恢复居民身份的原居民予以征税。此项税收适用于纳税人作为非居民期间实现的财产收益，但仅在恢复英国居民身份时计征。

Example

Country A imposes tax on capital gains at a rate of 15%; however, Country A does not impose tax on capital gains from the disposition of shares of resident companies (other than gains from the disposition of shares that derive their value principally from immovable property located in Country A) realized by nonresidents. A, a resident of Country A, owns shares of a company resident in Country A that originally cost 1 million and now have a value of 10 million. If A moves from Country A to Country B, which does not tax capital gains, A can avoid Country A's capital gains tax on the 9 million accrued gain. In order to prevent this type of tax avoidance, Country A may adopt a trailing tax. This trailing tax would apply to any capital gains in respect of property owned by former residents at the time they cease to be resident if the property is disposed of within five years after they cease to be resident. Therefore, under the trailing tax, if A disposes of the shares for 13 million within five years of ceasing to be resident in Country A, the entire 12 million gain would be subject to tax by Country A.

If Country A has an exit tax, A's accrued capital gain of 9 million at the time that A ceases to be resident in Country A would be subject to Country A tax at that time. When A sells the shares for 13 million, say, four years later, an additional capital gain of 3 million (proceeds of 13 million less deemed cost of 10 million) would be subject to tax under Country A's trailing tax. However, if A waits for more than five years after ceasing to be resident in Country A to sell the shares, the trailing tax would not apply.

Any tax treaties that a country enters into will prevent the application of the country's trailing tax unless those treaties contain special provisions allowing the imposition of such a tax. Article 13 of the OECD and UN Model Treaties does not allow the imposition of trailing taxes on capital gains realized by former residents. Therefore, on the facts of the preceding example, if at the time of the sale of the shares, Country A and Country B have a tax treaty with an article dealing with capital gains that is similar to Article 13 of the OECD or UN Model Treaties, A would be entitled to the benefits of the treaty as a resident of Country B, and Country A would not be entitled to tax A's capital gain from the sale of the shares (unless the value of the shares was derived primarily from immovable property situated in Country A or the shares represent a substantial interest in the company (UN Model Treaty only)). Some countries put special provisions in their tax treaties to allow them to impose trailing taxes on certain capital gains.

Some countries, such as the U.K., impose tax on former residents who resume their residence within a relatively short period (five years in the case of the U.K.). The tax applies to capital gains realized during the time that the taxpayer was a nonresident but applies only on the resumption of U.K. residence.

3.4.3 年度内居民

如果纳税人仅在一年的部分时间为一国居民，就可能需要适用特殊规定。一些国家对一年中任何时间为其居民的纳税人，对其全年的全球所得征税。尽管税收协定的双重居民加比规则可能在一定情形下提供救济，但这种结果似乎过于严厉，特别是如果纳税人的新居民国也采取同样措施。因此，一些国家制定了适用于年度内居民的规定，仅对其实际为居民相关年度中部分全球所得征税。这些规定可能对某些类型的所得不便执行，例如，通常按年计算的经营所得。纳税人的个人扣除、减免和抵免通常按其在相关年度实为居民的时间比例进行划分。理论上，纳税人的新居民国应就相关年度的剩余时间允许相应的各项个人税前扣除。

年度内居民的问题与认定居民的问题有所不同。例如，如第 2 章第 2.2.1 节所讨论，许多国家采用 183 **天规则**，根据此项规则，任何年度在该国停留超过 183 天的人都被认定为居民。这些居民通常被认定为全年的居民，而不仅是其该年度在该国停留期间的部分。但是，年度内居民被认为在一年的部分时间内成为居民，在当年的其余时间是非居民。

3.4.4 外汇损益

如 3.2.4.2 节所述，居民通常必须将其以外币计量的境外所得折算为居民国货币。这一货币折算过程通常可能导致确认归属于两种货币之间汇率波动的损益，即使相关财产与交易以外币核算时可能并没有产生损益。

在计算处置境外财产的资本收益和损失时，简单地将资本收益或损失的金额折算为本国货币是不恰当的，而应将外币核算的财产成本按照取得该财产时的汇率折算为本国货币，并将财产出售收益按照出售该财产时的汇率折算为本国货

3.4.3 Resident for Part of a Year

Special rules may be necessary if a taxpayer is a resident of a country for only part of a year. Some countries may impose tax on a taxpayer's worldwide income for the entire year if the taxpayer is resident at any time during the year. This result seems harsh, especially if the taxpayer's new country of residence follows the same practice, although the dual-residence tie-breaker rules in tax treaties may provide relief in some circumstances. As a result, some countries have rules to tax part-time residents on their worldwide income for only the portion of the year during which they are actually resident. These rules may be difficult to apply with respect to certain types of income, such as business income, that are usually calculated on an annual basis. A taxpayer's personal deductions, allowances, and credits are usually prorated to reflect the portion of time during the year that the taxpayer is actually resident. In theory, the taxpayer's new country of residence should provide the taxpayer with personal allowances for the balance of the year.

The problems of part-time residents are different from those of deemed residents. For example, as discussed in Chapter 2, section 2.2.1, many countries have **183-day rules** under which persons who are present in the country for more than 183 days in any year are deemed to be residents. These residents are typically deemed to be resident for the entire year, not just for the portion of the year during which they are present in the country. However, part-time residents are considered to be resident for part of a year and nonresident for the remainder of the year.

3.4.4 Foreign Exchange Gains and Losses

As mentioned in section 3.2.4.2 above, residents must generally translate their foreign source income from a foreign currency into the currency of the residence country. This process of currency translation may often result in recognition of gains and losses attributable to changes in the exchange rates between the two currencies, even though there may be no gain or loss with respect to the underlying property or transaction measured in the foreign currency.

For purposes of computing capital gains and losses from the disposal of foreign property, it is inappropriate to simply convert the amount of a capital gain or loss into domestic currency. Instead, the cost of the property in foreign currency should be translated into domestic currency at the exchange rate applicable at the time that the property was acquired, and the proceeds

币。这种外币折算方法的结果是将外币损益确认为财产处置的资本收益或损失的组成部分，具体如以下案例所示。

案例

X是R国居民，2000年10月20日以100000欧元（S国货币）的成本从S国取得一项资产。2000年10月20日欧元与R国货币的折算汇率是1欧元 = 1.5R元。2020年12月7日，X以100000欧元出售该资产。当日欧元与R国货币的折算汇率是1欧元 =1R元。R国税务损失计算如下：

收入	100000 欧元	=	100000 R 元
成本	100000 欧元	=	150000 R 元
损失			50000 R 元

虽然上述资产处置以欧元核算没有产生损益，但是，由于R国货币相对于欧元升值，因此，资产处置发生损失。如果R国货币相对于欧元出现贬值（即2000年10月20日汇率是1欧元 = 1R元，2020年12月7日汇率是1欧元 = 1.5R元），即使以欧元核算没有产生损益，但纳税人将获得50000R元的收益。

如果以外币核算损益（即成本和收益），仅将其按照出售当日汇率或出售当年平均汇率折算为本国货币，则不会产生外汇损益。如前例所示，虽然汇率发生显著变动，但以欧元核算将不会产生损益。

债务也可能产生外汇损益，例如，假设R国居民纳税人贷款1000欧元，R国货币为R元。贷款时汇率为1欧元 = 5R元，借款利息为每年10%。每次应付/应计/支付100欧元利息时，纳税人必须按照应付/应计/实际支付利息时的适用汇率将其折算为R国货币。偿还贷款时，纳税人将产生收益或损失，视R国货币对欧元升值或贬值而定。例如，如果偿还时1欧元 = 4R元，纳税人将

from the sale of the property should be translated into domestic currency at the exchange rate applicable at the time the property is sold. This method of foreign currency translation results in recognition of the foreign currency gains and losses as part of the capital gain or loss from the disposal of the property, as illustrated in the following simple example.

Example

X, a resident of Country R, acquired property in Country S on October 20, 2000, at a cost of EUR 100,000, the currency of Country S. On October 20, 2000, the exchange rate of the euro relative to Country R's currency was EUR 1 = 1.5 Country R dollars. X sells the property on December 7, 2020, for EUR 100,000. The exchange rate relative to Country R dollars on that date is EUR 1 = 1 Country R dollar. The loss for purposes of Country R tax might be calculated as follows:

Proceeds	EUR 100,000	100,000 Country R dollars
Cost	EUR 100,000	150,000 Country R dollars
Loss		50,000 Country R dollars

Because the dollar has appreciated against the euro, the disposal of the property produces a loss, although there is no gain or loss with respect to the property measured in euros. If the Country R dollar had depreciated relative to the euro (i.e., the exchange rate was EUR1=1 dollar on October 20, 2000, and EUR 1 = 1.5 dollars on December 7, 2020), the taxpayer would have realized a gain of 50,000 Country R dollars, although there would have been no gain or loss in terms of euros.

If the gain or loss is determined in the foreign currency (i.e., the cost and proceeds) and that amount is simply translated into domestic currency at the rate applicable on the date of sale, or perhaps at the average rate applicable for the year in which the sale occurs, foreign exchange gains and losses would not be realized at all. As shown in the previous example, there would be no gain or loss measured in euros despite significant movement in the exchange rate.

Foreign exchange gains and losses may also arise with respect to debt obligations. For example, assume that a taxpayer resident in Country R, whose currency is R dollars, borrows EUR 1,000. At the time of the borrowing, the exchange rate is EUR 1=5 Country R dollars. Interest on the loan is 10% annually. Each time that interest of EUR 100 becomes payable (or accrues or is paid), the taxpayer must convert that amount to Country R dollars at the exchange rate applicable at the time the interest becomes payable, or accrues, or is actually paid. When

实现 1000R 元的收益。实际上，纳税人贷了 5000R 元款，但仅需 4000R 元即可偿还该贷款。根据国内法，偿还或清算债务的外汇损益，可能被作为资本损益或者正常的收入或损失。

外币风险产生于实际以外币进行的交易，也产生于纳税人经营的其他方面。例如，向另一国居民销售产品的纳税人，可能面对对方国家货币走弱于纳税人所在国货币的风险，导致纳税人的产品对该另一国居民变得更为昂贵。

企业往往试图通过自然套期保值来管理和抵消外汇风险，例如，以经营所在地或持有资产所在地的货币借款，或者通过运用衍生品，即旨在产生抵消相关资产或负债损益的收益或损失的金融产品。这些套期保值的税收处理，取决于会计规则与本国税法的结合，税收协定通常不涉及套期保值。

the loan is repaid, the taxpayer will realize a gain or loss depending on whether the Country R dollar has appreciated or depreciated in relation to the euro. For example, if on repayment, the exchange rate is EUR 1 = 4 Country R dollars, the taxpayer will realize a gain of 1,000 Country R dollars. In effect, the taxpayer has borrowed 5,000 Country R dollars but needs only 4,000 Country R dollars to repay the loan. Under domestic law, foreign exchange gain or loss on the repayment or settlement of a debt obligation may be treated as a capital gain or loss or as ordinary income or loss.

Foreign currency risks arise with respect to actual foreign currency transactions as well as other aspects of a taxpayer's business. For example, a taxpayer that sells its products to residents of another country is exposed to the risk that the country's currency may weaken against the taxpayer's currency, with the result that the taxpayer's products become more expensive for residents of the other country.

Businesses often try to manage or hedge their foreign currency risks through natural hedges, such as borrowing in the currency of the country in which they carry on business or own assets, or through derivatives, which are financial products designed to produce a gain or loss that offsets a gain or loss in respect of an underlying asset or liability. The treatment of these hedges for tax purposes is dependent on a mixture of accounting rules and domestic tax law. Tax treaties do not generally deal with hedging.

4　消除双重征税

4.1　引言

正如本书第 2 章所阐释，大部分国家就本国税收居民的全球所得征税，对于非居民，仅就其来源于本国的所得征税。结果就是一国居民来源于境外的所得可能被所得发生的国家（来源国）和纳税人为其居民的国家（居民国）同时征税。20 世纪初所得税刚刚起步时，所得税税率较低，双重征税造成的低效率和不公平或许尚可容忍。随着所得税税率提高至目前的普遍水平，双重税收可能形成沉重负担，对国际贸易产生实质性影响。从公平和经济政策的角度来看，消除国际双重征税的必要性都是显而易见的。但是，什么类型的消除方式更为适当，是一个有争议的问题。

国际双重征税可以多种方式产生。以下三种类型的双重征税是由两个或两个以上国家对同一纳税人的同一所得征收所得税的主张发生重叠而产生的（称为**法律性双重征税**）：

（1）来源国——来源国主张。两个国家都认为某一纳税人的同一所得来源于本国而行使征税权。

（2）居民国——居民国主张。两个国家都认为某一纳税人为本国居民，并据此对该纳税人的同一所得行使征税权。一个纳税人被两个国家认定为税收居民，通常称为“双重居民纳税人”。

（3）居民国——来源国主张。一国因某一纳税人是该国居民，而对其来源

CHAPTER 4

Double Taxation Relief

4.1 INTRODUCTION

As discussed in Chapter 2, most countries tax their residents on their worldwide income and nonresidents only on their domestic source income. Consequently, foreign source income earned by a resident of a country may be taxed both by the country in which the income is earned (the source country) and by the country in which the taxpayer is resident (the residence country). If income tax rates are low, as they were in the early years of the 20th century when income taxes were in their infancy, the inefficiencies and unfairness caused by this double taxation might have been tolerable. But when tax rates reach the levels that now prevail, double-tax burdens can become onerous and interfere substantially with international commerce. The necessity for the relief of international double taxation is clear on the grounds of equity and economic policy. However, the type of relief that is appropriate is a controversial question.

International double taxation can arise in a variety of ways. The following three types of double taxation arise from overlapping claims by two or more countries to impose income tax on the same taxpayer on the same income (referred to as **legal double taxation**):

(1) *Source-source claims.* Two countries assert the right to tax the same income of a taxpayer because they both claim that the income is sourced in their country.

(2) *Residence-residence claims.* Two countries assert the right to tax the same income of a taxpayer because they both claim that the taxpayer is a resident of their country. A taxpayer that is a resident of two countries is commonly referred to as a "dual-resident taxpayer."

(3) *Residence-source claims.* One country asserts the right to tax foreign source income of a taxpayer because the taxpayer is a resident of that country, and another country

于境外的所得行使征税权；另一国则因该所得发生或来源于该国，而对同一所得行使征税权。

在这三种类型的国际双重征税中，最有可能发生的是居民国和来源国征税主张的重叠。在一定程度上，纳税人可以通过缜密的税收筹划，尽可能避免其他类型的双重征税，但是纳税人很难通过税收筹划避免居民国和来源国的双重征税。因此，国际税收界针对国际双重征税所作出的努力，主要集中于消除居民国和来源国的冲突。

由于各国对所得的定义不同，对所得实现时间的定义不同或在计算所得时采用的税收会计规则存在差异，也可能导致国际双重征税。如第 6 章所述，国际双重征税也可能因各国就关联方之间商品和服务跨境交易的独立交易价格存在争议而导致。此外，各国为打击避税而实行的其他规则，也可能引起双重征税。例如，如果一国根据资本弱化或收益剥离规则，不允许其居民企业税前扣除支付给另一国股东的利息，并将所支付的利息视为股息，那么，该笔利息就可能在两个国家被重复征税，即在一国作为股息征收预提税，在另一国作为利息计入居民企业的所得。

税收协定通常能够消除上述三种主要类型及一些其他类型的国际双重征税，尽管这种消除有时是不完全的。部分基于所得来源的征税主张重叠而导致的双重征税，可以通过关于所得来源的明确规则予以解决。例如，OECD 协定范本和联合国协定范本第 11 条第 5 款规定，利息应被认为是发生于（即来源于）支付方为其居民的国家。然而，如第 2 章第 2.3.1 节所述，大多数税收协定没有涵盖广泛的来源规则。涉及来源国——来源国的双重征税个案，如无法根据协定具体条款予以解决，可由协定缔约国双方主管当局通过协定相互协商程序解决。关于相互协商程序的讨论，参见第 8 章第 8.8.3 节。解决这些问题并不容易，因为大多数国家的主管当局本能地不愿意放弃对其认为来源于本国的所得的征税权。

个人纳税人通常通过税收协定中的加比规则，消除因双重居民身份而产生的

asserts the right to tax the same income because the income arises or has its source in that country.

Of these three types of international double taxation, overlapping residence-source claims are the most likely to occur. To some degree, taxpayers can minimize their exposure to the other types of double taxation through careful tax planning, but residence-source double taxation is difficult for taxpayers to avoid through tax planning. Therefore, the attempts of the international tax community to deal with international double taxation have focused primarily on the elimination of residence-source conflicts.

International double taxation can also occur due to differences in the way countries define income and the timing and tax accounting rules they adopt for computing income. As explained in Chapter 6, international double taxation may also occur due to disputes between countries about the proper arm's-length prices for cross-border transfers of goods and services between related parties. Other rules adopted to curtail tax avoidance can also produce double taxation. For example, if one country denies the deduction of interest paid by a resident corporation to a shareholder in another country pursuant to thin capitalization or earnings-stripping rules and treats the interest paid as a dividend, the amount may be taxable in both countries, as a dividend subject to withholding tax in one country and as interest included in the resident corporation's income by the other country.

Typically, tax treaties provide relief from the three major types of international double taxation and from some of the other types as well, although the relief is sometimes limited. Some cases of double taxation resulting from overlapping claims based on the source of income are dealt with by explicit rules for the source of income. For example, Article 11(5) of the OECD and UN Model Treaties provides that interest is deemed to arise (i.e., have its source) in the country in which the payer is resident. As noted in Chapter 2, section 2.3.1, however, most tax treaties do not contain extensive source rules. Cases involving source-source double taxation that are not resolved by the specific provisions of a treaty may be resolved through consultation between the competent authorities of the two treaty countries under the treaty's MAP. *See* Chapter 8, section 8.8.3, for a discussion of the MAP. Resolution of such issues is not easy because the competent authorities of most countries are naturally reluctant to give up their country's right to tax what they consider to be domestic source income.

Individual taxpayers almost always obtain relief from international double taxation resulting from dual residence through the tie-breaker rules in tax treaties. Cases involving the dual residence of legal entities may also be resolved by treaty. As discussed in section 2.2.3, Article

国际双重征税。涉及法律实体双重居民的个案，也可根据协定解决。如第 2.2.3 节所述，OECD 协定范本和联合国协定范本第 4 条第 2 款，规定了一系列的“加比”规则，以解决个人根据两个国家的国内法分别都构成居民的情况。2017 年以前，根据 OECD 协定范本和联合国协定范本第 4 条第 3 款，解决法律实体的双重居民身份问题，是将该实体视为其实际管理机构所在地国家的居民。然而，在 2017 年对两个协定范本的更新中，取消了在实践中被证实难以操作的实际管理机构所在地规则，法人实体的双重居民身份问题，留待主管当局通过协定相互协商程序予以解决。由于双重居民实体经常被用来避税，一些双边税收协定拒绝给予这类实体协定待遇。

居民国和来源国对同一所得项目征税而产生的双重征税通常由居民国予以消除。也就是说，来源国基于所得来源的征税权优先于居民国征税权。

部分或完全消除双重征税通常采用三种方法，即**扣除法**、**免税法**和**抵免法**。对“国际双重征税”这一概念进行解释后，下文第 4.3 节将讨论这三种方法。

4.2 国际双重征税的定义

“双重征税”在众多不同的情况下使用，难以有一个精确的定义涵盖所有的情形。尽管 OECD 协定范本和联合国协定范本的主要目的之一是“避免对所得和财产的双重征税”，但两个范本及其注释都未给出双重征税的定义。

“国际双重征税”可以定义为两个或两个以上主权国家在同一期间对同一纳税人的同一所得项目（包括财产收益）征收所得税。这一司法或法律性国际双重征税的定义有失宽泛，没有涵盖评论人士通常视为双重征税的许多情形，但它的确明确了国际双重征税的构成要素。即便如此，根据这一定义确定某一个案是否存在双重征税也并不容易。例如，人们面临两国所征的税收是否都是所得税，或被征税的所得项目是否相同等问题。

国际双重征税的法律界定要与广义的经济性重复征税的概念区分开。当同一

4(2) of the OECD and UN Model Treaties provides a series of "tie-breaker" rules to resolve cases in which an individual is resident in both countries under their domestic laws. Until 2017, the dual residence of a legal entity was resolved under Article 4(3) of the OECD and UN Model Treaties by deeming the entity to be resident in the country where its place of effective management was located. However, in the 2017 updates of both model treaties, the place-of-effective-management rule, which proved to be difficult to apply in practice, was eliminated, and the residence of dual-resident entities was left to the competent authorities to resolve pursuant to the MAP. Since dual-resident entities are often used to avoid tax, some bilateral tax treaties deny treaty benefits to such entities.

Ordinarily, the residence country grants relief from double taxation resulting from the imposition of tax on the same item of income by both the residence country and the source country. In other words, the source country's right to tax on the basis of the source of the income has priority over the residence country's right.

Three methods—the **deduction method**, the **exemption method**, and the **credit method**—are commonly used for providing full or partial relief from double taxation. These methods are discussed in section 4.3 below after a brief explanation of what is meant by the term "international double taxation."

4.2 INTERNATIONAL DOUBLE TAXATION DEFINED

"Double taxation" is used in so many different contexts that any precise definition of the term is not appropriate in all contexts. The term is not defined in the OECD or UN Model Treaties or the Commentary on those Models, although one of their main objectives is "the avoidance of double taxation with respect to taxes on income and on capital."

"International double taxation" can be defined as the imposition of income taxes by two or more sovereign countries on the same item of income (including capital gains) of the same taxable person for the same period. This juridical or legal definition of international double taxation is narrow and does not cover many situations that commentators frequently refer to as double taxation, although it does identify the essential ingredients of international double taxation. Even so, under this definition, it is not always easy to determine whether double taxation exists in a particular case. For example, questions may arise as to whether the taxes levied by the two countries are both income taxes or whether the items of income subject to tax are the same.

The legal definition of international double taxation should be distinguished from the

经济所得承受多重税收时即认为发生了经济性重复征税。按照法律界定，一国对子公司利润征税，而另一国就子公司向母公司支付的股息向母公司征税，不是国际双重征税，因为母公司与子公司是各自独立的法人实体。但从经济意义上讲，母子公司构成一个单独的企业，对子公司利润征税又对该利润的分配征税，显然构成了对这些利润的双重征税。对合伙企业和合伙人征税，或者对信托和信托受益人征税，也可能产生经济性双重征税，而不是法律性双重征税。

消除国际双重征税的方法主要针对法律性双重征税，而不是经济性双重征税。消除双重征税仅限于法律性双重征税，是因为经济双重征税的定义过于宽泛，难以准确地加以界定，以满足税法的准确性要求。例如，在所得取得和消费时都征税，会形成经济性双重征税，但没有任何国家准备对销售税和其他消费税消除双重征税。同样，也没有国家准备消除因征收所得税和遗产或财产税而产生的经济性双重征税。对公司而言，这些困难更为复杂，因为不完全清楚针对公司征收的税收，是否或在多大程度上由其股东、雇员或客户实际承担。双重征税的消除有时候也会扩大到税款由居民母公司的外国子公司和其他境外关联体缴纳的经济性双重征税的情形，即使税款不是由母公司缴纳。

应将国际双重征税与一国对同一所得项目的双重征税加以区分，后者或许可以称为“国内双重征税”。例如，按照公司税的**经典模式**，对于由公司取得并分配给国内股东的所得，就可能产生国内双重征税。当一个人的所得被一国中央政府和一个或多个的地方政府征税时，也可能形成国内双重征税。中央政府和地方政府的重复征税并不一定是不可接受的——实际上，如果合理规范税权级次以避免过重税收负担，这种双重征税可能是实行财政联邦制不可避免的。

broader economic concept of double taxation. **Economic double taxation** occurs whenever there is multiple taxation of the same item of economic income. Under the legal definition, taxation of the profits of a subsidiary company by one country and taxation of the parent company on a dividend from that subsidiary by another country is not international double taxation because the two companies are separate legal entities. In the economic sense, however, the parent and the subsidiary constitute a single enterprise and tax imposed on both the profits of the subsidiary and distributions of those profits clearly constitutes double taxation of the profits. Economic, but not legal, double taxation also may arise when income is taxed to a partnership and the partners or when it is taxed to a trust and the beneficiaries of the trust.

Methods for relieving international double taxation are primarily focused on legal double taxation rather than economic double taxation. The reason double taxation relief is limited to legal double taxation is that the definition of economic double taxation is exceedingly broad and difficult to specify with the precision needed for tax laws. For example, some economic double taxation occurs where income is taxed when earned and again when consumed, yet no country is prepared to extend double taxation relief to sales taxes or other consumption taxes. Similarly, countries are not prepared to grant relief from the economic double taxation resulting from the imposition of both an income tax and an estate or wealth tax. These difficulties are compounded with respect to corporations because it is not entirely clear whether or to what extent the tax on corporations is actually borne by its shareholders, employees, or customers. Double taxation relief is sometimes extended to economic double taxation, where taxes are paid by foreign subsidiaries and other foreign affiliates of a resident parent corporation despite the fact that the taxes are not paid by the parent.

International double taxation should be distinguished from the double taxation of an item of income by a single country, which might be termed "domestic double taxation." Domestic double taxation may arise, for example, with respect to income earned by a corporation and distributed to its domestic shareholders under the so-called **classical method** of corporate taxation. It may also arise when tax is imposed on the income of a person by both the central government of a country and one or more of its political subdivisions. Double taxation by national and subnational governments is not necessarily objectionable—indeed, when the levels of taxation are properly regulated to avoid excessive tax burdens, such double taxation may be an inevitable feature of fiscal federalism.

4.3 消除双重征税的机制

4.3.1 引言

对于消除国际双重征税的适当方法，尚无国际共识。通常使用的有以下三种方法。一国可能仅使用其中一种方法，也可能组合使用这三种方法；大部分国家区别不同类型的国际双重征税，对这三种方法均予采用。

（1）扣除法。居民国允许其纳税人在计算所得额时，扣除各种税收，包括就外国来源所得已向外国政府缴纳的所得税。

（2）免税法。居民国对本国居民取得的境外来源所得，免征居民国税收。

（3）抵免法。居民国允许其居民纳税人在本应缴纳的居民国税收中，抵减向外国政府缴纳的所得税。抵免法下，境外税收是在计算居民国应纳税额时扣除，而不是在计算纳税人的所得额时扣除。

采用扣除法时，对该国居民境外来源所得征税的实际税率高于抵免法或免税法。当境外实际税率高于或等于本国实际税率，免税法和抵免法的结果通常是相同的。一般情况下，如果境外实际税率低于本国实际税率，则免税法对纳税人最有利。以下案例说明了三种方法的基本结果。

案例

R 是 A 国居民，从 B 国取得所得 100 元，并就该所得向 B 国缴税 40 元。按照扣除法，R 应就净所得 60 元（100－40），向 A 国纳税，即在计算 A 国应税所得时，可以扣除向 B 国缴纳的境外税收 40 元。假设在 A 国应按照税率 50% 对 R 予以征税，则 R 向 A 国缴税 30 元，其 100 元的所得共缴税 70 元（境外和本国合计税率是 70%）。如果 A 国采用抵免法，R 在 A 国的应纳税额（境外税收

4.3 RELIEF MECHANISMS

4.3.1 Introduction

No international consensus has been reached on the appropriate method for granting relief from international double taxation. The following three methods are in common use. A country may use only one of these methods, or it may use some combination of methods; most countries use all three methods for different types of international double taxation:

(1) *Deduction method.* The residence country allows its taxpayers to claim a deduction in computing income for taxes, including income taxes, paid to a foreign government in respect of foreign source income.
(2) *Exemption method.* The residence country exempts from residence country tax foreign source income derived by its residents.
(3) *Credit method.* The residence country provides its resident taxpayers with a credit for income taxes paid to a foreign country against residence country taxes otherwise payable. Under the credit method, foreign taxes are deductible in computing the tax payable to the residence country, not in computing the taxpayer's income.

Foreign source income earned by residents of a country that uses the deduction method is taxable at a higher effective rate than it would be under either the credit method or the exemption method. The exemption method and the credit method typically give equivalent results whenever the effective foreign tax rate is equal to or greater than the domestic effective tax rate. The exemption method is generally the most favorable to the taxpayer when the foreign effective tax rate is less than the domestic effective tax rate. The basic results of the three methods are illustrated in the following example.

Example

R, a resident of Country A, earns 100 of income from Country B, on which R pays tax of 40 to Country B. Under the **deduction method**, R will pay tax to Country A on net income of 60 (100−40). The foreign tax paid to Country B of 40 is deductible in computing R's income subject to tax in Country A. Assuming that R is taxable in Country A at a rate of 50%, R will pay tax of 30 to Country A and a total tax of 70 on income of 100 (a combined foreign and

抵免前）为其全球净所得（100 元）的 50%，且不能在计算净所得时扣除已向 B 国缴纳的税额。但是 R 可以用已向 B 国缴纳的（40 元）抵减本应向 A 国缴纳的税收。即在境外缴纳的税额（40 元）可以抵免在 A 国的应纳税额。其结果是 R 只向 A 国缴税 10 元（50－40），纳税总额为 50 元（境外和本国合计实际税率是 50%）。最后，如果 A 国使用免税法，R 无须就其在 B 国取得的境外来源所得在 A 国缴税，对该所得的合计应缴税款为 40 元（境外和本国合计税率是 40%）。上述结果在表 4–1 中列示。

表 4–1　消除双重征税方法的比较

	扣除法	抵免法	免税法
境外来源所得	100	100	100
境外税收（40%）	40	40	40
扣除境外税收	40	—	—
本国净所得	60	100	—
抵免前本国税收（50%）	30	50	—
减：境外税收抵免	—	40	—
最终本国税收	30	10	—
合计境外和本国税收	70	50	40

以下第 4.3.2 节至第 4.3.4 节分别详述了扣除法、免税法和抵免法的运用，第 4.3.5 节对免税法和抵免法进行了对比分析。第 4.3.6 节则分析了税收协定对消除双重征税的若干作用。

4.3.2　扣除法

采用扣除法的国家对本国居民的全球所得征税，但允许纳税人在计算本国应税所得时，扣除其已缴境外税收，实际上是将已缴纳的境外税收——所得税和其他种类的税收——视作纳税人在境外从事经营活动或取得所得的成本或当期费

domestic rate of 70%). If Country A uses the **credit method**, R's tax liability to Country A (before any foreign tax credit) will be 50% of the total worldwide net income (100), with no deduction for the taxes paid to Country B. However, R will receive a credit against the tax otherwise payable to Country A for the taxes paid to Country B of 40. The foreign tax paid of 40 is deductible against the tax payable to Country A. The result is that R will pay tax to Country A of only 10 (50−40) and a total tax of 50 (a combined foreign and domestic effective tax rate of 50%). Finally, if Country A uses the **exemption method**, R will pay no tax to Country A in respect of the foreign source income earned in Country B, and the total tax payable on the income will be 40 (a combined foreign and domestic rate of 40%). These results are summarized in Table 4.1.

Table 4.1 Comparison of Methods for Relieving Double Taxation

	Deduction Method	*Credit Method*	*Exemption Method*
Foreign source income	100	100	100
Foreign tax (40%)	40	40	40
Deduction for foreign tax	40	nil	nil
Net domestic income	60	100	nil
Domestic tax beforec redit (50%)	30	50	nil
Less: foreign tax credit	nil	40	nil
Final domestic tax	30	10	nil
Total domestic and foreign tax	70	50	40

Additional information on the operation of the deduction, exemption, and credit methods is provided below in sections 4.3.2, 4.3.3, and 4.3.4, respectively, and the exemption and credit methods are compared in section 4.3.5. Section 4.3.6 examines some of the effects of tax treaties on double-taxation relief.

4.3.2 Deduction Method

Countries using the deduction method tax their residents on their worldwide income and allow those taxpayers to take a deduction for foreign taxes paid in the computation of their taxable income. In effect, foreign taxes—income taxes and other types of taxes—are treated as costs or current expenses of doing business or earning income in the foreign jurisdiction. As noted above, the deduction method is the least generous method of granting relief from

用。正如上文所述，扣除法是消除国际双重征税最不充分的方法。

许多国家在刚建立所得税制时采用扣除法，当时全球所得税率较低，扣除法尚可接受。而随着第二次世界大战后所得税率的提升，很多国家采用免税法或抵免法作为消除双重征税的基本方法。OECD 协定范本和联合国协定范本仅认可以免税法和抵免法作为消除双重征税方法。

但是，扣除法并没有消失。一些采用抵免法的国家保留扣除法作为消除双重征税的备用方法，用于处理由于特定原因不符合抵免要求的境外税收。此外，有些国家对外国组合投资所得的已纳税额采用扣除法。

各国在对居民从外国公司取得的股息征税时，假设该外国公司已缴纳一定数额的境外所得税，如对该所得税不允许境外税收抵免，则实际上是采用了扣除法。例如，假设 F 公司是一家外国公司，取得境外所得 100 元，并缴纳境外所得税 20 元。F 公司将其剩余的税后所得 80 元作为股息分配给其股东，其中包括给予 R 的股息 20 元。R 为 A 国居民，持有 F 公司 25% 的股权。基于上述事实，R 通过 F 公司，获得境外来源所得 25 元，并为此已经缴纳境外所得税 5 元（25% × 20）。如果 A 国对 R 就所得 20 元征税，就相当于允许 R 扣除由 F 公司缴纳的所得税 5 元。如果一国要求将相应税收加回到股息中，则称为对股息进行**“还原加计”**，这是为了还原支付股息的税前所得。还原加计规则的目的，是对直接取得外国所得的纳税人和通过外国公司间接取得此种所得的纳税人，实现等效的处理。参见第 4.3.3.3 节中的**间接境外税收抵免**。

扣除法的结果是，与适用于本国来源所得的税率相比，取得境外来源所得，并对其缴纳境外所得税的居民，将按较高的合并税率纳税。因此，只要外国投资可能会被征收境外所得税，扣除法就会造成有利于本国投资，不利于外国投资的偏向。于是，从国家间资源配置的角度来看，扣除法不符合中性原则。但从一国自身利益的角度考虑，这种处理方式可能自有其道理：不仅可以鼓励本国投资，而且取得同等的全球净所得的居民将被同等对待，因为他们将缴纳同样多的本国

international double taxation.

The deduction method was used by a number of countries in the formative years of their tax systems when worldwide tax rates were low, and at that time, it was an acceptable approach. As tax rates increased in the post-World War Ⅱ period, however, most countries adopted either the exemption method or the credit method as the basic method for relieving international double taxation. The OECD and UN Model Treaties authorize only the exemption method and credit method as methods for granting double-tax relief.

However, the deduction method has not disappeared. Several countries that have adopted the credit method have retained the deduction method as an optional form of relief and a way of dealing with foreign taxes that, for some reason, do not qualify for the foreign tax credit. In addition, some countries use the deduction method for taxes paid with respect to income derived from foreign portfolio investments.

In effect, countries use the deduction method whenever they tax residents on the amount of the dividends they receive from a foreign corporation, assuming that the foreign corporation has paid some foreign income tax and a foreign tax credit is not allowed with respect to that tax. For example, assume that FCo, a foreign corporation, earns 100 of foreign income and pays foreign income tax of 20. FCo pays its remaining after-tax income of 80 as dividends to its shareholders, including a dividend of 20 to R, a resident of Country A who owns 25% of the shares of FCo. On these facts, R has earned 25 of foreign source income through FCo, on which foreign income tax of 5 (25% × 20) has been paid. If Country A taxes R on income of 20, it is, in effect, allowing R a deduction for the 5 of income tax that was paid by FCo. A country that requires the associated tax to be added to dividends is said to "**gross up**" the dividends to approximate the before-tax income out of which the dividends were paid. The purpose of a gross-up rule is to provide equivalent treatment to taxpayers earning foreign income directly and taxpayers earning such income indirectly through a foreign corporation. *See* the discussion of the **indirect foreign tax credit** in section 4.3.3.3 below.

The effect of the deduction method is that residents earning foreign source income and paying foreign income taxes on that income are taxable at a higher combined tax rate than the rate applied to domestic source income. As a result, the deduction method creates a bias in favor of domestic investment over foreign investment whenever the foreign investment is likely to be subject to foreign income tax. Thus, the deduction method is not neutral with respect to the allocation of resources between countries. This treatment may be justified from the viewpoint of national self-interest: not only is domestic investment encouraged, but residents with equal net worldwide income are treated similarly in that they will pay the same amount of domestic

税收。当然，就纳税人全球所得的总体（本国和境外合计）税负而言，扣除法不能使得所有居民税收待遇平等。因为尽管取得同等全球净所得的居民会缴纳同等数额的本国税收，但他们需要支付千差万别的境外税收。

4.3.3 免税法

按照免税法，居民国只对其居民本国来源的所得征税，对其部分或全部境外来源的所得，免于征收本国税收。实际上，居民国放弃了其对境外来源所得的征税权，结果就是该所得仅由来源国征税。由于只有一国，即来源国，对该所得征税，免税法可以完全消除居民国和来源国之间的国际双重征税。

部分国家（地区）对其居民取得的大部分或全部境外来源所得适用免税法，中国香港是一个突出的例子。这些国家（地区）实际上仅对本国（地区）来源所得征税，为此经常被称为属地征税，而不是全球征税。但是，对于使用免税法的大多数国家（地区）而言，境外来源所得免税局限于特定类型的所得，最常见的是在境外取得的经营所得和从境外关联公司取得的股息。而且，免税法有时也只局限于境外已经予以征税的所得，或者境外税收达到某低限税率的所得。

尽管境外来源的所得，可以由采用免税法的居民国免于征收居民国税收，但在确定纳税人其他应税所得在居民国的适用税率时，可能会将这些境外来源的所得纳入计算。这种做法被称为“累进免税法”。按照这种方法，将境外来源所得计入所得，仅仅是为了确定假如该境外所得也应税时，纳税人适用的平均税率，然后使用该平均税率，计算纳税人其他（非免税）所得的实际应纳税额。包括比利时、芬兰、德国和荷兰在内的一些国家实行累进免税法。

案例

假设A国对所得10000元及以内的适用税率为20%；所得超过10000元的部分适用税率为40%。T是A国居民纳税人，取得10000元的本国来源

tax. Of course, from the perspective of the total (combined domestic and foreign) tax burden on a taxpayer's worldwide income, the deduction method does not achieve equal treatment of residents. Although residents with equal net worldwide income will pay the same amount of domestic tax, they may pay widely differing amounts of foreign tax.

4.3.3 Exemption Method

Under the exemption method, the country of residence taxes its residents on their domestic source income and exempts them from domestic tax on some or all of their foreign source income. In effect, the country of residence gives up its right to tax foreign source income, which consequently is taxable exclusively by the source country. The exemption method completely eliminates residence-source international double taxation because only one jurisdiction, the source country, imposes tax on the income.

Some countries—Hong Kong is a prominent example—have adopted the exemption method with respect to most or all foreign source income earned by their residents. In effect, these countries tax only income from domestic sources. For this reason, they are often said to tax on a territorial basis rather than a worldwide basis. For most countries using the exemption method, however, the exemption of foreign source income is limited to certain types of income, most commonly business income earned in foreign countries and dividends from foreign affiliates. Further, the exemption method is sometimes restricted to income that has been subject to tax or subject to a minimum rate of tax by the foreign country.

Although foreign source income may be exempt from residence country tax by countries using the exemption method, the income may be taken into account in determining the rate of domestic tax applicable to the taxpayer's other taxable income. This practice is referred to as "exemption with progression." In such systems, the foreign source income is included in income for the limited purpose of determining a taxpayer's average tax rate as if the foreign income were taxable; this average rate is then used to compute the actual tax due on the taxpayer's other (nonexempt) income. Several countries, including Belgium, Finland, Germany, and the Netherlands, use the exemption with progression method.

Example

Assume that Country A levies tax at a rate of 20% on the first 10,000 of income and 40% on income in excess of 10,000. T, a taxpayer resident in Country A, has 10,000 of domestic source income from Country A and 10,000 of exempt foreign source income. T would pay

所得和 10000 元的免税境外来源所得。按照常规免税法，T 应缴税 2000 元（10000×20%）。按照累进免税法，T 必须确定，如果其全部所得 20000 元都是本国来源所得时，应该适用的平均税率。在此例中，平均税率应为 30%［（10000×0.2 + 10000×0.4）/20000］。然后，将平均税率适用于本国来源所得 10000 元，即可确定应向 A 国缴纳的税收，得出应纳税额为 3000 元。

免税法可使税务机关的征管更加简单，且能有效消除国际双重征税。累进免税法更为复杂，它要求税务机关掌握居民纳税人境外来源所得的数额的信息。

尽管免税法被广泛采用，并被 OECD 协定范本和联合国协定范本所认可（参见两个范本的第 23 条），但它与税收政策的公平和效率目标相悖。如果境外税收低于本国税收，取得免税境外来源所得的居民纳税人就比其他居民纳税人享受更为优惠的税收待遇。而且，免税法鼓励本国居民向低税率国家，特别是避税地投资，并激励纳税人将本国来源的所得转移到此类国家。例如，实施免税法国家的居民纳税人，如从投资于本国的资金收取利息，会有强烈的愿望将资金转移到对利息所得征税较低或不征税的外国。

由于免税法存在上述缺陷，对所有境外来源所得采用免税法消除双重征税，也就是相当于实行属地征税，很难证明其合理性。为此，仅有少数国家（地区）对所有境外来源所得采用该方法。如果将免税法仅作为抵免法的简便替代方法使用，或者仅对特定所得类型适用，则相对合理。例如，一国可以对其居民纳税人来源于与本国征税税率及征税条件大体类似的境外所得免于征税。如果此种免税法适用得当，其结果与抵免法相类似；因为在这种情况下，境外来源所得缴纳的境外税收与居民国税收相当，则采用抵免法的居民国从中补征甚少或征不到任何税收。这一情形可通过以下案例予以说明。

案例

A 公司是 A 国居民企业，A 国所得税税率是 25%。A 公司分别从 B 国和 C

tax of 2,000 (20% of 10,000) under a regular exemption system. Under an exemption with progression system, T must determine the average tax rate that would apply if the total income of 20,000 were domestic source income. In this example, the average rate would be 30% ((10,000 × 0.20 + 10,000 × 0.40) divided by 20,000). The tax payable to Country A would then be determined by applying the 30% average rate to the domestic source income of 10,000, resulting in tax payable of 3,000.

The exemption method is relatively simple for the tax authorities to administer and is effective in eliminating international double taxation. The exemption with progression system is more complex because it requires the tax authorities to obtain information about the amount of foreign source income earned by resident taxpayers.

Although the exemption method is widely used and is authorized by both the OECD and UN Model Treaties (*see* Article 23A of both treaties), it is inconsistent with the tax policy objectives of fairness and economic efficiency. To the extent that foreign taxes are lower than domestic taxes, resident taxpayers with exempt foreign source income are treated more favorably than other residents. Moreover, an exemption system encourages resident taxpayers to invest abroad in countries with lower tax rates, especially tax havens, and encourages them to divert domestic source income to such countries. For example, a taxpayer residing in an exemption country who earns interest on funds invested in that country has a strong incentive to move the funds to a foreign country that imposes low or no taxes on interest income.

Because of these deficiencies, as noted above, the application of the exemption method for relieving double taxation to all foreign source income, which is equivalent to taxing on a territorial basis, is difficult to justify and is used by only a few countries. The exemption method can be justified if it is used as a convenient and simple proxy for the credit method or is limited to certain types of income. For example, a country might exempt resident taxpayers on income derived from foreign countries that impose tax at rates and under conditions that are roughly comparable to its own rates and conditions. If such an exemption system is properly enforced, the results are similar to those obtained under a credit system because, in such circumstances, a country using the credit method would collect little or no tax with respect to any foreign source income that is subject to foreign tax comparable to the residence country's tax. This point is illustrated in the following example.

Example

ACo is a resident in Country A, which levies income tax at a rate of 25%. ACo earns

国取得所得 1000 元，B 国和 C 国所得税税率分别为 25% 和 30%。A 国采用境外税收抵免法消除国际双重征税。B 国和 C 国已缴税收的抵免额分别为 250 元和 300 元，将完全冲抵对 A 公司全部境外来源所得 2000 元的 A 国税收 250 元[①]。只有 A 公司的实际境外税率低于 A 国的实际税率时，A 国才会在允许境外税收抵免后，向 A 公司征税。

当然，在上例中，即使 B 国和 C 国在总体上对境外公司征收较高的税收，实际境外税率仍有可能低于 A 国税率。例如，其中一国或两国实行一些特殊的税收优惠，或其税法存在一些漏洞，外国公司可以加以利用。在这种情况下，A 国就可能从 A 公司的境外来源所得获得一些税收收入。

目前，针对由居民公司通过境外分支机构或常设机构取得的积极经营所得，以及针对从由居民公司在其中拥有最低所有权权益（通常为 5% 或 10%）的外国公司取得的某些股息，有些国家实行免税法。针对股息的这种免税通常称为参股免税，下文第 4.3.3.1 节将作详细讨论。

一般认为，采用免税法消除国际双重征税的优点是简便性：它使得纳税人遵从成本和税务机关的征管成本最小化。当境外税收和居民国税收大致相当时，有理由以免税法作为境外税收抵免的替代方法。但是，如果境外税收显著低于居民国税收，基于国际竞争力及资本输入中性考虑，免税法有其合理性。如果对 A 国居民公司就其在 B 国获得的经营所得，或从在 B 国经营的 B 国居民子公司取得的股息不予征税，那么，这些公司就其从 B 国取得的所得缴纳的税收，将与 B 国的其他居民公司或在 B 国经营的其他国家的居民公司缴纳的税收相同。

尽管对境外来源所得采用免税法使税务机关易于管理，但需要制定严密的所得来源规则。还需要制定反避税规则，以预防纳税人利用免税制度将本国来源所得转移为境外来源所得。最后，还需要制定费用分摊规则或反避税规则，以预防纳税人在其本国所得中，扣除为取得免税境外来源所得所发生的费用。

① 原文为“250”，似应为“500”（2000 × 25%）。——译者注

income of 1,000 in each of Country B and Country C, which levy tax at rates of 25 and 30%, respectively. Country A has a foreign tax credit system to relieve international double taxation. Consequently, the credits for taxes paid to Countries B and C, 250 and 300, respectively, will completely offset Country A's tax of 250 on ACo's total foreign source income of 2,000. Country A will collect tax from ACo after allowing the credit for foreign taxes only if ACo's effective foreign tax rate is less than the effective tax rate of Country A.

Of course, in the example above, the effective foreign tax rate may be lower than the Country A rate, even if Country B and Country C generally impose substantial taxes on foreign corporations. For example, one or both countries may offer some special tax incentives, or their tax laws may contain some loopholes that foreign corporations are able to exploit. In such circumstances, Country A might collect some tax revenue from ACo in respect of its foreign source income.

Several countries use the exemption method for active business income earned by resident corporations through a foreign branch or PE and for certain dividends received from foreign corporations in which resident corporations have a minimum ownership interest, usually 5 or 10%. This exemption for dividends is often referred to as a participation exemption and is discussed in more detail in section 4.3.3.1 below.

The alleged virtue of the exemption method for relieving international double taxation is its simplicity: it minimizes compliance costs for taxpayers and administrative costs for tax authorities. An exemption system can be justified as a proxy for a foreign tax credit where foreign taxes are roughly comparable to residence country taxes. However, where foreign taxes are significantly lower than residence country taxes, exemption is usually justified on the basis of international competitiveness and capital-import neutrality. If corporations resident in Country A are not taxable on their business income earned in Country B or on dividends received from a subsidiary resident and carrying on business in Country B, those corporations will pay the same tax on their income earned from Country B as other corporations resident in Country B or elsewhere doing business in Country B.

Although an exemption system for foreign source income is relatively easy for the tax authorities to administer, it requires rigorous source-of-income rules. It also requires anti-avoidance rules to prevent taxpayers from diverting domestic source income to foreign sources in order to take advantage of the exemption. Finally, it requires expense allocation rules or anti-avoidance rules to prevent taxpayers from deducting expenses incurred to earn exempt foreign source income against their domestic income.

One often-overlooked weakness of an exemption system is its likely impact on the

免税法有一个经常被忽视的缺点，在特定情况下，它有可能产生将税负从收入方转移到付款方的结果。例如，假设A国公司税率为30%，对境外来源所得实行免税。B国对支付给非居民的利息，征收20%的预提税。A公司是A国居民，向B国居民B公司提供100000元的贷款。如果A公司向C国居民而不是B公司提供贷款可以获得10000元的免税利息，则A公司可能会要求B公司每年支付缴纳B国预提税后的净额10000元。为此，B公司只能对其向A公司的款项支付，进行还原加计，以使得在缴纳了B国20%的预提税后，A公司最终能够得到10000元。这一安排的结果是，B公司承担了B国就支付给A公司的款项所征收的预提税2000元。如果A国采用抵免法，就可以避免这种经济影响。在抵免法情况下，A公司无论在何处取得利息所得10000元，都需要就此利息所得缴纳3000元的税收。A公司没有机会获得10000元的免税所得，而且B国的预提税可以抵免A公司应向A国缴纳的税收，因此无须将B国的预提税转嫁给B公司。

4.3.3.1 参股免税

大多数外国直接投资采取的形式是投资获得外国公司或非居民公司的股权或股份。针对从外国公司取得的股息和处置外国公司股份产生的财产收益如何消除国际双重征税，存在一些特别考量。本节讨论对涉及实质性参股外国公司的股息或财产收益的免税。下文第4.3.4.4节讨论来源于外国公司的股息的间接或相关境外税收抵免。参股免税和间接抵免的比较，参见第4.3.4节。

不少国家采用免税法消除对外国公司股息的双重征税。虽然免税法是欧洲国家采用的传统方法，但近年来，澳大利亚、日本、英国，以及美国（2017年）也采用了参股免税法。

设计参股免税法有三个关键要素：

（1）获得免税资格所必需的持股水平；

（2）由外国公司取得并从中支付股息的所得的性质；以及

shifting of tax burdens from an income earner to the payer in some circumstances. Assume, for example, that Country A, which has a corporate tax rate of 30%, provides an exemption for foreign source income. Country B imposes a withholding tax of 20% on interest payments made to nonresidents. ACo, a resident of Country A, makes a loan of 100,000 to BCo, a resident of Country B. If ACo can earn 10,000 of interest free of tax by loaning money to a resident of Country C instead of BCo, ACo is likely to demand that it receive annual payments from BCo of 10,000 net of Country B's withholding tax. Therefore, BCo would be required to gross up its payments to ACo so that ACo ends up with 10,000 after Country B's 20% withholding tax. The effect of this arrangement is that the burden of the withholding tax of 2,000 imposed by Country B on the payment to ACo is borne by BCo. This economic effect would be avoided if Country A used the credit method. In that case, ACo would pay taxes of 3,000 on the interest of 10,000 wherever it earned that interest income. ACo would have no leverage to shift Country B's withholding tax to BCo because it would have no opportunity to earn 10,000 free of tax, and Country B's withholding tax would be creditable against ACo's tax payable to Country A.

4.3.3.1 Participation Exemption

Most foreign direct investment takes the form of equity or share investments in foreign or nonresident corporations. Special considerations apply to the relief of international double taxation with respect to dividends from foreign corporations and capital gains from the disposition of shares of foreign corporations. This section discusses the exemption of dividends and capital gains with respect to substantial participations in foreign corporations. The indirect or underlying foreign tax credit for dividends from foreign corporations is discussed in section 4.3.4.4 below. The participation exemption and the indirect credit are compared in section 4.3.4.

Several countries use the exemption method to eliminate the double taxation of dividends from foreign corporations. The exemption method has been the traditional method used by European countries; however, in recent years, Australia, Japan, the U.K., and the U.S., in 2017, have also adopted participation exemptions.

There are three key elements in the design of a participation exemption:

(1) the level of share ownership necessary to qualify for the exemption;
(2) the nature of the income earned by the foreign corporation out of which the dividends are paid; and

（3）针对外国公司上述所得的境外税收的数额。

如第 4.3.4.4 节所述，上述三个要素对于设计境外税收间接抵免制度也很重要。

参股免税仅适用于居民企业从其拥有实质所有权权益或参股的外国公司取得的股息。要求的持股比例从 5%（如荷兰）到 25%（如日本和欧盟母子公司指令）不等。许多国家采用 10% 的持股比例作为门槛。持股比例门槛的基数可以是有投票权的股份或股权价值（或两者兼具），或外国公司的股本。

理论上，针对股息的免税应仅限于来自外国公司取得的积极经营所得的股息。来自外国公司消极投资所得的股息不符合免税条件；否则，居民公司会愿意将消极所得转移到其外国子公司，以减少居民国税收。例如，假设 A 公司是 A 国居民企业，有可用于投资的资金，可取得消极所得 100 万元。如果 A 公司通过在 A 国投资，获得该消极所得，则需要向 A 国缴纳税收 30 万元，因为 A 国按照税率 30% 征收公司税。但是，如果 A 公司用该投资资金收购其全资子公司 B 公司的股份，B 公司是 B 国居民，且 B 国仅按 10% 的税率征税，则 B 公司取得消极所得 100 万元，仅需向 B 国缴税 10 万元。B 国随后将税后利润 90 万元分配给 A 公司，假设 A 国对股息免税，这个简单的税收筹划就可以使 A 公司实现节税 20 万元。

因此，一些国家将免税法限制于外国关联公司从特定类型所得（如积极经营所得）派发的股息。这种方法（有时候称为“篮子”系统）对纳税人产生较大的遵从负担，纳税人需要记录其外国关联公司取得的所得的类型，并要求制定规则，以确定所支付的股息应属于哪一类型的所得。由于这些不便，一些国家放弃尝试将参股免税局限于从居民公司的外国关联公司积极经营所得中支付的股息，而是转而依靠受控外国企业规则或其他反规避规则，来防止对参股免税的滥用。例如，根据受控外国企业规则，对居民公司的受控外国关联公司取得的任何消极所得，在由该受控外国关联公司取得之时，即对该居民公司予以征税，而不需要等到该所得以股息形式进行分配。如果对居民母公司在获取该消极所得时即征

(3) the amount of foreign tax on the income of the foreign corporation.

These same three elements are also important in the design of an indirect foreign tax credit, as discussed in section 4.3.4.4.

The participation exemption is limited to dividends received by a resident corporation from a foreign corporation in which the resident corporation has a substantial ownership interest or participation. The level of share ownership required varies from 5% (e.g., in the Netherlands) to 25% (e.g., in Japan and the Parent-Subsidiary Directive in the EU). Many countries use a 10% ownership threshold. The ownership threshold can be based on voting shares, the value of shares (or both votes and value), or the share capital of the foreign corporation.

In theory, an exemption for dividends should be limited to dividends out of the active business income earned by a foreign corporation. Dividends out of passive investment income should not qualify for exemption; otherwise, resident corporations would have an incentive to divert passive income to their foreign subsidiaries in order to reduce residence country tax. For example, assume that ACo, a company resident in Country A, has funds available for investment that could earn passive income of 1 million. If ACo earns the income by investing in Country A, it will pay tax to Country A of 300,000 because Country A imposes corporation tax at a rate of 30%. However, if ACo uses the funds to acquire shares in its wholly owned subsidiary, BCo, resident in Country B, which taxes at a rate of only 10%, and BCo earns passive income of 1 million, BCo will pay tax to Country B of only 100,000. BCo can then distribute its after-tax profits of 900,000 to ACo. Assuming that Country A exempts the dividend, this simple tax planning would result in tax savings for ACo of 200,000.

Therefore, some countries limit the exemption method to dividends paid out of certain types of income, such as active business income of foreign affiliates. Such an approach (which is sometimes referred to as a basket system) imposes significant compliance obligations on taxpayers to keep track of the type of income earned by their foreign affiliates and requires rules to determine the type of income from which dividends are considered to be paid. As a consequence of these problems, some countries have abandoned any attempt to limit their participation exemptions to dividends paid out of active business income of foreign affiliates of resident corporations and instead rely on CFC rules or other anti-avoidance rules to prevent the abuse of the participation exemption. For example, under CFC rules, any passive income earned by a controlled foreign affiliate of a resident corporation is taxable to the resident corporation when earned by the controlled foreign affiliate without waiting for the income to be distributed in the form of a dividend. If the passive income is taxable to the resident parent corporation when

税，则后续来自该所得的任何股息，都可以根据参股免税免于征税。第 7 章第 7.3 节讨论了受控外国企业规则。

如上所述，假设对居民公司实质性参股的外国关联公司的所得予以征收境外税收，且其税率加上对股息的预提税接近居民国征税的税率，那么即使采用抵免法，居民国也不会从外国关联公司的股息征收任何税收。为此，从税收政策角度看，如果将参股免税限制在来自应按照与居民国公司税率相当的税率缴纳外国税收（公司税和股息预提税）的所得的股息，则有理由将参股免税作为境外税收抵免的替代。

一些国家已将参股免税的范围限定于设立在列明的可比税收国家或者与本国签订了包含股息免税的双边税收协定国家的外国关联公司所分配的股息。其他一些国家为简便起见，则没有将其参股免税局限于缴纳与居民国税收相当的境外税收的所得。在这些国家，即使外国关联公司的股息来自低税收国家，也可以适用参股免税。这些国家大多借助其他规则，如受控外国企业规则，以防止参股免税的滥用。如上所述，如果受控外国企业的所得在取得时即对其居民母公司征税，则后续该所得构成的股息，就可以免于征收居民国税收。

对来自外国关联公司的股息适用参股免税的一些国家，还将免税范围扩大至处置这些外国关联公司股份产生的财产收益。将参股免税扩大到财产收益的理由是，从经济和商业角度考虑，在实质性参股前提下，股息往往是财产收益的替代品。因此，如果股东公司为其居民的国家对来自外国关联公司的股息免税，但对出售外国关联公司股份的财产收益不免税，股东公司可以在计划出售外国关联公司股份前，要求外国关联公司支付免税股息，来降低出售股份产生的财产收益。

例如，假设 A 公司是 A 国居民，拥有 B 国居民 B 公司的全部股份。A 国对居民公司在其中拥有 10% 及以上股份（按投票权和价值计算）的外国公司的股息适用参股免税。但是，A 国对财产收益，包括处置外国公司股份产生的财产收益，征收 20% 的税收。A 公司正在考虑将 B 公司的股份出售给一无关联购买方，并预计获得 1000 万元的财产收益［销售收入 1400 万元减去股份成本（400 万

earned, any subsequent dividend out of that income can be exempt from tax under the participation exemption. CFC rules are discussed in Chapter 7, section 7.3.

As noted above, if the income of a foreign affiliate in which a resident corporation has a substantial participation is subject to foreign tax at a rate that, when combined with any withholding tax on dividends, approximates the tax rate imposed by the residence country, the residence country will not collect any tax on dividends from foreign affiliates in that country even if it uses the credit method. Therefore, from a tax policy perspective, a participation exemption can be justified as a proxy for a foreign tax credit if the exemption is limited to dividends out of income that is subject to foreign tax (corporation tax and dividend withholding tax) at a rate that is comparable to the residence country's corporate tax rate.

Some countries have limited their participation exemptions to dividends from foreign affiliates established in listed comparable-tax countries or to countries with which they have concluded bilateral tax treaties that provide an exemption for dividends. In the interests of simplicity, other countries have abandoned any attempt to limit their participation exemptions to dividends that are paid out of income that has been subject to foreign tax comparable to residence country tax. In these countries, the participation exemption is available even for dividends from foreign affiliates in low-tax countries. Most of these countries rely on other rules, such as CFC rules, to prevent abuses of the participation exemption. As noted above, if the income of a CFC is taxable to its resident parent corporation when earned, any subsequent dividends out of that income may be exempt from residence country tax.

Some countries with a participation exemption for dividends from foreign affiliates also extend the exemption to capital gains on the disposition of the shares of those foreign affiliates. The rationale for extending the participation exemption to capital gains is that, from an economic and commercial perspective, dividends are often a substitute for capital gains with respect to substantial participations. Thus, if dividends from a foreign affiliate are exempt from tax by the country in which the shareholder corporation is resident but capital gains on the sale of the shares of a foreign affiliate are not exempt, the shareholder corporation can reduce the capital gain from a proposed sale of the shares of a foreign affiliate by requiring it to pay exempt dividends before the sale.

For example, assume that ACo, resident in Country A, owns all the shares of BCo, resident in Country B. Country A has a participation exemption for dividends from foreign corporations in which resident corporations own at least 10% of the shares (by votes and value). However, Country A imposes a tax of 20% on capital gains, including capital gains from the disposal of shares of foreign corporations. ACo is contemplating a sale of the shares of BCo to

元）］。这一收益将由 A 国按 1000 万元的 20% 征税，即 200 万元。如果 B 公司在出售前向 A 公司支付股息 1000 万元，该股息将降低股份价值、销售收入和财产收益。但是，B 国可能对该股息征收预提税。如果是这样，只有当来源国的预提所得税低于居民国对财产收益的税收时，通过支付股息以减少财产收益才有利可图。旨在减少或规避针对处置外国子公司股份的税收的交易通常称为股息或盈余剥离交易。

4.3.4 抵免法

根据抵免法，居民纳税人就境外来源所得缴纳的境外税收，一般会减少该所得应缴纳的本国税收，减少的数额即为境外税收的数额。例如，如果 P 就某个境外来源所得项目缴纳境外税收 10 元，该所得原本应缴纳本国税收 40 元，那么，境外税收抵免将本国应缴税收从 40 元减到 30 元。因此，抵免法完全消除了居民国和来源国间的这一类国际双重征税。根据抵免法，只要已缴纳境外税收少于应缴纳本国税收，就应对境外来源所得征收本国税收。在这种情况下，本国净税收数额等于境外来源所得乘以两国税率之差。实际上，假设本国税率高于境外税率，则境外税收应由本国税收“补足”，使得针对境外来源所得的本国和境外合并税率等于本国税率。

如果其居民境外来源所得缴纳的境外税收高于该所得的本国应纳的税收，任何采用抵免法的国家都不会将超出部分退还其居民，税收协定中的条款也无此要求（参见 OECD 协定范本和联合国协定范本第 23B 条）。类似地，采用境外税收抵免法的国家通常也不会允许以超出部分的境外税收抵消对本国来源所得应于征收的税收。也就是说，已缴境外税收的抵免通常仅限于境外来源所得的应缴本国税收。为了防止境外税收抵免的不当利用，各国根据自己的要求采用了各种限制规则，这些规则的实际使用有时相当复杂，如下文所讨论。由于这些抵免限制，只要境外税率高于本国税率，境外所得一般都按照境外税率被征税。总之，

an arm's-length purchaser and expects to make a capital gain of 10 million (proceeds of sale of 14 million less the cost of the shares (4 million)). The gain would be subject to tax by Country A of 20% of 10 million, or 2 million. If BCo pays a dividend of 10 million to ACo before the sale, the dividend will reduce the value of the shares, the proceeds of sale, and the capital gain. However, the dividend may be subject to withholding tax by Country B. If so, the payment of dividends to reduce the capital gain would be beneficial only to the extent that the source country's withhold- ing tax is less than the residence country's tax on the capital gain. Transactions that are intended to reduce or avoid tax on the disposition of the shares of a foreign subsidiary are often referred to as dividend- or surplus-stripping transactions.

4.3.4 Credit Method

Under the credit method, foreign taxes paid by a resident taxpayer on foreign source income generally reduce domestic taxes payable on that income by the amount of the foreign tax. For example, if P pays a foreign tax of 10 on an item of foreign source income and would otherwise be subject to domestic tax of 40 on that income, the foreign tax credit reduces the domestic tax payable from 40 to 30. Consequently, the credit method completely eliminates international double taxation of the residence-source type. Under the credit method, foreign source income is subject to domestic tax whenever the foreign tax paid is less than the domestic tax payable. In such circumstances, the net domestic tax is an amount equal to the foreign source income multiplied by the difference between the two tax rates. In effect, assuming that the domestic tax rate is higher than the foreign tax rate, the foreign taxes are "topped up" by domestic taxes so that the combined domestic and foreign tax rate on the foreign source income is equal to the domestic tax rate.

Invariably, countries using the credit method do not refund foreign taxes paid by their residents on foreign source income in excess of the domestic tax on that income, nor are they required to do so under the provisions of tax treaties (*see*, for example, Article 23B of the OECD and UN Model Treaties). Similarly, countries with foreign tax credit systems do not generally allow excess foreign taxes to offset taxes imposed on domestic income. In other words, the credit for foreign taxes paid is usually limited to the amount of the domestic tax payable on the foreign source income. Various limitation rules, sometimes quite complex in application, as discussed below, are used to prevent what are perceived to be inappropriate uses of foreign tax credits. As a result of these limitations on the credit, foreign income is typically taxed at the foreign tax rate whenever the foreign rate is higher than the domestic rate. In

按照抵免法，居民取得的境外来源所得，一般按照本国税率和境外税率中孰高者征税。

4.3.4.1 一般规则

抵免法避免了第 4.3.1 节所述扣除法的缺点：从境外来源所得的国内外总税负角度看，居民纳税人受到同样的税收处理，但境外税收超过国内税收的情况除外。此外，排除上述例外情况，抵免法对居民纳税人在国内或国外投资决策的影响是中性的。下面的例子说明了这些观点。

X 和 Y 都是 A 国的居民，各自取得境外来源所得 100 元。针对各自境外来源所得，X 缴纳境外税收为零，而 Y 缴纳 30 元。如果 A 国对 X 和 Y 都按照 40% 征税，则 X 需向 A 国缴税 40 元，Y 缴税 10 元。在这两种情况下，缴纳的本国税收和境外税收合计都是 40 元。但是，如果 Y 的已缴境外税收是 45 元，由于 A 国不会就 Y 境外来源所得已缴的境外税收（45 元）超过本国税收（40 元）的部分（5 元）给予抵免，则 Y 的本国税率和境外税率合计为 45%。结果就是，Y 缴税 45 元，X 缴税 40 元。

许多国家允许当年不能抵免的境外所得税（境外税收抵免的超额部分）向后结转，用于抵免以后年度的本国税收。各国的可结转年限各不相同。以后年度中对这些境外税收抵免的超额部分的抵减，有抵免限额的规定。例如，假设 R 是 A 国居民，A 国按照税率 30% 进行征税。第一年，R 取得境外来源所得 100 元，缴纳境外税收 50 元。允许境外税收抵免 A 国税收，限额为 30 元，即完全抵消了应向 A 国缴纳的税收。对于境外税收超过本国税收的部分（20 元），此境外税收无法抵免，因此，R 存在抵免的超额部分 20 元。第二年，假设 R 取得境外来源所得 100 元，并缴纳境外税收 25 元。允许 R 抵免 30 元，即第二年的境外税收 25 元，加上从第一年向后结转并用于以后年度的超额部分 5 元。由第一年向后结转，并用于第三年及以后年度的超额抵免数额从 20 元减到 15 元。

从税收政策的角度看，众多税务评论人士认为，理论上，抵免法是消除国

summary, under the credit method, foreign source income earned by residents is generally taxed at the higher of the domestic and foreign tax rates.

4.3.4.1 General Rules

The credit method avoids the shortcomings of the deduction method described in section 4.3.1: resident taxpayers are treated equally from the perspective of the total domestic and foreign tax burden on their foreign source income, except when foreign taxes exceed domestic taxes. Moreover, subject to the same exception, the credit method is neutral with respect to a resident taxpayer's decision to invest domestically or abroad. These points are illustrated by the following example.

X and Y, who are both residents of Country A, each earn 100 of foreign source income. The foreign tax on such income is nil for X and 30 for Y. If both X and Y are subject to tax by Country A at a rate of 40%, X will pay 40 and Y will pay 10 of tax to Country A. In both cases, the combined domestic and foreign tax paid will be 40. If the foreign tax paid by Y is 45, however, the combined domestic and foreign tax rate on Y would be 45% because Country A would not provide relief for 5 of the foreign taxes paid (45) in excess of domestic taxes (40) on the foreign source income. As a result, Y would pay tax of 45, and X would pay tax of 40.

Many countries allow foreign income taxes that cannot be credited in the current year (excess foreign tax credits) to be carried forward and credited against domestic taxes in future years. The carryforward period varies from country to country. The limitations on the credit apply to the deduction of these excess foreign tax credits in future years. Assume, for example, that R, a resident of Country A, which imposes tax at a rate of 30%, earns foreign income in year one of 100 and pays foreign tax of 50. The foreign tax is allowed as a credit against the Country A tax to the extent of 30, thereby eliminating the tax payable to Country A completely. To the extent that the foreign tax exceeds the Country A tax (20), the foreign tax is not creditable, and R has an excess credit of 20. In year two, assume that R earns foreign income of 100 and pays foreign tax of 25. R might be allowed a credit of 30—the foreign tax in year two of 25 plus 5 of the excess credit carried forward from year one for use in future years. The amount of the excess credit from year one that is available for carryforward to year three and subsequent years would be reduced from 20 to 15.

On tax policy grounds, the credit method is recognized by many tax commentators to be theoretically the best method for eliminating international double taxation. The credit method,

际双重征税的最佳方法。然而，抵免法并非没有问题。最重要的是，从税务机关和纳税人的角度来看，抵免制度的操作趋于复杂。在众多难题中，必须解决的包括：

——哪些境外税收可以抵免？

——如何计算抵免限额？是否区分来源、项目、一篮子项目、国家，或者是笼而统之辅之以针对各种所得类型的具体的规则？又或者是这几种方法的组合？

——采用什么所得来源和扣除规则？

——是否需要制定反避税规则？

要使抵免法有效运作，就必须制定详细、技术性强且非常复杂的法律条文，来解决上述问题和其他相关问题。复杂的法律条文给纳税人和税务机关带来遵从和管理方面的负担，但是对于从低税或无税国取得的所得而言，这也是必需且合理的。否则，就可以通过将本国来源所得转移至这些国家，规避本国税收。

如果居民纳税人就其境外来源所得，应予缴纳境外税收，且税率与本国税率相当，抵免法之复杂是否还有其价值是受到质疑的。这种情况下，一国在允许纳税人抵免境外税收后，不太可能就其境外来源所得，从纳税人征收到较大数额的本国税收。一国采用的境外税收抵免制度，可能会激励其他国家将对该国居民所取得所得的税收提高到该国的税收水平（所谓的**吸收税**）。这种税收的增加不会影响非居民投资者的税后收益，因此不会抑制外来投资。但是，这种做法会导致税收收入从采用抵免法的居民国向所得来源国的转移。例如，假设 A 国按照 40% 税率征税，并采用境外税收抵免制度，A 国居民在 B 国有大量投资。如果 B 国对 A 国居民取得的所得，按照 25% 税率征税，那么，A 国将对 A 国居民就其在 B 国取得的所得征税 15 元（40－针对 B 国缴纳税收的境外税收抵免额 25），则该所得的合计税收为 40 元（向 B 国缴纳 25 元，向 A 国缴纳 15 元）。但是，

however, is not free from difficulties. Most important, the operation of a foreign tax credit system can be complex from the perspectives of both tax authorities and taxpayers. Among the difficult questions that must be resolved are the following:

- What foreign taxes are creditable?
- How should the limitations on the credit be calculated? On a source-by-source, item-by-item, basket of items, country-by-country, or overall basis with various special rules applicable to certain types of income? Or some combination of these methods?
- What rules should be adopted for determining the source of income and deductions?
- Are any anti-avoidance rules necessary?

Detailed, technical, and highly complicated legislative provisions are needed to resolve these and other matters if the credit method is to operate effectively. The compliance and administrative burdens imposed on taxpayers and tax authorities as a result of these complex rules are probably both necessary and justifiable in respect of income earned in no-tax or low-tax countries—otherwise, domestic tax could be avoided by diverting domestic source income to these countries.

When resident taxpayers are subject to foreign tax on their foreign source income at a rate that is comparable to the domestic tax rate, it is questionable whether the complexity of a credit system is worthwhile. In such circumstances, a country is unlikely to collect a significant amount of domestic tax from those taxpayers with respect to their foreign source income after allowing them a credit for foreign taxes. A foreign tax credit system used by one country may encourage other countries to increase their taxes on income earned by residents of that country to the level of tax in that country (so-called **soak-up taxes**). Such a tax increase would not affect the after-tax return to nonresident investors and therefore would not discourage investment from abroad. It would, however, result in a shift of tax revenues from the residence country with the credit system to the source country in which the income is earned. For example, assume that Country A imposes tax at a rate of 40% and uses a foreign tax credit system and that residents of Country A have substantial investments in Country B. If Country B imposes tax on the income earned by residents of Country A at 25%, residents of Country A will be subject to tax by Country A on income earned in Country B of 15 (40 minus a foreign tax credit for Country B's tax of 25) and total taxes on the income of 40 (25 to Country B and 15 to Country A). However,

如果 B 国把对 A 国居民取得所得的征税提高至 40%，那么，对 A 国居民的所得的合计征税仍为 40 元，但全部税收都缴纳给 B 国。

如果一国绝大部分的外国投资都集中来自几个国家的居民，且这几个国家的税率大致相当，那么，这个国家很有可能实行与抵免的国家有差异的税收。有些国家在其境外税收抵免规则中加入了防止“吸收税”作为可抵免境外税收的规定。此外，大多数税收协定中的非歧视待遇条款将阻止缔约国征收“吸收税”（关于非歧视待遇条款的讨论，参见第 8 章第 8.8.1 节）。

很多国家至少针对一些特定纳税人和一些特定类型的境外来源所得，通过抵免法消除国际双重征税。有些国家单方面给予境外税收抵免，其他一些国家仅根据双边税收协定给予抵免。采用抵免法的大多数国家既单方面，也根据协定，给予抵免。还有一些国家将其境外税收抵免机制延伸至涵盖“**税收饶让**”。税收饶让将在第 4.5 节中讨论。

4.3.4.2　可抵免的境外税收

几乎所有实行抵免制国家，都将其境外税收抵免限于境外所得税。其他境外税收，如增值税和房地产税，不是所得税，不符合境外税收抵免的条件。但是，预提税尽管是对股息、利息和特许权使用费等款项支付的总额征税，也被视为所得税。

根据 OECD 协定范本和联合国协定范本第 23B 条的规定，一国必须就所得向另一国缴纳的税款给予抵免，只要该所得“根据本协定条款”可在另一国征税。因此，必须参考协定条款，以确定另一国是否对具体所得项目具有征税权。然而第 23B 条并未规定哪些税可以抵免。OECD 协定范本和联合国协定范本第 2 条对协定所涵盖的“对所得的征税”（以及对财产的征税）均作了宽泛但模糊的定义，包括对全部所得、某些项目所得、转让财产取得的收益、全部工资和薪金，以及资本增值征收的税收。对于不在第 2 条对所得的征税定义范围内的任何税收，根据第 23B 条都不可抵免。

if Country B increases its tax to 40% on income earned by the residents of Country A, those residents will still be subject to total tax on the income of 40, but the entire tax will be paid to Country B.

A country is most likely to impose a discriminatory tax on residents of credit countries where the overwhelming amount of foreign investment in the country is owned by residents of a few foreign countries, and those foreign countries have approximately equivalent tax rates. Some countries include provisions in their foreign tax credit rules to prevent soak-up taxes from qualifying as creditable foreign taxes. In addition, the nondiscrimination article in most tax treaties would prevent the contracting states from imposing a soak-up tax (*see* Chapter 8, section 8.8.1 for a discussion of the nondiscrimination article).

Many countries use the credit method to eliminate international double taxation with respect to at least certain taxpayers and certain types of foreign source income. Some countries grant a credit for foreign taxes unilaterally; others grant a credit only pursuant to their bilateral tax treaties. Most credit countries grant the credit both unilaterally and by treaty. Still others have extended their foreign tax credit mechanisms to encompass "**tax sparing**." Tax sparing is discussed in section 4.5 below.

4.3.4.2 Creditable Foreign Taxes

Virtually all countries with credit systems limit their credits for foreign taxes to foreign income taxes. Other foreign taxes, such as value-added taxes and estate taxes, are not income taxes and do not qualify for the foreign tax credit. However, withholding taxes are treated as income taxes despite the fact that they are imposed on the gross amount of payments, such as dividends, interest, and royalties.

Under Article 23B of both the OECD and UN Model Treaties, a country is required to allow a credit for tax paid to the other country on income that may be taxed in the other country "in accordance with the provisions of this Convention." Therefore, the provisions of the treaty must be consulted to determine whether the other country is entitled to tax the particular item of income. However, Article 23B does not provide any rules as to what taxes are creditable. Article 2 of the OECD and UN Model Treaties provides a broad but vague definition of the "taxes on income" (as well as taxes on capital) covered by the convention to include taxes on total income, elements of income, gains from the alienation of property, total wages and salaries, and capital appreciation. Any taxes not within the definition of taxes on income in Article 2 are not creditable under Article 23B.

一般来说，税收是出于公共目的根据法律强制征收的。例如，税收不包含付费人因费用而直接获益的使用者付费。判断各种税收是否属于所得税时，可能会出现解释方面的许多难题。例如，就在线广告和其他数字化产品和服务支付给非居民的款项所征收的数字服务税，实质上可以视为所得税，尽管征收这些税收的国家称其并非所得税。关于数字服务税的讨论，见第 9 章第 9.5.3 节。此外，一些国家参照替代物核算收入据以征收某些特殊税种，如涉及航运的吨位税、资产税、涉及农业活动的核定征税，以及对推算或核定收入征收的其他税收。出于税收协定的目的，这些税收是否属于所得税？另一个难题在于，在某些情况下，部分国家可能有意地将所得税化身为税收协定范围之外的间接税。

4.3.4.3 抵免限额的类型

如上所述，实行抵免法的国家将境外税收抵免局限于针对境外来源所得的本国税收数额。为此，各国规定了各种类型的抵免限额。

在综合或全球抵免限额下，将向所有境外国家缴纳的境外税收加总计算，抵免仅限于已缴纳境外税收合计与针对纳税人境外来源所得总额应缴纳本国税收两者之孰低。这一方法允许在向部分国家缴纳的较高境外税收与向其他国家缴纳的较低境外税收之间实现平均。

在分国抵免或逐国抵免限额下，抵免仅限于向特定境外国家缴纳的税收与纳税人该国来源所得应予缴纳的本国税收中的孰低者。这种方法避免向不同国家缴纳的较高和较低境外税收之间的平均，但允许向某个特定国家，就不同类型所得，缴纳境外税收的较高和较低税率之间的平均。

在分项抵免限额下，抵免仅限于就各个特定所得项目缴纳的境外税收与该所得项目应予缴纳的本国税收的孰低者。这种方法避免了高低拉平，从理论上说是最好的制度，但实践中只被很少国家采用。在此制度中，所得“项目”有时是指所得的特定类别或“篮子”，如利息所得或海运所得等。原则上，一国可以将某

In general, a tax is a compulsory levy imposed by law for public purposes. For example, a tax would not include user fees where the payer receives direct benefits from the payment of the fees. Many difficult issues of interpretation may arise as to the characterization of various taxes as income taxes. For example, DSTs on payments to nonresidents for online advertising and other digital goods and services can be considered to be income taxes in substance, although the countries imposing those taxes claim that they are not income taxes. DSTs are discussed in Chapter 9, section 9.5.3. In addition, several countries impose special types of taxes that use proxies to measure income, such as tonnage taxes on shipping, assets taxes, presumptive taxes on agricultural activities, and other taxes on imputed or deemed income. Are these taxes income taxes for the purpose of tax treaties? Another difficulty is that, in some circumstances, countries may intentionally convert income taxes into indirect taxes that are outside the scope of tax treaties.

4.3.4.3 Types of Limitations

As noted above, countries that use the credit method limit the credit for foreign taxes to the amount of domestic tax on the foreign source income. For this purpose, countries use a variety of limitations.

Under an overall or worldwide limitation, foreign taxes paid to all foreign countries are aggregated; in effect, the credit is limited to the lesser of the aggregate of foreign taxes paid and the domestic tax payable on the total amount of the taxpayer's foreign source income. This method permits the averaging of high foreign taxes paid to some countries with low foreign taxes paid to other countries.

Under a country-by-country or per-country limitation, the credit is limited to the lesser of the taxes paid to a particular foreign country and the domestic tax payable on the taxpayer's income from that country. This method prevents the averaging of high and low foreign taxes paid to different countries but permits the averaging of high and low rates of foreign tax paid to a particular country on different types of income.

Under an item-by-item limitation, the credit is limited to the lesser of the foreign tax paid on each particular item of income and the domestic tax payable on that item of income. This method prevents averaging and is probably the best method from a theoretical perspective, although few countries use it in practice. In this context, an "item" of income is sometimes defined as a category or "basket" of income, such as interest income or shipping income. In principle, a country might define an item of income as any category of income that is subject to a special

一所得项目，界定为在某个境外国家适用特殊税收制度的所得类别。例如，一国可以将来源于某个境外国家的经营所得和利息所得视为单独的所得项目，以确定其境外税收抵免限额，特别是针对境外国家对由非居民取得的利息所得，按照优惠（低）税率征税的情况。

以下例子比较了对境外税收抵免实行综合、分国和分项限额时的结果。如表4–2所示，A公司是A国居民，取得境外来源所得，并就该所得缴纳境外税收。

表4–2 案例：基本情况

	境外所得	境外税收
从X国取得的经营所得	100000	45000
从X国取得的股息	20000	1000
从Y国取得的经营所得	50000	10000
从Z国取得的利息	10000	1500
合计	180000	57500

A国的公司税率为30%。A公司从其在A国开展的经营活动，取得本国来源所得200000元。如果不存在境外税收抵免限额，则应向A国缴纳的税收数额为：

案例：无限额情形

总所得	380000
抵免前税收（30%）	114000
境外税收抵免	57500
应纳税额	56500

合计应缴税收为114000元（境外税收57500元，A国税收56500元）。如果A国采用综合、分国或分项抵免限额，应缴税收如表4–3所示。

tax regime in a foreign country. For example, a country might treat business income and interest income arising in a foreign country as separate items of income for purposes of imposing a limitation on its foreign tax credit, especially where foreign countries tax interest income derived by nonresidents at preferential (low) rates.

The results of the overall, per-country, and item-by-item limitations on the foreign tax credit are compared in the following example. ACo, a resident of Country A, earns foreign source income and pays foreign taxes on such income, as shown in Table 4.2.

Table 4.2 Example: Facts

	Foreign Income	*Foreign Tax*
Business income from Country X	100,000	45,000
Dividends from Country X	20,000	1,000
Business income from Country Y	50,000	10,000
Interest from Country Z	10,000	1,500
Total	180,000	57,500

The corporate tax rate in Country A is 30%. ACo earns 200,000 of domestic source income from its business carried on in Country A. If there is no limitation on the foreign tax credit, the amount of tax payable to Country A by ACo would be:

Example: No Limitation

Total income	380,000
Tax before credit (30%)	114,000
Foreign tax credit	57,500
Tax payable	56,500

Therefore, the total tax payable would be 114,000 (foreign tax of 57,500 and Country A tax of 56,500). In contrast, if Country A uses an overall, per-country, or item-by-item limitation, the tax payable would be as shown in Table 4.3.

表 4–3　案例：综合抵免限额情形

综合抵免限额	
抵免前 A 国税收	114000
抵免：	
以下两项孰低：	
（1）境外税收 57500，以及	
（2）针对境外所得的 A 国税收（180000×30%=54000）	54000
抵免后 A 国税收	60000
合计税收（57500+60000）	117500

案例：分国抵免限额情形

分国抵免限额	
抵免前 A 国税收	114000
抵免：	
（a）X 国	
以下两项孰低：	
（1）境外税收 46000，以及	
（2）针对 X 国所得的 A 国税收（120000×30%=36000）	36000
（b）Y 国	
以下两项孰低：	
（1）境外税收 10000，以及	
（2）针对 Y 国所得的 A 国税收（50000×30%=15000）	10000
（c）Z 国	
以下两项孰低：	
（1）境外税收 1500，以及	
（2）针对 Z 国所得的 A 国税收（10000×30%=3000）	1500
合计可抵免税收	47500
抵免后 A 国税收	66500
合计税收（66500+57500）	124000

Table 4.3 Example: Overall Limitation

Overall Limitation	
Country A tax before credit	114,000
Credit:	
Lesser of:	
(1) Foreign tax of 57,500,and	
(2) Country A tax on foreign income (180,000 × 30% = 54,000)	54,000
Country A tax after credit	60,000
Total tax (57,500+60,000)	117,500

Example: Per-country Limitation

Per-country Limitation	
Country A tax before credit	114,000
Credit:	
(a) Country X	
Lesser of:	
(1) Foreign tax of 46,000,and	
(2) Country A tax on Country X income (120,000×30%=36,000)	36,000
(b) Country Y	
Lesser of:	
(1) Foreign tax of 10,000,and	
(2) Country A tax on Country Y income (50,000×30%=15,000)	10,000
(c) Country Z	
Lesser of:	
(1) Foreign tax of 1,500, and	
(2) Country A tax on Country Z income (10,000×30%=3,000)	1,500
Total creditable taxes	47,500
Country A tax after credit	66,500
Total tax (66,500+57,500)	124,000

案例：分项抵免限额情形

分项抵免限额	
抵免前 A 国税收	114000
抵免：	
（a）X 国	
（i）经营所得	
以下两项孰低：	
（1）境外税收 45000，以及	
（2）针对经营所得的 A 国税收（100000 × 30% = 30000）	30000
（ii）股息	
以下两项孰低：	
（1）境外税收 1000，以及	
（2）针对股息的 A 国税收（20000 × 30% = 6000）	1000
（b）Y 国	
以下两项孰低：	
（1）境外税收 10000，以及	
（2）针对经营所得的 A 国税收（50000 × 30% = 15000）	10000
（c）Z 国	
以下两项孰低：	
（1）境外税收 1500，以及	
（2）针对利息的 A 国税收（10000 × 30% = 3000）	1500
合计可抵免税收	42500
抵免后 A 国税收	71500
合计税收（71500 + 57500）	129000

用于限制境外税收抵免的三种方法并不互相排斥。例如，一国可以使用综合抵免限额法为基础方法，并针对特定类型的所得，如积极经营所得和消极投资所得，使用分项法。一些国家实行这种混合方法，也有时被称为“分篮法”。

Example: Item-by-Item Limitation

Item-by-Item Limitation	
Country A tax before credit	114,000
Credit:	
(a) Country X	
(i) Business income	
lesser of:	
(1) Foreign tax of 45,000,and	
(2) Country A tax on business income (100,000×30%=30,000)	30,000
(ii) dividends	
lesser of:	
(1) Foreign tax of 1,000,and	
(2) Country A tax on dividends (20,000×30%=6,000)	1,000
(b) Country Y	
lesser of:	
(1) Foreign tax of 10,000,and	
(2) Country A tax on business income (50,000×30%=15,000)	10,000
(c) Country Z	
lesser of:	
(1) Foreign tax of 1,500, and	
(2) Country A tax on interest (10,000×30%=3,000)	1,500
Total creditable taxes	42,500
Country A tax after credit	71,500
Total tax (71,500+57,500)	129,000

The three methods for limiting the foreign tax credit are not mutually exclusive. For example, a country could use an overall limitation as the basic method and also use the item-by-item method for certain types of income, such as active business income and passive investment income. Several countries use this type of hybrid method, which is sometimes referred to as a separate-baskets approach.

由于境外税收抵免额的限制，纳税人有时可能会发现他们有超额的境外税收抵免额（即境外税收超过了纳税人在国内可抵免的税收）。许多国家允许纳税人将这种境外税收抵免的超额部分向后结转到未来年度。但是，未来年度对境外税收抵免额超额部分的使用将受到相同的限额限制，这可能意味着超额部分逐年增加，无法使用。为了利用超额抵免额，纳税人可以在账面制造无经济实质的境外来源所得以吸收超额抵免额，一些国家制定了相关的反避税规则以阻止这种税收筹划策略。

4.3.4.4 间接或越层抵免

一些国家规定了通常所称的“间接”或“越层”境外税收抵免。间接抵免是指当居民公司从其外国关联公司收取股息时，针对由外国关联公司缴纳的境外所得税，而给予居民公司的抵免。允许作为抵免的数额为由外国关联公司就从中支付股息的所得而缴纳的相关境外税收。在通常情况下，境外税收抵免只允许针对居民纳税人直接缴纳的境外所得税。间接抵免规则实际上只是为了允许抵免，从而忽略居民公司和外国关联公司是独立纳税主体这一事实。为了获得由外国关联公司所缴纳税收的抵免，居民公司通常必须拥有外国公司股本中的实质性权益，从 5% 至 25% 不等。

间接抵免的基本运作可以通过下面的例子（见表 4–4）说明。假设 A 公司是 A 国居民企业，拥有为 B 国居民的全资子公司 B 公司。B 公司年度取得所得 800 元，并就该所得向 B 国按照 30% 的税率缴税，即 240 元。B 公司将其全部税后利润 560 元（800 – 240）作为股息分配给 A 公司。A 公司在 A 国应就 800 元纳税，其中包括股息 560 元，以及 B 公司就从中支付股息的所得缴纳的相关税收 240 元（经常被称为“还原加计额”）。假设 A 国按照 40% 税率征税，并且不存在境外税收抵免限额，则 A 公司应向 A 国缴纳的税收为 80 元（320 元减去 B 公司就支付股息的所得缴纳的境外税收的间接境外税收抵免额 240 元）。

As a result of the limitation on the amount of the foreign tax credit, taxpayers may sometimes find that they have excess foreign tax credits (i.e., foreign taxes in excess of the amount that can be credited against the taxpayer's domestic tax). Many countries allow taxpayers to carry such excess foreign tax credits forward to future years. However, the use of the excess credit in future years would be subject to the same limitation in those years, which may mean that the excess credits increase from year to year and cannot be used. In an attempt to use excess credits, taxpayers have created notional, non-economic foreign source income to absorb the excess credits, and some countries have enacted anti-avoidance rules to prevent such tax planning strategies.

4.3.4.4 Indirect or Underlying Credit

Some countries provide what is often referred to as an "indirect" or "underlying" foreign tax credit. The indirect credit is a credit granted to a resident corporation for the foreign income taxes paid by a foreign affiliate of the resident corporation when the resident corporation receives a dividend distribution from its foreign affiliate. The amount allowable as a credit is the amount of the underlying foreign tax paid by the foreign affiliate on the income out of which the dividend is paid. Ordinarily, a foreign tax credit is allowable only for foreign income taxes that a resident taxpayer pays directly. In effect, for the limited purpose of allowing the credit, the indirect credit rules ignore the fact that the resident corporation and its foreign affiliate are separate taxable entities. To claim a credit for taxes paid by a foreign affiliate, the domestic corporation must usually own a substantial interest, varying from 5% to 25%, in the share capital of the foreign corporation.

The basic operation of an indirect foreign tax credit is illustrated in the following example (Table 4.4). Assume that ACo, resident in Country A, has a wholly owned subsidiary, BCo, resident in Country B. BCo's income for the year is 800, and it pays tax to Country B at a rate of 30%, or 240, on its income. BCo distributes all its after-tax profits of 560 (800−240) to ACo as a dividend. ACo is taxable in Country A on 800—the dividend of 560 plus the underlying tax of 240 (often referred to as the "gross-up amount") paid by BCo on the income out of which the dividends were paid. Assuming that Country A levies tax at a rate of 40% and there is no limitation on the foreign tax credit, the tax payable to Country A would be 80 (320 minus an indirect foreign tax credit of 240 for the foreign taxes paid by BCo on the income out of which the dividend was paid).

表 4–4 案例：间接或相关境外税收抵免

B 公司所得	800
B 国税收	240
税后利润	560
分配股息	560
A 公司所得：	
从 B 公司取得的股息	560
还原加计额	240
合计	800
抵免前 A 国税收（40%）	320
B 公司已缴 B 国税收的抵免额	240
A 国净税收	80

在上例中，如果 A 公司取得的股息须由 B 国征收预提税，则该预提税也可以抵免 A 公司应向 A 国缴纳的税收，但应符合适用的限额规则。预提税尽管是从股息的支付方征收，但其针对的是股息收取方，因此，对于预提税的抵免属于直接抵免，而不是间接抵免。

抵免法可能会抑制本国公司就其通过外国关联公司获得的利润将作为股息分配汇回本国的积极性。假设 A 公司是 A 国居民，拥有作为 F 国居民的全资子公司 F，A 国税率是 35%，F 国税率是 10%。F 公司在 F 国取得利润 100 元，并向 F 国缴纳税收 10 元。如果 F 公司将税后利润 90 元作为股息汇回 A 公司，那么，A 公司将就 F 公司缴纳的相关境外税收，获得境外税收抵免 10 元，但需要向 A 国缴纳净税收 25 元，如表 4–5 所示。

表 4–5 案例：抵免法的结果

A 公司获得的股息	90
还原加计额	10
A 公司所得额	100
抵免前 A 国税收（35%）	35
针对由 F 公司缴纳税收的间接境外税收抵免额	10
A 国税收	25

Table 4.4 Example: Indirect or Underlying Foreign Tax Credit

BCo's income	800
Country B tax	240
After-tax profit	560
Dividend paid	560
ACo's income:	
Dividend received from BCo	560
Gross-up amount	240
Total	800
Country A tax before credit (40%)	320
Credit for Country B tax paid by BCo	240
Net Country A tax	80

If the dividend received by ACo in the above example is subject to withholding tax by Country B, the withholding tax would usually also be creditable against ACo's tax payable to Country A, subject to any applicable limitation rule. The credit for withholding tax is a direct foreign tax credit, not an indirect credit, because the withholding tax is imposed on the recipient of the dividend even though it is collected from the payer of the dividend.

The credit method may have the effect of discouraging domestic corporations that have earned profits abroad through foreign affiliates from repatriating these profits as dividend distributions. Assume that ACo, resident in Country A, has a wholly owned affiliate, FCo, resident in Country F. The tax rate in Country A is 35%, and the rate in Country F is 10%. FCo earns profits in Country F of 100 and pays tax to Country F of 10. If FCo's after-tax profits are repatriated to ACo as a dividend of 90, ACo will get a foreign tax credit of 10 for the underlying foreign tax paid by FCo, but it will be required to pay a net tax to Country A of 25, as shown in Table 4.5.

Table 4.5 Example: Effects of the Credit Method

Dividend received from ACo	90
Gross-up amount	10
Income of ACo	100
Country A tax before credit (35%)	35
Indirect foreign tax credit for taxes paid by FCo	10
Country A tax	25

通过将利润留存在 F 公司，A 公司可以无限期递延潜在的 A 国税收 25 元。在美国于 2017 年对来自外国公司的股息实行参股免税之前，这种税收筹划策略被美国大型跨国企业广泛应用。

为避免造成不利于利润汇回的倾向，采用抵免法的国家可以按照权责发生制（即在由外国关联公司取得所得之时），对居民公司的外国关联公司的所得予以征税。按照权责发生制进行税收征收，能够避免居民**递延**其通过外国关联公司取得的境外来源所得的本国税收。人们不时提出全面实施权责发生制的建议，但迄今没有在任何国家得到实施，尽管在某些情况下存在权责发生制税收处理。按照如第 7.3 和 7.5 节所述的受控外国企业规则和外国投资基金规则，一些国家在认定存在潜在的滥用情形时，对由外国关联公司或外国基金取得的某些所得，在当期征收本国税收。

旨在规范间接境外税收抵免的规则，往往是非常复杂的。只有当居民公司从外国关联公司取得一笔股息时，才可获得间接抵免。允许作为抵免的数额，是可以恰当地归属于该笔股息的境外所得税额。为确定抵免数额，必须解决发生时间和所得计量的难题。例如，居民公司必须确定用以支付股息的是外国关联公司的哪些利润，以及可归属于这些利润的是哪些境外税收。因为这些利润可能是过去不同年份取得的，通常会以外币计算，所依据的税收会计规则可能迥异于居民公司所适用的税务会计规则。当这些规则与上文第 4.3.4.3 节讨论的境外税收抵免限制规则相结合，其复杂程度会导致严重的遵从和管理问题。但是，需要面对间接境外税收抵免规则复杂性的通常是具备处理这种复杂性能力的大企业。尽管如此，一些国家还是对来自外国关联公司的股息实行参股免税以规避境外税收抵免规则的复杂性。

4.3.5 免税法和抵免法的比较

关于免税法抑或抵免法更有利于消除国际双重征税的争论，常常是激烈且情绪化的。目前只有很少国家（地区）实行纯粹的免税法或抵免法。哥斯达黎加、

By retaining the profits in FCo, ACo can indefinitely defer the potential Country A tax of 25. This type of tax planning strategy was widely used by most large U.S. multinationals before the U.S. adopted a participation exemption for dividends from foreign corporations in 2017.

To avoid creating a bias against the repatriation of profits, a credit country could tax the income of foreign affiliates of resident corporations on an accrual basis (i.e., as the income is earned by the foreign affiliates). Accrual taxation would eliminate the **deferral** of residence country tax on the foreign source income earned by residents through foreign affiliates. Proposals for a comprehensive accrual system have surfaced from time to time but have not yet been adopted in any country, although accrual taxation is used in some circumstances. Under the CFC rules and the FIF rules described in sections 7.3 and 7.5, some countries impose domestic taxes currently on certain income earned by foreign affiliates and foreign funds in what are perceived to be potentially abusive situations.

The rules designed to govern the indirect foreign tax credit are often very complex. The indirect credit is available only when a resident corporation receives a dividend from a foreign affiliate. The amount allowable as a credit is the amount of foreign income tax properly attributable to the dividend. Difficult timing and income measurement issues must be resolved in order to determine the amount of the credit. For example, the resident corporation must determine the profits of the foreign affiliate out of which the dividend was paid and the foreign tax attributable to those profits. Those profits may have been earned over many years in the past and would usually have been computed in a foreign currency and under tax accounting rules that may differ significantly from the tax accounting rules applicable to the resident corporation. When these rules are combined with rules for limiting the foreign tax credit discussed in section 4.3.4.3 above, the level of complexity causes serious compliance and administrative problems. However, the taxpayers that face the complexity of an indirect foreign tax credit system are typically large corporations that are well equipped to handle the complexity. Nevertheless, several countries have adopted participation exemptions for dividends from foreign affiliates in order to avoid the complexity of an indirect foreign tax credit.

4.3.5 Comparison of the Exemption and Credit Methods

The debate about whether the exemption method or the credit method is better for relieving international double taxation is often vigorous and emotional. Few countries have either a pure exemption system or a pure credit system. Costa Rica, Hong Kong, and Panama are examples of jurisdictions that tax on a territorial basis; they tax only income earned or having its source

中国香港和巴拿马是实行属地制度国家（地区）；其仅对在本地取得或来源于本地的所得征税，一般对全部或大部分境外来源所得免于征税。然而，对于大多数采用免税法的国家，境外来源所得的免税通常仅限于居民公司的某些积极经营所得和来自外国关联公司的股息。因此，公司往往仅就其从境外来源取得的积极经营所得，以及从其外国关联公司的积极经营所得中收取的股息，获得免税。投资所得通常不能免税，因为这样的免税将使居民纳税人很容易通过将本国来源的投资所得转移到外国，从而避免就其投资所得缴税。

关于经营所得，对免税法和抵免法的分析显示：第一，两种方法都产生了本质上相同的结构性问题；第二，如果设计得当，两种方法可以合理地比较。以下内容比较了从外国关联公司积极经营所得中收取股息的参股免税和对由外国关联公司就积极经营所得所缴纳的相关境外税收给予间接抵免两种情形。

如果由外国关联公司缴纳的相关境外税收，加上涉及股息的预提税，等于或大于针对该股息的本国税收，那么，两种方法对消除国际双重征税的效果相同。按照免税法，对股息免于征收本国税收，因此，总的税收就是外国关联公司就用以支付股息的所得所缴纳的相关境外税收，与针对该股息的境外预提税之和。按照间接抵免法，相关境外税收和境外预提税可以抵免针对股息的本国税收。因此，如果这些境外税收之和等于或大于针对股息的本国税收，则无须再缴纳本国税收。以下示例说明这一结果。

假设母公司是 A 国居民企业，全资拥有为 B 国居民并在 B 国开展业务的外国子公司。A 国对公司利润按 35% 的税率征税。B 国对公司利润按 30% 的税率征税。外国子公司获得利润 100 元，向 B 国缴纳税收 30 元，并将其 70 元的全部税后利润作为股息分配给母公司。如果 A 国使用参股免税或间接抵免法来消除对股息的国际双重征税，税收结果如表 4–6 所示。

in their territory and generally exempt all or most foreign source income from tax. For most countries using the exemption method, however, the exemption of foreign source income is often restricted to certain active business income earned by resident corporations and dividends from foreign affiliates. Thus, a corporation is often exempt only from its active business income derived from foreign sources and dividends received out of the active business income of its foreign affiliates. An exemption is not generally available for investment income because such an exemption would make it easy for resident taxpayers to avoid paying taxes on their investment income by shifting the source of domestic investment income to a foreign country.

With respect to business income, an analysis of the exemption and credit methods indicates, first, that the two methods raise essentially the same structural issues, and, second, that the two methods are reasonably comparable if designed properly. The following material compares a participation exemption for dividends received out of active business income of foreign affiliates with an indirect credit for the underlying foreign taxes paid by foreign affiliates on active business income.

The first point is that the results of these two methods for relieving international double taxation are the same if the underlying foreign taxes paid by the foreign affiliate, plus any withholding taxes on the dividends, are at least equal to the domestic taxes on the dividends. Under the exemption method, the dividends are exempt from domestic tax, so the total tax is the sum of the underlying foreign taxes paid by the foreign affiliate on the income out of which the dividend is paid and any foreign withholding taxes on the dividend. Under the indirect credit method, the underlying foreign taxes and the foreign withholding taxes are creditable against the domestic tax on the dividend. Therefore, if the sum of those foreign taxes equals or exceeds the domestic tax on the dividend, no domestic tax is payable. This result is illustrated in the following example.

Assume that Parentco, a company resident in Country A, has a wholly owned subsidiary, Forco, resident and carrying on business in Country B. Country A imposes tax on corporate profits at a rate of 35%. Country B imposes tax on corporate profits at a rate of 30%. Forco earns profits of 100, pays tax to Country B of 30, and distributes its entire after-tax income of 70 to Parentco as a dividend. Where Country A uses a participation exemption or an indirect credit system for relieving international double taxation of dividends, the tax results are shown in Table 4.6.

表 4-6 抵免法和免税法的比较

	抵免法	免税法
外国子公司		
所得额	100	100
境外税收（30%）	30	30
向母公司分配的股息	70	70
预提税（10%）	7	7
母公司		
取得的股息	70	70
还原加计额	30	
应纳税所得额	100	0
抵免前 A 国税收	35	-
境外税收抵免额（37 与 35 之孰低）	35	-
本国净税收	0	0
合计税收	37	37

如果境外公司税和股息预提税之和小于本国税收，则差额为应向 A 国缴纳的税收，因为境外税收未能完全抵消 A 国税收。但是，需要留意的是，母公司应缴纳的本国税收被递延到取得股息之时。假设外国关联公司可以使用该部分资金，实现比母公司更高的税后回报率，股息支付被递延的时间越长，居民国对股息税收的现值就越小。

参股免税通常的理由与普遍免税制的理由相同：国际竞争力和简单易行。不管对纳税人还是税务机关，参股免税通常比间接抵免更简单。然而，简化的益处往往被夸大，或者只是通过牺牲免税制的完整性才得以实现。

如果意在以参股免税替代间接抵免，则其设计应确保免税仅适用于外国税率与本国税率相当的境外来源所得。合理的对股息免税制度需要复杂的规则，以确保其完整性。其中许多规则与涉及间接境外税收抵免的规则显著相似。例如，两种制度都需要涉及以下方面的规则：

Table 4.6 Comparison of Credit and Exemption Methods

	Credit	*Exemption*
Forco		
Income	100	100
Foreign tax (30%)	30	30
Dividend to parent	70	70
Withholding tax (10%)	7	7
Parentco		
Dividend received	70	70
Gross-up amount	30	–
Taxable income	100	0
Country A tax before credit	35	–
Foreign tax credit (lesser of 37 and 35)	35	–
Net domestic tax	0	0
Total tax	37	37

Where the sum of the foreign corporate tax and the dividend withholding tax is less than the domestic tax, the difference will be tax payable to Country A because the foreign taxes will not offset Country A's tax completely. However, it should be recalled that the domestic tax payable by Parentco is deferred until dividends are received. The longer the payment of dividends is deferred, the lower is the present value of the residence country taxes on the dividends, assuming that the foreign affiliate can earn a higher after-tax rate of return on the funds than its parent corporation.

The usual justifications for a participation exemption are the same as the justifications for an exemption system generally: international competitiveness and simplicity. A participation exemption is usually simpler than an indirect credit for both taxpayers and tax officials. However, the benefits of simplification are often overstated or achieved only by sacrificing the integrity of the exemption.

If the participation exemption is intended to be a proxy for an indirect credit, it should be designed to ensure that the exemption is restricted to foreign source income that is subject to foreign tax rates that are comparable to domestic tax rates. A properly designed exemption system for dividends requires complicated rules to protect its integrity. Many of these rules are strikingly similar to the rules with respect to an indirect foreign tax credit. For example, both systems require rules dealing with:

—— 符合免税或抵免条件的居民纳税人（通常情况下，免税或抵免资格仅限于居民公司在其中拥有实质性权益的外国关联公司，实质性权益一般定义为拥有外国关联公司 10% 或以上股份）；

—— 符合免税或间接抵免条件的所得类型（这些规则通常区分积极经营所得和其他类型的所得）；

—— 境外税收在符合免税或间接抵免条件的所得和其他所得之间的划分；

—— 所得来源的判定；

—— 费用分摊（参见 4.4 节）；

—— 对居民控制的外国公司的消极所得的税收，是采用实收制还是应计制（第 7 章第 7.3 节讨论的受控外国企业规则）；

—— 境外亏损的处理；以及

—— 如何按照本国税收规则计算外国关联公司的所得。

免税法和间接抵免法最重要的区别在于，间接抵免法要求界定可抵免的境外税收，而免税法则要求制定规则以确定境外来源所得应纳境外税收的水平是否与本国所得税税收相当（假设免税法被用以替代间接抵免法）。

如上所述，许多国家为了实现外国关联公司股息参股免税的简单易行，只能牺牲免税法的完整性。在很多参股免税制度中，从外国关联公司取得的股息并没有适用与本国税率水平相当的外国税率，但仍适用参股免税制度。这种情况的发生有时是疏忽，而非故意为之。例如，一国规定，如外国关联公司为与其签订税收协定国家的居民，则从该关联公司取得的股息享受免税。如果该国与低税收国家或实施优惠性低税制度的国家签署了税收协定，那么，股息免税即可适用于来自这些国家的外国关联公司的股息，尽管用以支付股息的所得并未按与本国税率相当的税率缴纳境外税收。

一些国家有目的地实行参股免税制度，其相关制度并不试图确保对外国关联公司所得按照与本国税率相当的境外税率纳税。对这些国家来说，免税法并不是

- the resident taxpayers qualifying for the exemption or credit (usually, the entitlement to the exemption or credit is limited to foreign affiliates in which resident corporations have a substantial interest, which is often defined as 10% or more of the shares of the foreign affiliate);
- the type of income that qualifies for the exemption or indirect credit (usually, these rules distinguish between active business income and other types of income);
- the allocation of taxes between income that qualifies for the exemption or indirect credit and other income;
- the source of income;
- the allocation of expenses (*see* section 4.4);
- the current or accrual taxation of passive income of foreign corporations controlled by residents (CFC rules, which are discussed in Chapter 7, section 7.3);
- the treatment of foreign losses; and
- the computation of the income of the foreign affiliate in accordance with domestic tax rules.

The most important difference between the exemption and indirect credit methods is that the indirect credit method requires a definition of creditable foreign taxes, whereas the exemption method requires rules to determine when foreign source income is subject to a level of foreign tax that is comparable to domestic income tax (assuming that the exemption system is a proxy for an indirect credit system).

As noted above, many countries achieve the benefits of simplification with respect to their participation exemptions for dividends from foreign affiliates only by sacrificing the integrity of the exemption. In many participation exemptions, the exemption is available for dividends received from foreign affiliates that have not been subject to foreign tax rates comparable to domestic tax rates. Sometimes this appears to happen inadvertently rather than intentionally. For example, a country may provide an exemption for dividends from foreign affiliates resident in countries with which it has entered into tax treaties. If the country enters into tax treaties with low-tax countries or countries that provide preferential low-tax regimes, the dividend exemption will be available for dividends from foreign affiliates in those countries, even though the income out of which the dividends are paid is not subject to foreign tax rates that are comparable to domestic tax rates.

Several countries have intentionally adopted participation exemption systems that do not even attempt to ensure that the income of the foreign affiliates is subject to foreign tax rates

抵免法的替代。这种免税制度背后的政策取向不仅仅在于消除国际双重征税（尽管也实现了这个目的），还在于提升本国居民跨国企业的国际竞争力。为此，一些国家实行免税制度，对居民公司从其拥有实质性利益的外国关联公司取得的全部股息，免于征收居民国税收。结果是，这些国家的居民跨国企业，由于仅在经营活动所在地国家纳税，就能更好地在境外与当地居民公司以及第三国居民公司竞争。

例如，假设 M 公司是 A 国的居民跨国企业，A 国按照 35% 的税率征收公司税。M 公司全资拥有为 B 国居民且在 B 国开展业务的子公司，B 国按照 12.5% 的税率征收公司税。如果 A 国对 M 公司从其位于 B 国的子公司收取的股息征税，则该项税收是 M 公司在 B 国开展经营的成本（尽管该成本被递延到股息支付之时），B 国居民公司或在 B 国开展经营的其他国家居民可能并不需要承担该成本（当然，假设这些其他国家对来自外国关联公司的股息免于征税）。因此，与在 B 国开展经营的其他公司相比，M 公司将处于竞争劣势。

4.3.6　协定方面

如上所述，抵免法和免税法得到了 OECD 协定范本和联合国协定范本第 23 条的认可，而扣除法没有得到这两个协定范本的认可。OECD 协定范本和联合国协定范本第 23 条确立了抵免法和免税法的一般原则，至于落实这些一般原则的各项具体规定，则留待各国在其国内法中制定。

除了在其签订的协定中纳入消除双重征税规定以外，一些国家根据其国内法，规定对境外来源所得免于征税，或对已缴（以及外国关联公司已缴纳）境外税收给予抵免。尽管如此，协定的消除规定仍然非常重要，这是因为协定规定可能比国内法中的单边规定更为优惠。而且还因为，协定限制了一国修改其国内法，撤销或限制给予其居民的双重征税救济的能力。

例如，假设 A 国在其国内税法中规定，对 A 国居民取得的特定境外来源所

comparable to domestic tax rates. For these countries, the exemption method is not a proxy for the credit method. The underlying policy of such an exemption system is not just to eliminate international double taxation (although it accomplishes that result) but also to promote the international competitiveness of a country's resident multinational corporations. Thus, several countries have adopted exemption systems under which all dividends received by resident corporations from foreign affiliates in which they have a substantial interest are exempt from residence country tax. As a result, multinationals resident in such countries are able to compete in other countries with corporations resident in those countries and third countries because they are subject to tax only by the country in which the business is carried on.

For example, assume that a multinational corporation, MCo, is resident in Country A, which imposes corporate tax at a rate of 35%. MCo has a wholly owned subsidiary that is resident and carries on business in Country B, which imposes corporate tax at a rate of 12.5%. If Country A taxes dividends received by MCo from its subsidiary in Country B, that tax represents a cost to MCo for carrying on business in Country B (although the cost is deferred until the dividends are paid) that corporations resident in Country B or resident in other countries that carry on business in Country B may not bear (assuming, of course, that those other countries exempt dividends from foreign affiliates from tax). Accordingly, MCo would be at a competitive disadvantage compared to other corporations doing business in Country B.

4.3.6 Treaty Aspects

As mentioned above, both the credit and exemption methods are authorized by Article 23 of the OECD and UN Model Treaties. The deduction method is not authorized by those model treaties. Article 23 of the OECD and UN Model Treaties establishes the general principles of exemption and credit, with each country left to establish detailed rules in its domestic law for the implementation of the general principle.

Some countries provide an exemption for foreign source income or a credit for foreign taxes paid (and paid by a foreign affiliate) under their domestic law in addition to providing relief in any treaties that they enter into. Treaty relief is still important, however, because it may be more generous than the unilateral relief provided in domestic law and because it constrains a country's ability to amend its domestic law to withdraw or restrict the double taxation relief afforded to its residents.

For example, assume that Country A provides an exemption in its domestic tax law for certain foreign source income earned by residents of Country A. Country A enters into

得免于征税。A 国和 B 国签订税收协定，其中体现了同样的免税规定。如果 A 国后来废除了其国内税法中的免税规定，只要没有修改或终止与 B 国的协定，则 A 国仍须对从 B 国取得所得的本国居民给予免税。

4.4 费用分摊

一国无论采用免税法或抵免法消除国际双重征税，都应制定规则，以在其居民纳税人境外来源的全部所得和本国来源的全部所得之间，合理地分摊该纳税人发生的费用。多数国家认识到，需要制定此类规则，以对非居民纳税人的本国来源所得征税。因此，如果非居民产生的费用与取得应税本国所得无关，就不予认可该费用。出于境外税收抵免的目的，也需要制定类似的规则，以便在本国来源所得和境外来源所得之间，合理地分摊居民纳税人的费用。

对于对境外来源所得免税的国家，不应允许扣除居民纳税人为取得此免税所得而发生的费用。这符合税法的基本原则，即为获得非应税或免税所得而发生的费用不应扣除。例如，不应允许纳税人扣除用于取得免税境外来源所得的借贷资金所发生的利息费用。一国如果允许扣除此种利息费用，实质上就相当于对居民纳税人提供税收优惠或补贴，鼓励他们取得免税境外来源所得，而不是应税本国来源所得。事实上，此些国家不仅对居民纳税人的境外来源所得给予免税，还对一部分本国来源所得也给予了免税。

大部分国家缺乏向境外来源所得归属费用的具体规定。归属费用通常采用两种方法，即追溯法和分配或分摊法。追溯法涉及对费用和境外来源所得之间的联系进行事实性调查；而分配或分摊法则涉及通过公式，向境外来源所得归属费用，其依据是纳税人的外国资产与总资产之比，或全部境外来源所得与合计全部所得之比。与追溯法不同，分配或分摊法所基于的假设是，相关费用的发生是均衡地支持了纳税人的所有资产或取得所得的经营活动。

在实行境外税收抵免的国家，通常允许居民纳税人扣除为取得境外来源所

a treaty with Country B that incorporates the same exemption. If Country A subsequently repeals the exemption in its domestic law, it must nevertheless continue to provide the exemption to its residents that earn income in Country B unless the treaty with Country B is modified or terminated.

4.4 ALLOCATION OF EXPENSES

Whether a country uses the exemption method or the credit method to provide relief from international double taxation, it should have rules for allocating a proper portion of the expenses incurred by its resident taxpayers between their foreign source gross income and their domestic source gross income. Most countries recognize the need for such rules for taxing nonresidents on their domestic source income. Thus, expenses incurred by nonresidents will be denied unless those expenses are properly related to the earning of the domestic income subject to tax. Similar rules are necessary to properly apportion the expenses of resident taxpayers between domestic source and foreign source income for purposes of the foreign tax credit.

For countries that exempt foreign source income, expenses incurred by a resident taxpayer to earn that income should not be deductible. This result follows from the fundamental principle of tax law that expenses incurred to earn nontaxable or exempt income should not be deductible. For example, a taxpayer should not be allowed to deduct interest expense on borrowed funds used to earn exempt foreign source income. A country that allows such interest expenses to be deductible is, in effect, providing its resident taxpayers with an incentive or subsidy to earn exempt foreign source income rather than taxable domestic source income. In effect, the country is providing an exemption not only for foreign source income but also for a portion of the domestic source income of its resident taxpayers.

Most countries lack specific rules for attributing expenses to foreign source income. Two approaches that are often used for that purpose are tracing and allocation or apportionment. A tracing approach involves a factual inquiry into the connection between the expenses and the foreign source income. In contrast, allocation or apportionment involves the attribution of expenses to foreign source income by formula on the basis of either the proportion of the taxpayer's foreign assets to its total assets or the proportion of its gross foreign income to its total gross income. Unlike tracing, allocation or apportionment is based on the assumption that the relevant expenses were incurred to support all of the taxpayer's assets or income-earning activities proportionately.

In countries that have a foreign tax credit system, resident taxpayers are usually allowed

得所发生的费用，因为该所得将作为纳税人全球所得的一部分，对纳税人征税。然而，正如上文所阐释的，外国境外税收抵免总是局限于对境外来源应税所得原本应予征收的本国税收。为此，必须合理地计算纳税人的境外来源应税所得，否则，会不适当地扩大抵免限额。为了准确地计算应税境外来源所得，应要求纳税人从其全部境外来源所得中扣除为取得该所得而发生的费用。

制定费用分摊规则的必要性可以通过一个简单的例子来说明（见表 4–7）。假设某居民公司以年利率 8% 借入资金 1000 元，并且将这笔贷款用于外国分公司的经营活动。外国分公司获得毛收入 280 元。在扣除利息费用 80 元后，外国分公司的净所得为 200 元。该所得需在外国按照 40% 的税率缴税 80 元。如果该公司的本国来源净所得为 2000 元，则该公司的全部净所得为 2200 元。假设本国税率为 30%，该公司在减去可允许的外国税收抵免前的应纳税额为 660 元（2200 × 30%）。该公司可以就其已缴境外税收获得抵免，但抵免仅限于 80 元（已缴纳境外税收）和 60 元（660 × 200/2200）（境外来源所得的本国税收）的孰低者。

表 4–7　费用分摊

境外毛收入	280
利息费用	80
境外净所得	200
境外税收（40%）	80
本国净所得	2000
合计所得（200+2000）	2200
按 30% 税率计算的本国税收	660
境外税收抵免（80 与 60 之孰低）	60
应缴本国税收	600

在上例中，80 元的利息费用完全对应于或分摊给境外来源所得。如果将其对应于本国来源所得，由于抵免限额为 80 元和 93.33 元（660 × 280/2200）之孰低者，则全部境外税收（80 元）都可以在本国税收中抵免。假设可以将利息合

to deduct expenses incurred to earn foreign source income because those taxpayers are taxable on that income as part of their worldwide income. As explained above, however, the foreign tax credit is invariably limited to the amount of a country's domestic tax otherwise imposed on foreign source taxable income. For this purpose, the amount of a taxpayer's foreign source *taxable* income must be computed properly; otherwise, the limitation on the credit will be improperly inflated. In order to compute foreign source *taxable* income properly, the taxpayer should be required to deduct from its gross foreign source income the expenses incurred to earn that income.

The need for expense allocation rules can be illustrated with a simple example (Table 4.7). Assume that a resident corporation borrows 1,000 with interest at 8% annually and uses the loan proceeds to finance the business activities of a foreign branch. The foreign branch produces gross income of 280. After deducting the interest payment of 80, the branch's net income is 200. The net income of 200 is subject to foreign tax of 40%, resulting in tax of 80. If the corporation's domestic source net income is 2,000, the corporation's total net income is 2,200. Assuming that the domestic tax rate is 30%, the tax payable, prior to subtracting the allowable foreign tax credit, is 660 (30% of 2,200). The corporation is entitled to a credit for the foreign taxes paid, but the credit is limited to the lesser of 80 (the foreign tax paid) and 60 (660 × 200/2,200) (the domestic tax on the foreign source income).

Table 4.7 Allocation of Expenses

Gross foreign income	280
Interest expense	80
Net foreign income	200
Foreign tax (40%)	80
Net domestic income	2,000
Total income (200+2,000)	2,200
Domestic tax of 30%	660
Credit for foreign tax (lesser of 80 and 60)	60
Domestic tax payable	600

In the above example, the interest expense of 80 was applied or allocated totally against the foreign source income. If it had been applied against domestic source income, the entire amount of foreign taxes (80) would have been creditable against the domestic tax because the credit would be limited to the lesser of 80 and 93.33 (660 × 280/2,200). Assuming that the interest is

理地归属于境外来源所得，则在计算抵免限额时，也应将利息分摊给该所得。其原因在于，否则，本国税收体系给予的境外税收抵免额将超过对境外来源净所得的本国税收。因此，为保护国内税基，将利息和其他费用恰如其分地在本国来源所得和境外来源所得之间分摊至关重要。

如第 4.3.4.4 节所述，为了计算间接境外税收抵免限额，也应当将适当数额的费用归属于境外来源所得。此外，境外税收间接抵免还会涉及居民母公司通过外国关联公司取得境外来源所得所发生费用的扣除时间问题。针对通过外国关联公司取得的境外来源所得的居民国税收，通常会推迟或递延到居民母公司取得股息或其他应税分配之时。至少从理论上来说，居民母公司为取得该递延所得发生的利息和其他费用，在与之相关的所得计征居民国税收之前，都不应该扣除，即这些费用应在居民纳税人从其外国关联公司取得相关所得的应税分配时，才可以扣除。由于其复杂性，实际上目前很少国家尝试触及此时间匹配问题。

4.5 税收饶让

有些税收协定规定了“税收饶让”，通常通过税收饶让抵免实现。税收饶让抵免是指居民国对于根据来源国通常的税收法规本应缴纳，但出于某种原因没有实际缴纳的境外税收，所给予的抵免。没有缴纳税收通常原因是，来源国为在该国投资或开展经营活动的外国投资者，规定了免税期或其他税收激励。如果没有税收饶让，来源国为吸引外国投资而给予的税收激励的实际受益者就可能是投资者为其居民的国家，而不是外国投资者。其结果（有时被称为税收或收入转移效应）是，来源国税收的减少转而成为居住国税收的增加。

以下示例即可说明，如果不存在税收饶让，税收激励的益处会从外国投资者转移到其母国的国库之中。A 国是发展中国家，其正常的公司税税率为 30%。外国公司如果在 A 国设立制造工厂，A 国即给予 10 年免税期。B 国居民企业 B 公司在 A 国设立一家制造厂。B 国按照 35% 税率征收公司税，并采用境外税收抵

properly attributable to the foreign source income, it should be allocated to that income in computing the limitation on the credit because otherwise, the domestic tax system would be giving a credit for foreign taxes in excess of the domestic taxes on the foreign source net income. Therefore, in order to protect the domestic tax base, it is crucial for interest and other expenses to be allocated properly between domestic source and foreign source income.

An appropriate amount of expenses should also be attributed to foreign source income for purposes of computing the limitation on the indirect foreign tax credit, discussed in section 4.3.4.4. In addition, the indirect foreign tax credit raises the issue of the timing of the deduction of expenses incurred by a resident parent corporation to earn foreign source income through a foreign affiliate. Residence country tax on foreign source income earned through a foreign affiliate is generally postponed or deferred until the resident parent receives dividends or other taxable distributions. Interest and other expenses incurred by the resident parent to earn that deferred income should not be deductible, at least theoretically, until the income to which the expenses relate is subject to residence country taxation. These payments should be deductible when the resident taxpayer receives taxable distributions out of the related income from its foreign affiliate. Few countries currently attempt to deal with this timing issue because of its complexity.

4.5 TAX SPARING

Some tax treaties provide for "tax sparing," typically through a tax-sparing credit. A tax-sparing credit is a credit granted by the residence country for foreign taxes that, for some reason, were not actually paid to the source country but that would have been paid under the source country's normal tax rules. The usual reason for the tax not being paid is that the source country has provided a tax holiday or other tax incentive for foreign investors to invest or conduct business in the country. In the absence of tax sparing, the actual beneficiary of a tax incentive provided by a source country to attract foreign investment might be the country in which the investor is resident rather than the foreign investor. This result (which is sometimes referred to as the tax or revenue transfer effect) occurs whenever the reduction in source country tax is replaced by an increase in residence country tax.

The shifting of the benefit of an incentive from a foreign investor to its home country's treasury in the absence of tax sparing is illustrated by the following example. Country A, a developing country whose normal corporate tax rate is 30%, offers foreign corporations a ten-year tax holiday if they establish a manufacturing enterprise in Country A. BCo, a resident of

免制度消除国际双重征税。B 公司第一年通过其制造厂（常设机构）在 A 国取得所得 1000 元。如果没有免税期，A 国将对 B 公司征税 300 元，B 国将对 B 公司征税 50 元，即从税收 350 元中减去对于本应缴纳的境外税收 300 元的抵免。免税期取消了 A 国税收 300 元，因此，B 公司应向 B 国缴纳的税收应是 350 元减去可允许的境外税收抵免，后者为零，其原因在于 B 公司由于免税期，未向 A 国实际缴纳任何税收。这样，A 国因给予 B 公司因免税期而放弃的税收 300 元，使得 B 国而不是 B 公司受益。

如果 B 国愿意就 A 国放弃的税收，给予 B 公司税收饶让抵免，B 公司就可以获得免税期的益处。B 公司在 A 国取得所得 1000 元，其向 A 国无须缴税。B 公司在 B 国原本的应纳税额为 350 元，但允许其从中减去 A 国放弃或饶让的税收 300 元，故而合计税收义务为 50 元。结果如表 4-8 所示。

表 4-8 案例：税收饶让

A 国	
从 A 国取得的所得	1000
没有免税期时 A 国税收	300
免税期抵免	300
A 国税收	0
B 国	
从 B 国取得的所得	1000
B 国税收	350
税收饶让抵免	300
合计 B 国税收	50

如该例所示，在没有税收饶让抵免的情况下，A 国的免税期不会对 B 国居民中的潜在投资者产生任何影响，因为其居民国的税收将增加，抵消了 A 国提供的税收优惠。

税收饶让主要存在于发达国家和发展中国家之间的税收协定。在过去，很

Country B, establishes a manufacturing plant in Country A. Country B imposes corporate tax at a rate of 35% and uses a foreign tax credit system to provide relief from international double taxation. BCo earns income through its plant (PE) in Country A of 1,000 in the first year. In the absence of the tax holiday, Country A would impose a tax of 300 on BCo, and Country B would impose a tax of 50 on BCo, determined by subtracting from the tax of 350 otherwise payable a foreign tax credit of 300. The tax holiday eliminates Country A's tax of 300. Therefore, BCo's tax liability to Country B would be 350 minus the allowable credit, which is zero because BCo did not actually pay any tax to Country A due to the tax holiday. Thus, the tax revenue of 300 forgone by Country A in granting the tax holiday to BCo goes to the benefit of Country B and not to BCo.

If Country B was willing to give a tax-sparing credit to BCo for the taxes forgone by Country A, then BCo would get the benefit of the tax holiday. BCo's income in Country A would be 1,000, and it would pay no tax to Country A. It would have an initial tax obligation of 350 in Country B but would be allowed to reduce that amount by the 300 of tax forgone or spared by Country A, for a total tax liability of 50. The results are shown in Table 4.8.

Table 4.8 Example: Tax Sparing

Country A	
Income from Country A	1,000
Country A tax before holiday	300
Tax holiday credit	300
Country A tax	0
Country B	
Income from Country B	1,000
Country B tax	350
Tax-sparing credit	300
Total Country B tax	50

As the example shows, in the absence of the tax-sparing credit, Country A's tax holiday would not have any impact on potential investors resident in Country B because their residence country tax would increase to offset the benefit of the tax incentive provided by Country A.

Tax sparing is primarily a feature of tax treaties between developed and developing

多发达国家会理所当然地通过协定，给予发展中国家某种形式的税收饶让，以此作为鼓励在这些国家进行投资的一种方式，但其他国家只是勉强准予税收饶让抵免。一些发展中国家传统上拒绝与发达国家签订税收协定，除非可以得到税收饶让抵免。

美国坚决反对税收饶让，在其所有税收协定中，都未准许税收饶让。因此多年以来，美国与发展中国家签订的税收协定为数不多。美国的立场是，对并不存在的税收，即并未实际缴纳的税收，给予抵免，与其境外税收抵免的效率和公平目标相悖，会鼓励发展中国家通过税收激励制度，进行以邻为壑式的竞相追逐。尽管这一立场被认为是"傲慢的""帝国主义的"和"骄傲自大的"，但它对税收饶让影响的评价自有其合理之处。近年来，许多发展中国家的强硬态度有所缓解，美国与发展中国家签订税收协定的数量也在增长。其他一些发达国家最近在与发展中国家的协定中，也不再同意税收饶让条款，或者采取了仅在严格条件下，才给予税收饶让的立场。

税收饶让抵免的价值与其所带来的税收激励的价值是一体的。税收激励尽管在政界颇有一些狂热的支持者，但是基于税收政策原则，却很难站得住脚。旨在实现某一既定目标的有针对性的激励措施，可能有其合理之处。但是为了防止受到滥用，这类激励措施的范围极为有限，往往因此不能带来政治支持。从大量关于税收激励的税收文献中得出的一般性结论是，税收激励的成本通常较大，其益处却永远是不确定的；只有在极为罕见的情况下，其潜在的益处能够证明值得为之付出的各种代价。

发展中国家即使在其税收协定中未能加入税收饶让条款，也不妨碍其实现利用税收激励吸引外国投资的愿望。如果潜在投资者的居民国像越来越多的发达国家一样，采用免税法消除国际双重征税，则显然并不需要税收饶让。因为对于其居民国采用免税法的投资者而言，来源国税收是仅有的税收。为此，来源国税收的降低会自然而然地使他们受益。下面的例子说明，即便投资者居民国使用抵免法，投资者也可以略作税收筹划，即可从来源国的税收激励措施中受益。

countries. In the past, as a matter of course, many developed countries granted some form of tax sparing to developing countries by way of treaty as a way of encouraging investment in those countries, although others granted tax-sparing credits only reluctantly. Some developing countries traditionally have refused to enter into a tax treaty with a developed country unless they obtained a tax-sparing credit.

The U.S. is adamantly opposed to tax sparing and has not granted it in any of its tax treaties. Consequently, for many years it concluded very few tax treaties with developing countries. The U.S. position is that granting a credit for phantom taxes—taxes not actually paid—is inconsistent with the efficiency and fairness goals of its foreign tax credit and encourages developing countries to engage in beggar-thy-neighbor bidding wars through their tax incentive programs. This position has been characterized as "arrogant," "imperialistic," and "patronizing," but it is a defensible assessment of the effects of tax sparing. In recent years, the hard-line view of many developing countries has softened, and the number of U.S. tax treaties with developing countries is growing. Several other developed countries have recently either stopped agreeing to tax-sparing provisions in their treaties with developing countries or adopted the position of granting tax sparing only under stringent conditions.

The merits of tax-sparing credits cannot be divorced from the merits of the tax incentives that they encourage. Although tax incentives have some enthusiastic supporters in the political arena, they are difficult to justify on the basis of tax policy principles. Certain targeted incentives aimed at achieving some identified goal may be justified, but those incentives are so narrowly drawn to prevent abuse that they tend to generate little political support. The general conclusion to be drawn from the voluminous tax literature dealing with tax incentives is that the costs of tax incentives are typically large, the benefits are always uncertain, and only rarely do the potential benefits justify the likely costs.

A developing country wishing to use tax incentives to attract foreign investment is not stymied by a failure to obtain a tax-sparing article in its tax treaties. Tax sparing obviously is not needed if the country of residence of the potential investors uses the exemption method to avoid double taxation, as developed countries are increasingly doing, because, for investors resident in an exemption country, the source country tax is the only tax. Thus, any reduction in source country taxation automatically accrues to their benefit. Even investors from credit countries may benefit from a source country incentive with a little tax planning, as the example below illustrates.

在前面的例子中，B 公司是 B 国居民投资者，希望从 A 国给予的免税期中获益。为此，B 公司在 A 国设立全资子公司 A 公司，从事符合免税期条件的生产活动。A 公司从其在 A 国的生产活动中取得所得 1000 元，B 国未对该所得征税，因为 A 公司不是 B[①] 国的居民，且该所得不是从 B[②]国取得。B 国可对 B 公司就其从 A 公司获得的股息予以征税，但 A 公司并无义务一定分配股息。事实上，在该安排中，A 国从其免税期政策中的获益，可能会超过从税收饶让的获益，因为支付给 B 公司的股息可能会被征税，使得 A 公司更愿意将其利润再投资于 A 国。但是，因为 B 公司如果不缴税就不能将其投资所产生的利润汇回，因此可能不愿意在 A 国投资。

在没有税收饶让的情况下，税收激励措施有可能通过多种途径，使采用抵免法国家的居民受益。以上例子说明的只是其中的一种途径。例如，由于综合外国税收抵免限额运作的方式，实行综合抵免限额的国家的跨国企业居民，通常能够从来源国的税收激励措施中获益。按照综合抵免限额，在一国缴纳了较高税收的公司，原本超过境外税收抵免限额而原本应在居民国补交的税额，可以用在另一国的境外经营利润缴纳较低境外税收来抵减。例如，假设 P 国居民 P 公司，从其在 A 国的经营中获得了外国税收抵免的超限额部分 35 元。P 公司在 B 国取得利润 100 元，该利润通常在 B 国应纳税 35 元，但此项税收因为 B 国规定的免税期而被免征。P 公司仍可以从该免税期中获益，因为 P 公司可以用来自 A 国的超限额部分 35 元，抵消 P 国原本对其在 B 国的利润应予征收的税收 35 元。

税收饶让的另一问题是有可能被滥用，以实现避税。例如，某一协定中较为宽松的税收饶让抵免，经常会鼓励第三国居民在给予税收饶让的国家设立导管实体。此外，由于税收饶让会鼓励纳税人将利润转移到提供税收激励的国家，因此会给一国转让定价规则的执行带来压力。

1998 年，OECD 发表了题为《税收饶让：再思考》的报告，报告表明，实行

①② 原文为“A”，似应为“B”。——译者注

BCo, the investor resident in Country B in the preceding example, wants to obtain for itself the benefits of the tax holiday offered by Country A. To that end, it organizes ACo, a wholly owned subsidiary, in Country A. ACo engages in manufacturing activities that qualify for the tax holiday. ACo earns 1,000 from its manufacturing activities in Country A, which is not taxable by Country B because ACo is not resident in Country A and the income is not earned in Country A. BCo would be taxable by Country B on any dividends received from ACo, but ACo has no obligation to pay such dividends. Indeed, Country A may benefit more from its tax holiday under this arrangement than it would from tax sparing because the potential tax on dividends paid to BCo will provide a strong incentive for ACo to reinvest its profits in Country A. However, BCo may be reluctant to invest in Country A if it cannot repatriate any profits generated by its investment without paying tax.

The above example illustrates only one of several ways that tax incentives may benefit residents of countries using the credit method in the absence of tax sparing. For example, multinationals resident in countries with an overall limitation on the foreign tax credit can often benefit from source country tax incentives because of the way the overall limitation operates. Under the overall limitation, corporations that pay high foreign taxes to one country can use what would otherwise be excess foreign tax credits to offset their residence country tax that would otherwise be imposed on foreign business profits subject to low foreign taxes in another country. Assume, for example, that PCo, resident in Country P, has an excess foreign tax credit of 35 from operations in Country A. PCo earns profits of 100 in Country B that ordinarily would be subject to tax in Country B of 35, but that tax is eliminated because of a tax holiday provided by Country B. PCo benefits from that tax holiday because it can eliminate the Country P tax of 35 that would otherwise be imposed on its profits in Country B with the excess credit of 35 from Country A.

Another problem with tax sparing is the potential for abusive tax avoidance. For example, generous tax-sparing credits in a particular treaty often encourage residents of third countries to establish conduit entities in the country granting tax sparing. Tax sparing also puts pressure on the enforcement of a country's transfer pricing rules because taxpayers are encouraged to shift profits to the country providing the tax incentives.

In 1998 the OECD published a report, *Tax Sparing: A Reconsideration*, which suggests that the case for tax sparing is not persuasive. It recommends that tax sparing be restricted to countries whose economic development is at a considerably lower level than that of OECD member countries. It also sets out some best practices for the design of tax-sparing provisions

税收饶让的理由并不具有说服力。报告建议，应将税收饶让局限于经济发展水平显著低于 OECD 成员国的国家。报告还列举了制定饶让条款的若干最佳实践，以确保饶让条款仅适用于真实的商业投资，并使其不易被滥用。详情参见 OECD 协定范本关于第 23 条的注释第 72 段至第 78.1 段。

拟议的支柱二全球最低税方案将对各国向外国跨国公司提供的税收优惠产生重大影响，税收饶让问题也将受到类似影响。如果来源国的税收优惠导致外国跨国公司在该国的子公司或常设机构的超额利润的实际税率低于 15%，则该跨国公司将被其居民国征收补足税，该补足税税率等于 15% 与来源国实际税率之差。补足税将产生抵消来源国提供的税收优惠的效应。各国可以通过征收国内最低补足税来避免将税收实际转移到跨国公司母公司所在国。第 9 章第 9.5.5.3 节讨论了支柱二的最低税收。

to ensure that the provisions are limited to genuine business investments and are not susceptible to abuse. *See* also paragraphs 72–78.1 of the Commentary on Article 23 of the OECD Model Treaty.

The proposed Pillar Two global minimum tax will have significant effects on tax incentives provided by countries to foreign multinationals, similar to the tax-sparing issue. To the extent that a source country's tax incentives result in an effective tax rate of less than 15% on the excess profit of a foreign multinational's subsidiary or PE located in the country, the multinational will be subject to a top-up tax by its country of residence equal to the difference between 15% and the source country's effective tax rate. The top-up tax will have the effect of offsetting the tax incentives provided by the source country. Countries can avoid effectively transferring tax revenue to the country in which the parent of the multinational is resident by imposing a domestic minimum top-up tax. The Pillar Two minimum tax is discussed in Chapter 9, section 9.5.5.3.

5 非居民税收

5.1 引言

如第 2 章所述，大多数国家对其居民的全球所得和非居民的本国来源所得（即在一国领土范围内取得的所得）征税。而一些国家只对本国来源的所得征税（属地税收），不管取得相关所得的是居民还是非居民。因此，公平地说，除纯粹的避税港外，所有国家对非居民来源于其领土范围内的所得均征税。对于就全球所得征税的国家，有必要制定区分居民和非居民的规则，因为非居民仅就其来源于该国的所得而不是全球所得负有纳税义务。第 2 章第 2.2 节讨论了如何确定某人是否为某国税收居民的规则。

如第 2 章和第 3 章所述，国际上已经达成共识——各国有权对来源于其领土范围的任何所得征税。第 2.3 节论述了确定所得来源的规则。一个国家对本国来源所得的征税权，通常优先于其他国家基于所得取得人的居民身份而拥有的征税权。因此，居民国有义务消除国际双重征税，以承认来源国的优先征税权。

本章将探讨一国对非居民就其本国来源所得征税涉及的主要问题。首先简要论述了对非居民征税的税收政策依据，然后讨论了对非居民征税的门槛要求、非居民营业利润和投资所得的征税，以及非居民税款征收等实际问题。

为了方便从概念上加以讨论，可将非居民税收分为以下几个步骤：

CHAPTER 5
Taxation of Nonresidents

5.1 INTRODUCTION

As noted in Chapter 2, most countries tax their residents on their worldwide income and nonresidents on their domestic source income (i.e., income earned or derived in a country's territory). A few countries impose tax exclusively on domestic source income (territorial taxation) irrespective of whether the income is derived by a resident or a nonresident. Thus, it is fair to say that all countries, other than pure tax havens, tax the income earned or derived in their territory by nonresidents. For countries that tax on a worldwide basis, it is necessary to have rules that distinguish between residents and nonresidents because nonresidents are taxable only on their domestic source income, not on their worldwide income. The rules for determining whether a person is a resident of a country for income tax purposes are discussed in Chapter 2, section 2.2.

As discussed in Chapters 2 and 3, the international consensus is that countries are entitled to tax any income that arises or has its source in their territory. The rules for determining the source of income are dealt with in Chapter 2, section 2.3. A country's right to tax domestic source income generally takes priority over the right of another country to tax that income based on the residence of the person deriving the income. For this reason, the residence country has an obligation to relieve international double taxation in recognition of the source country's prior right to tax.

This chapter examines the major issues involved in taxing nonresidents on their domestic source income. The chapter begins with a brief discussion of the tax policy justifications for taxing nonresidents and then deals with practical issues such as threshold requirements for taxing nonresidents, the taxation of business profits and investment income of nonresidents, and the collection of tax from nonresidents.

For conceptual purposes, it is convenient to divide the taxation of nonresidents into the

—— 一国必须确定非居民必须与该国建立何种联系（联结度）（在该国的活动、在该国的财产所有权、在该国的实际存在，以及从该国取得所得等），该国才能行使其税收管辖权。

—— 一国一旦确定拥有税收管辖权，必须决定是否只有在非居民达到某个最低门槛（如常设机构或固定基地）的情况下，才行使税收管辖权。

—— 如果达到门槛或该国确定不需要门槛，则该国必须制定规则来确定非居民取得的何种款项应予以征税；这些规则通常被称为来源规则。

—— 计算非居民所得和应纳税额所必需的规则。

—— 最后，非居民税款征收所必需的规则。

上述步骤紧密相连且经常交叉。例如，如果一国决定对居民支付给非居民的所有利息或股息征税，则依付款人居民身份所确定的所得来源，就是赋予该国税收管辖权的联系；因此，该国就没有必要设立任何门槛要求。同样，转让定价规则既可视为来源规则也可视为计算规则。这些步骤的划分旨在为非居民税收问题的思考提供一个分析框架，并不在于说明各国对非居民征税的实际方式。

就非居民税收而言，营业利润和投资所得之间的区分尤为重要。对经营所得征税通常以净额为基础，适用与居民纳税人相同的税率，因此，在另一国家取得经营所得的个人通常适用累进税率。相比之下，对投资所得征税通常以总额为基础，适用固定税率，而且，税款通常以预提方式征收（即向非居民付款的居民有义务从支付款项中扣留税款，并将税款缴至税务机关）。

5.2 对非居民征税的税收政策考量

回顾一下第 3 章第 3.2 节，对居民全球所得征税的主要税收政策依据是公平和中性。对非居民的征税则难以以公平为由，因为，在大多数情况下，来源国并

following stages:

- A country must determine what type of connection (nexus) a nonresident must have to the country (activities in the country, the ownership of property in the country, physical presence in the country, receipt of income from the country, etc.) in order for the country to be able to exercise its jurisdiction to tax.
- Once a country has decided that it has jurisdiction to tax, it must decide whether it should exercise that jurisdiction to tax only if the nonresident meets some minimum threshold such as a PE or fixed base.
- If the threshold is met or the country decides that a threshold is unnecessary, a country must have rules to determine what amounts derived by nonresidents are subject to tax; these rules are usually referred to as source rules.
- Rules are necessary to compute the nonresident's income and tax payable.
- Finally, rules are necessary with respect to the collection of tax from nonresidents.

These stages are intimately connected and often overlap. For example, if a country decides to tax any interest or dividends paid by a resident to a nonresident, the source of the income as represented by the residence of the payer is the connection that gives the country the jurisdiction to tax; accordingly, that country has rejected the necessity for any threshold requirement. Similarly, transfer pricing rules can be viewed as source rules or computational rules. These stages are set out to provide an analytical framework for thinking about the taxation of nonresidents; they do not attempt to describe the ways in which countries actually tax nonresidents.

The distinction between business profits and investment income is particularly important with respect to the taxation of nonresidents. Business income is typically taxed on a net basis at the same rates applicable to resident taxpayers so that individuals earning business income in another country are often subject to tax at progressive rates. In contrast, investment income is typically taxed at a flat rate on the gross amount; moreover, the tax is usually imposed by way of a withholding tax (i.e., there is an obligation on the resident person paying the amount to the nonresident to withhold the amount of the tax from the payment to the nonresident and to remit the tax to the tax authorities).

5.2 TAX POLICY CONSIDERATIONS IN TAXING NONRESIDENTS

It may be recalled from Chapter 3, section 3.2 that the major tax policy justifications for taxing residents on their worldwide income are equity and neutrality. It is difficult to justify taxing

不掌握非居民税收情况的完整信息。例如，非居民在来源国的所得可能只是其全部所得的一小部分，或者可能与其他国家的损失相抵消。一般来说，一国很难确定居民和非居民在税收地位上是否相似，除非非居民的全部或几乎全部所得都从同一个来源国取得。

然而，一般来说，在可能的情况下，对非居民的待遇不应优于或劣于情形类似的居民，这一说法是比较合理的。非居民从来源国获得了利益，可以以此为理由，解释对非居民就其本国来源的所得征税。例如，在一国开展经营活动的非居民，以与居民相同的方式，利用该国的基础设施及法律制度。即使非居民仅向一国的客户销售商品或提供服务，也可以认为，该非居民也是从该国提供的市场受益，这种受益足以构成税收的合理性。

非歧视原则——从一国取得所得的非居民不应受到比该国居民更差的待遇——是大多数国家遵循（或至少部分遵循）的一项重要原则。尽管可能存在诱因使一国以比居民更严苛的方式对非居民征税（非居民毕竟没有投票权），但其他国家可能会做出同样的反应，从而使先发歧视国家的居民处于不利地位。实践中，大多数国家的所得税制度中，令人意外地罕见对非居民的歧视做法。在某些情况下，许多国家反而为非居民提供优待；为了吸引外国投资，而向非居民提供免税期或其他税收优惠。尽管对于非居民的这种区别性优待受到了税收政策评论人士的广泛批评，但并不被认为具有冒犯性。参见第 4 章第 4.5 节中关于税收饶让的讨论。OECD 协定范本和联合国协定范本第 24 条均确认了非歧视原则。第 8 章第 8.8.1 节涉及税收协定的**非歧视条款**。

从收入的角度来看，各国显然有必要对非居民征税。然而，对于税收收入的需要必须与对于外国投资的需要相平衡。如果一国对非居民的征税过于严苛，其后果可能是阻止非居民在该国投资；而且，其他国家可能会采取同样严苛的方式对该国居民征税。因此，有资本进出并就全球所得征税的国家，同时作为居民国和来源国，相关利益必须加以平衡。作为居民国，他们希望尽量减少来源国对其居民境外来源所得的征税，并确保其居民相对于来源国居民，不受歧视。作为来

nonresidents on the basis of equity because, in most situations, the source country will not have complete information about the nonresident's tax situation; for example, the nonresident's income earned in the source country may be only a small part of the nonresident's total income or may be offset by losses incurred in other countries. It is generally impossible for a country to determine whether residents and nonresidents are similarly situated for tax purposes except in situations where all or almost all of a nonresident's income is derived from one source country.

In general, however, it is reasonable to say that, to the extent possible, nonresidents should not be treated better or worse than residents in similar situations. The taxation of nonresidents on their domestic source income can be justified on the basis that nonresidents derive benefits from the source country; for example, nonresidents doing business in a country take advantage of the country's infrastructure and its legal system in the same way as residents. It can also be argued that even if a nonresident simply sells goods or provides services to customers in a country, the nonresident is benefiting from the market provided by that country, and that benefit is sufficient to justify taxation.

The principle that nonresidents deriving income from a country should not be treated less favorably than residents of that country—the **nondiscrimination principle**—is an important principle that most countries follow, at least in part. Although it may be tempting for a country to tax nonresidents more harshly than residents—after all, nonresidents do not vote—the likely response of other countries would be to do the same, thus putting the first country's residents at a disadvantage. In practice, there is surprisingly little discrimination against nonresidents in the income tax systems of most countries. Many countries do, however, discriminate in favor of nonresidents in certain circumstances by providing them with tax holidays and other tax incentives in order to attract foreign investment. Discrimination in favor of nonresidents is not considered to be offensive, although it is widely criticized by tax policy commentators. *See* the discussion of tax sparing in Chapter 4, section 4.5. The nondiscrimination principle is recognized in Article 24 of both the OECD and the UN Model Treaties. The **Non-discrimination article** in tax treaties is dealt with in Chapter 8 in section 8.8.1.

From a revenue perspective, it makes obvious sense for countries to tax nonresidents. However, the need for tax revenue must be balanced against the need for foreign investment. If a country taxes nonresidents too harshly, the effect may be to discourage nonresidents from investing in the country; moreover, other countries can be expected to respond by taxing that country's residents equally harshly. Thus, countries that import and export capital and tax on a worldwide basis have interests as both residence countries and source countries that must be balanced. As residence countries, they want to minimize tax imposed by source countries on the

源国，他们既希望吸引外国投资，也希望尽可能多地对非居民征税。这些相互矛盾的利益不可能全部实现，因为可能导致其他国家不可避免地进行报复。

对非居民税收的另一个重要考虑是政策的执行。一方面，一国开征无法有效执行的非居民税收，显然毫无意义。另一方面，即使可以有效执行，一国对非居民取得的全部所得，也不能都征税。大多数国家并不采用对非居民能征税则征税的做法，其原因或许在于，正如上文所述，各国都不希望其他国家采取同样的做法，同时还希望吸引外国投资。然而，或许可以公平地说，各国一般都尽最大可能对非居民征税，除非有充分的理由不这么做。

5.3 门槛要求

尽管一国对非居民就其所有本国来源所得的征税权并没有法律限制，但没有国家这样做——大多数国家仅在满足最低门槛的情况下，对某些类型的所得征税。例如，许多国家仅在非居民的经营所得可归属于位于该国的常设机构时，才对该所得征税。OECD 协定范本和联合国协定范本第 7 条也采用了关于营业利润征税的常设机构门槛。即使在国内法中没有采用常设机构概念的国家，通常也仅在非居民的经营活动超过某个门槛时，才对非居民的经营所得征税，例如，美国仅对在其境内从事贸易或经营的非居民就其经营所得征税。

对非居民征税设定门槛有几个原因。首先，如果对非居民就全部本国来源所得征税，则可能出现严重的遵从和执行问题。税务机关很难确定从该国获得所得的所有非居民，也很难获得有关该所得的信息（如对在一国提供几天服务的咨询师征税存在困难）。此外，除非非居民在一国具有某种实质性、持续性的存在，否则，该国可能很难或不可能征收到税款。其次，如第 2 章第 2.3 节所述，很少有国家制定了详细的来源规则，因此设定门槛条件可以为非居民提供更多的确定性，以确定他们何时在一国纳税。最后，要求非居民就相对小额的所得，填

foreign source income of their residents and to ensure that their residents are not discriminated against relative to the residents of source countries. As source countries, they want to attract foreign investment but also want to tax nonresidents as heavily as possible. These competing interests cannot all be achieved fully because of the inevitable retaliation by other countries that might result.

Another important consideration in the taxation of nonresidents is enforcement. On the one hand, it obviously makes no sense for a country to impose tax on nonresidents that cannot be enforced effectively. On the other hand, it may not make sense for a country to tax all the income derived by nonresidents that can be enforced effectively. Most countries do not follow the practice of taxing nonresidents on everything that they can tax, probably because, as noted above, they do not want other countries to do the same, and they want to attract foreign investment. Nevertheless, it is probably fair to say that countries generally tax nonresidents to the maximum extent possible unless there is some good reason not to.

5.3 THRESHOLD REQUIREMENTS

Although there is no legal restriction on the authority of a country to tax any and all domestic source income derived by a nonresident, few countries do so—most countries tax nonresidents on certain types of income only if a minimum threshold is met. For example, many countries tax nonresidents on their business income only if the income is attributable to a PE in the country. This PE threshold for the taxation of business profits is also used in Article 7 of the OECD and UN Model Treaties. Even countries that do not use the PE concept in their domestic law usually tax nonresidents on their business income only if their business activities exceed some threshold; for example, in the U.S., nonresidents are taxable on their business income only if they are engaged in a trade or business in the U.S.

There are several reasons for the establishment of a threshold requirement for the taxation of nonresidents. First, serious compliance and enforcement problems may arise where nonresidents are taxable on all their domestic source income. It is difficult for tax authorities to identify all nonresidents earning income from the country and to get information about that income. (Consider, for example, the difficulties in taxing a consultant who performs services in a country for a few days.) Moreover, unless a nonresident has some type of substantial and continuing presence in a country, it may be difficult or impossible for the country to collect its tax. Second, as noted in Chapter 2, section 2.3, few countries have detailed source rules; as a result, a threshold requirement can provide more certainty for nonresidents as to when they

报纳税申报表，并缴税，可能会抑制跨境贸易和投资，或导致非居民忽视其纳税义务。

对非居民征税的门槛条件由国内法和税收协定规定，并根据所得类型而有所不同。下面介绍一些常见的门槛条件：

—— 营业利润：税收协定规定的门槛条件，是在一国存在常设机构。一般而言，常设机构是一个固定的经营场所，或在该国代表非居民行事的非独立代理人。某些类型的营业利润，如艺人和运动员的所得，通常适用较低的门槛条件。联合国协定范本对非居民提供服务所得的征税既适用固定基地的门槛条件，也适用183天的门槛条件，并对保险业务作出了特殊规定。

—— 不动产所得：一国有权对源自位于该国的不动产的所得征税。

—— 受雇所得：一般来说，门槛条件是雇员在一国实际存在，并在该国履行受雇职责，尽管根据税收协定，来源国无权向未在该国设立常设机构的非居民雇主所雇佣的非居民雇员征税除非该雇员在该国实际存在超过183天。

—— 投资所得：通常，根据国内法或协定，对于来源国对股息、利息和特许权使用费等的征税，不存在门槛条件。所需要的是由来源国居民或在来源国开展业务的非居民支付款项。如下文所述，来源国通常对支付款项总额按固定税率征收最终预提税。

一般而言，非居民征税的门槛采取以下形式：固定场所（固定经营场所或不动产）、非居民的实际存在、在该国代表非居民行事的代理人（有时规定具体期间）。国内法和税收协定很少基于非居民取得的收入或所得数额设定门槛。

对非居民来源于某国的营业利润征税设定门槛条件，必然意味着该国不能对无须任何实际存在即可从该国获得营业利润的非居民征税。例如，非居民零售商通过邮购向来源国的客户宣传和销售商品，除非其在来源国设有固定经营场所，

become subject to tax by a country. Third, requiring nonresidents to file tax returns and pay tax on relatively small amounts of income is likely to discourage cross-border trade and investment or result in nonresidents ignoring their tax obligations.

Threshold requirements for taxing nonresidents are provided by domestic law and tax treaties and differ depending on the type of income. Some common thresholds are described below:

- *Business profits*: The threshold provided by tax treaties is the existence of a PE in a country. In general, a PE is a fixed place of business or a dependent agent acting in the country on behalf of the nonresident. Certain types of business profits, such as income derived by entertainers and athletes, are usually subject to a lower threshold. The UN Model Treaty uses both a fixed base threshold and a 183-day threshold for the taxation of income from services derived by nonresidents and has a special provision for insurance businesses.
- *Income from immovable property*: A country is entitled to tax income from immovable property located in the country.
- *Employment income*: As a general rule, the threshold is the physical presence of the employee in the country and the performance of the duties of employment in the country, although, under tax treaties, the source country is precluded from taxing a nonresident employee of a nonresident employer without a PE in the source country unless the employee is physically present in the country for more than 183 days.
- *Investment income*: Typically, there is no threshold for source country taxation of dividends, interest, and royalties under domestic law or treaties. All that is necessary is for the payment to be made by a resident of the source country or by a nonresident carrying on business in the source country. As discussed below, the source country tax is usually imposed as a final withholding tax at a flat rate on the gross amount of the payment.

In general, thresholds for the taxation of nonresidents take the form of a fixed place (either a fixed place of business or immovable property) or the physical presence of the nonresident or an agent acting on behalf of the nonresident in the country (sometimes for a specified period). Thresholds based on the amount of revenue or income derived by a nonresident are rare in both domestic law and treaties.

The existence of a threshold requirement for taxing nonresidents on business profits derived from a country inevitably means that the country is unable to impose tax on nonresidents that derive business profits from the country without the need for any physical presence there. For example, a nonresident retailer who advertises and sells its goods by mail order to customers in

如零售店、仓库或销售代理，否则，来源国不得对其从该国获得的营业利润征税。这种对来源国征税的限制一度是可以接受或者至少可以容忍的。但随着互联网的发展和经济数字化使大型跨国企业数字商品和服务的远程销售成为经济中很大的一部分，一些国家因此摒弃了对非居民基于固定经营场所或实际存在的最低门槛要求，转而采用基于重大经济存在的门槛条件；其他国家则对向非居民支付的数字商品和服务款项，就总额征收流转税或预提税。有关数字经济税收的详细讨论，参见第 9 章第 9.5 节。

5.4 来源规则

一旦确定一国对非居民拥有税收管辖权，且已满足征税门槛条件，就有必要制定规则，来确定哪些款项应予征税，以及如何对这些款项征税。一般来说，各国只对非居民就其境内来源的所得征税。因此，有必要制定所得来源规则，以确定非居民的所得是否来源于该国境内。有时，这些来源规则是明确的。例如，一国的税法可能规定对非居民的境内来源所得征税，然后列举被视为境内来源所得的项目或款项。然而，更常见的情形是，各国只是规定非居民取得的应予征税款项，并没有明确提及这些款项的来源。例如，一国可能对居民公司支付给非居民的股息征税。在这种情况下，来源规则是含糊的——实际上，股息被视为来源于股息支付公司所属的居民国（无论该公司从何处取得所得）。除了按总额对所得征税的情形以外，在确定应予征税的境内所得时，还必须确定可以扣除的费用。第 2 章第 2.3 节更为详细地讨论了来源规则。

5.5 双重征税

在一国居民取得来源于另一国的所得的情况下，按照国际共识，所得来源国优先享有对该所得的征税权，而且，居民国有相应的义务，通过对该所得免于征

a source country would not be subject to tax by the source country on its sales profits derived from that country unless it has a fixed place of business, such as a retail store or warehouse or sales agents in that country. This limitation on source country taxation remained acceptable, or at least tolerable, until the Internet and the digitalization of the economy made remote selling of digital goods and services by large multinational enterprises such a large part of the economy. As a result, some countries have abandoned minimum threshold requirements for taxing nonresidents based on a fixed place of business or physical presence in favor of a threshold based on a significant economic presence; other countries have resorted to imposing gross-based turnover taxes or withholding taxes on payments for digital goods and services to nonresidents. *See* Chapter 9, section 9.5 for a more detailed discussion of the taxation of the digital economy.

5.4 SOURCE RULES

Once it has been determined that a country has jurisdiction to tax a nonresident and any threshold for taxation has been met, it is necessary to have rules to determine what amounts are subject to tax and how those amounts are taxed. In general, countries tax nonresidents only on their domestic source income. As a result, source-of-income rules are necessary to determine whether a nonresident's income is derived from sources inside the territory of the country. Sometimes these source rules are explicit: for example, a country's tax law might provide that a nonresident is taxable on domestic source income and then list items or amounts that are considered to be from domestic sources. More often, however, countries simply prescribe the amounts derived by nonresidents that are subject to tax without explicit reference to the source of those amounts. For example, a country might impose tax on dividends paid by a resident corporation to a nonresident. The source rule in this case is implicit—in effect, dividends are considered to have their source in the country in which the company paying the dividends is resident (irrespective of where the company derives its income). Except in cases where the income is taxed on a gross basis, it is also necessary to determine what expenses are deductible in determining the domestic income subject to tax. Source rules are discussed in more detail in Chapter 2, section 2.3.

5.5 DOUBLE TAXATION

In situations where a resident of one country earns income sourced in another country, by international consensus, the country in which the income is earned has the first right to tax

税或对来源国税收给予抵免等方式，消除国际双重征税。因此，在对非居民征税时，来源国不必关注消除此类双重征税的问题，因为居民国有义务消除此类双重征税。来源国应关注的唯一一种双重征税情形是，两国都主张相关所得项目来源于本国。因此，一国的来源规则范围越广，其来源主张与其他国家来源主张重叠的可能性就越大。

5.6 对非居民的过度征税

虽然除来源规则重叠的情形外，来源国不必关注消除双重征税的问题，但是，它们应关注对非居民的过度征税问题。如下文所述，对某些类型的所得，通常以对支付款项总额适用固定税率的方式，来征收预提税。在这些情况下，相对于非居民取得的净所得而言，来源国的税收可能过高。如以下情形，即非居民为在一国取得特许权使用费，发生了大额费用，如果来源国在不许扣除任何费用的情况下，对特许权使用费适用 30% 的固定税率，则该非居民从交易中即使可以获得税后利润，也所剩无几。如果居民国对境外来源的特许权使用费免税，则对来源国税收，不承担减轻负担义务。即使居民国提供境外税收抵免，但抵免限额可能导致纳税人仅就来源国税收获得部分抵减（有关境外税收抵免限额的讨论，参见第 4 章第 4.3.4 节）。总之，特许权使用费适用的实际税率可能大大高于纳税人所属居民国的税率。

税收协定通常通过确定预提税的最高限额，来有效地减少或消除来源国的过度税收（参见第 8 章第 8.7.3.5 节）。有时，为避免来源国过度征税，非居民可以要求居民支付人对支付款项进行含税还原加计，从而由居民实际承担来源国税收（参见第 4 章第 4.3.3 节案例）。否则，过度的来源国税收可能会阻碍外国投资。

the income, and the residence country has a corresponding obligation to relieve international double taxation by exempting the income from tax or providing a credit for the source country tax. Therefore, in taxing nonresidents, source countries do not need to be concerned about eliminating double taxation of this type because residence countries have responsibility for eliminating such double taxation. The only type of double taxation that source countries should be concerned about is one where two countries both claim that the relevant item of income has its source in their country. Accordingly, the more expansive a country's source rules are, the more likely it is that its source claims will overlap with other countries' source claims.

5.6 EXCESSIVE TAXATION OF NONRESIDENTS

Although source countries do not need to be concerned about the elimination of double taxation except in the case of overlapping source rules, they should be concerned about the excessive taxation of nonresidents. As discussed below, certain types of income are typically taxed by withholding at a flat rate on the gross amount of the payment. In these situations, there is a risk that the source country tax may be excessive relative to the net income derived by the nonresident. For example, consider a situation in which a nonresident incurs substantial expenses to earn royalties in a country. If the source country taxes the royalties at a flat rate of 30% without any recognition of the expenses, the nonresident may realize little, if any, after-tax profit from the transaction. If the residence country exempts foreign source royalties, it will not provide any relief for the source country tax, and even if the residence country provides a foreign tax credit, the limitation on the credit (*see* Chapter 4, section 4.3.4 for a discussion of the limitations on a foreign tax credit) will likely result in the taxpayer getting only partial relief for the source country tax. The overall result is that the royalties may be taxable at an effective rate that is considerably higher than the residence country tax rate on the taxpayer.

Tax treaties are often effective in reducing or eliminating excessive source country tax by establishing maximum limits on withholding tax (*see* Chapter 8, section 8.7.3.5). Sometimes nonresidents may be able to avoid excessive source country taxation by requiring the resident payers to effectively absorb the tax by grossing up the payments, with the result that the source country tax is borne by residents of the source country (*see* the example in Chapter 4, section 4.3.3). Otherwise, excessive source country taxation is likely to discourage foreign investment.

5.7 非居民境内来源所得的计算

一般来说，非居民与居民适用相同的所得计算规则。因此，确定哪些款项应当计入所得、允许哪些扣除项目，以及所得实现和扣除发生时点的规则，同样适用于居民和非居民。例如，如果一国只允许纳税人扣除部分招待费，则该规则将同样适用于发生了招待费的非居民。虽然一般来说，居民和非居民的所得计算规则相同，但也有一些例外。例如，转让定价规则适用于居民和非居民关联方之间的交易，而不适用于居民关联方之间的交易。第 6 章将论述转让定价规则。同样，资本弱化规则通常只适用于居民公司支付给非居民的利息，不过一些国家的规则也适用于支付给免税居民的利息。受控外国企业规则只适用于由一国居民控制的非居民公司。第 7 章第 7.2 和 7.3 节将分别详述资本弱化规则和受控外国企业规则。在这方面，应当指出的是，在诸如资本弱化或受控外国企业等问题上，欧盟法院的判例法严格限制欧盟成员国制定区别对待本国居民和其他欧盟成员国居民的规则，除非是针对完全人为操控的情形。

如以下第 5.8 节所述，适用的税收协定中的非歧视条款通常要求来源国允许非居民在计算可归属于常设机构的利润时，按与从事类似活动的居民相同的规则扣除费用。但是，如果对非居民按总额征收预提税，则不允许扣除。因此，量化区分营业利润和投资所得非常重要；前者系按净额予以征税，后者应予征收预提税。第 5.8.1 节将讨论此种区分。

对于非居民个人，来源国通常不提供个人扣除、减免、专项免除和抵减。例如，许多国家都规定了基本的个人或家庭免税额，这样，如果个人或家庭所得不超过最低数额，就不需要纳税。同样，许多国家对依赖纳税人赡养的家庭成员，都规定了扣除或免除。这些和其他类似的个人扣减一般不适用于非居民，而且，

5.7 COMPUTATION OF THE DOMESTIC SOURCE INCOME OF NONRESIDENTS

In general, the rules for computing the income of nonresidents are the same as the rules applicable to residents. Thus, the rules that determine what amounts are included in income, what deductions are allowable, and the timing of income and deductions are applicable equally to residents and nonresidents. For example, if a country allows a deduction for only a portion of a taxpayer's entertainment expenses, that rule will likely apply equally to nonresidents who incur entertainment expenses. Although, in general, the rules for computing the income of residents and nonresidents are the same, there are some exceptions. For example, transfer pricing rules apply to transactions between a resident and a related nonresident and not to transactions between related residents. Transfer pricing rules are discussed in Chapter 6. Similarly, thin capitalization rules are typically applicable only to interest paid by a resident corporation to nonresidents, although some countries' rules also apply to interest paid to tax-exempt residents. CFC rules apply only to nonresident companies that are controlled by residents of a country. Thin capitalization rules and CFC rules are dealt with in detail in Chapter 7, sections 7.2 and 7.3, respectively. It should be noted in this regard that the case law of the Court of Justice of the European Union (CJEU) has severely restricted the ability of an EU member country to have rules, such as thin capitalization rules or CFC rules, that apply differently to residents of that country and residents of another EU member country except in wholly artificial situations.

As discussed below in section 5.8, the non-discrimination article of an applicable tax treaty usually requires the source country to allow nonresidents to deduct expenses in computing the profits attributable to a PE on the same basis as residents engaged in similar activities. However, where nonresidents are subject to tax on a gross withholding basis, no deductions are allowed. Therefore, the distinction between amounts such as business profits, which are subject to net-based taxation, and investment income, which are subject to withholding tax, is very important. This distinction is discussed in section 5.8.1 below.

With respect to nonresident individuals, personal deductions, reliefs, allowances, and credits are not customarily provided by source countries. For example, many countries provide a basic personal or family exemption from tax so that if an individual's or family's income does not exceed the minimum amount, no tax is payable. Similarly, many countries provide deductions or allowances for family members who are dependent on the taxpayer for support. These and other similar personal allowances are not generally provided by countries to nonresidents,

税收协定中常用的非歧视条款也不要求将此类扣减延伸到非居民。

如前所述，没有法律阻止来源国给予非居民的待遇优于居民，特别是，许多发展中国家向非居民投资者提供的特殊税收优惠是居民所不能享受的。

如果一国对某些支付款项的总额（如股息、利息和特许权使用费）征收最终预提税，因为是对总额征税，就无须制定计算规则。但是，如果是就非居民的最终纳税义务而临时征收预提税，则有必要制定净所得计算规则。一些南美国家对向非居民支付的诸多款项征收最终预提税，但在许多情况下，对支付款项的固定百分比而不是对所得总额，按固定税率征税。这种核定的做法意味着在不需要征纳双方计算特定非居民实际净所得的前提下，对该非居民为取得某些所得而发生的费用给予扣除。

5.8 非居民各种所得的征税

5.8.1 经营所得

5.8.1.1 概述

非居民取得的经营所得通常按净额纳税，而投资所得则按总额纳税，因此，对这两类所得进行区分很重要。在一些大陆法系国家，法人实体取得的全部所得都被定性为经营所得，因此仅对个人有必要区分经营所得和其他所得。然而，在其他一些国家，法人实体和个人都可以取得各种类型的所得。有些国家按分类制度征税，这意味着他们按照不同的规则对不同类型的所得征税，有时甚至适用不同的税率。即使就全球所得征税的国家，往往针对经营所得和其他所得，也制定了不同的规则。通常，涉及诸如财产处置收益，利息、租金和特许权使用费等相关款项时，需要界定属于经营所得或是其他所得。

如何区分经营所得和其他所得？在许多英联邦国家中，存在大量的判例法，

and the typical nondiscrimination article in tax treaties does not require such allowances to be extended to nonresidents.

As mentioned above, there are no legal constraints to prevent a source country from treating nonresidents more favorably than residents. In particular, many developing countries provide nonresident investors with special tax incentives that are not available to residents.

Where a country imposes a final withholding tax on the gross amount of certain payments, such as dividends, interest, and royalties, no computational rules are necessary since the gross amount is taxable. However, where the withholding tax is imposed on an interim basis on account of a nonresident's final tax liability, rules for the computation of net income are necessary. Some South American countries impose final withholding taxes on a wide range of payments made to nonresidents; in many cases, the tax is imposed at a fixed rate on a fixed percentage of the payment rather than on the gross amount. Taxing a presumptive amount in this way represents an attempt to give relief for the expenses incurred to earn certain types of income without the necessity for either the taxpayer or the tax authorities to calculate a particular nonresident's actual net income.

5.8 TAXATION OF VARIOUS TYPES OF INCOME OF NONRESIDENTS

5.8.1 Business Income

5.8.1.1 In General

Because business income earned by nonresidents is usually taxed on a net basis and investment income is taxed on a gross basis, it is important to distinguish between the two types of income. In some civil law countries, all the income earned by a legal entity is characterized as business income, and therefore it is necessary to distinguish between business and other income only with respect to individuals. In other countries, however, both legal entities and individuals can earn various types of income. Some countries tax on a schedular basis, which means that they tax different types of income in accordance with different rules, and sometimes even at different rates. Even countries that tax on a global basis often have different rules for business income and other income. Typically, the characterization of an amount as income from business or other income arises with respect to capital gains from the disposal of property, interest, rent, and royalties.

How is the distinction between business and other income made? In many Commonwealth

涉及财产收益和普通经营所得之间的区分。这种判例法通常同样适用于非居民。各国也可能制定了区分这两种所得的法定规则。例如，有些国家的规则将对于财产收益的处理，局限于持有或拥有达到最短期限的财产；其他收益则被视为普通经营所得。有些国家可能更笼统地制定规则，定义经营所得。

经营所得和其他类型所得的区分，对税收协定也很重要，因为税收协定分类处理不同类型的所得。例如，经营所得、利息和财产收益适用不同的规则。大多数双边税收协定所依据的 OECD 协定范本和联合国协定范本，并未对“经营”作出全面的定义。2000 年，OECD 协定范本删除了涉及提供独立专业服务的第 14 条；此后，第 3 条第 1 款第（6）项规定，“经营”包括此类劳务。由于协定中缺乏完整的定义，对于“经营”一词的含义，有必要参考根据 OECD 协定范本和联合国协定范本第 3 条第 2 款而适用协定的国家的国内法。本书第 8 章第 8.6.3 节将讨论上述第 3 条第 2 款。

根据以 OECD 协定范本和联合国协定范本为基础的税收协定，还必须区分各种类型的经营所得。一般而言，根据第 7 条，一国居民从另一国或在另一国取得的经营所得，只有在通过常设机构进行经营且该所得可归属于常设机构的情况下，才由另一国征税。但是，根据第 8 条，国际海运和空运所得，只能由企业所属的居民国征税。相反，根据第 17 条，一国居民在另一国以演艺人员或运动员身份提供个人服务取得的经营所得由另一国征税，无须在该国设立常设机构或在该国停留的时间达到最低标准。实际上，根据税收协定，常设机构是对大多数经营所得征税的门槛条件，而仅对可归属于常设机构的利润予以征税，则在功能上相当于来源规则。为了准确起见，必须说明的是，根据第 7 条，可归属于常设机构的利润可包括来自常设机构所在国以外的利润。第 8 章第 8.8.5 节将进一步讨论这些协定规则。

非居民取得的经营所得，一般由取得该项所得所在的国家按净额征税，且用于计算经营所得的规则通常与适用于居民的规则相同。税收协定的非歧视条款（OECD 协定范本和联合国协定范本第 24 条第 3 款）要求：来源国对另一国居

countries, there is a substantial body of case law dealing with the distinction between capital gains and ordinary business income. This case law is usually equally applicable to nonresidents. Countries may also have statutory rules that distinguish between the two types of income. For example, some countries have rules that limit capital gains treatment to property that is held or owned for a minimum period; other gains are treated as ordinary business income. More generally, some countries may have rules that define business income.

The distinction between business and other types of income is also important for purposes of tax treaties because tax treaties deal with various types of income on a schedular basis. As a result, for example, business income, interest, and capital gains are subject to different rules. The OECD and UN Model Treaties, on which most bilateral tax treaties are based, do not provide a comprehensive definition of "business." Article 14 of the OECD Model Treaty, dealing with the performance of independent and professional services, was deleted in 2000; since then, Article 3(1)(f) has defined "business" to include such services. Because of the absence of a complete definition in the treaty, it is necessary to refer to the meaning of the term "business" under the domestic law of the country applying the treaty in accordance with Article 3(2) of the OECD and UN Model Treaties; *see* Chapter 8, section 8.6.3 for a discussion of Article 3(2).

Under tax treaties based on the OECD and UN Model Treaties, it is also necessary to distinguish between various types of business income. In general, under Article 7, business income derived by a resident of one country from or in the other country is taxable by the other country only if the business is carried on through a PE and the income is attributable to the PE. Under Article 8, however, income from international shipping and air transportation is taxable only by the country in which the enterprise is resident. In contrast, under Article 17, business income from personal services performed by a resident of one country in the other country as an entertainer or athlete is taxable by that other country without the need for a PE or a minimum period of presence in the country. In effect, under tax treaties, a PE is a threshold requirement for the taxation of most business income and the rule that only profits attributable to the PE are taxable is the functional equivalent of a source rule. In the interests of accuracy, it must be noted that under Article 7, the profits attributable to a PE can include profits from outside the country in which the PE is located. These treaty rules are discussed further in Chapter 8, section 8.8.5.

Business income derived by a nonresident is usually taxed by the country in which the income is earned on a net basis, and the rules for the computation of business income are generally the same as the rules for residents. The nondiscrimination article of tax treaties (Article 24(3) of the OECD and UN Model Treaties) requires the source country to tax a PE of a

民在其境内设立的常设机构所得的征税，不得劣于从事相同活动的来源国本国居民。第 8 章第 8.8.1 节将更详细地讨论非歧视条款。一旦非居民满足来源国征税的最低门槛要求（通常是在来源国存在常设机构），则适用国内税收规则，来确定应予征税的经营所得数额（收入额减去扣除额）。在一些国家，一旦非居民在来源国设立了常设机构，来源国将就非居民来源于其境内的全部所得征税。然而，大多数国家并没有采用这种**引力原则**，而只对从在来源国开展的经营活动取得的所得征税（尽管其他所得，如投资所得，可能按不同的方法征税）。OECD 协定范本并未采用引力规则；只有归属于常设机构的所得才由来源国征税。联合国协定范本则采用了有限的引力规则：授权来源国对其他国家居民从其境内取得的，所有与通过常设机构所取得利润相同或类似的营业利润征税。第 8 章第 8.8.5 节将讨论向常设机构归属利润的协定规则。

5.8.1.2 分支机构税收

正如本书多次提到（尤其是在第 1 章第 1.4 节中），纳税人通常可以选择在一国设立分支机构或独立法人实体（通常是公司）来开展业务。对于企业纳税人来说，这种选择通常被描述为分支机构和子公司之间的选择。如果一国的居民公司在另一国成立了子公司，该子公司可能被视为独立的法人实体和纳税实体，从而被视为另一国居民（在某些情况下，还要看该子公司的管理机构是否也位于该国）。如果公司在另一国设立了分支机构，那么，该分支机构只是公司的一部分。非居民公司的子公司，作为来源国居民，通常就其全球所得纳税，而分支机构通常仅就归属于该机构的境内来源所得，在来源国纳税。如果子公司仅获取境内来源的所得（即其全部所得均在子公司所属的居民国获得），则子公司与分支机构在此方面并无显著差异。

从分支机构或子公司汇回资金的税收结果存在显著差异。如果子公司向其非居民母公司支付股息，该子公司所属的居民国可对股息总额征收预提税。

resident of the other state no less favorably than a resident of the source country carrying on the same activities. The nondiscrimination article is discussed in more detail in Chapter 8, section 8.8.1. Once a nonresident has met the minimum threshold requirement for taxation in the source country (usually the existence of a PE in the source country), domestic tax rules apply in order to determine the amount of income from the business (revenue less deductions) that is subject to tax. In some countries, once a nonresident has a PE in the source country, all the nonresident's income from the source country becomes taxable. However, most countries do not follow this **force-of-attraction principle**. Instead, only the income from the business carried on in the source country is taxable (although other amounts, such as investment income, may be taxable on a different basis). Under the OECD Model Treaty, there is no force-of-attraction rule; only income that is attributable to the PE is taxable by the source country. Under the UN Model Treaty, there is a limited force-of-attraction rule: the source country is authorized to tax a resident of the other country on any business profits from the source country of the same or similar kind as those derived through a PE. The treaty rules for the attribution of profits to a PE are discussed in Chapter 8, section 8.8.5.

5.8.1.2 Branch Taxes

As noted several times in this Primer (including in particular Chapter 1, section 1.4), taxpayers generally have the choice of doing business in a country in the form of a branch or a separate legal entity, usually a company. For corporate taxpayers, this choice is usually described as a choice between a branch and a subsidiary. If a corporation resident in one country forms a subsidiary corporation in another country, the subsidiary will likely be treated as a separate legal and taxable entity and, therefore, as a resident of the other country (in some cases only if the subsidiary's place of management is also located in that country). If a corporation establishes a branch in another country, the branch is simply a part of the corporation. As a resident of the source country, a subsidiary of a nonresident corporation is ordinarily taxable on its worldwide income, whereas only the domestic source income attributable to a branch is usually taxable by the source country. If, however, the subsidiary earns exclusively domestic source income (i.e., all its income is earned in the country in which it is resident), there is no significant difference between the subsidiary and a branch in this regard.

There is a significant difference with respect to the tax consequences of the repatriation of funds from a branch or subsidiary. If a subsidiary pays a dividend to its nonresident parent, the country in which the subsidiary is resident may impose a withholding tax on the gross amount

相反，如果资金是从分支机构提取，并汇回非居民公司总部，则不存在来源国可以征税的股息或其他款项。因此，非居民可能更愿意通过分支机构而不是子公司在一国开展业务，以避免股息和其他公司间款项的预提税。一些国家（如加拿大和美国）已经开征特殊的分公司税，以平等地对待分支机构和子公司。这类分公司税可能相当复杂，因为要以某种股息替代物为基础，计征相当于股息预提税的税收。一些其他国家则对以分支机构形式开展经营的非居民适用稍高的税率，以弥补分支机构汇回资金所或缺的预提税。尽管从税收政策的角度来看可以说具有合理性，上述两项措施似乎都违反了典型税收协定中的非歧视条款。

如果借款用于资助分支机构的活动，根据国内法和税收协定，在计算分支机构的利润时，通常允许扣除与借贷资金相关的利息支出。这种利息支出侵蚀了分支机构所在国家的税基，而且，由于利息由分支机构所属的非居民纳税人支付，而非由分支机构本身支付，可能无法对该利息征预提税。一些国家对这种利息征收所谓的分支机构层面的预提税。

5.8.1.3 经营性服务所得

尽管某些国家以与其他经营所得相同的方式，对经营性服务所得按净额征税，但大多数国家对某些类型的服务所得制定了特殊规则。例如，一些国家对非居民从事保险、娱乐或体育活动而取得的所得，未设立最低门槛条件；一些国家通过吨位税而不是所得税，对非居民从海运或空运取得的所得征税；一些国家对非居民通过向该国客户提供技术和特定数字服务而取得的所得，按总额征收预提税。

以 OECD 协定范本和联合国协定范本为基础的税收协定包含了若干规定（除第 7 条外，第 7 条一般性地适用于经营性服务），适用于各种服务，包括：保险（仅对联合国协定范本）、国际海运和空运、独立个人劳务（仅对联合国协定范

of the dividend. In contrast, if funds are withdrawn from a branch and repatriated to the head office of the nonresident corporation, there is no dividend or other payment on which the source country can levy tax. Therefore, nonresidents may prefer to do business in a country through a branch rather than a subsidiary in order to avoid withholding taxes on dividends and other inter-corporate payments. Some countries (e.g., Canada and the U.S.) have adopted special branch taxes in order to equalize the treatment of branches and subsidiaries. These branch taxes can be quite complex because of the need to impose a tax that is equivalent to a withholding tax on dividends on the basis of some type of proxy for dividends. Some other countries impose a slightly higher rate of tax on nonresidents carrying on business in the form of a branch in order to make up for the lack of withholding tax on the repatriation of funds from branches. Both of these measures appear to violate the nondiscrimination article of a typical tax treaty, although they are arguably justifiable on tax policy grounds.

If borrowed funds are used to finance the activities of a branch, the interest expense incurred with respect to the funds is ordinarily deductible in computing the profits of the branch under both domestic law and tax treaties. Such interest expense erodes the tax base of the country in which the branch is located; however, the interest may not be subject to withholding tax because the interest is paid by the nonresident taxpayer of which the branch is a part, not the branch itself. Some countries subject such interest to what is known as branch-level withholding tax.

5.8.1.3 Income from Business Services

Although some countries tax income from business services on a net basis in the same way as other business income, most countries have special rules for certain types of income from services. For example, some countries have no minimum threshold for taxing nonresidents earning income from insurance, entertainment, or athletic activities; some countries tax income of nonresidents from shipping or air transportation through tonnage taxes rather than income taxes; and some countries impose grossbased withholding taxes on nonresidents earning fees for technical and certain digital services provided to customers in their countries.

Tax treaties based on the OECD and UN Model Treaties contain several provisions applicable to various types of services (in addition to Article 7, which applies to business services generally), including insurance (UN Model only), international shipping and air transportation, professional and independent services provided by individuals (UN Model only), construction, entertainment, and athletic activities. Thus, as discussed above, it is necessary for these treaties

本）、建筑、娱乐和体育活动。因此，如上所述，这些协定有必要确定所提供服务的性质和服务提供者的法律地位。关于对国际海运和空运所得，以及娱乐和体育活动所得的处理的讨论，参见第 8 章第 8.7.3.2 节；关于独立个人劳务的讨论，参见第 8 章第 8.7.3.3 节；关于税收协定项下的咨询、技术及管理服务费的讨论，参见第 9 章第 9.3 节；关于数字商品和服务所得的讨论，参见第 9 章第 9.5 节。

5.8.2 不动产所得

非居民拥有或使用位于一国的不动产，显然足以证明该国征税权的合理性。此外，不动产的存在既是一项门槛条件，也是一项来源规则。不动产所在国有权就从该不动产取得的任何所得或处置该不动产取得的任何财产收益，向非居民所有人征税。OECD 协定范本和联合国协定范本第 6 条和第 13 条第 1 款据此确认了来源国对不动产所得和收益的征税权。

根据 OECD 协定范本和联合国协定范本，不动产所得与经营所得的税收处理不同。尽管根据第 6 条规定，不动产在某国的坐落可能被视为相当于常设机构的联结度，但没有要求类似于根据第 7 条对营业利润征税，对不动产所得按净额征税。如果第 6 条和第 7 条发生冲突，显然应该适用第 6 条（参见 OECD 协定范本第 6 条第 4 款和第 7 条第 4 款；联合国协定范本第 6 条第 4 款和第 7 条第 6 款）。因此，税收协定通常并不阻止各国以总额为基础对不动产所得征税；而且事实上，一些国家对某些类型的不动产所得按核定的方法征税。因此，了解一国如何根据其国内法对不动产所得进行界定和征税，十分重要。从事经营中涉及不动产的使用，该所得一般不认定为不动产所得。

5.8.3 受雇所得

非居民雇员在一国从事受雇工作，或从该国取得所得，或者甚至是其受雇工作产生的收益在该国被使用、消费，都使得该国有权对该非居民雇员征税。在大

to determine the nature of the services provided and the legal status of the service provider. *See* Chapter 8, section 8.7.3.2 for a discussion of the treatment of income from international shipping and air transportation and income from entertainment and athletic activities; Chapter 8, section 8.7.3.3 for independent personal services; Chapter 9, section 9.3 for fees for consulting, technical, and management services under tax treaties; and Chapter 9, section 9.5 for income from digital goods and services.

5.8.2 Income from Immovable Property

The ownership or use by a nonresident of immovable property situated in a country is clearly sufficient to justify jurisdiction to tax by that country. In addition, the existence of the immovable property operates as both a threshold requirement and a source rule. The country in which immovable property is situated is entitled to tax the nonresident owner on any income derived from the property or any capital gains derived from the disposal of the property. Articles 6 and 13(1) of the OECD and UN Model Treaties confirm the source country's right to tax income and gains from immovable property on this basis.

Income from immovable property is treated differently from income from business under the OECD and UN Model Treaties. Although the location of immovable property in a country may be seen as the equivalent of a PE in terms of nexus, under Article 6, there is no requirement for income from immovable property to be taxed on a net basis, as there is for business profits under Article 7. In any case of conflict between Articles 6 and 7, Article 6 clearly prevails (*see* Article 6(4) and Article 7(4) of the OECD Model Treaty and Article 6(4) and Article 7(6) of the UN Model Treaty). As a result, there is nothing in a typical tax treaty to prevent a country from taxing income from immovable property on a gross basis, and, in fact, some countries tax some types of income from immovable property on a presumptive basis. It is important, therefore, to understand how a country defines and taxes income from immovable property under its domestic law. Income from a business that involves the use of immovable property is not generally considered to be income from the immovable property.

5.8.3 Income from Employment

A country has jurisdiction to tax nonresident employees if the employment activities are performed in the country, the income is derived from the country, or even if the benefits from the employment activities are used or consumed in the country. In most countries, there is no

多数国家中，对非居民雇员征税，没有设定最低门槛，不过，美国对其非居民雇主支付的报酬不超过 3000 美元且在美国停留时间不超过 90 天的非居民雇员，规定免税。如果居民雇主雇用非居民，则对于雇员的征税相对易于执行，因为可要求雇主扣缴税款。即使雇主是非居民，如果雇主在来源国设立了常设机构，税款也能得以有效地征收。在其他情况下，则可能难以实现对非居民雇员为其非居民雇主在一国提供几天服务的情形予以征税。

根据 OECD 协定范本和联合国协定范本，非居民雇员取得的受雇所得，只有在雇员为提供受雇服务，而在来源国停留的情况下，才可由该国征税。只有在非居民雇员在来源国停留的时间少于 183 天，且其工薪不是由居民雇主支付的，而且，在计算非居民雇主设立于来源国的常设机构的所得时，非居民雇员的工薪不予扣除，则对该非居民雇员予以免税。

5.8.4　投资所得：股息、利息和特许权使用费

大多数国家对非居民取得的某些投资所得征税。为此，有必要对应税的投资所得类型进行界定，特别是如第 5.8.1.1 节中所讨论的，需要区分经营所得和投资所得。这种区分不能仅仅基于所得的性质，因为，如金融机构从贷款中赚取的利息显然是经营所得，而个人投资者赚取的利息则是投资所得。

这种区分很重要，因为通常情况下，投资所得由来源国就支付给非居民的款项总额，按固定税率，征收预提税，而经营所得通常通过核算，对净额征税。将以总额为基础的预提税作为所得税的一部分，这是否合适可能会受到质疑。但是，由于实践中难以执行对非居民投资所得的征税，使得预提税能够被广泛接受，前提是对税率有所限制，以使这种扣缴的税额，能够接近于对净所得按一般税率计征的税款。这就解释了为什么预提税一般仅限于非居民不太可能为之发生大量费用的款项。

如第 5.6 节所述，在某些情况下，对利息、租金或特许权使用费按总额征收

minimum threshold for the taxation of nonresident employees, although the U.S. provides an exemption for nonresident employees who are paid by a nonresident employer, earn not more than USD 3,000, and are present in the U.S. for not more than ninety days. If a nonresident is employed by a resident employer, any tax on the employee is relatively easy to enforce by requiring the employer to withhold the tax. Even if the employer is a nonresident, the tax can be effectively enforced if the employer has a PE in the source country. In other situations, any tax imposed on a nonresident employee who spends a few days in a country performing services for a nonresident employer may be difficult to enforce.

Under the OECD and UN Model Treaties, income from employment derived by a nonresident employee is taxable by the source country only if the employee is present in the country to perform the employment services. An exemption is provided for nonresident employees if they are present in the source country for less than 183 days, they are not paid by a resident employer, and their remuneration is not deductible for purposes of computing the income of a PE that the nonresident employer has in the source country.

5.8.4 Investment Income: Dividends, Interest, and Royalties

Most countries tax certain investment income derived by nonresidents. For this purpose, it is necessary to define the types of investment income that are taxable and, in particular, to distinguish between business income and investment income, as discussed in section 5.8.1.1. This distinction cannot be made solely on the basis of the nature of the income because, for example, interest earned by a financial institution from lending money is clearly income from business, whereas interest earned by an individual investor is investment income.

The distinction is important because, typically, investment income is taxable by source countries through a withholding tax at a flat rate on the gross amount paid to nonresidents, while business income is usually taxable on a net basis by way of an assessment. It may be questioned whether a gross-based withholding tax is appropriate as part of an income tax; however, in practice, the difficulty of enforcing tax imposed on the investment income of nonresidents makes withholding taxes generally acceptable if the rate is limited so that the withholding tax approximates the tax that would be imposed at ordinary rates on net income. This explains why withholding tax is generally limited to amounts in respect of which the nonresident is unlikely to have incurred substantial expenses to earn those amounts.

The imposition of tax on the gross amount of interest, rent, or royalties can be excessive in certain circumstances, as explained in section 5.6 above.

的税款有可能过多。

根据国内法或税收协定，对非居民取得的投资所得征税通常没有任何门槛条件；一般而言，投资所得被视为来源于付款人所属的居民国。OECD 协定范本和联合国协定范本第 10 条至第 12 条采用了相同的来源规则。然而，一些国家对某些类型的投资所得，制定了特殊的来源规则，如利息和特许权使用费可以被视为来源于资金或资产的使用地。

5.8.5 财产收益

对非居民实现的财产收益征税，对将此类收益区别于经营所得征税的国家，提出了很多特殊的问题。许多国家对非居民处置下列财产所取得的资本收益征税：位于该国的不动产、在该国开展经营活动（通常通过常设机构）的财产，以及对居民公司、合伙企业和其他法人实体的实质性参股。大多数国家不对非居民处置股份取得的资本收益征税，除非被处置股份属于持有大量房地产的企业（即居民和非居民公司的资产主要由位于该国的不动产组成）以及属于对居民公司的实质性参股。这一模式反映在 OECD 协定范本和联合国协定范本第 13 条中，其中的不同之处在于，根据 OECD 协定范本，不允许来源国对处置实质性参股产生的资本收益征税。

对非居民财产收益税收的执行特别困难。如果非居民出售位于一国的不动产，该国应征的资本收益税，可以通过要求买方从价款中扣缴卖方应缴的税额来实现，除非该非居民预缴了税款或提供了纳税担保，如银行担保。如果预缴税款过多，该非居民通常有权申请退税。即使非居民将不动产出售给另一非居民，通常可以规定，如果不缴纳税款买方将不得对该财产进行所有权登记，从而实现税款的征收。

当非居民实现与公司股份或其他实体权益相关的收益时，如果这些公司或实体拥有坐落于来源国的某些资产，则会遇到特殊问题。拥有资产的公司或其他

Investment income derived by nonresidents is typically taxed without any threshold requirement under either domestic law or tax treaties; in general, it is considered to have its source in the country in which the payer is resident. The same source rule is used in Articles 10 through 12 of the OECD and UN Model Treaties. Several countries, however, have special source rules for certain types of investment income. For example, interest and royalties may be considered to be earned where the funds or property are used.

5.8.5 Capital Gains

The taxation of capital gains realized by nonresidents presents special problems for countries that tax such gains differently from business income. Many countries tax capital gains derived by nonresidents from the disposal of immovable property situated in their countries, property of a business carried on (often through a PE) in their countries, and substantial participations in resident companies, partnerships, and other legal entities. Most countries do not tax nonresidents on capital gains from the disposal of shares of companies other than land-rich companies (resident and nonresident companies whose assets consist primarily of immovable property located in the country) and substantial participations in resident companies. This pattern is reflected in Article 13 of the OECD and UN Model Treaties, except that, under the OECD Model Treaty, source countries are not allowed to tax capital gains from substantial participations.

The enforcement of tax on the capital gains of nonresidents raises special difficulties. If a nonresident sells immovable property situated in a country, that country's tax on the capital gain can be enforced by requiring the purchaser to withhold an amount on account of the seller's tax from the purchase price unless the nonresident prepays the tax or provides security for the payment of the tax, such as a bank guarantee. If the prepayment is excessive, the nonresident is usually entitled to file a return to claim a refund of the excess. Even if the nonresident sells the property to another nonresident, the tax can usually be enforced in this way by refusing to allow the purchaser to register the ownership of the property unless the tax has been paid.

Special problems are encountered where nonresidents realize gains with respect to shares of companies or interests in other entities where those companies or entities own certain assets located in a source country. The company or other entity that owns the asset may be resident in the country in which the asset is located, in the country in which the nonresident owner is

实体可能是资产所在国的居民，也可能是其非居民持股者所属居民国的居民或第三国的居民。而且，可能通过多层公司或实体，间接拥有不动产。例如，假设 A 国居民公司 A 拥有 B 国居民公司 B 的所有股份，而 B 公司拥有 C 国居民公司 C 的所有股份，C 公司拥有位于 C 国的不动产。如果 C 公司出售不动产，C 国可以对与财产有关的收益向 C 公司征税。但是，当 B 公司出售 C 公司股份，或 A 公司出售 B 公司股份时，如果 C 国不对相关收益征税，那么，这些所谓的**间接转让**或出售，便成为非居民规避来源国税收的一种简单易行的方法。

因此，对持有不动产的公司股份或其他实体权益（如信托和合伙企业）的财产收益征税，对于防止通过以下形式，轻易规避针对处置不动产所产生收益的税收很有必要，即通过公司或其他实体持有不动产，然后出售公司股份或实体权益，而不是不动产本身。OECD 协定范本和联合国协定范本第 13 条第 4 款规定，如果一家公司股份或一家实体权益的价值，在处置前 365 天内的任何时间，有 50% 以上可直接或间接地归属于位于一国的不动产，则该国有权对从出售该公司股份或该实体权益所获得的财产收益征税。对于出售持有大量房地产的企业或重大参股居民公司的股份而获得的资本收益，唯一有效的征税方式，是让买方负担从购价中预提税款的义务。比起股份处置，这种方式对不动产的处置更有效，因为在不动产的情况下，税款可以作为对不动产的留置权。

针对因出售非居民公司股份或其他类型非居民实体权益所产生收益的征税问题，并不局限于持有大量房地产的企业或实体的股份或权益，还波及其他资产，如采矿许可证、电信许可证和其他类似资产。如果非居民处置其在某一实体中的权益，而该实体并非资产所在国家的居民，则该资产所在国可以对涉及相关资产的收益征税，可以认定在资产所有者的控制权直接或间接发生变化时，发生了资产转让。在这种情况下，有两种征税方式。一是该国可以认定在资产控制权发生变化时，实现了相关资产的转让，对资产的直接所有人（在上例中为 C 公司）征税。二是该国可以认定相关收益来源于本国，从而对出售股份或其他权益的实际非居民卖方征税。希望对这些间接转让征税的国家可以通过以下方式，执行此项

resident, or in a third country. Moreover, the asset may be owned indirectly through multiple tiers of companies or entities. For example, assume that ACo, a company resident in Country A, owns all the shares of BCo, a company resident in Country B, and BCo owns all the shares of CCo, a company resident in Country C, which owns immovable property situated in Country C. If CCo sells the immovable property, Country C can impose tax on CCo on any gain with respect to the property. However, if Country C does not tax the gain where BCo sells the shares of CCo or where ACo sells the shares of BCo, these so-called **indirect transfers** or sales are an easy way for nonresidents to avoid source country tax.

Thus, the taxation of capital gains in respect of shares of companies or interests in other entities (such as trusts and partnerships) holding immovable property is necessary to prevent the easy avoidance of the tax on gains from the disposal of immovable property by holding the property in a company or other entity and then selling the shares or interests rather than the immovable property itself. The rule in Article 13(4) of the OECD and UN Model Treaties provides that a country is entitled to tax gains from the sale of shares of a company or interests in another entity if more than 50% of the value of the shares of the company or interest in the entity is attributable, directly or indirectly, to immovable property situated in the country at any time during the 365-day period before the disposition. For capital gains from the sale of shares of land-rich companies or substantial participations in resident companies, the only effective method of enforcing the tax is to place an obligation on the purchaser to withhold the tax from the purchase price. This method of enforcement is not as effective for shares as for the disposal of immovable property because, in the case of immovable property, the tax can be registered as a lien against the property.

The problem of taxing gains from the sale of shares of a nonresident company or interests in other types of nonresident entities extends beyond shares or interests in land-rich companies or entities to other assets, such as mining licenses, telecommunications licenses, and other similar property. Where a nonresident disposes of interests in an entity that is not resident in the country in which the asset is located, that country can impose tax on the gain in respect of the underlying asset by deeming a disposition of the underlying asset to occur when there is a change of control, directly or indirectly, of the owner of the asset. There are two ways to impose tax in this situation. First, the country can tax the direct owner of the asset (CCo in the above example) by deeming a disposition of the underlying asset to occur when a change of control occurs. Second, the country can tax the actual nonresident seller of the shares or other interests by deeming such a gain to have its source in the country. Countries that wish to tax these indirect transfers can enforce the tax by requiring the purchaser to withhold an amount on

征税，即要求买方预提某一款项，作为卖方的应缴税款，或要求资产的直接所有人作为实际非居民卖方的代理人来缴纳税款。参见税收合作平台，离岸间接转让的税收征收工具包，网址：www.tax-platform.org。

如果非居民出售其在一国用于经营的资产，对处置经营资产所产生的财产收益的征税，与对企业经营所得的征税方式相同，尽管当遇到非居民出售全部经营资产的情形，税款征收会有困难。

5.9 非居民的税收征管

5.9.1 引言

在对涉及居民和非居民的跨境交易和投资的征税方面，税收征管的各种困难都被放大。对取得本国来源所得的非居民征税，不同于对居民征税，因为居民通常存在于一国之中（或与该国有实质性联系），并受其法律制度的约束。对于一个国家来说，对非居民开征其无力实际执行的税收是毫无意义的。本节研究两个主要问题：获取必要的信息和税款征收。

5.9.2 获取非居民境内来源所得的信息

这里的基本问题是：来源国需要什么信息，才能有效地向非居民实施税款征收？第一，来源国需要基本信息，如名称、地址和纳税人识别号（如有），以识别获得境内来源所得的非居民。第二，来源国需要信息，以确定非居民是否在境内开展经营活动、是否在境内设有常设机构、是否从境内获得投资所得。第三，需要信息，以确定或核实非居民境内来源所得的计算（收入和支出）。第四，需要涉及与关联方之间交易，特别是与来源国居民关联方交易的信息。第五，如果非居民根据适用的税收协定，要求减免来源国税收，则来源国应掌握足够的信息，来判断是否应该给予其协定待遇。

account of the tax payable by the seller or by requiring the direct owner of the asset to pay the tax as the agent of the actual nonresident seller. *See* the Platform for Collaboration on Tax, *The Taxation of Offshore Indirect Transfers—A Toolkit*, available at www.tax-platform.org.

In the case of the sale of the property of a business carried on in a country by a nonresident, the tax on any capital gains from the disposal of the business assets can be enforced in the same way as tax on the income from the business, although the tax may be difficult to collect where the nonresident sells all the assets of the business.

5.9 ADMINISTRATIVE ASPECTS OF TAXING NONRESIDENTS

5.9.1 Introduction

The difficulties of tax administration are exacerbated with respect to the taxation of cross-border transactions and investment involving both residents and nonresidents. Collecting tax from nonresidents earning domestic source income is different from collecting tax from residents because, unlike nonresidents, residents are usually present in a country (or have substantial connections with the country) and are subject to its legal system. It makes little sense for a country to impose a tax on nonresidents that it cannot collect. In this section, two major problems are examined: obtaining the necessary information and collecting the tax.

5.9.2 Obtaining Information about Domestic Source Income of Nonresidents

The basic question here is: what information do source countries need to collect tax effectively from nonresidents? First, they need basic information, such as name, address, and taxpayer identification number, if available, to identify nonresidents earning domestic source income. Second, they need information to determine whether nonresidents are carrying on business in their countries, or have PEs there, or are earning investment income there. Third, information is necessary to determine or verify the computation of a nonresident's domestic source income (revenue and expenses). Fourth, information is necessary concerning transactions with related persons, especially with related persons who are residents of the source country. Fifth, if the nonresident is claiming a reduction of or exemption from source country tax under an applicable tax treaty, the source country should have sufficient information to verify whether the benefits of the treaty should be granted.

在某些情况下，可以对非居民提出主动报告的要求，来获得必要的信息。然而，理想情况下，税务机关应该掌握独立的信息，以便核实非居民提供的信息。

在其他情况下，可以从与非居民有关系或交易的居民获得信息。例如，可以要求向非居民支付股息、利息、特许权使用费或其他款项的居民，报告有关非居民收款人、付款金额以及付款性质等基本信息。向第三方提出此类报告要求，可能会导致其产生高额的遵从成本，因此，在提出这种报告要求时，来源国必须仔细权衡信息需求与第三方承受的遵从成本。一国不应该索要其不能有效利用的信息。

如果税务机关掌握了必要的技术来使用电子信息，则应要求纳税人以电子格式提供信息。税务机关如果有电子格式的信息和纳税人识别号，就能够比对不同来源的信息。应该要求纳税人每年以一致的格式报告信息，既可以与非居民的纳税申报表一起申报（如果申报表属必需），也可以单独申报，或者由纳税人留存，以备税务机关可能的检查。

在许多情况下，要从来源国之外取得必要的信息。如果纳税人掌握信息，但不及时提供，可以对其进行处罚。一些国家制定了专门的规则，禁止纳税人在后续法律程序中，提供之前未按税务机关要求披露的存放于境外的信息；如果纳税人披露了所有有利于自身的信息，这种规则就不太可能有效。如果信息由无关联的第三方掌握，纳税人则不应该因为不提供该信息而受到处罚。但是，如果信息由关联方掌握，在某些情况下实施处罚则是合理的。

如果来源国和非居民所属居民国之间存在协定，则可通过协定中的信息交换条款获得境外信息。以 OECD 协定范本和联合国协定范本为基础的双边税收协定包含了信息交换条款（第 26 条），该条款授权税务机关应另一国的具体请求，交换多种类型的信息，并且可以自动进行。此外，一些国家与尚未缔结全面税收协定的国家（如避税地）签订了《税收信息交换协定》。虽然没有必要与这些国家缔结全面税收协定，但是，交换信息对居民国和来源国都有益

In some cases, the necessary information can be obtained by imposing reporting requirements on the nonresidents themselves. Ideally, however, the tax authorities should have independent information to verify information provided by nonresidents.

In other cases, information can be obtained from residents who have relationships or transactions with nonresidents. For example, residents paying dividends, interest, royalties, or other amounts to nonresidents can be required to report basic information about the nonresident recipients and the amount and nature of the payments. Imposing these types of reporting requirements on third persons may result in their incurring significant compliance costs. As a result, in adopting such reporting requirements, a source country must carefully balance the need for information against the compliance costs imposed on third parties. A country should not ask for information that it cannot use effectively.

Information should be provided in electronic format if the tax authorities have the necessary technology to use information in this format. If the tax authorities have information in electronic format and have taxpayer identification numbers, they will be able to match information from various sources. The information should be provided in a consistent format from year to year. It can be filed with the nonresident's tax return (assuming that a return is required) or filed separately, or retained by the taxpayer for possible inspection by the tax authorities.

In many situations, the necessary information is located outside the source country. If the information is in possession of the taxpayer, a penalty can be imposed on the taxpayer for failing to produce the information on a timely basis. Some countries have adopted special rules to preclude a taxpayer from introducing in any subsequent legal proceedings foreign-based information that is not disclosed to the tax authorities when requested; such a rule is unlikely to be effective if the taxpayer discloses all the information favorable to the taxpayer's case. If the information is in possession of an unrelated third party, the taxpayer should not be penalized for not producing the information. If the information is held by a related party, however, it may be appropriate to impose penalties in certain circumstances.

If there is a treaty in place between the source country and the country in which the nonresident is resident, foreign-based information may be obtained through the exchange-of-information provision in the treaty. Bilateral tax treaties based on the OECD or UN Model Treaties contain an exchange-of-information article (Article 26), which authorizes the tax authorities to exchange many types of information in response to a specific request from the other country and to do so automatically. In addition, several countries have entered into Tax Information Exchange Agreements (TIEAs) with countries (such as tax havens) with which they do not have comprehensive tax treaties. Comprehensive tax treaties with these countries are not necessary,

处。北欧国家及欧盟的多边协定和欧洲理事会与 OECD 签署的《多边税收征管互助公约》（1995 年生效，起步较慢，但截至 2022 年 9 月，146 个国家已签署）都涵盖了信息交换。第 8 章第 8.8.4 节更加详细地讨论了税收协定中的信息交换。

5.9.3 非居民的税款征收

确定非居民应纳税额的基本方法有两种：计征和扣缴。计征通常适用于非居民按净额纳税的情形，而扣缴通常适用于按总额征税的消极投资所得。计征通常以提交纳税申报表的方式核算非居民的应纳税所得额和应纳税额。如果非居民不缴纳任何应缴税款，则来源国可以根据国内法对税款采取强制执行措施。

扣缴则通过赋予向非居民支付某一款项的人（通常是居民）相关义务，让其按照所支付款项的一定百分比扣留税款，并代表非居民将税款缴给税务机关。有两种类型扣缴。临时或暂时扣缴仅是一种税款征收手段。扣留并以非居民纳税人的名义缴纳给税务机关的款项实际上视同非居民分期缴纳的税款。非居民有义务提交纳税申报表，缴纳应纳税额中超过已扣缴的部分，或就超过应纳税额的已扣款项获得退税。如果非居民未提交纳税申报表，税务机关则将已扣款项充抵非居民的应纳税额。

各国经常利用雇主的临时扣缴，从对支付给雇员的薪金和工资中征收税款。最终预提税是对支付给非居民的某些款项的总额（或总额一定的百分比）征收的一种税。这就是最终缴纳的税款，因为非居民无权按实际净所得提交纳税申报表。虽然最终预提税在形式上不是所得税，但由于对非居民征税困难，只要税率设置得当，则被国际社会公认为所得税的替代方式。

显然，如果非居民在来源国拥有资产或实际存在于来源国，则来源国可直接对非居民采取征税措施。在这些情况下，包括在一国开展经营的非居民，来源国

but exchange of information can be useful for both residence and source countries. Exchange of information is also covered by multilateral agreements among the Nordic countries, the EU, and the joint Convention on Mutual Administrative Assistance in Tax Matters of the Council of Europe and the OECD, which entered into force in 1995; after a slow start, 146 countries had signed this Convention as of September 2022. Exchange of information under tax treaties is discussed in more detail in Chapter 8, section 8.8.4.

5.9.3 Collection of Tax from Nonresidents

There are two basic ways of determining the tax payable by nonresidents: assessment and withholding. Assessment is typically used in situations in which nonresidents are taxed on a net basis, whereas withholding is typically used for passive investment income taxed on a gross basis. Assessment involves the determination of a nonresident's income subject to tax and tax payable, usually by way of filing a tax return. If the nonresident does not pay any tax owing, the source country can take action to enforce the tax in accordance with its domestic law.

Withholding operates by the imposition of an obligation on persons (usually residents) paying certain amounts to nonresidents to withhold tax at a specified percentage of those payments and remit the tax to the tax authorities on behalf of the nonresident. There are two types of withholding. Provisional or interim withholding is purely a collection device. The amounts withheld are remitted to the tax authorities on account of the nonresident taxpayer; they are treated, in effect, like installments of tax paid by the nonresident. The nonresident is under an obligation to file a return and either pay any tax owing in excess of the amount withheld or receive a refund of the amount withheld in excess of the tax payable. If the nonresident does not file a return, the tax authorities will have access to the amounts withheld to satisfy the nonresident's tax liability.

Provisional withholding by employers is often used to collect tax from salary and wages paid to employees. Final withholding is a tax imposed on the gross amount (or a percentage of that amount) of certain payments to a nonresident. It is final because the nonresident is not entitled to file a return on the basis of its actual net income. Although a final withholding tax is not, in form, an income tax, if the rate of withholding tax is set appropriately, it is recognized as an internationally accepted proxy for an income tax because of the difficulties in collecting tax from nonresidents.

Obviously, if a nonresident has assets in the source country or is physically present in the source country, collection action can be taken by the source country directly against the

通常通过计征方式对非居民征税。在实行自行报缴制度的国家，非居民应提交纳税申报表，申报其收入和支出，并确定其应纳税额。来源国可以审核非居民的纳税申报表，并以基本上与居民相同的方式，来实现非居民税款的征收。通常情况下，此类非居民可能需要在整个纳税年度内定期分期缴纳税款，也可能需要对向其支付和由其支付的某些款项实行临时扣缴。

但是，如果非居民未存在于来源国，并且在来源国没有重大资产，则来源国必须采取特别措施对其征税。第一，来源国可以考虑就非居民的未缴税款，从本国法院获得判决，然后请求非居民所属居民国的法院强制执行该判决。这种做法的问题在于，许多国家不会执行其他国家的刑事和税收判决（这被广泛称为收入规则）。第二，来源国可根据两国之间的税收协定，就未缴税款向非居民所属居民国请求征收协助，但前提是该协定根据 OECD 协定范本和联合国协定范本第 27 条，包含涉及征收协助的相关条款。第三，如果来源国和居民国是诸如《多边税收征管互助公约》（第 5.9.2 节在论述信息交换时提及）等涉税事项征管协助多边公约的缔约国，则来源国可以要求居民国代为征收来源国的税款，视同居民国应征税款。

许多国家认为：预提税是向在该国没有显著存在的非居民征税的最有效方法。由于净所得可能远远低于总收入，因此，对受雇所得、来自服务的其他所得、租金和特许权使用费等所得的扣缴，有时是临时的。非居民有权提交纳税申报表，并就任何超额扣缴的税款申请退税。然而，实际执行中临时扣缴经常会成为最终预提税，因为非居民可以选择不提交纳税申报表，除非已扣税额远远超过应纳税额。此外，遗憾的是，一些国家的税收征管效率低下，可能会有意或无意地使非居民难以获得退税。

对某些支付款项的总额征收最终预提税，是对非居民征税的一种方便有效的方法，特别是对于缺乏足够征管资源的发展中国家。但是，除非税率很低，

nonresident. In these circumstances, which may include nonresidents carrying on business in a country, source countries typically impose tax by means of an assessment levied on the nonresident. In countries with self-assessment systems, nonresidents are expected to file tax returns in which they report their revenue and expenses and determine their tax payable. Source countries can audit nonresidents' tax returns and enforce tax payable by nonresidents in largely the same way as with residents. Often such nonresidents may be required to pay periodic installments of tax throughout a taxation year; they may also be subject to interim or provisional withholding on certain amounts paid to them and by them.

If, however, the nonresident is not present and does not have significant assets in the source country, the source country must take special measures to collect its tax. First, the source country might consider obtaining a court judgment for the unpaid tax against the nonresident from the country's courts and then seeking enforcement of that judgment by the courts in the nonresident's country of residence. The problem with this course of action is that many countries will not enforce other countries' criminal and tax judgments (this is widely known as the revenue rule). Second, the source country may consider requesting assistance in the collection of the unpaid tax from the country of residence pursuant to the tax treaty between the two countries if that treaty has an article dealing with Assistance in Collection based on Article 27 of the OECD and UN Model Treaties. Third, if the source and residence countries are parties to a multilateral convention dealing with administrative assistance in tax matters, such as the Convention on Mutual Administrative Assistance in Tax Matters, referred to above in section 5.9.2 in connection with exchange of information, the source country can request the residence country to collect the source country's tax as if it were tax owing to the residence country.

Many countries have concluded that withholding is the most effective method of collecting tax from nonresidents that do not have a significant presence in the country. The withholding is sometimes provisional with respect to amounts such as employment income, other income from services, and rents and royalties because the net income may be significantly less than the gross amount. Nonresidents have the right to file a return and obtain a refund of any excess tax withheld. Often, however, as a practical matter, provisional withholding operates as a final withholding tax because the nonresident may choose not to file a return unless the amount withheld is substantially in excess of the amount of tax payable. Also, unfortunately, some countries may make it difficult, either deliberately or inadvertently, through inefficient tax administration, for nonresidents to obtain refunds.

A final withholding tax on the gross amount of certain payments is a convenient and effective method of collecting tax from nonresidents, especially for developing countries that

否则，最终预提税对非居民可能发生重大费用的款项并不合适。如果非居民的营业利润系由股息、利息、特许权使用费或服务费等款项构成，就可能属于这种情况。

缓解过高预提税的另一种方法，是允许非居民选择以净额计税。如果选择了此种方式，非居民可以提交纳税申报表，并就净所得缴纳税款。一些国家就不动产所得提供了这种方式以供选择。非居民从位于一国的不动产取得的租金，通常要按总额适用预提税。尽管对不动产的租金所得征收此种预提税，符合 OECD 协定范本和联合国协定范本第 6 条，但非居民可能已就不动产发生了大量费用，如抵押利息、财产税和维护费等。因此，即使税率相对较低，基于总额的预提税也可能过高；如果非居民可以选择以净额纳税，问题则得以缓解。

说明最终预提税的有效性和适当性之间矛盾的一个例子，是发展中国家对咨询费、技术费和管理费的税收处理。根据 OECD 协定范本和联合国协定范本，只有非居民在来源国停留超过 183 天，或在来源国设有常设机构或固定基地，且上述款项可归属于常设机构或固定基地时，这些款项才是来源国应予征税的营业利润。在大多数情况下，纳税人可以通过策划安排，在避免在来源国构成常设机构或固定基地的情况下（或避免在来源国停留如联合国协定范本第 14 条第 1 款第 2 项所规定的 183 天），仍可获取巨额收费。

发展中国家往往无法接受这一结果，有的认为，技术费和管理费属于特许权使用费，应征预提税。一些国家，如印度、牙买加、肯尼亚、蒙古国、坦桑尼亚和越南，在其税收协定中加入了特殊条款，允许来源国按总额，适用限制税率，对咨询费、技术费和管理费征税。2017 年，联合国协定范本增加了关于技术服务费的第 12A 条。该条款允许来源国通过预提税对技术服务费总额征税，税率由协定双方商定，前提是费用的支付人为来源国居民，或在来源国设有常设机构或固定基地的非居民。技术服务费被定义为，针对咨询、技术或管理服务支付的款项，但不包括支付给雇员的款项、支付给个人劳务的款项、支付给教育机构用

lack sufficient administrative resources. However, unless the rate of tax is quite low, a final withholding tax is inappropriate for amounts in respect of which a nonresident is likely to have incurred significant expenses. This may be the case where amounts such as dividends, interest, royalties, or fees for services constitute profits of a business carried on by a nonresident.

Another method of providing relief from excessive withholding taxes is allowing nonresidents to elect to pay tax on a net basis; if this election is made, the nonresident can file a return and pay tax on the net income. Several countries provide this type of election with respect to income from immovable property. A nonresident deriving rent from immovable property located in a country will often be subject to withholding tax on the gross amount of the rent. Although such a withholding tax on rental income from immovable property is in accordance with Article 6 of the OECD and UN Model Treaties, the nonresident may have incurred significant expenses with respect to the immovable property, such as mortgage interest, property taxes, and maintenance. As a result, a gross-basis withholding tax, even at a relatively low rate, may well be excessive, and the ability of the nonresident to make an election to pay tax on a net basis can provide relief.

An example of the tension between the effectiveness and the appropriateness of final withholding is the taxation of consulting, technical, and management fees by developing countries. Under the OECD and UN Model Treaties, such fees are business profits that are taxable by the source country only if the nonresident spends more than 183 days in the source country or has a PE or fixed base in the source country and the fees are attributable to the PE or fixed base. In most cases, taxpayers can arrange their affairs so that they can earn substantial fees without having a PE or fixed base in the source country (or without spending more than 183 days in the source country under Article 14(1)(b) of the UN Model Treaty).

This result is often unacceptable to developing countries, and some of them have taken the position that technical and management fees are royalties subject to withholding tax. Several countries, such as India, Jamaica, Kenya, Mongolia, Tanzania, and Vietnam, have included special articles in their tax treaties allowing them to tax consulting, technical, and management fees on a gross basis but at a limited rate. In 2017, Article 12A dealing with fees for technical services was added to the UN Model Treaty. This article permits a source country to tax such fees through a withholding tax on the gross amount of the fees at a rate to be agreed on by the parties to the treaty where the payer of the fees is a resident of the source country or a nonresident with a PE or fixed base in the source country. Fees for technical services are defined to be payments for consulting, technical, or management services but do not include payments to employees, payments for personal services, and payments to and by educational institutions for

于教学的款项和教育机构支付的用于教学的款项。来源国有权对技术服务费征税，即使服务是在该国境外提供的。第 9 章第 9.3.3 节将对第 12A 条展开更广泛的论述。

针对因自动数字服务而支付款项的税款扣缴，也存在类似的问题。根据联合国协定范本第 12B 条，此类服务应由来源国征税。第 12B 条是联合国协定范本 2021 年新增的条款，第 9 章第 9.5.4 节将予以讨论。

teaching. The source country is entitled to tax fees for technical services even where the services are rendered outside that country. Article 12A is dealt with more extensively in Chapter 9, section 9.3.3.

Similar issues arise with respect to withholding taxes on payments for automated digital services, which are taxable by source countries under Article 12B of the UN Model Treaty. Article 12B was added to the UN Model Treaty in 2021 and is discussed in Chapter 9, section 9.5.4.

6 转让定价

6.1 引言

转让价格是在关联方之间交易中确定的价格。例如，如果 A 公司在 A 国生产商品，并将商品出售给其外国关联公司 B 公司，B 公司是 B 国居民公司，则此项销售据以发生的价格即称为转让价格。转让价格可能会不同于市场价格。市场价格是指市场上非关联方之间，为了转让商品和服务而设定的价格。通常而言，在非关联方之间的商品或服务销售中，双方利益的冲突能够确保针对商品或服务所收取的价格，不会人为地过高或过低。然而，关联方之间不存在利益冲突，因此，关联方之间交易中收取的价格可能与市场价格存在显著差异。

跨国公司将转让价格用于在其企业集团内销售和其他方式转让商品和服务。这些集团内转让价格是最重要的一类转让价格。个人也可使用转让价格，与其控制下的公司或其他实体交易，或是与其近亲进行交易。

除非受到阻止，从事跨境交易的关联方可以通过操纵转让价格来避税。例如，在前文的例子中，A 公司可以通过设定向 B 公司销售的由其制造商品的价格，导致 A 公司获利偏低或为零，从而避免在 A 国缴纳所得税。如果 B 国的实际税率低于 A 国的实际税率，则利用不恰当的转让价格，将会造成 A 公司和 B 公司的总体税负减少。如果 B 国是低税率国家，A 公司和 B 公司将就其合并利润少纳税或不纳税。

CHAPTER 6
Transfer Pricing

6.1 INTRODUCTION

A transfer price is the price established in a transaction between related persons. For example, if ACo manufactures goods in Country A and sells them to its foreign affiliate, BCo, resident in Country B, the price at which that sale takes place is called a transfer price. A transfer price may be different from the market price, which is the price set in the marketplace for transfers of goods and services between unrelated persons. In a sale of goods or services between unrelated parties, the conflicting interests of the parties usually ensure that the price charged for the goods or services is neither artificially high nor low. However, related parties do not have conflicting interests, and therefore, the prices charged in transactions between related parties may be significantly different from market prices.

Multinational companies use transfer prices for sales and other transfers of goods and services within their corporate group. These intercompany transfer prices are the most important category of transfer prices. Transfer prices may also be used by individuals dealing with corporations or other entities under their control and by individuals dealing with close family members.

Unless prevented from doing so, related persons engaged in cross-border transactions can avoid tax through their manipulation of transfer prices. For example, in the example above, ACo might avoid paying income taxes in Country A by setting a price on the sale of its manufactured goods to BCo that results in its earning little or no profit. If the effective tax rate in Country B is lower than the effective tax rate in Country A, the total tax burden on ACo and BCo would be reduced through the use of inappropriate transfer prices. If Country B is a low-tax country, ACo and BCo will pay little or no tax on their combined profits.

在完善的所得税制度下，如果关联方设定的转让价格与市场价格不同，税务机关应有权调整转让价格。此种权力包括在关联方之间分配收入、扣除、抵免和其他列支款项，从而防止相关国家的本国税基受到侵蚀，征收合理份额的税收收入。

一般而言，关联方包括由共同利益方直接或间接拥有或控制的各方。此种关系的一个有力标识，是有能力设定不同于市场价格的转让价格。

如上所述，税务机关应有权调整转让价格，以防止纳税人将所得转移至位于避税地或在某些国家享受税收优惠的关联方。税收优惠包括相对较低的税率、免税期或其他税收激励措施，以及可税前扣除的亏损。尽管纳税人通常不会将所得转移到法定税率较高的国家，但当其附属集团的成员在该国有亏损，或者如果纳税人能够利用该高税率国家税收制度中的一些漏洞或税收优惠制度，则纳税人会做出如此选择。纳税人也可以通过将可扣除费用从低税率国家的实体转移到高税率国家的关联实体来实现节税，因为此种扣除在高税率国家，会产生更多节税。

一个国家的税务机关应有权调整转让价格的另一个原因，是防止其他国家过于激进地实施其转让定价规则，从跨境交易的所得中获取非合理份额的税收收入。如果某个国家在转让价格调整方面态度激进，而另一个国家趋于温和，那么，在这两个国家进行交易的纳税人可能会将所得转移至激进的国家，以降低双重征税的风险。

当多个国家对相同的交易适用各自的转让定价规则时，极有可能导致双重征税。例如，假设A公司在A国以60元的成本生产商品，并将商品出售给B国的一家关联公司B公司，B公司再以150元的价格，将商品出售给B国的零售客户。A公司就其生产利润在A国缴税，B公司就其销售利润在B国缴税。由A公司和B公司组成的公司集团的净利润为90元（150－60）。假设A国认定，A公司向B公司销售商品的合理转让价格为90元，而B国却认为，合理转让价格应为50元。在这种情况下，虽然集团合并所得为90元，但却就130元的所得纳税，因此导致了双重征税。如下所示：

In a well-designed income tax system, the tax authorities should have the power to adjust the transfer prices set by related persons where those prices differ from market prices. This authority should include the power to allocate revenue, deductions, credits, and other allowances among related persons so that the country is able to prevent the erosion of its domestic tax base and collect its fair share of tax revenue.

In general, related persons include persons that are owned or controlled, directly or indirectly, by the same interests. A good indicator of such a relationship is the ability to set transfer prices that differ from market prices.

As suggested above, the tax authorities should be given the power to adjust transfer prices to prevent taxpayers from shifting income to related persons resident in tax havens or in countries where they enjoy some preferential tax treatment. Examples of preferential tax treatment include relatively low tax rates, tax holidays or other tax incentives, and tax-deductible losses. Although taxpayers generally do not seek to deflect income to a country that has high statutory tax rates, they may do so when a member of their affiliated group has losses in that country or if they are able to exploit some loophole or preferential tax regime in the high-tax country's tax system. Taxpayers can also obtain tax savings by shifting deductible expenses from an entity in a low-tax country to a related entity in a high-tax country since the deduction in the high-tax country generates more tax savings.

The tax authorities of a country also need the power to adjust transfer prices in order to prevent other countries from obtaining an unfair share of the tax revenue on income derived from cross-border transactions through overly aggressive enforcement of their transfer pricing rules. When one country is aggressive in making transfer price adjustments and another country is not, taxpayers engaged in transactions in both countries may divert income to the aggressive country in order to mitigate their risks of double taxation.

Double taxation is a serious possibility when multiple countries apply their transfer pricing rules to the same transactions. For example, assume that ACo manufactures goods in Country A at a cost of 60 and sells them to a related company, BCo, that is resident in Country B. BCo then sells the goods to retail customers in Country B for 150. ACo is taxable in Country A on its manufacturing profits, and BCo is taxable in Country B on its sales profits. The corporate group (consisting of ACo and BCo) has a net profit of 90 (150−60). Assume that Country A concludes that the proper transfer price on the sales from ACo to BCo is 90, whereas Country B takes the position that the proper price for the sales is 50. In that event, double taxation will result because the combined group will have income of 90 but will be taxable on income of 130, as follows:

A 公司在 A 国的应纳税所得额：	
销售额	90
商品成本	60
所得	30
B 公司在 B 国的应纳税所得额：	
销售额	150
商品成本	50
所得	100
A 公司与 B 公司的合计所得	130

如果两国执行统一的规则以调整不当的转让价格，并在所有情况下以同样方式运用这些规则，则可以消除以上示例中的双重征税。仍以上述情形为例，如果 B 国接受 A 国 90 元的转让价格（那么 B 国将只能对 B 公司的 60 元所得征税），或者 A 国接受 B 国 50 元的转让价格（那么 A 国会将 A 公司视为亏损 10 元），就可以消除双重征税。

为了实现一定程度的一致性，OECD 协定范本和联合国协定范本第 9 条均规定，应调整转让价格，以反映在独立运营的非关联企业之间的同一交易中可能使用的价格。这一**独立交易方法（标准、原则或方式）**已为世界大多数国家所采用。然而，对独立交易方法的广泛接受，掩盖了对该方法在实践中应用方式的重大分歧。下文第 6.4 节详述了为实施独立交易标准所采用的主要转让定价方法。

有的国家会在转让定价争议实际产生之前，设法与纳税人就其在设定转让价格过程中所使用的方法达成一致意见。此类方法的主要目的，是降低纳税人和税务机关将涉及转让价格的争议付诸诉讼通常会产生的高额成本。如果纳税人希望其事关一项或多项交易的定价方法在事先得到认可，则通常会向税务机关提交申请，要求达成通常所谓的“**预约定价安排**”。纳税人必须详细说明其计划应用于预约定价安排所涵盖交易的转让定价方法，并且必须解释该方法会产生合理结果

Income of ACo taxable in Country A:	
Sales	90
Cost of goods	60
Income	30
Income of BCo taxable in Country B:	
Sales	150
Cost of goods	50
Income	100
Total income of ACo and BCo	130

The double taxation illustrated in the above example would be eliminated if both countries had uniform rules for adjusting inappropriate transfer prices and applied those rules in the same way in all cases. Thus, on the facts of the example, double taxation would be eliminated either if Country B accepted Country A's transfer price of 90 (because Country B would then tax BCo on income of only 60) or if Country A accepted Country B's transfer price of 50 (because then Country A would treat ACo as having a loss of 10).

In an attempt to achieve some degree of uniformity, Article 9 of both the OECD and UN Model Treaties provides that transfer prices should be adjusted to reflect the prices that would have been used in the same transaction between unrelated enterprises acting independently. This so-called **arm's-length method (standard, principle, or approach)** has been adopted by most countries worldwide. The broad acceptance of the arm's-length method, however, masks substantial disagreements over the way the method is applied in practice. The main transfer pricing methods employed for implementing the arm's-length standard are described in section 6.4 below.

Some countries try to reach an agreement with taxpayers on the methodologies to be used by them in setting their transfer prices before a transfer pricing dispute actually arises. A major objective of this type of approach is to reduce the high costs that taxpayers and tax authorities typically incur in litigating disputes over transfer prices. A taxpayer that wants advance approval of its pricing methodology with respect to one or more transactions typically submits a request to the tax authorities for what is generally known as an *Advance Pricing Agreement* (APA). The taxpayer must give details about the transfer pricing methodology that it intends to apply to the transactions covered by the APA and must explain

的原因。在某些情况下，两个或两个以上国家的政府，可以利用其税收协定中的争端解决机制，共同议定纳税人使用的定价方法。OECD 已为双多边预约定价安排发布了指南。

6.2 《OECD 转让定价指南》

从 20 世纪 60 年代开始，美国率先提出限制滥用转让定价的方法。在早期，《美国国内收入法典》第 482 节对独立交易标准的定义曾引发争议，如今已获广泛认可。第 482 节细则提出了确定独立交易价格的三种方法：可比非受控价格法、再销售价格法及成本加成法。1995 年，美国出台新的转让定价细则，允许使用一些其他的方法，主要针对所销售或许可的产品包含无形资产的情形。尽管这些方法起初饱受争议，但现在已被许多国家所接受，并在符合一定条件的情况下，得到了 OECD 的认可。

多年来，OECD 一直不懈努力，争取就转让定价规则达成国际共识。1979 年，OECD 出版题为《转让定价与跨国企业》的报告，主张采用独立交易原则来确定关联企业之间交易的价格。1984 年，《转让定价与跨国企业：三个税收问题》报告对 1979 年的报告进行了补充，补充报告涉及相互协商程序、银行业务以及总部管理与服务成本的分摊。1992 年，OECD 成立工作组，梳理美国转让定价的发展。1993 年 OECD 成立另一工作组，修订 1979 年及 1984 年关于转让定价的报告。上述种种努力终于使转让定价问题得到全面和根本性的审视，并于 1995 年发布了 OECD《跨国企业与税务机关转让定价指南》（以下简称《OECD 转让定价指南》）。

自 1995 年以来，《OECD 转让定价指南》已数次修订。2022 年，依据 BEPS 项目形成的数份报告，对指南再次进行了最新修订，涉及交易利润分割法的运用、难以估值的无形资产和金融交易等议题。

why that methodology would produce an appropriate result. In some instances, two or more governments may use the dispute- resolution mechanism in their tax treaties to agree jointly on the pricing methodology to be used by a taxpayer. The OECD has issued guidelines for countries in developing joint APAs.

6.2 THE OECD TRANSFER PRICING GUIDELINES

Beginning in the 1960s, the U.S. took the lead in developing techniques for limiting transfer pricing abuses. The definition of the arm's-length standard under section 482 of the U.S. Internal Revenue Code was initially controversial but is now widely accepted. The regulations under section 482 promoted three methods for determining the arm's-length price: the **Comparable Uncontrolled Price (CUP) method,** the **resale price method**, and the **cost-plus method**. In 1995, the U.S. adopted new transfer pricing regulations that endorsed some additional methods to be applied primarily when products embodying intangible property are sold or licensed. Although initially quite controversial, those methods have now been accepted by many other governments and, with some qualifications, have been endorsed by the OECD.

The OECD has been working steadily for many years to achieve an international consensus on transfer pricing rules. In 1979, the OECD published a report, *Transfer Pricing and Multinational Enterprises*, which advocated the adoption of the arm's- length standard to determine the prices of transactions between associated enterprises. The 1979 report was supplemented by a 1984 report, *Transfer Pricing and Multinational Enterprises: Three Taxation Issues*, which dealt with the MAP, banking, and the allocation of central management and service costs. In 1992, the OECD established a task force to review transfer pricing developments in the U.S.; another task force was established in 1993 to revise the 1979 and 1984 reports on transfer pricing. These efforts culminated in a comprehensive and fundamental review of transfer pricing issues and the publication, in 1995, of the OECD's *Transfer Pricing Guidelines for Multinational Enterprises and Tax Administrations* (OECD Guidelines).

Revisions to the Guidelines have been made on several occasions since 1995, most rece ntly in 2022, to incorporate several reports resulting from the BEPS Project dealing with the application of the transactional profit-split method, hard-to-value intangibles, and financial transactions.

6.3 联合国《发展中国家转让定价实务手册》

2013年，联合国国际税收专家委员会出版了《发展中国家转让定价实务手册》（纽约：联合国，2013年）（以下简称《联合国手册》），并在第二版（2017年）和第三版（2021年）中有修订和扩展。修订和扩展新章节涉及无形资产、集团内服务、成本分摊协议、利润分割、金融交易和可比性问题。联合国手册旨在为发展中国家税务机关应用独立交易原则提供实务支持，并考虑了发展中国家的特殊需求以及管理能力。联合国手册总体上与《OECD转让定价指南》相一致。除了转让定价方法、文档要求、可比性分析，以及《OECD转让定价指南》中同样触及的相似内容外，《联合国手册》还涉及发展中国家处理转让定价问题的能力建设、调查和风险评估技术、争议解决程序，以及对巴西、中国、印度、肯尼亚、墨西哥和南非转让定价实践的描述。

6.4 独立交易原则

6.4.1 引言

按照国际惯例，合理的转让价格需符合独立交易原则。如果纳税人在与关联方的交易中设定的转让价格，与纳税人在与非关联方的类似交易中使用的价格可比，则转让价格可被视为符合独立交易原则。

然而，关于独立交易原则的上述定义，并未就在特定情况下如何确定转让价格提供指导。各国为赋予独立交易原则实质内容而采用了一些基本规则，概述如下。第6.4.2节描述了识别符合独立交易原则的可比交易或企业，用以确定关联企业之间交易合适的独立交易价格。第6.5节描述了在关联公司组成集团并共享资源的情况下，适用于设定转让价格的规则。第6.6节描述了适用于成本分摊协议的规则，关联方可依据这些规则，分摊由其共同开发的无形资产所产生

6.3 UN, PRACTICAL MANUAL ON TRANSFER PRICING FOR DEVELOPING COUNTRIES

In 2013, the UN Committee of Experts published a *Practical Manual on Transfer Pricing for Developing Countries* (New York: UN, 2013), revised and expanded in the second (2017) and third (2021) editions, which contain new chapters dealing with intangibles, intragroup services, cost contribution arrangements, profit splits, financial transactions, and comparability issues. The UN Manual is intended to provide practical assistance to the tax authorities of developing countries in applying the arm's-length standard while recognizing the particular needs and administrative capacities of those countries. It is generally consistent with the OECD Guidelines. In addition to material on transfer pricing methods, documentation requirements, comparability analysis, and similar material that is also dealt with in the OECD Guidelines, the UN Manual deals with building capacity to handle transfer pricing issues in developing countries, audits and risk assessment techniques, and dispute-resolution procedures, as well as a description of transfer pricing practices in Brazil, China, India, Kenya, Mexico, and South Africa.

6.4 THE ARM'S-LENGTH STANDARD

6.4.1 Introduction

According to international custom, an appropriate transfer price is one that meets the arm's-length standard. This standard is met if a taxpayer sets its transfer prices in its transactions with related persons so that those prices are comparable to the prices used in similar transactions with unrelated persons.

The above definition of the arm's-length standard provides little guidance as to how transfer prices should be established in particular situations. Some of the basic rules that countries have adopted to give content to the arm's-length standard are summarized below. Section 6.4.2 describes the identification of comparable arm's- length transactions or enterprises that are used to determine the appropriate arm's- length price for transactions between associated enterprises. Section 6.5 describes rules applicable for setting transfer prices where a group of related corporations shares common resources. Section 6.6 describes the rules that apply to cost contribution arrangements, under which related persons share the profits from the exploitation of intangible

的利润。

《OECD 转让定价指南》大力倡导独立交易原则。与此同时，指南也坦承，独立交易原则的实施有时会为纳税人和税务机关带来严重困难。针对判断非关联方之间的交易是否与公司集团成员间实际进行的交易相类似时需考虑的因素，指南进行了有价值的探讨。然而，与大多数关于独立交易原则的研究论著一样，指南似乎更多的是揭示了在确定受控和非受控交易之间的可比性方面存在的问题，而不足以就如何应对这些问题，向税务机关提出切实可行的建议。

纵观整个税收领域，人们采用许多方法，确定有形个人资产销售的独立交易价格。以下讨论五种方法。前三种方法，即可比非受控价格法、再销售价格法和成本加成法，有时被称为传统方法，在国际税务界得到广泛认可。然而，在许多重要的情况下，特别是在当所销售的产品包含有价值的无形资产的情况下，这些方法的应用即使并非全无可能，但也极为困难。第 6.4.3 节至第 6.4.5 节描述了这些传统方法，第 6.4.6 节则对其进行了比较。

另外两种独立交易方法在《OECD 转让定价指南》中被称为“交易利润法”，可以适用于更多情形。其中，**利润分割法**经常被税务机关在通过内部申诉程序解决与纳税人之间的争议时，非正式地使用。美国在 1994 年修订第 482 节细则时，正式批准了**交易净利润法**，又称为**可比利润法**。利润分割法和交易净利润法侧重于关注关联企业之间受控交易的利润，与类似情况下非受控交易的利润之间的比较。在 1995 年的转让定价报告中，OECD 建议，利润分割法和交易净利润法只能作为最后的手段使用。然而结果是从此取消了对这两种方法使用的限制。现行《OECD 转让定价指南》（第 2.2—2.12 段）承认，在某些情况下，基于交易利润的方法可能比传统方法更为合适。实际上，无论在何种情况下，找到最合适的转让定价方法才是最终目标。第 6.4.7 节和第 6.4.8 节分别对交易利润法进行了描述。

《OECD 转让定价指南》指出，纳税人可以使用指南认可的传统方法和交易利润法以外的其他方法，前提是这些方法符合独立交易原则，并且比指南认可的

property that they have developed jointly.

The OECD Guidelines on transfer pricing strongly endorse the arm's-length standard. At the same time, they acknowledge frankly that the application of that standard sometimes presents serious difficulties for taxpayers and tax administrations. The Guidelines provide a valuable discussion of the factors to be considered in determining whether transactions between unrelated persons are comparable to the transactions actually entered into by members of a corporate group. Like most of the literature on the arm's-length approach, however, the OECD Guidelines are arguably better at highlighting the problems of establishing the comparability of controlled and uncontrolled transactions than they are at giving practical advice to tax administrators on how to cope with these problems.

Many methods are used throughout the tax world for determining the arm's- length price for sales of tangible personal property. Five methods are discussed below. The first three methods—the CUP method, the resale price method, and the cost-plus method—are sometimes referred to as traditional methods and are widely accepted by the international tax community. Unfortunately, these methods are extremely difficult, if not impossible, to apply in many important cases, especially cases in which the products being sold incorporate valuable intangible property. The traditional methods are described in sections 6.4.3 through 6.4.5 and compared in section 6.4.6.

The two other arm's-length methods referred to in the OECD Guidelines as "transactional profit" methods can be applied in more situations. The **profit-split method** is frequently used on an informal basis by tax authorities in settling disputes with taxpayers through internal appeal procedures. The **Transactional Net Margin Method** (TNMM), also known as the **Comparable Profits Method** (CPM), was formally approved by the U.S. in revisions to the section 482 regulations in 1994. Both the profit-split and TNMM methods focus on the profits from controlled transactions between associated enterprises compared to the profits from uncontrolled transactions in similar circumstances. In its 1995 Report on transfer pricing, the OECD suggested that the profit-split and TNMM methods should be used only as a last resort; however, that limitation on their use has since been eliminated. The current OECD Guidelines (paragraphs 2.2–2.12) recognize that transactional profit methods may be more appropriate than traditional methods in certain cases. In every case, the objective is to find the transfer pricing method that is most appropriate. The transactional profit methods are described in sections 6.4.7 and 6.4.8.

The OECD Guidelines recognize that taxpayers may use methods other than the traditional and transactional profit methods authorized by the OECD Guidelines as long as they

方法更加合适。

6.4.2 可比性分析

转让定价的本质是基于可比的独立交易，为非独立交易确定合适的价格。用于比较的独立交易可以是纳税人（即需对其非独立交易进行定价的一方）与独立交易方之间的交易（即内部可比对象），也可以是非关联独立交易方之间的交易（即外部可比对象）。例如，一家企业可能同时向关联方和非关联方销售相同的商品，因此，针对非关联方销售所收取的价格即构成较好的可比对象，用以确定关联方销售的独立交易价格。然而，如果企业未向非关联方出售相同商品，则有必要寻找在相同市场或行业中经营，且向独立交易方出售相同商品的独立企业，作为可比对象。

在大多数情况下，由于独立交易价格体现了诸多考量因素（例如，销售数量、商品质量、销售条款、市场条件和市场地理位置），因此，完美的可比对象几乎不存在。但是，只要有可能对交易进行调整，并在调整后使之成为可比对象，就不必苛求精确的可比对象。

下文讨论的所有转让定价方法，都需要进行某种类型的可比性分析（参见《OECD 转让定价指南》第 3 章）。在传统方法（可比非受控价格法、再销售价格法和成本加成法）的情况下，关键在于寻找独立交易方之间可比交易的价格；而在利润分割法或交易净利润法下，寻找的则是可比交易的利润而非可比交易的价格。在这两种情况下，可比性分析都被用于选择最合适的转让定价方法，并运用该方法来确定独立交易价格或利润。

关联（或受控）交易与独立（或非受控）交易的可比性通常基于以下五个因素：

（1）所转让财物或服务的特性；

（2）交易各方的功能分析；

（3）合同条款；

are in accordance with the arm's-length principle and an authorized method is not more appropriate.

6.4.2 Comparability Analysis

The essence of transfer pricing is determining the appropriate price for a non-arm's- length transaction based on a comparable arm's-length transaction. The arm's-length transaction used for comparison may be a transaction between the taxpayer (the person whose non-arm's-length transaction is being priced) and an arm's-length person (internal comparable) or between unrelated arm's-length persons (external comparable). For example, an enterprise may sell the same goods to both related and unrelated persons; therefore, the prices charged for the sales to unrelated persons may provide good comparables for determining the arm's-length price for the related-party sales. However, if the enterprise does not sell the same goods to unrelated parties, it is necessary to search for an independent enterprise operating in the same market or industry that sells the same goods to arm's-length parties.

In most cases, it is impossible to find perfect comparables because arm's-length prices reflect many considerations (e.g., the quantity sold, the quality of the goods, the terms of sale, the conditions of the market, and the location of the market). However, it is not necessary to identify precise comparables as long as it is possible to make adjustments to a transaction so that, with the adjustments, it becomes comparable.

All the transfer pricing methods discussed below require some type of comparability analysis (*see* Chapter Ⅲ of the OECD Guidelines). In the case of the traditional methods—CUP method, resale price method, and cost-plus method—the key is to find the price in a comparable transaction between arm's-length parties; however, in the case of a profit split or TNMM, the search is for the profits from a comparable transaction rather than the price of a comparable transaction. In both cases, comparability analysis is used to select the most appropriate transfer pricing method and apply that method in order to determine the arm's-length price or profits.

The comparability of a related-party or controlled transaction and an arm's-length or uncontrolled transaction is usually based on five factors:

(1) the characteristics of the transferred property or services;

(2) a functional analysis of the parties to the transaction;

(3) the terms of the contract;

（4）经济情况；以及

（5）交易各方执行的经营策略。

从这些因素可以明显看出，可比性分析需要准确了解纳税人及其业务以及所涉交易的信息。

功能分析是甄别有效的可比交易的关键因素。这也是根据 OECD 协定范本第 7 条向常设机构归属利润的关键因素（参见本书第 8 章，第 8.8.5 节）。功能分析包括考察相关交易各方履行的功能、使用的资产和承担的风险，这三个因素决定各方预期从交易中获得的回报。功能包括研发、制造、采购、运输、储存、营销和管理服务；资产包括有形资产和无形资产；风险包括财务、产品、收款、市场、国家 / 地区和一般商业风险。

自《OECD 转让定价指南》于 1995 年首次出版以来，跨国企业一直利用合同约定的风险承担，在企业集团成员之间转移利润。2017 年，OECD 对指南进行了修订，明确仅在集团中某个公司能够对风险进行控制，并具备承担风险的财务能力时，该公司由合同约定的风险承担才应予以考虑。

在许多情况下，由于种种原因，如缺少相关信息或交易涉及新技术，不存在可比对象，故而可能无法找到可靠的可比交易或可比企业。

6.4.3　可比非受控价格法

可比非受控价格法参照非关联方之间在类似情况下类似产品的销售，确定独立交易价格。如果存在可比销售交易，则可比非受控价格法是首选方法。此法广泛用于对石油、铁矿石、小麦和其他在公开商品市场上出售的商品进行定价。2017 年，《OECD 转让定价指南》修订版进一步澄清，假设受控和非受控交易的特征具有可比性，则可以将商品挂牌价作为衡量独立交易价格的指标。定价日期是运用挂牌价时的重要因素。可比非受控价格法也适用于对其价值基本不依赖于特殊专有技术或品牌的产成品进行定价。不过，此法不适用于某些半成品（如通

(4) the economic circumstances; and

(5) the business strategies pursued by the parties.

It is apparent from these factors that comparability analysis requires good information about the taxpayer and its business, as well as the transactions involved.

Functional analysis is a key element in identifying useful comparable transactions. (It is also a key element in the attribution of profits to PEs under Article 7 of the OECD Model Treaty (*see* Chapter 8, section 8.8.5).) Functional analysis involves an examination of the functions performed, assets used, and risks assumed by the parties to the relevant transaction since these factors should determine the returns that the parties should expect from the transaction. Functions include research and development, manufacturing, purchasing, transportation, storage, marketing, and management services; assets include both tangible and intangible assets; risks include financial, product, collection, market, country/locational, and general business risks.

Since the OECD Guidelines were first published in 1995, multinational enterprises have used the contractual assumption of risk to shift profits among members of the corporate group. In 2017, the Guidelines were revised to clarify that contractual risks assumed by a group company should be taken into account only if that company can exercise control over the risk and has the financial capacity to assume the risk.

In many situations, reliable comparable transactions or enterprises may not be available for one reason or another, such as a lack of information or transactions involving new technology for which there are no comparables.

6.4.3 Comparable Uncontrolled Price Method

The CUP method establishes an arm's-length price by reference to sales of similar products made between unrelated persons in similar circumstances. The CUP method is the preferred method if comparable sales exist. It is widely used for pricing oil, iron ore, wheat, and other goods sold on public commodity markets. The OECD Guidelines were revised in 2017 to clarify that quoted commodity prices may be relied on as indicators of arm's-length prices, assuming that the characteristics of the controlled and uncontrolled transactions are comparable. The pricing date is an important factor in using quoted prices. The CUP method is also useful for pricing manufactured goods that do not depend substantially for their value on special know-how or brand names. However, it is not suitable for pricing

常不向非关联方进行销售的定制零部件），也不适合为其价值高度依赖生产商商标的商品进行定价。下面的例子列示了可比非受控价格法的实际运用。

假设在 X 国成立，并且是 X 国居民的 X 公司，以 40 元的成本在 X 国生产木椅，并以 47 元的单价将其销售给非关联外国分销商。同时，X 公司向其为 Y 国居民的全资子公司 Y 公司销售几乎完全相同的椅子。Y 公司将从 X 公司购得的椅子，以 70 元的价格转销给非关联客户。如果向 Y 公司和非关联分销商进行销售的条款和条件基本相同，那么，向 Y 公司销售椅子的独立交易价格为 47 元。因此，X 公司将从关联销售中获得 7 元（47 – 40）的利润，Y 公司将获得 23 元（70 – 47）的利润。

即使关联方销售的条款和条件与非关联销售的条款和条件并不完全相同，只要可以针对差异进行调整，就也可以适用可比非受控价格法。例如，在前面的例子中，假设 X 公司与非关联分销商之间的售价不包括交货成本，而与 Y 公司之间的售价包括交货成本，那么上述销售仍可被视为可比，只不过必须针对运费和装卸费进行必要的调整。

6.4.4 再销售价格法

再销售价格法是从最终销售给非关联方的售价中，减去适当的利润，以此设定关联方之间销售的独立交易价格。典型的再销售价格法的应用场景为：纳税人将其产成品出售给作为分销商的关联方，后者未对商品进行任何加工，将其再销售给非关联客户。适当的利润加成即为毛利，体现为再销售价格的一定百分比，这是分销商通常在与非关联方的类似交易中能取得的利润。

假设在上述示例中，X 公司未向非关联方销售家具，因此，不能取得可比非受控价格。另假设 Y 公司开展的唯一活动是在外国市场再销售椅子。在这些假设条件下，再销售价格法适合于确定椅子的独立交易价格。根据再销售价格法，第一步是确定与 Y 公司从事类似活动的分销商的常规利润加成。如果独立的外国分销商在购销与木制椅子可比的产品时，赚取 20% 的佣金，那么，可以使用

many intermediate goods, such as custom-made parts that are not generally sold to unrelated parties. Nor is it suitable for setting the price on sales of goods that are highly dependent for their value on the trade name of the producer. The operation of the CUP method is illustrated by the following example.

Assume that XCo is a corporation organized and resident in Country X. It manufactures wooden chairs in Country X at a cost of 40 and sells them to unrelated foreign distributors for 47 each. It also sells nearly identical chairs to YCo, a wholly owned foreign subsidiary resident in Country Y. YCo resells the chairs purchased from XCo to unrelated consumers at 70. If the terms and conditions of the sales to YCo and the unrelated distributors are essentially equivalent, the arm's-length price for the sale of the chairs to YCo is 47. Thus, XCo would have a profit of 7 (47−40) from the intercompany sales, and YCo would have a profit of 23 (70−47).

The CUP method may be used even if the terms and conditions of the related- party sales are not identical to the sales to unrelated parties, as long as adjustments can be made to account for those differences. For example, if in the previous example, the sales by XCo to unrelated distributors do not include delivery costs, whereas the sales to YCo do include delivery costs, the sales may still be considered to be comparable, although some adjustment must be made for freight and handling costs.

6.4.4 Resale Price Method

The resale price method sets the arm's-length price for the sale of goods between related parties by subtracting an appropriate markup from the price at which the goods are ultimately sold to unrelated parties. The paradigm case for its application is the sale by a taxpayer of its manufactured goods to a related party acting as a distributor, followed by resale to unrelated customers without any further processing of the goods. The appropriate markup is the gross profit, expressed as a percentage of the resale price that distributors would typically earn from similar transactions with unrelated parties.

Assume that in the previous example, XCo does not make any sales of furniture to unrelated parties and that no CUP is available. Assume also that the only activity performed by YCo is to resell the chairs in foreign markets. Under these assumptions, the resale price method might be appropriate for determining an arm's-length price for the chairs. Under the resale price method, the first step is to determine the normal markup for a distributor engaging in activities similar to those performed by YCo. If independent foreign distributors earn commissions of

20% 的加成，以确定 X 公司向 Y 公司销售椅子的独立交易价格。因此，如果 Y 公司以 70 元的价格（再销售价格）向客户出售椅子，那么根据再销售价格法，X 公司与 Y 公司之间受控销售的独立交易价格则为 56 元，即 70 – 14（即 70 元的 20%）。于是，按照再销售价格法，X 公司的独立交易利润为 16 元（56 – 40），Y 公司的利润为 14 元（70 – 56）。

6.4.5 成本加成法

成本加成法以关联销售方的制造成本和其他成本作为出发点，确定独立交易价格。销售方的成本乘以适当的利润率，其结果加上销售方的成本，即可确定独立交易价格。利润率的确定，可参照销售方在与非关联方的交易中、或可比非关联方在与非关联方的类似交易中所获取的毛利率。成本加成法典型的应用场景为：商品制造商向关联方销售商品，关联方将其商标附着于商品之上，并将其再销售给非关联客户。

假设在上述示例中，X 公司向 Y 公司出售家具，家具未贴商标。Y 公司将其有价值的商标贴在家具上，并再销售给外国市场的客户。在这种情况下，成本加成法可用来确定适当的独立交易价格。例如，假设家具制造业的标准毛利率是生产成本的 25%，X 公司生产家具的平均成本，根据一般公认会计准则核算为 40 元。那么，根据这些假设条件，按照成本加成法，X 公司向 Y 公司销售家具的独立交易价格为 50 元（40 × 125%）。

只要可以通过调整毛利率，以反映出不同业务或活动之间的差异，那么毛利率不一定需要来自从事相同活动的其他纳税人。

6.4.6 传统方法比较

在上述示例中，X 公司和 Y 公司从事的是存在风险的经营活动；可能会产生整体收益或整体亏损。在可比非受控价格下，经营的收益或亏损通过参照独立交

20% on the purchase and sale of products comparable to the wooden chairs, a 20% markup might be used to determine the arm's-length price on sales of chairs by XCo to YCo. Thus, if YCo sells the chairs to customers for 70 (the resale price), then the arm's-length price of the controlled sale between XCo and YCo under the resale price method would be 56 (70−14 (20% of 70)). Thus, under the resale price method, XCo would have an arm's-length profit of 16 (56−40), and YCo would have a profit of 14 (70−56).

6.4.5 Cost-Plus Method

The cost-plus method uses the manufacturing and other costs of the related seller as the starting point in establishing the arm's-length price. The seller's costs are then multiplied by an appropriate profit percentage, and the result is added to the seller's costs to determine the arm's-length price. The profit percentage is determined by reference to the gross profit percentage earned by the seller in transactions with unrelated parties or by comparable unrelated parties in similar transactions with unrelated parties. A paradigm case for the application of the cost-plus method is a sale by a manufacturer of goods to a related party, with the related party affixing its brand name to the goods and reselling them to unrelated customers.

Assume that in the previous example, XCo sells furniture to YCo without any brand name affixed to the furniture. YCo affixes its valuable brand name to the furniture and resells it to customers in foreign markets. In such circumstances, the cost-plus method may provide the appropriate arm's-length price. Assume, for example, that the standard gross profit margin practice in the furniture manufacturing industry is 25% of the costs of production. XCo's average cost of producing furniture, determined under Generally Accepted Accounting Principles (GAAP), is 40. Under these assumptions, the arm's-length price under the cost-plus method on sales of furniture by XCo to YCo is 50 (125% of 40).

It is not necessary for the gross profit margin to be based on the gross profit margins of other taxpayers engaged in the same activities as long as adjustments are made to take into account any differences between the different businesses or activities.

6.4.6 Comparison of Traditional Methods

In the examples above, XCo and YCo were engaged in entrepreneurial activities that could result in an overall gain or an overall loss. Under the CUP method, the entrepreneurial gain or loss is allocated between XCo and YCo by reference to comparable transactions between arm's-

易方之间的可比交易，在 X 公司和 Y 公司之间进行分配。在再销售价格法下，分销商 Y 公司确保获得利润，所有的经营风险，剩余利润或亏损均归属于制造商 X 公司。在成本加成法下，X 公司确保获利，所有的经营风险，剩余利润或亏损均归属于Y公司。根据三种传统方法，归属于X公司与Y公司的收入如表6–1 所示。

表 6–1 三种传统方法下可归属于 X 公司与 Y 公司的收入

	可比非受控价格法	再销售价格法	成本加成法
（1）X 公司的商品销售成本	40	40	40
（2）Y 公司对非关联客户的销售价格	70	70	70
（3）独立交易转让价格	47	56	50
（4）X 公司利润［第（3）行 – 第（1）行］	7	16	10
（5）Y 公司利润［第（2）行 – 第（3）行］	23	14	20
（6）X 公司及 Y 公司的合计利润	30	30	30
（7）风险性盈亏归属方	共享	X 公司	Y 公司

当跨国企业集团从事制造和销售包含有价值的无形资产的产品时，通常能够获得高额的风险回报性利润。如果出售的商品包含有价值的无形资产，则通常不能使用可比非受控价格法，因为此种商品往往是独特的，不存在可比交易。然而，在某些情况下，可能满足使用再销售价格法或成本加成法所要求的条件。如果制造商（上例中的 X 公司）在低税率国家生产商品，而分销商（上例中的 Y 公司）在高税率国家销售商品，公司集团可能倾向于采用再销售价格法，因为该方法可将企业利润分配至位于低税率国家的制造商。相反，如果生产国是高税率国家，而销售国是低税率国家，企业集团就会更倾向于使用成本加成法，该方法将企业利润归属于销售国。

length parties. Under the resale price method, the distributor, YCo, is guaranteed a profit and all the entrepreneurial or residual profit or loss is allocated to XCo, the manufacturer. Under the cost-plus method, XCo is guaranteed a profit and the entrepreneurial or residual profit or loss is allocated to YCo. Table 6.1 summarizes the income attributable to XCo and YCo under the three traditional methods.

Table 6.1 Income Attributable to PCo and SCo under the Three Traditional Methods

	CUP Method	*Resale Price Method*	*Cost-Plus Method*
(1) XCo's cost of goods sold	40	40	40
(2) YCo's sales price to related	70	70	70
Customers			
(3) Arm's-length transfer price	47	56	50
(4) Profit for XCo (Line (3)−Line (1))	7	16	10
(5) Profit for YCo (Line (2)−Line (3))	23	14	20
(6) Total profits to PCo and SCo	30	30	30
(7) Recipient of entrepreneurial profit	shared	PCo	Sco

When a multinational group of corporations is engaged in the manufacture and sale of products that embody valuable intangible property, it usually earns substantial entrepreneurial profits. The CUP method generally cannot be applied when the goods sold embody valuable intangible property because the goods sold are usually unique—there are no comparable transactions. In some cases, however, the conditions required for applying the resale price method or the cost-plus method may be met. If the manufacturer (XCo in the above example) is producing the goods in a low-tax country and the distributor (YCo in the above example) is selling those goods in a high-tax country, the corporate group is likely to favor the application of the resale price method because that method allocates the entrepreneurial profits to the manufacturer in the low-tax country. In contrast, if the country of production is a high-tax country and the country of sale is a low-tax country, the corporate group would prefer to use the cost-plus method, which allocates the entrepreneurial profit to the country of sale.

6.4.7 利润分割法

在利润分割法下，在同一业务链开展业务活动的关联方的全球应税收入，根据各关联方对取得该收入所做的贡献，在各关联方之间进行分配。当上述三种传统方法都不适用时，通常采用利润分割法。如果关联企业集团有一条以上的产品线，利润分割法可以分别应用于每条产品线。事实上，利润分割法有很多种应用方式。此方法的显著特点，是适用于一组交易（而非单个交易）的合计利润。与之相反，传统方法全都基于单个交易。以下示例说明了利润分割法的应用。

X 公司和 Y 公司是从事药品生产和销售的关联公司。X 公司从事大量研究活动，使用专利流程制造药品，并将药品出售给 Y 公司。Y 公司对产品进行再包装用于零售，贴上其有价值的商标，并通过大量营销活动，进行药品的再销售。X 公司不向非关联方进行任何销售，其他制药公司也不存在同类产品的可比销售。

在这些条件下，有的国家可能会使用利润分割法，来确定适当的药品转让价格。假设 X 公司在产品制造过程中产生的成本为 300 元，Y 公司包装、营销和销售药品所发生的成本为 100 元，另假设 Y 公司向非关联客户销售药品的总销售收入为 600 元。基于这些事实，该公司集团的净利润为 200 元［600－（300+100）］。如果 X 公司对企业的贡献约占净利润总额的 75%，则利润按 75/25 分割比较合适。因此，X 公司的利润为 150 元，Y 公司的利润为 50 元。

利润分割法可能存在多种形式变化，包括可将其与一种或多种传统方法相结合。例如，传统方法可以用来分配常规活动带来的平均利润，而用利润分割法分配因利用有价值的无形资产所获得的剩余利润。

在上述示例中，假设 X 公司从事常规生产活动，Y 公司从事常规销售活动。X 公司的生产总成本为 300 元。从事可比制造活动的非关联公司赚取成本加成 20% 的毛利润。基于这些事实，按照成本加成法，分配至 X 公司的利润为 60 元（300 × 20%）。Y 公司的销售总收入为 600 元。从事类似活动的非关

6.4.7 Profit-Split Method

Under the profit-split method, the worldwide taxable income of related parties engaging in a common line of business is allocated among the related parties in proportion to their contributions to earning the income. This method typically is employed when none of the three traditional methods can be applied. If a group of affiliated companies has more than one product line, the profit-split method might be applied separately to each product line. Indeed, a profit-split method may be applied in a wide variety of ways. A distinctive feature of the method is that it applies to aggregate profits from a group of transactions and not to individual transactions. The traditional methods, in contrast, are all based on individual transactions. The following example illustrates the application of a profit-split method.

XCo and YCo are related companies engaged in the production and sale of pharmaceuticals. XCo engages in extensive research activities and uses patented processes to manufacture the pharmaceutical products which it sells to YCo. YCo repackages the products for retail sale, attaches its valuable trade name, and resells them through an extensive marketing operation. XCo does not make any sales to unrelated parties, and there are no comparable sales of equivalent products by other pharmaceutical companies.

Under these conditions, some countries might use a profit-split method to establish an appropriate transfer price for the pharmaceuticals. Assume that XCo incurs costs of 300 in manufacturing the products and YCo incurs costs of 100 in packaging, marketing, and selling them. Assume also that the sales proceeds from aggregate sales by YCo to unrelated customers are 600. On these facts, the corporate group has net profits of 200 (600−(300 + 100)). If XCo's contribution to the enterprise accounts for approximately 75% of the total net profits, then a 75/25 split of the profits might be appropriate. Thus, XCo would have profits of 150 and YCo would have profits of 50.

There are many possible variations of the profit-split method, including combining it with one or more of the traditional methods. For example, traditional methods might be used to allocate average profits from routine activities, and the profit-split method might be reserved for dividing entrepreneurial profits from the exploitation of valuable intangible property.

Assume in the example above that XCo engages in routine production activities and YCo engages in routine sales activities. XCo has gross costs of production of 300. Unrelated companies engaged in comparable manufacturing activities earn gross profit margins of 20% of costs. On these facts, XCo would have profits of 60 (20% of 300) allocated to it under the cost-plus

联公司的毛利率为 10%。因此，按照再销售价格法，分配至 Y 公司的利润为 60 元（600 × 10%）。80 元［200 –（60+60）］的剩余利润将按照利润分割法进行分配。假设按 75/25 分割，根据利润分割法，X 公司可获得的剩余利润为 60 元（80 × 75%），总利润为 120 元（60+60）；Y 公司按照利润分割法可获得的利润为 20 元（80 × 25%），总利润为 80 元（20+60）。

采用公平有效的方法来确定适当的利润分割比例，是公平有效地运用利润分割法的必要前提。OECD 采用的一种方法是，考察从事可比交易或可比活动的非受控方之间的利润分割比例。不过，此类信息通常难以获取。由于利润分割法常用于涉及有价值的无形资产的情形，因此，根据关联方对相关无形资产开发的相对贡献来确定分割比例，可能较为合适。

2018 年，《OECD 转让定价指南》对其中涉及利润分割法的内容进行了广泛修订。修订后的指南指出，利润分割法适宜于关联方均对经营活动做出独特且有价值贡献的情形，也适宜于经营活动高度一体化的情形（如共同履行功能、共同使用资产或分担风险）。在这些情形下，较少可以获取可比交易。

利润分割法要求确定待分割的利润，这需要界定相关交易，并确定各方的相关收入和费用项目。为此目的，应统一各方使用的会计标准。一般来说，营业利润被用作利润分割的基础，但在各方仅分担部分风险的情况下，可以使用毛利润。然后，必须基于合理的经济依据，对相关利润进行分割，其中涉及客观数据（如对独立方的销售）应当是可以验证的，并有可比对象或内部数据支持，或两者兼而有之。通常用于此目的的因素包括资产、资本、成本、增量销售额和关键员工的薪酬。

6.4.8 交易净利润法

在交易净利润法下，纳税人必须为自己或关联方（被测试方），针对一系列交易，确定符合独立交易原则的利润区间。如果被测试方这些交易所获得的利润

method. YCo has gross sales revenue of 600. Unrelated companies engaged in similar activities earn gross profit margins of 10%. Under the resale price method, therefore, YCo would have profits allocated to it of 60 (10% of 600). The remaining profits of 80 (200–(60 + 60)) would be allocated under the profit-split method. Assuming that a 75/25 split is applied, XCo would be considered to have profits of 60 (75% of 80) under the profit-split method and total profits of 120 (60 + 60). YCo would be considered to have profits of 20 (25% of 80) under the profit-split method and total profits of 80 (20 + 60).

For the profit-split method to operate fairly and effectively, some fair and effective method must be applied to determine the appropriate profit split. One approach used by the OECD is to examine profit splits between uncontrolled persons that are engaged in comparable transactions or activities. Unfortunately, such information is typically not available. Because the profit-split method is most likely to be applied when valuable intangible property is involved, a profit split based on the relative contributions of the related parties to the development of that intangible property might be appropriate.

The OECD Transfer Pricing Guidelines dealing with the profit-split method were revised extensively in 2018. The revised Guidelines indicate that the profit-split method may be appropriate in situations where related parties both make unique and valuable contributions to the business activities and where the business activities are highly integrated (e.g., functions are performed jointly, assets are used jointly, or risks are shared). Comparable transactions are seldom available in these situations.

The profit-split method requires the determination of the profits to be split, which requires the delineation of the relevant transactions and the identification of the relevant income and expense items for each party. The accounting standards used by the parties should be harmonized for this purpose. In general, operating profits are used as the basis for a profit split, although gross profits may be used where only some risks are shared by the parties. The relevant profits must then be split on an economically valid basis, which involves objective data (such as sales to independent parties), is verifiable, and is supported by comparables or internal data, or both. The factors commonly used for this purpose are assets, capital, costs, incremental sales, and the compensation of key employees.

6.4.8 Transactional Net Margin Method

Under the TNMM, the taxpayer must establish, either for itself or a related party (the tested party), an arm's-length range of profits for a set of transactions. If the tested party's

位于该区间内，则其转让价格可以作为符合独立交易原则，从而得到税务机关的认可。如果其利润不在该区间之内，税务机关可能会调整转让价格，使利润位于该区间内（通常调整至中位值）。尽管“交易净利润法”名称中使用了“交易”一词，但交易净利润法并非是基于交易来确定符合独立交易原则的转让价格的方法。相反，交易净利润法着眼于某个实体从一组交易中获得的利润，而非传统转让定价方法所关注的特定交易的价格。

一般来说，被测试方利润的确定，是通过确定某个非关联方的利润与特定经济指标的比率，然后应用该比率计算被测试方的利润。例如，假设某非关联方的应税所得为 80 元，投入资本为 800 元，该投入资本被选作交易净利润法使用的经济指标。非关联方的应税所得与投入资本的比率为 80 ： 800，即 10%。如果被测试方的投入资本为 500 元，那么按照简化的交易净利润法，其符合独立交易原则的利润应为 50 元（500 × 80/800）。

为完善交易净利润法的应用，纳税人或税务机关可能会对一个以上非关联方进行交易净利润法计算。这种计算越多，结果就越可靠。被测试方的独立交易利润应位于根据若干计算而确定的利润区间内。可以应用统计学方法，来选择该区间内的具体数值，并将其视为被测试方的独立交易利润。如果被测试方是关联方而非纳税人本身，那么，纳税人的利润等于两家公司的合并利润减去按照交易净利润法得出的被测试方的利润。

究竟以纳税人还是某个关联方作为被测试方，视各特定个案的具体情况而定。目的是确保作为被测试方的关联公司，其业务功能与作为可比对象的非关联公司的业务功能最为相似。例如，假设 A 公司在 A 国制造商品，并将该商品出售给其全资子公司 B 公司，B 公司将商品贴上其有价值的商标，并在 B 国销售。如果无法获取足够信息来对 A 公司使用传统定价方法或交易净利润法，而对 B 公司使用交易净利润法所需要的信息可以取得，那么 B 公司无论是否为纳税人本人，都将成为被测试方。

为了使用交易净利润法，纳税人必须确定从事可比交易的非关联方预期赚

reported profits from those transactions fall within that range, its transfer prices will be accepted by the tax authorities as being in accordance with the arm's-length standard. If its profits fall outside that range, the tax authorities may adjust transfer prices so that the profits fall within the range, typically at the midpoint. Despite the use of the term "transactional" in the name TNMM, TNMM is not a transactional method for determining arm's-length transfer prices. Instead, TNMM is based on an entity's profits from a group of transactions and not on the prices for particular transactions, which is the focus of the traditional transfer pricing methods.

In general terms, the profits of a tested party are established by determining the ratio of profits to some economic indicator for an unrelated person and then applying that ratio to calculate the profits of the tested party. Assume, for example, that an unrelated person has taxable income of 80 and invested capital of 800 and that invested capital is the economic indicator used in applying TNMM. The ratio of taxable income to invested capital for the unrelated person is 80:800 or 10%. If the tested party has invested capital of 500, then under a simplified version of TNMM, its arm's-length profits will be 50 (500 × 80/800).

To refine the application of TNMM, the taxpayer or the tax authorities might make TNMM calculations for more than one unrelated person. The more such calculations are made, the more reliable the results are likely to be. The arm's-length profits of the tested party are an amount falling within the range of profits determined under several calculations. Statistical techniques might be applied to select the point within that range that would be deemed to be the tested party's arm's-length profits. If the tested party is a related corporation rather than the taxpayer, then the profits of the taxpayer are determined by subtracting the profits of the tested person, as determined under TNMM, from the combined profits of the two corporations.

Whether the taxpayer or a related person is used as the tested party depends on the facts and circumstances of each particular case. The objective is to have, as the tested party, the related corporation whose business functions are most similar to the business functions of unrelated corporations that are used as comparables. For example, assume that ACo manufactures goods in Country A, sells the goods to BCo, its wholly owned subsidiary, and BCo sells the goods in Country B after affixing its valuable trade name to those goods. If information necessary for applying the traditional pricing methods or TNMM to ACo is not available, such information might be available for applying TNMM to BCo. If so, BCo would be the tested party, whether or not it is the taxpayer.

To apply TNMM, a taxpayer must determine a range of profits that unrelated persons

取的利润区间。纳税人可以通过多种方法建立这一区间。一种方法即如上所述，计算从事与纳税人大体相似活动的两个或多个非关联方的资本回报率，然后将每个非关联方的资本回报率乘以纳税人（或被测试方，视具体情形而定）的资本金额。纳税人可以采用的另一种方法是，计算两个或两个以上可比非关联方的营业利润与销售总收入的比率，然后将该比率乘以纳税人（或被测试方）的销售收入。第三种方法是计算两个或两个以上非关联方的毛利与营业费用的比率，并将该比率乘以纳税人或被测试方的营业费用。也可以使用其他经济指标。

例如，假设被测试方 A 公司从事的业务活动在复杂程度和性质方面与 X 公司和 Y 公司的活动类似，X 公司和 Y 公司与 A 公司之间没有关联，且 X 公司与 Y 公司彼此之间亦无关联。X 公司与 Y 公司的营业利润与总收入的比率分别为 0.2 和 0.3。A 公司的总收入为 200000 元。在交易净利润法下，A 公司的独立交易利润区间为 40000 元（200000 × 0.2）至 60000 元（200000 × 0.3）。假设使用交易净利润法的各个条件均满足，则 A 公司的独立交易利润应视为位于 40000 元至 60000 元。

在确定了交易净利润法的利润区间之后，需要选择该区间内的某一数值作为被测试方的独立交易利润。一般来说，如果纳税人账载的转让价格所确定的利润位于交易净利润法的利润区间内，那么，该转让价格很可能得到税务机关的认可。如果纳税人报告的利润位于这一区间之外，那么，税务机关可能会将区间的中位值视为独立交易利润。如果使用两个以上非关联方的数据来计算利润区间，则所得利润数额的加权平均值可用于计算区间中位值。

纳税人或税务机关能够通过对可比公司的选择，来人为控制交易净利润法的应用结果。因此，为了防止得出有利于纳税人或税务机关的系统性偏差，需要制定选择适当可比公司的标准。此外，应根据中性的规则来剔除会产生不合理结果的可比公司，并在交易净利润法的利润区间内确定独立交易利润。

would be expected to earn from engaging in comparable transactions. The taxpayer can establish this range in a variety of ways. One way, illustrated above, is to determine the rate of return on capital employed by two or more unrelated parties engaging in activities that are broadly similar to the activities of the taxpayer. This rate of return on capital for each unrelated person is then multiplied by the amount of capital of the taxpayer (or the tested party, as the case may be). An alternative approach for the taxpayer is to determine the ratio of operating profits to gross sales receipts for two or more comparable related persons and then apply these ratios to its own (or the tested party's) sales. A third way is to determine the ratio of gross profit to operating expenses for two or more related persons and apply these ratios to the taxpayer's or the tested party's operating expenses. Other economic indicators might also be used.

Assume, for example, that ACo, the tested party, is engaged in business activities similar in complexity and character to the activities of XCo and YCo, corporations unrelated to ACo and one another. XCo and YCo have ratios of operating profits to gross receipts of 0.2 and 0.3, respectively. ACo has gross receipts of 200,000. Under TNMM, ACo's arm's-length range of profits would be from 40,000 (200,000 × 0.2) to 60,000 (200,000 × 0.3). Assuming that the various conditions for application of TNMM are met, ACo's arm's-length profits would be considered to be in the range of 40,000 to 60,000.

Once the TNMM range has been established, it is necessary to select some amount within that range as the arm's-length profits of the tested party. In general, the tax authorities would probably accept the transfer prices shown in the taxpayer's books and records if the profits determined by using those prices fall within the TNMM range. If the taxpayer's reported profits fall outside the range, the tax authorities are likely to treat the midpoint of the range as the arm's-length profits. If data for more than two unrelated persons is used to establish the TNMM range, then a weighted average of the resulting profit numbers could be used to establish the midpoint of the range.

TNMM can be manipulated, by the taxpayer or the tax authorities, through the choice of comparable companies. To prevent systemic biases in favor of either the taxpayer or the tax authorities, criteria need to be developed for selecting appropriate comparable companies. In addition, neutral rules should be applied to eliminate comparable companies that yield unreasonable results and to select the arm's-length profits from within the TNMM range.

6.5 公司资源共享

6.5.1 引言

关联公司经常共享资金、信用额度、公司总部、专有技术、商标、员工和其他公司资源。独立交易原则要求对于共享资源的所有者的征税，是视同其向关联方因使用这些资源而收取了符合独立交易原则的使用费。理论上，使用费应该等于同等资源的所有者向非关联方收取的金额。而实际上，难以确定合理的公平成交价格，部分原因是非关联公司通常不共享类似的资源。

6.5.2 公司间贷款或预付款

从事商业贷款安排的集团公司，对于向关联方发放的贷款或预付款，应该使用能够反映当前借款成本的利率。对于不从事贷款发放业务的集团公司，某些国家规定了安全港利率，如果贷款利率位于安全港内，则对该利率不做调整。例如，一国可能允许纳税人使用与政府借款平均成本挂钩的利率。2017 年发布的《OECD 转让定价指南》明确规定，如果金融公司除了随时按要求向集团公司预付资金外、几乎不从事其他活动，且不承担集团内贷款产生的金融风险，则其仅有权获得无风险的资金回报率。这一规定旨在防止利用所谓的“现金盒”将利润转移到低税率国家。

2020 年，对《OECD 转让定价指南》中关于公司间贷款的内容进行了修订，涉及借款方的信用度、信用评级的使用、集团成员的隐性支持，以及针对转贷的情形使用资金成本法。总的来说，指南要求采用基于具体事实和情况的方法，这导致难以寻找可比交易，并且不允许使用替代品或安全港。针对公司间贷款确定独立交易利率的困难在于，集团成员可以在其公司间债务中增设条件，如不需要担保或担保不充分、规定较长的期限、将相关债务从属于其他债务，以及不提供任何限制性契约，从而增加了风险，并为较高的利率提供了理由。

6.5 SHARING OF CORPORATE RESOURCES

6.5.1 Introduction

Related corporations frequently share funds, credit lines, corporate headquarters, know-how, trade names, employees, and other corporate resources. The arm's-length standard requi res the owner of the shared resources to be taxed as if it charged related parties an arm's-length fee for their use. In theory, the fee should equal the amount that the owner of an equivalent resource would charge an unrelated party for its use. In practice, the appropriate arm's-length price is difficult to determine, in part because unrelated corporations do not often share comparable resources.

6.5.2 Intercompany Loans or Advances

A group company engaged in the business of making commercial loans should be required to use a rate of interest for loans or advances to related parties that reflects the current cost of borrowing. For a group company that is not in the business of making loans, some countries provide a safe harbor interest rate so that the interest rate charged on the loan will not be adjusted if it is within the safe harbor. For example, a country may allow taxpayers to use an interest rate pegged to the average cost of government borrowing. The OECD Guidelines clarify that finance companies that perform few activities, other than advancing funds to group companies whenever requested to do so, and that do not control the financial risks arising from their intragroup loans, are entitled only to a risk-free rate of return. This clarification is intended to prevent the use of so-called cash boxes to shift profits to low-tax countries.

The OECD Guidelines dealing with intercompany loans were revised in 2020 to deal with the creditworthiness of the borrower, the use of credit ratings, the implicit support of group members, and the use of a cost-of-funds approach for on-lending situations. In general, the Guidelines require a facts-and-circumstances approach, which makes finding comparable transactions difficult and does not allow the use of proxies or safe harbors. The difficulty with establishing an arm's-length interest rate for intercompany loans is that group members can add terms to their intercompany debt, such as requiring no or inadequate security, providing a long term, subordinating the debt to other debts, and not providing any restrictive covenants, to increase risk and justify higher interest rates.

6.5.3 服务提供

如果一方为了关联方的利益，提供营销、管理、行政、技术或其他服务，则应当认为服务提供方根据独立交易原则，收取了独立服务提供商针对相同服务所收取的同等费用。如不存在可比独立交易服务，那么，独立交易服务费用可基于提供服务的成本加上适当的利润。然而，在此类情况下，设定适当的独立交易价格困难重重。

《OECD 转让定价指南》（第 7 章，第 7.43—7.65 段）针对低附加值集团内服务提供了一种具体可选的简易方法。低附加值集团内服务被定义为由一家集团公司为同一集团内一家或多家其他公司提供的服务，这些服务是支持性的，不属于该跨国集团核心业务范畴，也不涉及使用或创造有价值的无形资产，服务提供商亦不承担重大风险。低附加值服务的例子包括会计和审计、账目处理、人力资源活动、内部信息技术活动，以及法律服务。这种简易方法涉及计算所有集团公司就每一类低附加值服务产生的成本，而非仅为某一家集团公司提供此类服务产生的成本。然后，应根据每类服务的合理要素（如针对信息服务时的用户总数、针对会计服务时的总资产或营业额、针对人力资源活动时的员工人数），在受益于这些服务的集团公司之间分摊成本。无论低附加值服务的具体类别，独立交易服务费用的确定，均可按所有低附加值服务的成本加成 5%。税务机关有权将简易方法的适用范围，限定在未超过基于某些比率（如总服务成本占营业额的一定百分比）的情况。

6.5.4 有形资产的使用

如果一方向关联方提供办公室或设备等有形资产，那么，资产所有者应当被认为向使用者收取了符合独立交易原则的租赁费。有形资产转租适用同样的规则。

6.5.3 Performance of Services

If marketing, managerial, administrative, technical, or other services are performed by one person for the benefit of a related person, the person providing the services should be considered to charge an amount in accordance with the arm's-length standard that an independent service provider would charge for the same services. If no comparable arm's-length services are available, the arm's-length fee might be based on the cost of providing the services plus an appropriate profit. However, the problem of setting an appropriate arm's-length price in these circumstances is formidable.

The OECD Guidelines (Chapter VII, paragraphs 7.43–7.65) provide a special elective simplified method for dealing with low-value intragroup services. Low-value intragroup services are defined to be services provided by one group company for one or more other companies of the same group where the services are supportive, but not part of the core business of the multinational group, and do not involve the use or creation of valuable intangibles or involve significant risks for the service provider. Examples of low-value services include accounting and auditing, processing accounts, human resource activities, internal information technology activities, and legal services. The simplified method involves a calculation of the costs incur red by all group companies with respect to each category of low-value services other than such services provided for only one other group company. The costs should then be allocated among the group companies that benefit from the services in accordance with appropriate factors for each category of services (e.g., the total number of users for IT services, total assets or turnover for accounting services, and number of staff for human resource activities). The arm's-length amount for low-value services is then determined by applying a 5% markup to the costs of all low-value services, irrespective of the particular category. Tax administrations are entitled to limit the application of the simplified method to situations where a threshold based on some ratio, such as total service costs as a percentage of turnover, is not exceeded.

6.5.4 Use of Tangible Property

If tangible property, such as an office or equipment, is made available by a person to a related person, the owner of the property should be considered to charge the user an arm's-length rental fee. The same rule should apply to subleases of tangible property.

6.5.5 无形资产的使用或转让

如果向关联方提供专利或商标等无形资产，那么，资产所有者应当被认为收取了在类似情况下，对非关联方因其使用该资产应收取的费用。这一收费的确定，可参照资产所有者向非关联方提供相同或类似资产所收取的特许权使用费费率。然而，无论是税务机关还是纳税人，经常难以获取必要的数据来确定符合独立交易原则的特许权使用费，跨国公司常被指控通过使用不适当的特许权使用费来避税。而税务机关也常难以评估纳税人使用的涉及无形资产交易的定价信息（即所谓的“信息不对称”）。

如果向关联方出售无形资产，那么可以参照资产使用寿命内，符合独立交易原则的预期特许权使用费折现价值，来确定符合独立交易原则的销售价格。然而，拥有独特且有价值无形资产的跨国企业不可能将此种资产出售或租赁给非关联方，却不保有收益或特许权使用费调整机制，以反映该项无形资产未来可产生的利润。如下文第 6.7 节所述，对于由关联企业实际实施的交易，如果这些交易缺乏商业合理性，税务机关可以不予认可。

无形资产的处理，毫无疑问是最棘手的转让定价问题之一。《OECD 转让定价指南》第 6 章用了 73 页、212 段文字，包括带有 29 个示例的一个附录，来说明相关指引的运用。2017 年发布的 BEPS 第 8 项行动计划最终报告《无形资产转让定价指引》，大幅修订了《OECD 转让定价指南》第 6 章，即关于无形资产转让定价处理的基本方法。此番修订阐释了无形资产的定义，并就涉及无形资产交易的识别，以及涉及无形资产个案独立交易条件的确定等问题，提供了指导性意见。修订版指南强调，无形资产的所有权并不足以支持所有者应获得无形资产的全部回报。

对指南关于无形资产最重要的一处修订，或许是要求对履行与无形资产开发、价值提升、维护、保护和利用（DEMPE）相关功能的关联企业，必须针对

6.5.5 Use or Transfer of Intangible Property

If intangible property, such as a patent or trademark, is made available to a related party, the owner of the property should be considered to charge whatever amounts would be charged to an unrelated person for the use of the property in similar circumstances. This charge might be set by reference to royalty rates charged by the owner on the same or similar property made available to unrelated parties. However, obtaining the data necessary to determine the proper arm's-length royalty is often difficult, both for the tax authorities and the taxpayer, and multinational companies are commonly accused of avoiding tax through the use of inappropriate royalty rates. Often, the tax authorities have difficulty in evaluating the information used by taxpayers to price transactions involving intangibles (so-called information asymmetry).

If intangible property is sold to a related person, the arm's-length sales price can be established by reference to the discounted value of the arm's-length royalties anticipated over the life of the property. However, it is unlikely that a multinational enterprise with unique and valuable intangible property would sell or lease that property to an unrelated party without some mechanism to adjust the proceeds or royalty to reflect future profits generated by the intangible. As discussed in section 6.7 below, the tax authorities are permitted to disregard the actual transactions entered into by associated enterprises where those transactions lack commercial rationality.

It is not surprising that dealing with intangibles is one of the most difficult transfer pricing issues. Chapter VI of the OECD Guidelines consists of 212 paragraphs and 73 pages, including an annex with 29 examples to illustrate the application of the guidance. In 2017, pursuant to the BEPS Action 8 Final Report: *Guidance on Transfer Pricing Aspects of Intangibles*, extensive revisions were made to Chapter VI of the OECD Guidelines dealing with the basic treatment of intangibles for transfer pricing purposes. These revisions clarify the definition of intangibles and provide guidance for identifying transactions involving intangibles and determining the arm's-length conditions for cases involving intangibles. The revised guidance emphasizes that ownership of an intangible is not sufficient to justify the owner's entitlement to all or any of the return from the intangible.

Perhaps the most important change to the Guidelines with respect to intangibles is the requirement that an associated enterprise that performs functions related to the Development, Enhancement, Maintenance, Protection or Exploitation (DEMPE) of an intangible must

这些功能，给予其符合独立交易原则的补偿。此外，承担与无形资产 DEMPE 功能相关风险的关联企业，只有在其对风险进行实际控制，并拥有承担风险的财务能力时，才有权就此类风险获得符合独立交易原则的补偿。仅提供与无形资产相关的资金、但不履行任何 DEMPE 功能的关联企业，只能获得无风险或调整风险因素后的回报。

在难以估值的无形资产方面，《OECD 转让定价指南》第 6 章于 2018 年进行了修订，增加了 D.4 节和附录二，为税务机关处理与此类无形资产相关的信息不对称问题提供了指引。难以估值的无形资产是指不存在可靠可比对象的无形资产，并且在交易之时，关于该种无形资产的价值，或该种财产的未来收入或现金流，存在重大不确定性。这种难以估值的无形资产包括部分得到开发的财产、预计几年内不会得到商业利用或预计将以新颖的方式加以利用的财产，一次性付款方式转让的财产，以及根据成本分摊协议使用或开发的财产。税务机关经常难以确定未来的动向或事项，这些动向或事项可能会影响难以估值的无形资产的转让价格，而这些动向和事项也可能在转让时是合理的可预见的。例如，纳税人可能会在其开发的早期阶段转让此类无形资产，其特许权使用费并不完全反映其价值，然而纳税人事后所持的立场是，价值的增加是由于转让时无法预见的后续开发。在这种情况下，税务机关在很大程度上依赖于纳税人提供的信息。

《OECD 转让定价指南》中建议的方法是，税务机关使用后续证据，来评估纳税人在转让时用于确定转让价格的信息的可靠性。

6.6 成本分摊协议

如果公司集团计划开发有价值的无形资产，并将在两个或两个以上成员之间分享收益，那么，公司集团可以通过**成本分摊协议**，由无形资产的所有潜在用户共同开发无形资产，从而避免转让定价问题。在这种协议中，对开发无形资产做出贡献的所有各方都有权按其贡献比例，获得相关无形资产所产生的利润，无须

receive arm's-length compensation for those functions. Further, an associated enterprise assuming risks related to the DEMPE of an intangible is entitled to arm's-length remuneration for such risks only if the enterprise exercises control over the risk and has the financial capacity to assume the risk. Associated enterprises that provide funding related to intangibles but do not perform any of the functions (DEMPE) are entitled only to a risk-free or risk-adjusted return.

With respect to hard-to-value intangibles, Chapter VI of the OECD Guidelines was revised in 2018 to add section D.4 and Annex II to provide guidance to tax administrations in dealing with the problem of information asymmetry with respect to such intangibles. Hard-to-value intangibles are intangibles for which no reliable comparables exist and for which there is significant uncertainty at the time of the transaction as to the value of the intangible or the future income or cash flows from the property. Such hard-to-value intangibles include partly developed property, property that is not expected to be commercially exploited for several years or that is expected to be exploited in a novel fashion, property transferred for a lump sum, and property used or developed under a cost contribution arrangement. Tax administrations frequently experience difficulty in establishing future developments or events that might affect the transfer price for a hard-to-value intangible and that might have been reasonably foreseeable at the time of the transfer. For example, taxpayers may transfer such intangibles at an early stage in their development with a royalty that does not fully reflect the value but later take the position that the increase in value was attributable to subsequent developments that were not foreseeable at the time of the transfer. In such situations, tax administrations are largely dependent on information provided by the taxpayer.

The approach recommended in the OECD Guidelines is for tax administrations to use subsequent evidence to assess the reliability of the information used by the taxpayer to determine the transfer price at the time of the transfer.

6.6 COST CONTRIBUTION ARRANGEMENTS

If a group of corporations intends to develop valuable intangible property and share the benefits among two or more of its members, it can avoid transfer pricing issues by having all the prospective users of the intangible property jointly develop that property through a **cost contribution arrangement**. In such an arrangement, all the contributors to the development of the property have rights to the profits generated by the property in proportion to their contributions, and no transfer of the property or rights to the use of the property between members of

在公司集团的成员之间转让相关资产或相关资产的使用权。《OECD 转让定价指南》第 8 章对成本分摊协议进行了讨论。总体来讲，OECD 的规则旨在认可真实的成本分摊协议，但限制将其用于避税目的。

为了使成本分摊协议符合独立交易原则，其应具备以下特征：

—— 协议应以在法律上可以实施的书面合同呈现，在成本分摊安排确定之时签署，列明成本分摊安排的性质、期限，并应包括实施与修正条款；
—— 仅允许可以合理预期从成本分摊安排受益的成员成为参与方；
—— 合同应要求安排的各参与方，按照其可以合理预期从无形资产使用中获得收益的比例，分摊该无形资产的开发成本；
—— 成本分摊协议的参与方应留存适当的记录，记载其成本，并解释其预期收益的计算方法。

例如，假设 A 公司和 B 公司是从事小型电器制造的关联公司。A 公司在 A 国开展业务，B 公司在 B 国开展业务。A 公司和 B 公司计划开发新技术，这一技术将实现以较低成本制造电器产品。两家公司签订书面合同。合同规定，A 公司拥有在 A 国利用依据协议所开发无形资产的权利，B 公司取得在 B 国的类似权利。目前，A 公司在 A 国的电器销售额为 400 元，B 公司在 B 国的销售额为 600 元。这一总体格局未来有望继续维持。根据成本分摊协议，A 公司同意支付 40% 的成本，B 公司同意支付剩余 60% 的成本。二者均同意，对其各自的成本和销售额进行详细的会计记录。

假设 A 国针对成本分摊协议，采用了类似于《OECD 转让定价指南》中的规则，那么，A 公司与 B 公司之间的安排将被视为真实的成本分摊协议。根据一般适用于以开发无形资产为目的所支付款项的规则，A 国应允许 A 公司扣除其按照成本分摊协议所支付的款项。此外，A 公司应被视为所形成无形资产的共同所有者。因此，根据 A 国的转让定价法规，A 公司不应被视为向 B 公司支付视同特许权使用费。如果 A 公司向 B 公司实际支付了特许权使用费，则该费用不可扣除。

the corporate group is required. Cost contribution arrangements are dealt with in Chapter VIII of the OECD Guidelines. In general, the OECD rules are designed to recognize bona fide cost contribution arrangements but limit their use for tax avoidance purposes.

For a cost contribution arrangement to be consistent with the arm's-length standard, it should have the following characteristics:

- The arrangement should be embodied in a legally enforceable written contract entered into at the time the arrangement is established that clearly sets out the nature of the arrangement, its duration, and the terms for its enforcement and amendment.
- Only persons with a legitimate expectation of benefiting under the arrangement should be permitted to be participants.
- The contract should require the participants to the arrangement to contribute to the costs of development of the intangible property in proportion to the benefits that they might reasonably be anticipated to derive from the use of that property.
- The participants in the arrangement should be required to keep adequate records documenting their costs and explaining how their anticipated benefits are calculated.

Assume, for example, that ACo and BCo are related corporations engaged in manufacturing small electrical appliances. ACo is engaged in business in Country A, and BCo is engaged in business in Country B. ACo and BCo intend to develop new technology that would allow them to manufacture their appliances at a lower cost. They enter into a written contract that assigns to ACo the rights to exploit any intangible property developed under the agreement in Country A. BCo receives similar rights with respect to Country B. ACo has current sales of appliances in Country A of 400, and BCo has sales in Country B of 600; that general pattern is expected to continue in the future. Under the cost contribution arrangement, ACo agrees to pay 40% of the costs, and BCo agrees to pay the remaining 60%. They both agree to keep detailed accounting records with respect to their costs and their sales.

Assuming that County A has adopted rules for cost contribution arrangements similar to those in the OECD Guidelines, the arrangement between ACo and BCo would qualify as a bona fide cost contribution arrangement. Country A should permit ACo to take a deduction for payments made under that arrangement under the rules generally applicable to amounts paid to develop intangible property. In addition, ACo should be treated as a co-owner of the resulting intangible property; therefore, ACo should not be treated as paying a deemed royalty to BCo under the transfer pricing rules of Country A. If ACo makes an actual royalty payment to BCo, that payment should not be deductible.

2017年，由于BEPS第8项行动计划最终报告的建议，OECD修订了涉及成本分摊协议的《OECD转让定价指南》第8章。概括而言，修订后的指南明确指出，成本分摊协议同样受制于其他合同安排所适用的转让定价分析框架，包括确定相关交易、评估无形资产价值、否定缺乏商业合理性的安排。独立交易原则要求，成本分摊协议中每个参与方的贡献，必须与其预期从协议中获得的收益份额相一致。鉴于此，修订后的指南要求，每个参与方的贡献应基于价值而非投入成本计算，除非在少数特定情况下，成本可被视为衡量贡献价值的可靠指标。修订后的指南同时强调，成本分摊协议不应用于规避2017年修订的关于风险和无形资产的指南。

关联方之间成本分摊协议的规则，应允许参与方修改协议，以反映经济环境的变化。然而，为了符合独立交易原则，此种规则应该要求，参与方应能获得与其可能放弃权利的公允市场价值相等的款项，以及为其获得的新权利支付相应的公允市场价值。如果新的参与方加入成本分摊协议，则应要求该参与方对其他参与方就其被稀释利益的公允市场价值予以补偿。对现有成本分摊协议的任何修订都应以书面形式进行，或满足一份新的成本分摊协议的要求。

为了防止避税，当关联方之间的经济行为实为成本分摊协议的安排时，税务机关有权将关联方视作已签署成本分摊协议。例如，假设A公司和B公司是关联方，共同开发无形资产，但尚未签署成本分摊协议。A公司在A国经营中使用无形资产，并为此向B国居民B公司支付特许权使用费。根据A国与B国之间的税收协定，特许权使用费不必在A国缴纳预提所得税，因为该协定包含了类似于OECD协定范本第12条的条款，将对特许权使用费的专属征税权赋予了居民国。A公司在计算其在A国的应纳税所得额时，要求扣除支付的特许权使用费。然而，A国有权视同A公司和B公司实为签订了成本分摊协议，从而不允许A公司扣除向B公司支付的特许权使用费。

In 2017, as a result of the recommendations in the BEPS Action 8 Final Report, changes were made to Chapter VIII of the OECD Guidelines dealing with cost contribution arrangements. In general terms, the revised Guidelines clarify that cost contribution arrangements are subject to the same transfer pricing analytical framework that applies to other contractual arrangements, including determining the relevant transactions, valuing intangibles, and disregarding arrangements that lack commercial rationality. The arm's-length standard requires that each participant's contribution to a cost contribution arrangement must be consistent with its share of the expected benefits from the arrangement. For this purpose, the revised Guidelines require each participant's contribution to be based on its value rather than on its cost unless, in certain limited circumstances, cost is a reliable indicator of the value of contributions. The revised Guidelines also emphasize that cost contribution arrangements should not be used to circumvent the 2017 revised guidance on risks and intangibles.

The rules governing cost contribution arrangements among related persons should permit the participants to modify an arrangement to reflect changed economic circumstances. In order to conform to the arm's-length standard, however, those rules should require that the participants receive a payment equal to the fair market value of any rights that they may have relinquished and pay fair market value for any new rights obtained. If a new participant is brought into a cost contribution arrangement, that participant should be required to compensate the other participants for the fair market value of the dilution of their interests in the arrangement. Any revision of a qualifying cost contribution arrangement should be in writing and otherwise conform to the requirements for a new cost contribution arrangement.

To prevent tax avoidance, governments should have the authority to treat related persons as if they had entered into a cost contribution arrangement when their economic behavior is consistent with such an arrangement. Assume, for example, that ACo and BCo are related persons and have jointly developed some intangible property. However, they have not entered into a cost contribution arrangement. ACo makes use of the intangible property in its business in Country A and pays a royalty for that use to BCo, a resident of Country B. Under the tax treaty between Country A and Country B, the royalty is not subject to withholding tax by Country A because the treaty contains an article similar to Article 12 of the OECD Model Treaty, giving the exclusive right to tax royalties to the residence country. ACo claims a deduction for the royalty payment in computing its taxable income in Country A. Country A should have the authority to treat ACo and BCo as having entered into a constructive cost contribution arrangement, with the result that ACo would not be permitted to take a deduction for the royalty payment to BCo.

成本分摊协议被广泛用于将利润转移到低税率国家。造成这一现象，很大程度上是因为跨国企业能掌握其自身的知识产权和研发活动信息，而税务机关却难以获得此类信息。因此，举例来说，某一低税率国家的集团公司可能与另一高税率国家的集团公司签订成本分摊协议，高税率国家允许低税率国家的公司获得与集团所有研发活动相比不匹配的科研权益，从而使低税率国家的公司获得过高的利润。

6.7 不予认可的交易

《OECD 转让定价指南》（第 1 章，第 1.122—1.228 段）强调，税务机关应承认关联企业进行的实际交易，并对这些交易适用转让定价规则。然而，如果实际交易缺乏独立交易方之间交易的“商业合理性”，《OECD 转让定价指南》允许税务机关否定关联企业进行的实际交易，并另行在各企业之间分配利润。

例如，拥有有价值无形资产的跨国企业通常不会向非关联方出售或长期出租该资产，却不保有某种价格调整机制，允许出让人可以分享未来的利润。因此，如果此类销售活动发生在关联企业之间，税务机关可以不予认可。如果非关联方之间实际存在类似的交易，税务机关则不应对关联交易予以否认。然而，未在非关联方之间观察到类似交易，并不一定意味着实际交易缺乏商业合理性。

如果某项关联交易被否定，税务机关可以选择不同的交易替代被否定的交易。但是，所选替代交易应尽可能地符合实际交易的情况，能够得出商业上合理的结果。

税务机关可以否定实际交易的特殊情形，与反避税规则极其相似，这种反避税规则允许税务机关否定纳税人实际交易的税收利益。一些国家的税务机关是否有权，如《OECD 转让定价指南》所述，在未经国内法明确授权情况下，对交易重新定性，仍有待商榷。

Cost contribution arrangements have been widely used to shift profits to low-tax countries. This result is possible largely because multinational enterprises have access to information about their intellectual property and research and development activities that is not available to the tax authorities. Therefore, for example, a group company in a low-tax country might enter into a cost contribution arrangement with another group company in a high-tax country; the high-tax country would allow the first company to acquire rights to research that is disproportionately profitable compared to all the research and development activities of the group.

6.7 DISREGARDED TRANSACTIONS

The OECD Guidelines (Chapter 1, paragraphs 1.122–1.228) emphasize that the tax authorities must accept the actual transactions entered into by associated enterprises and apply the transfer pricing rules to those transactions. However, the OECD Guidelines permit the tax authorities to ignore the actual transactions entered into by related enterprises and allocate the profits between the enterprises on a different basis where the actual transactions lack the "commercial rationality" of transactions between arm's-length parties.

For example, a multinational enterprise with valuable intangible property would not sell or lease that property on a long-term basis to an unrelated enterprise without some price-adjustment mechanism allowing the transferor to share in future profits. Therefore, if such a sale takes place between related enterprises, the tax authorities can disregard the sale. It is inappropriate for the tax authorities to disregard transactions where similar transactions can be observed between arm's-length parties. However, simply because similar arrangements between arm's-length parties cannot be observed does not necessarily mean that the actual transactions lack commercial rationality.

Where a transaction is disregarded, the tax authorities may substitute a different transaction; however, the substituted transaction should conform as closely as possible to the facts of the actual transaction and achieve a commercially rational result.

The exceptional circumstances in which the tax authorities can disregard actual transactions are strikingly similar to anti-avoidance rules, which allow tax authorities to deny the tax benefits of a taxpayer's actual transactions. It is questionable whether the tax authorities in some countries have the power to recharacterize transactions, as provided in the OECD Guidelines, without explicit statutory authority in domestic law.

6.8 转让定价文档要求

当认识到转让定价滥用的存在时，为了应对，许多国家要求跨国公司向税务机关提供翔实的同期资料，以支持其转让定价的方法。此处的理念是，通过要求跨国公司提前确定其转让价格，一国可以防范“事后”为避税目的而转移收入。纳税人若未能提供必要的转让定价文档，则可能面临严重的处罚。

例如，假设 A 公司在 A 国经营，向在 B 国经营的关联公司 B 公司出售商品。A 国的公司税税率为 40%，B 国为 20%。A 公司和 B 公司通过对其公司间销售设定转让价格，使 A 国利润较低而 B 国利润较高。在确定此种价格，并向 A 国提供文档后，A 公司发现，由于一些非关联业务，将在 A 国出现巨额税务亏损。如果其定价方法没有在事先得到确定，那么，A 公司很可能会试图修改定价方法，将 B 国部分收入转移到 A 国，从而充分利用在 A 国的税务亏损。然而，同期资料的相关规定可能会阻止公司修改转让定价方法。

《OECD 转让定价指南》支持双重策略，即提出同期资料要求，并处罚未遵从同期资料要求的纳税人。然而，指南也建议税务机关在采取上述策略时要格外谨慎，以避免对诚信经营的纳税人增加不公平或负担过重的义务。

BEPS 第 13 项行动计划最终报告《转让定价文档和国别报告》在国别报告方面提出了若干建议，其结果是强化了现行的转让定价文档要求。目前，跨国企业必须向其开展业务活动所在的所有国家税务机关提交一份主体文档，主体文档包含其业务运营的一般信息，以及其转让定价实践和政策。此外，跨国企业还须向每个国家提交本地文档，本地文档包含涉及在该国发生的所有关联交易信息。最重要的是，要求跨国企业向其业务开展所在国家提交年度报告，披露企业在该国的收入、利润、应缴和已缴税款的数额。虽然国别报告不要求对各个实体逐一提供信息，但仍为税务机关提供了一个重要工具，使其更有效地开展审计风险评估

6.8 TRANSFER PRICING DOCUMENTATION REQUIREMENTS

Many countries have attempted to deal with perceived transfer pricing abuses by requiring multinational companies to provide tax authorities with extensive, contemporaneous documentation to support the methods used to establish their transfer prices. The idea is that by forcing multinational companies to establish their transfer prices in advance, a country can prevent after-the-fact shifting of income for tax avoidance purposes. Taxpayers failing to provide the requisite documentation may be subject to substantial penalties.

For example, assume that ACo, operating in Country A, is selling goods to BCo, a related corporation operating in Country B. The corporate tax rate is 40% in Country A and 20% in Country B. ACo and BCo set the transfer prices for their intercompany sales so that there is a small profit in Country A and a large profit in Country B. After setting those prices and providing the documentation to Country A, ACo discovers that it will suffer a large tax loss in Country A from some unrelated operations. If its pricing methodology had not been previously established, ACo might have been strongly tempted to revise the methodology to deflect some income from Country B to Country A so that it could fully utilize the Country A loss. The contemporaneous documentation rules, however, may prevent such a revision in a company's transfer pricing methodology.

The OECD Guidelines support the dual strategy of requiring contemporaneous documentation and penalizing taxpayers for failure to comply with the documentation requirements. However, tax administrators are advised to pursue that strategy with extreme caution so as to avoid imposing unfair or excessively burdensome obligations on taxpayers acting in good faith.

The existing transfer pricing documentation requirements were enhanced as a result of the recommendations in the BEPS Action 13 Final Report: *Transfer Pricing Documentation and Country-by-Country Reporting* with respect to country-by-country reporting. Multinational enterprises must now provide the tax authorities of all countries in which they do business with a master file containing general information about their business operations and their transfer pricing practices and policies. In addition, each country must be provided with a local file containing information with respect to any related-party transactions occurring in the country. Most important, multinationals are required to provide an annual report to each country in which they operate, setting out the amount of revenue, profit, and taxes accrued and paid with respect to that country. Although these country-by-country reports do not require information to be provided on an entity-by-entity basis, they should nevertheless provide the tax authorities with

和运用转让定价规则。

各国可以通过给予税务机关适当的自由裁量权和资源，对不能诚信地设定转让价格的纳税人施以严厉处罚，从而限制最为恶劣的转让定价行为。税务机关可以通过将本国的边际税率设置在从国际标准来看的适中水平，以消除转让定价滥用的一些诱因。出台针对避税地的具体立法，也可以消除转让定价滥用的一些诱因，因为纳税人通常会设定不适当的转让价格，以便将其收入转移到位于避税地的关联实体。第 7 章描述了此类反避税法规。各国还可以通过与其税收协定伙伴国，尤其是近邻国家开展合作，在控制转让定价滥用方面获得帮助。然而，尽管各国税务机关不懈努力，并与贸易伙伴国加强合作，转让定价仍然是一个严重的问题。

6.9 转让定价的协定视角

OECD 协定范本和联合国协定范本中的条款并未详细触及转让定价问题。这两项协定范本的第 9 条第 1 款都授权调整与另一家企业有关联关系的企业的利润，前提是“两个企业之间达成或施加的条件不同于独立企业之间可以达成的条件”。因此，从字面上讲，第 9 条第 1 款侧重于关联方交易的条款和条件，而不是特定交易中收取的价格。

第 9 条（关联企业）适用于缔约国一方企业直接或间接参与缔约国另一方企业的管理、控制或资本，或者同一方直接或间接参与缔约国双方两个或两个以上企业的管理、控制或资本。除了这一用语之外，第 9 条并没有定义“关联企业”；因此，企业之间是否属于关联企业，需要根据各国的国内法来确定。大多数国家将其转让定价法规适用于一家企业控制另一家企业，或者两家企业同为另一方控制时，这两家企业之间的交易。拥有某一实体 50% 以上的股份或利益，即被视为控制。

OECD 协定范本和联合国协定范本第 9 条第 1 款指出，本由一个企业发生，但因为与关联企业之间的非独立交易而未发生的利润，“可以计入”该企业的利

an important tool with which to perform audit risk assessments and apply their transfer pricing rules more effectively.

Countries can limit the most egregious forms of transfer pricing abuses by giving appropriate discretion and resources to their tax departments and imposing stiff penalties on taxpayers that have not set their transfer prices in good faith. They can take away some of the incentives for transfer pricing abuses by setting their marginal tax rates at levels that are moderate by international standards. Adoption of specific legislation targeted at tax havens can also take away some of the incentives for transfer pricing abuses because taxpayers commonly set improper transfer prices in order to shift their income to affiliated entities in tax havens. Chapter 7 describes such anti-avoidance provisions. Countries can also obtain help in controlling transfer pricing abuses through cooperation with their tax treaty partners, particularly their close neighbors. However, despite determined efforts by national tax authorities and increased cooperation with their trading partners, transfer pricing continues to be a serious problem.

6.9 TREATY ASPECTS OF TRANSFER PRICING

The provisions of the OECD and UN Model Treaties do not deal with the problem of transfer pricing in any detailed way. Article 9(1) of both Model Treaties authorizes an adjustment to the profits of an enterprise that is associated with another enterprise if "conditions are made or imposed between the two enterprises which differ from those which would be made between independent enterprises." Literally, therefore, Article 9(1) focuses on the terms and conditions of related-party transactions rather than just on the prices charged in specific transactions.

Article 9 (Associated Enterprises) applies where an enterprise of one contracting state participates directly or indirectly in the management, control, or capital of another enterprise in the other contracting state or where the same persons participate directly or indirectly in the management, control, or capital of two or more enterprises in the contracting states. Beyond this wording, Article 9 does not define "associated enterprises"; as a result, whether enterprises are associated must be determined in accordance with domestic law. Most countries apply their transfer pricing rules to transactions between enterprises where one enterprise controls the other or where they are both controlled by another person, and control is considered to be the ownership of more than 50% of the shares or interests in an entity.

Article 9(1) of both the OECD and UN Model Treaties provides that the profits that would have accrued to an enterprise, but did not because of non-arm's-length transactions with

润。因此，从字面上理解（且与协定其他条款不同），第 9 条第 1 款的措辞并不是各缔约国必须实行的强制性条款（如“应予计入”）。一些评论者认为，由于第 9 条第 1 款允许性措辞，缔约国有权对居民企业可能高于或低于独立交易原则之要求的利润征税。例如，如果 A 国居民 A 公司以 100 元的价格向其作为 B 国居民的子公司 B 公司出售其制造的商品，而该商品的独立交易价格为 75 元，第 9 条第 1 款并未要求 A 国单方面调减价格至 75 元。相反，如果商品或服务的独立交易价格为 125 元，第 9 条第 1 款也未要求 A 国调增价格至 125 元，虽然大部分情况下，A 国希望如此。

由此看来，第 9 条第 1 款仅仅是对原则的阐述，即根据独立交易原则确定关联企业的利润。然而，OECD 协定范本和联合国协定范本第 9 条第 2 款规定，如果转让价格已被缔约国另一方依据独立交易原则调整，则缔约国一方也应对用于计算其纳税人应税所得的转让价格进行调整。

仍以上述情形为例，假设 A 国将 A 公司向外国关联公司 B 公司出售其制造商品的价格，从 100 元（实际销售价格）调整至 125 元（A 国认为独立交易方应收取的价格）。由此，A 国将增加 A 公司的应纳税所得额 25 元。如果 B 国接受了 A 国对合理转让价格的认定，则应允许 B 公司将购买商品的实际成本上调 25 元（100+25=125），并相应减少 B 公司的应纳税所得额 25 元。一方纳税人考虑到另一国对关联纳税人使用的转让价格所做的调整，而对其自身所使用的转让价格进行的调整，被称为“**相应调整**”。

基于利润的转让定价方法，如利润分割法和交易净利润法，是否与第 9 条第 1 款的用语内容相一致，存在一定争议。第 9 条第 1 款提及的利润，可以指全部利润，也可以仅指特定交易或业务所获得的利润。无论如何，《OECD 转让定价指南》认可基于利润的方法，明确了根据第 9 条，在某些情况下，这些方法是可接受的。

尽管各国在其双边税收协定中均赞成坚持独立交易原则，各国之间因转让定价而产生的争议仍然十分常见。大多数税收协定规定，因转让价格不一致而遭受

associated enterprises, "may be included" in the profits of the enterprise. Thus, read literally (and unlike other treaty provisions), Article 9(1) is not worded as a mandatory provision ("shall be included") that the contracting states must apply. Some commentators argue that, as a result of the permissive wording of Article 9(1), contracting states are entitled to tax resident enterprises on profits that are more or less than their profits in accordance with the arm's-length standard. For example, if ACo, a resident of Country A, charges its subsidiary, BCo, resident in Country B, 100 for manufactured goods that have an arm's-length price of only 75, Country A is not required by Article 9(1) to unilaterally reduce the price to 75. Conversely, if the arm's-length price of the goods or services is 125, Country A is not required by Article 9(1) to increase the price to 125, although in most circumstances it will want to do so.

On this view, Article 9(1) is merely a statement of principle about the determination of the profits of associated enterprises in accordance with the arm's-length standard. However, Article 9(2) of both the OECD and UN Model Treaties requires a country to make adjustments to the transfer prices used to compute taxable income of their taxpayers where those prices have been adjusted by the other contracting state in accordance with the arm's-length standard.

Assume, on the facts of the previous example, that Country A adjusts the price at which ACo sells its manufactured goods to its foreign affiliate, BCo, from 100 (the actual sales price) to 125 (the price that Country A considers that arm's-length parties would have charged). Therefore, Country A will increase ACo's taxable income by 25. If Country B concurs with Country A's determination of the proper transfer price, it should allow BCo to increase its actual cost of acquiring the goods by 25 (100 + 25 = 125) and reduce its taxable income accordingly by 25. An adjustment of a transfer price used by one taxpayer to take into account an adjustment made by another country to the transfer price used by an affiliated taxpayer is refer red to as a "**corresponding adjustmen**t."

It is arguable whether profit-based transfer pricing methods, such as the profit-split method and TNMM, are consistent with the language of Article 9(1). The reference to profits in Article 9(1) could be a reference to all profits or just the profits from particular transactions or types of business. In any event, by endorsing the profit-based methods, the OECD Guidelines clarify that those methods are acceptable in certain circumstances under Article 9.

Conflicts between countries over transfer prices are commonplace, despite the fact that all countries have agreed in their bilateral tax treaties to adhere to the arm's-length standard. Most tax treaties provide that an enterprise that is subject to double taxation because of inconsistent transfer prices may seek redress through the MAP. Under that procedure, the competent

双重征税的企业，可以通过相互协商程序寻求救济。这项程序要求主管当局设法处理纳税人的申诉，但是，在通常情况下，主管当局没有义务一定要解决争议。若干近期的协定包含解决此种争议的约束性仲裁程序。有关通过相互协商程序解决协定争议和仲裁的讨论，请分别参见第 8 章第 8.8.3 节和第 9 章第 9.5 节。

6.10 税收政策考量：公式分配和独立交易原则的未来

坦白地说，尽管已经历数十年的实践和完善，目前基于独立交易原则的转让定价规则仍无法有效运行。独立交易转让定价规则之所以失灵，原因有很多，最根本的原因是其基本假设存在明显的谬误：即可以将跨国企业各个单独的组成部分视为相互独立而开展各自的活动。跨国企业之所以存在，是因为通过整合其各项经济活动，能实现经济和财务上的优势。然而，基于独立交易原则的转让定价忽略了跨国企业商业活动的经济一体化，却固守其法律结构和集团内关联交易的法律形式。

独立交易原则一直受到学术界、直接受其影响的纳税人和税务机关的大量批评。纳税人抱怨该原则经常给纳税人施加不合理的举证负担；给他们带来主管当局通过税收协定也不能解决的双重征税问题；并且，税务机关在调查过程中也经常不遵守独立交易原则。税务机关则抱怨，独立交易原则纵容跨境交易的纳税人的税负偏低；鼓励纳税人对于其纳税申报采取冒险激进的立场，以避免被发现，或者能够在调查中达成对自己有利的结果；此外，独立交易原则的执行非常耗时，需要投入大量成本。一些学者认为，在某些情况下，使用独立交易原则的方法必然会产生不恰当的结果，因为它不能核算关联公司通常从整合的业务中能获得的利润。上述所有批评意见都有道理。

虽然普遍认为独立交易原则的转让定价方法存在着严重且不可弥补的缺陷，但它有一个非常重要的优势，即，这一原则已被广泛接受。向另一套不同的、即便是更好的体系转变，其过渡成本可能是巨大的。更何况，是否存在一套更好的

authorities are required to try and deal with the taxpayer's complaint, but they are not generally obligated to resolve it. Several recent treaties include a procedure for binding arbitration to resolve such disputes. For a discussion of the MAP for resolving treaty disputes and arbitration, *see* Chapter 8, section 8.8.3 and Chapter 9, section 9.4, respectively.

6.10 TAX POLICY CONSIDERATIONS: FORMULARY APPORTIONMENT AND THE FUTURE OF THE ARM'S-LENGTH METHOD

To be blunt, the current transfer pricing rules based on the arm's-length standard do not work effectively, despite decades of practical experience and refinement. Although there are many reasons for the failure of arm's-length transfer pricing rules, the most fundamental reason is that the underlying assumption—that the separate parts of a multinational enterprise can be considered to behave as if they were independent—is patently false. Multinational enterprises exist because there are economic and financial advantages to the economic integration of their activities. However, transfer pricing in accordance with the arm's-length standard ignores the economic integration of a multinational enterprise's activities but respects its legal structure and the legal form of its intercorporate transactions.

The arm's-length standard has received considerable criticism from academic commentators, taxpayers directly affected by the standard, and tax administrators. Taxpayers complain that it often imposes unreasonable burdens of proof on them, that it presents them with problems of double taxation not resolved by the competent authority mechanism of tax treaties, and that frequently it is not followed by the tax authorities during audits. The tax authorities complain that the arm's-length standard allows considerable under-taxation of taxpayers engaged in cross-border transactions, that it encourages taxpayers to take aggressive positions on their tax returns in the hope of avoiding detection or of striking a favorable bargain on audit, and that it is extremely time-consuming and expensive to enforce. Some academics contend that, in some cases, the arm's-length method necessarily produces improper results because it cannot account for the profits that related corporations typically enjoy from conducting an integrated business. All of these criticisms are valid.

Although arm's-length transfer pricing is generally acknowledged to be seriously and irreparably flawed, it has one very important advantage—namely, that it is widely accepted. The transitional costs of moving to a different, even if better, system would likely be enormous. Moreover, it is not clear that there is a better system. Some commentators argue that the profits of multinational groups should be allocated among the members of the group based

体系，现在还是未知数。一些评论者认为，跨国集团的利润应该根据利润分割法分配给集团成员。事实上，如前所述，《OECD 转让定价指南》目前认可在某些情况下使用利润分割法，并在实践中也似乎越来越多地使用利润分割法来解决转让定价争议。利润分割法的难点在于，现在并不清楚应以什么为基础，将跨国企业的利润分配给跨国企业在其中开展业务的各个国家。

呼声很高的可用于替代独立交易原则的另一个方法，是全球**公式分配体系**。在公式分配体系中，将同一企业中的所有关联实体视为一个单独的实体进行征税。该企业在世界范围内的所得，会按预先设定的公式，在企业从事有价值经济活动的所有国家间进行分配。假设所有国家都同意使用这一体系，并就应纳税所得额的合理且统一的定义达成一致，那么，跨国公司的全球所得将被征税一次，且仅被征税一次。

例如，对于从事商品制造和销售的跨国企业，公式分配法可能会根据各个国家的销售额，将企业收入的一部分（可能是收入的一半），在这些国家中进行分配。收入的剩余部分将在生产商品的国家之间进行分配，分配的依据是全部生产性资产或企业人员薪资，或这两个因素的某种组合。很少或根本没有收入应分配给位于避税地的集团实体，除非在该避税地国家发生了销售或制造活动。

显而易见，使用公式分配法作为在关联公司间分配利润的方式，存在诸多问题。事先确定公式的武断性，难以兼顾每个跨国企业的具体情况。这一方法高度依赖国外信息。几乎可以肯定，即使企业诚信记账，并严格遵循会计准则，分配给跨国集团各成员的利润额会与其账载利润不同，有时甚至相差很大。为解决这些问题，各国政府之间必须开展实质性的合作，而各国不太可能就通用的分配公式达成一致。

然而，公式分配法具有一些吸引人的特点。精心设计的公式化分配体系可以在不依赖复杂且难以管理的受控外国企业法规的情况下，消除低税收国家的税务优势。公式分配法还可以避免在独立交易原则下经常发生的一些高难度转让定价调查问题。与独立交易原则不同的是，公式分配法不需要另就总收入和扣除额的

on profit-split methods. In fact, as noted above, the OECD Guidelines currently recognize the use of profit splits in certain circumstances, and, in practice, it would appear that they are used increasingly to resolve transfer pricing disputes. The difficulty with profit-split methods is that it is unclear on what basis the profits of a multinational enterprise should be allocated to the countries in which it does business.

The alternative to the arm's-length approach that is most frequently advanced is a global **formulary apportionment system**. In a formulary apportionment system, affiliated entities engaged in a common enterprise are taxed as if they were a single entity. The worldwide income of the enterprise is attributed by a predetermined formula among all the countries where the enterprise engages in meaningful economic activity. Assuming that all countries could agree on the use of this system and also agree on a reasonably uniform definition of taxable income, multinational corporations would be taxable once, and only once, on their worldwide income.

For example, in the case of a multinational enterprise engaged in the manufacture and sale of goods, an apportionment formula might allocate some fraction—perhaps one-half—of the income of the enterprise among the countries in accordance with the sales in those countries. The remaining part of the income would be apportioned among the countries where the manufacturing is conducted, with the allocation based on the total manufacturing assets or the payroll of the enterprise, or some combination of these two factors. Little or no income would be apportioned to any group entity in a tax haven unless sales or manufacturing activities take place in that country.

There are obviously many problems with the use of formulary apportionment as a means of allocating profits among related corporations. The arbitrariness of predetermined formulas makes it difficult to take into account the particular circumstances of each multinational enterprise. It relies heavily on access to foreign-based information. It almost guarantees that the amount of profits attributed to each member of a multinational group will differ, sometimes markedly, from the income shown on its books of account, even if those books are kept in good faith and in accordance with approved accounting methods. Substantial cooperation among governments is necessary to solve these problems, and it is unlikely that countries would be able to agree on a common apportionment formula.

Nevertheless, formulary apportionment has some attractive features. A welldesigned system can eliminate the tax advantages of low-tax countries without the need for complex, difficult-to-administer CFC rules. Formulary apportionment also avoids some of the difficult audit problems that frequently arise under the arm's-length approach. Unlike the arm's-length

来源问题达成一致，以避免双重征税的发生，因为来源规则已经隐含在分配公式中。虽然有人认为相比于独立交易原则，公式分配法可能对发展中国家更有利，但这种说法有待商榷，因为公式计算所用的销售额、资产额、员工人数或者工资等因素，都不大可能导致发展中国家分配到与现行独立交易规则的情况相比，明显更多的所得。

在比较公式分配法和独立交易法时，有必要比较两种方法对于无形资产收益的处理方式。在公式分配法下，所有收益，包括来自无形资产的收益，都将被分配给生产和销售商品的每个国家。相反，在独立交易法下，无形资产收益被分配至实际执行 DEMPE 功能或者承担 DEMPE 风险的企业。然而，分配 DEMPE 功能和风险的难度很大，且存在不确定性。

公式分配法遭遇了其不应得的恶评，很大程度是出于政治原因。理性地讨论这一方法及其替代方法，需要避免贴标签，摒弃先入之见。此外，独立交易原则和公式分配法不应被看作两个极端；相反，它们均应被看作并行不悖的方法谱系的组成部分，从可比非受控价格法到预设公式法，不一而足。

公式分配法在某些情形下会运用独立交易原则，独立交易原则下有时也使用公式（如利润分割）。对独立交易原则的最近几次修订，越来越依赖于公式，而且，这种趋势似乎正在得到国际认可。因此，有时难以划分独立交易原则和公式分配法之间的起止界限。为其中任何一种方法贴上贬义和误导性的标签都不是建设性的做法。

尽管独立交易原则存在着缺陷，但除了某些特殊情况以外，该原则很可能仍然是国际间可接受的转让定价问题解决之道。然而，正如先前关于定价方法的讨论所示，独立交易原则的边界模糊不清，其解释可以包容诸如利润分割法和交易净利润法之类的定价方法，而这两种方法似乎更接近于公式分配法，而非独立交易方法。

在一些联邦制国家（如加拿大和美国），公式分配法被用于在各个州政府之间分配实体的所得。同时，这一方法也已被提议在美国 – 墨西哥 – 加拿大协定

approach, it does not require separate agreement on the source of gross income and deductions in order to avoid double taxation because source rules are implicitly incorporated into the apportionment formulas. Although it is sometimes argued that formulary apportionment would be better for developing countries than arm's-length transfer pricing, this claim is questionable. The use of factors such as sales, property, and employees or payroll in the formula is unlikely to result in the allocation of significantly more income to developing countries than the current arm's-length rules.

In comparing the formulary apportionment method to the arm's-length method, it is useful to contrast the treatment of income from intangible property under the two approaches. Under formulary apportionment, all income, including income derived from intangibles, would be apportioned to the countries in which goods are produced and sold. In contrast, under the arm's-length method, such income is allocated to the entities performing DEMPE functions or assuming DEMPE risks with respect to the intangible property. Allocating DEMPE functions and risks is difficult and uncertain.

Formulary apportionment has an undeservedly bad reputation, largely for political reasons. A sensible discussion of that method and the alternatives to it must go beyond labels and preconceived ideas. Moreover, the arm's-length standard and formulary apportionment should not be seen as polar extremes—instead, they should be viewed as parts of a continuum of methods ranging from CUPs to predetermined formulas.

A formulary apportionment system uses an arm's-length approach in some circumstances, and the arm's-length approach sometimes uses formulas (profit splits). Recent refinements in the arm's-length approach rely increasingly on formulas, and that trend seems to be gaining international acceptance. Consequently, it is sometimes unclear where the arm's-length principle ceases and formulary apportionment begins. Applying pejorative and misleading labels to either approach is counterproductive.

Despite its deficiencies, the arm's-length standard is likely to continue to be the internationally accepted approach for resolving transfer pricing issues, except in special circumstances. As the earlier discussion of pricing methodologies indicates, however, the arm's-length standard is vague and has been interpreted to accommodate pricing methodologies, such as the profit-split method and TNMM, that seem closer to formulary apportionment than to an arm's-length approach.

Formulary apportionment is used in some federal countries (e.g., Canada and the U.S.) to allocate the income of an entity among the subnational governments. It has been proposed for internal use within the U.S.-Mexico-Canada Agreement (formerly the North America Free

（即原先的北美自由贸易协定）和欧盟内部使用。近年来，欧盟一直在探索采用某种类型的公式分配法的可能性，以处理欧盟成员国在确定企业从其境内活动所获所得的数额时遇到的复杂问题。然而，关于共同合并税基却一直难以达成一致意见。

OECD 已经批准使用公式分配法，来分配从事全球贸易、银行业和保险业的企业集团的所得。因此，现行的转让定价规则实为各种独立交易方法和公式分配法的混合体。

关于采用公式分配法的最新提案是 OECD 包容性框架的支柱一提案。支柱一的目的是，当大型盈利跨国公司在不构成实质性应税存在的市场国向消费者出售商品和服务时，为相关市场国创设额外的征税权。据此，符合收入和盈利阈值的大型跨国公司，根据其合并财务报表计算的剩余全球利润（超过其收入 10% 的全球利润的 25%，称为金额 A），在市场国纳税。一跨国公司的金额 A 将在其当地收入超过 100 万欧元的市场国家之间，按照在每个市场国家的销售收入的比例，进行分配。跨国公司的其他利润则根据现行转让定价规则确定。因此，即使是拟议的支柱一，也是公式分配规则（金额 A）和传统的转让定价规则的一种令人颇为尴尬的混合体。支柱一提案在第 9 章第 9.5.5.2 节中有更详细的讨论。

考虑独立交易方法和公式分配法各自的缺陷，以及改变现有体系的难度，转让定价似乎有可能将继续杂糅各种规则，尽管不断完善，但在解决存在的问题时，总是难以令人满意。

Trade Agreement) and the EU. For several years, the EU has been exploring the possibility of adopting some type of formulary apportionment to deal with the complex problems that member states encounter in determining the amount of income derived by corporations from activities occurring within their borders. However, agreement on a common consolidated tax base has been elusive.

The OECD has approved the use of formulas for apportioning the income of corporate groups engaged in global trading, banking, and insurance. Therefore, current transfer pricing rules are a mix of arm's-length methods and formulary apportionment methods.

The most recent proposal for the adoption of a formulary apportionment method is the OECD Inclusive Framework's Pillar One proposal. Pillar One is intended to create additional taxing rights for market countries in which goods and services are sold to consumers by large profitable multinationals without any substantial taxable presence in those countries. Market countries will be entitled to tax large multinationals meeting revenue and profitability thresholds on their residual global profits (25% of global profits in excess of 10% of their revenue, called Amount A) computed in accordance with their consolidated financial accounts. A multinational's Amount A will be allocated among the market countries in which the multinational earns revenue of at least EUR 1 million in proportion to the sales revenue derived from each market country. A multinational's other profits are determined in accordance with the existing transfer pricing rules. Thus, even the proposed Pillar One consists of an uncomfortable mixture of formulary apportionment rules (Amount A) and traditional transfer pricing rules. The Pillar One proposals are discussed in more detail in Chapter 9, section 9.5.5.2.

Given the deficiencies of both the arm's-length method and formulary apportionment, as well as the difficulty of changing the existing system, it seems likely that transfer pricing will continue to be a complex mixture of rules that, despite continuous refinement, will never deal with the underlying problem in a satisfactory manner.

7 反避税措施

7.1 引言

国际交易为避税提供了诸多机会。在这方面，必须将避税与逃税加以区分。逃税是非法的，通常涉及故意隐瞒收入或欺诈行为。避税则较难准确地加以定义，不过它通常是指纳税人实施的交易或安排，其目的在于以合法的方式，最大限度地减少应缴税额。

通过国际交易进行避税的方式众多，难以逐一列举。但是，以下示例说明了产生避税行为的各种可能性：

—— 纳税人将其居民身份从一国迁移至征税较低或不征税的另一国。

—— 纳税人将其来源于本国的所得转移至设立在避税地的受控外国实体，诸如信托或公司。

—— 纳税人在避税地设立子公司，由其取得来源于境外的所得，或由其收取设于其他国家的子公司的股息。

—— 在存在可利用的协定的情况下，纳税人可以通过在外国设立的子公司，转移股息、利息、特许权使用费和其他款项，以减少这些款项的预提税数额。

毫不奇怪，大多数国家都制定了反避税规则，以应对国际避税，还有一些国家仍然利用外汇管制，来管控其居民的外国投资和交易。尽管外汇管制可以有效地防止国际避税，但在过去几十年中，大多数国家都放弃了外汇管制，为资本的

CHAPTER 7
Anti-avoidance Measures

7.1 INTRODUCTION

International transactions provide many opportunities for the avoidance of tax. In this context, tax avoidance must be distinguished from *tax evasion,* which is illegal and usually involves the intentional nondisclosure of income or fraud. Tax avoidance is difficult to define precisely, but it generally means transactions or arrangements entered into by a taxpayer in order to minimize the amount of tax payable in a lawful manner.

The various ways of avoiding tax through international transactions are far too numerous to itemize. The following examples, however, illustrate the range of possibilities:

- A taxpayer can shift his or her residence from one country to another country that levies lower or no taxes.
- A taxpayer can divert domestic source income to a controlled foreign entity, such as a trust or a corporation, established in a tax haven.
- A taxpayer can establish a tax haven subsidiary to earn foreign source income or to receive dividends from subsidiaries in other foreign countries.
- If advantageous treaties exist, a taxpayer can route dividends, interest, royalties, and other amounts through subsidiaries established in foreign countries in order to reduce the amount of withholding tax on such amounts.

Not surprisingly, most countries have anti-avoidance rules to deal with certain types of international tax avoidance, and some countries still use exchange controls to regulate foreign investments and transactions by residents. Although exchange controls can be effective in preventing international tax avoidance, over the past several decades, most countries have abandoned exchange controls in favor of the free movement of capital.

自由流动创造有利条件。

不实行外汇管制的国家，采用各种税收措施，打击国际避税。下面简要介绍此类措施的一些重要示例。关于部分措施，在本书其他章节中有更为详细的描述。

反避税规则和原则。许多国家都形成了司法反避税原则或法定反避税规则，可以据以在计征所得税时推翻相关交易。这些原则和规则普遍适用于各种避税交易或安排，包括国际交易。司法反避税原则包括虚假交易、实质重于形式、商业目的、分步交易，以及法律滥用理论。例如，根据虚假交易原则，对于设立在避税地的控股公司，如果其不从事任何真实的商业活动，则可将其视为虚假设立予以否定。法定反避税规则包括特别反避税规则和一般反避税规则。特别反避税规则包括转让定价规则、资本弱化和收益剥离规则、受控外国企业规则、非居民信托规则、外国投资基金规则、盈余剥离规则、反混合规则，以及背对背或反导管规则。一般反避税规则的初衷在于使其覆盖面足够宽泛，能够应对所有或大多数类型的滥用型避税行为，包括国际避税交易。在一般情况下，如果一项交易或一系列交易的主要目的或主要目的之一在于避税，导致相关税收法规被滥用，形同虚设或无法执行，或者导致与相关税收法规的目的和宗旨不一致的结果，那么，就可以适用一般反避税规则。

针对避税地的特别规定。部分国家制定了具体的规定，旨在应对特定的滥用避税地行为。例如，德国针对将其居所迁移至避税地的人，征收了一项特别的税收。其他国家则不允许扣除支付给避税地实体的利息和特许权使用费款项或针对服务的款项，除非纳税人能够证明交易是真实的。实际上，此类扣除正当性的举证责任在纳税人一方。

转让定价规则。大多数国家制定了公司间或转让定价规则，防止关联纳税人在交易中人为抬高或压低价格，以将收入和费用从一国转移至另一国。这些规则应归类为国际反避税规则，或仅是一个国家基本税制的组成部分，还有待商榷。本书第 6 章详细讨论了转让定价规则。

受控外国企业规则。有为数不少的国家采用受控外国企业规则，以防止向设

Countries that do not use exchange controls employ a wide variety of tax measures to combat international tax avoidance. Some important examples of such measures are described briefly below, with references in some instances to more detailed treatment elsewhere in the Primer.

Anti-avoidance rules and doctrines. Many countries have judicial anti-avoidance doctrines or statutory anti-avoidance rules under which transactions may be disregarded for income tax purposes. These doctrines and rules generally apply to tax avoidance transactions or arrangements, including international transactions. Judicial anti-avoidance doctrines include the sham transaction, substance over form, business purpose, step transactions, and abuse of law doctrines. For example, under the sham transaction doctrine, the existence of a holding company established in a tax haven may be disregarded as a sham if it does not engage in any genuine commercial activities. Statutory anti-avoidance rules include specific and General Anti-avoidance Rules (GAARs). Specific anti-avoidance rules include transfer pricing rules, thin capitalization and earnings-stripping rules, CFC rules, nonresident trust rules, FIF rules, surplus-stripping rules, anti-hybrid rules, and back-to-back or anti-conduit rules. GAARs are intended to be sufficiently broad to deal with most or all types of abusive tax avoidance, including international tax avoidance transactions. Typically, GAARs apply when the principal purpose or one of the principal purposes of a transaction or a series of transactions is to avoid tax and the transaction abuses, frustrates, or defeats, or is inconsistent with the object and purpose of the relevant tax legislation.

Special tax haven provisions. Some countries have specific provisions designed to deal with particular tax haven abuses. For example, Germany imposes a special tax on persons who move their domicile to a tax haven. Other countries disallow the deduction of interest and royalty payments or payments for services made to a tax haven entity unless the taxpayer can establish that the transactions are genuine; in effect, the onus of proof is placed on the taxpayer to justify such deductions.

Transfer pricing rules. Most countries have intercompany or transfer pricing rules to prevent related taxpayers from carrying out transactions at artificially high or low prices in order to shift income and expenses from one country to another. It is arguable whether these rules are properly classified as international anti-avoidance rules or whether they are just part of a country's basic tax system. Transfer pricing rules are discussed in detail in Chapter 6.

CFC rules. Several countries have adopted CFC rules to prevent the diversion of passive and certain other income to, and the accumulation of such income in, a CFC established in a

立在低税收国家的受控外国企业转移消极所得和某些其他类型的所得，以及防止此类所得在这些受控外国企业滞留。稍后的第 7.3 节将讨论受控外国企业规则。有些国家针对非居民信托制定了类似的规则，第 7.4 节将加以论述。

外国投资基金规则。不少国家实行外国投资基金规则，以防止通过投资外国共同基金、单位信托或类似实体的居民推迟国内税收。第 7.5 节将讨论这些规则。

反择协避税规则。不少国家坚持在其税收协定和 / 或其国内法中，加入防止择协避税的条款。择协避税一般涉及由非居民在一国设立法律实体，借以获得该国税收协定待遇。本书第 8 章第 8.8.2.2 节将讨论择协避税。

资本弱化和收益剥离规则。不少国家通过资本弱化或收益剥离规则，限制居民公司和其他法律实体的利息扣除。资本弱化规则旨在防止居民公司的非居民股东，采用超额借贷资本，从而在抽取公司利润时得以作为利息支出在税前扣除，而回避作为不可税前扣除的股息支付。与资本弱化规则相比，收益剥离规则更广泛地针对那些申报扣除不合比例的高额利息的居民公司和其他实体。接下来的第 7.2 节将讨论这些规则。

针对对外转让财产收益和放弃国籍应计收益的税收。当向关联非居民转让增值财产（有应计收益的财产）时，一些国家将该财产视为按其公允市场价值出售，因此对应计收益予以征税。否则，针对相关收益的国内税收会被完全规避。此外，有些国家在纳税人终止居民身份时，或在终止居民身份后的特定一段时间内，对其应计收益征税。第 3 章第 3.4.1 节和第 3.4.2 节讨论了此类退出或出境税和延续税。

背对背安排。**背对背安排**或**导管安排**经常被用作税收筹划策略，其目的在于使纳税人获得其原本并不能直接获得的税收利益。例如，有时可以通过在关联方之间增加独立交易的中间方，来规避一国针对关联方交易的规则。同样，可以通过背对背安排，不当获得一国的协定待遇，如降低预提税。这种安排在金融交易方面尤其常见，因为资金可以较为容易地经由非关联金融机构转手。例如，假设

low-tax country. These rules are discussed in section 7.3 below. Some countries have similar rules with respect to nonresident trusts, which are discussed in section 7.4 below.

FIF rules. Several countries have adopted FIF rules to prevent the deferral of domestic tax by residents through investments in foreign mutual funds, unit trusts, or similar entities. These rules are discussed in section 7.5 below.

Anti-treaty shopping rules. Several countries insist on the inclusion of provisions in their tax treaties and/or in their domestic legislation to prevent treaty shopping. Treaty shopping typically involves the establishment of a legal entity in a country by nonresidents in order to obtain the benefits of that country's tax treaties. Treaty shopping is discussed in Chapter 8, section 8.8.2.2.

Thin capitalization and earnings-stripping rules. Several countries have adopted thin capitalization or earnings-stripping rules to limit the deduction of interest by resident corporations and other legal entities. Thin capitalization rules are intended to prevent non-resident shareholders of resident corporations from using excessive debt capital to extract corporate profits in the form of deductible interest rather than non-deductible dividends. Earnings-stripping rules are more broadly targeted at resident corporations and other entities that claim disproportionately large interest deductions. These rules are discussed in section 7.2 below.

Taxation of gains on transfers of property abroad and on expatriation. When appreciated property—property with an accrued gain—is transferred to a related nonresident, some countries deem the property to have been sold for its fair market value so that the accrued gain is subject to tax; otherwise, domestic tax on the gain might be avoided entirely. Further, some countries impose tax on accrued gains when a taxpayer ceases to be resident or for a temporary period after a taxpayer ceases to be resident; such exit or departure taxes and trailing taxes are discussed in Chapter 3, sections 3.4.1 and 3.4.2.

Back-to-back arrangements. **Back-to-back arrangements** or **conduit arrangements** are commonly used as a tax planning device to obtain tax benefits that would not otherwise be available to a taxpayer directly. For example, a country may have rules dealing with related-party transactions; these rules can sometimes be avoided by inserting an arm's-length intermediary between the related parties. Similarly, the benefits of a country's treaties, such as reductions in withholding taxes, may be inappropriately obtained through back-to-back arrangements. Such arrangements are particularly common with respect to financial transactions since funds can be funneled through an arm's-length financial institution with relative ease. For example, assume that Country A exempts interest payments by corporations

A 国对居民公司向无关联非居民支付利息免于征收利息预提税，而居民公司 A 向作为 B 国居民的关联公司 B 支付利息，则该利息应缴纳 A 国预提税。但是，如果 B 公司将资金存入与 A 公司和 B 公司均无关联的金融机构，并由该金融机构向 A 公司发放同等数额的贷款，则 A 国预提税将不适用于由 A 公司向该金融机构支付的利息，因为 A 公司和该金融机构进行的是独立交易。下文第 7.6 节将讨论背对背或反导管规则。

盈余剥离。“盈余剥离”一词通常所指的交易事项是，将公司的盈余或税后利润，以股息或其他应税分配以外的形式，有效地分配给公司的股东。盈余剥离交易可以是纯粹的国内交易或跨境交易（居民公司与其非居民股东之间）。在跨境盈余剥离的情形下，其目的通常是避免股息预提税（在许多国家中，预提税也适用于居民公司清算时所做的分配）。通常，这些交易涉及出售盈余被剥离公司的股份，其目的是将股息转变为财产收益，而财产收益将免于征税（免税的原因或许是适用的税收协定的规定）。各国可能试图通过特别反规避规则或一般反避税规则，来防止跨境盈余剥离交易。

混合实体和混合金融工具。“混合”安排是指，由于两国对各种实体、交易或安排的处理存在差异，纳税人利用这些差异获得税收利益。例如，一国对居民公司发行的优先股，按其法律属性视为股权，可以据以支付股息；但另一国将这类股权视为债务，可以据以支付利息。那么这种处理上的差异，可以被利用来实现节税。如果前述公司为其居民的国家将与股份相关的款项支付视为利息，则该款项支付可以在税前予以扣除，从而减少了该国的税基。如果该款项收取方为其居民的国家将该款项视为股息，则可以依据参股免税规定予以免税。以下第 7.7 节将更为详尽地讨论混合安排。

resident in Country A to arm's-length nonresidents from its withholding tax on interest. If ACo, a corporation resident in Country A, pays interest to BCo, a related corporation resident in Country B, the interest would be subject to Country A's withholding tax. However, if BCo puts funds on deposit with a financial institution that deals at arm's length with both ACo and BCo and the financial institution loans an equivalent amount to ACo, Country A's withholding tax would not apply to the interest payments by ACo to the financial institution because ACo and the financial institution deal at arm's length. Back-to-back or anti-conduit rules are discussed in section 7.6 below.

Surplus stripping. The term "surplus stripping" is commonly used to refer to transactions whereby the surplus or after-tax profits of a corporation are effectively distributed to its shareholders in a form other than dividends or other taxable distributions. Surplus-stripping transactions can be purely domestic or cross-border (i.e., a resident corporation with nonresident shareholders). In a cross-border surplus strip, the objective is usually the avoidance of withholding tax on dividends (which in many countries also applies to distributions on the liquidation of a resident corporation). Often, these transactions involve a sale of the shares of the corporation whose surplus is being stripped in order to convert dividends into capital gains, which will be exempt from tax (perhaps because of the provisions of an applicable tax treaty). Countries may attempt to prevent cross-border surplus-stripping transactions through specific anti-avoidance rules or a GAAR.

Hybrid entities and hybrid financial instruments. A "hybrid" arrangement refers to situations in which two countries treat entities, transactions, or arrangements differently, and the different treatment is exploited to produce tax benefits. For example, if one country treats preferred shares issued by a resident corporation in accordance with their legal form as shares on which dividends are paid, but another country treats the shares as debt on which interest is paid, this inconsistent treatment can be exploited to produce tax savings. If the country in which the corporation is resident treats the payments on the shares as interest, the payments will be deductible and reduce that country's tax base. If the country in which the recipient of the payments is resident treats the payments as dividends, it may exempt those dividends from tax as a result of its participation exemption. Hybrid arrangements are discussed in more detail below in section 7.7.

7.2 针对利息扣除的限制：资本弱化和收益剥离规则

7.2.1 引言

当居民公司向非居民支付利息时，支付方在计算其所得时，通常可以扣除该利息，除非另有特殊规定。利息支付可能需要缴纳预提税，但是，根据适用的税收协定，预提税率可能会大幅降低或完全免除。非居民贷款人为其居民的国家，可能会对该利息征税，也可能不征税。如果非居民贷款人也是居民公司的控股股东，则非居民贷款人 / 股东通常可以选择向其子公司提供债务或权益融资，并通过收取股息或利息来分享子公司的利润。

与利息不同，居民公司支付的股息一般不可以税前扣除。因此，由居民公司取得并向其股东进行分配的所得，会在两个层面发生税收：公司取得所得时征收的公司税收，和所得作为股息向股东分配时征收的股东税收。如果股东是非居民，股东税收通常是作为预提税进行征收的。

与上述情况不同，当居民公司取得的所得以利息的形式，向同时也是公司股东的非居民贷款人进行分配时，只会在一个层面上发生税收。由于利息可以由公司税前扣除，因此来源国仅就向非居民支付的利息款项征收预提税；但是，许多国家都单方面或者依据其税收协定，降低或免除了对利息的预提税。与向非居民股东支付股息相比，支付利息更为有利，于是无可避免地使非居民投资者更青睐于向居民公司提供债务融资。以下举例说明这种倾向性。

非居民公司 N 拥有居民公司 R 的全部股份。R 公司需要向其经营活动注资 100 万元。为了提供这一资金，N 公司可以追加认购 R 公司股份 100 万元，或者可以向 R 公司提供贷款 100 万元（也可以是债务和权益的某种组合）。假设 R 公司支付利息或股息之前所得为 100000 元，并将其全部税后所得作为股息进行分配。进一步假设贷款应支付利息的独立交易利率为 10%，股息预提税的适用税

7.2 RESTRICTIONS ON THE DEDUCTION OF INTEREST: THIN CAPITALIZATION AND EARNINGS-STRIPPING RULES

7.2.1 Introduction

When a resident corporation pays interest to nonresidents, the interest is usually deductible by the payer in computing its income unless there are special rules to the contrary. The interest payments may be subject to withholding tax, but the rate of withholding tax may be substantially reduced or completely eliminated pursuant to an applicable tax treaty. The nonresident lender may or may not be subject to tax on the interest in its country of residence. If the nonresident lender is also the controlling shareholder of the resident corporation, the nonresident lender/shareholder will usually have a choice of financing its subsidiary with debt or equity and extracting the profits of the subsidiary by receiving either dividends or interest.

Unlike interest, dividends paid by a resident corporation generally are not deductible. Accordingly, income earned by a resident corporation and distributed to its shareholders is subject to two levels of tax—corporate tax when the income is earned by the corporation and shareholder tax when the income is distributed to the shareholders as a dividend. If the shareholder is a nonresident, the shareholder tax is usually imposed as a withholding tax.

In contrast, income earned by a resident corporation and distributed in the form of interest to a nonresident lender who is also a shareholder of the corporation is subject to only one level of tax. Because the interest is deductible by the corporation, usually the only source country tax is the withholding tax on the interest payment to the nonresident; however, many countries have reduced or eliminated their withholding taxes on interest, either unilaterally or under their tax treaties. The advantage of paying interest to nonresident shareholders compared to paying dividends constitutes an inherent bias in favor of debt financing of resident corporations by nonresident investors. This bias is illustrated in the following example.

NCo, a nonresident corporation, owns all the shares of RCo, a resident corporation. RCo requires capital of 1 million to finance its business activities. To provide that capital, NCo can either subscribe for 1 million in additional shares of RCo or loan RCo 1 million (or some combination of debt and equity). Assume that RCo earns income, before the payment of interest or dividends, of 100,000 and distributes its entire after-tax income as a dividend. Assume further that the arm's-length interest rate payable on loans is 10%, and the applicable rates of

率为 5%，利息预提税率为 10%，表 7-1 比较了分别以债务和权益方式筹措资金所产生的税收结果。

表 7-1　债务和权益融资优劣比较

	债务	权益
支付利息或股息前的公司收入	100000	100000
利息扣除额	100000	不适用
应税所得	0	100000
公司税（30%）	0	30000
股息	不适用	60000
预提税（10%，5%）	10000	3000
税款合计	10000	33000

如此例所示，与权益融资相比，以债务的形式为居民公司提供资金，能够更为有效地减少来源国税收。其中的主要原因在于利息可以扣除，而股息不能扣除。此外，居民公司可以随时偿还贷款，同时并不引发税收问题。然而居民公司在偿还权益投资（赎回股份或减少资本）时，难以回避应税股息问题。

由居民向非居民支付的所有可扣除利息，都减少或侵蚀了一国的税基。然而，并非所有减少税基的款项都是不合理的，居民向非居民支付的包括利息在内的许多可扣除款项，都是为取得收入而产生的合法费用。

为了解决上述权益融资与债务融资之间对后者的倾向性，许多国家对向非居民支付利息的税前扣除加以限制，有的则更为普遍地对利息扣除实行限制。根据"资本弱化"规则，对于由居民公司支付给非居民控股股东（或某些情况下的实质性控股股东）的利息，如果居民公司要求扣除的利息被认定为数额过大，则其扣除将拒绝。根据此类规则，如果居民公司的债务相比于其权益，超过了规定的比值（通常为 1.5：1 或 2：1），即可认定利息数额过大。"资本弱化"一词所表述的规则仅适用于公司权益资本较之其债务偏低的情形。

withholding tax are 5% on dividends and 10% on interest. A comparison of the tax results of advancing funds by way of debt and equity is set out in Table 7.1.

Table 7.1 Relative Advantages of Debt and Equity Finance

	Debt	*Equity*
Corporate income before payment of interest or dividends	100,000	100,000
Deduction of interest	100,000	not applicable
Taxable income	nil	100,000
Corporate tax (30%)	nil	30,000
Dividends	not applicable	60,000
Withholding tax (10%, 5%)	10,000	3,000
Total tax	10,000	33,000

As this example illustrates, financing a resident corporation with debt is considerably more effective in reducing source country tax than financing with equity. The major reason is that interest is deductible, whereas dividends are not deductible. In addition, a resident corporation can repay a loan at any time without triggering tax, whereas it may not be able to repay equity investments (redeem shares or reduce capital) without triggering a taxable dividend.

All deductible interest payments by residents to nonresidents reduce or erode a country's tax base. However, not all base-eroding payments are objectionable; many deductible payments by residents to nonresidents, including interest, represent legitimate income-earning expenses.

In response to the bias in favor of debt compared with equity, several countries have adopted restrictions on the deduction of interest paid to nonresidents or on the deduction of interest more generally. Under "thin capitalization" rules, the deduction for interest paid by a resident corporation to a nonresident controlling (or sometimes substantial) shareholder is denied to the extent that interest deductions claimed by the corporation are considered to be excessive. Under these rules, interest is considered to be excessive to the extent that the corporation's debt relative to its equity exceeds a fixed debt:equity ratio (often 1.5:1 or 2:1). The term "thin capitalization" is apt because the rules apply only when a corporation's equity capital is small in relation to its debt.

各国的法定资本弱化规则之间存在着明显的差异。在一些国家，资本弱化规则被视为专门的转让定价规则，局限于向关联方或非独立交易方支付的利息款项。在其他一些国家，此类规则针对被认定为变相股息的利息款项支付；换言之，规则仅适用于非居民股东持有居民公司实质性权益情形下的债务。还有一些国家的此类规则普遍适用于利息支付。稍后的第 7.2.2 节讨论资本弱化规则。

根据收益剥离规则，如果利息超过了公司收益的一定财务比例（通常是扣除利息、税款、折旧和摊销前的收益，即“EBITDA”，的 25% ~ 30%），则可认定利息数额过大，不予扣除。BEPS 第 4 项行动计划报告建议各国采用收益剥离规则，并认为此规则优于资本弱化规则。第 7.2.3b 节讨论 BEPS 第 4 项行动计划报告和收益剥离规则。

有些国家选择依托征管方面的操作手册或操作实务，来解决超额利息扣除问题。还有些国家则通过运用其转让定价规则或一般反避税规则。

超额利息扣除的问题不仅存在于上述向非居民支付的利息，当取得免税所得或减税所得过程中发生利息费用，利息扣除问题一样存在。这种情形经常出现在采取如下做法的国家之中，即对归属于外国常设机构的所得实行免税，或对居民公司从其拥有实质性权益的外国公司收取的股息实行免税。从理论上来说，用于取得非应税所得的借贷资金的利息费用不应扣除。然而，许多国家允许在这些情况下扣除利息。即使在拒绝或限制此类利息扣除的国家，将利息费用划分到各种来源所得的规则时常被纳税人规避。在这些情况下允许扣除利息，其实际效果就是补贴居民公司的对外投资，鼓励纳税人到税率低于居民国的国家投资。

少数国家对上述问题直接加以处理。澳大利亚和新西兰采用所谓的对外资本弱化规则。根据该规则，如果居民公司的债务超过其国内净资产成本或价值的一定百分比（如 75%），则居民公司将不得扣除利息。如下文第 7.2.3 节所述，将收益剥离规则适用于居民公司发生的所有利息费用的国家，可以限制但不能完全消除与取得免税境外来源所得相关的利息费用的扣除问题。

关于利息费用的另一个问题涉及“债务下推安排”。这种安排通常用于跨

The statutory thin capitalization rules of countries differ considerably. In some countries, thin capitalization rules are seen as specific transfer pricing rules that are limited to interest payments to related or non-arm's-length parties. In other countries, the rules are targeted at interest payments that are viewed as disguised dividends: in other words, debt held by nonresident shareholders with a substantial interest in a resident corporation. Other countries consider the rules to be aimed at interest payments generally. Thin capitalization rules are discussed in section 7.2.2 below.

Under earnings-stripping rules, interest is considered to be excessive and its deduction is denied where it exceeds a financial formula based on the earnings of the corporation (often 25%–30% of Earnings Before Deduction of Interest, Taxes, Depreciation, and Amortization, ("EBITDA")). The BEPS Action 4 Report recommended that countries adopt earnings-stripping rules in preference to thin capitalization rules. The BEPS Action 4 Report and earnings-stripping rules are discussed in section 7.2.3 below.

Some countries try to deal with the problem of excessive interest deductions by relying on administrative guidelines or practices. Still others apply their transfer pricing rules or GAARs.

Excessive interest deductions are a problem not only where, as described above, interest is paid to nonresidents but also where interest expenses are incurred to earn exempt or preferentially taxed income. This situation often arises in countries that exempt income attributable to a foreign PE or exempt dividends from foreign corporations in which resident corporations own a substantial interest. Theoretically, interest expenses on borrowed funds used to earn income that is not taxable should not be deductible. However, many countries allow the deduction of interest in these circumstances and even for countries that deny or limit the deduction of interest, the rules for allocating interest expenses to sources of income can often be avoided by taxpayers. The effect of allowing the deduction of interest in these circumstances is to provide a subsidy for foreign investment by resident companies in foreign countries that impose tax at rates lower than the tax rate in the residence country.

Few countries deal with this problem directly. Australia and New Zealand have adopted so-called outbound thin capitalization rules under which resident companies are denied interest deductions to the extent that their debt exceeds a percentage (say, 75%) of the cost or value of their net domestic assets. Countries that have adopted earnings-stripping rules that apply to all interest expenses incurred by resident corporations, as described in section 7.2.3 below, may limit, but will not eliminate completely, interest expenses incurred to earn exempt foreign source income.

Another problem with interest expenses involves "debt push-down arrangements," which

境收购之中，即将因收购某一特定国家的居民公司股份而产生的债务转移给该被收购公司。以下示例用以说明实现债务下推的不同途径。A 国居民 A 公司正在收购 B 国居民 B 公司的全部股份。如果 A 公司借贷此项收购所需的资金，则在计算 A 公司的所得时，可以扣除借款的利息，从而减少了 A 国的税基。由于各种原因（如 A 公司所得不足以冲抵利息扣除，或因 B 国税率较高利息扣除更具价值），A 公司希望用上述利息扣减 B 国 B 公司的利润。为此，A 公司在 B 国设立一家新公司 Newco，由其收购 B 公司的股份。A 公司将借入的资金转借给 Newco，由 Newco 用以收购 B 公司的股份。Newco 支付给 A 公司的利息会被计入 A 公司的收入之中，但又被其利息扣除所抵消。虽然 Newco 可以正常扣除由其支付给 A 公司的利息，但由于 Newco 是控股公司，因此可能并无任何所得，用于冲抵利息费用。这时，Newco 和 B 公司有可能合并成为一个公司实体，于是在计算合并后公司的利润时得以扣除利息费用。另外，B 国可能实行相关规则，允许居民公司提交合并纳税申报表；在合并纳税申报表中，可以用 Newco 的利息费用扣减 B 公司的利润。这样，就可以在 B 公司的利润中扣除 Newco 的利息费用。

虽然资本弱化规则或收益剥离规则可以限制居民公司所提出涉及债务下推安排的利息扣除数额，但这些规则并不专门针对债务下推安排，也不能否定所有涉及此种债务的利息扣除。为此，有些国家有针对性的反避税规则或尝试通过其一般反避税规则，来否定因不合理债务下推安排而造成的利息扣除。

7.2.2 资本弱化规则的结构性特征

在一般情况下，资本弱化规则（及针对支付给国内公司非居民股东的利息的收益剥离规则）都具有大部分如下所列的结构性特征。

非居民出借方。资本弱化规则一般仅适用于支付给拥有居民公司较高比例股份的非居民的利息。对上述拥有居民公司股份比例，各国规定不尽相同，有的限

are often used in cross-border acquisitions to shift the debt used to acquire the shares of a corporation resident in a particular country to that corporation. Although debt push-downs can be accomplished in many ways, consider the following example. ACo, resident in Country A, is acquiring all the shares of BCo, resident in Country B. If ACo borrows the necessary funds to finance the acquisition, the interest on the borrowed funds will be deductible in computing ACo's income and reducing Country A's tax base. For a variety of reasons (e.g., ACo does not have sufficient income to absorb the interest deductions or the interest deductions are more valuable because of higher tax rates in Country B), ACo may wish the interest to be deductible against the profits of BCo in Country B. Therefore, ACo may cause the incorporation of a new company in Country B, Newco, to make the acquisition of the shares of BCo. ACo might use its borrowed funds to lend to Newco, and Newco could then use those funds to acquire the shares of BCo. The interest paid by Newco to ACo will be included in ACo's income but will be offset by its interest deductions. The interest paid by Newco to ACo would ordinarily be deductible by Newco. Since Newco is a holding company, it may not have any income against which to deduct the interest expenses. However, it may be possible for Newco and BCo to merge into one corporate entity, in which case the interest expenses will be deductible in computing the profits of the merged corporation. Alternatively, Country B may have rules to allow resident companies to file consolidated tax returns in which the interest expense of Newco would be deductible against the profits of BCo. As a result, the interest expenses of Newco will be deductible against the profits of BCo.

Thin capitalization rules or earnings-stripping rules will limit the amount of interest deductions claimed by resident corporations through debt push-down arrangements; however, those rules are not targeted specifically at debt push-down arrangements and will not deny all interest deductions on such debt. Alternatively, some countries may adopt specific anti-avoidance rules or attempt to apply their GAARs in order to deny interest deductions resulting from inappropriate debt push-down arrangements.

7.2.2 The Structural Features of Thin Capitalization Rules

Typically, thin capitalization rules (and earnings-stripping rules that are targeted at interest paid to nonresident shareholders of domestic corporations) have most of the following structural features.

Nonresident lenders. Thin capitalization rules generally apply only to interest paid to nonresidents who own a significant percentage of the shares of a resident corporation. The

于实质性持股（10% ~ 25%），有的限于控制性持股（占股 50% 以上）。但是，如上所述，有些国家，如澳大利亚和新西兰，也将其规则适用于以债务融资为其外国投资筹措资金的居民公司（即所谓的对外资本弱化规则）。正如下文第 7.2.3 节中所讨论的，欧洲国家和美国所采用的收益剥离规则，则同时适用于支付给居民和非居民出借方的利息。

适用规则的实体。大多数国家的资本弱化规则仅适用于居民公司。但是，对于合伙企业、信托和非居民公司的分支机构（常设机构），也可能产生通过向关联非居民支付超额利息而剥离利润，因此越来越多的国家将资本弱化规则的适用范围扩大到这些实体。

超额利息的确定。一般来说，资本弱化规则仅适用于由居民公司向非居民支付的某些"超额"利息。各国使用不同的方法，确定何者构成超额利息，对此并不存在国际共识。最为常见的方法是使用某个固定债务权益比。按照此方法，只有当公司债务相比公司权益被人为扩大，且其利息被支付给控股股东或主要股东时，即实际上权益被伪装成债务时，方不允许扣除相关利息。OECD 建议税收协定使用的另一种方法，是通过分析所有相关事实和情形，包括居民公司的债务权益比，来对债务和权益加以定性。根据 OECD 的看法，这一方法符合转让定价领域中普遍运用的独立交易标准，避免了运用固定债务权益比时存在的不灵活和武断性。

债务权益比的计算。关于资本弱化规则设定的债务权益比，有以下两种：

—— 以主观方式确定的比率，即不考虑公司间债务和权益，在合并的基础上计算的比率；或

—— 依据所有居民公司或某一特定行业或门类的所有居民公司的债务权益比的平均值。

大多数国家似乎都以主观的方式，在 1.5 : 1 至 3 : 1 之间选择一个债务权益比，有的针对金融机构确定较高的比率。在计算作为该比率组成部分的债务和权

level of share ownership varies from a substantial interest in the shares (10%–25%) to control (more than 50% of the shares) of the resident corporation. However, as noted above, some countries, such as Australia and New Zealand, also apply their rules to resident corporations that use debt to finance foreign investment (so-called outbound thin capitalization rules). In contrast, as discussed below in section 7.2.3, the earnings-stripping rules adopted by European countries and the U.S. apply to interest paid to resident and nonresident lenders.

Entities subject to the rules. The thin capitalization rules of most countries apply only to resident corporations. However, the stripping of profits through the payment of excessive interest to related nonresidents may also arise with respect to partnerships, trusts, and branches (PEs) of nonresident corporations. As a result, countries are increasingly extending the application of their thin capitalization rules to these entities.

Determination of excessive interest. Generally, thin capitalization rules apply only to certain "excessive" interest paid to nonresidents by resident corporations. Countries use a variety of different approaches to determine what constitutes excessive interest; there is no international consensus on this issue. The most common approach is the use of a fixed debt/equity ratio, under which only interest on a corporation's debt that is artificially large in relation to its equity and paid to a controlling or substantial shareholder—in effect, debt that is disguised equity—is not deductible. An alternative approach, recommended by the OECD for tax treaties, attempts to characterize debt and equity by reference to all the facts and circumstances, including the debt:equity ratio of the resident corporation. According to the OECD, this approach is consistent with the arm's-length standard used for transfer pricing generally and avoids the inflexibility and arbitrariness of applying a fixed debt: equity ratio.

Computation of debt: equity ratio. A debt:equity ratio for purposes of thin capitalization rules can be established either:

- as an arbitrary ratio, computed on a consolidated basis, ignoring any inter-company debt and equity; or
- by reference to the average debt:equity ratio for all resident corporations or all resident corporations engaged in a particular industrial or commercial sector.

Most countries seem to use an arbitrary debt:equity ratio of 1.5:1 to 3:1, sometimes with a higher ratio for financial institutions. The calculation of debt and equity as components of the ratio raises many subsidiary tax policy decisions. For example, should all debt held by nonres-

益时，导致了许多相关的税收政策决策。例如，债务应包括非居民持有的所有债务，还是只包括实质性持股非居民股东的债务？权益应包括实缴盈余，还是只包括股本和留存收益？优先股等混合证券应如何归类？是否应包括非居民股东担保的债务？公司的总债务中是否应减去留存现金，尤其是因为这些现金可能会产生利息收入？

影响。适用资本弱化规则或收益剥离规则的结果，一般是对超额利息不予扣除。某些国家将此种超额利息视为股息。在其他一些国家，某一年度不可扣除的超额利息可以结转，在后续年度扣除，但前提是在该后续年度，该超额利息没有受到利息扣除规定的限制。

税务机关必须意识到，纳税人可以通过与国际银行和其他独立交易金融中介机构的背对背安排，掩盖公司间贷款，从而规避资本弱化规则。因此，有些国家在其资本弱化规则中作出规定，尽力防止使用背对背贷款和类似的避税策略。关于背对背或反导管规则的相关讨论，参见第 7.6 节。

资本弱化规则的着重点是向非居民支付的利息。支付给居民的利息通常没有问题，因为收到利息款项的居民通常要就这些款项纳税。然而，欧盟成员国被禁止歧视其他欧盟成员国的居民。欧洲法院裁定，仅适用于支付给非居民的利息的资本弱化规则，在适用于其他欧盟成员国的居民时无效。因此，如下文第 7.2.3 节所述，2016 年，欧盟发布了一项反避税指令，要求欧盟成员国采用收益剥离规则，并将其适用于由居民公司所做的所有利息支付，包括对居民的此类支付。

基于收益确定超额利息，相比依据固定债务权益比确定超额利息，二者的显著差异在于，前者对利率波动敏感，而后者不敏感。在低利率时期，公司能够比在高利率时期承担更多的债务，但基于固定债务权益比的资本弱化规则不因利率高低发生变化。解决这个问题，可以通过定期调整债务权益比来反映利率的重大变化。

idents be taken into account, or just debt held by substantial nonresident shareholders? Should equity include contributed surplus or only share capital and retained earnings? How should hybrid securities such as preferred shares be classified? Should debt that is guaranteed by a nonresident shareholder be taken into account? Should a corporation's gross debt be reduced by any cash on hand, especially since such cash may be earning interest income?

Consequences. The effect of the application of thin capitalization or earnings-stripping rules is generally that excessive interest is not deductible. In some countries, this excessive interest is treated as a dividend. In other countries, excessive interest that is not deductible in one year can be carried forward and deducted in a subsequent year, assuming that it is not subject to the limitation on the deduction of interest in that year.

Tax authorities must be aware that their thin capitalization rules can be avoided if taxpayers channel their intercompany loans through back-to-back arrangements with international banks and other arm's-length financial intermediaries. Therefore, some countries' thin capitalization rules contain provisions that attempt to prevent the use of back-to-back loans and similar tax avoidance devices. *See* section 7.6 for a discussion of back-to-back or anti-conduit rules.

Thin capitalization rules focus on payments of interest to nonresidents. Interest payments to residents are not generally problematic because the residents receiving the payments are usually taxable on those payments. However, EU countries are prohibited from discriminating against residents of other EU countries, and the Court of Justice of the European Union (CJEU) has ruled that thin capitalization rules that are applicable only to interest payments to nonresidents are invalid insofar as they apply to residents of other EU countries. Consequently, as described below in section 7.2.3, in 2016, the EU issued an anti-tax avoidance directive requiring EU countries to adopt earnings-stripping rules that apply to all interest payments by resident corporations, including such payments to residents.

One significant difference between the determination of excessive interest on the basis of earnings or a fixed debt:equity ratio is that earnings are sensitive to fluctuations in interest rates, whereas a fixed debt:equity rule is not. In periods of low interest rates, corporations can carry more debt than in periods when interest rates are high. Thin capitalization rules based on a fixed debt:equity ratio apply irrespective of whether interest rates are high or low. This difficulty can be dealt with by adjusting the debt:equity ratio periodically to reflect significant changes in interest rates.

7.2.3 收益剥离规则

BEPS 第 4 项行动计划最终报告反对资本弱化规则，而赞成收益剥离规则。这主要是因为该报告认为收益能够更好地衡量一个实体履行偿息义务的能力，同时也因为资本弱化规则存在前述没有考虑利率波动问题。相比之下，收益法鼓励纳税人在利率上升期间减少其债务，以避免对利息扣除的限制。

BEPS 第 4 项行动计划报告中提出的建议并非强制性的，各国可以选择是否采纳这些建议。值得注意的是，欧盟和美国都采用了与该报告建议类似的收益剥离规则。

简言之，BEPS 第 4 项行动计划报告中建议的收益剥离规则具有如下主要特征：

只有当实体的利息费用超过最低金额限制时，该规则才适用。此举旨在减轻该规则的管理和遵从负担。欧盟指令规定最低限额为 300 万欧元，该限额必须在跨国集团成员之间分配。

允许一个实体扣除的净利息费用（利息费用超出利息收入的部分），最多不超过其净利息费用与 EBITDA 的基准比率。实体的净利息费用和 EBITDA 的计算系根据一国的税收法规，而不是其财务会计制度。上述基准比率设定在实体 EBITDA 的 10% ~ 30%。欧盟和美国采用的基准比率均为 EBITDA 的 30%，不过，美国的规则针对 2022 年以后年度，转为基于 EBIT 的比率。超过允许数额的利息费用将不可扣除，但可结转至以往或今后年度。

上述规则适用于实体的净利息费用（实体的利息费用多于其总利息收入的部分），目的在于将集团内部的利息支付考虑在内。

作为一种可选的救济措施，如果实体所属跨国集团的独立交易净利息费用与 EBITDA 的比率大于实体的比率，则允许该实体扣除超出其 EBITDA 允许百分

7.2.3 Earnings-Stripping Rules

The BEPS Action 4 Final Report rejects thin capitalization rules in favor of earnings-stripping rules, largely because, according to the Report, earnings provide a better measure of an entity's ability to meet its interest obligations and also because, as noted above, thin capitalization rules do not take interest rates into account. In contrast, under an earnings approach, taxpayers have an incentive to reduce their debt during periods of rising interest rates in order to avoid restrictions on the deduction of interest.

The recommendations in the BEPS Action 4 Report are not mandatory; countries may or may not choose to adopt them. However, the EU and the U.S. have adopted earnings-stripping rules similar to the rules recommended in the Report.

In simple terms, the major features of the earnings-stripping rules recommended in the BEPS Action 4 Report are described below:

> The rules would apply only if an entity's interest expenses exceed a *de minimis* monetary threshold, which is intended to reduce the administrative and compliance burden of the rules. The EU Directive establishes a *de minimis* threshold amount of 3 million Euros, which must be allocated among the members of a multinational group.

An entity would be permitted to deduct its net interest expense up to a benchmark ratio of its net interest expenses (interest expenses in excess of interest income) to EBITDA. An entity's net interest expenses and EBITDA would be calculated in accordance with a country's tax rules, not its financial accounting rules. The benchmark ratio would be set within a range of 10% to 30% of an entity's EBITDA. Both the EU and the U.S. have adopted a benchmark ratio of 30% of EBITDA, although the U.S. rules moved to a ratio based on Earnings Before Interest and Taxes (EBIT) for years after 2022. Interest expenses in excess of the allowable amount would not be deductible but could be carried over to past or future years.

The rules would apply to an entity's net interest expense (its interest expenses in excess of its gross interest receipts) in order to accommodate intergroup payments of interest.

As an optional relief measure, an entity would be allowed to deduct interest expenses in excess of the allowable percentage of its EBITDA if the net arm's-length interest expense to EBITDA ratio of the multinational group of which the entity is a part is greater than the entity's ratio. The rationale for this alternative worldwide group rule is that if a resident

比的利息费用。这种全球集团替代规则的基本原理是，如果某个居民实体的杠杆比率接近全球集团的杠杆比率，则该居民实体所要求的利息扣除导致的税基侵蚀是可以接受的，不属于超额利息。这一可选的全球集团规则要求纳税人汇集有关于跨国集团整体的财务信息，并由税务管理人员对其进行审计，为此必须使用的是财务会计信息而非税务信息。欧盟的收益剥离规则允许属于合并集团的各个实体扣除其超额利息，但不得超过集团的净利息费用与 EBITDA 之比。此外，如果实体的权益与总资产之比加上 2 个百分点，等于或高于整个集团的这一比率，则实体可以扣除其所有利息费用。美国的收益剥离规则没有规定任何全球集团救济规则。

这些规则旨在适用于利息和所有其他经济上等同于利息的款项支付，即采用经济实质原则。

对于不属于跨国集团的国内实体，可选择是否适用收益剥离规则。如果不适用，此种单独的实体可以扣除所有的利息费用。

允许实体将不予扣除的利息费用结转至以往或今后年度，也可将任何未使用的利息扣除额度从某一年结转至其后续年度。

为长期公共利益项目融资所产生的利息费用可以除外，前提是该项目通过无追索权债务进行融资，项目所得按章纳税，所借入资金不得出借给其他实体。欧盟的规则对符合公共利益的长期公共基础设施项目，作了例外规定。

各国可能希望通过有针对性的规则，防止人为安排，并解决金融服务和保险公司方面的特殊考虑。有针对性的反规避规则的例子，包括资本弱化规则和涉及背对背融资安排的规则。

与大多数国家的资本弱化规则不同，BEPS 第 4 项行动计划所建议的和欧盟及美国采用的收益剥离规则，并非仅仅适用于支付给非居民的利息，而是适用于居民实体的所有利息费用，但有少数例外。因此，这些收益剥离规则普遍性地针对超额利息费用扣除，而不是专门针对跨境税基侵蚀。正如上文已经指出的，欧盟收益剥离规则的广泛运用，其原因在于避免与欧盟法律的非歧视保护规定相

entity is leveraged at a ratio approximating the global group's leverage ratio, the base erosion resulting from the interest deductions claimed by the resident entity is acceptable and not excessive. The optional worldwide group rule requires taxpayers to assemble, and tax administrators to audit, the financial information with respect to the multinational group as a whole; it would be necessary to use financial accounting information rather than tax information for this purpose. The EU earnings-stripping rules allow entities that are part of a consolidated group to deduct their excessive interest up to the group's ratio of net interest expense to EBITDA. Further, an entity is entitled to deduct all its interest expenses where the entity's equity to total assets ratio plus two percentage points is equal to or higher than the equivalent ratio of the group as a whole. The U.S. earnings-stripping rules do not provide any worldwide group relief rule.

The rules are intended to apply to interest and all other payments that are economically equivalent to interest, applying an economic substance approach.

The application of earnings-stripping rules to domestic entities that are not part of a multinational group is optional. If the rules are not applied to such stand-alone entities, they would be entitled to deduct all their interest expenses.

Entities are allowed to carry over disallowed interest expenses to past or future years as well as carry forward any unused interest deductibility room from one year to future years.

An exception for interest expenses incurred to finance long-term public benefit projects could be adopted as long as the project is financed with nonrecourse debt, the income from the project is subject to tax, and the borrowed funds are not loaned to another entity. The EU rules provide an exception for long-term public infrastructure projects that are in the general public interest.

Countries may wish to adopt targeted rules to prevent artificial arrangements and to address the special considerations of financial services and insurance companies. Examples of targeted anti-avoidance rules include thin capitalization rules and rules to deal with back-to-back financing arrangements.

Unlike most countries' thin capitalization rules, the earnings-stripping rules recommended in BEPS Action 4 and adopted by the EU and U.S. apply to all interest expenses of resident entities, subject to certain narrow exceptions, rather than just to interest paid to nonresidents. Thus, these earnings-stripping rules are targeted at the deduction of excessive interest expenses generally, not at cross-border base erosion specifically. As noted above, the reason for the broad application of the EU earnings- stripping rules is to avoid any conflict with the nondiscrimination protections of EU law. Other countries may also decide to adopt broad earnings-stripping

抵触。其他国家也可以决定采用覆盖面广的收益剥离规则，以避免与其税收协定中的非歧视条款产生冲突。根据 OECD 协定范本和联合国协定范本第 24（4）和（5）条，禁止缔约国一方对支付给缔约国另一方居民的利息（和其他款项）的处理劣于对支付给其本国居民的类似款项的处理，并禁止缔约国一方对由缔约国另一方居民拥有或控制的居民公司的处理劣于其他居民公司。第 8 章第 8.8.1 节将讨论 OECD 协定范本和联合国协定范本的非歧视条款。

收益剥离规则的一项重要优势是，如果跨国公司集团将利润从高税收国家转移到低税收国家，那么，高税收国家的税基中可扣除的利息将相应减少。

以收益为基础对利息扣除加以限制，存在着一个重要的问题，即如何处理一个实体在某一年度出现亏损的情形。一般来说，无论借贷资金的使用是否实际产生应税所得，利息都应该可以扣除。人们普遍认为，以实际产生所得作为利息扣除的先决条件，并不是妥善的税收政策，因为这会阻碍纳税人从事有风险的投资活动。因此，为了避免使承受较大风险或具有周期性的企业处于不利地位，各国可以规定允许结转所有未予扣除的利息。

各国自行选择收益的某一固定百分比，作为允许扣除利息的限额。规则的目的是允许跨国集团扣除所有属于从事经营活动合理成本的独立交易第三方的利息费用，但不允许扣除侵蚀一个国家的税基的超额利息费用。大多数国家采用的限额是收益的 25% ~ 30%。

7.3 受控外国企业规则

7.3.1 引言

如第 3 章第 3.3.1 节所述，居民避免其全球所得受到征税的最有效方法之一，是使用 CFC 和其他法律实体收取来源于境外的所得。通过设立外国公司或其他法律实体（如信托），并由其获得境外来源所得，可以轻而易举地推迟或完全规

rules to avoid any conflict with the Non-discrimination article of their tax treaties. Under Article 24(4) and (5) of the OECD and UN Model Treaties, one contracting state is prohibited from treating interest (and other disbursements) paid to residents of the other contracting state less favorably than similar payments to its own residents and from treating resident corporations owned or controlled by residents of the other contracting state less favorably than other resident corporations. The nondiscrimination article of the OECD and UN Model Treaties is discussed in Chapter 8, section 8.8.1.

One important advantage of an earnings-stripping rule is that if a multinational group of companies shifts profits from a high-tax country to a low-tax country, the deduction of interest against the high-tax country's tax base is reduced accordingly.

One serious problem in restricting interest deductions on the basis of earnings is how to deal with situations in which an entity has a loss for a year. Typically, interest is deductible whether or not taxable income actually results from the use of borrowed funds. It is generally accepted that it would not be good tax policy to make interest deductions dependent on the actual production of income because that would discourage taxpayers from engaging in risky ventures. Therefore, to avoid penalizing businesses that are very risky or cyclical in nature, countries can provide a carryover for any disallowed interest.

The selection of a specific percentage of earnings as an allowable limit for interest deductions is arbitrary. The objective is to allow deductions for all the arm's-length third-party interest expenses of a multinational group that are reasonable costs of doing business but to disallow deductions for interest expenses that are excessive and represent an unacceptable erosion of a country's tax base. Most countries have adopted a limitation of 25% to 30% of earnings.

7.3 CFC RULES

7.3.1 Introduction

As noted in Chapter 3, section 3.3.1, one of the most effective ways for residents to avoid tax on their worldwide income is the use of CFCs and other legal entities to earn foreign source income. Domestic tax on foreign source income can easily be deferred or avoided completely by establishing a foreign corporation or other legal entity, such as a trust, to earn the income. Because the foreign corporation or trust is generally considered to be a separate taxable entity

避对境外来源所得的国内税收。由于外国公司或信托通常被视为单独的应纳税实体，而不是其控股股东或受益人为其居民的国家的居民，因此当该外国公司或信托取得所得时，对这些股东或受益人并无纳税义务。

当上述公司或信托支付分配款项时，相关股东或受益人的居民国应对这些股东或受益人予以征税。但是，如果居民公司在外国公司中存在实质性权益，那么，许多国家对因此外国公司分配的股息免于征收居民国税收。即使对分配款项应该予以征税，居民国税收也会被推迟至收到相关分配款项之时，这可能是在外国实体实现所得之后若干年。因此，通过外国实体获取所得，有可能导致推迟或完全规避居民国税收。上述外国公司或信托应付的外国税收较低或为零时，这种好处得以最大化。因此，这一问题产生的关键是在避税地设立的 CFC 或信托。

通过利用受控外国实体避税和递延纳税的问题，在消极投资所得方面最为突出，因为很容易将此类所得转移到设在避税地的离岸实体，或累积在这些实体之中。例如，假设 A 国某居民公司从债券中获得 1000 元的利息所得，A 国的税率为 40%。如果该公司在不征税的避税地设立全资子公司，并将其债券转让给该子公司，则该公司就可以递延纳税 400 元。子公司获得的利息所得可能不会被征 A 国预提税，或者因为该利息并非来源于 A 国，或者 A 国对该利息免征预提税。即使利息需要缴纳 A 国预提税，只要公司税税率和预提税率之间存在差异（这·差异有可能相当可观），该公司也可以推迟缴纳 A 国税收。如果 A 国对从外国公司获得的股息规定了参股免税，那么，通过债券转让给子公司所得到的税收利益将更大。

如果居民国对居民从外国公司和其他实体取得的分配款项予以征税，居民国税收会被推迟，但不会被完全规避。如果外国子公司将股息分配给其居民母公司或母公司转让其在外国子公司的股份，则居民国可能会对分配款项或转让收益征税。因此，在某个具体情形下，递延纳税的利益取决于国内和国外税率之间的差异、递延税款的回报率和递延的时间。根据标准现值计算，无限期递延纳税几乎等同于免税。

and not resident in the country where its controlling shareholders or beneficiaries are resident, those shareholders or beneficiaries are not taxable when the income is earned by the foreign corporation or trust.

When distributions from the corporation or trust are paid, the shareholders or beneficiaries may be taxable by the residence country. However, many countries exempt dividends from foreign corporations from residence country tax if the dividends are received on shares owned by a resident corporation with a substantial interest in the foreign corporation. Even if the distributions are taxable, the residence country tax is postponed until distributions are received, which may be several years after the foreign entity earns the income. Thus, earning income through a foreign entity may result in deferral or complete avoidance of residence country tax. The benefit is greatest when the foreign tax on the income of the foreign corporation or trust is low or nil. Therefore, the problem arises primarily from the establishment of CFCs or trusts in tax havens.

The problem of tax avoidance and deferral through the use of controlled foreign entities is most pronounced with respect to passive investment income because such income can easily be diverted to or accumulated in an offshore entity in a tax haven. For example, assume that a corporation resident in Country A earns interest income of 1,000 from bonds and the tax rate in Country A is 40%. If the corporation establishes a wholly owned subsidiary in a tax haven that does not impose tax, it can defer tax of 400 by transferring the bonds to the subsidiary. The interest income derived by the subsidiary may not be subject to Country A's withholding tax because either the interest is not sourced in Country A or the interest is exempt from withholding tax. However, even if the interest is subject to Country A's withholding tax, the corporation can defer Country A's tax to the extent of the difference between the corporate tax rate and the withholding tax rate (which may be substantial). The tax benefit from the transfer of the bonds to the subsidiary will be even greater if Country A provides a participation exemption for dividends received from foreign corporations.

Where a residence country imposes tax on distributions received by residents from foreign corporations and other entities, residence country tax is deferred but not avoided entirely. Where a foreign subsidiary distributes dividends to its resident parent corporation or the parent corporation disposes of its shares in the foreign subsidiary, the residence country will presumably tax the distribution or gain. Therefore, the benefit of deferral in any particular case depends on the difference between the domestic and foreign tax rates, the rate of return on the deferred taxes, and the period of deferral. Under standard present value calculations, indefinite deferral is nearly equivalent to exemption.

不少国家制定了详尽的法规制度，防止或限制利用 CFC 递延或规避国内税收。美国率先在 1962 年实施了 CFC 规则（F 分部）；这些规则的基础是 1937 年针对个人利用外国公司而制定的类似规则（个人控股外国公司规则）。关于 F 分部规则的制定，各方观点众说纷纭。最初的提议是要针对所有的 CFC 所得，消除递延纳税；美国的跨国公司则认为，只应该针对确切无疑的消极所得，不予递延纳税。最终获得通过的法规，在上述两种观点之间，采取了折中的做法。关于 F 分部的相关规定，时至今日仍然争议不断。多年以来，美国的跨国公司一直表示，与其他国家的 CFC 规则相比较而言，F 分部规则更为宽泛，且过于严厉，将美国的跨国公司置于不利的竞争地位。2001 年 1 月，美国财政部发布了一份关于 F 分部的报告（《通过美国受控外国企业推迟取得所得：政策研究》，2000 年 12 月）。该报告得出结论，F 分部的基本政策是恰当的，并不存在具有说服力的证据能够说明，美国跨国公司的国际竞争力受到了 F 分部规则的不利影响。

自美国于 1962 年实行 F 分部规则以来，若干其他资本输出国家也制定了 CFC 规则，以保护其税基。根据 OECD 的统计，截至 2019 年中，接近 50 个国家颁布了 CFC 规则，这些国家中包含所有欧盟成员国。这是一个稳定的发展趋势，很可能会继续下去。

CFC 法规的基本格局在所有国家中都大同小异。对于设立在零征税或低征税国家的外国公司，具有控制权或拥有实质性权益的居民股东，应就其在外国公司的全部或部分所得中相应比例的所得份额，当期缴纳居民国税收，无论此所得是否已实际向居民股东进行了分配。如果外国公司从事正当的离岸商业活动，那么，CFC 规则并不普遍适用于由这些活动产生的所得。例如，假设 A 国居民 A 公司拥有低税收国家居民 CFC 的所有股份。该 CFC 获得 1000 元消极所得，并就该所得向其居民国缴纳税款 100 元。该 CFC 没有将其任何税后所得分配给 A 公司。如果 A 国实行 CFC 规则，则 A 公司应就 CFC 的所得 1000 元，在 A 国纳税（尽管 A 公司尚未从 CFC 获得该所得的任何分配），并将因 CFC 缴纳的 100 元税款获得抵免。因此，如果 A 国以 30% 的税率征税，那么，A 公司将缴纳税款 200

Several countries have adopted detailed statutory rules to prevent or restrict the use of CFCs to defer or avoid domestic tax. The U.S. was the first country to adopt CFC rules (Subpart F) in 1962; the rules were based on similar rules (the foreign personal holding company rules) adopted in 1937 that were targeted at the use of foreign corporations by individuals. The adoption of the Subpart F rules was very controversial. The rules that were finally enacted represented a compromise between the original proposal to eliminate deferral for all income of CFCs and the arguments of U.S.-based multinationals that deferral should be eliminated only with respect to clearly passive income. Subpart F remains controversial today. For many years, U.S. multinationals have argued that the Subpart F rules are broader and tougher than the CFC rules of other countries and that they put U.S. multinationals at a competitive disadvantage. In January 2001, the U.S. Treasury issued a report on Subpart F (*The Deferral of Income Earned Through U.S. Controlled Foreign Corporations: A Policy Study*, December 2000), which concluded that the basic policy of Subpart F was appropriate and there was no convincing evidence that the international competitiveness of U.S. multinationals was adversely affected by the rules.

Since the U.S. adopted Subpart F in 1962, several other capital-exporting countries have enacted CFC rules to protect their tax base. According to the OECD, as of mid-2019, almost fifty countries, including all EU member countries, had enacted CFC rules. This is a well-established trend that will likely continue.

The basic pattern of CFC legislation is similar in all countries. Resident shareholders that control, or have a substantial interest in, a foreign corporation established in a no-tax or low-tax country are subject to residence country tax currently on their proportionate share of all or some of the income of the foreign corporation, whether or not the income is actually distributed to them. If a foreign corporation is engaged in legitimate commercial activities offshore, the CFC rules do not generally apply to the income generated by those activities. For example, assume that ACo, a resident of Country A, owns all the shares of a CFC resident in a low-tax country. The CFC earns passive income of 1,000 and pays tax of 100 on that income to its country of residence. The CFC does not distribute any of its after-tax income to ACo. If Country A has CFC rules, ACo would be subject to tax by Country A on the CFC's income of 1,000 (despite the fact that ACo has not received any distribution of that income from the CFC) and would receive credit for the tax paid by the CFC of 100. Thus, if Country A imposes tax at a rate of 30%, ACo would pay tax of 200 (300 less a foreign tax credit of 100), which is exactly the amount of tax that ACo would have paid

元（300 元减去外国税款抵免 100 元），这正是 A 公司若是直接获得该项所得本应缴纳的税款数额。

CFC 法规的基本结构反映了两项相互矛盾的政策。首先是希望防止避税，并推进第 1 章第 1.3 节讨论的公平和经济效率的传统目标。与此同时，各国一般并不希望不合理地干预居民公司在国外市场的竞争能力。在采取了 CFC 措施的每一个国家，都存在这两项政策之间的平衡，尽管每个国家实现这种平衡的方式不尽相同。除巴西外，没有任何国家全面消除使用 CFC 所产生的利益，大多数国家将其 CFC 规则局限于设立在低税收国家的 CFC 和 CFC 获得的消极收入。与此相反，巴西的 CFC 规则适用于巴西居民拥有 20% 或更多股份的所有 CFC 的全部（积极和消极）所得，与 CFC 为其居民的国家无关。新西兰最初的 CFC 规则也与其他国家有显著差异，几乎完全消除递延纳税；这些规则适用于由新西兰居民控制的所有 CFC 的全部（积极和消极）所得，但设立在七个列明国家者除外。然而，新西兰的 CFC 规则在 2010 年进行了修订，将积极经营所得排除在 CFC 规则的适用范围之外。

2017 年，美国异乎寻常地采取措施，对美国纳税人的 CFC 所得中，超过 CFC 有形资产被认定的 10% 回报率以上的部分，征收 10.5% 的最低税（2026 年增至 13.25%）。此项新最低税所适用的所得被称为“全球无形资产低税所得”，即 GILTI。因此，F 分部规则下未按美国公司税完整税率纳税的 CFC 所得（多数积极经营所得），将受制于该最低税率，并且，CFC 针对该所得缴纳的外国税款中，只有 80% 可用于抵免该最低税。

7.3.2 CFC 规则的结构性特征

虽然各国的 CFC 规则存在着明显的差异，但是，在大多数国家中，此类规则在若干基本结构要素还是具有相同之处。以下讨论 CFC 税收规则的这些方面。

if it had earned the income directly.

The basic structure of CFC legislation reflects two competing policies. First, there is a desire to prevent tax avoidance and to advance the traditional goals of fairness and economic efficiency discussed in Chapter 1, section 1.3. At the same time, countries generally do not want to interfere unreasonably in the ability of resident corporations to compete in foreign markets. In every country with CFC measures, there is a balancing of these two policies, although the balance is struck differently in every country. Other than Brazil, no country entirely eliminates the benefits from the use of CFCs, and most countries limit the application of their CFC rules to CFCs established in low-tax countries and passive income earned by CFCs. In contrast, the Brazilian CFC rules apply to all the income, active and passive, of all CFCs in which Brazilian residents own 20% or more of the shares, irrespective of the country in which the CFCs are resident. The original New Zealand CFC rules also differed markedly from other countries' CFC rules and came close to eliminating deferral entirely; they applied to all the income, active and passive, of all CFCs controlled by New Zealand residents, except those established in seven listed countries. However, the New Zealand CFC rules were revised in 2010 to exclude active business income from the application of the CFC rules.

In 2017, the U.S. took the extraordinary step of imposing a minimum tax of 10.5% (increasing to 13.25% in 2026) of the income of CFCs of U.S. taxpayers in excess of a deemed 10% rate of return on a CFC's tangible assets. The income subject to this new minimum tax is called GILTI. Thus, income of a CFC that is not subject to the full U.S. corporate tax rate under the Subpart F rules (most active business income) will be subject to this minimum tax, and only 80% of the foreign tax paid by the CFC on that income is creditable against the minimum tax.

7.3.2 Structural Features of CFC Rules

Although CFC rules vary considerably, several fundamental structural aspects of the rules are the same in most countries. These aspects of the taxation of CFCs are discussed below.

7.3.2.1 CFC 的定义

除少数例外，各国都将其 CFC 规则的范围限定为如下实体获得的所得：（1）非居民实体，（2）与其所有者分别纳税的公司或类似实体，以及（3）由国内股东控制，或国内股东在其中拥有实质性权益的实体。依据导管或穿透税收规则而应予纳税的实体（如合伙企业），则不在 CFC 规则的范围之内，但前提是外国合伙企业的居民合伙人就其在合伙企业所得中所占的份额在居民国纳税。实体的非居民身份根据居民国通常的法律实体居民身份判定规则（公司注册地或管理机构所在地，或两者同时满足）确定的。第 2 章第 2.2.2 节讨论了公司和法律实体的居民判定规则。

尽管貌似奇怪，但有些国家，如法国，将其 CFC 规则适用于外国分支机构或常设机构。将 CFC 规则扩展到外国分支机构或常设机构，在以下情况下是有必要的，即一国对通过外国分支机构或常设机构取得的所得免税，并且免税所得包括消极所得，而该消极所得若是由 CFC 取得，则将受制于该国的 CFC 规则。如果免于征税的经由外国分支机构或常设机构获得的所得仅限于积极经营所得（即如该所得由 CFC 获得，也不受制于 CFC 规则），就没有必要对外国分支机构或常设机构适用 CFC 规则。

并不意外的是，正如“受控外国企业”规则的名称所示，大多数 CFC 法规仅适用于受某些国内股东控制的外国公司。出于此目的，控制一般是指拥有超过 50% 的已发行有表决权股份。一些国家扩展了控制概念，将拥有价值等于或超过公司已发行股份总价值 50% 的股份包括在内。还有一些国家的规定将拥有少于 50% 的有表决权股份的一些情形也视同居民控制一家外国公司。例如，澳大利亚和新西兰的 CFC 规则认定，如果没有非居民拥有该外国公司的表决控制权，居民持有外国公司 40% 或以上的有表决权股份，即为对该外国公司的控制。

只有少数国家采用了实际控制标准，以此作为对基本法律控制标准的补充。

7.3.2.1 Definition of a CFC

With a few exceptions, countries restrict the scope of their CFC rules to income derived by entities (1) that are nonresident, (2) that are corporations or similar entities taxed separately from their owners, and (3) that are controlled by domestic shareholders or in which domestic shareholders have a substantial interest. Entities (such as partnerships) that are taxable on a conduit or flow-through basis are not within the scope of the CFC rules if the resident partners of a foreign partnership are subject to residence country tax on their share of the partnership's income. The status of an entity as a nonresident is established in accordance with the residence country's normal residence rules for legal entities (place of incorporation or place of management, or both). The residence rules for corporations and legal entities are discussed in Chapter 2, section 2.2.2.

Although it may seem strange, some countries, such as France, apply their CFC rules to foreign branches or PEs. The extension of CFC rules to foreign branches or PEs is necessary where a country exempts income earned through a foreign branch or PE and the exempt income includes passive income that, if earned by a CFC, would be subject to the country's CFC rules. The application of the CFC rules to foreign branches or PEs is not necessary if the exemption for income earned through foreign branches or PEs is limited to active business income (i.e., income that would not be subject to the CFC rules if it were earned by a CFC).

Not surprisingly, given the title of "controlled foreign company" rules, most CFC legislation applies only to foreign corporations that are *controlled* by certain domestic shareholders. For this purpose, control generally means the ownership of more than 50% of the outstanding voting shares. Some countries extend the concept of control to include ownership of shares having a value equal to more than 50% of the total value of the outstanding shares of the corporation. Other countries have rules that presume residents to control a foreign corporation in certain circumstances, even if they own less than 50% of the voting shares. For example, the Australian and New Zealand CFC rules deem a resident to control a foreign corporation if the resident owns 40% or more of the voting shares of the foreign corporation and no nonresident person has voting control of the corporation.

Only a few countries have adopted a de facto control test as a supplement to the basic de jure control test. Under a de facto control test, a resident taxpayer is considered

在实际控制标准中，如果根据所有的事实和情形，居民纳税人即使没有表决控制权，也有途径控制外国公司的事务，则该居民纳税人也被视为控制该外国公司。例如，如果某纳税人持有某公司 20% 的股份，而其余股份的持有十分分散，则该纳税人可能实际上拥有该公司的控制权。实际控制标准对纳税人来说具有相当大的不确定性，税务机关也很难应用。

在控制方面设置条件的理由是体现公平。如果外国公司的居民股东并不具备足够的法律或实际权力或者影响力，来决定外国公司从事的活动（即外国公司是否取得适用 CFC 规则的收入），或要求外国公司分配其收入，那么，就外国公司的未分配收入，向居民股东征税就是不公平的。

巴西、丹麦和葡萄牙等部分国家，不愿接受在控制判定上的复杂性和局限性。这些国家将其 CFC 规则适用于居民在其中拥有实质性所有权权益的外国公司（巴西为 20%，葡萄牙和丹麦为 25%）。在 2004 年之前，法国将其 CFC 规则适用于持有 CFC10% 或更多股份的法国居民。

CFC 规则中的控制通常包括间接控制。因此，一家避税地公司的股份由另一家由居民控制的外国公司所拥有，那么，CFC 规则就是无可避免的。例如，如果某居民拥有 A 公司 60% 的有表决权股份，而 A 公司又拥有第二家外国公司 B 公司 50% 以上的有表决权股份，则 B 公司即被视为该居民的 CFC。间接控制比例通常是通过将纳税人在一家公司中的权益比例与该公司在其他公司中的权益比例相乘来确定的，如此延续至更多层级。例如，如果 A 公司拥有 B 公司 40% 的股份，而 B 公司拥有 C 公司 30% 的股份，则认为 A 公司拥有 C 公司 12% 的股份。但是，如果一家公司控制了另一家公司，则第二家公司应被视为拥有后者所拥有的任何其他公司的所有股份。例如，如果 A 公司拥有 B 公司 51% 的股份，而 B 公司拥有 C 公司 51% 的股份，则应认为 A 公司拥有 B 公司拥有的 C 公司的所有股份，而不仅仅是 26.01%（51%×51%）。因此，应将 A 公司视为控制 B 公司和 C 公司（以及由 C 公司控制的任何公司）。

大多数国家还制定了推定所有权规则，防止纳税人通过将股份持有分散在关

to control a foreign corporation if, based on all the facts and circumstances, the taxpayer has the means to control the affairs of the corporation even where it does not have voting control. For example, a taxpayer that owns 20% of the shares of a corporation may have de facto control of the corporation if the rest of the shares are widely held. A de facto control test involves considerable uncertainty for taxpayers and is also difficult for the tax authorities to apply.

The rationale for the control requirement is fairness. It would be unfair to tax resident shareholders on the undistributed income of a foreign corporation if they do not have sufficient legal or actual power or influence over the foreign corporation to determine the activities it engages in (i.e., whether it earns income subject to the CFC rules) or to require it to distribute its income.

A few countries, such as Brazil, Denmark, and Portugal, have rejected the complexity and the limitations of a control test. They apply their CFC rules to foreign corporations in which a resident has a substantial ownership interest (20% in the case of Brazil and 25% in Portugal and Denmark). Until 2004, France applied its CFC rules to French residents owning 10% or more of the shares of a CFC.

Control for purposes of CFC rules usually includes indirect control. Thus, the CFC rules cannot be avoided by having the shares of a tax haven corporation owned by another foreign corporation that is controlled by residents. For example, if a resident owns 60% of the voting shares of ACo, which in turn owns more than 50% of the voting shares of a second foreign corporation, BCo, BCo is considered to be a CFC of the resident. Indirect control is usually determined by multiplying a taxpayer's interest in one corporation by the corporation's interest in other corporations, and so on. For example, if ACo owns 40% of the shares of BCo and BCo owns 30% of the shares of CCo, ACo is considered to own 12% of CCo. However, if one corporation controls another corporation, the second corporation should be considered to own all the shares of any other corporations owned by it. For example, if ACo owns 51% of the shares of BCo and BCo owns 51% of the shares of CCo, ACo would be considered to own all the shares of CCo owned by BCo, rather than just 26.01% (51% × 51%). Therefore, ACo would be considered to control BCo and CCo (and any corporations controlled by CCo).

Most countries also have constructive ownership rules to prevent taxpayers from avoiding the CFC rules by fragmenting the ownership of shares among related persons. For example, if one resident corporation owns 40% and another resident corporation owns 20% of the voting shares of a foreign corporation, the foreign corporation will be a CFC of both resident

联方之间，以规避 CFC 规则。例如，如果一家居民公司拥有某外国公司 40% 的有表决权的股份，而另一家居民公司拥有该外国公司 20% 的有表决权的股份，那么，如果这两家居民公司存在关联关系（如同为另一家居民公司的全资子公司），则上述外国公司将成为这两家居民公司的 CFC。在此，各方之间是否具有关联关系，系根据相关国家的国内法确定。

在一些国家中，控制必须集中于少量居民股东时，才能适用 CFC 规则。例如，澳大利亚、加拿大和新西兰要求外国公司的控制必须集中在五个或更少的居民股东。根据美国 F 分部规则，只有持有外国公司至少 10% 股份的美国股东才被计算在内，以确定该外国公司是否为 CFC。与此不同的是，在其他国家，如挪威和德国，即使是众多居民股东持有的外国公司，也被视为 CFC。

集中所有权操作与控制标准的基本原理有关。如果外国公司的股份被众多居民股东分散持有，这些股东就不可能对公司行使足够的权力，来决定其盈利活动或要求公司进行分配。集中所有权操作需要制定推定所有权规则，也许还需依据反规避规则。

7.3.2.2 指定管辖区或全球方法

CFC 规则的主要焦点是低税收实体。因此，大多数国家的 CFC 规则局限于位于被认定和指定为避税地的国家的 CFC（**“指定管辖区方法”**）。然而，一些国家，如巴西、加拿大和美国，将其 CFC 规则应用于 CFC 取得或收到的某些特定类型的所得，无论 CFC 是避税地居民还是高税收国家居民（**“全球方法”**）。

在指定管辖区方法中，外国公司在指定避税地的居民身份对 CFC 规则的适用至关重要。法律通常对避税地的性质作出一般性定义。然后，税务机关通过发布被视为避税地的国家或不被视为避税地的国家的清单，来补充该定义。然而，有些国家只是使用避税地或非避税地国家的清单，而对于何为避税地并没有任何法律定义。由于设立在未被指定为避税地国家的所有外国公司都不受 CFC 规则

corporations if they are related because, for example, they are both wholly owned subsidiaries of another resident corporation. Whether persons are related for this purpose is determined under the country's domestic law.

In some countries, control must be concentrated in a small number of resident shareholders in order for the CFC rules to apply. For example, Australia, Canada, and New Zealand require that control of a foreign corporation must be concentrated in five or fewer resident shareholders. Under the U.S. Subpart F rules, only U.S. shareholders owning at least 10% of the shares of the foreign corporation are counted in determining whether the foreign corporation is a CFC. In contrast, in other countries, such as Norway and Germany, even foreign corporations that are widely held by resident shareholders are considered to be CFCs.

The concentrated-ownership requirement is related to the rationale for a control test. Where the shares of a foreign corporation are widely held by resident shareholders, those shareholders are unlikely to be able to exercise sufficient power over the corporation to determine its income-earning activities or require it to make distributions. A concentrated-ownership requirement requires constructive ownership rules and perhaps anti-avoidance rules.

7.3.2.2 Designated Jurisdiction or Global Approach

The primary focus of CFC rules is low-taxed entities. As a result, the CFC rules of most countries are limited to CFCs located in countries that are defined and designated to be tax havens (the "**designated jurisdiction approach**"). However, a few countries, such as Brazil, Canada, and the U.S., apply their CFC rules to certain specified categories of income earned or received by a CFC, regardless of whether the CFC is resident in a tax haven or a high-tax country (the "**global approach**").

Under the designated jurisdiction approach, the residence of a foreign corporation in a designated tax haven is crucial to the application of the CFC rules. The legislation usually provides a general definition of what constitutes a tax haven; the tax authorities then supplement that definition by issuing a list of countries that are regarded as tax haven countries or that are not regarded as tax havens. However, some countries simply use a list of tax haven or nontax haven countries without any statutory definition of what constitutes a tax haven. Because all foreign corporations established in countries that are not designated as tax havens are exempt from the CFC rules, the compliance and administrative burden of the rules is reduced compared to the

的约束，因此，与全球方法相比，此种规则的遵从和管理负担都相对较轻。而在全球方法中，外国公司的居民身份并不相关；规则适用于全球范围，但仅适用于特定的收入类型。这种方法背后的理论是，所有国家，即使在总体属于高税收的国家，税收制度的某些方面也存在享受税收优惠或适用低税率的所得。

避税地的一般定义总是基于对外国和居民国征收的税收的比较。如果某外国相关税种税率实际上与居民国大致相同，则不应将该外国视为避税地，因为纳税人不能将其用于推迟或避免大量的居民国税收。国内税率和外国税率的比较可以基于：

—— 名义税率；

—— 实际税率；或

—— 某个 CFC 实际缴纳的外国税款。

使用名义税率来确定避税地是有问题的，因为它忽略了外国可能提供的各种优惠的扣除、豁免、抵免或专项减除。实际税率的使用也存在问题，因为很难确定实际税率，而且必须每年针对居民公司的 CFC 为其居民的每个国家确定实际税率。此外，仅仅因为一个国家的实际税率很高，并不一定意味着作为该国居民的某个 CFC 不会只需要缴纳较低的外国税收。虽然有些国家采用实际税率法，但大多数国家都将重点放在由一个 CFC 实际缴纳的外国税款上。

将一个 CFC 实际缴纳的外国税款与假如该 CFC 为居民公司而应缴纳的名义国内税款进行比较，是理论上正确的方法，因为此方法着重于每个特定 CFC 的情况。但是，这种方法给纳税人带来了沉重的遵从负担，因为必须根据居民国的规则，重新计算 CFC 的所得，以确定名义国内税款的数额。

外国税收与居民国税收的具体关系，在各国之间存在着较大的差异。一些国家将避税地定义为其税率低于居民国税率 55%（瑞典）、60%（芬兰）、662/3%（法国和挪威），或 75%（西班牙和英国）的国家。其他国家仅通过依据国外税率来定义避税地。例如，德国和日本将避税地定义为税率低于 25% 的

global approach. In contrast, under the global approach, the residence of the foreign corporation is irrelevant; the rules apply on a worldwide basis but only to specific categories of income. The theory behind this approach is that all countries, even generally high-tax countries, have aspects of their tax system that permit the earning of preferentially taxed or low-taxed income.

The general definition of a tax haven is invariably based on a comparison of the taxes levied in the foreign country and the residence country. If the foreign country actually levies taxes at approximately the same rates as the residence country, the foreign country should not be considered to be a tax haven because it cannot be used to defer or avoid a significant amount of residence country tax. The comparison of domestic and foreign tax rates can be based on:

– nominal tax rates;
– effective tax rates; or
– the actual foreign tax paid by a particular CFC.

The use of nominal tax rates to identify tax havens is problematic because it ignores generous deductions, exemptions, credits, or allowances that may be provided by a foreign country. The use of effective tax rates is also problematic because effective tax rates are difficult to determine and would have to be determined annually for every country in which a CFC of a resident corporation is resident. Moreover, just because a country has high effective tax rates does not necessarily mean that a particular CFC resident in that country may not be subject to low foreign taxes. Although some countries use the effective-tax-rate approach, most countries focus on the actual foreign tax paid by a CFC.

The comparison of the actual foreign tax paid by a CFC and the notional domestic tax that the CFC would have paid as a resident corporation is the theoretically correct approach because it focuses on the situation of each particular CFC. However, this approach imposes onerous compliance burdens on taxpayers because the income of a CFC must be recomputed in accordance with residence country rules in order to determine the amount of the notional domestic tax.

The specific relationship between the foreign tax and the residence country tax varies considerably. Some countries define a tax haven as a country whose tax rate is less than 55% (Sweden), 60% (Finland), 66 2/3% (France and Norway), or 75% (Spain and the U.K.) of the residence country rate. Other countries define a tax haven simply by reference to the foreign rate. For example, Germany and Japan define a tax haven as a country that levies tax of less than 25%; Korea uses 15%. It should be noted that even a small difference between the foreign

国家；韩国使用的标准是 15%。应当指出的是，即使外国税率和国内税率之间存在微小差异，也足以促使居民纳税人将（很容易转移的）消极所得转移到位于外国的 CFC。

由于难以通过比较避税地的税率与国内税率来界定避税地，特别是为了避免给征纳双方带来的不确定性，大多数采用指定管辖区方法的国家，都对其避税地定义辅之以避税地国家或非避税地国家或两者的清单。这种清单可以是法律性的（包括在构成 CFC 规则的法律之中）或管理性的（由税务机关发布）。这种清单旨在为纳税人和税务官员，针对设立在某一特定国家的 CFC 是否应当适用 CFC 规则，提供具体的指引。这种清单差异很大：有些清单约束性地将一国列为避税地或非避税地（即具有法律约束力），而另一些只是建立有讨论余地的推定。更为复杂的清单则承认，总体来说属于高税收的某个国家，仍然可能对某些类型的所得或实体很少征税或不征税。因此，这些国家可能被列入非避税地名单，但附明享受优惠性的所得或实体的某些例外。所以，不享受这些国家低税收制度的 CFC，才得以免于适用 CFC 规则。

与指定管辖区方法相比，全球方法更为精确。如上所述，全球方法不关注 CFC 的居民国，而具体考察所有居民纳税人的所有 CFC 从事的每一项交易，以确定从此交易中产生的所得的性质。如果该公司具有**“污点”所得**（稍后讨论），则该所得应归属于公司的国内股东，由其承担纳税义务，同时，通常可以抵免该所得所缴纳的外国税款。因此，如果位于高税收国家的 CFC 取得污点所得，则有可能对其适用 CFC 规则。相比之下，虽然指定管辖区法并非如此精确，但大幅度降低了 CFC 规则的遵从和管理负担。

7.3.2.3 可归属所得的定义和计算

有些国家在对国内股东就其 CFC 所得进行征税时，采用所谓的**实体法**。根据这种方法，CFC 规则通常会规定，对主要从事真实经营活动的某些 CFC 予以

and domestic tax rates may be sufficient to induce resident taxpayers to shift passive income (which is easily shifted) to a CFC in a foreign country.

As a result of the difficulties that arise in defining a tax haven by comparing its tax rate to the domestic tax rate—in particular, uncertainty for both taxpayers and tax authorities—most countries that use a designated jurisdiction approach have supplemented their definition of a tax haven with a list of tax haven countries, or nontax haven countries, or both. The list may be either legislative (included in the legislation making up the CFC rules) or administrative (issued by the tax authorities). Such a list is intended to provide taxpayers and tax officials with concrete guidance as to whether CFCs established in particular foreign countries will be subject to the CFC rules. The lists vary widely: some are determinative (legally binding) as to a country's status as a tax haven or a nontax haven, while others merely establish rebuttable presumptions. The more sophisticated lists recognize that a country that generally is a high-tax country may nevertheless impose little or no tax on certain types of income or entities. Consequently, such countries may be placed on a nontax haven list, subject to certain exceptions for preferentially taxed income or entities. As a result, CFCs that do not qualify for those countries' low-tax regimes will be exempt from the CFC rules.

The global approach is more precise than the designated jurisdiction approach. As mentioned above, under the global approach, the country of residence of the CFC is irrelevant, and therefore every transaction engaged in by all CFCs of all resident taxpayers must be examined in order to determine the nature of the income from the transaction. If the corporation has **"tainted" income**, as discussed below, the income is attributed to the domestic shareholders of the corporation and is subject to tax in their hands, usually with a credit for any foreign taxes on the income. Consequently, the CFC rules potentially apply even to CFCs in high-tax countries if they earn tainted income. In contrast, although the designated jurisdiction approach is not as precise, it minimizes the compliance and administrative burdens of the CFC rules.

7.3.2.3 *Definition and Computation of Attributable Income*

Some countries employ what may be called an *entity approach* in taxing the income of a CFC to its domestic shareholders. Under this approach, the CFC rules usually provide an exemption for certain CFCs that are engaged primarily in genuine business activities. This exemption is discussed in section 7.3.2.4 below. If a CFC does not qualify for the exemption, all its income is attributable to its domestic shareholders. If, however, the CFC

豁免。以下第 7.3.2.4 节讨论此种豁免规定。如果 CFC 不满足此种豁免的条件，则将其全部所得都归属于其国内股东。但是，如果 CFC 符合豁免条件，则其所得，即使是消极所得均不归属于其国内股东。这种非此即彼的结果是实体法的本质特征。

与此不同的是，其他一些国家遵循**交易法**。按照这种方法，只有 CFC 取得的某些种类的所得（被称为“污点所得”）才会被归属于国内股东。按照交易法，必须逐项分析 CFC 实施的交易，以确定 CFC 是否产生了污点所得或其他所得。在确定污点所得时，运用的是居民国计算所得的法规。虽然实体法没有交易法精确，但是，实体法大幅度降低了 CFC 规则的遵从和管理负担。有些国家则使用混合方法，综合了交易法和实体法的特点。例如，澳大利亚、新西兰和美国等一些国家采用交易法，但对污点所得低于其总所得特定百分比的 CFC 提供豁免。

污点所得通常包含消极投资所得和**基地公司所得**。消极所得包括股息、利息、租金、特许权使用费，以及财产收益。实行 CFC 规则的所有国家尽管对消极所得存在不同的定义，但都将消极所得视为污点所得。为实施 CFC 规则而确定消极所得时，最为困难的问题或许在于辨别消极所得应该属于积极经营所得的情形。例如，真实的金融机构收取的利息，一般被视为积极经营所得，故而应免于适用 CFC 规则。租金和特许权使用费也存在类似的问题。

为 CFC 规则目的，“基地公司所得”一词系指，除消极所得以外，其他可以被视为污点所得的任何所得。基地公司所得的定义通常相当复杂；各国 CFC 规则定义基地公司所得的范围也存在着显著的差异。

一般来说，存在三类主要的基地公司所得：

（1）CFC 从其控股股东居民国取得的所得。如果居民国对此所得未予征税，则该国的税基受到了侵蚀。许多国家认为，CFC 以这种方式侵蚀其税基是不合理的，尤其是因为在许多情形下，相关所得本可由 CFC 的母公司直接取得。

qualifies for the exemption, none of its income, even its passive income, is attributable to its domestic shareholders. This all-or-nothing result is the essential characteristic of the entity approach.

In contrast, other countries follow a **transactional approach**, under which only certain types of income (referred to as "tainted income") derived by a CFC are subject to attribution. Under a transactional approach, each transaction entered into by a CFC must be analyzed to determine whether it produces tainted or other income, and, for this purpose, tainted income is determined by applying the residence country's rules for computing income. Although the entity approach is less precise than the transactional approach, it minimizes the compliance and administrative burden of CFC rules. Some countries use a hybrid approach that combines elements of the transactional and entity approaches. For example, some countries, such as Australia, New Zealand, and the U.S., use a transactional approach but provide an exemption for CFCs whose tainted income is less than a specified percentage of their total income.

Tainted income usually consists of passive investment income and **base company income**. Passive income consists of dividends, interest, rents, royalties, and capital gains. All countries with CFC rules consider passive income to be tainted income, although they define passive income differently. Perhaps the most difficult issue in defining passive income for purposes of CFC rules is identifying situations in which passive income should be classified as active business income. For example, interest earned by a genuine financial institution is generally considered to be active business income and therefore exempt from CFC rules. Similar issues arise with respect to rents and royalties.

The term "base company income" is used to refer to any income, other than passive income, that is considered to be tainted income for purposes of CFC rules. The definition of base company income is often quite complex, and the scope of the definition for purposes of countries' CFC rules varies considerably.

In general, there are three major components of base company income:

(1) *Income derived by a CFC from the country in which its controlling shareholders are resident*. If such income is not taxable by the residence country, that country's tax base is eroded. Many countries consider the erosion of their tax base by a CFC in this manner to be inappropriate, especially since, in many situations, the income could be earned directly by the parent of the CFC.

(2) *Income derived by a CFC from transactions with related parties*. The treatment of

（2）CFC 从关联交易中取得的所得。将来自关联方交易的所得视为污点所得，其目的通常在于强化一国的转让定价规则。转让定价规则旨在防止通过对销售、服务和其他交易的非独立交易定价，将所得转移至关联外国公司（参见第 6 章）。这些规则的执行之难，是众所周知的。CFC 规则将上述所得视为污点所得，各国则无须依赖运用其转让定价规则。

（3）CFC 从其居民国之外的交易中取得的所得。将从 CFC 的当地市场以外的交易产生的所得视为污点所得，个中缘由涉及对国际竞争力的考量。当地市场交易取得的所得通常免于适用 CFC 规则，因为对 CFC 的此类所得当期征收居民国税收，将对 CFC 所属跨国企业在该国的竞争能力产生不利影响。但是，如果 CFC 在其当地市场之外获得所得，则没有必要为了 CFC 在当地市场的竞争而免除或推迟居民国税收。此外，CFC 在其居民国开展经营活动，也许为其设立提供充分的商业理由。

基地公司的以上三类所得并不相互排斥。因此，例如，一些国家将基地公司所得的定义限定为来自 CFC 居民国以外的关联方交易的所得，或者来自控股股东为其居民的国家，因关联方交易而产生的所得。

污点所得定义的一个关键问题涉及来自 CFC 之间的集团内交易所得。例如，如果高税收国家的居民 CFC 向作为低税收国家居民的关联 CFC 支付利息、特许权使用费或其他可扣除金额，则可以实现显著的节税。在没有特别规则的情况下，CFC 取得的利息、特许权使用费和其他款项，可能被视为消极所得，应受制于 CFC 规则。然而，许多国家的特别规则将此类集团内款项支付排除在污点所得范围之外。因此，一般来说，跨国企业可以设立集团财务公司或知识产权控股公司，不受 CFC 规则的约束，以减少外国税收。

应根据国内税收规则和本国货币，计算 CFC 应归属于其国内股东的任何污点所得。由于国内外税法的不同，这项要求存在许多困难。一般而言，CFC 不得

income from related-party transactions as tainted income is usually intended to reinforce a country's transfer pricing rules. Transfer pricing rules are intended to prevent the diversion of income to related foreign corporations through the non-arm's-length pricing of sales, services, and other transactions (*see* Chapter 6). These rules are notoriously difficult to enforce. By treating such income as tainted income for purposes of CFC rules, countries can avoid the necessity of relying on the application of their transfer pricing rules.

(3) *Income derived by a CFC from transactions outside the country in which it is resident.* The rationale for treating income from transactions outside the CFC's local market as tainted income relates to considerations of international competitiveness. Income from local market transactions is usually exempt because the current imposition of residence country tax on such income of a CFC would adversely affect the ability of the multinational enterprise of which the CFC is part to compete in that country. Where, however, the CFC derives income outside its local market, the exemption or deferral of residence country tax is not necessary for the CFC to compete in its local market. Moreover, where a CFC does business in its country of residence, there are probably good commercial reasons for it to be established there.

These three categories of base company income are not mutually exclusive. Thus, for example, some countries limit the definition of base company income to income derived from related-party transactions outside a CFC's country of residence or to income from the country in which the controlling shareholders are resident as a result of related-party transactions.

One key aspect of the definition of tainted income concerns income from intercompany transactions between CFCs. For example, significant tax savings can be achieved if a CFC that is resident in a high-tax country pays interest, royalties, or other deductible amounts to a related CFC resident in a low-tax country. In the absence of special rules, interest, royalties, and other amounts received by a CFC would likely be considered to be passive income subject to the CFC rules. However, many countries have adopted special rules to exclude such intercompany payments from the scope of tainted income. Thus, in general, multinational enterprises can establish group finance companies or holding companies for intellectual property in order to reduce foreign taxes without becoming subject to the CFC rules.

Any tainted income of a CFC that is attributable to its domestic shareholders should be computed in accordance with domestic tax rules and in domestic currency. This obligation presents many difficulties because of differences between foreign and domestic tax laws.

将其损益与其同一国内股东的其他 CFC 的损益合并。

7.3.2.4 豁免的性质和范围

各国可以规定各种豁免，限制其 CFC 规则的范围，这里将讨论其中最重要的豁免。豁免的方式多种多样，取决于一国是采用前述的实体法还是交易法。所有实行 CFC 法规的国家都至少规定了其中部分豁免。

真实营业活动或积极经营所得豁免。对于主要或专门从事真实营业活动的 CFC，或者对于 CFC 获得的积极经营所得，通常都会明确或隐含地给予豁免。使用交易法的国家只对 CFC 的污点所得征税。这种方法一个内在特点，是对经营所得给予豁免，因为这种所得不被认为是污点所得。采用实体法的其他国家，考察每一个 CFC，并将其全部所得完全归属于其国内股东，或完全不归属于其国内股东。采用实体法时，各国对主要或几乎完全从事真实营业活动的 CFC，均有豁免规定。这项豁免一般只有在以下情况下才可以获得：（1）CFC 从事特定的积极营业活动或不从事投资活动；（2）CFC 在外国具有实质性存在；（3）其所得中低于一定百分比（通常为 50%）部分为污点所得（一般为消极所得和基地公司所得）。

瑞典和巴西的 CFC 规则不区分积极经营所得和其他所得。根据两国的 CFC 规则，CFC 的所有非豁免所得都应归属于其国内股东。但是，瑞典规定了广泛的豁免，不受 CFC 规则的约束；设立在与瑞典签订了税收协定国家的，以及其他高税收国家的几乎所有 CFC，都在豁免之列。

分配豁免。如果 CFC 以其当期利润，向其居民股东分配股息，且这些股东应予缴纳居民国税收，则应无须适用 CFC 规则，因为居民国税收既未避免也未递延。尽管分配豁免在理论上站得住脚，但目前没有任何国家的 CFC 规则，给予此类豁免。不实行分配豁免的部分原因在于，许多国家对 CFC 的股息免税。另一个原因是分配豁免异常复杂，一些国家最初采用了后又取消了这

Generally, a CFC is not allowed to consolidate its profits and losses with the profits and losses of other CFCs of the same domestic shareholders.

7.3.2.4 Nature and Scope of Exemptions

Countries may provide a variety of exemptions that limit the scope of their CFC rules; the most important of these exemptions are described below. The exemptions vary depending on whether a country uses an entity or transactional approach, as described above. All countries with CFC legislation provide at least some of these exemptions.

Exemption for genuine business activities or active business income. An exemption is usually granted, expressly or implicitly, for CFCs engaged primarily or exclusively in genuine business activities or for active business income earned by CFCs. Countries that use a transactional approach impose tax only on the tainted income of a CFC. Inherent in this approach is the exemption of active business income since such income is not considered to be tainted income. Other countries use an entity approach, under which each CFC is tested, and either all or none of its income is attributed to its domestic shareholders. Under the entity approach, an exemption is invariably provided for CFCs engaged primarily or almost exclusively in genuine business activities. This exemption is generally available only if: (1) the CFC is engaged in certain defined active businesses or is not engaged in investment activities; (2) it has a substantial presence in the foreign country; and (3) less than a certain percentage (usually 50%) of its income is tainted income (generally passive income and base company income).

The CFC rules of Sweden and Brazil do not distinguish between active business income and other income. Under their CFC rules, all the income of a CFC that is not exempt is attributable to its domestic shareholders. However, Sweden provides broad exemptions from the CFC rules: virtually all CFCs established in countries with which Sweden has a tax treaty, as well as other high-tax countries, are exempt.

Distribution exemption. To the extent that a CFC distributes dividends out of its current profits to its resident shareholders that are subject to residence country tax, there is arguably no need to apply the CFC rules since residence country tax is neither avoided nor deferred. Despite the theoretical justification for a distribution exemption, no country currently provides such an exemption from the CFC rules. Part of the reason for the absence of a distribution exemption is that many countries exempt dividends from CFCs; another reason is that distribution exemptions are surprisingly complex, and some countries that had initially adopted such exemptions later eliminated them.

些豁免。

最低豁免。如果 CFC 的所得（或污点所得）不超过最低数额，则通常会给予最低豁免。各国最低豁免的差别很大，也有一些国家没有规定此类豁免。在加拿大，仅在 CFC 的污点所得为 5000 加元（约为 3800 美元，是一个毫无意义的小数额）或更少时，才给予豁免。其他一些国家尽管很难从税收政策的角度证明其合理性，但仍然规定了数额较大的最低豁免。最低豁免似乎主要是出于政治考虑，以减轻 CFC 规则在应税所得较小的情形时，给纳税人造成明显遵从负担的担忧。

其他豁免。一些国家对不以避税或减税为目的的 CFC 给予豁免（"动机"豁免）。虽然动机豁免可能与 CFC 法规的反避税目的相一致，但它给予税务机关相当大的自由裁量权。这可能是对 CFC 规则的范围有所限制的简单方法，避免了更为具体的例外规定带来的法律方面的复杂性。

7.3.2.5 应税居民纳税人

在大多数国家中，个人股东和公司股东都要根据 CFC 规则纳税，但在一些国家中，CFC 规则只适用于居民公司。似乎没有任何好的理由，解释为什么这些规则不应适用于个人，除非一国制定了其他规则，禁止富裕个人设立 CFC，以推迟或规避居民国税收。

在大多数国家，CFC 的未分配收入归属于在其纳税年度结束时，拥有公司股份的居民股东。这种做法似乎并不公平，因为这种方法按股东在 CFC 全年收入中所占的比例对其征税，尽管股东可能仅在一年的部分时间持有股份。然而，这种方法虽然不那么精确，但比确定纳税人在一年的部分时间内所持有 CFC 所得的份额，要简单得多。此外，一旦了解年终规则，收购 CFC 股份的人在确定股份购买价格时，将考虑这一因素。

在大多数国家中，如果为达到最低持股要求（通常为 10%），CFC 的居民股东不应就其在外国公司未分配收入中的份额纳税。对小规模投资 CFC 的股东实

De minimis exemption. A *de minimis* exemption is frequently granted for CFCs whose income (or tainted income) does not exceed a minimum amount. *De minimis* exemptions vary widely, and several countries do not provide any such exemption. The Canadian exemption is available only if the CFC's tainted income is CAD 5,000 (approximately USD 3,800—a meaninglessly small amount) or less. Other countries provide sizeable *de minimis* exemptions, although they are difficult to justify on tax policy grounds. *De minimis* exemptions appear to be largely motivated by political considerations in order to allay fears that CFC rules will impose significant compliance costs on taxpayers in respect of relatively small amounts of income subject to tax.

Other exemptions. A few countries provide an exemption for CFCs that are not used for the purpose of avoiding or reducing tax (a "motive" exemption). Although a motive exemption is perhaps consistent with the anti-avoidance purpose of CFC legislation, it gives the tax authorities considerable discretion. It may be a simple way of limiting the scope of the rules without the legislative complexity necessitated by more specific exceptions.

7.3.2.5 Resident Taxpayers Subject to Tax

In most countries, both individual and corporate shareholders are subject to tax under the CFC rules; in a few countries, the rules apply only to resident corporations. There does not appear to be any good reason why the rules should not apply to individuals unless a country has other rules to prevent wealthy individuals from establishing CFCs to defer or avoid residence country tax.

In most countries, the undistributed income of a CFC is attributed to resident shareholders who own shares in the corporation at the end of its taxation year. This approach may appear to be unfair because it taxes shareholders on their pro rata share of the CFC's income for the entire year despite the possibility that they may have owned their shares for only part of the year. However, this approach is much simpler, although less precise, than determining a taxpayer's share of the income of a CFC for part of a year. In addition, once the end-of-the-year rule is well understood, persons acquiring shares of a CFC can be expected to take the rule into account in setting the purchase price of the shares.

In most countries, resident shareholders of a CFC are not taxable on their share of the undistributed income of the foreign corporation unless they meet a minimum share ownership requirement (usually 10%). The reason for this exemption for shareholders with small investments in a CFC is that they may not have sufficient influence over the

行此种豁免的原因是，这些股东可能对外国公司没有足够的影响力，无法要求外国公司分配收入，或获取计算其所得份额所需的信息。然而，在判定外国公司是否由居民股东控制时，可以将这些小股东考虑在内。

7.3.2.6　救济规定

通常情况下，各国对因实施其 CFC 规则可能产生的双重征税给予某种形式的救济。因为 CFC 规则下的基本征税机制，是对 CFC 的居民股东在其未分配所得中所占的份额征税，所以，大多数国家允许将 CFC 缴纳的外国税收，在对居民股东及相关所得征税时予以抵免。如果 CFC 的所得需要缴纳外国税收，而后股东从 CFC 获得股息或转让其在 CFC 的股份，则也可能产生双重征税。大多数国家针对外国税收和随后来自 CFC 已征税所得的股息提供救济，但很少有国家针对转让 CFC 股份产生的财产收益，为 CFC 已征税所得缘故提供救济。下面的例子说明了这些双重征税问题。

P 公司是 P 国居民，拥有 S 国居民 S 公司的全部股份，2020 年，S 公司在 S 国取得消极所得 1000 元，向 S 国就该所得纳税 100 元。根据 P 国的 CFC 规则，P 公司应就 S 公司所得 1000 元，按 40% 的税率纳税（即 400 元），并符合条件，就 S 公司缴纳给 S 国的税款 100 元，抵免外国税款 100 元。2022 年，S 公司向 P 公司支付 900 元。如果该股息根据 P 国法律为应税所得，但由于 P 公司已经就从中支付股息的所得纳税，则应免于征收该 P 国税收。如果 S 国对该股息征收 10% 的预提税，则 P 国还应针对该预提税给予抵免；具体方式可以通过允许其向既往年度结转，作为 2020 年（当时由 CFC 最初取得该所得）的外国税收抵免，或通过允许其抵免对 2022 年或未来年度 CFC 所得征收的任何税收。

如果 P 公司在 2022 年出售 S 公司的股份，没有收取股息，则此项出售收益应该反映 S 公司 2020 年税后收入 900 元。由于 P 公司已经就该金额向 P 国缴纳了税款，因此不应要求就出售 S 公司股份所实现的财产收益缴纳税款，但前提是

foreign corporation to require it to distribute its income or obtain access to the information necessary to compute their share of the income. Nevertheless, these small shareholders may be counted in determining whether a foreign corporation is controlled by resident shareholders.

7.3.2.6 Relief Provisions

Typically, countries provide some relief from double taxation that may otherwise occur from the operation of their CFC rules. Because the basic taxing mechanism under CFC rules is to tax the resident shareholders of a CFC on their share of its undistributed income, most countries allow a credit for the foreign tax paid by a CFC on the income that is taxable in the hands of a resident shareholder. The possibility of double taxation also arises where the CFC's income is subject to foreign tax and a shareholder receives dividends from the CFC or disposes of its shares in the corporation. Most countries provide relief for foreign taxes and subsequent dividends out of previously taxed income of a CFC, but few countries provide relief for capital gains from the disposal of shares of a CFC that reflect previously taxed income of the CFC. These double taxation issues are illustrated in the following example.

PCo, a resident of Country P, owns all the shares of SCo, a resident of Country S. In 2020, SCo earns passive income of 1,000 in Country S and pays tax of 100 to Country S on its income. Under Country P's CFC rules, PCo is taxable on SCo's income of 1,000 at a rate of 40% (or 400) and qualifies for a foreign tax credit of 100 for the tax paid by SCo to Country S of 100. In 2022, SCo pays a dividend to PCo of 900. Since PCo has already been taxed on the income out of which the dividend was paid, the dividend should be exempt from Country P tax if it is otherwise taxable under the laws of Country P. If Country S imposes withholding tax of 10% on the dividend, Country P should also provide relief for that withholding tax, perhaps by allowing it to be carried back and claimed as a foreign tax credit in 2020 (when the income was originally earned by the CFC) or by allowing it to be claimed against any tax on CFC income for 2022 or future years.

If PCo sells the shares of SCo in 2022 without receiving a dividend, the proceeds of sale will presumably reflect SCo's after-tax income for 2020 of 900. Since PCo has already paid tax to Country P on that amount, it should not be required to pay tax on the capital gain realized on the sale of the shares of SCo to the extent that the gain is attributable to the previously taxed income of 900. If no relief is provided by Country P in this situation, PCo is likely to consider

该收益可归属于先前已纳税的收入 900 元。如果 P 国在这种情况下没有提供任何救济，P 公司可能会考虑让 S 公司支付股息 900 元（如上文所述，该股息可能由 P 国免税），以减少出售股份的财产收益。

一般并不将 CFC 的亏损归属于其居民股东。大多数国家允许将这类亏损向前结转，在计算未来年度 CFC 的可归属所得时予以扣除。

对于因适用两个或两个以上国家的 CFC 规则而产生的双重征税，大多数国家的 CFC 规则并没有规定具体的救济办法。例如，假设 A 国居民 A 公司拥有 B 国居民 B 公司的所有股份。B 公司拥有设立在避税港并获得消极所得的某公司的所有股份。如果 A 国和 B 国都实行 CFC 规则，避税地公司的消极所得可以由 A 国向 A 公司征税，B 国向 B 公司征税。虽然 A 国似乎应该对 B 国根据其 CFC 规则征收的税收给予抵免，但 A 国可能会认为，避税地公司的消极所得系被从 A 国转移，应由 A 国征税。一些国家通过扣除或抵免的方式，对根据另一国家的 CFC 规则征收的外国税收，规定了具体的救济措施。其他一些国家则不予救济，尽管根据适用的税收协定，通过相互协商程序，可以获得救济。随着越来越多的国家采用 CFC 规则，这种双重征税问题正在变得越来越严重。

7.3.3 税收协定和 CFC 规则

税收协定与 CFC 规则之间的关系存在着争议。在巴西、芬兰、法国、日本、瑞典和英国，纳税人对向外国子公司适用 CFC 规则提出质疑，称其违反了适用的税收协定。纳税人认为，标准的税收协定营业利润条款（OECD 协定范本和联合国协定范本第 7 条）规定，一国（实行 CFC 规则的国家）不能对另一国居民公司的营业利润征税（即使该公司受控于第一个国家的居民），除非公司在第一个国家有一个常设机构，而利润应归属于该常设机构。作为回应，税务机关认为，根据 CFC 规则，税收是对外国公司的居民股东征收的，而不是对 CFC 征收的，而且，税收协定中没有任何规定阻止一国对其居民征税。（注意，2017 年，

having SCo pay a dividend of 900 (which will probably be exempt from tax by Country P, as explained above) to reduce the capital gain on the sale of the shares.

Losses of a CFC are not generally attributable to its resident shareholders. Most countries permit such losses to be carried forward and deducted in computing the attributable income of the CFC in future years.

Most countries' CFC rules do not provide specific relief from double taxation resulting from the application of the CFC rules of two or more countries. For example, assume that ACo, resident in Country A, owns all the shares of BCo, resident in Country B. BCo owns all the shares of a corporation that is established in a tax haven and earns passive income. If Country A and Country B both have CFC rules, the passive income of the tax haven corporation may be subject to tax to ACo by Country A and to BCo by Country B. Although it may appear that Country A should give credit for the tax levied by Country B pursuant to its CFC rules, Country A may take the position that the passive income of the tax haven corporation was shifted from Country A and should be taxable in Country A. Some countries provide specific relief, by way of deduction or credit, for foreign taxes levied pursuant to another country's CFC rules. Other countries provide no relief, although relief might be available under the MAP of an applicable tax treaty. This double-tax problem is becoming more serious as more countries adopt CFC rules.

7.3.3 Tax Treaties and CFC Rules

The relationship between tax treaties and CFC rules is controversial. In Brazil, Finland, France, Japan, Sweden, and the U.K., taxpayers have challenged the application of CFC rules to foreign subsidiaries as a violation of an applicable tax treaty. The taxpayers have argued that the business profits article of the typical tax treaty (Article 7 of the OECD and UN Model Treaties) provides that a country (the country with CFC rules) cannot impose tax on the business profits of a corporation resident in the other country (even if controlled by residents of the first country) except to the extent that the corporation has a PE in the first country and the profits are attributable to the PE. In response, the tax authorities have argued that under CFC rules, tax is imposed on the resident shareholders of the foreign corporation, not the CFC, and nothing in a tax treaty prevents a country from taxing its own residents. (Note that, as of 2017, Article 1(3) of the OECD and UN Model Treaties confirms the principle that tax treaties do not restrict countries from taxing their own residents except to the extent that the treaty expressly provides otherwise.)

OECD 协定范本和联合国协定范本第 1 条第 3 款确认了税收协定不限制各国对其本国居民征税的原则，除非协定另行明确规定。）

这些观点的可靠程度各不相同，取决于特定国家的 CFC 规则和所适用协定的具体规定。如上所述，大多数国家的 CFC 规则并不适用于积极经营所得；此外，一些国家不对协定国居民适用 CFC 规则。因此，税收协定与 CFC 规则之间的潜在冲突是有限的。截至 2023 年，对于这类个案的裁定支持税务机关的观点，但巴西和法国除外。在法国，法国最高法院认定，法国—瑞士协定第 7 条禁止法国 CFC 规则适用于法国公司的瑞士子公司。

2003 年对 OECD 协定范本第 1 条的注释进行了修订。修订后的注释澄清，根据 OECD 的观点，CFC 规则与基于 OECD 协定范本的税收协定的规定之间，并不存在冲突；因此，税收协定不应妨碍 CFC 规则的适用。此外，对注释所作的修订说明，实行 CFC 规则的国家不必在其协定中明确规定允许适用 CFC。一些国家——比利时、卢森堡、荷兰和瑞士——对注释的这一说法提出了异议。该注释的确提醒各国，如果协定国征收的税收与本国相近，则不宜将 CFC 规则适用于作为该协定国居民公司。

7.3.4 CFC 规则与支柱二全球最低税

CFC 规则与提议中的支柱二全球最低税之间存在着一些相似之处。根据全球最低税，跨国集团的母公司对于其位于其他国家的 CFC 和 PE 的“超额利润”，需要缴纳补足税，前提是此类 CFC 或 PE 所在国征收的实际税率低于 15%。因此，CFC 规则和全球最低税采用了相同的基本征税机制：居民公司对其外国 CFC 和 PE 的部分所得应当缴纳居民国税收。出于这一理由，OECD 采取的立场是，基于 OECD 协定范本的双边税收协定的规定不会妨碍征收全球最低税，正如其并不妨碍根据 CFC 规则实行税收征收。关于支柱二全球最低税收的讨论，参见第 9.5.5.3 节。

The strength of these arguments varies depending on the particular country's CFC rules and the specific provisions of the applicable treaty. As noted above, most countries' CFC rules do not apply to active business income; moreover, several countries do not apply their CFC rules to CFCs resident in treaty countries. As a result, the potential conflict between tax treaties and CFC rules is limited. Up to 2023, the cases have been decided in favor of the tax authorities, except in Brazil and France. In France, the highest French court held that Article 7 of the France-Switzerland treaty prevented the application of the French CFC rules to a Swiss subsidiary of a French corporation.

The Commentary on Article 1 of the OECD Model Treaty was revised in 2003 to clarify that, according to the OECD, there is no conflict between CFC rules and the provisions of tax treaties based on the OECD Model Treaty; therefore, tax treaties should not prevent the application of CFC rules. Further, the revisions to the Commentary clarified that it is not necessary for countries with CFC rules to put an explicit provision in their treaties allowing the application of CFC rules. A few countries—Belgium, Luxembourg, the Netherlands, and Switzerland—have registered their disagreement with this aspect of the Commentary. The Commentary does caution countries not to apply their CFC rules to companies resident in treaty countries that are subject to tax in those countries comparable to the tax imposed by the resident country.

7.3.4 CFC Rules and the Pillar Two Global Minimum Tax

There are some similarities between CFC rules and the proposed Pillar Two global minimum tax. Under the global minimum tax, the parent entity of a multinational group is subject to a top-up tax on the "excess profit" of its CFCs and PEs in other countries to the extent that the effective tax rate imposed by the countries in which such CFCs and PEs are located is less than 15%. Thus, the same basic taxing mechanism is used for CFC rules and the global minimum tax: resident companies are subject to residence country tax on some of the income of their foreign CFCs and PEs. For this reason, the OECD has taken the position that the provisions of bilateral tax treaties based on the OECD Model Treaty would not prevent the imposition of the global minimum tax, just as they do not prevent the imposition of tax under CFC rules. See Chapter 9.5.5.3 for a discussion of the Pillar Two global minimum tax.

7.4 非居民信托

信托是一种法律关系。在这种关系下，财产的法定所有权和管理权与其受益所有权相分离。信托起源于英国法，作为英美法系的一部分，并在大多数英美法系国家的法律下得到承认。一些大陆法系国家已通过立法，允许建立信托或类似信托的关系。通常，信托涉及**委托人**［设立信托并将财产转让（清算）给信托的人］和**受托人**［为一个或多个财产的受益人（财产的受益所有人）的利益，对财产拥有合法所有权和管理权的人］。信托是一种特别灵活的安排，因为信托的委托人也可以是受托人和受益人。信托可以是自主信托，也可以是非自主裁量信托。在非自主裁量信托中，受益人的利益是固定的，未经修改信托，不得变更。相比而言，在自主信托下，受托人对应付给任何特定受益人的收入或资金的数额具有决定权。

信托的灵活性带来对其征税的困难，而且对于非居民信托来说，难度更大。许多承认信托的国家，将其作为实体征税，至少是对积累所得的信托。

受益人通常在收取向其分配信托所得时负有纳税义务，而信托的税后收入作为信托资本的分配（换言之，信托在一年内获得或收取的所得，如果在当年不向受益人进行分配，通常并入信托资金），受益人收取时无纳税义务。

如果 A 国某居民，为了 A 国居民的家庭成员的利益，在某避税地设立信托（许多避税地，特别是前英国殖民地，都实行灵活的信托立法，为设立信托提供便利）。在没有特殊规则的情况下，除非受益人收取该信托对当前所得的分配，A 国就不能对该信托的所得征税。信托本身不是 A 国居民，因此在 A 国不应纳税，除非其从 A 国取得所得。在大多数情况下，信托在一年内取得的任何收入都将被累积在信托中，并仅在后续年度，作为免予纳税的资本，或在受益人终止 A 国居民身份之后，分配给受益人。

为了防止这种类型的避税，一些国家采取了特殊规则，据以在居民将财产

7.4 NONRESIDENT TRUSTS

Trusts are legal relationships under which the legal ownership and management of property are separated from its beneficial ownership. Trusts originated under English law as part of the common law and are recognized under the laws of most common law countries. Some civil law countries have adopted legislation to allow the establishment of trusts or trust-like relationships. Typically, a trust involves a **settlor** (the person who establishes the trust and transfers (settles) property to the trust) and a **trustee** (the person who has legal ownership and management of the property for the benefit of one or more **beneficiaries** (the persons who are the beneficial owners of the property)). A trust is a particularly flexible arrangement because the settlor of the trust may also be a trustee and a beneficiary. Trusts may be either discretionary or nondiscretionary. Under a nondiscretionary trust, the interests of the beneficiaries are fixed and cannot be altered without the amendment of the trust. In contrast, under a discretionary trust, the trustee has discretion with respect to the amount of income or capital payable to any particular beneficiary.

The flexibility of trusts makes them difficult to tax, and the difficulty is magnified with respect to nonresident trusts. In many countries that recognize trusts, they are taxed as entities, at least to the extent that they accumulate their income.

Beneficiaries are generally taxable on trust income that is distributed to them but not on distributions of the capital of the trust, which usually includes the after-tax income of the trust (in other words, the income earned or received by a trust in a year is usually added to the trust's capital if it is not distributed to the beneficiaries in the year).

If a resident of Country A establishes a trust in a tax haven (and many tax havens, especially former U.K. colonies, have adopted flexible trust legislation to facilitate this practice) for the benefit of family members who are also resident in Country A, in the absence of special rules, Country A may be unable to tax the income of the trust unless the beneficiaries receive current distributions out of the trust's income. The trust itself is not a resident of Country A and therefore is not taxable by Country A except to the extent that it derives income from Country A. In most cases, any income earned by the trust in a year will be accumulated in the trust and distributed to the beneficiaries only in subsequent years as tax-free capital distributions or after the beneficiaries have ceased to be resident in Country A.

To prevent this type of tax avoidance, some countries have adopted special rules that attempt to impose tax if a resident transfers property to a nonresident trust with resident

转让给拥有居民受益人的非居民信托时予以征税。纳税人也可以设法规避此种规则，即设立外国信托，以被认可的国际慈善机构，作为唯一的指定受益人，但受托人或保护人（通常是可信任的非居民朋友或顾问）在任何时候都有权为信托增加新的受益人。类似避税途径还有，一些避税地允许设立无指定受益人的目的性信托。作为回应，一些国家拓展了其非居民信托规则，对居民委托人（任何将财产转让给非居民信托的居民）就相关信托所得征税。此举可能被认为颇为严厉，因为在法律上，委托人无权从信托中获得任何资金。然而，由于认识到无论是通过对信托或其居民受益人征税，各国在对此类信托的所得征税都存在困难，因此，该种措施的目的在于先行遏制居民将资金转移到非居民信托。

7.5 外国投资基金

如上文第 7.3.2.1 节所述，CFC 法规一般只适用于由居民股东控制的外国公司，在某些国家，仅适用于由一小批居民股东控制的外国公司。此外，有几个国家的 CFC 规则仅适用于持有外国公司股份至少达一定百分比（通常为 5% ~ 10%）的居民股东。因此，可以在低税收国家建立外国投资公司、共同基金或单位信托，相对容易地规避一国 CFC 规则的约束。此种 FIF 使相关国家的居民纳税人得以推迟其消极投资所得的国内税收。FIF 还使纳税人得以将原本属于普通所得的收入，通过转让基金中的权益，转变为财产收益。

一些国家已经制定了详细的法规，防止通过使用 FIF 推迟国内税收。对于一些国家来说，这些规则的目的是防止规避 CFC 法规。对于其他一些国家，FIF 规则有着更为广泛的目的：旨在针对所有投资于消极外国公司和不受 CFC 规则约束的其他实体的活动，消除递延纳税的利益。

在思考 FIF 规则时，比较三种不同投资方式的税务后果是很有帮助的：（1）投资于 FIF；（2）投资于国内投资基金；以及（3）直接外国投资（如购买外国债券或租赁位于海外的不动产）。居民投资于国内投资基金，与投资

beneficiaries. Taxpayers may attempt to avoid these rules by establishing foreign trusts with a recognized international charity as the only named beneficiary, but with a power in the trustee or a protector (usually a trusted friend or adviser who is a nonresident) to add new beneficiaries to the trust at any time. Alternatively, some tax havens allow the establishment of purpose trusts, which do not require any named beneficiaries. In response, some countries have exten ded their nonresident trust rules to tax the resident settlor (any resident who transfers property to a nonresident trust) on the income of the trust. This measure may be considered to be draconian because, legally, the settlor has no right to obtain any funds from the trust. However, it is intended to stop residents from transferring funds to nonresident trusts in the first place in recognition of the difficulty that countries have in taxing the income of such trusts, either by taxing the trust or its resident beneficiaries.

7.5 FOREIGN INVESTMENT FUNDS

As discussed in section 7.3.2.1 above, CFC legislation generally applies only to foreign corporations that are controlled by resident shareholders, and in some countries, only to foreign corporations that are controlled by a small group of resident shareholders. Moreover, the CFC rules of several countries apply only to resident shareholders that own a minimum percentage (usually 5%–10%) of the shares of the foreign corporation. As a result, it is relatively easy for foreign investment companies, mutual funds, or unit trusts to be established in low-tax countries without being subject to a country's CFC rules. Such FIFs allow taxpayers resident in the country to defer domestic tax on their passive investment income. FIFs may also permit taxpayers to convert what would otherwise be ordinary income into capital gains on the disposition of interests in the fund.

Several countries have enacted detailed legislation to prevent the deferral of domestic tax through the use of FIFs. For some countries, the purpose of these rules is to prevent the avoidance of CFC legislation. For some other countries, the FIF rules have a much broader purpose: they are intended to eliminate the benefit of deferral for all investments in passive foreign corporations and other entities that are not subject to the CFC rules.

When thinking about FIF rules, it is useful to compare the tax consequences of three alternative investments: (1) an investment in a FIF; (2) an investment in a domestic investment fund; and (3) a direct foreign investment (e.g., the purchase of a foreign bond or rental real property located offshore). The essential difference between the tax consequences for a resident investing in a domestic investment fund as compared to a FIF is that residence country tax is deferred

于 FIF 相比，两者税收后果之间的本质差异在于，对于外国基金而言，居民国税收被推迟至居民收到基金的分配款项或处置基金权益之时。而对于通过国内投资基金取得的收入，通常是按年缴纳国内税收。

与直接外国投资相比，投资 FIF 的利益在于，如果该基金累积其收入，那么，来自基金的收入实际上可以转变为财产收益。投资于居民公司的股份，也可以使投资所得转化为财产收益。但是，居民公司就其所得当期缴纳居民国的公司税，而外国公司则不必。

因此，只要（1）针对外国公司所得的外国税收低于针对居民公司同等所得的国内税收，以及（2）外国公司至少积累其部分收入，则相关国家的税收制度其实都鼓励居民个人投资于外国公司，而不是投资于居民公司。这种情形不在少数。如果外国公司建立在避税地，并积累其全部所得时，这种鼓励作用就最为突出。

各国使用若干不同方法来处理对 FIF 的投资；在某些情况下，有些国家使用不止一种方法。下面简要介绍这些方法。

CFC 规则。在一些国家，如德国，FIF 规则属于 CFC 规则的组成部分。CFC 规则适用于主要取得消极所得的外国公司和受居民控制的其他实体的小型投资者。

目的标准。有些国家，如加拿大，制定了基于目的的特别反避税规则，适用于在 FIF 中拥有权益的居民。因此，对于持有 FIF 权益的居民，如果购买 FIF 或在其中持有权益的主要目的在于避税，则应按推定所得予以征税。

市值调整法。市值调整法实质上是一种应计财产收益税，根据这种方法，居民纳税人在外国基金中权益价值的任何增加或减少，在计算纳税人每年的所得时，都必须包括在内。例如，如果纳税人在 FIF 中的权益年初价值为 300 元，年末为 500 元，则纳税人将就 200 的收益纳税。如果权益的价值在次年年底下降到 200 元，纳税人在该年度将发生亏损 300 元。

如果 FIF 在证券交易所进行活跃交易，或者基金提供有关基金当前权益价值

with respect to a foreign fund until the resident receives distributions or disposes of the interest in the fund. In contrast, domestic tax is customarily imposed annually on the income derived by a domestic investment fund.

The benefit of an investment in a FIF compared to a direct foreign investment is that the income from the fund can be effectively converted into capital gains if the fund accumulates its income. This conversion of investment income into capital gains may also occur with respect to investments in shares of resident corporations. However, resident corporations are subject to current corporate tax in the residence country on their income, whereas foreign corporations are not.

As a result, the tax systems of many countries contain an incentive for resident individuals to invest in foreign corporations as compared to resident corporations whenever (1) foreign taxes on the foreign corporation's income are less than the domestic taxes on the equivalent amount of income of a resident corporation, and (2) the foreign corporation accumulates at least part of its income. The incentive is greatest where the foreign corporation is based in a tax haven and accumulates all of its income.

Countries use several different approaches to deal with investments in FIFs, and in certain circumstances, some countries use more than one method. The methods are described briefly below.

CFC rules. In some countries, such as Germany, the FIF rules form part of the CFC rules. The CFC rules apply to small investors in foreign corporations and other entities controlled by residents where the entities earn primarily passive income.

Purpose test. Some countries, such as Canada, have a purpose-based specific anti-avoidance rule to deal with residents that own interests in a FIF. Thus, residents who hold an interest in a FIF are taxable on imputed income if one of the primary purposes for the acquisition or holding of the interest in the fund is to avoid tax.

Mark-to-market method. A mark-to-market method is essentially an accrual-based capital gains tax under which any increase or decrease in the value of a resident taxpayer's interest in a foreign fund must be included in computing the taxpayer's income for each year. For example, if a taxpayer's interest in a FIF has a value of 300 at the start of a year and 500 at the end of the year, the taxpayer would be subject to tax on a gain of 200. If the value of the interest declined to 200 at the end of the following year, the taxpayer would have a loss of 300 for that year.

The mark-to-market method is easy to apply if the FIF is actively traded on a stock exchange or the fund provides information on the current value of interests in the fund (usually

的信息（通常是为了赎回投资者的权益），那么，按市值调整法很容易应用。在其他情况下，除非在出售 FIF 之时，可能很难对 FIF 的权益进行估值。

核定所得法。根据核定所得法或核定回报率法，无论基金实际所得如何，居民纳税人均被视为以特定的比率，从其在海外基金中投资获得回报。例如，如果规定的回报率为 10%，则在基金中投资 10000 元的个人将就 1000 元核定所得纳税。某一年度的任何核定所得将被计入基金权益的成本。因此，假设基金没有进行分配，上述个人将对下一年度按 1100 元（11000 的 10%）的核定所得纳税。

核定所得法的优点在于，由于纳税人和税务机关不需要获得有关 FIF 实际收入的具体信息，因此此法简便易行，可以最大限度地降低纳税人的遵从负担和税务机关的管理负担。但是，核定所得法可能导致对投资者征税不足或过高。

视同分配法。根据这种方法，无论基金收入是否分配，都应对居民股东按其在外国基金所得中所占的比例予以征税。这种方法与 CFC 规则下的征税方法相同：它要求纳税人能够获得足够的信息，以便计算其在 FIF 所得中所占的份额。因此，这种方法有时只局限于在外国实体中拥有实质性权益的纳税人。

递延加征法。根据这种方法，在收到分配款项或实现收益之前，不征收居民国税收。但是，在此项税收征收之时，还将加收利息，以消除纳税人享受的推迟征税的好处。

大多数制定了 FIF 规则的国家，一般仅将其规则适用于主要获得消极所得，或其资产主要由消极资产（如有价证券）组成的外国实体。对于主要从事积极营业的外国实体，或在当期几乎分配其所有收益的外国实体，通常规定了豁免。令人满意地区分积极和消极所得或资产，通常存在困难且需要复杂的规则。大多数国家对外国税收、实际分配和处置基金所有权的财产收益，提供双重征税救济。这些救济机制类似于可比情况下通过 CFC 取得的所得所规定的救济（参见上文第 7.3.2.6 节）。

for the purpose of redeeming investors' interests). In other circumstances, it may be quite difficult to value interests in a FIF except when they are sold.

Imputed-income approach. Under an imputed-income or deemed rate of return approach, the resident taxpayer is considered to have earned income on the amount invested in the offshore fund at a specified rate, irrespective of the actual income earned by the fund. For example, if the specified rate of return is 10%, an individual who invests 10,000 in the fund would be taxable on deemed income of 1,000. Any deemed income for a year would then be added to the cost of the interest in the fund. Thus, assuming no distributions from the fund are made, the individual would be taxable on deemed income of 1,100 (10% of 11,000) for the following year.

The advantage of the imputed-income method is that it is simple to apply and minimizes the compliance burden on taxpayers and the administrative burden on the tax authorities because it is unnecessary for them to obtain specific information about the actual income of the FIF. However, the imputed-income method may result in the under-or over-taxation of investors.

Deemed distribution approach. Under this approach, resident shareholders are subject to tax on their pro rata share of the income of the foreign fund regardless of whether the income of the fund is distributed. This approach is the same as the method of taxation under CFC rules: it requires taxpayers to have access to sufficient information in order to compute their share of the FIF's income. As a result, it is sometimes limited to taxpayers who own a substantial interest in the offshore entity.

Deferral charge approach. Under this approach, residence country tax is not imposed until distributions are received or gains are realized. However, at that time, an interest charge is impo sed to eliminate the benefits of deferral that the taxpayer has enjoyed.

Most countries that have FIF rules generally apply their rules only to foreign entities that earn primarily passive income or whose assets consist primarily of passive assets such as marketable securities. Exemptions are often provided for foreign entities that are principally engaged in an active business or that distribute virtually all of their income currently. The distinction between active and passive income or assets is a difficult one to make in a satisfactory manner and usually requires complex rules. Most countries provide double-tax relief for foreign taxes, actual distributions, and capital gains on the disposition of ownership rights in the fund. These relief mechanisms are similar to those provided in comparable circumstances for income derived through CFCs (*see* section 7.3.2.6 above).

7.6 背对背或反导管规则

在许多国家，利息预提税只针对非居民支付的利息款项，而且支付方与此非居民之间的交易并非独立交易。同样，根据资本弱化规则，这些国家仅在向控制居民公司或拥有居民公司实质性权益的非居民股东支付利息的情况下，才拒绝扣除利息。在这些和其他类似情形下，有必要确定利息收取方的身份。因此，纳税人有机会通过背对背或导管安排来规避这些规则。特许权使用费等其他款项也可能出现类似的机会。

这个问题在国内法和税收协定下都很重要。在协定的情况下，识别贷款人至关重要，由此才能确认贷款人是否为利息的受益所有人，以及是否有权享受协定待遇（并可能适用降低了的预扣税）。根据国内法，正确识别贷款人，对于信息报告目的，以及预提税和适用关于利息扣除的限制（如资本弱化规则或收益剥离规则），都很重要。

在背对背安排的情况下，当中间方（如金融机构）与其他各方无关联关系时，正确识别贷款人的难度就更大。例如，假设 A 国居民 A 在 B 国居民某银行存款 1000 元，然后，该银行将 1000 元借给 C 国居民 C 公司，后者是 A 公司的全资子公司。出于 C 国国内法和 B 国与 C 国之间的税收协定的目的，C 国是否应将给予 C 公司的贷款视为系由 A 公司所提供?

基于上述简单的事实，可能很容易回答这个问题，特别是如果 C 公司直接向 A 公司支付的利息，需要缴纳 25% 预提税，但向独立交易的金融机构支付的利息不需要缴纳预提税。然而，在其他情况下，答案可能很难确定。例如，如果前后贷款的金额或条款或资金计价的货币并不完全相同，将会如何? 如果中间方支付款项的性质不同于中间方收取款项的性质（例如，中间方收取利息，但向最终受益人支付租金或特许权使用费），将会如何? 一般来说，这一问题取决于若干因素，诸如两笔交易的金额、它们在时间上的紧密关系程度，以及包括利率在

7.6 BACK-TO-BACK OR ANTI-CONDUIT RULES

Withholding taxes on interest are often imposed only on payments of interest to nonresidents with whom the payer does not deal at arm's length. Similarly, under thin capitalization rules, the deduction of interest may be denied only with respect to interest payments to nonresident shareholders that control or have a substantial interest in a resident company. In these and other similar situations, it is necessary to determine the identity of the recipient of interest payments, and, as a result, taxpayers have opportunities to avoid the rules through back-to-back or conduit arrangements. Similar opportunities may also arise with respect to other amounts, such as royalties.

This issue is important under both domestic law and tax treaties. In the case of treaties, identifying the lender is essential for determining whether the lender is the beneficial owner of the interest and entitled to treaty benefits (and possibly reduced withholding tax). Under domestic law, proper identification of the lender can be important for information-reporting purposes as well as for withholding tax and the application of any restrictions on the deduction of interest, such as thin capitalization rules or earnings-stripping rules.

The difficulty of identifying the correct lender in the case of back-to-back arrangements is even more challenging when the intermediary, such as a financial institution, is not related to the other parties. For instance, assume that ACo, a resident of Country A, makes a deposit of 1,000 in a bank resident in Country B. That same bank then lends 1,000 to CCo, a resident of Country C, that is, a wholly owned subsidiary of ACo. Should the loan to CCo be treated by Country C as a loan by ACo for the purposes of Country C's domestic law and for purposes of the tax treaty between Country B and Country C?

This question may be easy to answer on these simple facts, especially if, for example, interest payments from CCo to ACo directly would be subject to a 25% withholding tax, but interest payments to arm's-length financial institutions are exempt from withholding tax. However, in other situations, the answer may be difficult to determine. For example, what if the amounts or terms of the loans or the currency in which the funds are denominated are not exactly the same? What if the nature of the payment by the intermediary is different from the nature of the payment received by the intermediary (e.g., the intermediary receives interest but pays rent or royalties to the ultimate beneficiary?) In general, the issue depends on factors such as the amounts of the two transactions, how closely related they are in time, and the terms of the two

内的两笔交易的条款等。如果第一笔交易是以最终贷款或债务为条件的，这很可能明确说明两笔交易形成背对背安排。

一些国家制定了具体的反避税规则，以防止利用背对背安排。例如，加拿大实行全面但非常复杂的规则来处理背对背安排。其他一些国家则依靠如实质重于形式或虚假交易等司法反避税规则，或依据一般反避税规则，来解决这一问题。

对于一些国家来说，可能十分需要采用背对背规则，以满足 BEPS 第 6 项行动计划报告关于协定滥用的最低标准。如第 8 章第 8.8.2 节所述，除非一国采用 OECD 协定范本和联合国协定范本第 29 条第 9 款中的一般反滥用规则，否则，就必须采用简化或详细的利益限制条款，即如 OECD 协定范本和联合国协定范本第 29 条第 1 ~ 7 款中的条款，并在其协定或国内法中对这些条款辅之以反导管规则（关于应当适用反导管规则的安排的示例，参见关于 OECD 协定范本第 29 条的注释第 187 段）。

7.7 混合安排

7.7.1 什么是混合安排？

“混合安排”一词通常用于描述两个国家在一项安排某些方面的税收处理采取不同和不一致立场的情况。这种不一致的处理可能会给纳税人带来有益或有害的后果。例如，转让价格立场不一致可能导致双重征税；而针对某些款项支付性质的立场不一致，则可能导致在一个国家可以扣除，在另一个国家并不征税。当然，经过深思熟虑的纳税人，如跨国公司，会做出筹划，避免针对混合安排的有害后果，并利用混合安排来产生税收利益。

如上宽泛定义的混合安排涉及所得税制度的所有基本特征：纳税人、产生所得的活动类型（受雇、商业和投资），以及与计算净所得相关的款项支付类型。然而，最重要的混合安排类型是混合实体和混合金融工具。

transactions, including the interest rates. If the first transaction is conditional on the ultimate loan or indebtedness, that will likely be a clear indication that the two transactions form a back-to-back arrangement.

Some countries have enacted specific anti-avoidance rules to prevent the use of back-to-back arrangements. For example, Canada has comprehensive but very complicated rules to deal with back-to-back arrangements. Other countries rely on judicial anti-avoidance doctrines, such as substance over form or sham, or GAARs to deal with the problem.

It may be important for some countries to adopt back-to-back rules in order to satisfy the BEPS Action 6 Report's minimum standard on treaty abuse. As discussed in Chapter 8, section 8.8.2, unless a country adopts the general anti-abuse rule in Article 29(9) of the OECD and UN Model Treaties, it must adopt simplified or detailed **Limitation-on-Benefits (LOB)** provisions such as those in Article 29(1)–(7) of the OECD and UN Model Treaties and supplement those provisions with anti-conduit rules either in its treaties or in domestic law (*see* paragraph 187 of the Commentary on Article 29 of the OECD Model for examples of the arrangements to which anti-conduit rules should apply).

7.7 HYBRID ARRANGEMENTS

7.7.1 What Is a Hybrid Arrangement?

The term "hybrid arrangement" is generally used to describe situations in which two countries take different and inconsistent positions with respect to the tax treatment of some aspect of an arrangement. This inconsistent treatment may result in either beneficial or harmful consequences for a taxpayer. For example, inconsistent positions on transfer prices may result in double taxation, whereas inconsistent positions on the character of certain payments may result in a deduction in one country and no taxation in the other country. Of course, well-advised taxpayers, such as multinational corporations, will plan to avoid the harmful consequences of hybrid arrangements and use them to generate tax benefits.

Hybrid arrangements, as broadly defined above, include all the fundamental features of an income tax system: the persons subject to tax, the type of activities giving rise to income (employment, business, and investment), and the types of payments relevant to the computation of net income. However, the most important types of hybrid arrangements are hybrid entities and hybrid financial instruments.

混合安排通常被用来替代涉及避税地实体的税收筹划安排。例如，避税地实体通常被用作中介，从位于高税收来源国的实体收取可税前扣除的款项，然后，以非应税的形式，将这些款项支付给位于高税收居民国的关联实体。混合安排可以在不使用避税地的情况下，实现同样的结果。例如，如果作为高税收来源国居民的某个混合实体被视为穿透实体或透明实体，则高税收来源国家可能将向该混合实体支付的可扣除款项，视为向该实体所有者 A 公司支付的款项，而 A 公司可能也是高税收来源国的居民。根据其国内法或税收协定的规定，对向该混合实体支付的款项可能免于征收来源国税收；这些款项支付也可能没有在居民国征税，因为居民国将该混合实体视为一个单独的应税实体。因此，就居民国而言，A 公司没有收到这些款项支付。

7.7.2 混合实体

混合实体是一种法律关系，在一个管辖区被视为单独的应税实体，在另一个管辖区被视为透明或穿透实体。例如，根据 A 国的法律，可以建立一种商业组织形式，其成员在其中拥有利益并承担有限责任。出于税收目的，A 国可以将这类组织视为合伙企业，其结果就是，该组织的成员或合伙人应就其在该组织收入中所占的份额纳税，但该组织本身不纳税。然而，根据 B 国的税法，该组织可以被定性为公司，即独立于其成员或股东的法律实体，因此该组织本身需要就其收入纳税。因此，如果该组织的一名或多名成员是 B 国居民，则该组织在这两个国家的不同处理会产生许多税收筹划机会。

混合实体可以采用许多不同的外表和形式。某一特定实体是否为混合实体，取决于相关国家的国内法，特别是相关国家如何处于税收目的，对实体进行定性。例如，信托和其他类似的信托关系可能是混合实体，因为它们被一些普通法国家视为实体，但被一些大陆法系国家所忽略。

混合实体也可能包括一些避税地法律承认的特殊实体或安排，如担保有限公

Hybrid arrangements are often used as substitutes for tax-planning arrangements involving tax haven entities. For example, tax haven entities are often used as intermediaries to receive deductible payments from an entity in a high-tax source country and then pay those amounts in a nontaxable form to a related entity in a high-tax residence country. A hybrid arrangement can achieve the same result without the use of a tax haven. For example, if a Hybrid Entity (HE) resident in a high-tax source country is treated as a flow-through or transparent entity, the high-tax source country may treat deductible payments to HE as payments made to the owner of the entity, ACo, which might also be resident in a high-tax country. The payments to HE might be exempt from source country tax, either under its domestic law or under the provisions of a tax treaty; the payments also might not be taxable by the residence country because it treats HE as a separate taxable entity. Therefore, as far as the residence country is concerned, the payments are not received by ACo.

7.7.2 Hybrid Entities

A hybrid entity is a legal relationship that is treated as a separate taxable entity in one jurisdiction and as a transparent or flow-through entity in another jurisdiction. For example, under the laws of Country A, it may be possible to establish a form of business organization in which the members own interests and have limited liability. Country A may treat this type of organization as a partnership for tax purposes, with the result that the members or partners are taxable on their share of the income of the organization, but the organization itself is not subject to tax. On the other hand, under the tax laws of Country B, the organization may be characterized as a corporation—that is, as a legal entity separate from its members or shareholders—with the result that the organization itself is subject to tax on its income. Accordingly, if one or more of the members of the organization is resident in Country B, the different treatment of the organization in the two countries creates many tax-planning opportunities.

Hybrid entities may take many different shapes and forms. Whether or not a particular entity is a hybrid entity depends on the domestic laws of the countries involved and, in particular, how they characterize entities for tax purposes. For example, trusts and other similar fiduciary relationships may be hybrids because they are treated as entities by some common law countries but are ignored by some civil law countries.

Hybrid entities may also include special entities or arrangements, such as corporations limited by guarantee, that are recognized under the laws of some tax havens. The "owners" of the value of the company (the guarantors) have rights and obligations pursuant to a contract

司。公司价值的“所有者”（担保人）根据合同享有权利和义务，但无权投票或收取股息。公司的股份由有权选举董事但只有有限权利获得股息的股东所有。股息可以支付给与公司没有关系的人（即与担保人有关联关系的人）。股东通常是提供财富管理和房地产规划服务的信托公司。一些避税地颁布了允许设立这类实体的立法，这些实体具有生前信托的许多特征。

一些国家承认隐名合伙，这种合伙关系基本上是合同安排。隐名合伙人向管理合伙人注入资产，以换取企业利润中的某一份额。隐名合伙不被视为实体；管理合伙人拥有隐名合伙人转让的资产。在计算管理合伙人的收入时，向隐名合伙人支付的款项通常可以扣除，尽管这些款项可能需要缴纳预提税。如果隐名合伙人为其居民的国家将隐名合伙视为合伙企业，并且其基于属地对营业收入征税，那么，除了可能征收预提税之外，在任何一个国家都不存在征税。

在 1998 年英国的一项个案 Memec PLC 诉 IRC［1998］STC754（上诉法院）中，Memec 是一家英国公司，拥有一家德国公司的股份，后者又拥有两家德国运营公司的股份。当 Memec 从其第一层德国子公司获得股息时，运营公司支付的德国贸易税无法抵减英国税收。因此，Memec 与这家德国公司建立了隐名合伙关系，然后称其作为合作人，直接从运营公司获得了股息，因此贸易税是可以抵减的。英国上诉法院认定，根据英国法律，德国的隐名合伙不是合伙企业，上述收入的来源是合同安排。

在过去的 15 年到 20 年里，由于美国的勾选规则，通过使用混合实体进行税收筹划的机会激增。在 1997 年之前，根据美国税法，实体根据六个因素被归类为公司或合伙企业，包括有限责任、持续经营、集中管理和利益可自由转让。税收筹划者能够操纵这些因素，以实现其既定的实体地位。例如，使用有限责任公司作为透明的投资工具变得非常常见。根据特殊国家的法规，创建有限责任公司作为避税工具，针对投资者规定了有限的责任，但出于美国税收目的，被视为透明实体。

1997 年，美国政府通过了勾选规则，使纳税人可以选择许多商业实体的分

but have no rights to vote or receive dividends. The shares of the company are owned by shareholders who have the right to elect the directors but only limited rights to receive dividends. Dividends can be paid to persons who have no relationship with the company (i.e., persons related to the guarantor). The shareholders are typically trust companies that provide wealth management and estate planning services. Several tax havens have enacted legislation allowing the establishment of these types of entities, which have many of the characteristics of inter vivos trusts.

Several countries recognize silent partnerships, which are essentially contractual arrangements. The silent partners contribute assets to a managing partner in consideration for a share of the profits from a business. Silent partnerships are not treated as entities; the managing partner owns the assets transferred by the silent partners. The payments made to the silent partners are usually deductible in computing the income of the managing partner, although they may be subject to withholding tax. If the country in which a silent partner is resident treats the silent partnership as a partnership, and if it taxes business income on a territorial basis, then there will be no tax, except possibly withholding tax, in either country.

In a 1998 case in the U.K., *Memec PLC v. IRC* [1998] STC 754 (Court of Appeal), Memec, a U.K. company, owned shares of a German company, which in turn owned shares of two German operating companies. The operating companies paid German trade taxes that were not creditable against U.K. tax when Memec received dividends from its top-tier German subsidiary. Therefore, Memec entered into a silent partnership with the German corporation and then claimed that it had received dividends as a partner directly from the operating companies so that the trade taxes were creditable. The U.K. Court of Appeal held that the German silent partnership was not a partnership under U.K. law and that the source of the income was the contractual arrangement.

In the last fifteen to twenty years, tax-planning opportunities through the use of hybrid entities have proliferated as a result of the U.S. **check-the-box rules**. Before 1997, entities were classified as corporations or partnerships under U.S. tax law based on six factors, including limited liability, continuity of life, centralized management, and free transferability of interests; tax planners were able to manipulate these factors to achieve the desired status for an entity. For example, the use of Limited Liability Companies (LLCs) as transparent investment vehicles became very popular. LLCs were created under special state statutes as vehicles for tax shelters, providing limited liability for investors but treatment as transparent entities for U.S. tax purposes.

In 1997, the U.S. government adopted check-the-box rules, which made the classification

类。纳税人只需在规定的表格上勾选一个框，即可简便地选择将一个实体视为公司、合伙企业或可忽略的实体（如果该实体只有一名成员），而无须人为操纵上述六个因素来实现其希望的定性。如果单个所有者是个人，则可忽略的实体被视为独资企业；如果单个所有者为公司，则可忽略的实体被视为分支机构。这种选择可以针对有限责任公司、合伙企业、合资企业、分支机构和其他商业实体，也可以针对根据外国法律设立的实体。选择一经做出，5 年内不得更改。不能针对某些明确为公司（所谓的本身公司）和包含某个管辖区内商业公司的标准形式的实体进行这种选择。

美国勾选规则的动因是简化国内税收筹划和管理的愿望。也许是无意之中，勾选规则还使混合实体用于进出美国的投资变得更有吸引力和确定性。例如，针对收购或扩张美国企业，可以按以下方式构建两头沾利融资安排。

A 公司（ACo）是 A 国居民，提出收购美国公司（USCo）的所有股份。USCo 是一家在美国从事积极经营活动的美国公司。ACo 根据美国法律，或 ACo 在其中拥有所有部门或权益的避税地的法律，成立了一个混合实体（如有限责任公司）。根据 A 国的税法，该混合实体被视为公司。然而，根据美国的勾选规则，选择将该混合实体视为可忽略的实体或透明实体。ACo 还成立了一家全资美国子公司 USHoldco，以收购 USCo 的股份。ACo 从 A 国的一家银行借入用于收购 USCo 股份的价款，并将所借资金注入该混合实体。该混合实体将这些资金贷款给 USHoldco，后者用这些资金收购 USCo 的股份。

此类安排的税收后果如下：

—— USHoldco 支付的利息可在计算由 USHoldco 和 USCo 组成的美国合并集团的收入时扣除；

—— 混合实体不需要对收到的利息支付缴纳美国税收，因为出于美国税收目的，该实体是被忽略了的（即被视为透明）；

—— USHoldco 向混合实体支付的利息需缴纳美国预提税，因为出于美国税收的目的，这些利息被视为由 USHoldco 直接支付给 ACo；

of many business entities elective for taxpayers. Instead of manipulating the six factors to achieve the desired characterization, taxpayers can simply elect to have an entity treated as a corporation, a partnership, or a disregarded entity (if the entity has only one member) by checking a box on a prescribed form. A disregarded entity is treated as a sole proprietorship if the single owner is an individual or as a branch if the single owner is a corporation. The election can be made with respect to LLCs, partnerships, joint ventures, branches, and other business entities, and it can be made with respect to entities created under foreign laws. Once made, an election cannot be altered for five years. The election cannot be made for certain entities that are clearly corporations (so-called per se corporations) and include the standard form of business corporation in a jurisdiction.

The U.S. check-the-box rules were motivated by a desire to simplify domestic tax planning and administration. Perhaps inadvertently, they also made the use of hybrid entities for investment into and out of the U.S. much more attractive and certain. For example, a double-dip financing arrangement for the acquisition or expansion of a U.S. business might be structured in the following way.

ACo, a resident of Country A, proposes to acquire all the shares of USCo, a U.S. corporation engaged in an active business in the U.S. ACo forms a hybrid entity (e.g., an LLC) under the laws of the U.S. or a tax haven in which ACo owns all the units or interests. Under the tax law of Country A, the hybrid entity is treated as a corporation. However, an election is filed under the U.S. check-the-box rules to treat the hybrid entity as a disregarded or transparent entity. ACo also establishes a wholly owned U.S. subsidiary, USHoldco, to acquire the shares of USCo. ACo borrows the purchase price of the USCo shares from a bank in Country A and contributes the borrowed funds to the hybrid entity. The hybrid entity loans the funds to USHoldco, which uses them to acquire the shares of USCo.

The tax consequences of this type of arrangement are as follows:

- the interest paid by USHoldco is deductible in computing the income of the U.S.-consolidated group consisting of USHoldco and USCo;
- the hybrid entity is not subject to U.S. tax on the interest payments received because it is disregarded (i.e., treated as transparent) for U.S. tax purposes;
- the interest payments from USHoldco to the hybrid entity are subject to U.S. withholding tax because they are considered to be paid directly by USHoldco to ACo for U.S. tax purposes;

—— 混合实体不需要缴纳A国税收，因为它被视为非居民公司（假设根据A国的CFC规则，利息无须纳税）；以及

—— ACo支付的利息在出于A国税收的目的计算其收入时可以扣除。

最初，美国对支付利息的预提税率是美国和A国间协定规定的低税率，在某些情况下为零。然而，1997年，美国通过了规则，对于另一国将混合实体视为单独的应税实体而不对此种款项支付征税的情况，否定了低预提税率的协定利益。因此，该结构将不再对美国有效，因为利息将被征收30%的美国预提税。

几年来，一些纳税人使用在美国被称为“反向混合”的安排，来规避美国的预提税。

以前一个例子的事实为基础，反向混合涉及ACo根据美国法律构成混合实体，其出于美国税收目的选择被视为公司。该混合实体从一家美国银行借款，并用所借资金收购USCo的股份，USCo是一家从事积极经营活动的美国居民公司。这种安排之所以被称为反向混合，仅仅是因为出于美国税收目的，该混合实体被视为公司，而不是合伙或可忽略的实体。

这种反向混合安排的税收后果如下：

—— 在计算混合实体和由混合实体和USCo组成的美国合并集团的收入时，支付给银行的利息可以出于美国税收的目的予以扣除；

—— 无须缴纳美国预提税，因为利息系支付给美国银行；

—— 在计算ACo和ASub的收入时，支付给银行的利息可以出于A国税收的目的予以扣除，因为混合实体被视为ACo和ASub之间的合伙企业。

2001年，美国通过了针对反向混合安排规则，根据该规则，混合实体无权扣除向关联非居民方支付的利息。出于美国税收目的和美国税收协定的目的，此类款项支付被视为股息。这种股息处理仅适用于混合实体从关联美国公司收取股息的情况。

- the hybrid entity is not subject to Country A tax because it is treated as a nonresident corporation (assuming that the interest is not taxable under Country A's CFC rules); and
- the interest paid by ACo is deductible in computing its income for purposes of Country A tax.

Originally, the rate of U.S. withholding tax on the interest payments was the reduced rate provided in the treaty between the U.S. and Country A, which in some cases was zero. However, in 1997 the U.S. adopted rules to deny the benefit of any reduced rate of withholding under a treaty where the other country did not tax the payment because it treated the hybrid entity as a separate taxable entity. Thus, the structure would no longer be effective with respect to the U.S. because the interest would be subject to a 30% U.S. withholding tax.

For several years, some taxpayers used what were referred to in the U.S. as "reverse hybrid" arrangements to avoid U.S. withholding tax.

On the facts of the previous example, a reverse hybrid would involve ACo forming a hybrid entity under the laws of the U.S. that elects to be treated as a corporation for U.S. tax purposes. The hybrid entity would borrow from a U.S. bank and use the borrowed funds to acquire the shares of USCo, a U.S.-resident corporation engaged in active business. This arrangement is referred to as a reverse hybrid simply because, for U.S. tax purposes, the hybrid entity is treated as a corporation rather than a partnership or disregarded entity.

The tax consequences of this reverse hybrid arrangement are as follows:

- the interest paid to the bank is deductible for U.S. tax purposes in computing the income of the hybrid entity and the U.S.-consolidated group consisting of the hybrid entity and USCo;
- no U.S. withholding tax is payable because the interest is paid to a U.S. bank;
- the interest paid to the bank is deductible in computing the income of ACo and ASub for purposes of Country A tax because the hybrid entity is treated as a partnership between ACo and ASub.

In 2001, the U.S. adopted rules for reverse hybrid arrangements, under which a hybrid entity is not entitled to deduct interest payments made to related nonresident persons. Such payments are treated as dividends for U.S. tax purposes and U.S. tax treaties. This dividend treatment applies only to the extent that the hybrid entity receives dividends from related U.S. corporations.

利用混合实体进行税收筹划，不适合懦弱胆小者。其中涉及本国和外国税收规则、本国和外国公司法和商法，以及税收协定之间复杂的相互作用。不过，这种筹划的回报可能是巨大的，可是也存在着严重的风险。例如，在上面讨论的第一个混合示例中，如果该混合实体被视为 A 国居民，或者该混合实体被视为 ACo 在美国的常设机构，则该安排的利益将被化解于无形。此外，向混合实体所支付款项缴纳的任何美国税收，都不可抵免 ACo 根据 A 国 CFC 规则，应缴纳的任何 A 国税收，因为美国税收是由 ACo 而非混合实体缴纳的。

7.7.3 混合金融工具

一般来说，混合金融工具是指两个国家对其作出不同定性的金融工具。例如，具有债务和股权特征的工具可能被一个国家视为债务，而被另一个国家则视为股权（股份）。与混合实体一样，这些混合金融工具被广泛用于税收筹划目的。如果来源国将某个公司发行的某种金融工具视为债务，则其通常会将因该债务而支付的款项定性为利息，并允许这些款项支付作为扣除项。然而，此种款项收取方为其居民的国家有可能将该金融工具定性为发行方公司的股份，并将针对该股份所支付的款项视为免于征税的股息。

作为在居民国和来源国都产生扣除的混合金融工具的一个例子，可以设想以下出售和回购安排。A 国居民 ACo 拥有 B 国居民公司 BCo 的所有股份。BCo 又拥有同样作为 B 国居民的 CCo 的所有普通股和优先股。ACo 利用借贷资金，向 BCo 收购了 CCo 的优先股。与此同时，ACo 和 BCo 签订了一项协议，根据该协议，BCo 同意在 5 年后，以固定的价格，回购 CCo 的优先股。

A 国对于这些交易的处理与其法律形式相一致。因此，ACo 有权扣除其利息支付，但假设 A 国针对来自外国公司的股息实行参股免税，则 ACo 对收到的 CCo 优先股的股息无须缴税。相比之下，B 国根据其经济实质，将该安排视为 ACo 向 BCo 提供的 5 年期贷款，并以 ACo 持有 CCo 优先股作为担保。因此，B

Tax planning with hybrid entities is not for the fainthearted. It involves the complex interplay of domestic and foreign tax rules, domestic and foreign corporate and commercial law, and tax treaties. The rewards of such planning may be substantial; however, there are also serious risks. For example, in the first hybrid example dealt with above, if the hybrid entity is considered to be resident in Country A or the hybrid is considered to be a PE of ACo in the U.S., the benefits of the arrangement will be nullified. Moreover, any U.S. tax on the payments to the hybrid entity will not be creditable against any Country A tax payable by ACo pursuant to Country A's CFC rules because the U.S. tax is payable by ACo, not the hybrid entity.

7.7.3 Hybrid Financial Instruments

In general, a hybrid financial instrument is a financial instrument that is characterized differently by two countries. For example, an instrument with characteristics of both debt and equity may be treated as debt by one country but as equity (a share) by another country. Like hybrid entities, these hybrid financial instruments are widely used for tax-planning purposes. If a source country treats an instrument issued by a corporation as debt, it will usually characterize the payments on the debt as interest and allow a deduction for those payments. However, the country in which the recipient of the payments is resident may characterize the instrument as a share of the corporate issuer and treat the payments on the share as tax-exempt dividends.

As an example of a hybrid financial instrument that results in a deduction in both the residence and source countries, consider the following sale and repurchase ("repo") arrangement. ACo, a resident of Country A, owns all the shares of BCo, a corporation resident in Country B. In turn, BCo owns all the common and preferred shares of CCo, which is also resident in Country B. ACo borrows money to acquire the preferred shares of CCo from BCo. At the same time, ACo and BCo enter into an agreement under which BCo agrees to repurchase the preferred shares of CCo in five years at a fixed price.

Country A treats these transactions in accordance with their legal form. Thus, ACo is entitled to deduct its interest payments, but, assuming that Country A has a participation exemption for dividends from foreign corporations, ACo is not taxable on any dividends received on the preferred shares of CCo. In contrast, Country B treats the arrangement in accordance with its economic substance as a five-year loan by ACo to BCo, with the preferred shares of CCo held by ACo as security. Thus, Country B allows BCo to deduct

国允许 BCo 作为利息，扣除 CCo 就优先股支付的股息。因此，该安排在 A 国和 B 国都产生了利息扣除，但没有对应的收入入账。

7.7.4 BEPS 第 2 项行动计划关于混合错配安排的报告

BEPS 第 2 项行动计划最终报告《消除混合错配安排的影响》仅针对混合实体、混合金融工具和转让，而不是所有类型的混合安排。更具体地说，该报告侧重于造成在一个国家出现扣除而没有在另一个国家计入收入的混合安排，或者造成在两个国家都出现扣除的混合安排。该报告的建议并非针对可归因于外币损益的金融工具的时间差异或支付款项的价值差异。

关于混合金融工具，该报告侧重于针对金融工具或相关财产（如债务或股权）的款项支付所做定性（如利息或股息）之间的差异。为此目的，金融工具应根据国内法进行定义，在一些国家，国内法可能基于国际财务报告准则或其他会计规则。

关于混合实体，该报告针对的是混合实体支付的款项，所涉及的两个国家认为该款项是由不同实体支付的，或者其中一个国家认为根本不存在此款项支付。作为第二类混合错配的一个例子，设想 A 国居民 ACo 向其全资子公司 B 国居民 BCo 提供贷款的情况。B 国将 BCo 视为应税实体，并允许扣除支付给 ACo 的贷款利息。然而，A 国将 BCo 视为透明实体，并认为 ACo 在 B 国存在分支机构或常设机构。因此，A 国没有确认 BCo 向 ACo 支付的利息，并且可能对 ACo 的外国分支机构利润免于征收 A 国税收。

该报告还针对“反向混合”和“输入错配”，前者涉及混合实体收到的款项支付，后者是根据两国法律创建并转移（输入）到第三国的混合安排。作为输入混合错配安排的一个例子，考虑以下例子。B 国居民 BCo 向其母公司 A 国居民 ACo 发行混合金融工具。BCo 向 ACo 支付的款项可由 BCo 在 B 国扣除，但在 A 国不向 ACo 征税。BCo 然后将资金贷款给位于 C 国的关联公司 CCo。针对该

any dividends paid by CCo on the preferred shares as interest. In the result, the arrangement gives rise to interest deductions in both Country A and Country B with no offsetting income inclusion.

7.7.4 BEPS Action 2 Report on Hybrid Mismatch Arrangements

The BEPS Action 2 Final Report: *Neutralising the Effects of Hybrid Mismatch Arrangements* is targeted only at hybrid entities and hybrid financial instruments and transfers rather than at all types of hybrid arrangements. More specifically, the Report focuses on hybrids that result in a deduction in one country without any income inclusion in the other country or that result in a deduction in both countries. The Report's recommendations are not aimed at timing differences or differences in the value of payments with respect to financial instruments that are attributable to foreign-currency gains and losses.

With respect to hybrid financial instruments, the Report focuses on differences in the characterization of payments (e.g., interest or dividends) on a financial instrument or the underlying property (e.g., debt or shares). For this purpose, a financial instrument is intended to be defined under domestic law, which in some countries may be based on International Financial Reporting Standards or other accounting rules.

With respect to hybrid entities, the Report targets payments made by a hybrid entity where the two countries involved view the payment as being made by different entities or where one country does not consider a payment to have been made at all. As an example of the second type of hybrid mismatch, consider a situation in which ACo, resident in Country A, loans funds to a wholly owned entity, BCo, resident in Country B. Country B treats BCo as a taxable entity and allows a deduction for the interest paid to ACo on the loan. However, Country A treats BCo as transparent and considers ACo to have a branch or PE in Country B; as a result, Country A does not recognize any payment of interest by BCo to ACo and may exempt ACo's foreign branch profits from Country A tax.

The Report also targets "reverse hybrids," which involve payments received by hybrid entities, and "imported mismatches," which are hybrid arrangements created under the laws of two countries and shifted (imported) into a third country. As an example of an imported hybrid mismatch arrangement, consider the following example. BCo, resident in Country B, issues a hybrid financial instrument to its parent, ACo, resident in Country A. The payments by BCo to ACo are deductible by BCo in Country B but are not taxable to ACo in Country A. BCo then loans funds to a related company, CCo, in Country C. The interest payments on the loan are

项贷款所支付的利息，可由 CCo 在 C 国扣除，并计入 BCo 的收入，抵消 BCo 向 ACo 支付的可扣除款项。实际上，A 国和 B 国之间混合安排的利益被转移到了第三国，即 C 国。

为了应对上述不同类型混合安排使纳税人可以从中获益的税收结果，该报告建议制定一系列具体规则，而不是就此作出全面的一般性回应。这些规则非常复杂，许多国家（特别是发展中国家）的税务机关很难适用。

该报告的建议包括由各国单方面加以采用的国内规则，以及虽然是由各国单方面加以采用，但需要与其他国家的规则相协调的其他国内规则。为此，一个国家被视为对目标混合安排采取行动的主要国家，而另一个国家则被视为次要国家，其反混合规则只有在主要国家不处理此种混合安排的情况下才应得到适用。

如果混合安排涉及在一个国家出现扣除，但在另一个国家没有计入收入，则支付方为其居民的国家是主要国家。然而，关于混合金融工具，该报告建议，针对支付方可以扣除的款项支付，收款方为其居民的国家（次要国家）应不予扣除或免税。在任何一种情况下，为了适当地适用混合安排规则，各国都有必要获得有关另一国针对混合金融安排相关款项支付所做处理的详细信息。在这方面，大多数国家的税务机关一般都不具备太多的经验。

在涉及双重扣除的混合实体款项支付的情况下，主要国家是该款项收款方为其居民的国家，该国应当对此种款项不予扣除。类似的方法也适用于出现一国允许扣除而另一国未计收入情形的混合实体款项支付，以及反向混合和输入错配。在这些情况下，主要国家是所支付款项的收款方为其居民的国家。因此，收款方为其居民的国家应对此种款项支付不予免税或扣除，并在对方国家允许扣除时，要求收款方将其计入收入。然而，如果主要国家不照此办理，次要国家即应对此种款项支付不予扣除。尽管 BEPS 第 2 项行动计划报告主要关注修改国内法，以应对混合安排，但该报告也建议对 OECD 协定范本进行一次修改，该修改已被纳入范本在 2017 年的更新之中。

根据 OECD 和联合国协定范本第 1 条第 2 款，通过透明实体获得的所得仅在

deductible by CCo in Country C and are included in BCo's income, offsetting the deductible payments by BCo to ACo. In effect, the benefits of the hybrid arrangement between Country A and Country B are shifted to a third country, Country C.

To counter the beneficial tax results of the different types of hybrid arrangements described above, the Report recommends a series of specific rules rather than a comprehensive general response. The rules are very complex and will be difficult for the tax authorities of many countries, especially developing countries, to apply.

The Report's recommendations consist of domestic rules to be adopted by countries unilaterally and other domestic rules that, although adopted unilaterally, are intended to be coordinated with the rules of other countries. For this purpose, one country is considered to be the primary country taking action against the targeted hybrid arrangement and the other country is considered to be the secondary country whose anti-hybrid rules should apply only if the primary country does not deal with the hybrid arrangement.

In the case of hybrid arrangements involving deductions in one country but no income inclusion in another country, the country in which the payer is resident is the primary country. However, with respect to hybrid financial instruments, the Report recommends that the country in which the recipient is resident (the secondary country) should deny any deduction or exemption for payments that are deductible by the payer. In either case, in order to apply the hybrid arrangement rules properly, it will be necessary for countries to obtain detailed information about the treatment of payments on hybrid financial instruments in another country. This is not typically something with which the tax authorities of most countries have much experience.

In the case of hybrid entity payments involving double deductions, the primary country is the country in which the recipient of the payment is resident, and it is expected to deny a deduction for the payments. A similar approach applies to hybrid entity payments involving a deduction in one country but no income inclusion in the other country, reverse hybrids, and imported mismatches. In these situations, the primary country is the country in which the recipient of the payment is resident. Thus, the country in which the recipient is resident is expected to deny any exemption or deduction for the payment and to require it to be included in income if the other country allows a deduction. If, however, the primary country does not do so, the secondary country is expected to deny any deduction for the payment. Although the BEPS Action 2 Report focused primarily on changes to domestic law to deal with hybrid arrangements, it also recommended one change to the OECD Model Treaty, which was added in the 2017 update.

Under Article 1(2) of the OECD and UN Model Treaties, income earned through a transparent entity is treated as income of a resident for purposes of the treaty only to the extent that

缔约国一方国内税收将该收入视为其居民的所得时，才在协定上将其视为居民的所得。例如，假设A国居民ACo向B国的实体支付利息。A国将该实体视为公司，并根据A国和B国之间协定第11条，对该项利息征收预提税。然而，B国将该实体视为透明的合伙企业，而对合伙人征税。假设该实体有两个平等的成员或合伙人，则第1条第2款的适用取决于这些合伙人为哪一国的居民。一方面，如果两个合伙人都不是B国居民，则由ACo向该实体支付的利息都不符合条件，不能享受第11条所规定的较低税率的协定待遇，因为B国没有将此种利息视为B国居民的所得。另一方面，如果合伙人之一是B国居民，则该合伙人收到的利息的一半将有权取得第11条规定的利益。第1条第2款反映了1999年OECD合伙企业报告（将OECD协定范本适用于合伙企业）相关原则的延伸。

实际上，合伙企业报告和第1条第2款要求缔约国一方为了给予协定待遇，接受缔约国另一方对某个实体所做的定性。因此，在上述例子中，尽管A国将相关实体视为公司，但A国必须接受B国将该实体作为透明的合伙企业的定性。

a contracting state treats that income as income of a resident for purposes of its domestic tax. For example, assume that ACo, a resident of Country A, pays interest to an entity in Country B. Country A treats the entity as a company and imposes withholding tax on the interest in accordance with Article 11 of the treaty between Country A and Country B. However, Country B treats the entity as a transparent partnership and imposes tax on the partners. Assuming that the entity has two equal members or partners, the application of Article 1(2) depends on where those partners are resident. On the one hand, if both partners are not resident in Country B, none of the interest paid by ACo to the entity would qualify for the benefits of the lower rate of tax under Article 11 because Country B does not consider any of the interest to be income of a resident of Country B. On the other hand, if one of the partners is a resident of Country B, then half of the interest received by that partner would be entitled to the benefits of Article 11. Article 1(2) reflects an extension of the principles underlying the 1999 OECD Partnership Report (*The Application of the OECD Model Convention to Partnerships*).

In effect, the Partnership Report and Article 1(2) require a contracting state to accept the characterization of an entity by the other contracting state for purposes of granting the benefits of the treaty. Thus, in the example above, Country A must accept Country B's characterization of the entity as a transparent partnership despite Country A's treatment of the entity as a corporation.

8 税收协定简介

8.1 引言

双边税收协定是国际税收领域的重要内容，是缔约国双方税收制度之间的桥梁。目前世界上有效执行的所得税协定共有 3500 多个，且这一数字还在不断增长。大多数双边税收协定均在很大程度上以 OECD 协定范本和联合国协定范本为基础，联合国协定范本与 OECD 协定范本大体相似，但通过一些条款的增加和修改，允许来源国征收比 OECD 协定范本所允许的更多的税收。后续将讨论这两个范本。

第 8.2 节至第 8.6 节概述了税收协定的若干最重要的普遍性特点，包括税收协定的法律性质、其与国内法的关系、其目的，以及协定的解释等。第 8.7 节概括了颇具影响力的 OECD 协定范本和联合国协定范本的主要特征，让读者基本了解典型的税收协定中的各个条款。第 8.8 节考察若干具体问题，包括协定滥用、非歧视、争议解决、征管合作，以及旨在落实 BEPS 项目对协定所做修改的多边公约。

虽说本章完全着重于所得税协定，但是，还有其他一些类型的协定会涉及税收问题。例如，征收继承税或遗产税的国家，可能会达成对这类税种消除双重征税的协议。此外，截至 2022 年 9 月，共有 146 个国家签署了《多边税收征管互助公约》，该公约由 OECD 与欧洲委员会共同发起，于 1995 年正式生效，并于 2011 年进行了大幅修改。该公约涉及信息交换、税收征收协助、争议解决等

CHAPTER 8
An Introduction to Tax Treaties

8.1 INTRODUCTION

Bilateral tax treaties are an important feature of the international tax landscape that serve as a bridge between the tax systems of the contracting states. Over 3,500 bilateral income tax treaties are currently in effect, and the number is growing. Most bilateral tax treaties are based in large part on the OECD Model Treaty or the UN Model Treaty. The UN Model Treaty is substantially similar to the OECD Model Treaty but includes some additional and different provisions that permit source countries to impose more tax than is permitted by the OECD Model Treaty. Both of these models are discussed below.

Sections 8.2 through 8.6 below provide an overview of several of the most important general aspects of tax treaties, including the legal nature of tax treaties, their relationship with domestic law, their objectives, and the interpretation of treaties. The main features of the influential OECD and UN Model Treaties are summarized in section 8.7 in order to give readers a basic understanding of the provisions of a typical tax treaty. Some special topics, including treaty abuse, nondiscrimination, resolution of disputes, administrative cooperation, and the multilateral treaty to implement the treaty changes of the BEPS Project, are examined in section 8.8.

Although this chapter focuses exclusively on income tax treaties, several other types of treaties deal with tax issues. For example, countries that impose estate or inheritance taxes may have treaties to eliminate double taxation with respect to those taxes. In addition, as of September 2022, 146 countries had signed the Multilateral Convention on Mutual Assistance in Tax Matters, sponsored by the OECD and the Council of Europe, which entered into force in 1995 and was significantly revised in 2011. This Convention deals with tax administration issues, such as exchange of information, assistance in the collection of taxes, and dispute resolution. There are also many types of treaties that deal primarily with nontax matters but also

税收征管问题。另外还存在很多其他类型的协定，这些协定虽然主要解决非税问题，但也包括税收条款。这些非税协定包括航空运输协定、贸易投资协定等；此类协定大多数包括例外条款，规定任何所得税问题都应完全按照各国间的所得税协定予以处理。《关税与贸易总协定》（1994 年重新进行了谈判）与《服务贸易总协定》都包含关于所得税的重要条款，其主要目的是防止将所得税的相关规定作为变相的贸易壁垒或出口补贴。这两项协定于 1994 年并入了《世界贸易组织成立协议》。

近年来的一项重要进展是信息交换协定数量的大幅增加。信息交换协定一般是在高税国家与低税或不征税国家间签署的，因为高税国家与低税或不征税国家不会签署全面的所得税协定。总体而言，信息交换协定要求低税或不征税国家同样按照 OECD 协定范本和联合国协定范本第 26 条的规定，进行信息交换。

所得税协定通常都是双边的，而不是多边的。尽管不时有关于签署多边所得税协定的提议，但目前多边协定仅限于征管领域。各国似乎仍倾向于与每一个协定伙伴国达成定制化的协定，此等协定能够虑及两国的所得税制度，以及两国之间的跨境贸易和投资流动。但是，《关税与贸易总协定》《服务贸易总协定》等贸易和投资协定都是多边协定，因此关于多边所得税协定，并不存在法律障碍。事实上，相比目前各国通过重新谈判、逐一修订其协定的做法，多边协定是修订广泛的双边协定网络更为有效的方法。为此，BEPS 第 15 项行动计划《制定用于修订双边税收协定的多边协议》，催生了一项多边公约，以落实 BEPS 项目中所建议的对税收协定的修订。该公约于 2018 年 7 月 1 日生效，截至 2022 年 10 月，共有 100 个国家签署了该公约（参见下文第 8.8.6 节）。

8.2 税收协定的法律性质和效力

8.2.1 维也纳条约法公约

包括税收协定在内的所有条约都受制于《维也纳条约法公约》（以下简称

include tax provisions. These nontax treaties include air transportation agreements and trade and investment treaties; most of these agreements contain carve-out provisions indicating that any income tax issues will be dealt with exclusively under the income tax treaties between countries. The General Agreement on Tariffs and Trade (GATT), as renegotiated in 1994, and the General Agreement on Trade in Services (GATS), both of which were consolidated as part of the Agreement Establishing the World Trade Organization in 1994, contain some important provisions relating to income taxation that are primarily designed to prevent the use of income tax provisions as disguised trade barriers or export incentives.

An important recent development is the proliferation of TIEAs, typically between high-tax countries and low-or no-tax countries with which the high-tax countries would not otherwise have a comprehensive income tax treaty. In general, TIEAs require the low-or no-tax countries to exchange information on the same basis as provided in Article 26 of the OECD and UN Model Treaties.

Income tax treaties are typically bilateral rather than multilateral. Although proposals have been made from time to time for a multilateral income tax treaty, to date, multilateral agreements have been limited to administrative issues. Countries seem to prefer customized agreements with each treaty partner that take into account their income tax systems and cross-border trade and investment flows between the two countries. However, trade and investment treaties, such as the GATT and the GATS, are multilateral agreements, and there is no legal impediment to a multilateral income tax treaty. In fact, a multilateral agreement is a much more efficient method of revising the vast network of bilateral treaties than the current system of countries renegotiating each of their treaties separately. In this regard, pursuant to BEPS Action 15: *Developing a Multilateral Instrument to Modify Bilateral Tax Treaties*, a multilateral treaty to implement the changes to tax treaties that were recommended as part of the BEPS project entered into force on July 1, 2018 and has been signed by one hundred countries as of October 2022 (*see* section 8.8.6 below).

8.2 LEGAL NATURE AND EFFECT OF TAX TREATIES

8.2.1 *Vienna Convention on the Law of Treaties*

All treaties, including tax treaties, are governed by the *Vienna Convention on the Law of Treaties* ("Vienna Convention"), which was concluded on May 23, 1969, and entered into force on January 27, 1980. Although the Vienna Convention has not been signed by some

《维也纳公约》）。《维也纳公约》于 1969 年 5 月 23 日签署，1980 年 1 月 27 日生效。尽管一些国家（最值得注意的是美国）没有签署《维也纳公约》，但一般认为《维也纳公约》对所有国家都有约束力，因为它的条款是国际惯例法原则中涉及条约问题的法典化。一般认为，所有国家都受国际惯例法原则的约束。

条约是主权国家间达成的协定。根据《维也纳公约》第 2 条：

> 条约系国家间所缔结而以国际法为准之国际协定，不论其载于一项单独文书或两项以上文书内，亦不论其名称如何。

因此，有些税收协定名称为“convention（协议）”，有些则为“agreement（协定）”，这一点无关紧要。

税收协定将权利赋予协定缔约方或签署方，并明确其义务，缔约方或签署方在协定中称为“**缔约国双方**”。在大多数国家，除非通过某种方式将协定规定纳入其国内法，否则协定不会向其公民或居民赋予权利。各国将协定纳入国内法的方法不尽相同：在大多数英联邦国家中，通过国内立法将税收协定纳入国内法；对很多其他国家来说，税收协定是自动生效的，一经政府官员代表签署并批准后，就会成为国内法的一部分；而在另一些国家，协定生效要经过特殊的立法程序，例如在美国，行政部门（即总统，通过财政部执行）达成税收协定后，必须征求参议院的意见，经其同意后协定才能生效。

《维也纳公约》第 26 条包含有约必守原则。根据该原则，条约对缔约国双方均有约束力，各国必须善意履行条约。这一基本原则的意义不言自明：条约是主权国家之间具有约束力的协定，各国必须对其予以尊重；任何国家都不希望与不履行义务的国家达成协议。不幸的是，尽管有约必守原则对税收协定的正常执行来说至关重要，但确实存在相关国家不遵守其税收协定规定的情况。

对等是税收协定的另一项重要的基本原则，尽管其准确的含义并不十分明确。几乎所有税收协定的条款都是对等的。例如，如果根据某项协定，股息、利息、特许权使用费的预提税率被限制为 10% 或 15%，则该税率始终同样适用于

countries (most notably, the U.S.), it is generally considered to be binding on all nations because its provisions are a codification of the principles of customary international law dealing with treaties. All nations are considered to be subject to the principles of customary international law.

Treaties are agreements between sovereign nations. According to Article 2 of the Vienna Convention:

> A treaty is an international agreement (in one or more instruments, whatever called) concluded between states and governed by international law.

Thus, it does not matter that some tax treaties are called "conventions" and others are called "agreements."

Tax treaties confer rights and impose obligations on the parties or signatories to the treaty, who are referred to in the treaties as the **contracting states**. In most countries, they do not confer rights on citizens or residents of the two states unless and until the provisions of the treaty have been incorporated in some manner into the domestic law of the contracting states. The methods for incorporating treaties into domestic law vary from country to country. In most Commonwealth countries, tax treaties are usually incorporated into domestic law by means of domestic legislation. In many other countries, tax treaties are self-executing; they become part of domestic law once they are concluded and ratified by responsible government officials. In other countries, treaties are subject to a special legislative process; for example, in the U.S., tax treaties entered into by the executive branch (the President, acting through the Department of the Treasury) must receive the advice and consent of the U.S. Senate before they become effective.

Article 26 of the Vienna Convention contains *the pacta sunt servanda* principle, under which treaties are binding on the contracting states and must be performed by them in good faith. Such a fundamental principle is self-evident. Treaties are binding agreements between sovereign states and must be respected by them—countries are unlikely to be interested in entering into treaties with countries that do not adhere to their obligations. Unfortunately, although *the pacta sunt servanda* principle is essential for treaties to operate as intended, there have been instances where countries have not respected the provisions of their tax treaties.

Reciprocity is a fundamental underlying principle of tax treaties, although its precise meaning is unclear. The provisions of almost all bilateral tax treaties are reciprocal. For example, if the rate of tax on dividends, interest, and royalties under a treaty is limited to 10

缔约国一方居民支付给缔约国另一方居民的此类款项，以及缔约国另一方居民支付给缔约国一方居民的此类款项。另外，尽管缔约国双方之间支付股息、利息、特许权使用费的数量可能并不相当，但这些款项的预提税率对双方仍对等适用。在信息交换、税收征收协助等条款适用对等原则尤其困难，因为这些条款给各国增添了可能代价颇高的义务。尽管这些条款同样适用于缔约国双方，但存疑的是：对等原则是否要求双方对这些条款的使用必须大体相等，或者是否可以接受大部分甚至所有情况下是由其中一方使用？

虽然并不完全确定，但对等原则似乎源于国际法中一个更为基本的原则，即主权国家平等原则。对等原则有时被理解为两个国家开展税收协定谈判的动机是实现互利互惠。在税收协定条款的解释方面，对等意味着缔约国双方享有同样的法定权利并承担同样的义务，但并不意味着税收协定要在缔约国双方产生同样的法律效果。由于对等原则的法律含义并不宽泛，它对税收协定的解释和执行产生很少影响，甚至不产生影响。

8.2.2 税收协定与国内法的关系

税收协定与国内税收法规之间关系的复杂程度，远远超过许多评论人员和税务专业人士的认识。他们中有许多人认为，税收协定与国内法的关系用一项基本原则尽可以概括，即在协定与国内法规定出现冲突的情况下，协定应优先适用。事实上，税收协定与国内法的关系要比上述观点更为复杂，主要涉及以下问题：

——税收协定对各国地区性税收的影响；

——税收协定是否会限制国内征税、分配征税权或创设征税权；

——税收协定的影响有限，不会完全取代国内法；

——国内法用语的含义纳入税收协定；

——税收协定用语纳入国内法；以及

——国内法律优于税收协定条款适用。

or 15%, that rate invariably applies equally to payments of these amounts by residents of one contracting state to residents of the other contracting state and by residents of the other state to residents of the first state. Moreover, the reciprocal limitation on the rates of tax imposed on dividends, interest, and royalties by the contracting states applies, notwithstanding that the flows of these payments between the two contracting states may be unequal. The application of the principle of reciprocity is especially difficult with respect to provisions such as exchange of information and assistance in the collection of tax. These provisions impose potentially costly obligations on states. Although the provisions apply in the same manner in both states, does the principle of reciprocity require that both states make reasonably equal use of the provisions, or is it acceptable for one state to make disproportionate or even exclusive use of the provisions?

Although it is not completely clear, the principle of reciprocity appears to be derived from the even more fundamental principle of international law—the principle of the equality of sovereign states. The principle of reciprocity is sometimes used to mean the achievement of mutual benefits as motivation for two states to negotiate a tax treaty. With respect to the provisions of tax treaties, reciprocity means that both contracting states are subject to the same legal rights and obligations; it does not mean that tax treaties are intended to have the same legal effect in both states. As a result of this narrow legal meaning of reciprocity, it should have little or no impact on the interpretation or application of tax treaties.

8.2.2 The Relationship Between Tax Treaties and Domestic Law

The relationship between tax treaties and domestic tax legislation is much more complex than many commentators and tax professionals realize. Many of them think that the relationship consists of nothing more than the basic principle that a treaty prevails in the event of a conflict between the provisions of domestic law and the treaty. In fact, the relationship between tax treaties and domestic law is more complex, involving the following issues:

– the effect of tax treaties on subnational taxes;
– whether tax treaties limit domestic tax, allocate taxing rights, or impose tax;
– the limited impact of tax treaties in that they do not displace domestic law entirely;
– the incorporation of meanings of terms in domestic law into tax treaties;
– the incorporation of tax treaty terms into domestic law; and
– domestic laws that override the provisions of tax treaties.

下面简要讨论这几个问题。

总体而言，税收协定适用于缔约国双方征收的所有所得税税种，包括省（州）级、地方和其他国家层级以下的政府征收的税收。但是，在一些联邦制国家，宪法和既定传统禁止中央政府达成的税收协定限制地方政府的征税权。因此，加拿大、美国等一些联邦国家的税收协定仅适用于国家层级征收的税收。在这种情况下，尽管中央政府不能开征违背税收协定规定的税收，但地方政府不受此限制。

总体而言，税收协定并不创设征税权，也不在缔约国双方之间分配征税权，征税权来自一国的国内法。税收协定对一国征收的税收加以限制，其产生的效果从性质上来说，是减轻纳税人的负担。在这一方面，法国和采取法国做法的一些非洲国家是值得注意的例外，因为即使根据国内法并没有征收此种税收，也可以根据协定条款开征。也就是说，只要协定允许，这些国家就可以对某些款项进行征税，尽管按照国内法对这些款项不应予以征税。与此相反，对于大部分国家而言，如果按照国内法，某一款项不应予以征税，那就到此为止，不必再提及协定。

税收协定条款并不完全取代国内法条款。例如，如果按照A国和B国国内法，某人被视为两国税收居民，但按照A国和B国之间协定的加比规则，该人被认定为A国居民。OECD协定范本和联合国协定范本第4条第2款规定了一系列加比规则，以便为了上述协定的目的，将双重居民个人仅认定为其中一国的居民。尽管出于协定的目的，该个人被认定为A国居民，但出于不受协定影响的所有目的，按照B国国内法，该个人仍然是B国居民。例如，如果该个人向非居民支付股息、利息或特许权使用费款项，其应承担B国对B国居民支付此类款项所规定的扣缴义务。

很多税收协定条款明确应参考一些用语在国内法中的含义，因此，这些用语在税收协定中的含义取决于其在运用协定的缔约国一方国内法中的含义。例如，根据OECD协定范本和联合国协定范本第6条（不动产所得），从位于一方的不

These issues are discussed briefly below.

In general, tax treaties apply to all income taxes imposed by the contracting states, including taxes imposed by provincial (state), local, and other subnational governments. In some federal states, however, the central government is prevented by the constitution or established tradition from entering into tax treaties that limit the taxing powers of their subnational governments. Accordingly, the tax treaties of some federal states, such as Canada and the U.S., apply only to national taxes. In such circumstances, a subnational government may impose taxes that contravene the provisions of an applicable tax treaty despite the fact that the central government could not impose similar taxes.

In general, tax treaties do not impose tax, nor do they allocate taxing rights between the contracting states—the right to tax is derived from the domestic law of a state. Tax treaties limit the taxes otherwise imposed by a state; in effect, they are primarily relieving in nature. France and several African countries that follow the French practice are notable exceptions in this regard because taxes may be imposed pursuant to treaty provisions even where they are not imposed under domestic law. In other words, these countries may impose tax on amounts that a treaty allows them to tax, despite the fact that those amounts may not be taxable under their domestic law. In contrast, for most countries, if an amount is not taxable under domestic law, that is the end of the matter; it is unnecessary to refer to the treaty.

The provisions of tax treaties do not displace the provisions of domestic law entirely. For example, a person who is considered to be a resident of both Country A and Country B under their domestic laws may be deemed to be a resident of Country A pursuant to the tie-breaker rule in the treaty between Country A and Country B. Article 4(2) of both the OECD Model and UN Model Treaties provides a series of tie-breaker rules to make a dual-resident individual a resident of only one country for purposes of the treaty. However, although the individual may be considered to be a resident of Country A for purposes of the treaty, the individual will remain a resident of Country B under its domestic law for all purposes not affected by the treaty. If, for example, the individual makes payments of dividends, interest, or royalties to nonresidents, the person may be subject to any withholding obligations imposed by Country B on such payments made by residents of Country B.

Many tax treaty provisions include explicit references to the meaning of terms under domestic law. As a result, the meanings of those terms in a tax treaty are determined by reference to their meanings under the domestic law of the contracting state applying the treaty. For example, under Article 6 (Income from Immovable Property) of both the OECD and UN Model Treaties, income from immovable or real property located in a country is taxable by that

动产或房地产取得的所得应在该国征税。为此，第 6 条第 2 款规定，“不动产”一语具有根据该项财产所在国家的国内法所具有的含义。另外，第 3 条（一般定义）第 2 款规定，未经协定明确定义的用语，除上下文另有解释外，应具有适用协定的国家国内法所规定的含义，这一点后续将进行讨论。反过来说，在一些国家中，国内法使用了同样用于协定之中的用语，对于这些用语出于国内法目的的解释，可能依据这些用语在协定中的含义。实际上，在这类情况下，协定的含义就被纳入了国内法。

前面提到，一般情况下，如果协定条款与国内法条款出现冲突，协定条款应优先适用。在有些国家中，该原则被纳入了宪法；在其他一些国家，这一原则被确立为法定原则；还有一些国家则将协定视为特别法，而优先于其他法律。在美国，解决国内法和协定冲突的基本规则是时间上的后法优先。除了赋予协定宪法意义上的优先权的国家之外，一国有可能通过优先于其税收协定的法律。这种法律通常称为“**优于协定适用**”。例如，有些国家通过了法律规定，修改或推翻由国内法院对税收协定所做的解释，其所基于的考虑可能是法院判决与关于 OECD 协定范本或联合国协定范本的注释，或缔约国双方的初衷不一致。这一立法如系善意制定，可能并不违背该国根据其税收协定所承担的义务。但是，意欲优于协定适用的国家可能需要提前与其缔约伙伴国协商，显示其善意，避免误解。

个别情况下，一些国家的立法包含了优于协定适用的规定，以防止纳税人在法庭上提出该国税收协定导致无法适用国内法规定。这种优于协定适用的做法颇具争议。税收协定是非常严肃的义务，除特殊情况外不能无视。如果一国对协定条款不满意，恰当的补救措施是重谈或终止协定。同时，各国必须有能力适时修订国内税法规定，使之与时俱进、考虑最新进展，并澄清涉及协定和国内法关系的解释性疑难。

country. For this purpose, the term "immovable property" is defined in Article 6(2) to have the meaning that it has under the domestic law of the country in which the property is located. In addition, Article 3(2) (General Definitions), which is discussed below, provides that any undefined terms in a treaty should be given the meaning that they have under the law of the country applying the treaty unless the context requires otherwise. Conversely, in some countries where the domestic law uses terms that are also used in the treaty, the meaning of those terms for purposes of domestic law may be interpreted in accordance with the meaning of the terms for purposes of the treaty. In effect, in these circumstances, treaty meanings are incorporated into domestic law.

As noted above, as a general rule, the provisions of tax treaties prevail in the event of a conflict with the provisions of domestic law. In some countries, this principle is enshrined in the constitution; in other countries, it is enacted as a statutory rule; in yet other countries, treaties prevail over other laws because they are considered to be special (*lex specialis*). In the U.S., the basic rule for resolving conflicts between statutes and treaties is that the later in time prevails. Except in countries that give constitutional priority to treaties, it is possible for countries to adopt legislation that takes priority over their tax treaties. Such legislation is often referred to as a **treaty override**. For example, some countries have passed legislation to modify or overturn the interpretation of a tax treaty by their domestic courts, perhaps on the basis that the court decisions are inconsistent with the Commentary on the OECD or UN Model Treaties or the intentions of the contracting states. Such legislation, adopted in good faith, may not violate a country's obligations under its tax treaties. However, a country contemplating a treaty override may want to consult with its treaty partners in advance to demonstrate good faith and prevent misunderstandings.

Occasionally, some countries have included treaty overrides in legislation to prevent taxpayers from arguing in court that the countries' tax treaties prevent the application of the legislation. This type of treaty override is very controversial. Tax treaties are solemn obligations that should not be disregarded except in extraordinary circumstances. If a country becomes dissatisfied with the provisions of a tax treaty, the appropriate remedy is the renegotiation or termination of the treaty. At the same time, countries must have the ability to amend the provisions of their domestic tax legislation to keep it current to deal with new developments and to clarify interpretive difficulties concerning the relationship between the treaty and domestic law.

8.3 OECD 协定范本和联合国协定范本

目前存在两项有影响力的税收协定范本，即 OECD《关于所得和财产的税收协定范本》（参见 www.oecd.org）和联合国《发达国家与发展中国家间避免双重征税协定范本》（参见 www.un.org/development/desa/financing/sites/www.un.org.development.desa.financing/files/2022-03/UN%20Model_2021.pdf）。两个范本都分别于 2017 年、2021 年发布了最新版本。有些国家有其自己的税收协定工作文本，通常并不公布，但会提供给其他国家，用于商谈税收协定。美国公布了数版税收协定工作文本，最新（2016 年）版参见 www.irs.gov。联合国协定范本和各国的工作文本大体与 OECD 协定范本类似，可以视为 OECD 协定范本的修订版，而不是单独制定的范本。

OECD 协定范本历史悠久，起源于 19 世纪早先的一些外交条约。这些条约的目的非常有限，即保证一国在另一国工作的外交官不会受到歧视。20 世纪初，各国广泛施行所得税后，外交条约的适用范围得到扩大，涵盖了所得税。第一次世界大战后，国际联盟开始研究制定专门处理所得税问题的协定范本。这项工作的最终成果是分别在 1943 年和 1946 年初步拟就的伦敦范本和墨西哥范本。这两个范本并未得到普遍认可，而后 OECD 承担了起草能被广泛接受的范本这一工作。目前，OECD 有 38 个成员国，其中包括大部分主要的工业化国家。OECD 成员国最近扩大到智利、哥伦比亚、哥斯达黎加、爱沙尼亚、以色列、斯洛文尼亚和立陶宛。

OECD 协定范本于 1963 年首次以草案的形式公布，1977 年出版了正式版本，1992 年进行了修订。1992 年，OECD 决定以更灵活的方式处理协定范本，更频繁地定期更新，而不是偶尔全面翻新。因此，1992 年以后，OECD 协定范本修订了 10 次，最近一次是在 2017 年。由成员国资深税务专家组成的 OECD 财政事务委员会，通过几个工作组开展工作，其中第一工作组负责税收协定范本，持续密切关注协定问题。关于对 OECD 税收工作组织架构的说明，参见第 1 章第 1.5 节。

8.3 THE OECD AND UN MODEL TAX TREATIES

There are two influential model tax treaties—the OECD *Model Tax Convention on Income and on Capital* (available at www.oecd.org) and the UN *Model Double Taxation Convention Between Developed and Developing Countries* (available at www.un.org/ development/desa/ financing/sites/www.un.org.development.desa.financing/files/2022-03/UN%20Model_2021.pdf), the most recent versions of which were published in 2017 and 2021, respectively. Some countries have their own model tax treaties, which are often not published but are provided to other countries for the purpose of negotiating tax treaties. The U.S. has published several versions of its model treaty; the most recent (2016) version is available at www.irs.gov. The UN Model Treaty and the various country models are broadly similar to the OECD Model Treaty and can be viewed as modified versions of the OECD Model Treaty rather than as separate models.

The OECD Model Treaty has a long history, beginning with early diplomatic treaties of the nineteenth century. The limited objective of those treaties was to ensure that diplomats of one country working in another would not be discriminated against; they were extended to cover income taxation once income taxes began to be widely adopted in the early part of the twentieth century. After the First World War, the League of Nations commenced work on the development of a model treaty dealing exclusively with income tax issues. This work culminated in draft model conventions in 1943 (the London Model) and 1946 (the Mexico Model). These conventions were not unanimously accepted, and the work of creating an acceptable model treaty was taken over by the OECD. Currently, the OECD has thirty-eight members, consisting of most of the major industrialized countries. Membership in the OECD has recently been extended to Chile, Colombia, Costa Rica, Estonia, Israel, Slovenia, and Lithuania.

The OECD Model Treaty was first published, in draft form, in 1963. The first official version was issued in 1977 and was revised in 1992. In 1992, the OECD decided that the Model Treaty should be ambulatory, with more frequent periodic updates rather than complete revisions at less frequent intervals. Consequently, since 1992 the OECD Model Treaty has been revised ten times, most recently in 2017. The OECD Committee on Fiscal Affairs, which consists of senior tax officials from the member countries, operates through several Working Parties, including Working Party No. 1, which is responsible for the Model Treaty and examines issues related to the treaty on an ongoing basis. See Chapter 1, section 1.5 for a description of the organizational structure of the OECD's tax work.

1968 年，联合国经济和社会理事会（ECOSOC）设立了联合国发达国家与发展中国家间税收协定特别专家组，联合国关于协定范本的工作由此开始。该专家组拟定了《发达国家与发展中国家间双边税收协定谈判手册》，联合国《发达国家与发展中国家间税收协定范本》也随之于 1980 年发布。联合国协定范本于 2001 年、2011 年、2017 年有过修订，最近一次修订是在 2021 年。2004 年，上述专家组转变为国际税收合作专家委员会。关于联合国的税收工作和该专家委员会的介绍，参见第 1 章第 1.5 节。

联合国协定范本采用了 OECD 协定范本设定的体例，其中的很多条款与 OECD 协定范本的条款相同或基本相同。这两个范本的主要区别在于，联合国协定范本对发展中国家可能征收的税收设置了较少的限制，以反映发展中国家主要作为来源国的利益。例如，联合国协定范本没有具体限制来源国设定的关于股息、利息、特许权使用费、技术服务费和自动化数字服务所得的预提税率，而是交由缔约国双方通过双边谈判确定。同样，联合国协定范本在特定情形下降低了构成常设机构的门槛，相比 OECD 协定范本，允许来源国对更多的跨境营业利润征税，第 8.7.3.2 节将讨论这一点。

OECD 协定范本和联合国协定范本都附有详细的注释，按照协定条款逐项编排。值得一提的是，OECD 协定范本注释对税收协定解释和适用的重要性日益提升，对于非 OECD 成员之间的税收协定亦是如此。为了把一些非成员国的意见考虑在内，OECD 将范本注释于 1997 年向非成员国开放，把这些国家关于 OECD 协定范本条款及其注释的立场记录注明。截至 2022 年，已有 33 个非 OECD 成员表达过立场。

一般而言，相比联合国协定范本，OECD 协定范本有利于资本输出国（居民国）而非资本输入国（来源国）。通常，OECD 协定范本消除或减轻双重征税的方式，是要求来源国放弃其针对缔约国对方居民取得的特定类型所得的部分或全部征税权。如果两国贸易和投资往来大致相当，并且居民国对来源国免税的所得都予以征税，那么，OECD 协定范本的这种处理方式尚为恰当。下面的例子将说

The work of the UN on a model treaty commenced in 1968 with the establishment by the UN Economic and Social Council (ECOSOC) of the UN Ad Hoc Group of Experts on Tax Treaties Between Developed and Developing Countries. The Group of Experts produced a *Manual for the Negotiation of Bilateral Tax Treaties Between Developed and Developing Countries*, which led to the publication of the UN *Model Taxation Convention Between Developed and Developing Countries* in 1980. The UN Model Treaty was revised in 2001, 2011, 2017, and, most recently, in 2021. In 2004, the Group of Experts became the Committee of Experts on International Cooperation in Tax Matters. See Chapter 1, section 1.5 for a description of the Committee of Experts and the UN's tax work.

The UN Model Treaty follows the pattern set by the OECD Model Treaty, and many of its provisions are identical, or nearly identical, to those of the OECD Model Treaty. The chief difference between the two models is that the UN Model Treaty imposes fewer restrictions on the taxes that may be imposed by developing countries to reflect their interests as primarily source countries. For example, the UN Model Treaty does not contain specific limitations on withholding tax rates on dividends, interest, royalties, fees for technical services, and income from automated digital services imposed by source countries; instead, the withholding rates are left to bilateral negotiations between the contracting states. Similarly, as discussed in section 8.7.3.2 below, the UN Model Treaty allows source countries to tax more cross-border business profits than the OECD Model Treaty by lowering the threshold for a PE in certain circumstances.

A detailed Commentary, organized on an article-by-article basis, accompanies both the OECD and the UN Model Treaties. In particular, the OECD Commentary has become increasingly important with respect to the interpretation and application of tax treaties, including treaties between countries that are not members of the OECD. To take into account the positions of some nonmember states, the OECD opened up the Commentary in 1997 for nonmember countries to register their positions on the provisions of the OECD Model Treaty and its Commentary. As of 2022, thirty-three countries have done so.

In general and in comparison to the UN Model Treaty, the OECD Model Treaty favors capital-exporting (residence) countries over capital-importing (source) countries. Often it eliminates or mitigates double taxation by requiring the source country to give up some or all of its taxing rights on certain categories of income earned by residents of the other treaty country. This aspect of the OECD Model Treaty is appropriate if the flow of trade and investment between the two countries is reasonably equal and the residence country taxes any income that the source country exempts from tax. The following example

明这一点。

A 国和 B 国均为发达国家，正在考虑谈签税收协定。两国都对其居民的全球所得征税，并对其居民就外国来源所得缴纳的预提税给予外国税收抵免。假设 A 国有一个纳税人 A，从 B 国取得 1000 元特许权使用费。同样，B 国也有一个纳税人 B，从 A 国取得 1000 元特许权使用费。在没有协定的情况下，B 国会对支付给纳税人 A 的特许权使用费征收 15% 的预提税，A 国对支付给纳税人 B 的特许权使用费也做同样处理。B 国允许纳税人 B 对支付给 A 国的预提税，提出外国税收抵免，A 国允许抵免由纳税人 A 支付给 B 国的类似税款。如果两国在其税收协定中商定，针对缔约国另一方居民，将特许权使用费源泉预提税率降为零，那么，每个国家将因此损失来源国税收收入 150 元（1000 × 0.15），但是，两国额外向其本国居民征税 150 元，即可弥补损失的来源国税收收入。

通过上例可以得出两个重要结论。第一，放弃对来源于其境内所得的本国税收的国家，如果适用免税方法消除国际双重征税，其就不能指望通过扩大其居民管辖权，来弥补损失的税收收入。

第二，以基于所得来源的国内税收，换取基于纳税人居民身份的税收，对于资本净输入国来说可能是不利的。当然，缔约国双方之间的投资往来肯定不会像上例中那样精准吻合；与严格的对等略有偏差是可以接受的，对于税收协定网络较大的国家来说尤为如此。如果一组国家都基于 OECD 协定范本达成双边协定，重要的是这组国家之间的投资往来应大体平衡。这样，一国在其某些协定下损失的税收收入，有望可以从其他协定中得到补偿。

发展中国家都是资本净输入国，其中很多国家适用免税法为其居民纳税人消除双重征税。因此，与发达国家缔结税收协定的发展中国家，按照 OECD 协定范本所述，以基于所得来源的征税来换取基于纳税人居民身份的征税，并不能从中获益。如前所述，OECD 协定范本的这些缺点，使得发展中国家在联合国的主持下，制定自己的协定范本。

OECD 协定范本的成功是引人注目的，几乎所有双边税收协定都以该范本作

illustrates this point.

Country A and Country B are both developed countries contemplating a tax treaty. Both countries tax their residents on a worldwide basis, and both provide their residents with a foreign tax credit for withholding taxes paid with respect to foreign source income. Country A has one taxpayer, Taxpayer A, who earns royalties of 1,000 from Country B. Country B likewise has one taxpayer, Taxpayer B, who earns royalties of 1,000 from Country A. Absent a treaty, Country B would impose a 15% withholding tax on royalties paid to Taxpayer A, and Country A would do the same with respect to royalties paid to Taxpayer B. Country B would allow Taxpayer B to claim a foreign tax credit for the withholding taxes paid to Country A, and Country A would allow a credit for the comparable taxes paid by Taxpayer A to Country B. If the two countries agree in their tax treaty to reduce withholding at source on royalties to a rate of zero for residents of the other contracting state, each country would thereby lose source-tax revenue of 150 (1,000 × 0.15). However, they would recoup the lost source-tax revenue by collecting 150 in additional tax from their own residents.

Two important points may be drawn from this example. First, a country that gives up the domestic tax that it imposes on income derived from its territory cannot expect to recoup the lost revenue from an expansion of its residence jurisdiction if it uses an exemption system to relieve international double taxation.

Second, a trade-off of domestic tax based on the source of income for tax based on the residence of the taxpayer is likely to be unfavorable for a country that is a net importer of capital. Of course, investment flows between two contracting states are never as exact as in the above example; some deviations from strict reciprocity are acceptable, especially for countries with a network of tax treaties. If a group of countries enters into bilateral treaties based on the OECD Model Treaty, what is important is that the investment flows within that group be roughly in balance. In such circumstances, a country that loses revenue under some of its treaties can expect to recoup the revenue under other treaties.

Developing countries are net capital importers, and many of them use the exemption method for granting double taxation relief to their resident taxpayers. Consequently, developing countries entering into a tax treaty with a developed country would not benefit from the trade-off of taxation based on the source of income for taxation based on the residence of taxpayers contained in the OECD Model Treaty. As noted above, the shortcomings of the OECD Model Treaty led to developing countries devising their own model treaty under the auspices of the UN.

The success of the OECD Model Treaty has been remarkable—virtually all existing

为基础。如上所述，联合国协定范本和美国协定范本都遵循了 OECD 协定范本的基本体例。OECD 协定范本得到广泛接受，众多国际税收规则随之标准化，已成为缓解国际重复征税、促进国际贸易和投资的重要因素。

尽管如此，OECD 协定范本也有一些不足之处。例如，有些条款故意含混不清，以遮掩 OECD 成员国之间的分歧。其次，该协定范本完全没有涉及国际税收的许多重要内容，如外汇损益、复杂的财务安排、跨境重组和企业合并方法等。再次，从某种意义上讲，OECD 协定范本也是其自身成功的受害者；修订 OECD 协定范本条款，来纠正缺陷、回应变化极为困难。造成这种困难的原因之一，是各国只能通过重新商谈其现有协定，来纳入 OECD 协定范本的更新内容，这非常消耗时间，对于协定网络较大的国家来说尤为如此。

存在困难的原因之二在于 OECD 的传统做法，即只有在所有成员国一致同意的情况下，才能修订该协定范本。但是，一致同意规则的实际意义已有所降低，因为对协定范本的任何方面有不同意见的成员国，可以提出针对 OECD 协定范本某项具体条款的**保留意见**，并将之记录在案，表明该国不愿意在其税收协定中认同 OECD 协定范本的某项具体条款。在 OECD 协定范本的注释中可以看到这些保留意见，大部分国家都对该协定范本的部分内容提出了保留。例如，14 个 OECD 成员国对涉及特许权使用费的第 12 条提出了保留，表明其希望对特许权使用费征收预提税。

注释还包含一些国家对注释的具体内容的**意见备注**。这些意见通常用于表明，某个国家对协定范本某项条款或注释中部分内容的解释，不同于大多数成员国的解释。一国发表意见，并不意味着该国拒绝采纳协定范本的某项条款；相反，意见的目的在于表明该国同意在其协定中纳入该条款，但是，对该条款的解释和适用，将不同于范本注释表达的观点。如果注释列举多种不同立场，一国采用其中一种立场，该国就不应在注释中提出意见备注。

与协定范本的条款本身相比，OECD 协定范本的注释的修改要更容易得多。

bilateral tax treaties are based on it. As noted above, even the UN Model Treaty and U.S. Model Treaty follow the basic pattern of the OECD Model Treaty. This wide acceptance of the OECD Model Treaty, and the resulting standardization of many international tax rules, has been an important factor in reducing international double taxation and facilitating international trade and investment.

Nevertheless, the OECD Model Treaty has several deficiencies. For example, some provisions are intentionally vague in order to mask disagreements among OECD member countries. Also, many important aspects of international tax, such as foreigncurrency gains and losses, sophisticated financial arrangements, cross-border reorganizations, and corporate integration methods, are not dealt with in the Model Treaty at all. Moreover, in some ways, the OECD Model Treaty is a victim of its own success. Changing the articles of the OECD Model Treaty to correct flaws and respond to new developments is extremely difficult. One source of this difficulty is that countries can adopt revisions of the OECD Model Treaty only by renegotiating their existing treaties, which is time-consuming, especially for countries with large treaty networks.

Another source of difficulty is the OECD tradition of amending the Model Treaty only with the unanimous consent of all OECD members. The practical significance of the consensus rule is diminished because member countries that disagree with any aspect of the Model Treaty can register a reservation on the particular provision of the Model Treaty, indicating that the country does not intend to agree to the particular provision of the OECD Model Treaty in its tax treaties. These **reservations** are found in the Commentary on the OECD Model Treaty. Most countries have entered reservations on some aspects of the Model Treaty. For example, fourteen member countries have entered reservations on Article 12 dealing with royalties by asserting their intention to levy withholding taxes on royalties.

The Commentary also contains **observations** by particular countries on specific aspects of the Commentary. Observations are usually used to indicate that a particular country's interpretation of a provision of the Model Treaty or a part of the Commentary differs from the interpretation of the majority of the member countries. A country making an observation does not reject the particular article of the Model Treaty; rather, the purpose of the observation is to indicate that the country will agree to include the provision in its treaties but will interpret and apply the provision in a manner different from the view expressed in the Commentary. A country is not expected to enter an observation if the Commentary sets out alternative positions and the country adopts one of those positions.

The Commentary on the OECD Model Treaty is much easier to change than the articles of

如注释所述，注释中所表达的观点，除存在保留或不同意见的情况外，在解释和适用成员国之间的所有税收协定时，都应予以遵循，对于在注释修订前签署的协定也不例外。将对注释的修订适用于之前即已存在的税收协定，这种做法给协定解释带来了一些很有意思的问题，第 8.6 节将讨论这些问题。

8.4 谈签和修订税收协定的过程

税收协定谈判通常始于两国初步接触。在确定是否与对方国家开展税收协定谈判时，一国通常会考虑很多因素，包括与对方国家的贸易和投资水平。一旦两国决定进行谈判，负责官员就会交换工作文本（如果没有工作文本，也可以交换其最近签署的协定），并安排当面谈判或视频谈判（因新冠肺炎疫情）。

就传统而言，协定谈判需要进行两轮，即在双方国家各进行一轮。在第一轮谈判中，双方谈判团队同意采用某个文本（通常是 OECD 协定范本或联合国协定范本）作为谈判基础。双方介绍各自国内税法体系后，再逐条进行谈判。双方无法达成一致的文本内容一般放入方括号内，后续再进行讨论。一旦就某一条款的措辞达成一致，双方将对该条款进行草签[①]。双方谈判人员商定所有条款后，即安排被授权的官员（通常是大使或政府官员）签署协定。签字之后，各国必须根据各自国内的批准程序，批准该协定。各国交换批准文书后，即为达成该协定[②]。协定的生效以协定中的具体条款［OECD 协定范本和联合国协定范本第 30 条（生效）］为准。

因此，税收协定的缔结过程包含了若干单独的步骤或阶段：签署、批准、达成和生效。每个步骤都有特殊的含义和特定的影响。

协定一经缔结，经缔约国双方同意，可以对其进行细微或重大修订。修订税收协定的常见方式是双方签订协定的议定书。如上文第 8.2.1 节所述，按照《维

① 按照我国税收协定谈判惯例，谈判双方就协定所有条款达成一致后，再对协定文本整体进行草签。——译者注

② 按照我国税收协定谈判惯例，双方通过谈判就协定所有条款达成一致后，即视为达成协定。——译者注

the Model Treaty itself. According to the Commentary, the views expressed in the Commentary, subject to any reservations or observations, should be taken into account in interpreting and applying all treaties between member states, even those treaties entered into before the revisions to the Commentary. This practice of applying revisions of the Commentary to previously existing tax treaties raises some interesting questions of interpretation that are dealt with in section 8.6 below.

8.4 THE PROCESS OF NEGOTIATING AND REVISING TAX TREATIES

The negotiation of a tax treaty typically begins with initial contacts between the countries. Usually, a country will consider many factors, including the level of trade and investment with another country, in deciding whether to enter into negotiations for a tax treaty with that country. Once the countries have decided to negotiate, the responsible officials exchange their model treaties (or their most recent tax treaties if they do not have a model treaty) and schedule face-to-face or virtual (in light of the COVID-19 pandemic) negotiations.

Traditionally, treaties are negotiated in two rounds, one in each country. During the first round of negotiations, the negotiating teams agree on a particular text—usually the OECD Model or UN Model Treaty—to use as the basis for the negotiations. After presentations by both sides about their domestic tax systems, the negotiations proceed on an article-by-article basis. Aspects of the text that cannot be agreed on are usually placed in square brackets to be dealt with later. Once the wording of an article is agreed on, the parties initial it. Once all the articles have been agreed on by the treaty negotiators, arrangements are made for the treaty to be signed by an authorized official (often an ambassador or government official). After signature, each state must ratify the treaty in accordance with its own ratification procedures. The treaty is concluded when the countries exchange instruments of ratification. The treaty enters into force in accordance with the specific rules in the treaty (Article 30 (Entry into Force) of the OECD and UN Model Treaties).

Thus, the process for the adoption of a tax treaty involves several separate steps or stages: signature, ratification, conclusion, and entry into force. Each of these steps has a special meaning and particular consequences.

Once a treaty has been adopted, it may be modified in minor or major ways by the mutual consent of the contracting states. It is common for a tax treaty to be amended by the parties

也纳公约》的规定，被称为议定书的协议也是一种条约，只不过是名称不一样。因此，正如此前讨论的那样，必须根据适用于协定的规则，对议定书予以批准之后，议定书方能生效。

税收协定和国内税法一样需要更新。事实上，修订过程非常缓慢，也非常困难。议定书谈判花费与协定谈判一样多的时间，这种情况并非罕见。通常，一旦协定的某个方面可以重新谈判，那么，其他方面也可以进行协商。因此，如果一国具有广泛的协定网络（有些国家与 100 多个国家之间存在税收协定），重新谈判所有协定将耗费几十年的时间。

在有限的范围之内，税收协定可以通过解释进行更新，而无须正式的修订程序。例如，第 8.3 节已经提到，OECD 注释频繁更新，以明确协定条款的含义。OECD 认为，对注释的更新应适用于做出更新前已经签署的协定（参见 OECD 协定范本引言第 33 段至第 36.1 段）。但是，很多国家的法院似乎都不认同 OECD 的观点。此外，OECD 协定范本和联合国协定范本第 25 条（相互协商程序）都授权缔约国双方主管当局解决解释方面的问题。协定解释的一般规则将在以下第 8.6 节中讨论。

8.5 税收协定的目的

总体而言，税收协定的根本目的是通过消除对于跨境贸易和投资的税收障碍以促进跨境往来。这一宽泛的目标被辅之以若干具体的操作性目标。

从纳税人的角度来说，双边税收协定最重要的操作性目标是消除双重征税，典型双边税收协定的一些条款即为实现此目的。例如，税收协定包含“加比规则”（OECD 协定范本和联合国协定范本第 4 条第 2 款、第 3 款），出于协定的目的，将按照缔约国双方各自国内法，作为双方居民的纳税人，认定为仅为其中一方的居民。另外，税收协定还限制或取消来源国对某些类型所得的征税（OECD 协定范本和联合国协定范本第 10 条、第 11 条、第 12 条），并要求居

entering into a Protocol to the treaty. Under the provisions of the Vienna Convention, as discussed in section 8.2.1 above, an agreement designated as a Protocol is simply a treaty under a different name. Thus, as described above, it must be ratified under the rules applicable to treaties before it becomes effective.

Tax treaties require updating, just like domestic tax laws. In practice, the amendment process is often exceedingly slow and difficult—it is not uncommon for a Protocol to take as long to negotiate as a treaty. Often, once one aspect of a treaty is opened up for renegotiation, other aspects of the treaty become negotiable. Consequently, if a country has a broad network of tax treaties—some have tax treaties with over one hundred countries—the renegotiation of the entire network could take decades.

To a limited degree, tax treaties may be updated without a formal amendment procedure through the interpretive process. For example, as discussed in section 8.3 above, the OECD Commentary is frequently updated to "clarify" the meaning of the articles of the treaty. The OECD takes the position that the revisions to the Commentary should be applied to tax treaties that were entered into before those revisions were made (*see* paragraphs 33–36.1 of the Introduction to the OECD Model Treaty); however, the courts of many countries do not appear to follow the OECD position. In addition, Article 25 (MAP) of both the OECD and UN Model Treaties authorizes the competent authorities of the two states to resolve issues of interpretation. The general rules for interpreting treaties are discussed below in section 8.6.

8.5 OBJECTIVES OF TAX TREATIES

The fundamental objective of tax treaties, broadly stated, is to facilitate cross-border trade and investment by eliminating the tax impediments to these cross-border flows. This broad objective is supplemented by several more specific operational objectives.

From the perspective of taxpayers, the most important operational objective of bilateral tax treaties is the elimination of double taxation. Several provisions of the typical bilateral tax treaty are directed at the achievement of this goal. For example, tax treaties contain tie-breaker rules (Article 4(2) and (3) of the OECD and UN Model Treaties) to deem a taxpayer who is otherwise resident in both countries under their domestic law to be a resident of only one of the countries for purposes of the treaty. They also limit or eliminate the source country tax on certain types of income (Articles 10, 11, and 12 of the OECD and UN Model Treaties) and require residence countries to provide relief for source country taxes, either by way of a foreign tax credit or an exemption for the foreign source income (Article 23 of the OECD and

民国通过外国税收抵免，或对外国来源所得免税，以纾解来源国税收带来的重复征税（OECD 协定范本和联合国协定范本第 23 条）。第 4 章第 4.3 节讨论避免双重征税的机制。

20 世纪中叶，税收协定的焦点几乎完全在于解决双重征税的问题。1963 年和 1977 年的 OECD 协定范本的标题《A 国和 B 国关于对所得和财产避免双重征税的协定》即反映了这一焦点。当时，跨国企业面临严重双重征税的风险，对双重征税给予单边救济的国家非常少，大范围的税收协定网络刚刚开始形成。其实，大多数重大双重征税问题的协定解决方法，是在 20 世纪 50 年代和 60 年代初形成的，如今各国谈签税收协定时已广泛接受了这些方法。

历史上对消除双重征税的重视，不应掩盖大多数税收协定另外一个同等重要的操作性目标，即防止逃避税，这一目标是消除双重征税的反面。税收协定旨在消除对跨境所得的双重征税，但无意为双重不征税提供便利。税收协定所基于的假设是应当对跨境所得予以征税，但只能征税一次。

起初，OECD 协定范本和联合国协定范本序言指出，税收协定旨在消除双重征税和防止偷漏税。“偷漏税”一语的含义并不明确，有些国家将其宽泛地解释为包括避税，但是，包括瑞士在内的其他国家将该用语仅限于构成犯罪的逃税行为。OECD 协定范本和联合国协定范本分别于 1992 年和 2001 年删除了序言中提及避免双重征税和防止偷漏税的内容，将其移至脚注之中。但是，OECD 于 2003 年修订了关于协定范本的注释，其中明确表示“防止逃避税也是税收协定的目的之一”。

对利用税收协定为避税提供便利的关注越来越多，使得 OECD 在 BEPS 项目中，建议修改 OECD 协定范本的标题和序言，明确提及防止避税（参见 BEPS 第 6 项行动计划最终报告《防止不当情形下的协定待遇授予》，可浏览 www.oecd.org，第 8.8.2.3 节将进行讨论）。2017 年，OECD 协定范本的标题修改为《A 国和 B 国关于对所得和财产消除双重征税和防止逃避税的协定》。新的序言明确提及双重不征税和择协避税：“愿意缔结一项协定，以消除对所得和财产的双重征

UN Model Treaties). The mechanisms for granting relief from double taxation are discussed in Chapter 4, section 4.3.

In the mid-twentieth century, the focus of tax treaties was almost exclusively on solving the problem of double taxation. This focus was reflected in the title of the 1963 and 1977 OECD Model Treaties: "Convention between (State A) and (State B) for the avoidance of double taxation with respect to taxes on income and on capital." At that time, multinational enterprises were facing risks of substantial double taxation, few countries provided unilateral relief for double taxation, and widespread treaty networks were just starting to develop. Treaty solutions to most of the major double-tax problems were worked out in the 1950s and early 1960s, however, and they are now routinely accepted by states when they enter into tax treaties.

The historical emphasis on the elimination of double taxation should not obscure the fact that most tax treaties have another equally important operational objective—the prevention of tax evasion and avoidance. This objective is the converse of the elimination of double taxation. Tax treaties are intended to eliminate double taxation of cross-border income but are not intended to facilitate double nontaxation. The underlying assumption of tax treaties is that cross-border income should be taxed but taxed only once.

Originally, the OECD and UN Model Treaties included a preamble stating that the treaty was intended to eliminate double taxation and prevent fiscal evasion. The meaning of the term "fiscal evasion" was unclear; some countries interpreted it broadly to include tax avoidance, while others, such as Switzerland, restricted the term to criminal tax evasion. The references in the preamble to the avoidance of double taxation and prevention of fiscal evasion were eliminated from the OECD and UN Model Treaties and moved to a footnote in 1992 and 2001, respectively. However, in 2003 the Commentary on the OECD Model Treaty was revised to include an explicit statement that "[I]t is also a purpose of tax conventions to prevent tax avoidance and evasion."

The increasing focus on the use of tax treaties to facilitate tax avoidance led the OECD, as part of the BEPS project, to recommend changes to the title and preamble of the OECD Model Treaty to refer explicitly to the prevention of tax avoidance (*see* BEPS Action 6 Final Report: *Preventing the Granting of Treaty Benefits in Inappropriate Circumstances,* available at www.oecd.org and discussed in section 8.8.2.3). In 2017, the title of the OECD Model Treaty was revised to "Convention between (State A) and (State B) for the elimination of double taxation with respect to taxes on income and on capital and the prevention of tax evasion and avoidance." The new preamble includes explicit references to double nontaxation and treaty shopping: "*Intending to conclude a Convention for the elimination of double taxation with respect*

税，同时防止通过逃避税（包括第三国居民通过择协避税安排，取得本协定规定的税收优惠而间接获益）造成的不征税或少征税。”联合国协定范本 2017 年修订时也采用了同样的标题和序言。

尽管消除逃避税是大部分税收协定的明确目标，但在这些协定中，为实现这一目标设计的条款并不多。OECD 协定范本和联合国协定范本都包含信息交换（第 25 条）和税收征收协助（第 27 条）条款，这些条款为缔约国双方提供了防止逃避税的两个重要工具。但是，在 2017 年之前，这两个协定范本都不包含任何一般反避税规则，包含具体反避税规则的协定也很少。OECD 发布的 BEPS 第 6 项行动计划最终报告提出增加详细的防止择协避税的规则，与美国税收协定所含的利益限制条款类似。该报告还提出增加一般反滥用条款，根据该条款，如果一项交易或安排的主要目的之一是避税，那么，将否定其协定待遇，除非给予该待遇符合协定的宗旨和目的。关于协定滥用、择协避税（包括利益限制条款），以及 2017 年 OECD 协定范本和联合国协定范本新增加的一般反滥用条款的讨论，参见第 8.8.2 节。

除了以上两个主要的操作性目的外，税收协定还有其他一些辅助性目的。一项辅助性目的是消除对外国国民和非居民的歧视，第 8.8.1 节将讨论这一点。缔结税收协定的大部分国家都希望保证其居民得到与缔约国对方居民同等的待遇（即国民待遇），当然也不能比任何第三国居民的待遇差（即最惠国待遇）。另一项辅助性目的是将在第 8.8.4 节讨论的缔约国双方之间的信息交换和税收征收协助。如上所述，允许各国获得纳税人取得积极所得相关信息，是打击逃避税的重要工具，且在更为广泛的意义上，有助于确保协定条款正确适用。同样，要求各国协助其协定伙伴国实施其税收征收，可以防止纳税人通过迁移至另一国或在另一国隐匿资产或资金而进行逃避税。最后，大部分国家在其协定中建立了解决涉及协定适用争议，尤其是转让定价争议的机制。争议解决机制在以下第 8.8.3 节中讨论。

税收协定的一个重要作用——也是其暗含的目的，是为纳税人提供跨境投

to taxes on income and on capital without creating opportunities for non-taxation or reduced taxation through tax evasion or avoidance (including through treaty-shopping arrangements aimed at obtaining reliefs provided in this Convention for the indirect benefit of residents of third states)." The UN Model Treaty adopted the same title and preamble in its 2017 update.

Although the elimination of tax avoidance and evasion is an explicit objective of most tax treaties, few provisions in those treaties are designed to achieve that objective. Both the OECD and UN Model Treaties contain provisions for the exchange of information (Article 25) and assistance in the collection of taxes (Article 27). These provisions give the contracting states two important tools to prevent tax avoidance and evasion; however, until 2017, neither Model Treaty contained any general anti-avoidance rule, and few contained specific anti-avoidance rules. The OECD BEPS Action 6 Final Report proposed to add a detailed anti-treaty shopping rule similar to the limitation-on-benefits (LOB) provision included in U.S. tax treaties; it also proposed adding a general anti-abuse provision, under which treaty benefits would be denied if one of the principal purposes of a transaction or arrangement was to avoid tax unless the treaty benefits were in accordance with the object and purpose of the treaty. *See* section 8.8.2 for a discussion of treaty abuse, treaty shopping (including the LOB provision), and the general anti-abuse provision added to the OECD and UN Model Treaties in 2017.

In addition to the two principal operational objectives of tax treaties, there are several other ancillary objectives. One ancillary objective, which is discussed in section 8.8.1 below, is the elimination of discrimination against foreign nationals and nonresidents. Most countries entering into tax treaties want to ensure that their residents are treated the same as residents of the other contracting state (national treatment) and certainly no worse than residents of any third state (most-favored-nation treatment). Other ancillary objectives, discussed in section 8.8.4 below, are the exchange of information between the contracting states and assistance in the collection of taxes. As noted above, allowing countries to obtain information about the income-earning activities of taxpayers is an important tool in combating tax evasion and avoidance and, more generally, in ensuring that the provisions of the treaty are applied properly. Similarly, requiring countries to provide assistance in collecting the taxes imposed by their treaty partners can prevent taxpayers from avoiding and evading tax by moving to another country or hiding assets or funds in another country. Finally, most contracting states provide a mechanism in their treaties for resolving disputes with respect to the application of the treaty and, in particular, transfer pricing disputes. Dispute-resolution mechanisms are discussed in section 8.8.3 below.

An important effect of tax treaties—and an implicit purpose—is to provide certainty for

资税收结果方面的确定性。投资者都很喜欢确定性。税收协定的平均寿命大约为15年。因此，非居民投资者明白，尽管来源国税法的变化不可避免，但协定对其征税权作出了基本限制，将防止未来国内税法的变化改变这些限制。例如，如果A国居民公司A投资B国居民公司B的股票，A公司清楚，即使B国根据其国内法，提高对股息的预提税率，A国与B国之间的协定对B国所征股息预提税率的限制将继续适用。

税收协定的另外一个重要作用和隐含的目的，是将跨境活动所带来的税收收入在缔约国双方之间分配。税收协定条款规定决定了来自两国之间的跨境活动的所得中，有多少应在这两国的任一方予以征税。例如，如果A国同意在其与B国的协定中，纳入与OECD协定范本中涉及特许权使用费的第12条类似的条款，那么，A国居民向B国居民支付的特许权使用费应仅由B国征税，反之亦然。如果A国和B国之间的特许权使用费往来基本持平，那么从这些往来中取得的税收收入的分配也基本持平。但是，如果这种往来不成比例，以A国居民向B国的支付居多（如果A国是发展中国家，B国是发达国家，情况通常如此），那么税收收入分配也将不成比例，以分配给B国的居多。A国可能会试图避免出现这一结果，坚持协定第12条允许来源国对由其居民支付给另一国居民的特许权使用费，按照限制税率（如15%）征税。在这种情况下，A国获得的税收收入相当于其居民向B国居民支付的特许权使用费的15%，B国获得的税收收入相当于其居民从A国居民取得的特许权使用费的应征税款减去该特许权使用费的15%（假设B国对A国税收实施抵免）。

8.6 税收协定的解释

8.6.1 引言

在某些方面，税收协定的解释与国内税法的解释类似。用语的含义、使用这些用语的上下文、协定相关条款的目的，以及相互矛盾的不同解释所产生的结

taxpayers with respect to the tax consequences of cross-border investment. Investors like certainty. Tax treaties have an average life of approximately fifteen years. As a result, nonresident investors know that, despite changes that will inevitably be made to the tax laws of the source country, the basic limitations in the treaty on the source country's right to tax will prevent future changes from affecting those limitations. For example, if Company A, a resident of Country A, makes an investment in the shares of Company B, a resident of Country B, Company A knows that the limit provided in the treaty between Country A and Country B on the rate of withholding tax imposed by Country B on dividends will continue to apply even if Country B increases the rate of withholding tax on dividends under its domestic law.

Another important effect, and an implicit objective, of a tax treaty is the allocation of tax revenues from cross-border activity between the two contracting states. The provisions of tax treaties determine how much tax revenue from the cross-border activity between the two states will be subject to tax by each of those states. For example, if Country A agrees to include in its treaty with Country B a provision similar to Article 12 of the OECD Model Treaty dealing with royalties, any royalties paid by residents of Country A to residents of Country B will be taxable exclusively by Country B, and vice versa. If royalty flows between Country A and Country B are relatively equal, the allocation of the tax revenues from those flows will also be relatively equal. However, if the flows occur disproportionately from residents of Country A to Country B (as would usually be the case if Country A is a developing country and Country B is a developed country), the tax revenues would be allocated disproportionately to Country B. Country A might attempt to avoid this result by insisting that Article 12 of the treaty allow the source country to tax royalties paid by its residents to residents of the other country at a limited rate of, say 15%. In this case, Country A would derive tax revenues equal to 15% of any royalties paid by its residents to residents of Country B, and Country B would derive tax revenues equal to its tax rate on royalties derived by its residents from residents of Country A less 15% of those royalties (assuming that Country B provides a credit for Country A's tax).

8.6 INTERPRETATION OF TAX TREATIES

8.6.1 Introduction

In certain respects, the interpretation of tax treaties is similar to the interpretation of domestic tax legislation. The meaning of the words of the treaty, the context in which they are used, the purpose of the relevant provisions of the treaty, and the consequences of competing

果，一般都是解释协定和国内税法的重要因素。因此，各国税务机关和法院似乎有可能按照与解释国内税法相同的方式，来解释税收协定。但是，在税收协定与国内税法之间，存在着若干重要差异：

（1）税收协定是双边的，因此，解决解释方面的问题，应参考缔约国双方的意图。

（2）税收协定针对两国政府和两国纳税人，比国内税法的范围更为宽泛。

（3）税收协定的拟定，通常使用不同于国内法的用语。例如，OECD 协定范本和联合国协定范本都使用了“企业”一语，此用语在于许多国家的国内法中并不存在。

（4）与国内法不同，税收协定一般并不创设征税权；协定对缔约国双方所征收的税收予以限制。

（5）OECD 协定范本及注释和联合国协定范本及注释对双边协定颇具影响，但在国内税法的背景中，不存在类似的影响。

这些差异可能意味着税收协定的解释方式不同于国内法。但是，包括税收协定条款和国内税收规则在内的所有表述的解释都是一种判断，不应沦为机械的规则，应当谨记这一点。

8.6.2　《维也纳条约法公约》的解释条款

税收协定的解释受国际惯例法的制约，这些惯例包含在《维也纳条约法公约》中。《维也纳公约》的解释规则适用于所有协定，而不仅仅是税收协定。第 8.2.1 节已经提到，《维也纳公约》的条款对所有国家都有约束力，因为其体现了国际惯例法。

《维也纳公约》第 31 条第 1 款规定了协定解释的基本规则：

> 条约应依其用语按其上下文并参照条约之目的及宗旨所具有之通常意义，善意解释之。

interpretations are generally important factors in interpreting both treaties and domestic tax legislation. As a result, it seems likely that a country's tax authorities and its courts will interpret tax treaties in the same manner as domestic tax legislation. There are, however, several important differences between tax treaties and domestic tax legislation:

(1) Because tax treaties are bilateral, questions of interpretation should be resolved by reference to the intentions of both states.
(2) Tax treaties are addressed both to the governments and the taxpayers of both countries, whereas domestic tax legislation has a narrower scope.
(3) Tax treaties are often drafted using different terms from those used in domestic legislation. For example, the OECD and UN Model Treaties use the term "enterprise," which is not used in the domestic legislation of many countries.
(4) Unlike domestic tax legislation, tax treaties do not generally impose tax; they limit the taxes imposed by the contracting states.
(5) The influential OECD Model Treaty and Commentary and the UN Model Treaty and Commentary have no counterparts in the context of domestic tax legislation.

These differences may suggest that tax treaties should be interpreted differently from domestic tax legislation. However, it should be kept in mind that the interpretation of all language, including the provisions of tax treaties and domestic tax rules, is a matter of judgment that cannot be reduced to mechanical rules.

8.6.2 The Interpretive Provisions of the *Vienna Convention on the Law of Treaties*

The interpretation of tax treaties is governed by customary international law, as embodied in the *Vienna Convention on the Law of Treaties*. The interpretive rules of the Vienna Convention apply to all treaties, not just tax treaties. As discussed in section 8.2.1 above, the provisions of the Vienna Convention are binding on all nations because they represent a codification of customary international law.

Article 31(1) of the Vienna Convention provides a basic rule for the interpretation of treaties:

> A treaty shall be interpreted in good faith in accordance with the ordinary meaning to be given to the terms of the treaty in their context and in light of its object and purpose.

第 31 条第 2 款规定，协定的上下文包括协定文本、双方签署的与达成协定相关的协议，以及由一方订立、另一方认可的文书。例如，美国对其每一项税收协定，均作出了技术性解释；加拿大公开表示，其接受美国对美加协定的技术性解释。根据第 31 条第 3 款，协定双方后续签署的协议、关于协定解释的后续做法、国际法的适用规则等，都应和上下文一同予以考虑。第 31 条第 4 款规定，协定用语可以具有其通常含义以外的特殊含义，前提是确定协定缔约双方有此意愿。有的用语有意采用特殊含义，OECD 协定范本和联合国协定范本注释对此予以证明。

《维也纳公约》第 31 条第 1 款的基本解释规则在直觉上也有道理。对协定用语作出解释，首先必须仔细考虑其通常含义，这一点不言而喻。这些用语必须在其上下文，也就是用语所在的特定条款和整个协定中进行理解，因为用语的含义总是取决于其所处的上下文。参照相关条款和整个协定的目的来解释协定术语，也是有意义的，因为缔约国双方缔结协定，并就协定用语达成一致，显然是为了实现特定的目的。

尽管《维也纳公约》第 31 条第 1 款很有道理，但其规定含混不清，未能给纳税人、税务机关和法院提供关于协定解释方面的清晰、有意义的指引，这一点我们必须承认。最重要的是，它没有说明在具体情况下，应当分别给用语的通常含义、上下文和协定相关条款的目的多少权重。例如，如果用语的通常含义和相关条款的目的出现冲突，第 31 条第 1 款并没有说明如何予以解决。虽然大部分法院和评论员都认为，不应为达到未明确表达的、不确定的目的，而忽略某一用语相对明确的含义，但要就特定情况下各相关因素的权重作出解释性规定实属不易。

根据《维也纳公约》第 32 条，被称作补充性解释途径的其他材料，包括协定的准备工作，应仅在为了确认已按照第 31 条确定的含义，或如果应用第 31 条得出的结果模糊、晦涩、荒谬或不合理的情况下，才予以考虑。

Under Article 31(2), the context of a treaty includes the text of the treaty, any agreements between the parties made in connection with the conclusion of the treaty, and any instrument made by one party and accepted by the other party. For example, the U.S. produces a technical explanation for each of its tax treaties, and Canada publicly announced its acceptance of the U.S. technical explanation of the U.S.-Canada treaty. Under Article 31(3), subsequent agreements between the parties to the treaty and their subsequent practice with respect to the interpretation of the treaty, and any applicable rules of international law, must also be taken into account together with the context. Article 31(4) provides that a treaty term may have a special meaning rather than its ordinary meaning if it is established that the parties so intend. The Commentary on the OECD or UN Model Treaty may provide evidence that a term is intended to have a special meaning.

The basic interpretive rule in Article 31(1) of the Vienna Convention makes intuitive sense. Obviously, the first step in any interpretive exercise must be to carefully consider the ordinary meaning of the words of the treaty. And those words must be read in their context—the particular provision in which the words are used and the treaty as a whole—because the meaning of words is always dependent on the context in which they are used. It also makes sense to interpret the terms of a treaty in light of the purpose of the provision and the treaty as a whole because, obviously, the contracting states are trying to accomplish something by entering into the treaty and agreeing on its terms.

Although Article 31(1) of the Vienna Convention makes sense, it must also be acknowledged that it is vague and does not provide any clear, meaningful guidance for taxpayers, tax authorities, or courts about how to interpret treaties. Most importantly, it does not indicate how much weight to give to the ordinary meaning of the words, the context, and the purpose of the relevant provisions of the treaty in any particular case. For example, if there is a conflict between the ordinary meaning of the words and the purpose of the relevant provision, Article 31(1) does not indicate how the conflict should be resolved. Although most courts and commentators would take the position that words with a relatively clear meaning should not be disregarded in order to carry out an unexpressed, uncertain purpose, it is difficult to write an interpretive rule as to how all the relevant factors should be weighed in any particular case.

Under Article 32 of the Vienna Convention, other material, referred to as supplementary means of interpretation, which includes the *travaux préparatoires* (preparatory work) of the treaty, should be considered only to confirm the meaning established pursuant to Article 31, or to establish the meaning if applying Article 31 produces an ambiguous, obscure, absurd, or unreasonable result.

虽然关于 OECD 协定范本和联合国协定范本的注释对于税收协定的解释非常重要，但按照《维也纳公约》规定，其法律地位并不明确。初步看来，范本注释似乎是第 32 条所称的补充解释途径。若是如此，范本注释只能用以确认已按照第 31 条的基本解释规则确定的含义，或在第 31 条确定的含义模糊、晦涩、荒谬或不合理的情况下，才能得以应用。范本注释的作用如此有限，这并不是 OECD 的初衷。注释的引言指出，注释"对税收协定的适用和解释，特别是对争议的解决，大有裨益"（第 29 段）。但是，按照《维也纳公约》第 31 条，难以说明可以将注释作为协定上下文的一部分，特别是如果需要解释的协定是在注释修订前达成，或者如果缔约国一方不是 OECD 成员国，且未参与注释的拟定。

尽管 OECD 协定范本和注释在《维也纳公约》下的地位是国际税收学者争论的话题，但是，这一问题似乎并无实际影响。在几乎所有国家的协定案件中，法院无不赋予 OECD 协定范本及注释实质性的权重。

税收协定条款在缔约国双方应当以同样的方式予以解释（即共同解释原则），否则相关所得可能会被双重征税，或者根本没有被征税。例如，假设 A 国居民 A 公司在 B 国为 B 国居民 B 公司提供劳务。该劳务产生的工作成果由 B 公司使用。A 公司收到 B 公司支付的款项。根据 B 国的法律，该款项被定性为因在 B 国提供劳务而得到的报酬。与此不同的是，A 国将其认定为因允许 B 公司使用 A 公司的工作成果而支付的特许权使用费。按照这两个国家之间的税收协定，个人劳务费由来源国征税，但是，特许权使用费仅由居民国征税。在这种情况下，如果两国主管当局不解决这一问题，A 公司将面临双重征税。B 国将按照协定第 7 条，对 A 公司的所得征税（假设 A 公司在 B 国设有常设机构）；而 A 国将按照协定第 12 条，对 A 公司收到的款项，作为特许权使用费予以征税。由于 B 国的税收并非针对特许权使用费，故而 A 国可能不会对 B 国税收予以抵免。

Although the Commentaries on the OECD and UN Model Treaties are very important for the interpretation of tax treaties, their legal status under the provisions of the Vienna Convention is unclear. At first glance, they appear to be supplementary means of interpretation under Article 32. If so, they are relevant only to confirm the meaning otherwise established by the application of the basic interpretive rule in Article 31 or to establish the meaning if the meaning under Article 31 is ambiguous, obscure, absurd, or unreasonable. The OECD does not intend for the Commentary to have such a limited role. In the Introduction to the Commentary, it is stated that the Commentary "can be ... of great assistance in the application and interpretation of the conventions and, in particular, in the settlement of any disputes" (paragraph 29). It is difficult, however, to justify including the Commentary as part of the context of a treaty under Article 31 of the Vienna Convention, especially if the treaty being interpreted was entered into before the Commentary was revised or if one of the contracting states is not a member of the OECD and therefore had no part in the preparation of the Commentary.

Although the status of the OECD Model Treaty and Commentary under the Vienna Convention is a controversial topic among international tax scholars, the issue appears to be of little practical significance. In treaty cases from virtually all countries, the courts invariably give the OECD Model Treaty and Commentary substantial weight.

The provisions of tax treaties should be interpreted in the same way in both countries (the principle of common interpretation) because otherwise, income may either be taxed twice or not at all. Assume, for example, that Company A, a resident of Country A, performs services in Country B for the benefit of Company B, a resident of Country B. The services result in the creation of some work product used by Company B. Company A receives a payment from Company B that is characterized under the laws of Country B as compensation for services performed in Country B. In contrast, Country A characterizes the payment as a royalty for allowing Company B to use Company A's work product. Under the tax treaty between the two countries, fees for personal services are taxable in the source state, but royalties are taxable exclusively by the residence state. Under these circumstances, Company A will be subject to double taxation unless the competent authorities of the two countries can resolve the matter. Country B will impose tax on Company A's income in accordance with Article 7 of the treaty (assuming that Company A has a PE in Country B); in contrast, Country A will impose tax on the payments received by Company A as royalties under Article 12 of the treaty. Country A may not provide any relief for the tax imposed by Country B because Country B's tax is not imposed on the royalties.

有些国家具有多种官方语言。当这些国家达成税收协定时，可能存在不同语言的多个正式文本。《维也纳公约》第33条规定，以多种语言签署的税收协定，所有版本同等作准，除非协定条款明确规定，在出现冲突的情况下，以其中一个版本为准。中国等以多种语言签署税收协定的国家规定，在不同版本出现冲突的情况下，以英语版本为准。

8.6.3 按照国内法对协定未定义的用语进行解释：第3条第2款

除《维也纳公约》的规定外，基于OECD协定范本和联合国协定范本的税收协定还包含了一条内在解释规则。OECD协定范本和联合国协定范本第3条第2款规定如下：

> 关于缔约国一方在任何时候对本协定的实施，除上下文另有要求外，未经本协定定义的用语应当具有协定实施时，该国针对本协定所适用税种的法律规定的含义，此用语根据该国适用税法的含义优先于该国其他法律赋予该用语的含义。

实际上，第3条第2款规定，协定中使用的未定义用语，应当具有实施协定的国家国内法所规定的含义，除非上下文另有要求。为此，一国采取与协定相关的措施，如颁布裁定、作出纳税评定等，都是在实施协定。第3条第2款的适用涉及三个步骤：

（1）协定是否定义了某用语？

（2）如果协定未定义该用语，该用语的国内法含义是什么？

（3）协定上下文是否要求该用语的含义与国内法含义不同？

第一个步骤并非看似那么简单，部分原因是因为税收协定中的有些定义是包含式的，有些则是排他式的。例如，第3条第1款第（1）项将“人”定义为包含个人、公司和人的其他团体。然而，第3条第1款第（2）项对“公司”的定

Several countries have multiple official languages. When these countries enter into tax treaties, there may be multiple official versions of the treaty in different languages. Article 33 of the Vienna Convention provides that all versions of tax treaties concluded in multiple languages are considered to be equally authentic unless the provisions of the treaty specify that one version is to govern in the event of a conflict. Some countries that conclude their tax treaties in multiple languages, such as China, provide that the English-language version of the treaty will prevail where the versions conflict.

8.6.3 The Interpretation of Undefined Terms in Accordance with Domestic Law: Article 3(2)

In addition to the provisions of the Vienna Convention, tax treaties based on the OECD and UN Model Treaties contain an internal rule of interpretation. Article 3(2) of the OECD and UN Model Treaties provides as follows:

> As regards the application of the Convention at any time by a contracting state, any term not defined therein shall, unless the context requires otherwise, have the meaning that it has at that time under the law of that State for the purposes of the taxes to which the Convention applies, any meaning under the applicable tax laws of that State prevailing over a meaning given to the term under other laws of that State.

In effect, Article 3(2) provides that undefined terms used in the treaty have the meaning that they have under the domestic law of the country applying the treaty unless the context requires otherwise. For this purpose, a country "applies" a treaty when it takes any relevant action with respect to the treaty, such as issuing a ruling or an assessment of tax.

The application of Article 3(2) involves a three-stage process:

(1) Does the treaty provide a definition of the term?

(2) If the treaty does not provide a definition of the term, what is its domestic meaning?

(3) Does the context of the treaty require a meaning different from the domestic meaning?

The first step is not as simple as it appears, in part because some definitions in tax treaties are inclusive, while others are exclusive. For example, Article 3(1)(a) defines a "person" to include an individual, a company, and any other body of persons. In contrast, the definition of "company" in Article 3(1)(b) is exclusive ("company means … "). Generally, an

义则是排他式的（“公司”一语是指……）。一般而言，包含式的定义表示该用语具有其常用含义，再加上特别指出的内容。那么，是否可以适用第3条第2款，对包含式定义用语，如“人”，按照国内法确定其常用含义呢？我认为，这种情况下可以适用第3条第2款，这样，“人”这一用语将包括按照适用协定的一国国内法认定为“人”的任何法律实体。另一个难题是，税收协定的定义中经常包括没有定义的用语；例如，第3条第1款第（1）项中的“个人”“人的团体”等用语都没有定义。我认为，这些用语同样可以按照第3条第2款，采用其国内法含义。

按照国内法来确定用语的含义有时也很困难。第3条第2款规定，未定义用语在国内税法中的含义优先于在其他国内法中的含义。但是，在一国税法中，某个未定义的用语可能有不止一种含义。在这种情况下，出于协定的目的，就要采纳最合适的国内含义。此外，第3条第2款指的是未定义用语在国内法中的“含义”而非其定义。一个用语未必为一国税法而被定义，但总应该有其含义。

适用第3条第2款的最后一个步骤，是考虑协定上下文是否要求赋予该用语与国内法不同的含义。为了实现这一目的，有必要考虑该用语出于协定目的的可替代含义，以及就协定上下文来说，这些其他含义是否比国内法含义更为合适。按照第3条第2款的注释，这一分析过程中应考虑的因素包括：

—— 与其在国内税法中的含义相比而言，该用语的常用含义；

—— 该用语在另一国税法中的含义；

—— 税收协定相关规定的目的；以及

—— 参考外部资料，比如OECD协定范本或联合国协定范本注释。

有些国际税收学者认为，在适用第3条第2款时，对于未定义的用语，应尽可能赋予其独立于国内法的含义，使用国内法的含义只能是最后选择，并认为这样可以规避或最大限度地减少缔约国双方国内法的冲突。其他学者则认为，第3条第2款有优先选择国内法含义的意思，因为只有“上下文另有要求”时，才能

inclusive definition means that the term has its ordinary meaning plus the items that are specifically mentioned. Does Article 3(2) apply to determine the ordinary meaning under domestic law of terms that are defined inclusively, such as "person?" In my view, Article 3(2) should apply in these circumstances so that the term "person" would include any legal entity that is considered to be a person under the domestic law of the state applying the treaty. A further difficulty is that definitions in a treaty often contain terms that are undefined; for example, the terms "individual" and "body of persons" in Article 3(1)(a) are not defined. Again, in my view, these terms should take their meaning from domestic law by virtue of Article 3(2).

The determination of the meaning of a term under domestic law may also be difficult. Article 3(2) provides that the meaning of an undefined term under a country's tax law prevails over the meaning under other domestic laws. An undefined term, however, may have more than one meaning for purposes of a country's tax law. In this situation, the domestic meaning that is most appropriate should be used for purposes of the treaty. Further, Article 3(2) refers to the "meaning" of an undefined term, not to its definition, under domestic law. A term may not be defined for purposes of a country's tax law, but it should have a meaning.

The final step in the application of Article 3(2) is to consider whether the context of the treaty requires a term to be given a different meaning from its meaning under domestic law. For this purpose, it is necessary to consider alternative meanings for the term for purposes of the treaty and whether one of these meanings is more appropriate in the context of the treaty than the domestic law meaning. According to the Commentary on Article 3(2), matters that should be considered in this analysis include:

- the ordinary meaning of the term as compared to the meaning under the domestic tax law;
- the meaning of the term under the other country's tax law;
- the purpose of the relevant provision of the treaty; and
- extrinsic material such as the Commentary on the OECD or UN Model Treaty.

Some international tax scholars argue that in applying Article 3(2), if at all possible, undefined terms should be given a meaning that is independent of domestic law and that a domestic law meaning should be used only as a last resort. In this way, they argue that conflicts between the domestic laws of the contracting states can be avoided or minimized. Other scholars argue that Article 3(2) contains a preference for domestic law meanings because

用协定含义代替国内法含义。后者还指出，使用“要求”一语，为人们寻求确立一个协定含义设置了实质性的障碍。

我认为，对于未定义的用语，第 3 条第 2 款并未明确体现倾向于国内法含义还是协定含义。另外，并没有充分的理由，来说明对于未定义的用语，应该是国内法含义优先还是协定含义优先。如上所述，税收协定中未定义用语的含义，应在参考所有相关信息后确定。

关于 OECD 协定范本和联合国协定范本第 3 条第 2 款的解释，还有一个颇具争议的重要问题，即用语是否具有签署协定时，其根据国内法所具有的含义（静态方法），或是其根据不时修订后的国内法所具有的含义（动态方法）。1995 年 OECD 对其协定范本第 3 条第 2 款进行修订，明确应根据动态方法适用第 3 条第 2 款。联合国协定范本也在 2001 年作出了类似修订。动态方法允许协定适应国内法发生的变化，而不必重新进行协定谈判。因此，动态方法实质上允许一国通过修改国内法，来单方面修订其与另一国签署的协定。可以认为，如果对于国内法的修改在很大程度上改变了两国之间的协议，而且两国在协定谈判时并未对此有过考虑，那么，这项修改就等同于推翻协定。

8.7 OECD 协定范本和联合国协定范本条款概述

8.7.1 引言

本节讨论 OECD 协定范本和联合国协定范本的主要条款。第 8.7.2 节将介绍界定协定双方和纳税义务受协定影响的人，确定协定范围，以及协定批准、终止、修订的条款；第 8.7.3 节将介绍典型税收协定对各类所得的处理，这些条款也被称为协定的分配规则；第 8.7.4 节介绍与征管事项和协定伙伴国之间合作相关的规则。

每个税收协定都包括纾解或消除双重征税的条款。在 OECD 协定范本和联合

those meanings are displaced by treaty meanings only if "the context requires otherwise." The use of the word "requires," they argue, places a substantial onus on those seeking to justify a treaty meaning.

In my view, Article 3(2) does not establish any clear preference for domestic law meanings or treaty meanings for undefined terms. Furthermore, there are no strong arguments for establishing any residual presumption in favor of either a domestic or treaty meaning of an undefined term. As noted above, the meaning of undefined terms in a tax treaty should be determined by reference to all the relevant information.

Another important and controversial issue of interpretation in connection with Article 3(2) of the OECD and UN Model Treaties is whether a term has its meaning under domestic law at the time that the treaty was entered into (the static approach) or its meaning under domestic law as amended from time to time (the ambulatory approach). Article 3(2) of the OECD Model Treaty was amended in 1995 to clarify that Article 3(2) should be applied in accordance with the ambulatory approach. A similar conforming amendment was made to the UN Model Treaty in 2001. The ambulatory approach allows treaties to accommodate necessary changes to domestic law without the need to renegotiate the treaty. As a result, the ambulatory approach also effectively permits a country to unilaterally amend its tax treaty with another country by changing its domestic law. However, an amendment to domestic law that significantly alters the bargain between the two countries and was not contemplated by both countries when the treaty was negotiated is equivalent to a treaty override.

8.7 SUMMARY OF THE PROVISIONS OF THE OECD AND UN MODEL TREATIES

8.7.1 Introduction

This section describes the major provisions of the OECD and UN Model Treaties. Section 8.7.2 describes the provisions that identify the parties to a treaty and the persons whose tax obligations are affected by it, that establish the scope of the treaty, and that govern its ratification, termination, and amendment. Section 8.7.3 describes the treatment of various categories of income under a typical tax treaty; these provisions are known as the distributive rules of a treaty. Section 8.7.4 describes the rules dealing with administrative matters and cooperation between the treaty partners.

Every tax treaty includes some provision for relieving or mitigating double taxation. In the

国协定范本中，第 23A 条（免税法）和第 23B 条（抵免法）规定了双重征税的救济办法。消除双重征税的方法已在第 4 章中进行了讨论。

为防止通过转让定价进行避税，大多数国家的国内税法都赋予税务机关调整关联方之间交易价格的权力，以反映若是此种交易系与非关联方按照独立交易原则进行时，本应确定的价格。OECD 协定范本和联合国协定范本第 9 条（关联企业）规定，允许（实际是“期望”）缔约国双方，按照所谓的独立交易原则，对关联方之间的交易价格进行调整，并重新计算由其产生的利润。转让定价和独立交易原则已在第 6 章中进行了讨论。

8.7.2 涵盖的内容、范围和法律效力

签署双边所得税协定的两个国家被称为“缔约国双方”。根据 OECD 协定范本和联合国协定范本第 1 条（人的范围），协定的各项条款适用于“缔约国一方或同时为双方居民”的人。第 4 条（居民）出于协定的目的，将缔约国一方“居民”定义为按照该国国内法，基于居所、住所、管理机构所在地及其他类似标准等一些关联因素，在该国负有纳税义务的人。如第 2 章第 2.2.3 节所述，第 4 条还包括加比规则，防止出于协定目的，将某人同时认定为缔约国双方的居民。第 3 条（一般定义）将“人”定义为包括“个人、公司和人的其他团体”。OECD 注释指出，慈善基金属于第 3 条意义中的“人”。的确，在适用协定时，缔约国法律认可的任何法人实体都可能被作为“人”对待。虽然合伙企业很可能是人的团体，因此也是 OECD 协定范本和联合国协定范本所规定的“人”，但是，如果合伙人就其按持股份额从合伙企业取得的所得在缔约国一方负有纳税义务，而不是合伙企业在该国负有纳税义务，那么合伙企业可能不构成该国居民。

OECD 协定范本和联合国协定范本第 2 条（税种范围）规定，协定适用于“缔约国一方、其行政区或地方当局对所得和财产征收的税收”。有些协定并不延伸涵盖国家层面以下的所得税税收。虽然存在第 2 条的限制，但是，OECD 协定范

OECD and UN Model Treaties, relief from double taxation is provided either by Article 23A (Exemption Method) or Article 23B (Credit Method). Methods of providing relief from double taxation are discussed in Chapter 4.

To prevent tax avoidance through transfer pricing, the domestic tax laws of most countries give the tax authorities the power to adjust prices in transactions between related persons to reflect the prices that would have prevailed if the transaction had taken place at arm's length with an unrelated person. Article 9 (Associated Enterprises) of the OECD and UN Model Treaties provides that the contracting states are permitted (indeed, expected) to adjust prices and recompute profits from related-party transactions in accordance with this so-called arm's-length standard. Transfer pricing and the arm's-length standard are discussed in Chapter 6.

8.7.2 Coverage, Scope, and Legal Effect

The two countries that enter into a bilateral income tax treaty are called the "contracting states." Under Article 1 (Personal Scope) of the OECD and UN Model Treaties, the provisions of the treaty apply to persons who are "residents of one or both of the contracting states." Article 4 (Resident) defines a "resident" of a contracting state for purposes of the treaty as a person who is liable to tax under the domestic laws of that contracting state on the basis of certain connecting factors, such as residence, domicile, place of management, or other similar criteria. As discussed in Chapter 2, section 2.2.3, Article 4 also includes tie-breaker rules that prevent a person from being a resident of both contracting states for purposes of the treaty. A "person" is defined in Article 3 (General Definitions) to include "an individual, a company and any other body of persons." The OECD Commentary indicates that a charitable foundation is a "person" within the meaning of Article 3—indeed, any legal entity that is recognized under the laws of a contracting state is likely to be treated as a "person" for tax treaty purposes. Although a partnership is probably a body of persons and therefore a person for purposes of the OECD and UN Model Treaties, it may not be a resident of a contracting state if the partners rather than the partnership are liable to tax in that state on their share of the income of the partnership.

Article 2 (Taxes Covered) of the OECD and UN Model Treaties specifies that the treaty applies "to taxes on income and on capital imposed on behalf of a contracting state or of its political subdivisions or local authorities." Some treaties do not extend coverage to subnational income taxes. Despite any limitations in Article 2, Articles 24, 26, and 27 of the OECD and UN

本和联合国协定范本第 24 条、第 26 条和第 27 条分别涉及非歧视待遇、信息交换和税收征收协助，不仅适用于第 2 条所述的税收，而是适用于由缔约国双方征收的所有税收。

典型的税收协定会列举其适用的缔约国双方的全国性税收（有时也包括国家层面以下征收的税收）。各国的个人所得税和企业所得税总是会被列举。大部分税收协定还规定，协定适用于对所列税收的变动，也适用于嗣后征收的与所列税收相同或实质性相似的税收。有些协定还列出了协定不涵盖的一些所得或财产税；比如，很多税收协定将政府因筹集退休金而征收的工资和社会保险税排除在协定范围之外。

当前和税收协定所适用的所得税种相关的一个问题是数字服务税是否属于第 2 条的范围之中。征收数字服务税的国家不希望其税收协定涵盖此种数字服务税，因为协定会妨碍其征收数字服务税。第 9 章第 9.5.3 节将讨论数字服务税。

根据 OECD 协定范本和联合国协定范本第 30 条（生效），协定在批准后生效，缔约国双方通常约定尽快交换批准文书。每个缔约国都有其批准协定的国内程序，必须予以履行。例如，很多国家规定，由政府谈判的税收协定必须经过立法机关同意才能生效。这些内部程序完成后，缔约国双方将交换批准文书。税收协定中按照纳税年度适用的条款，如第 7 条（营业利润）等，通常会自双方互换批准文书的下一公历年度 1 月 1 日起生效。协定的其他条款，如涉及针对股息、利息和特许权使用费等支付款项征收预提税的条款，则可能早于或晚于协定其他内容生效。此外，OECD 协定范本和联合国协定范本的一些条款还可能追溯适用。例如，信息交换或税收征收协助的请求，可能与协定生效之前的年度有关。此类请求只要在协定生效后提出，都是有效的。

虽然税收协定伙伴国可能认为其关系会无限期延续，但是协定都规定，应其中任一方的要求，可以终止协定。根据 OECD 协定范本和联合国协定范本第 31 条（终止），缔约国一方通过在当年度结束前至少 6 个月内书面通知其协定伙伴国，可以单方面自下一公历年度之初起终止协定。经双方同意，缔约国双方可以

Model Treaties dealing with nondiscrimination, exchange of information, and assistance in the collection of taxes, respectively, apply to all taxes imposed by the contracting states and not just those taxes described in Article 2.

A typical tax treaty expressly lists the national taxes (and sometimes the subnational taxes) of the contracting states to which the treaty applies. Each country's personal income tax and corporate income tax are invariably listed. Most treaties also provide that the treaty applies to amendments of the listed taxes and to subsequently imposed taxes that are identical or substantially similar to the listed taxes. Some treaties also list certain income and capital taxes that are not to be covered by the treaty; for example, many tax treaties exclude from their scope payroll and social security taxes earmarked for government pensions.

One current issue involving the income taxes covered by tax treaties is whether DSTs are within the scope of Article 2. Countries imposing DSTs do not want those taxes to be covered by their tax treaties because the treaties would prevent them from levying such taxes. DSTs are discussed in Chapter 9, section 9.5.3.

According to Article 30 (Entry into Force) of the OECD and UN Model Treaties, tax treaties become effective on ratification, and the states usually agree to exchange instruments of ratification as soon as possible. Each contracting state has its own internal procedures for ratifying treaties that must be satisfied. For example, many countries provide that a treaty negotiated by the government must receive legislative approval to be effective. Once these internal procedures have been satisfied, the contracting states will exchange instruments of ratification. Generally, tax treaties become effective on the first day of the calendar year following the exchange of the instruments of ratification with respect to provisions of the treaty that apply on the basis of taxation years, such as Article 7 (Business Profits). Other provisions of the treaty, such as the provisions dealing with withholding taxes imposed on payments such as dividends, interest, and royalties, may take effect earlier or later than the rest of the treaty. In addition, certain provisions of the OECD and UN Model Treaties may apply retrospectively. For example, a request for information or for assistance in the collection of taxes may relate to a year before the treaty entered into force. Such a request is valid as long as it is made after the treaty becomes effective.

Although tax treaty partners may contemplate that their relationship will last indefinitely, their treaties provide for the termination of the treaty at the request of either party. Under Article 31 (Termination) of the OECD and UN Model Treaties, a contracting state may unilaterally terminate a treaty as of the beginning of the next calendar year by giving notice of termination to its treaty partner at least six months before the end of the current

随时终止协定，但是有些协定规定，新协定在生效后，必须在一段最低时限内保持有效。

8.7.3 分配规则：第 6 条至第 21 条

8.7.3.1 引言

OECD 协定范本和联合国协定范本第 6 条至第 21 条涉及各类所得的处理，包括营业利润等范围较宽的所得，也包括董事费和退休金等范围较窄的所得。这一方法不可避免地意味着，出于协定的目的，如何对所得进行分类会出现冲突。这类冲突常常被称为定性冲突，有时可以通过相关条款的定义解决。例如，第 10 条第 3 款将股息定义为从股份或其他“非债权”权利取得的所得，第 11 条第 3 款将利息定义为“从各种债权取得的所得”。因此，第 10 条和第 11 条不可能适用于同一款项——如果某一款项是来自债权的所得，即为利息，而不可能是股息。有些冲突则可以按照协定的具体条款得以解决。例如，如果第 7 条和另一条款都适用，则按照 OECD 协定范本第 7 条第 4 款（联合国协定范本第 7 条第 6 款）规定，其他条款优先适用。有些冲突的解决则不是通过具体规则。如果一项所得并不被任何具体条款（第 6 条至第 20 条）所涵盖，则应通过第 21 条（其他所得）予以处理。

OECD 协定范本和联合国协定范本分配规则的措辞非常一致。如果某个条款使用了“应仅在”缔约国一方征税的表述，则意味着缔约国另一方不能对该所得征税。例如，根据第 8 条第 1 款，企业以船舶或飞机经营国际运输取得的利润“应仅在”该企业的居民国征税。相反，如果使用的是“可在”缔约国一方征税的表述，那么，就意味着该国可以对相关款项征税，但是这并不意味着缔约国另一方不能对该款项征税。换句话说，“可在”一国征税的措辞意味着，根据协定，缔约国双方均有权对相关款项征税。在这种情况下，来源国优先征税，并且第 23 条要求居民国通过对所得免征居民国税收，或在该所得的居民国税收中，对来源

year. The contracting states may terminate a treaty at any time by mutual consent, although some treaties provide that a new treaty must remain in effect for a minimum period after it enters into force.

8.7.3 The Distributive Rules: Articles 6 Through 21

8.7.3.1 Introduction

Articles 6 through 21 of the OECD and UN Model Treaties deal with the treatment of various types of income, from broad categories such as business profits to quite narrow categories such as directors' fees and pensions. This approach inevitably means that conflicts arise as to how amounts should be categorized for purposes of the treaty. These conflicts, often referred to as conflicts of qualification, are sometimes resolved by definitions in the relevant articles. For example, Article 10(3) defines dividends as income from shares or other rights "not being debt-claims," and Article 11(3) defines interest as "income from debt-claims of every kind." Consequently, Articles 10 and 11 cannot both apply to the same amount—if an amount is income from a debt claim, it is interest and cannot be a dividend. Sometimes conflicts are resolved pursuant to specific provisions in the treaty. For example, where Article 7 and another article both apply, Article 7(4) of the OECD Model (Article 7(6) of the UN Model) gives priority to the other article. Some conflicts are not resolved by specific rules. Where an item of income is not covered by any of the specific articles (Articles 6–20), it is dealt with in Article 21 (Other Income).

The wording of the distributive rules of the OECD and UN Model Treaties is remarkably consistent. Where an article uses the words "shall be taxable only" in one of the contracting states, it means that the other state is precluded from taxing the relevant income. For example, under Article 8(1), profits from the operation of ships or aircraft in international traffic "shall be taxable only" in the country of which the enterprise is a resident. In contrast, where the words "may be taxed" in a contracting state are used, it means that the relevant amount may be taxed by that country; however, it does not mean that the amount is not taxable by the other contracting state. In other words, the words "may be taxed" mean that the contracting states are both entitled to tax the relevant amount under the treaty. In these circumstances, the source country's tax takes priority, and Article 23 requires the residence country to provide relief from double taxation by exempting the income from residence country tax or granting a credit for the source country tax against

国税款给予抵免，从而消除双重征税。

8.7.3.2 经营所得

OECD 协定范本和联合国协定范本区分了各种经营所得。例如，第 6 条、第 8 条、第 17 条分别涉及来自不动产、国际海运和空运，以及演艺和体育活动的利润。OECD 协定范本和联合国协定范本第 7 条适用于其他更为具体的条款没有涵盖的营业利润。第 7 条（营业利润）规定，“缔约国一方企业”在缔约国另一方开展营业活动取得的所得，应在缔约国另一方免税，除非该营业活动系通过位于该缔约国另一方的常设机构进行，且利润应归属于该常设机构。第 2 章讨论了这种对一国的来源管辖权的限制。第 5 条（常设机构）定义了常设机构，后续会讨论该定义。第 3 条（一般定义）将“缔约国一方企业”定义为缔约国一方居民经营的企业，第 4 条定义了“缔约国一方居民”。

如果缔约国一方的企业在缔约国另一方设有常设机构，那么，缔约国另一方仅应对归属于常设机构的利润征税。OECD 协定范本和联合国协定范本第 7 条第 2 款规定，常设机构利润的确定应基于如下假设，即将常设机构视同独立分设实体，并独立地与其所属企业的其他部门进行交易。第 7 条第 2 款中此种假设的效果就是，将根据第 9 条适用于关联企业的转让定价规则也类比适用于确定常设机构利润归属。第 8.8.5 节讨论将独立交易原则用于确定可归属于常设机构的利润时所存在的困难。

OECD 协定范本第 7 条没有采用所谓的引力方法，按照该方法，如果纳税人在一国设有常设机构，则其从该国取得的所有所得都要由该国征税。根据第7条，如果纳税人在一国设有常设机构，该国仅应对纳税人来自应归属于该常设机构营业活动的利润征税。其他所得可以按照协定的其他条款征税，但不是按照第7条。

在确定应归属于常设机构的所得时，联合国协定范本第 7 条第 1 款采用了有限的引力原则。按照该原则，如果企业在缔约国一方设有常设机构，那么，该国

the residence country tax on that income.

8.7.3.2 Business Income

The OECD and UN Model Treaties distinguish between several types of business income. For example, profits from immovable property, profits from international shipping and air transportation, and profits from entertainment and athletic activities are dealt with under Articles 6, 8, and 17, respectively. Article 7 of the OECD and UN Model Treaties applies to business profits that are not covered by a more specific article. Article 7 (Business Profits) provides that "an enterprise of a contracting state" is exempt from tax by the other contracting state on its profits derived from business carried on in the other state unless the business is carried on through a PE located in that other state and the profits are attributable to the PE. This limitation on a country's source jurisdiction is discussed in Chapter 2. The definition of a PE is provided in Article 5 (PE) and is discussed below. Article 3 (General Definitions) defines "an enterprise of a contracting state" as an enterprise carried on by a resident of a contracting state as defined in Article 4.

If an enterprise of a contracting state has a PE in the other contracting state, it is taxable by the other state only on the profits attributable to the PE. Article 7(2) of the OECD and UN Model Treaties provides that the profits of a PE should be determined on the assumption that the PE is a separate and distinct entity dealing independently with the other parts of the enterprise of which the PE is a part. The effect of these assumptions in Article 7(2) is that the transfer pricing rules applicable to associated enterprises under Article 9 also apply, by analogy, for the purpose of determining the profits attributable to a PE. The difficulties that arise in applying the arm's-length principle to determine the profits attributable to a PE are addressed in section 8.8.5 below.

Article 7 of the OECD Model Treaty does not use a so-called force-of-attraction approach, under which all of a taxpayer's income derived from a country is subject to tax by that country if it has a PE in that country. Under Article 7, if a taxpayer has a PE in a country, only the taxpayer's profits from the business that are attributable to the PE are subject to tax by that country. Other income may be taxable under other articles of the treaty but not under Article 7.

Article 7(1) of the UN Model Treaty employs a limited force-of-attraction principle in determining the income attributable to a PE. Under that principle, if an enterprise has a PE in a contracting state, it is taxable by that state not only on the profits attributable to

对于该常设机构的征税，不仅针对归属于该常设机构的利润，也针对在该国销售与通过常设机构销售商品类似的商品，或在该国开展与通过常设机构开展的经营活动类似的经营活动，所产生的利润。

常设机构的定义

根据 OECD 协定范本和联合国协定范本第 5 条第 1 款，将常设机构定义为“企业进行全部或部分营业的固定营业场所”。在几乎所有税收协定中，这一表述都以实质上相同的形式得到了使用。

为在缔约国一方拥有“固定营业场所”，一个企业必须在一个特定的地理位置开展经营活动，且其在该地点的活动必须持续不止一段短暂的时间（一般为 6 个月以上）。因此，如果纳税人在一国多个地点开展经营活动，时间总计不超过 6 个月，那么该纳税人在该国不拥有固定营业场所常设机构。设备（如抽油机）使用所在的场所可能会构成固定营业场所，即使该设备并无该企业人员值守。但有些国家认为，人员参与是营业场所构成常设机构的必要条件。

按照关于 OECD 协定范本和联合国协定范本第 5 条的注释，为了使营业场所在地理意义上实现“固定”，必须同时存在地理和商业上的一致性。例如，如果企业定期在市场开展经营活动，那么，该市场可以成为该企业的固定营业场所，即使企业每次使用的摊位不一样，因为市场本身具有地理上和商业上的一致性。相反，如果室内设计师在某客户办公室为其提供 4 个月的服务，该客户办公室是某大型办公楼的一个楼层。之后，该设计师为在同一办公楼占有另一楼层的另一家客户也提供 4 个月的服务，则不能认为该办公楼构成该设计师的常设机构。虽然该办公楼提供地理上的一致性（其为一个固定场所），但是，该设计师开展工作所在的办公室系由不同客户租用，因此并不存在商业上的一致性。因此，这两个办公楼层是独立的固定营业场所，且均未达到 6 个月的最低时间门槛。同样，如果设计师在同一客户拥有的两个办公楼开展工作，这两个办公楼也不会构成该设计师的常设机构，因为这两个办公楼虽然有商业上的一致性，却没有地理上的一致性（它们是不同的固定场所）。但是，如果几个办公楼是构成一个单独地点

the PE but also on the profits derived from sales in that state of goods similar to those sold through the PE or from business activities in that state similar to the activities conducted through the PE.

The Definition of a Permanent Establishment

Under Article 5(1) of the OECD and UN Model Treaties, a PE is defined as "a fixed place of business through which the business of an enterprise is wholly or partly carried on." This language is used in essentially identical form in almost all tax treaties.

For an enterprise to have a "fixed place of business" in a contracting state, it must operate at a specific geographical location, and its activities at that location must continue for more than a temporary period (generally for more than six months). Thus, a taxpayer that does business at various locations in a country for an aggregate of more than six months does not have a fixed place of business PE in that country. The place where equipment (such as an oil-pumping machine) is used can constitute a fixed place of business, even where the equipment is unattended by human agents of the enterprise. However, some countries take the position that human intervention is necessary for a place of business to constitute a PE.

According to the Commentary on Article 5 of the OECD and UN Model Treaties, in order for a place of business to be "fixed" in a geographical sense, it must have both geographical and commercial coherence. For example, a marketplace can be the fixed place of business of an enterprise where the enterprise operates within that marketplace on a regular basis, even though it may use a different stall from time to time, because the marketplace has both geographical and commercial coherence. In contrast, if an interior designer provides services for a client in the client's office occupying a floor in a large office building for four months and then provides services for a different client with an office on a different floor in the same building for another four months, the office building cannot be considered to be the designer's PE. Although the building has geographical coherence (it is a fixed place), the offices where the designer works do not have commercial coherence because they are leased by different clients. As a result, those two office floors are separate fixed places of business, and neither meets the minimum time threshold of six months. Similarly, if the designer does work in two different buildings owned by the same person, those buildings are not the designer's PE since the buildings do not have geographical coherence (they are different fixed places), although they do have commercial coherence. However, multiple buildings may have geographical coherence if they are part of a campus or office complex that consti-

的校园或办公综合体的一部分，那么，就可能存在地理上的一致性。

在确定某一场所是否构成常设机构时，该场所是企业租用的还是自有的不重要，重要的是该场所是否由企业支配（参见 OECD 协定范本注释第 11 段）。某一场所由纳税人“支配”的概念带来不少问题。显然，纳税人不需要有合法的使用权，但是仅仅“使用”该场所超过 6 个月，似乎不足以构成常设机构。例如，OECD 协定范本注释指出，如果企业雇佣的销售人员每天都到客户办公室拜访并接受订单，客户办公室不受该企业支配，不构成该企业的常设机构。OECD 协定范本注释第 12 段在 2017 年进行了修订，明确固定场所是否受纳税人支配，取决于纳税人使用该场所的“实际权力”、纳税人在该场所存在的程度，以及在该场所开展活动的性质。例如，如果纳税人并未使用某场所，或没有任何权利在该场所出现，就不能将该场所视为由该纳税人支配。同样，如果纳税人定期访问某个场所，但并未长时间在此工作，该场所也不由该纳税人支配。对这种情况，注释举了一个例子：某合同制造商拥有一家工厂，为某纳税人生产商品，该纳税人偶尔到工厂视察。但是，如果某公司雇员被允许使用，且实际上在长期使用其关联公司拥有的场所，则应认为该场所由首先提及的公司支配控制。

OECD 协定范本和联合国协定范本规定，建筑工地、建筑或安装工程将构成常设机构，其前提是项目持续时间满足 OECD 协定范本（第 5 条第 3 款）要求的至少 12 个月，联合国协定范本［第 5 条第 3 款第（1）项］要求项目持续至少 6 个月。这两个条款也适用于与建筑或安装工地有关而开展的安装和监督活动。这些活动在联合国协定范本第 5 条第 3 款第（1）项有明确表述，但 OECD 协定范本未予表述，而是在注释（关于第 5 条的注释第 50 段）中有所提及。

发展中国家一般会在其税收协定中采用联合国协定范本规定的 6 个月期限（或针对建筑工地，采用更低的时间门槛），如印度—美国税收协定中的时间门槛为 4 个月。发达国家间的有些协定将时间门槛提高到一年以上，例如日本—美国协定设置了 24 个月的时间门槛。

OECD 协定范本和联合国协定范本中的建筑工地条款通常被误解为“视同条

tutes a single location.

In determining whether the premises constitute a PE, it is immaterial whether an enterprise rents or owns its premises as long as the place is at its disposal (*see* paragraph 11 of the OECD Commentary). This concept of a place being at the taxpayer's disposal is problematic. It is clear that the taxpayer does not need to have a legal right to use the place; however, it appears that the mere use of a place for more than six months is not sufficient to constitute a PE. For example, the OECD Commentary indicates that if a salesperson employed by an enterprise visits a client's office every day to take orders, the client's office is not at the disposal of the enterprise and is not a PE of the enterprise. Paragraph 12 of the OECD Commentary was amended in 2017 to clarify that whether a fixed place is at a taxpayer's disposal depends on the taxpayer's "effective power" to use the place, the extent of the taxpayer's presence at the place, and the nature of the activities it performs there. For example, where a taxpayer does not use a place or have any right to be present there, the place cannot be considered to be at the taxpayer's disposal. Similarly, if a taxpayer visits a place periodically but does not work there for an extended period, the place is not at the taxpayer's disposal. In this regard, the Commentary gives the example of a plant owned by a contract manufacturer that produces goods for a taxpayer who may visit that plant occasionally. However, where employees of a company are allowed to use, and in fact use, premises owned by a related company for an extended period, those premises should be considered to be at the disposal of the first company.

Both the OECD and UN Model Treaties provide that a building site or construction or installation project constitutes a PE if the project continues for at least twelve months in the case of the OECD Model Treaty (Article 5(3)) and six months in the case of the UN Model Treaty (Article 5(3)(a)). Both provisions apply to assembly and supervisory activities conducted in connection with a building or assembly site. These activities are explicitly included in Article 5(3)(a) of the UN Model Treaty but not in the OECD Model Treaty, where they are dealt with in the Commentary (paragraph 50 of the Commentary on Article 5).

Developing countries typically adopt the six-month period in the UN Model Treaty (or an even shorter minimum period for construction sites) in their tax treaties; for example, the minimum period in the India-U.S. treaty is four months. A few treaties between developed countries extend the minimum period beyond one year. For example, the Japan-U.S. treaty has a twenty-four-month period.

The construction site provisions in the OECD and UN Model Treaties are commonly misunderstood as deeming provisions. In my view, they are properly interpreted as an

款”。我认为，这些条款应该恰当地解释为是附加条件，必须满足这些条件，才能将建筑工地认定为构成常设机构。换句话说，建筑工地必须满足第 5 条第 1 款的固定营业场所条件，还必须持续至少 12 个月（OECD 协定范本）或 6 个月（联合国协定范本）。因此，如果一项工程涉及在某个国家的不同地点开展建筑活动，时间总计超过 12 个月，但如果在每个地点的活动持续时间不到 12 个月，那么该工程就没有构成常设机构。每个开展建筑活动的场所必须单独对待，除非相关场所有上文所述的地理和商业上的一致性。

如果常设机构的定义仅限于固定营业场所，就会太过狭隘，无法适用于很多不需要通过固定场所开展的营业活动。因此，OECD 协定范本和联合国协定范本都将常设机构定义扩展为包括代表企业开展活动的人，即通常所称的非独立代理人。根据两个协定范本的第 5 条第 5 款，如果某人（通常称为非独立代理人）经常代表缔约国一方一居民在缔约国另一方订立合同，或对于按常规订立的合同，经常在合同得以订立的过程中发挥主要作用，该居民无须对合同进行实质性修改，且合同对该居民具有约束力，则应认为该居民在缔约国另一方拥有常设机构。代理人必须“以该企业的名义”订立合同，且合同针对由该企业提供的服务，或者针对转让由该企业拥有或有权使用的财产的所有权或使用权。代理人必须代表另一国居民企业在来源国开展活动，且必须经常（即定期或重复地）开展此类活动。“以该企业的名义”一语不应按字面意思理解，合同对该企业具有法律约束力即可。

在 2017 年更新 OECD 协定范本和联合国协定范本前，非独立代理人条款仅适用于有权订立对其委托人有约束力的合同，并经常行使这种权力的代理人。因此，例如，在 2008 年加拿大 the Knights of Columbus v.The Queen，2008 TCC 307 一案中，加拿大税务法庭认定，通过 200 多个代理人在加拿大开展活动的美国保险公司，在加拿大不拥有常设机构，因为这些加拿大代理人没有代表该美国公司签署合同。虽然加拿大代理人负责开发客户、向客户展示各种保险产品，并招揽投保申请，但保险申请的承保和接受（90% 以上都是按照常规接受）均由 the Knights

additional condition that must be met in order for a construction site to constitute a PE. In other words, a construction site must satisfy the conditions of a fixed place of business under Article 5(1) and must also last for at least twelve months (OECD) or six months (UN). Thus, a project that involves construction activities at different locations in a country for an aggregate of more than twelve months is not a PE if the activities at each location do not last for at least twelve months. Each place at which construction occurs must be treated as a separate place unless the places have geographical and commercial coherence, as discussed above.

If the definition of a PE were limited to fixed places of business, it would be too narrow and would not apply to many types of businesses that do not need to be carried on through a fixed place of business. Consequently, both the OECD and UN Model Treaties extend the definition of a PE to include certain persons, often referred to as dependent agents, acting on behalf of an enterprise. Under Article 5(5) of both Model Treaties, a resident of one contracting state is deemed to have a PE in the other contracting state if a person (often referred to as a dependent agent) habitually concludes contracts or plays the principal role leading to the conclusion of contracts that are routinely concluded, without material modifications, by the resident and that are binding on the resident. The agent must conclude contracts "in the name of the enterprise" for the services provided by the enterprise, or for the transfer of the ownership of or the right to use property that is owned by the enterprise or that the enterprise has the right to use. The agent must act in the source country on behalf of the enterprise resident in the other country and must also do so habitually, which means regularly or repeatedly. The phrase "in the name of the enterprise" is not intended to have a literal meaning; it is sufficient if the contracts are legally binding on the enterprise.

Before the 2017 update of the OECD and UN Model Treaties, the dependent-agent provision was limited to agents who had and habitually exercised an authority to conclude contracts binding on their principals. Thus, for example, in a 2008 Canadian case—*Knights of Columbus v. The Queen*, 2008 TCC 307—the Tax Court of Canada held that a U.S.-resident insurance enterprise with over 200 agents operating in Canada did not have a PE in Canada because the Canadian agents did not conclude contracts on behalf of the U.S. enterprise. Although the Canadian agents found clients, presented the various insurance products, and solicited applications for insurance, the underwriting and acceptance of the applications (over 90% were routinely accepted) were done at the head office of the Knights of Columbus in the U.S. Under the revised version of Article 5(5) of the OECD and UN Model Treaties, the of Columbus 公司的美国总部进行。根据修订后的 OECD 协定范本和联合国协定范本第 5 条第 5 款，the Knights of Columbus 可能会被认为在加拿大存在常设机构，因为加拿大代理人在未被实质性修改的合同的订立过程中，发挥了主要作用。

如果代表企业开展活动的人是具有独立地位的代理人，且其在常规经营过程中开展活动（OECD 协定范本第 5 条第 6 款和联合国协定范本第 5 条第 7 款），则不适用第 5 条第 5 款中的视同常设机构规则。然而，如果代理人专门或者几乎专门代表与其“紧密关联”的人从事活动，那么，该代理人不符合作为独立代理人的条件。为此，OECD 协定范本第 5 条第 8 款和联合国协定范本第 5 条第 9 款规定，如果基于所有相关事实和情况，认定某人与某企业中的一方控制另一方，或双方被相同的人或企业控制，则应认为该人与该企业紧密关联。但是，如果一方直接或间接拥有另一方超过 50% 的受益权，或者第三方直接或间接拥有上述两方超过 50% 的受益权，则会自动认为双方紧密关联。在涉及公司的情况下，受益权意味着超过 50% 的合计表决权和其股权价值，或 50% 的公司受益股权价值。公司股份的“合计表决权和价值”或公司的“受益股权价值”的确切含义并不清晰，注释也没有作出说明。

某人是否属于独立代理人，取决于所有事实和情况，尤其取决于该人对于企业承担义务的程度。关于 OECD 协定范本第 5 条第 6 款的注释（第 104 段）指出，如果该人代表企业的活动受制于“具体指导”和“全面控制”或者该人不承担或几乎不承担经营风险，就不能将该人认定为独立代理人。因此，公司雇员无一例外都是非独立代理人，接受类似控制的人大多数情况下可能会被认定为非独立代理人。

相比 OECD 规则，联合国协定范本的代理人规则范围稍显宽泛；该规则延伸至经常保有货物库存，并从中代表企业进行货物交付的非独立代理人。

很多跨国企业都通过**佣金代理安排**，规避在一国构成常设机构。佣金代理安排是得到民法承认的一种法律关系。根据此种安排，一人以另一人的名义或代表另一人达成合同，但合同对该另一人并没有约束力。因此，跨国公司可以对其业务进行筹划，使位于低税国的集团一成员公司，将位于高税国的集团另一成员公司作为自

Knights of Columbus would likely be considered to have a PE in Canada because the Canadian agents played the principal role leading to the conclusion of contracts without material modifications.

The deemed PE rule in Article 5(5) does not apply if the person acting on behalf of an enterprise is an agent of independent status who is acting in the ordinary course of business (Article 5(6) of the OECD Model Treaty and Article 5(7) of the UN Model Treaty). However, where an agent acts exclusively or almost exclusively on behalf of a "closely related" person, that agent cannot qualify as an independent agent. For this purpose, Article 5(8) of the OECD Model and Article 5(9) of the UN Model Treaty provide that a person is closely related to an enterprise if, based on all the relevant facts and circumstances, one controls the other or both are controlled by another person or enterprise. However, parties are automatically considered to be closely related if one party owns, directly or indirectly, more than 50% of the beneficial interests of the other party or a third person owns, directly or indirectly, more than 50% of the beneficial interests in both parties. Where a company is involved, beneficial interest means more than 50% of the aggregate vote and value of its shares or beneficial equity interest in the company. The precise meaning of the "aggregate vote and value" of a company's shares or the "beneficial equity interest" in a company is unclear, and no clarification is provided in the Commentary.

Whether a person is an independent agent depends on all the facts and circumstances, and in particular, on the extent of the obligations that the person has with respect to an enterprise. The Commentary on Article 5(6) of the OECD Model (paragraph 104) indicates that where the person's activities on behalf of the enterprise are subject to "detailed instructions" or "comprehensive control," or the person bears little or no entrepreneurial risk, the person cannot be regarded as an independent agent. Thus, an employee is invariably a dependent agent, and a person who is subject to similar control is likely to be considered a dependent agent in most circumstances.

The agency rule in the UN Model Treaty is slightly more expansive than the OECD rule; it extends to dependent agents that habitually maintain a stock of goods from which they make deliveries on behalf of an enterprise.

Many multinational corporations have used **commissionaire arrangements** to avoid having a PE in a country. A commissionaire arrangement is a legal relationship recognized under civil law, under which one person enters into contracts in the name of or on behalf of another person, but those contracts are not legally binding on that other person. Therefore, multinational corporations were able to structure their affairs so that a group

己的佣金代理人，并向高税国的顾客销售自己的产品。佣金代理人并不拥有商品，其与顾客签订的合同对拥有商品的集团成员没有法律约束力。结果是，作为佣金代理人开展活动的集团成员因其活动仅获得了一小部分利润，并仅就这一小部分利润在其作为居民的高税国征税。同时，位于低税国的集团公司获得了销售产品的大部分利润，但因其在高税国不存在常设机构，就无须在高税国纳税。

戴尔计算机公司通过这种佣金代理安排，在一些高税欧洲国家进行避税。设立在爱尔兰的一家戴尔集团成员公司向设立在挪威的另一家集团成员公司销售计算机，后者再将这些计算机销售给位于挪威的客户。挪威最高法院认定，戴尔爱尔兰公司在挪威不拥有常设机构［参见荷兰财税文献局税收协定判例 Dell Productsv. The State，December 2，2011（Tax East），HR–2011–02245–A（Case No. 2011.755）］。法国最高行政法院在 Zimmer 一案得出了同样的结论（参见荷兰财税文献局税收协定判例 Société Zimmer Limited，March31，2010，Case No. 304715 and No. 308525）。

在 OECD 协定范本和联合国协定范本于 2017 年更新后，典型的佣金代理安排被第 5 条第 5 款涵盖为非独立代理人而视同构成常设机构。理由是：为了销售委托人拥有的商品，佣金代理人洽谈了合同的实质性内容，尽管这些合同对委托人没有法律约束力（即代理人发挥了主要作用，使合同得以订立）；并且由于代理人全部或几乎全部代表与其紧密关联的企业，因此不构成独立代理人。

如果代理人的活动仅限于范本第 5 条第 4 款所列举的豁免活动（一般的准备性或辅助性活动），两个协定范本第 5 条第 5 款中的代理人视同构成常设机构规则就不适用，这一点将在后面讨论。

根据联合国协定范本第 5 条第 6 款，如果从事保险销售业务的公司在缔约国一方收取保费，或为存在于该国的风险提供担保，则应视同该公司在该国拥有常设机构。然而，如果这些活动由独立代理人按其常规业务进行，则该规则不适用。联合国协定范本第 5 条第 3 款第（2）项规定，如果企业通过雇员或其他人员，在缔约国一方从事劳务，且在任何 12 个月内超过了 183 天，则应认为该企业在该

company in a low-tax country could sell its products through another group company in a high-tax country to customers in that country as a commissionaire for the low-tax group company. The commissionaire did not own the goods, and the contracts it entered into with customers were not legally binding on the group company that owned the goods. The result was that the group company acting as a commissionaire earned only a small profit from its activities; that profit was taxable in the high-tax country in which it was resident. However, the group company in the low-tax country earned most of the profit from the sale of the products, and it was not taxable in the high-tax country because it did not have a PE there.

Dell computers used this type of commissionaire arrangement to avoid tax in several high-tax European countries. A Dell group company established in Ireland sold computers to another group company established in Norway that resold the computers to customers in Norway. The Norwegian Supreme Court held that Dell Ireland did not have a PE in Norway (*see Dell Products v. The State*, December 2, 2011 (*Tax East*), HR-2011-02245-A (Case No. 2011.755), Tax Treaty Case Law International Bureau of Fiscal Documentation (IBFD)). The French Conseil d'Etat reached the same result in the Zimmer case (*see Société Zimmer Limited*, March 31, 2010, Case No. 304715 and No. 308525, Tax Treaty Case Law IBFD).

After the 2017 update of the OECD and UN Model Treaties, a typical commissionaire arrangement is covered by Article 5(5) because the commissionaire negotiates the material elements of the contracts for the sale of the goods owned by the principal even though those contracts are not legally binding on the principal (i.e., it plays the principal role leading to the conclusion of contracts) and since the commissionaire deals exclusively or almost exclusively with a closely related enterprise, it cannot qualify as an independent agent.

The deemed-agency PE rule in Article 5(5) of both Model Treaties does not apply where an agent's activities are limited to the exempt activities (generally preparatory or auxiliary activities) listed in Article 5(4), which is discussed below.

Under Article 5(6) of the UN Model Treaty, an enterprise engaged in the sale of insurance in a contracting state is deemed to have a PE in that state if it collects premiums in that state or ensures risks located in that state. This rule does not apply, however, if these activities are conducted by an independent agent acting in the ordinary course of business.

Article 5(3)(b) of the UN Model Treaty provides that an enterprise is deemed to have a PE in a contracting state if it performs services in that state through employees or other

国拥有常设机构。在联合国协定范本于 2017 年更新前，第 5 条第 3 款第（2）项要求劳务是为同一或相关联项目提供，这大大限制了这一条款的适用范围。2017 年的更新取消了这一要求。OECD 协定范本中没有与联合国协定范本第 5 条第 3 款第（2）项类似的条款，但是 OECD 注释包含了供各国选用的另一劳务型常设机构条款（参见 OECD 关于第 5 条的注释第 144 段）。

按照联合国协定范本，从事独立个人劳务取得的所得应按照第 14 条征税，而不是按照第 7 条。OECD 协定范本此前也采用了这一做法，但在 2000 年删除了第 14 条。第 8.7.3.3 节将讨论对独立个人劳务的征税。

OECD 协定范本和联合国协定范本第 5 条第 4 款将完全用于某些准备性或辅助性活动的固定营业场所，排除在常设机构的定义之外。按照这两个范本，如果某企业的固定营业场所仅用于从事下列活动，且这些活动单独或整体的性质为准备性或辅助性，则不应认为该固定营业场所构成常设机构：

—— 存储或展示本企业拥有的货物；
—— 为储存、陈列或为另一企业加工的目的而保存本企业拥有的货物；
—— 为本企业采购货物或收集信息；以及
—— 具有准备性、辅助性的其他活动。

OECD 协定范本第 5 条第 4 款还适用于仅用来交付企业拥有的商品的固定营业场所。因此，如果企业在一国拥有或租用仓库，将该仓库用于储存其拥有的商品，并将这些商品交付给客户，则该仓库不构成该企业的常设机构。与此相反，按照联合国协定范本，该仓库将构成常设机构，因为商品交付活动并非豁免活动（注意，根据这两个协定范本，如果将仓库用来储存其他企业的商品，则不符合豁免条件）。

2017 年的更新修订了第 5 条第 4 款，以确保真正具有准备性或辅助性的活动才可以豁免。因此，如果企业拥有的大型仓库用来存储通过在线网站销售的商品，则应将该仓库认定为常设机构，尽管这些活动仅限于存储和交付。

personnel for a period of at least 183 days in any twelve-month period. Before the 2017 update of the UN Model Treaty, Article 5(3)(b) required the services to be provided for the same or a connected project, which limited the scope of the provision significantly. This requirement was deleted in the 2017 update. The OECD Model Treaty does not contain any provision comparable to Article 5(3)(b), although the OECD Commentary contains an alternative services PE provision that countries may adopt (*see* paragraph 144 of the OECD Commentary on Article 5).

Under the UN Model Treaty, income from the performance of independent personal services is taxable under Article 14 and not under Article 7. This approach was also followed under the OECD Model Treaty until 2000 when Article 14 was deleted. The taxation of independent personal services is discussed in section 8.7.3.3 below.

Article 5(4) of the OECD and UN Model Treaties provides an exemption from the definition of a PE for fixed places of business that are used exclusively for certain preparatory or auxiliary activities. Under both models, a fixed place of business of an enterprise used solely for the following activities is deemed not to be a PE if, taken alone or together, the activities are preparatory or auxiliary in nature:

- the storage or display of goods owned by the enterprise;
- the maintenance of a stock of goods owned by the enterprise for storage or display or for processing by another enterprise;
- purchasing goods or collecting information for the enterprise; and
- other activities of a preparatory or auxiliary character.

Article 5(4) of the OECD Model also applies to a fixed place of business used solely for the delivery of goods owned by an enterprise. Therefore, if an enterprise owns or rents a warehouse in a country that it uses to store goods owned by it and to deliver those goods to customers, the warehouse would not be a PE of the enterprise. In contrast, under the UN Model Treaty, the warehouse would be a PE because delivery of goods is not an exempt activity. (Note that under both Model Treaties, if a warehouse is used to store goods owned by other enterprises, it will not qualify for the exemption.)

In the 2017 update, Article 5(4) was revised to ensure that the exemption for the listed activities is available only if they are truly preparatory or auxiliary. Thus, a large warehouse owned by an enterprise and used to store goods that are sold through online shopping websites would be considered to be a PE even though the activities are limited to storage and delivery.

按照 OECD 协定范本第 5 条第 7 款和联合国协定范本第 5 条第 8 款，作为一国居民或在一国开展营业活动的子公司，不会仅因受母公司控制，而构成母公司在该国的常设机构。同样，母公司也不是其子公司的常设机构。因此，如果 A 国居民公司在 B 国拥有子公司，该子公司为 B 国居民或在 B 国开展营业活动，该公司不会仅仅因为控制其子公司，而在 B 国拥有常设机构。但是，如果子公司经常代表其母公司在 B 国订立合同，或由母公司支配子公司拥有或租用的设备，并由母公司使用超过 6 个月，则母公司可能在 B 国拥有常设机构。关于 OECD 协定范本和联合国协定范本的注释指出，对于跨国集团，必须针对集团中的各个公司，单独判定是否存在常设机构；仅仅因为某个集团成员在一国设有常设机构，并不意味着任何其他集团成员在该国也拥有常设机构。

在判定某企业是否由于在一国销售数字商品或服务而在该国拥有常设机构的过程中，出现了很多难题。第 9 章第 9.5 节将讨论这些问题。

国际海运和空运

2017 年之前，根据 OECD 协定范本第 8 条和联合国协定范本第 8 条（选项 A），缔约国一方居民企业以船舶和飞机经营国际运输取得的营业利润，应仅在该企业实际管理机构所在国征税。企业实际管理机构所在地的确定有很大的不确定性。由于这种不确定性，第 4 条第 3 款关于双重居民身份的“加比规则”和第 8 条都删除了实际管理机构所在地的要求。

由于 2017 年删除了实际管理机构所在地的要求，第 8 条适用于“缔约国一方企业”开展国际海运和空运“取得的利润”。按照第 3 条第 1 款（d）项规定，“缔约国一方企业”是由缔约国一方居民经营的企业，因此，开展国际海运和空运取得的利润应仅在纳税人的居民国征税，而不是在纳税人的实际管理机构所在国征税。第 8 条第 2 款进一步明确，第 8 条也适用于参加合伙经营、联合经营或者国际经营机构取得的利润。

第 8 条涉及的“国际运输”的定义［第 3 条第 1 款第（5）项］极其宽泛，

According to Article 5(7) of the OECD Model Treaty and Article 5(8) of the UN Model Treaty, a subsidiary resident in a country or carrying on business in a country does not constitute a PE of its parent company in that country simply because the parent controls it. Similarly, a parent company is not a PE of its subsidiary. Thus, a company resident in Country A that owns a subsidiary resident or carrying on business in Country B does not have a PE in Country B simply because it controls the subsidiary. However, the parent company might have a PE in Country B if its subsidiary habitually acts on its behalf in Country B with respect to the conclusion of contracts or if facilities owned or leased by the subsidiary are at the disposal of the parent company and used by it for more than six months. The Commentary on both the OECD and UN Model Treaties indicates that, with respect to a multinational group, the determination of whether a PE exists must be made separately for each company in the group; just because one group company has a PE in a country does not mean that any other group company has a PE in that country.

Many difficult issues arise in determining whether an enterprise has a PE in a contracting state as a result of selling digital goods or services in that state. Those issues are addressed in Chapter 9, section 9.5.

International Shipping and Air Transportation

Until 2017, under Article 8 of the OECD Model Treaty and Article 8 (Alternative A) of the UN Model Treaty, business profits derived by an enterprise resident in one contracting state from the operation of ships or aircraft in international traffic were taxable exclusively by the state in which the enterprise had its place of effective management. The determination of the place of effective management of an enterprise involves significant uncertainty. As a result of this uncertainty, the place-of-effective-management requirement was eliminated in both the dual-resident tie-breaker test in Article 4(3) and in Article 8.

As a result of the elimination of the place-of-effective-management requirement in 2017, Article 8 applies to "profits of an enterprise of a Contracting State" from international shipping and air transport. Since "an enterprise of a Contracting State" is defined in Article 3(1)(d) to mean an enterprise carried on by a resident of a contracting state, profits from international shipping and air transport are taxable exclusively by the country in which the taxpayer is resident, not by the country in which the taxpayer's place of effective management is located. Article 8(2) also clarifies that profits from participation in a pool, joint business, or international operating agency are covered by Article 8.

The definition of "international traffic" (Article 3(1)(e)) for purposes of Article 8 is

包括除了仅在一国两地之间运输货物或乘客的所有其他运输活动。因此，第 8 条不允许一国对缔约国另一方居民企业在该国承载货物或乘客，或者在该国卸载货物或乘客，而取得的利润征税。例如，如果某航空公司是 A 国居民，其航程始于 B 国境外，在 B 国停留并卸载和承载乘客，航程的终点也在 B 国之外，则 B 国不应对该航空公司征税。但是，如果该航空公司经营的航班在 B 国停留并承载乘客，之后终止于 B 国另一地点，则应允许 B 国就该航班完全发生在其境内的部分所产生的利润征税。

如果海运活动（不包括空运）“并非随意发生的”，联合国协定范本第 8 条（B 选项）则允许来源国对由其产生的所得征税。按照注释，并非随意发生指的是任何前往一国承载货物或乘客的有计划的行程。

演艺和体育活动所得

根据 OECD 协定范本和联合国协定范本第 17 条，缔约国一方居民作为演艺人员或运动员，在缔约国另一方从事演艺和体育活动取得的所得，可以在该缔约国另一方征税，没有任何门槛要求或限制。因此，对在一国短暂停留的演艺人员和运动员，该国有权对其从该国取得款项的总额征税，且对税率没有限制。

第 17 条与第 7 条形成了鲜明的对比。按照第 7 条，来源国仅在非居民在该国设有常设机构，且净利润应归属于常设机构的情况下，才有权对其营业利润征税。很难按照任何原则对第 17 条进行解释。一些演艺人员和运动员能够在相对较短的时间里取得巨额款项，各国都想从中分一杯羹。但是，其他一些纳税人，如咨询顾问和名人，也能够在相对较短的时间里获得大量金钱，但如果其在另一国没有常设机构，或没有位于该国的固定基地，那么另一国就不会对他们在该国取得的所得征税。另外，很多演艺人员和运动员仅从其演艺或体育活动中仅取得有限数额的款项，但是按照第 17 条的规定，其开展活动所在的国家可以不受限制地对其征税。

第 17 条第 2 款包含了一项反避税规定，即使演艺人员或运动员转由其他人来取得所得，也允许一国对源自在该国发生的演艺或体育活动的所得征税。例

extremely broad and includes all transport other than transport of goods or persons solely between places within a country. Thus, Article 8 does not permit a country to tax the profits derived by an enterprise resident in the other contracting state from taking goods or passengers on board in the country or unloading goods or passengers in the country. For example, an airline resident in Country A that starts flights outside Country B, stops in Country B to drop off passengers and take on passengers and completes the flights outside Country B would not be subject to tax by Country B. However, if the airline operates a flight that stops in Country B to pick up passengers and then stops at another location in Country B, Country B is allowed to tax the profits from the portion of the flight that takes place solely in Country B.

Article 8 (Alternative B) of the UN Model Treaty permits the source country to tax income derived from shipping (but not air transportation) activities if such activities are "more than casual." According to the Commentary, more than casual means any planned trip to a country to pick up goods or passengers.

Income from Entertainment and Athletic Activities

Under Article 17 of both the OECD and UN Model Treaties, income derived by an entertainer or athlete resident in one contracting state from entertainment or athletic activities performed in the other state is taxable in that other state without any threshold requirement or any limitations. Thus, a country is entitled to tax an entertainer or athlete who is present in the country for only a short period on the gross amount received by the entertainer or athlete without any limit on the rate of tax.

Article 17 provides a sharp contrast with Article 7, under which a source country is entitled to tax a nonresident on business profits only if the nonresident has a PE in the source country and the net profits are attributable to the PE. It is difficult to justify Article 17 on any principled basis. Some entertainers and athletes can make large sums of money in a relatively short time, and countries want their share of that money. However, other taxpayers, such as consultants and celebrities, who can also earn large sums in a relatively short time, are not subject to tax if they earn income in another country without any PE or fixed base in that country. Moreover, many entertainers and athletes earn only modest amounts from their entertainment and athletic activities; nevertheless, under the terms of Article 17, they are subject to tax without any limitations by the country in which their activities are exercised.

Article 17(2) contains an anti-avoidance rule that allows a country to tax income from entertainment or athletic activities occurring in the country even if the income is assigned by the entertainer or athlete to another person. For example, an entertainer might perform in a country

如，某演艺人员可能作为个人劳务公司（通常称为“租星公司”）的雇员在一国从事演艺活动，这样，演艺活动的所得大部分都由公司而不是该演艺人员收取。第 17 条第 2 款允许该国既对演艺人员也对公司征税。

租赁所得

1992 年之前，出于 OECD 协定范本第 12 条的目的，特许权使用费的定义中包含租赁设备取得的所得。1992 年之后，这些租赁所得系按照 OECD 协定范本第 7 条进行征税，因此只有在纳税人在来源国设有常设机构，且该所得应归属于该常设机构时，来源国才能对该所得征税。相反，联合国协定范本第 12 条允许来源国将设备租赁所得作为特许权使用费征税。因此，即使纳税人在来源国未拥有常设机构，其因租赁商业、科学或工业设备而取得的所得，来源国可按照商定的税率，对租金总额征税。如果纳税人的确在来源国设有常设机构，且设备租赁与常设机构实际相关，则应适用第 7 条。

从位于一国的不动产取得的租金，应由该国根据 OECD 协定范本和联合国协定范本第 6 条征税，无论纳税人在该国是否设有常设机构。例如，出租公寓楼取得的所得，可以由该公寓楼所在的缔约国征税。第 8.7.3.4 节将讨论第 6 条。

管理、技术、咨询服务费和自动化数字服务所得

按照联合国协定范本的特殊规定，来源国可以按照总额，对咨询、技术、管理服务费和自动化数字服务所得，征收预提税，尽管提供服务的非居民在来源国并不存在常设机构。第 12A 条适用于缔约国一方居民或在该国有常设机构或固定场所的非居民向缔约国另一方居民支付的咨询、技术和管理服务费。第 9 章第 9.3.3 节详细讨论第 12A 条。第 12B 条适用于缔约国一方居民或在该国有常设机构或固定场所的非居民向缔约国另一方居民支付的自动化数字服务相关款项。第 12B 条是联合国协定范本 2021 年新增加的内容，第 9 章第 9.5.4 节将讨论该条款。

as an employee of a personal services corporation (often referred to as a "rent-a-star" company) so that most of the income from the performance is derived by the corporation rather than the entertainer. Article 17(2) allows the country to tax both the entertainer and the corporation.

Leasing Income

Until 1992, rental income derived from leasing equipment was included in the definition of royalties for purposes of Article 12 of the OECD Model Treaty. Since 1992, such rental income has been taxable in accordance with Article 7 of the OECD Model Treaty; as a result, the income is subject to tax by a source country only if the taxpayer has a PE in the country and the income is attributable to the PE. In contrast, Article 12 of the UN Model Treaty permits the source country to tax income from equipment rentals as royalties; therefore, income from leasing commercial, scientific, or industrial equipment is subject to tax by the source country at an agreed rate on the gross rental payments even if the taxpayer does not have a PE in the source country. If the taxpayer does have a PE in the source country and the leasing equipment is effectively connected with the PE, then Article 7 applies.

Rent derived from immovable property situated in a country is taxable by that country in accordance with Article 6 of the OECD and UN Model Treaties, irrespective of whether the taxpayer has a PE in that country. For example, income derived from renting an apartment building would be taxable in the contracting state where the building is located. Article 6 is discussed in section 8.7.3.4 below.

Fees for Management, Technical, and Consulting Services and Income from Automated Digital Services

Under special provisions of the UN Model Treaty, fees for consulting, technical, and management services and income from automated digital services are taxable by source countries through gross-based withholding taxes, despite the fact that the nonresident service provider does not have a PE in the source country. Article 12A applies to fees for consulting, technical, and management services paid by a resident of one contracting state or a nonresident with a PE or fixed base in that state to a resident of the other contracting state. Article 12A is discussed in detail in Chapter 9, section 9.3.3. Article 12B applies to payments for automated digital services by a resident of one contracting state or a nonresident with a PE or fixed base in that state to a resident of the other contracting state. Article 12B of the UN Model Treaty, which was added in 2021, is discussed in Chapter 9, section 9.5.4.

8.7.3.3 受雇和个人劳务所得

OECD 协定范本和联合国协定范本的多项条款涉及从各种劳务取得的所得。这些条款差异很大，因此，区分各类劳务非常重要。例如，第 15 条是对受雇所得征税的基本规则。然而，演艺和体育活动所得、董事费、高级管理人员报酬、退休金和政府服务所得等一些其他种类的受雇所得却适用特殊规则。

经常需要区分受雇所得和独立个人劳务，以确定对于一个特定个案，应适用第 15 条处理受雇所得的规则，还是适用第 7 条（或联合国协定范本第 14 条）处理独立个人劳务的规则。这种区分之所以重要，是因为两种规则差异很大。例如，如果缔约国一方居民个人受雇于缔约国另一方居民雇主，则应由该缔约国另一方对其在该另一方从事受雇活动取得的任何所得征税。相反，如果该个人为独立承包商，则只有其在缔约国另一方设有经常使用的固定基地或常设机构，或在缔约国另一方停留超过 183 天的情况下，缔约国另一方才能对其征税。

根据联合国协定范本第 14 条（独立个人劳务），缔约国一方居民在缔约国另一方从事“专业劳务或具有独立性的其他活动”，该缔约国另一方不应对其征税，除非其在缔约国另一方设有经常使用的固定基地，或在任何 12 个月内在该缔约国另一方停留超过 183 天。“专业劳务”一语包括医师、律师、工程师、牙医师和会计师所提供的劳务，以及独立的科学、文学、艺术、教育或教学活动。OECD 于 2000 年删除了协定范本第 14 条。因此，在缔约国一方从事独立个人劳务的个人和公司，只有其在该国设有常设机构，且其所得应归属于该常设机构时，才应在该国纳税。

联合国协定范本第 14 条和 OECD 协定范本 2000 年之前版本中的固定基地概念，旨在与第 5 条常设机构概念中的固定营业场所概念相对应。但是，第 5 条中的代理视同常设机构规则和对准备性、辅助性活动的豁免，在按第 14 条确定企业是否设有固定基地时并不适用。

8.7.3.3 *Employment and Personal Services Income*

Many provisions of the OECD and UN Model Treaties deal with a wide variety of income from services. The provisions differ significantly, and therefore it is important to distinguish among the various types of services. For example, the basic rule for the taxation of income from employment is Article 15. However, some types of income from employment—such as income from entertainment and athletic activities, directors' fees, remuneration of top-level managerial officials, pensions, and income from government service—are subject to special rules.

It is frequently necessary to distinguish between employment income and independent personal services income in order to determine whether the rules for the treatment of employment income under Article 15 or the rules for the treatment of independent personal services income under Article 7 (or Article 14 of the UN Model Treaty) apply in a particular case. This distinction is important because the rules differ significantly. For example, an individual resident in one contracting state who is employed by an employer resident in the other contracting state is taxable by that other state on any income derived from employment exercised in that state. In contrast, if the individual is an independent contractor, the individual is taxable by the other contracting state only if the individual has a regularly available fixed base or PE in that state or stays in that state for more than 183 days.

Under Article 14 (Independent Personal Services) of the UN Model Treaty, a resident of a contracting state who performs "professional services or other activities of an independent nature" in the other contracting state is not taxable in that State unless he or she has a "fixed base" in the state that is regularly available or stays in the state for more than 183 days in any twelve-month period. The term "professional services" includes the services of physicians, lawyers, engineers, architects, dentists, and accountants, as well as independent scientific, literary, artistic, educational, and teaching activities. Article 14 of the OECD Model Treaty was deleted in 2000; as a result, individuals and companies engaged in the performance of independent personal services in a contracting state are taxable in that state only if they have a PE in that state and their income is attributable to the PE.

The concept of a fixed base in Article 14 of the UN Model Treaty and the pre-2000 version of the OECD Model Treaty is intended to be equivalent to the concept of a fixed place of business in the definition of a PE in Article 5. However, the deemed-agency PE rules and the exception for preparatory and auxiliary activities in Article 5 are not applicable in determining whether an enterprise has a fixed base for purposes of Article 14.

在一国从事受雇活动取得的所得，在该国可以按照 OECD 协定范本和联合国协定范本第 15 条（非独立个人劳务）征税，无论受雇人员在该国是否拥有固定基地。但是，如果所得系由在来源国未设立常设机构的非居民雇主支付的，且受雇人员在任何 12 个月内在来源国停留不超过 183 天，则来源国应对该项所得免税。

就专业人员和受雇人员对来源国征税权的限制，一般不适用于演艺人员和运动员（参见 OECD 协定范本和联合国协定范本第 17 条），也不适用于作为居民企业董事收取费用，或作为居民企业的高层管理人员收取报酬的非居民（参见 OECD 协定范本和联合国协定范本第 16 条）。按照第 16 条，公司董事或高级管理人员取得的所得是否来自在该公司的居民国从事的劳务并不重要。

除了某些例外，为缔约国一方政府从事受雇劳务的个人，应仅由该国征税（参见 OECD 协定范本和联合国协定范本第 19 条）。作为政府外交使团成员在外国工作的外交官和领事官员，应按照特别协定或国际法原则予以免税，税收协定不应对该免税待遇产生影响（参见 OECD 协定范本和联合国协定范本第 27 条）。

按照 OECD 协定范本第 18 条，个人因以前的雇佣关系而取得的退休金，一般应仅由其目前为其居民的国家征税。相反，联合国协定范本规定，退休金支付方为其居民的国家享有有限范围的征税权。政府退休金一般由支付退休金的缔约国征税，除非收取退休金的个人既是缔约国另一方居民，又是其国民（参见 OECD 协定范本和联合国协定范本第 19 条第 2 款）。

为接受教育或培训的目的而访问缔约国一方的学生、学徒和实习生，其为了维持生活、接受教育或培训的目的而从缔约国另一方居民收到的款项，一般不应在该缔约国一方征税（参见 OECD 协定范本和联合国协定范本第 20 条）。有些协定也为客座教授和教师规定了对等的免税。

Income from employment performed in a country may be taxable in the country under Article 15 (Dependent Personal Services) of the OECD and UN Model Treaties whether or not the employee has a fixed base in the country. However, such income is exempt from tax in the source country if an employee is paid by a nonresident employer without a PE in the source country and the employee is present in the source country for not more than 183 days in any twelve-month period.

The limitations on source country taxation of professionals and employees do not generally apply to entertainers and athletes (*see* Article 17 of the OECD and UN Model Treaties). Nor do they apply to nonresidents receiving fees as corporate directors of resident corporations (*see* Article 16 of the OECD and UN Model Treaties) or remuneration as top-level managers of resident corporations (*see* Article 16 of the UN Model Treaty). Under Article 16, it is immaterial whether the income of the directors or top-level officials of a company arises from services performed in the contracting state in which the company is resident.

With certain exceptions, individuals performing employment services for the government of a contracting state are taxable only by that state (*see* Article 19 of the OECD and UN Model Treaties). Diplomats and consular officials who work in a foreign country as members of their government's diplomatic missions are exempt from tax under special agreements or under the rules of international law. A tax treaty would not affect such exemptions (*see* Article 27 of the OECD and UN Model Treaties).

Under Article 18 of the OECD Model Treaty, individuals receiving pensions on account of past employment are generally taxable only by the contracting state in which they are resident. In contrast, the UN Model Treaty provides some limited scope for taxation by the country where the payer of the pension is resident. Government pensions generally are taxable by the contracting state making the pension payment unless the individual receiving the pension is both a resident and a national of the other contracting state (*see* Article 19(2) of the OECD and UN Model Treaties).

Students and certain business apprentices or trainees who visit a contracting state for educational or training purposes are generally not taxable in that contracting state on payments for their maintenance, education, or training received from persons resident in the other state (*see* Article 20 of the OECD and UN Model Treaties). Some tax treaties also provide reciprocal exemptions for visiting professors and teachers.

8.7.3.4 不动产所得和收益

大部分国家都希望保留对因出租、销售位于本国境内的不动产或开采位于本国境内的自然资源取得所得的征税权。为反映这一共同观点，OECD 协定范本和联合国协定范本第 6 条允许来源国对从位于该国的“不动产”取得的所得征税。“不动产”一语的含义按照其所在国家的法律确定；该用语还包括农业和林业所使用的牲畜和设备，以及开发矿藏和其他自然资源的权利。两个协定范本第 13 条都允许来源国对处置不动产产生的收益征税。

由于来源国对不动产相关所得和不动产处置收益均有征税权，出于协定范本的目的，将不动产收益定性为所得还是财产收益无关紧要；这一定性问题留待国内法解决。OECD 协定范本和联合国协定范本对不动产之外的其他财产相关所得和收益也采用了同样的处理方法。

OECD 协定范本和联合国协定范本第 13 条第 4 款规定，对于处置公司股份、合伙企业或其他实体的权益取得的收益，如果该公司、合伙企业或其他实体的价值主要来自位于一国的不动产 (即所谓的“持有大量不动产的实体”)，则该来源国有权对该收益征税。该规定的目的是防止纳税人将不动产转让给受控公司、合伙企业或其他实体，然后通过一项交易处置其在该公司、合伙企业或实体中的权益，从而规避来源国对该不动产收益的征税。如果没有第 13 条第 4 款规定，按照税收协定，该交易将在来源国免税。

8.7.3.5 特定投资所得预提税率的降低

大部分税收协定的主要目的之一，是降低来源国对支付给缔约国另一方居民的股息、利息和特许权使用费的预提税率。降低预提税率的目的是在来源国和居民国之间分享税收收入。

8.7.3.4 *Income and Gains from Immovable Property*

Most countries want to retain the right to tax income derived from the sale and rental of immovable property and from the extraction of natural resources located within their territory. Reflecting this consensus view, Article 6 of the OECD and UN Model Treaties allows the country of source to tax income derived from "immovable property" situated in the country. The meaning of the term "immovable property" is determined in accordance with the law of the country in which the property is situated; the term also includes livestock and equipment used in agriculture and forestry, and rights to work mineral deposits, and other natural resources. Article 13 of both Model Treaties allows gains from the disposition of immovable property to be taxed by the source country.

Because the source country is entitled to tax both the income derived from immovable property and gains from the disposition of such property, it does not generally matter for purposes of the model treaties whether a gain from the disposition of immovable property is characterized as income or capital gain; this characterization issue is left to domestic law. The same approach is used under the OECD and UN Model Treaties for income and gains from property other than immovable property.

Article 13(4) of the OECD and UN Model Treaties provides that a source country is entitled to tax gains from the disposition of shares of a company or an interest in a partnership or other entity if the value of the company, partnership, or other entity is derived primarily from immovable property situated in the country (so-called **land-rich entities**). This provision is intended to prevent a taxpayer from avoiding source country taxation on gains derived from immovable property by transferring the property to a controlled corporation, partnership, or other entity and then disposing of the interests in the corporation, partnership, or entity in a transaction that would otherwise be exempt from source taxation under the tax treaty.

8.7.3.5 *Reduced Withholding Rates on Certain Investment Income*

A major objective of most tax treaties is to provide for reduced rates of withholding tax levied by the source country on dividends, interest, and royalties paid to residents of the other contracting state. The goal of these reduced rates is to provide for some sharing of the tax revenue between the source and residence countries.

OECD 协定范本规定，来源国对股息、利息和特许权使用费征收的预提税应限于如表 8-1 所示的税率。

表 8-1　OECD 协定范本认可的最高预提税率

	向实质持股公司支付的股息	向其他人支付的股息	利息	特许权使用费
最高税率	5%	15%	10%	0

来源：OECD 协定范本第 10 条（股息）、第 11 条（利息）和第 12 条（特许权使用费）。

大多数发展中国家和很多发达国家无法接受 OECD 协定范本建议的最高税率，特别是特许权使用费条款的零税率。联合国协定范本没有对预提税率提出具体的限制，而将其留待缔约国双方谈判确定。发展中国家签署的税收协定，大部分都允许特许权使用费最高预提税率大幅度超过 OECD 协定范本规定的零税率；例如，发展中国家同意特许权使用费最高预提税率低于 15% 的情况并不常见。

与 OECD 协定范本所提议的简单模式相比，很多税收协定所规定的最高预提税率要复杂得多。例如，税收协定通常针对工业特许权使用费、与文学作品版权相关而支付的特许权使用费，以及因播放动画影片而支付的特许权使用费，规定了不同的预提税率限制。

OECD 协定范本和联合国协定范本第 10 条、第 11 条和第 12 条中分别适用于股息、利息和特许权使用费的规定，优先于第 7 条关于营业利润的征税规定适用。例如，按照第 11 条规定，缔约国一方居民支付给缔约国另一方居民的利息可在缔约国一方征税，即使该利息构成缔约国另一方居民的营业利润。但是，如果缔约国另一方居民在缔约国一方拥有常设机构，且据以支付利息的债权与该常设机构实际相关，缔约国一方则应按照第 7 条而不是第 11 条对该利息进行征税（参见 OECD 协定范本第 7 条第 4 款和第 11 条第 4 款、联合国协定范本第 7 条第 6 款和第 11 条第 4 款）。OECD 协定范本和联合国协定范本第 10 条第 4 款、第 11 条第 4 款和第 12 条第 4 款的规定被称为“抛回规则”，因为股息、利息和特许权使用

The OECD Model Treaty provides that the withholding taxes imposed by a source country on dividends, interest, and royalties will be limited to the rates shown in Table 8.1.

Table 8.1 Maximum Withholding Rates Endorsed by OECD Model Treaty

	Dividends Paid to Corporations with a Substantial Interest	*Dividends Paid to Other Persons*	*Interest*	*Royalties*
Maximum Rate (%)	5	15	10	0

Source: OECD Model Treaty, Article 10 (Dividends), Article 11 (Interest), and Article 12 (Royalties).

The maximum rates proposed in the OECD Model Treaty, especially the zero rate on royalties, are unacceptable to most developing countries and many developed countries. The UN Model Treaty does not provide any specific limits on withholding rates, leaving those limits to be negotiated by the contracting states. Most tax treaties with developing countries allow maximum withholding rates on royalties that are substantially in excess of the zero rate provided in the OECD Model Treaty; for example, it is uncommon for developing countries to agree to a maximum withholding rate on royalties lower than 15%.

Many tax treaties provide for a more complicated set of maximum withholding rates than the simple pattern proposed in the OECD Model Treaty. For example, it is common for tax treaties to impose separate limitations on the withholding rates applicable to industrial royalties, royalties paid with respect to copyrights of literary works, and royalties paid for the showing of motion picture films.

The rules for the taxation of dividends, interest, and royalties under Articles 10, 11, and 12 of the OECD and UN Model Treaties, respectively, take priority over the rules for the taxation of business profits in Article 7. For example, under Article 11, interest paid by a resident of one contracting state to a resident of the other contracting state is taxable by the first state, even if the interest forms part of the business profits of the resident of the other state. However, if the resident of the other state has a PE in the first state and the debt claim in respect of which the interest is paid is effectively connected with the PE, the interest is taxable by the first state in accordance with Article 7 rather than Article 11 (*see* Articles 7(4) and 11(4) of the OECD Model Treaty and Articles 7(6) and 11(4) of the UN Model Treaty). The rules in Articles 10(4), 11(4), and 12(4) of the OECD and UN Model Treaties are known as "throwback rules" because, in the first instance, Article 7 applies to dividends, interest, and royalties that constitute business profits; Article 7 then gives priority to Articles 10, 11, or 12, but those articles then make

费首先因构成营业利润而适用第 7 条，第 7 条又规定第 10 条、第 11 条和第 12 条应优先适用，但第 10 条、第 11 条和第 12 条又规定最终还是适用第 7 条。

股息、利息或特许权使用费的收款人只有在既是缔约国一方居民，又是股息、利息或特许权使用费受益所有人的情况下，才有权享受 OECD 协定范本和联合国协定范本第 10 条、第 11 条和第 12 条规定的低税率。第 8.8.2.2 节将对受益所有人的要求进行讨论。OECD 协定范本第 10 条第 2 款规定，如果缔约国一方居民公司从缔约国另一方居民公司取得股息，且收款方在股息支付日之前的 365 天期间均持有支付方公司至少 25% 的资本，则所征税款不应超过股息的 5%。联合国协定范本第 10 条第 2 款的规定与此类似，只是预提税率必须通过缔约国双方谈判确定。

8.7.3.6 其他所得类型

除上述各类所得外的其他所得，大部分税收协定并未限制一国对其居民取得所得的征税权。（参见 OECD 协定范本和联合国协定范本第 1 条第 3 款的保留条款，其中指出，除特定情况外，协定范本的条款并不限制一国对其居民的征税权。第 1 条第 3 款已在第 3 章进行讨论。）OECD 协定范本和联合国协定范本第 13 条都规定，除了处置位于来源国的常设机构的资产、位于来源国的不动产、用于国际运输的船舶和飞机，以及价值主要来源于位于一国的不动产的公司、合伙企业和其他实体的权益的相关收益外，财产收益应由居民国独享征税权。联合国协定范本第 13 条第 5 款规定，公司或其他实体的居民国有权对处置该公司或实体的实质性权益产生的收益征税。

OECD 协定范本第 21 条（其他所得）包含兜底规定，明确协定其他条款未作规定的所得，应由居民国独享征税权。与此相反，联合国协定范本第 21 条允许来源国对这些其他所得征税，只要其发生于来源国。OECD 协定范本第 21 条对通过金融工具取得的所得来说非常重要，因为对于一些与传统所得类型相似、

Article 7 applicable once again.

The recipient of dividends, interest, or royalties is entitled to the benefit of the reduced rate of tax provided in Articles 10, 11, or 12 of the OECD and UN Model Treaties, respectively, only if the recipient is both a resident of a contracting state and the beneficial owner of the dividends, interest, or royalties. This beneficial ownership requirement is discussed in section 8.8.2.2. Article 10(2) of the OECD Model Treaty provides for a maximum 5% rate of tax on dividends received by a company resident in one contracting state from a company resident in the other contracting state where the recipient owns at least 25% of the capital of the payer company throughout the 365-day period preceding the date on which the dividend is paid. Article 10(2) of the UN Model Treaty is similar, except that the rate of tax must be established pursuant to the negotiations of the contracting states.

8.7.3.6 Other Types of Income

Most tax treaties do not impose limits on the rights of the contracting states to tax income, other than those types of income discussed above, derived by their own residents. (*See* the saving clause in Article 1(3) of both the OECD and UN Model Treaties, which indicates that, subject to certain circumstances, the provisions of the model treaties do not limit a country's right to tax its own residents; Article 1(3) is discussed in Chapter 3.) Article 13 of the OECD and UN Model Treaties generally provides that capital gains, other than gains from the disposal of the assets of a PE in the source country, immovable property situated in the source country, ships and aircraft used in international traffic, and interests in corporations, partnerships, and other entities the value of which is derived primarily from immovable property situated in the country, are taxable exclusively by the residence country. Under Article 13(5) of the UN Model Treaty, the country in which a company or other entity is resident is entitled to tax gains from the disposal of a substantial interest in the company or other entity.

The residual rule contained in Article 21 (Other Income) of the OECD Model Treaty provides that items of income not dealt with in other articles of the treaty are taxable exclusively by the residence country. In contrast, Article 21 of the UN Model Treaty allows the source country to tax such other income as long as it arises in the source country. Article 21 of the OECD Model is important with respect to income derived from financial instruments since it precludes taxation at source of income items that may resemble various traditional types of

但通过合同安排却构成协定未涉及的所得类型的所得项目，OECD 协定范本第 21 条不允许来源国征税。

8.7.4 征管合作

OECD 协定范本和联合国协定范本都制定了促进缔约国双方征管合作的若干条款。OECD 协定范本和联合国协定范本第 24 条（非歧视待遇）要求缔约国双方不能不公平地对待缔约国对方的居民和国民。虽然非歧视这一目标很有价值，但却并不容易实现。以下第 8.8.1 节将讨论非歧视待遇条款相关问题。

OECD 协定范本和联合国协定范本第 25 条（相互协商程序）确立了一项机制，以解决因缔约国双方税制相互作用或因适用税收协定本身而产生的争议。以下第 8.8.3 节将讨论相互协商程序，包括税收争议的仲裁。

几乎所有税收协定都规定，缔约国双方要在执行税收协定及国内税法过程中，开展一定程度的合作。OECD 协定范本和联合国协定范本第 26 条（信息交换）规定，缔约国双方应交换“可以预见的与执行本协定条款相关的信息，或与执行本协定适用税种的国内税法相关的信息”。最近，OECD 协定范本和联合国协定范本都增加了第 27 条（税收征收协助），规定在税收征收或执行方面相互协助。以下第 8.8.4 节将讨论信息交换和相互协助。

8.8 特殊协定问题

8.8.1 非歧视待遇

一般来说，对一国的税收管辖权并不存在重大的法律限制。因此，一国就可能考虑对非居民实行比居民更严厉的征税措施。但实际上，大部分国家都在所得税方面给予非居民与居民同等或更优的待遇。制约各国不能对非居民给予不平等待遇最重要的因素，或许是其他国家可能予以报复，以及需要吸引非居民投资。

income but that are modified by contractual arrangements to constitute a type of income that is not mentioned in the treaty.

8.7.4 Administrative Cooperation

Several provisions in the OECD and UN Model Treaties are designed to promote administrative cooperation between the contracting states. Article 24 (Non- discrimination) of the OECD and UN Model Treaties requires each contracting state not to discriminate unfairly against the residents and nationals of the other contracting state. Although nondiscrimination is a worthy objective, it is not easily attained. Issues arising under the Non-discrimination article are addressed in section 8.8.1 below.

Article 25 (MAP) of the OECD and UN Model Treaties establishes a mechanism for resolving disputes that arise from the interaction of the tax systems of the contracting states or from the operation of the treaty itself. The MAP, including arbitration of tax disputes, is discussed in section 8.8.3 below.

Virtually all tax treaties provide for some cooperation between the contracting states in the administration of the tax treaty and their domestic tax systems. Article 26 (Exchange of Information) of the OECD and UN Model Treaties provides for the exchange of "such information as is foreseeably relevant for carrying out the provisions of this Convention or of the domestic laws of the Contracting States concerning taxes covered by the Convention." Article 27 (Assistance in the Collection of Taxes) is a recent addition to both the OECD and UN Model Treaties, which provides for mutual assistance in the collection or enforcement of taxes. Exchange of information and mutual assistance are dealt with in section 8.8.4 below.

8.8 SPECIAL TREATY ISSUES

8.8.1 Nondiscrimination

In general, there are no significant legal restrictions on a country's jurisdiction to tax, and consequently, a country could consider taxing nonresidents more harshly than residents. In fact, however, most countries generally treat nonresidents in the same way as, or more favorably than, residents for income tax purposes. Probably the most important constraints on the unequal treatment of nonresidents are the possibility of retaliation by other countries and the need to attract investment from nonresidents.

双边税收协定的非歧视待遇条款是防止税收歧视最重要的一类法律保护。《关税与贸易总协定》《服务贸易总协定》和其他贸易与投资协定的非歧视待遇条款一般规定，税收歧视问题应通过双边税收协定解决。OECD 协定范本和联合国协定范本第 24 条禁止缔约国一方对缔约国另一方公民或居民造成的税收结果，比其公民或居民的税收结果受益较少或更为不利。协定范本并没有定义歧视和非歧视，但是，歧视一般意味着以不合理、不相关或随意的理由，在各类人之间做出不利的区分。相反，非歧视则意味着平等（在功能方面等同的）或中性的待遇。在非歧视的案例中，最重要的问题是确定要进行比较的确切情形。

OECD 协定范本和联合国协定范本第 24 条禁止在以下方面歧视外国国民和非居民：

（1）第 24 条第 1 款禁止国籍歧视。由于大多数国家并非基于国籍对个人进行征税（美国是主要的例外），本条款对法人实体比较重要。

（2）第 24 条第 3 款禁止歧视通过常设机构在一国开展营业活动的非居民。这些非居民的待遇不应次于该国从事类似活动的居民的待遇。

（3）第 24 条第 4 款要求对于缔约国一方居民支付给缔约国另一方居民的款项，各缔约国应根据与支付给本国居民的款项相同的原则予以扣除。该条款实际是间接反对歧视，因为这一法律保护的直接受益人是本国居民企业。第 7 章第 7.2 节所讨论的资本弱化和收益剥离规则，如果其适用仅仅是为了不允许扣除支付给非居民的利息，则将被普遍视为在这一方面违反了非歧视待遇条款。

（4）第 24 条第 5 款保证，作为缔约国一方居民的公司、合伙企业或其他实体，如果其资本由缔约国另一方居民拥有或控制，则其待遇不应次于由本国居民拥有或控制的企业的待遇。与第 24 条第 4 款类似，这种免遭歧视的保护系直接针对居民实体，间接针对这些实体的非居民所有者。

The most important type of legal protection against discrimination for tax purposes is the Non-discrimination article of bilateral tax treaties. The nondiscrimination provisions of the GATT, the GATS, and other trade and investment treaties generally provide that tax discrimination is to be dealt with in accordance with bilateral tax treaties. Article 24 of the OECD and UN Model Treaties prohibits the contracting states from imposing tax consequences on the citizens or residents of the treaty partner that are less favorable or more adverse than the tax consequences imposed on their own citizens or residents. The model treaties do not define discrimination or nondiscrimination. In general, however, discrimination means distinguishing between persons adversely on the grounds that are unreasonable, irrelevant, or arbitrary. Conversely, nondiscrimination means equal (functionally equivalent) or neutral treatment. In any nondiscrimination case, the crucial issue is to determine the precise situations that are to be compared.

Article 24 of the OECD and UN Model Treaties prohibits discrimination against foreign nationals and nonresidents in several respects:

(1) Article 24(1) prohibits discrimination on the basis of nationality. Because most countries do not tax individuals on the basis of nationality (the U.S. is a major exception), this provision is primarily important with respect to legal entities.
(2) Article 24(3) prohibits discrimination against nonresidents carrying on business in a country through a PE. Such nonresidents must be treated no less favorably than residents of the treaty country engaged in similar activities.
(3) Article 24(4) requires countries to allow the deduction of amounts paid by residents of a contracting state to residents of the other contracting state on the same basis as amounts paid to residents of the first state. In effect, this provision provides protection against discrimination indirectly because the direct beneficiaries of the legal protection are resident enterprises. Thin capitalization and earnings-stripping rules, which are discussed in Chapter 7, section 7.2, are widely considered to violate this aspect of a nondiscrimination article if they apply only to deny the deduction of interest paid to nonresidents.
(4) Article 24(5) ensures that corporations, partnerships, and other entities resident in a contracting state whose capital is owned or controlled by residents of the other contracting state must be treated no less favorably than enterprises owned or controlled by residents. As with Article 24(4), protection against discrimination is provided directly to resident entities and only indirectly to the nonresident owners of those entities.

OECD 协定范本和联合国协定范本第 24 条规定的防止税收歧视的保护措施非常重要，但也较为有限。加拿大等一些国家拒绝同意对非居民给予与居民同等税收待遇（即**国民待遇**）的非歧视待遇条款。这些国家仅同意在其与具体国家税收协定中，为对方国家的居民提供**最惠国待遇**。最惠国待遇保证协定国家的居民与其他外国居民享受同等待遇，但并不保证其与居民纳税人享受同等或类似待遇。

8.8.2 协定滥用

8.8.2.1 引言

一般而言，税收协定限制了缔约国双方的税收。因此，纳税人普遍利用税收协定进行避税，这一点并不奇怪。本节主要探讨各国如何保护自己免受滥用和不当适用协定所造成的影响。第 8.8.2.2 节讨论一种特殊的协定滥用形式，即择协避税，以及 OECD 协定范本和联合国协定范本为应对择协避税，于 2017 年新增的利益限制条款。第 8.8.2.3 节讨论按照 BEPS 第 6 项行动计划，为防止协定滥用，于 2017 年对 OECD 协定范本和联合国协定范本所做的其他修订。第 8.8.2.4 节讨论关于 OECD 协定范本和联合国协定范本第 1 条的注释涉及协定滥用的内容，这些内容对尚未修订，并纳入一般反避税规则的税收协定同样重要。第 8.8.2.5 节讨论第 29 条第 8 款应对第三国常设机构问题的特殊反避税规定，OECD 协定范本和联合国协定范本于 2017 年增加了该规定。

如上文第 8.5 节所述，基于 OECD 协定范本和联合国协定范本的税收协定，其最明显的两个目的是消除双重征税和防止逃避税。2017 年，两个协定范本通过增加新的标题和序言的方式[①]，体现了这两个目的。标题和序言都明确税收协

① 此为英文原文本意。事实上，2017 年，两个协定范本对原有标题和序言进行了修改，而非新增标题和序言。——译者注

Article 24 of the OECD and UN Model Treaties provides important but limited protection against tax discrimination. Some countries, such as Canada, refuse to agree to a nondiscrimination article that guarantees the same treatment to nonresidents as that provided to residents (**national treatment**) for tax purposes. Instead, they agree in their tax treaties only to provide **most-favored-nation treatment** to the residents of a particular treaty country. Most-favored-nation treatment ensures that the residents of a treaty country are treated the same as residents of other foreign countries. It does not guarantee that they will be treated the same or as well as resident taxpayers.

8.8.2 Treaty Abuse

8.8.2.1 Introduction

In general, tax treaties limit the taxes imposed by the contracting states. Not surprisingly, therefore, tax treaties have been widely used by taxpayers to avoid tax. This section examines the ways in which countries protect themselves from the abuse or improper use of their tax treaties. Section 8.8.2.2 deals with one particular aspect of treaty abuse, the problem of treaty shopping and the limitation-on benefits (LOB) provisions added to the OECD and UN Model Treaties in 2017 to counter treaty shopping. Section 8.8.2.3 describes the other changes made to the OECD and UN Model Treaties in 2017 to deal with treaty abuse pursuant to BEPS Action 6. Section 8.8.2.4 discusses the Commentary on Article 1 of both the OECD and UN Model Treaties dealing with treaty abuse, which remains important for tax treaties that are not modified to include a general anti-abuse rule. Section 8.8.2.5 examines Article 29(8), a special anti-avoidance rule added to the OECD and UN Model Treaties in 2017 to deal with PEs in third states.

As discussed in section 8.5 above, the two most obvious purposes of tax treaties based on the OECD and UN Model Treaties are the elimination of double taxation and the prevention of tax avoidance and evasion. In 2017, these purposes were incorporated into the model treaties through the addition of a new title and preamble, both of which recite that a fundamental purpose of a tax treaty is to prevent tax avoidance. The new title and preamble are discussed in section 8.8.2.3.

定的根本目的之一是防止避税。第 8.8.2.3 节将讨论新的标题和序言。

虽然协定范本都包括若干明确的条款，旨在消除或防止双重征税，但是，在 2017 年之前，协定范本中实际涉及避税的条款为数不多。此前协定范本中具体的反滥用规则仅有关于转让定价的第 9 条、第 13 条第 4 款（允许来源国对处置持有大量房地产的实体相关权益的收益进行征税），以及第 17 条第 2 款（允许来源国对由演艺人员或运动员以外的人取得的演艺或体育活动所得进行征税）。但是，OECD 协定范本和联合国协定范本在 2017 年增加了下列具体的反避税规则：

—— 第 1 条第 2 款规定，出于协定的目的，通过透明实体取得的所得可视为缔约国一方居民取得的所得，但仅以该缔约国一方在税收上将所得作为该居民取得的所得为限（参见第 7 章第 7.7 节）。

—— 修订了第 4 条第 3 款针对法人实体的加比规则，拒绝对拥有双重居民身份的法人实体给予协定利益（参见第 2 章第 2.2.3 节）。

——第 1 条第 3 款的保留条款，防止一国居民利用协定条款，限制该国对其征税的权利（参见第 2 章第 2.2.3 节）。

——第 5 条第 4 款中从事准备性或辅助性活动不构成常设机构的情形，仅限于单独或合并考虑时，具有准备性或辅助性的活动（参见上文第 8.7.3.2 节）。

—— 第 5 条第 4.1 款中的反拆分规则，防止纳税人通过在紧密关联企业间拆分活动，来利用第 5 条第 4 款关于准备性或辅助性活动不构成常设机构的规定（参见上文第 8.7.3.2 节）。

—— 扩展了非独立代理型常设机构规则，使之涵盖佣金代理人安排和非独立代理人本身虽然没有订立合同，但在合同订立的过程中发挥主要作用，且合同对被代理人有约束力的情况（参见上文第 8.7.3.2 节）。

—— 第 10 条第 2 款第（1）项关于股息适用 5% 预提税率，增加了持股 365 天的条件（参见第 8.7.3.5 节）。

—— OECD 协定范本第 13 条第 4 款是关于持有大量房地产的公司股票收益

Although the model treaties contain several explicit provisions aimed at eliminating or preventing double taxation, prior to 2017, they had few provisions that actually dealt with tax avoidance. Article 9 dealing with transfer pricing, Article 13(4) (allowing source countries to tax gains from the disposal of interests in land-rich entities), and Article 17(2) (allowing source countries to tax income from entertainment and athletic activities that accrue to a person other than the entertainer or athlete) were the only specific anti-abuse rules found in the model treaties. However, in 2017 the following specific anti-avoidance rules were added to the OECD and UN Model Treaties:

- Under Article 1(2), income derived through a transparent entity is considered to be income of a resident of a contracting state for purposes of the treaty only to the extent that it is treated as income of the resident for purposes of taxation by that state (*see* Chapter 7, section 7.7).
- The tie-breaker rule for legal entities in Article 4(3) was revised to deny treaty benefits for dual-resident legal entities (*see* Chapter 2, section 2.2.3).
- The saving clause in Article 1(3) prevents residents of a country from relying on the provisions of a treaty to limit that country's right to tax them (*see* Chapter 2, section 2.2.3).
- The exception for a PE engaged in preparatory or auxiliary activities in Article 5(4) is limited to activities that, taken alone or in combination, are preparatory or auxiliary (*see* section 8.7.3.2 above).
- The anti-fragmentation rule in Article 5(4.1) prevents taxpayers from taking advantage of the exception for preparatory or auxiliary activities in Article 5(4) by splitting the activities among closely related enterprises (*see* section 8.7.3.2 above).
- The dependent-agency PE rule has been expanded to cover commissionaire arrangements and situations in which dependent agents play the principal role leading to the conclusion of contracts binding on the persons for whom they act even though they do not conclude such contracts themselves (*see* section 8.7.3.2 above).
- A 365-day holding period has been added as a condition for entitlement to the 5% rate of tax on dividends under Article 10(2)(a) (*see* section 8.7.3.5).
- The anti-avoidance rule for gains on shares of land-rich companies in Article 13(4) of the OECD Model Treaty has been extended to comparable interests such as interests in partnerships and trusts, and the rule applies if more than 50% of the value of the shares

的反避税规则，将该规则扩展至包括合伙企业或信托等的类似权益；如果在转让前 365 天内的任一时间（不仅仅是转让时），该股份价值 50% 以上来自位于一国的不动产，则适用该规则（参见第 5 章第 5.8.5 节）。

—— 第 29 条第 1 款至第 7 款增加了利益限制条款，将协定待遇局限于缔约国双方真正的居民（参见以下第 8.8.2.2 节）。

—— 按照第 29 条第 8 款，对于采用免税法避免双重征税的国家，如果其居民在第三国设立了常设机构，一些情形下则不能享受协定待遇（参见以下第 8.8.2.5 节）。

对于税收协定数量众多的国家，重谈其所有协定，来纳入所建议的一般反滥用规则和所建议的其他反避税条款，将耗费很长时间。同时，仅将这些修改纳入一国的部分税收协定，可能会产生消极影响，即不能对没有纳入这些条款的协定进行防止协定滥用的解读。因此，OECD 协定范本 2017 年与协定滥用相关的修订，其有效性取决于能否通过签署多边公约快速高效地实现。BEPS 第 15 项行动计划报告《制定用于修订双边税收协定的多边工具》即以该多边公约为主题，该公约已于 2018 年生效，第 8.8.6 节将讨论该公约。

8.8.2.2 防止择协避税的措施（利益限制条款）

只有缔约国居民和（一些情况下的）国民才有权取得所得税协定所规定的待遇。OECD 协定范本和联合国协定范本第一条规定，协定适用于缔约国一方或同时为缔约国双方居民的人。并非为缔约国一方居民或国民的纳税人，经常通过在缔约国双方中的任一方设立公司或其他法律实体，作为从缔约国另一方取得所得的导管，寻求获得该税收协定的优惠。这一做法通常被称为择协避税。虽然纳税人可以通过实施择协避税，获得原本无法获得的任何协定优惠，但是，大多数择协避税都涉及纳税人试图适用股息、利息、特许权使用费条款更低的预提税率，或规避对资产处置收益的征税。择协避税只是协定滥用的一种形式。

is derived from immovable property located in a country at any time during the 365 days before the disposition of the shares (not just at the time of the disposition) (*see* Chapter 5, section 5.8.5).

- A LOB provision has been added in Article 29(1)–(7) to limit treaty benefits to genuine residents of a contracting state (*see* section 8.8.2.2 below).
- Under Article 29(8), treaty benefits are denied in some circumstances where a resident of a country that uses the exemption method to relieve double taxation establishes a PE in a third country (*see* section 8.8.2.5 below).

It would take a long time for countries with numerous tax treaties to renegotiate all their treaties to include the proposed general anti-abuse rule and the other proposed anti-avoidance provisions. In the meantime, if the changes are included in only some of a country's tax treaties, a negative implication may arise that treaties without those provisions cannot be interpreted to prevent treaty abuse. Therefore, a key issue with respect to the 2017 changes to the OECD Model dealing with treaty abuse is that their effectiveness depended on the conclusion of a multilateral treaty to implement the changes quickly and efficiently. Such a multilateral treaty was the subject of the BEPS Action 15 Report, *Developing a Multilateral Instrument to Modify Bilateral Tax Treaties*, and the treaty entered into force in 2018. The multilateral treaty is discussed in section 8.8.6 below.

8.8.2.2 *Anti-treaty Shopping Measures (LOB)*

Only residents and (in some cases) nationals of a contracting state are entitled to benefits under an income tax treaty. Article 1 of the OECD and UN Model Treaties provides that a treaty applies to persons who are residents of one or both of the contracting states. Taxpayers who are not residents or nationals of a contracting state have frequently sought to obtain the benefits of a tax treaty by organizing a corporation or other legal entity in one of the contracting states to serve as a conduit for income earned in the other contracting state. This practice is commonly referred to as treaty shopping. Although a taxpayer may engage in treaty shopping to obtain any treaty benefits not otherwise available, most treaty shopping involves attempts by taxpayers to obtain reduced withholding rates on dividends, interest, and royalties or to avoid the taxation of gains on the disposal of property. Treaty shopping is just one form of treaty abuse.

择协避税的一个简单形式是，来源国居民将款项支付给作为未与来源国签订税收协定的国家居民的被指定人、代理人或纳税人的导管公司，但该被指定人、代理人或导管公司是与该来源国签订了协定的国家的居民。为防止这种简单形式的择协避税，OECD 协定范本和联合国协定范本第 10 条、第 11 条、第 12 条均要求收到股息、利息或特许权使用费的缔约国一方居民是该所得的受益所有人。关于这些条款的注释均明确，代理人和被指定人虽收取相关款项，但不符合该款项的受益所有人的条件。类似，如果导管公司使用或享有相关款项的权利受到合同义务或法律义务的约束，需将该款项转交给另一方，那么，导管公司就不符合作为该款项的受益所有人的条件（参见如 OECD 协定范本第 10 条注释第 12.4 段）。

择协避税的传统形式之一，是利用缔约国一方境内的非关联财务公司作为中介，来为本身并不具备享受协定待遇资格的纳税人开展投资活动。例如，假设 T 是 TH 国的居民，TH 国是一避税辖区，与 A 国没有税收协定。不过，A 国和 B 国之间有税收协定，按照该协定，对于支付给 B 国居民的利息，A 国将其通常的预提税率从 30% 降至零。T 向 B 公司投资 100 万元，B 公司是独立的财务中介，且为 B 国居民。B 公司用这 100 万元购买由非关联的 A 国居民公司 A 发行的债券。A 公司就该债券向 B 公司支付利息 10 万元。B 公司称，按照 A 国与 B 国的税收协定，应对此笔利息免于征收 A 国预提税。B 公司对这 10 万元款项，扣除适当佣金后，作为对原始投资的回报，支付给 T。

该示例利用通常称为“背对背安排”的方法，来最大限度地降低税收负担。B 公司作为财务中介，利用与 B 国之间的税收协定，规避了 A 国的税收，同时也大幅规避了在 B 国的税收，因为通过扣除向 T 支付的款项，抵消了其从 A 公司取得的 10 万元利息。第 7 章第 7.6 节讨论了“背对背安排”。

择协避税的另一种传统形式，涉及利用在缔约国一方设立的受控公司。例如，上例中，假设 T 在 C 国设立了全资子公司 C。T 认购 C 公司的股份 200 万元，C 公司用此款项购买在 A 国证券交易所上市的多家 A 国居民公司的股份。C 公司取得这些股份的股息 40 万元。根据 A 国与 C 国之间的税收协定，A 国对向 C 国

One simple form of treaty shopping involves payments by a resident of a source country to a nominee, agent, or conduit of a taxpayer resident in a country that does not have a treaty with the source country; however, the nominee, agent, or conduit is resident in a country with which the source country does have a treaty. To prevent this simple form of treaty shopping, Articles 10, 11, and 12 of the OECD and UN Model Treaties require a resident of a contracting state that receives dividends, interest, or royalties to be the beneficial owner of the income. The Commentary on those articles clarifies that an agent or nominee cannot qualify as the beneficial owner of the amounts the agent or nominee receives. Similarly, a conduit company cannot qualify as the beneficial owner of an amount where its right to use and enjoy the amount is constrained by a contractual or legal obligation to pass on the amount to another person (*see*, for example, paragraph 12.4 of the OECD Commentary).

A classic form of treaty shopping involves the use of an unrelated financial intermediary located in a treaty country to make investments for taxpayers who are not themselves eligible for treaty benefits. For example, assume that T is a resident of Country TH, a tax haven jurisdiction that does not have a tax treaty with Country A. However, Country A has a tax treaty with Country B, under which Country A reduces its normal withholding tax rate from 30% to zero on interest paid to residents of Country B. T invests 1 million with BCo, an independent financial intermediary that is resident in Country B. BCo uses the 1 million to purchase a bond issued by ACo, an unrelated corporation resident in Country A. ACo pays BCo 100,000 of interest on the bond. BCo claims that the 100,000 is exempt from County A's withholding tax under the treaty with Country B. BCo pays 100,000 to T, minus some commission, as a return on T's original investment in BCo.

This example utilizes what is commonly referred to as a back-to-back arrangement to minimize taxes. BCo, the financial intermediary, avoids tax in Country A under the tax treaty with Country B and avoids paying significant tax in Country B because the 100,000 of interest received from ACo is offset by the deduction of the amount paid to T. Back-to-back arrangements are discussed in Chapter 7, section 7.6.

Another classic form of treaty shopping involves the use of a controlled corporation organized in a treaty country. For example, assume that T, in the example above, organizes a wholly owned corporation, CCo, in Country C. T subscribes 2 million for shares of CCo, and CCo uses that money to purchase shares of stock in various companies that are resident in Country A and listed on Country A's stock exchange. CCo receives dividends of 400,000 on the shares. Country A has a tax treaty with Country C that reduces Country A's

居民支付股息征收的预提税率从 30% 降为 15%。作为 C 国居民，C 公司申请协定待遇，将其就 40 万股息原本应向 A 国缴纳的税收从 12 万元降至 6 万元。假设 C 国国内法对从外国公司取得的股息不征税，则 C 公司这笔所得在 C 国免税，从而，纳税人利用此择协避税安排少缴 6 万元税款。

国际税收界在遏制择协避税方面行动迟缓。直到 2017 年，OECD 协定范本和联合国协定范本才纳入针对上述择协避税滥用协定的措施。很明显，一些国家认为，作为吸引外国投资的措施，容忍择协避税符合其国家利益。对于美国这样在不同税收协定中规定差异极大的预提税率的国家，择协避税问题更加严重，因为纳税人趋于利用最为有利可图的协定。美国一直率先倡导采取积极主动的国际行动，遏制择协避税行为。

美国近年签署的所有税收协定都包含旨在打击择协避税的利益限制条款。利益限制条款的基本方针是，对虽为缔约国任一方居民，但实质上作为某第三国居民导管的公司，拒绝其享受协定待遇。可以这么理解，利益限制条款的目的，是把协定优惠局限于真正的缔约国任一方居民。

2017 年，OECD 协定范本和联合国协定范本都增加了利益限制条款（第 29 条第 1 款至第 7 款）。新的利益限制条款的特殊性体现在两个方面。第一，第 29 条第 1 款至第 7 款并没有精准的措辞，因为具体表述会因缔约国双方如何落实 BEPS 项目防止协定滥用的最低标准而有所不同。如第 8.8.2.3 节所述，各国可通过以下方式满足最低标准：

—— 第 29 条第 9 款的一般反滥用规则；或者

—— 简化版利益限制条款，加上第 29 条第 9 款的一般反滥用规则；或者

—— 详细版或完整版的利益限制条款，并辅以如注释所述之反导管规则。

第二，简化版利益限制条款和详细版利益限制条款显然都是 OECD 协定范本和联合国协定范本最为复杂的条款。

根据简化版和详细版利益限制条款，缔约国一方居民只有在申请协定待遇时

withholding tax on dividends paid to residents of Country C from 30% to 15%. As a resident of Country C, CCo claims the benefit of the treaty to reduce its tax otherwise payable to Country A on the 400,000 of dividends from 120,000 to 60,000. Assuming that CCo is exempt from tax in Country C because Country C does not tax dividends from foreign corporations under its domestic tax law, this type of treaty shopping results in a tax saving of 60,000.

The international tax community was slow to take action to curtail treaty shopping. Anti-treaty shopping measures to combat the types of treaty shopping abuses illustrated in the above examples were not added to the OECD and UN Model Treaties until 2017. Some countries apparently concluded that tolerance of treaty shopping was in their national interest as a means of attracting foreign investment. The problem of treaty shopping is exacerbated for countries, like the U.S., that enter into tax treaties with widely varying withholding rates because taxpayers have an incentive to take advantage of the most favorable treaty. The U.S. has been the leading proponent of aggressive international action to curtail treaty shopping.

All recent tax treaties entered into by the U.S. include LOB provisions intended to curtail treaty shopping. The basic policy of the LOB provisions is to deny treaty benefits to a corporation that is resident in one of the contracting states but is, in effect, serving as a conduit for residents of some third country. One way of thinking about LOB provisions is to consider them as an attempt to limit treaty benefits to genuine residents of a contracting state.

In 2017, a LOB provision—Article 29(1)–(7)—was added to both the OECD and UN Model Treaties. The new LOB provision is special for two reasons. First, the precise wording of the provision is not set out in Article 29(1)–(7) because the wording will vary depending on how the contracting states agree to implement the BEPS minimum standard with respect to treaty abuse. As explained in section 8.8.2.3 below, countries can satisfy the minimum standard by adopting:

– the general anti-abuse rule in Article 29(9); or
– a simplified version of the LOB and the general anti-abuse rule in Article 29(9); or
– a detailed or comprehensive version of the LOB and an anti-conduit rule, as described in the Commentary.

Second, both the simplified and detailed versions of the LOB are clearly the most complex provisions of the OECD and UN Model Treaties.

Under both the detailed and simplified versions of the LOB, the benefits of the treaty (other

属于“合格的人”，才可以享受协定优惠（第 4 条第 3 款的加比规则、第 9 条第 2 款对应调整的权利和第 25 条提起相互协商的权利除外）。第 29 条第 2 款的简化版利益限制条款界定了“合格的人”，其中包括：

—— 个人；

—— 缔约国双方、其行政区和政府机构；

——其主要类型的股份或权益经常在被认可的股票交易所进行交易的公司和其他实体（第 29 条第 7 款定义了“股份”“主要类型的股份”和“被认可的证券交易所”等用语）；

—— 非营利公司；

—— 养老基金；以及

—— 其股份或权益直接或间接由属于上述“合格的人”的居民拥有的实体。

对于并非“合格的人”的居民企业，如果其满足积极经营标准，或符合“衍生优惠”的条件，也可以获得协定待遇。根据第 29 条第 3 款，如果居民实体在其居民国“从事积极经营活动”，且其所得“来源于或附属于该活动”，则该居民实体有权就该所得获得协定待遇。如果居民企业从在来源国开展的经营活动或从“关联方”取得所得，那么，基于所有事实和情况，相对于由该居民或其关联方在来源国开展的活动，其在居民国的经营活动必须具有实质性。如果一方持有另一方，或第三方同时持有此双方 50% 或以上的受益权（在公司的情况下为合计表决权和股权价值），一方控制另一方或双方同时被第三方控制，则认为上述双方为关联方（第 29 条第 7 款）。上述积极经营标准不适用于控股公司、管理公司，以及进行投资或投资管理的财务公司或企业（银行、保险企业和注册的证券交易商除外）。

根据第 29 条第 4 款，并非“合格的人”的缔约国一方居民实体，如果在其需享受协定待遇期间的任何 12 个月中至少一半的天数里，其股份或权益的至少 75% 由（如第 29 条第 7 款所定义的）“等同受益人”持有，该居民企业依然可以享受协定待遇。这一所谓的衍生待遇条款在实体自身不符合协定待遇条件时，

than the tie-breaker rule in Article 4(3), the right to a corresponding adjustment under Article 9(2), and access to the MAP in Article 25) are not available to a resident of a contracting state unless that resident is a "qualified person" at the time a treaty benefit is claimed. Article 29(2) of the simplified version defines a qualified person to include:

- individuals;
- the contracting states, their political subdivisions, and governmental bodies;
- companies and other entities whose principal class of shares or interests is regularly traded on a recognized stock exchange; the terms "shares," "principal class of shares," and "recognized stock exchange" are defined in Article 29(7);
- nonprofit corporations;
- pension funds; and
- entities whose shares or interests are owned directly or indirectly by residents who are qualified persons listed above.

Even if a resident entity is not a qualified person, it may nevertheless obtain treaty benefits if it satisfies an active business test or qualifies for "derivative benefits." Under Article 29(3), a resident entity is entitled to treaty benefits with respect to an item of income where the resident "is engaged in the active conduct of a business" in the residence country and the income "emanates from, or is incidental to, that business." Where the income is derived from business activity in the source country or a "connected person," the business activity in the residence country must be "substantial," based on all the facts and circumstances in relation to the business carried on in the source country by the resident or the connected person. Persons are connected if one owns 50% or more of the beneficial interests (or aggregate votes and value in the case of a company) in the other person or if a third person owns 50% or more of both persons, or if one controls the other or both are controlled by a third person (Article 29(7)). This active business test does not apply to holding, management, and finance companies or businesses of making or managing investments (except by banks, insurance enterprises, and registered securities dealers).

Under Article 29(4), resident entities of a contracting state that are not qualified persons may nevertheless obtain treaty benefits if, for at least half of the days in any twelve-month period in which the benefit arises, "equivalent beneficiaries" (as defined in Article 29(7)) own, directly or indirectly, at least 75% of the shares or interests in the resident entities. This so-called derivative benefits provision allows treaty benefits to be granted where an entity does not qualify for treaty benefits itself but is owned by persons who would qualify for these

如其拥有人直接取得相关所得能够满足享受待遇的条件，则允许该实体享受协定待遇。

举个简单的例子。假设 A 国居民公司 A 从 B 国一家居民公司取得股息。按照 B 国国内法，居民公司向非居民股东支付的股息应适用 25% 的预提税。但是，按照 A 国与 B 国的税收协定，股息预提税率降到了 10%。A 公司不是该协定中利益限制条款所规定的“合格的人”，因为其股份并没有公开上市交易。但是，A 公司股份全部由 C 国居民公司 C 持有。按照 B 国与 C 国的税收协定，股息应按 10% 征收预提税。因此，如果将由 B 公司支付给 A 公司的股息直接支付给 C 公司，则 B 国应按照 10% 的税率对该股息征收预提税。B 国的税基没有被侵蚀，在 B 公司和 C 公司之间插入 A 公司也没有减少 B 国的税收收入。因此，A 公司有权享受 A 国与 B 国间股息适用 10% 预提税的协定待遇。

第三，如果纳税人无权作为“合格的人”，或根据积极经营或衍生待遇的例外而享受协定待遇，缔约国一方主管当局仍可酌情给予其协定待遇。这种特殊待遇的必要前提是符合协定的宗旨和目的，且纳税人的主要目的之一不是获取协定优惠。

相比简化版，详细版利益限制条款的刚性更强，包括一些更为复杂的规则和附加条款。例如，根据简化版，如果公司或其他实体主要类型的股份或权益经常在被认可的股票交易所交易，则该公司或实体即为“合格的人”。然而根据详细版，公司作为“合格的人”不仅要求其主要类型的股份经常在被认可的股票交易所交易，还要求其“主要类型的股份”主要在其居民国被认可的股票交易所交易，或其（如第 29 条第 7 款所定义的）主要管理和控制机构位于其居民国。另外，该公司（如第 29 条第 7 款所定义的）不成比例的股份必须满足上述条件，且必须在整个相关纳税期间满足上述条件。不成比例的股份指的是任何通过股息或其他款项支付，使股东不成比例地、过高地分享该公司收益的股份。

如果一国决定不通过采用一般反滥用规则，来满足 BEPS 行动计划最低标准，那么，就必须以反导管规则辅助其利益限制条款。反导管规则之所以有其

benefits if they received the item of income directly.

To take a simple example, assume that ACo, a company resident in Country A, receives dividends from a company resident in Country B. Under the domestic law of Country B, dividends paid by resident companies to nonresident shareholders are subject to a withholding tax of 25%. However, under the tax treaty between Country A and Country B, the withholding tax on dividends is reduced to 10%. ACo is not a qualified person for the purpose of the LOB provision in the treaty because its shares are not publicly traded. However, all the shares of ACo are owned by CCo, a company resident in Country C. Under the treaty between Country B and Country C, dividends are subject to withholding tax of 10%. Therefore, if the dividends paid by BCo to ACo had been paid directly to CCo, they would have been subject to withholding tax of 10% by Country B. Country B's tax base is not eroded, nor is its tax reduced through the interposition of ACo; as a result, ACo is entitled to the benefit of the 10% rate of withholding tax on dividends under the treaty between Country A and Country B.

Finally, where a taxpayer is not entitled to the benefits of the treaty as a qualified person or under the active business or derivative benefits exceptions, the competent authority of the country may grant the benefits on a discretionary basis. This discretionary relief is intended to be granted only if it is consistent with the purpose of the treaty and none of the taxpayer's principal purposes was to obtain the benefits of the treaty.

The detailed version of the LOB is more robust than the simplified version and contains more complicated rules and additional provisions. For example, under the simplified version, a company or other entity is a qualified person if its principal class of shares is regularly traded on a recognized stock exchange. In contrast, under the detailed version, a company is a qualified person if its principal class of shares is not only regularly traded on a recognized stock exchange but also either "primarily traded" on a recognized stock exchange in its country of residence or its primary place of management and control (as defined in Article 29(7)) is located in its country of residence. In addition, the conditions must be met for any disproportionate class of shares (as defined in Article 29(7)) and throughout the relevant taxable period. A disproportionate class of shares is any class of shares that entitles a shareholder to a disproportionately higher participation in the company's earnings through dividends or other payments.

Where a country decides to meet the BEPS minimum standard with respect to treaty abuse without adopting a general anti-abuse rule, it must supplement the LOB provision with anti-conduit rules. Anti-conduit rules are necessary because neither the simplified nor

必要性，是因为简化版和详细版的利益限制条款都没有阻止利用导管安排来获取协定待遇。当不存在反导管规则时，如果缔约国一方居民公司进行积极经营活动，或其主要类型的股份在被认可的证券交易所公开交易，该公司即有权获得协定待遇。这种公司有可能被用作导管公司，就与其积极经营活动无关的一项所得，获得协定待遇。例如，假设 A 国居民公司 A 从 B 国居民公司 B 取得股息、利息或特许权使用费，A 公司和 B 公司同为一家跨国集团的成员，A 国与 B 国缔结的税收协定与 OECD 协定范本完全相同。进一步假设 A 公司是“合格的人”，或从事积极经营活动，故而符合协定待遇的条件。因此，A 公司有权就其从 B 国取得的股息、利息或特许权使用费，适用较低的预提税率。但是，如果 A 公司将收到的款项转交给另一家关联公司，该公司是与 B 国没有税收协定的第三国居民，则可通过该安排不当取得了协定待遇，这并不符合协定的目的。

一国可以在其税收协定或国内法中纳入应对导管安排所需要的规则。OECD 协定范本注释（第 29 条注释第 187 段）列举若干示例，说明了恰当和不恰当的导管安排，但并没有就可以纳入税收协定的反导管条款提出表述建议。

8.8.2.3 OECD 协定范本和联合国协定范本涉及协定滥用的条款

2015 年发布的 BEPS 第 6 项行动计划最终报告《防止不当情形下的协定待遇授予》提出了应对协定滥用的全面的一系列建议，包括修改 OECD 协定范本标题和序言，若干具体的反避税规则（参见第 8.8.2.1 节），以及新增一般反滥用规则。在 2017 年更新 OECD 协定范本和联合国协定范本时，将这些建议全部纳入了协定范本之中。上一节讨论了防止择协避税条款。本节讨论协定范本的新标题和序言，以及一般反滥用规则。

OECD 协定范本和联合国协定范本的新标题明确，缔约国双方签署税收协定是“为了在针对所得和财产的税收方面消除双重征税，以及防止逃避税”。最初

detailed LOB provisions prevent the use of conduit arrangements to obtain treaty benefits. In the absence of anti-conduit rules, a company resident in one contracting state would be entitled to treaty benefits if its principal class of shares is publicly traded on a recognized stock exchange or it is engaged in the active conduct of a business. Such a company could be used as a conduit to derive treaty benefits with respect to an item of income unrelated to its active business. For example, assume that ACo, a company resident in Country A, receives dividends, interest, or royalties from a company resident in Country B that is part of the same multinational group as ACo. Country A and Country B have concluded a tax treaty that is identical to the OECD Model Treaty. Assume further that ACo qualifies for treaty benefits as a qualified person or as engaged in the conduct of an active business; as a result, ACo would be entitled to the reduced rate of withholding tax on dividends, interest, or royalties received from Country B. However, if ACo passes the funds on to another related company resident in a third country that does not have a treaty with Country B, the arrangement would be successful in obtaining treaty benefits inappropriately and contrary to the purpose of the treaty.

The rules necessary to deal with conduit arrangements can be included in a country's tax treaties or its domestic law. The OECD Commentary (paragraph 187 of the Commentary on Article 29) provides a series of examples to illustrate appropriate and inappropriate conduit arrangements but does not provide suggested wording for an anti-conduit provision that could be included in tax treaties.

8.8.2.3 Provisions of the OECD and UN Model Treaties Dealing with Treaty Abuse

The BEPS Action 6 Final Report: *Preventing the Granting of Treaty Benefits in Inappropriate Circumstances* (2015) presented a comprehensive set of proposals to deal with treaty abuse, ranging from amendments to the title and preamble of the OECD Model Treaty to several specific anti-avoidance rules (*see* section 8.8.2.1 above), to the addition of a general anti-abuse rule. The 2017 updates to the OECD and UN Model Treaties incorporated all these proposals into the model treaties. The preceding section dealt with anti-treaty shopping provisions. This section deals with the new title and preamble and the general anti-abuse rule.

The new title to the OECD and UN Model Treaties provides that the convention between the two named contracting states is "for the elimination of double taxation with respect to taxes on income and on capital and the prevention of tax evasion and avoidance." The title of the original 1977 OECD Model referred only to the elimination of double taxation and the

的 1977 年版 OECD 协定范本的标题仅提到了消除双重征税和防止偷漏税。2003 年，修改了范本注释，明确表示税收协定的目的之一是防止避税。2017 年更新后的 OECD 协定范本和联合国协定范本将 2003 年注释中的这项声明纳入协定范本正文，重申了注释中的观点。

另外，2017 年的更新增加了新的序言，更为明确地指出，OECD 协定范本和联合国协定范本的核心目的是消除双重征税和防止避税。新的序言表示，协定旨在消除双重征税，“防止逃避税造成的不征税或少征税（包括第三国居民通过择协避税安排，取得本协定规定的税收优惠而间接获益的情况）”。

OECD 协定范本和联合国协定范本的新标题和序言，对于解释税收协定各项条款来说可能至关重要。根据《维也纳公约》第 31 条，协定的上下文包括其标题和序言，而解释协定的一般原则是赋予协定用语在其上下文中通常的含义，并考虑协定的目的。第 8.6 节已详细讨论了税收协定的解释。上述修改的意图在于提供依据，以便各国税务机关和法院在解释双边协定的具体条款时，将防止避税考虑在内。OECD 协定范本导言第 16.2 段阐明，标题和序言“应在协定条款的解释上，发挥重要作用”。

OECD 协定范本和联合国协定范本 2017 年更新中最重要的增订，可能是第 29 条第 9 款中所包含的新的一般反滥用规则。这项一般反滥用规则常常被错误地称为主要目的测试（本书没有使用这一名称，因为实际上一般反滥用规则涉及主要目的之一测试，与主要目的测试存在很大差异）。第 29 条第 9 款内容如下：

> 虽有本协定的其他条款，如果在考虑了所有相关事实和情况后，可以合理地认定，就某项所得或财产，获取本协定所规定的某项优惠，是直接或间接导致该优惠的交易或安排的主要目的之一，则不应对该项所得或财产给予该优惠，除非能够证明在此种情况下，给予该优惠符合本协定相关条款的宗旨和目的。

prevention of tax evasion. In 2003, the Commentary was amended to include a clear statement that one of the purposes of tax treaties was to prevent tax avoidance. The 2017 updates of the OECD and UN Model Treaties incorporate the statement in the 2003 Commentary into the model treaties themselves, thus reaffirming the position taken in the Commentary.

In addition, the 2017 updates add a new preamble that spells out even more explicitly that the central purposes of the OECD and UN Model Treaties are to eliminate double taxation and prevent tax avoidance. The new preamble recites that the convention is intended to eliminate double taxation "without creating opportunities for non-taxation or reduced taxation through tax evasion or avoidance (including through treaty-shopping arrangements aimed at obtaining reliefs provided in this Convention for the indirect benefit of residents of third States)."

The addition of the new title and preamble to the OECD and UN Model Treaties may be significant for purposes of the interpretation of the provisions of tax treaties. Under Article 31 of the Vienna Convention, the title and preamble form part of the context of a treaty, and the general rule for the interpretation of treaties is that the terms of the treaty should be given their ordinary meaning in their context and in light of the purpose of the treaty. The interpretation of tax treaties is discussed in detail in section 8.6. The intention behind these changes is to provide a basis for tax authorities and national courts to take the prevention of tax avoidance into account in interpreting the provisions of actual bilateral treaties. Paragraph 16.2 of the Introduction to the OECD Model Treaty expresses the view that the title and preamble "should play an important role in the interpretation of the provisions of the Convention."

Perhaps the most important addition to the OECD and UN Model Treaties in the 2017 updates is the new general anti-abuse rule contained in Article 29(9). This general anti-abuse rule is commonly referred to, mistakenly, as the Principal-Purpose Test (PPT). (This name is not used here because, in fact, the general anti-abuse rule involves a one-of-the-principal purposes test, which is significantly different from a PPT.) Article 29(9) reads:

> Notwithstanding the other provisions of this Convention, a benefit under this Convention shall not be granted in respect of an item of income or capital if it is reasonable to conclude, having regard to all relevant facts and circumstances, that obtaining that benefit was one of the principal purposes of any arrangement or transaction that resulted directly or indirectly in that benefit, unless it is established that granting that benefit in these circumstances would be in accordance with the object and purpose of the relevant provisions of this Convention.

实际上，第 29 条第 9 款将关于第 1 条的注释中所包含的指导原则纳入了协定范本的正文之中，以下第 8.8.2.4 节将讨论这一指导原则。虽然注释被视为具有说服价值，对各国法院明显没有约束力，但协定本身所包含的一项规则却是不能轻易忽略的。在实际的双边税收协定中纳入此种一般反滥用规则，有助于抑制涉及税收协定的滥用型避税行为，但也容易产生纳税人和税务机关之间的诸多争议。

第 29 条第 9 款中的一般反滥用规则包括一个由两个部分组成的测试。第一，交易或安排的主要目的之一必须是获得协定待遇。第二，如果测试证实了上述主要目的的存在，则纳税人有责任证明其在此特定情况下，获得协定待遇符合协定有关条款的目的，否则协定待遇将遭拒绝。

第 29 条第 9 款相当有争议，对于国内法中没有一般反避税规定的国家尤为如此。该规则含义模糊又宽泛，无疑将为纳税人和税务机关带来很大的不确定性。尽管关于第 29 条第 9 款的注释列举了一系列简单例子，来说明应该如何适用该一般反滥用规则，但这些例子的帮助很有限。

第 29 条第 9 款采用主要目的之一测试，导致该规则非常宽泛。任何带来重大协定优惠的交易或安排，似乎都可以合理地得出结论，其主要目的至少有一个是为了获得该项优惠。换句话说，很难得出这样的结论，即实际带来重大协定优惠的交易或安排，其都不是为了获得该项优惠（即纳税人仅仅是走运而已）。

若是如此，几乎在所有情况下，适用第 29 条第 9 款的关键问题在于，协定待遇是否符合协定有关条款的目的。确定一项交易或安排符合或有悖协定有关条款，需要按照两个步骤进行分析。第一，必须明确协定有关条款的目的。为此，可以基于对有关条款的措辞、OECD 或联合国关于这些条款的注释（假设这项条款采用了 OECD 协定范本或联合国协定范本对应条款的表述），以及包括协定准备工作在内的外部材料的分析。对于习惯按照字面意思解释国内税法的法院来说，通过目的解释法来适用第 29 条第 9 款可能有很大挑战，他们很可能简单地

In effect, Article 29(9) incorporates the guiding principle included in the Commentary on Article 1, discussed in section 8.8.2.4 below, into the Model Treaties themselves. Although the Commentary is considered to be of persuasive value, it is clearly not binding on domestic courts; however, a rule contained in the treaty itself cannot be easily ignored. The inclusion of such a general anti-abuse rule in actual bilateral tax treaties may have the effect of discouraging abusive tax avoidance involving tax treaties but is also likely to generate many disputes between taxpayers and tax authorities.

The general anti-abuse rule in Article 29(9) consists of a two-part test. First, one of the principal purposes of a transaction or arrangement must be to obtain treaty benefits. Second, if the purpose test is met, the onus is on the taxpayer to establish that obtaining the treaty benefits in the particular circumstances is in accordance with the purpose of the relevant provisions of the treaty; otherwise, the benefits of the treaty are denied.

Article 29(9) is quite controversial, especially for countries that do not have a general anti-avoidance rule in their domestic law. The rule is vague and potentially broad and will undoubtedly cause considerable uncertainty for both taxpayers and tax authorities. Although the Commentary on Article 29(9) provides a series of simple examples to illustrate how the general anti-abuse rule should be applied, the examples are of limited assistance.

The use of a one-of-the-principal purposes test in Article 29(9) makes the rule potentially very broad. It seems reasonable to conclude that at least one of the principal purposes of any transaction or arrangement that results in a significant treaty benefit was to obtain that benefit. To put it somewhat differently, it would be difficult to conclude that none of the purposes of a transaction or arrangement that actually results in a significant treaty benefit was to obtain that benefit (i.e., the taxpayer was just lucky).

If this is so, then the crucial issue with respect to the application of Article 29(9) in almost every case will be whether the treaty benefits are in accordance with the purpose of the relevant provisions of the treaty. The determination of whether a transaction or arrangement is in accordance with or contrary to the purpose of the relevant provisions of the treaty requires a two-step analysis. First, the purpose of the relevant provisions must be ascertained. This can be done based on an analysis of the words of those provisions, the OECD or UN Commentary on those provisions (assuming that they follow the wording of the comparable provisions of the OECD or UN Model Treaty), and other extrinsic material, such as the *travaux préparatoires* of the treaty. For national courts that are accustomed to interpreting domestic tax legislation literally, applying a purposive approach to the application of Article 29(9) may be quite challenging, and they may be tempted simply to equate the purpose of a treaty provision with its literal meaning.

将协定条款的目的等同于其字面含义。第二，必须对相关交易或安排进行研究，确定其是否符合按照第一个步骤所确定的协定的目的：如果两相符合，则纳税人可以获得协定待遇；如果与协定目的相悖，则应拒绝协定待遇。虽然第 29 条第 9 款并未详细说明如何实施第二步，但是，似乎有理由认为，应将交易或安排的经济后果和开展方式考虑在内。

OECD 协定范本和联合国协定范本纳入一般反滥用规则，可以将其视为对协定滥用的重要回应，但很明显，该规则需要纳入双边税收协定才能产生作用。但是，为纳入一般反滥用规则而重谈税收协定，可能会耗费几十年的时间，对于协定网络较大的国家尤为如此。另外，仅将该规则纳入一部分协定，可能会产生消极影响，即不能对未纳入该规定的协定进行可以防止协定滥用的解读。BEPS 项目预料到了这一问题，建议拟定多边公约，由此修订现行双边税收协定，从而体现旨在防止协定滥用的 BEPS 税收协定修订内容。第 8.8.6 节将讨论多边公约。

8.8.2.4 关于 OECD 协定范本和联合国协定范本第 1 条涉及协定滥用的注释

虽然关于 OECD 协定范本和联合国协定范本第 1 条涉及协定滥用的注释对各国法庭没有法律约束力，但是，该注释对于从防止协定滥用的角度解释协定的相关度和潜在重要性都很高，对于未纳入类似于第 29 条第 9 款的一般反滥用规则的协定来说尤为如此。这些年来，关于两个协定范本第 1 条的注释都做了很多修订。根据 OECD 协定范本导言第 33 段至第 36.1 段，现行版本的注释适用于解释所有以 OECD 协定范本为基础的双边税收协定，甚至包括注释修订前达成的协定。也就是说，2017 年版 OECD 协定范本关于第 1 条的注释应适用于解释 2017 年之前和之后签署的税收协定。但是，很多学者（和一些法院）不认可这一观点，主要是因为在签署某项协定的时候，缔约国双方税务人员和纳税人都不可能预知嗣后的注释。协定条款的解释应该参考当前的注释版本还是该协定签署时的注释版本，这一问题在大部分国家都未能解决。因此，确定在解释一国税收协定

Second, the transaction or arrangement in question must be examined to determine whether it is in accordance with the purpose of the treaty as determined in the first step, in which case the taxpayer will get the benefits of the treaty, or contrary to the treaty, in which case the treaty benefits will be denied. Although Article 29(9) does not provide any details as to how this second step should be applied, it seems reasonable to assume that the economic consequences of the transaction or arrangement and the manner in which it is carried out should be taken into account.

Although the inclusion of a general anti-abuse rule in the OECD and UN Model Treaties may be seen as an important response to treaty abuse, that rule obviously needs to be incorporated into actual bilateral tax treaties in order to have any effect. However, the renegotiation of tax treaties to include a general anti-abuse rule could take decades, especially for countries with large treaty networks. Moreover, the inclusion of such a rule in a few treaties might create a negative implication that treaties without such a rule cannot be interpreted to prevent treaty abuse. The BEPS Project foresaw this problem and proposed a multilateral treaty that would modify existing bilateral tax treaties in order to incorporate the BEPS tax treaty changes aimed at preventing treaty abuse. This multilateral treaty is discussed in section 8.8.6.

8.8.2.4 The Commentary on Article 1 of the OECD and UN Model Treaties with Respect to Treaty Abuse

Although the Commentary on Article 1 of the OECD and UN Model Treaties with respect to treaty abuse is not legally binding on a country's courts, it is relevant and potentially important for the interpretation of tax treaties to prevent treaty abuse, especially for tax treaties that do not contain a general anti-abuse rule similar to Article 29(9). The Commentary on Article 1 of both Model Treaties has been revised extensively over the years. According to paragraphs 33–36.1 of the Introduction to the OECD Model Treaty, the current version of the Commentary applies for the purpose of interpreting all bilateral tax treaties based on the OECD Model Treaty, even those treaties entered into before the time the Commentary was revised. For example, the 2017 OECD Commentary on Article 1 should be applied to interpret tax treaties entered into both before and after 2017. However, many scholars (and some courts) disagree with this position, mainly because neither the tax officials of the contracting states nor taxpayers could possibly have known about the subsequent Commentary at the time the particular treaty was concluded. In most countries, the issue of whether the provisions of a treaty should be interpreted by reference to the current version of the Commentary or the version of the

时，应适用哪个注释版本非常重要。一般来说，关于OECD协定范本和联合国协定范本第1条注释的较早版本，尤其是关于联合国协定范本第1条注释2011年之前的版本和OECD协定范本注释2003年之前的版本，在防止协定滥用方面的效力都弱于之后的版本。

关于1977年版OECD协定范本第1条的注释表明，税收协定不应为避税提供帮助。但是，通过其国内法中应对避税，并在其税收协定中维护国内反避税规则的适用，是各国的职责。OECD协定范本注释于1992年进行了修订，规定税收协定并不限制诸如实质重于形式和受控外国企业规则等国内反避税规则的适用。

如第9章第9.2.2节所述，2003年，OECD依据其有害税收竞争项目对协定范本第1条的注释进行了大规模修订，第一次在注释中明确表示“防止逃避税也是税收协定的目的之一”。另外，2003年版OECD协定范本注释还涉及对相关协定条款的解释，以防止在滥用情况下授予协定待遇，以及说明国内反避税规则和税收协定之间的关系。关于第一个问题，OECD协定范本注释第9.5段实际上以如下“指导原则”的名义，提出了一项一般反滥用规则：

> 指导原则是，如果从事某些交易或安排的主要目的，是为了获得更为有利的税收地位，而且，在此等情形下，取得更为有利的待遇，有悖于有关条款的目的和宗旨，则不应给予避免双重征税协定的待遇。

与第29条第9款中的一般反滥用规则一样，该指导原则也涉及以上第8.8.2.3节所述的两步分析法。

关于第二个问题，OECD协定范本注释第22.1段再次强调了国内反避税规则不受税收协定影响的原则。因此，一般情况下，国内反避税规则和税收协定条款不会出现冲突，其结果就是，税收协定并不妨碍国内反避税规则的适用。

2017年版OECD关于协定范本第1条的注释保留了2003年版OECD协定范本注释中关于协定滥用的基本处理方法。虽然有些国家认为，任何协定滥用都是

Commentary as it read at the time the particular treaty was concluded remains unresolved. Therefore, it may be important to determine which version of the Commentary applies for the purpose of interpreting a country's tax treaties. In general, earlier versions of the OECD and UN Commentary on Article 1, especially versions of the UN Commentary on Article 1 before 2011 and versions of the OECD Commentary before 2003, are less effective in preventing treaty abuse than subsequent versions of the Commentary.

The OECD Commentary on Article 1 in the 1977 OECD Model Treaty stated that tax treaties should not facilitate tax avoidance but that it was the responsibility of states to deal with tax avoidance in their domestic law and then to protect the application of their domestic anti-avoidance rules in their tax treaties. The OECD Commentary was revised in 1992 to provide that tax treaties did not limit the application of domestic anti-avoidance rules such as substance-over-form and CFC rules.

The OECD Commentary on Article 1 was revised extensively in 2003 pursuant to the OECD's Harmful Tax Competition Project, which is described in Chapter 9, section 9.2.2. For the first time, the Commentary stated explicitly that "[I]t is also a purpose of tax conventions to prevent tax avoidance and evasion." In addition, the 2003 OECD Commentary dealt with the interpretation of the provisions of tax treaties to prevent the granting of treaty benefits in abusive cases and with the relationship between domestic anti-avoidance rules and tax treaties. With respect to the first issue, the Commentary (paragraph 9.5) adopted, in effect, a general anti-abuse rule in the guise of the following "guiding principle":

> A guiding principle is that the benefits of a double taxation convention should not be available where a main purpose for entering into certain transactions or arrangements was to secure a more favourable tax position and obtaining that more favourable treatment in these circumstances would be contrary to the object and purpose of the relevant provisions.

This guiding principle involves the same two-step analysis as the general anti-abuse rule in Article 29(9), as discussed in section 8.8.2.3 above.

With respect to the second issue, the Commentary (paragraph 22.1) reiterated the principle that domestic anti-avoidance rules are not affected by tax treaties. In general, therefore, there is no conflict between domestic anti-avoidance rules and the provisions of tax treaties, with the result that tax treaties do not prevent the application of domestic anti-avoidance rules.

The fundamental approach to treaty abuse in the 2003 OECD Commentary has been retained in the 2017 OECD Commentary on Article 1. Although some countries consider any

对国内法的滥用，而其他国家则对协定滥用和国内法滥用进行了区分。注释重申，在这两种情况下，各国都有权按照上述指导原则，拒绝给予协定待遇。

2011 年之前，联合国关于协定范本第 1 条的注释中涉及协定滥用的内容，大致遵循 2003 年以前版本的 OECD 注释。但是，联合国关于协定范本第 1 条的注释于 2011 年进行了大规模修订，在 2003 年版 OECD 注释的基础上，确定并讨论了应对协定滥用的六种方式：

（1）国内法中的具体反避税规则；

（2）国内法中的一般反避税规则；

（3）司法反避税规则及解释方式；

（4）税收协定中的具体反避税规则；

（5）税收协定中的一般反避税规则；以及

（6）从防止滥用的角度解释协定条款。

联合国注释作出了这样的解释，即虽然在出现冲突的情况下，税收协定一般优先于国内法，但是，通常可以避免国内反避税规则和税收协定之间的冲突。至于何种行为构成协定滥用，联合国注释认可（前文中引述的）OECD 指导原则。联合国注释进一步指出，注释中关于指导原则的说明不具有约束力，对于不希望以该指导原则为依据的国家，可以其为基础在协定中纳入一般反滥用规则。2017 年 OECD 协定范本和联合国协定范本新增第 29 条第 9 款就是将该指导原则纳入了协定范本。

2017 年联合国关于协定范本第 1 条的注释中涉及协定滥用的内容有所完善，但没有根本性修改，其中明确表示，希望与 OECD 关于第 1 条的注释中涉及协定滥用的内容保持一致。2017 年联合国关于协定范本第 1 条的注释提供了一些有用的示例，以说明协定滥用的各种潜在形式和为了处理这些滥用所需要的规则。

8.8.2.5 针对设于第三国常设机构的反避税规则

OECD 协定范本和联合国协定范本于 2017 年进行了修订，在第 29 条第 8 款

treaty abuse also to be an abuse of domestic law, other countries distinguish between abuses of a treaty and abuses of domestic law. In either case, the Commentary reiterates that countries are entitled to deny treaty benefits in accordance with the same guiding principle refer red to above.

Until 2011, the UN Commentary on Article 1 dealing with treaty abuse simply followed the pre-2003 OECD Commentary. However, in 2011 the UN Commentary on Article 1 was revised extensively and, building on the 2003 OECD Commentary, it identified and discussed six approaches to deal with treaty abuse:

(1) specific anti-avoidance rules in domestic law;
(2) GAARs in domestic law;
(3) judicial anti-avoidance rules and approaches to interpretation;
(4) specific anti-avoidance rules in tax treaties;
(5) GAARs in tax treaties; and
(6) the interpretation of treaty provisions to prevent abuse.

The UN Commentary explained that although tax treaties generally prevail over domestic law in the event of a conflict between them, conflicts between domestic anti-avoidance rules and tax treaties can often be avoided. It also endorsed the OECD guiding principle (quoted above) as to what constitutes an abuse of a treaty. Further, it indicated that, for countries that prefer not to rely on a nonbinding statement of the guiding principle in the Commentary, the guiding principle could form the basis for a general anti-abuse rule to be included in the treaty—which is precisely what happened in 2017 when Article 29(9) was added to both the OECD and UN Model Treaties.

The 2017 UN Commentary on Article 1 dealing with treaty abuse has been refined without any fundamental changes and states explicitly that it is intended to be consistent with the OECD Commentary on Article 1 dealing with treaty abuse. The 2017 UN Commentary on Article 1 provides several useful examples to illustrate the wide variety of potential treaty abuses and the rules necessary to deal with them.

8.8.2.5 *Anti-avoidance Rule for PEs in Third States*

In 2017, the OECD and UN Model Treaties were amended to add a specific anti- avoidance rule in Article 29(8) to deal with tax avoidance through certain triangular situations involving a PE located in a third state. Where a resident of one contracting state (Country B) pays

增加了一项具体反避税规则，以应对通过位于第三国的常设机构等三角架构避税的问题。如果缔约国一方（B 国）居民向缔约国另一方（A 国）居民支付股息、利息、特许权使用费等款项，通常可以在 B 国适用更低的预提税率的协定待遇。但是，如果该款项的接收方（A 国居民）在第三国（C 国）设有常设机构，A 国对归属于外国常设机构的利润免于征税，并且，A 国将所支付的款项视为可归属于位于 C 国的常设机构，这种情况下，不应要求 B 国给予协定减税待遇，因为 A 国将不对该款项征税。

为应对这种形式的税收协定滥用，第 29 条第 8 款规定，在此例中，如果 C 国（常设机构所在国）对该款项的征税少于如果该常设机构位于 A 国的情形下 A 国对该款项征税的 60%，则不要求 B 国（来源国）给予协定待遇。但是，该规则有两个例外情况：

（1）如果该所得附属于常设机构开展的积极经营活动，不包括为企业自身开展的投资活动（银行、保险或证券交易业务除外）；或者

（2）应 A 国居民请求并经与 A 国主管当局协商，B 国主管当局认为给予协定待遇是恰当的。

例如，如果 A 国居民产生了亏损，因此即使该常设机构位于 A 国，A 国也不对该所得征税，这种情况下按照第 29 条第 8 款不否定协定待遇是恰当的。

8.8.3 争议解决

大多数税收协定都规定了相互协商程序，以解决协定项下发生的争议。如果缔约国一方居民认为，缔约国一方或双方所采取的措施，将导致不符合协定的征税，则可以向缔约国任何一方“主管当局”申请救济。主管当局一般是一国税务部门负责国际税收事务的高级官员。主管当局判断纳税人的请求是否合理，如果合理的话，则应尽量提供恰当的救济。如果主管当局没有权力单方面解决争议，可设法通过与缔约国另一方主管当局协商，以解决争议。

an amount, such as dividends, interest, or royalties, to a resident of the other contracting state (Country A), the benefits of the treaty in the form of reduced rates of withholding tax imposed by Country B would ordinarily be available. However, where the recipient of the amount (the resident of Country A) has a PE in a third country (Country C), Country A provides an exemption for profits attributable to foreign PEs, and Country A considers the amount paid to be attributable to the PE in Country C, it is inappropriate to require Country B to provide treaty benefits by reducing its tax, since Country A is not imposing any tax on the amount.

Article 29(8) deals with this form of tax treaty abuse by providing that Country B in this example (the source country) is not required to grant the benefit of the treaty where the tax imposed by Country C (where the PE is located) on the amount is less than 60% of the tax that would be imposed on the amount by Country A if the PE were located in Country A. However, this rule is subject to two exceptions where:

(1) the income is incidental to an active business carried on by the PE other than an investment business for the enterprise's own account (except a banking, insurance, or securities-trading business); or
(2) the competent authority of Country B considers that it is appropriate to provide treaty benefits at the request of the resident of Country A and after consultation with the competent authority of Country A.

For example, it might be appropriate not to deny treaty benefits under Article 29(8) where the resident of Country A has losses so that Country A would not impose tax on the income even if the PE were located in Country A.

8.8.3 Resolution of Disputes

Most tax treaties provide a MAP for resolving disputes that arise under the treaty. A person resident in a contracting state who believes that the actions of one or both contracting states will result in taxation that is not in accordance with the treaty may request relief from the "competent authority" of either state. The competent authority is typically a senior official in the country's tax department who is responsible for international tax matters. The competent authority makes a determination whether the taxpayer's request appears justified and, if so, attempts to provide an appropriate remedy. If the competent authority does not have the power to resolve a dispute on its own, it may attempt to resolve the dispute through consultations with the competent authority of the other contracting state.

OECD 协定范本和联合国协定范本的争议解决机制在于第 25 条（相互协商程序）。该条款规定，缔约国双方主管当局“应设法”解决向其提出的争议。需要注意的是，即使结果将对纳税人带来不符合协定规定的双重征税，该条款也没有要求主管当局必须达成一致。因此，2008 年，OECD 协定范本在第 25 条第 5 款增加了强制仲裁，以解决双方主管当局未能在两年内达成一致的问题。第 9 章第 9.4 节将讨论仲裁。

虽然纳税人有权将案情提交给缔约国任何一方的主管当局（即提起相互协商），但不允许其直接参与缔约国双方主管当局的协商过程，因为相互协商是政府间程序。

向主管当局提交的请求涉及不同种类的争议。其中有些争议涉及协定表述的恰当解释，有些涉及纳税人的纳税义务所依据的事实情况。提交给主管当局的争议中，最常见的（也是最复杂的）涉及对跨境交易中的转让价格，如何恰当地适用独立交易原则。导致此类争议难以解决的原因很多，其中一个原因是所涉及的税收收入数额巨大。OECD 协定范本和联合国协定范本第 9 条第 2 款规定，如果缔约国一方按照独立交易原则，调整关联企业使用的转让价格（并且，缔约国另一方也同意该调整），那么，缔约国另一方必须对关联企业的利润进行对应调整，以避免重复征税。转让定价已在第 6 章讨论。

BEPS 第 14 项行动计划报告《使争议解决机制更有效》承认，并不存在各国主管当局必须解决相互协商个案的明确义务，并且对于强制仲裁尚缺乏共识。因此，该报告建议，采取辅助措施，改善对于相互协商程序的利用，提高相互协商程序的效率和效力，保证争议在启动相互协商程序后都能得到解决。总体而言，第 14 项行动计划建议，制定针对相互协商程序个案的最低标准，并建立监督程序保证各国遵守最低标准。相互协商程序的最低标准包括所有成员国的税收协定都纳入 OECD 协定范本第 25 条第 1 款至第 3 款、承诺在 24 个月内解决相互协商个案、改善纳税人使用相互协商程序的渠道，以及保证相互协商结果的实施不受国内法时间限制的影响。

The dispute-resolution mechanism of the OECD and UN Model Treaties is set out in Article 25 (MAP), which provides that the competent authorities "shall endeavor" to resolve matters referred to them. Thus, it is notable that the competent authorities are not required to reach an agreement, even if the result is that a taxpayer is subject to double taxation not in accordance with the treaty. For this reason, mandatory arbitration was added to Article 25(5) of the OECD Model Treaty in 2008 for the resolution of issues that the competent authorities are unable to agree on within two years. Arbitration is discussed in Chapter 9, section 9.4.

Although a taxpayer is entitled to present its case to either competent authority (i.e., to initiate a MAP), it is not allowed to participate directly in the consultative procedure between the competent authorities of the two contracting states because the MAP is a government-to-government process.

A variety of disputes may be referred to the competent authorities. Some of these disputes involve the proper interpretation of treaty language, while others involve disputes over the facts on which a taxpayer's tax liability is based. The most common (and complex) disputes referred to the competent authorities involve the proper application of the arm's-length standard to transfer prices in cross-border transactions. These disputes are sometimes difficult to resolve for a variety of reasons, including the large amounts of tax revenue frequently at stake. Article 9(2) of the OECD and UN Model Treaties provides that if one country adjusts the transfer prices used by related corporations in accordance with the arm's-length standard (and the other country agrees with the adjustment), the other country must make a corresponding adjustment to the profits of the related corporation in order to avoid double taxation. Transfer pricing is discussed in Chapter 6.

The BEPS Action 14 Report: *Make Dispute Resolution Mechanisms More Effective* acknowledged the absence of a clear obligation on the competent authorities to resolve MAP cases and the lack of consensus on mandatory arbitration. Therefore, the Report recommended that complementary steps be taken to improve access to the MAP and to make the MAP more efficient and effective in order to ensure that disputes are resolved once a MAP has been initiated. In general, Action 14 recommends that minimum standards for MAP cases should be established and also that a monitoring process should be established to ensure that participating countries adhere to the minimum standard. The minimum standards for MAP consist of the inclusion of Article 25(1)–(3) of the OECD Model Treaty in all member countries' tax treaties, a commitment to resolve MAP cases within twenty-four months, improvement of taxpayers' access to MAP, and the implementation of MAP agreements despite any time limits in domestic law.

根据很多国家的国内法，跨国公司可以就其集团内交易价格的定价方法，事先征得税务机关的正式批准。按照该程序达成的征管裁定，通常被称为预约定价安排。如有可能，跨国企业很多情况下都希望利用主管当局间的协商程序，由其营业活动所在的多个国家共同签署预约定价安排。

8.8.4 征管合作

在获取居民的境外活动信息及确定信息的准确性方面，各国税务机关经常面临困难。此前，由于很多国家存在银行保密法，避税地不愿意与税率较高的国家交换信息，更进一步加重了这种困难。

OECD 协定范本和联合国协定范本第 26 条（信息交换）规定，应交换“可以预见的与执行本协定的规定相关的信息，或与执行缔约国双方各种税收的国内法律相关的信息”。OECD 于 2005 年修订了协定范本第 26 条，将信息交换的标准由“必要的”信息改为“可以预见相关的”信息，且要求交换与缔约国双方征收的所有税种相关的信息，而不仅仅是协定所涵盖的税种。这些修改的目的，在于明确本条款的含义，而非改变其主旨。

按照 OECD 协定范本和联合国协定范本，可以应协定伙伴国的具体请求、通过自动信息交换安排或由缔约国一方自行主动发起，进行信息交换。对于缔约国一方请求的信息，缔约国另一方必须予以提供，即使出于该缔约国另一方自身税收的目的，该信息可能并无必要性或相关性（即该信息对于缔约国另一方来说，可能没有国内利益）。

缔约国一方税务机关按照信息交换条款收到的信息应当作为密件处理，但一般允许在法庭诉讼程序中披露该信息。根据信息交换条款，缔约国一方没有义务代表其协定伙伴国采取与其自身法律和惯例相违背的行政措施、提供按照其国内法或在双方国家正常行政管理过程中不能得到的信息，或提供泄露贸易秘密之类的信息。如果被请求信息的披露会“违反公共政策”，则免除条款一般都允许缔

Under the domestic laws of many countries, multinational companies may request formal advance approval from the tax authorities of their methodology for establishing prices in their intergroup transactions. An administrative ruling entered into under this procedure is commonly referred to as an APA. In many situations, multinational enterprises prefer, if possible, to use the competent authority procedure to arrange for the joint issuance of an APA by several of the countries in which they do business.

8.8.4 Administrative Cooperation

The tax authorities of a country often experience difficulty in obtaining information concerning the foreign activities of residents and verifying that the information is correct. In the past, this difficulty was exacerbated by bank secrecy laws in many countries and the unwillingness of tax havens to exchange information with high-tax countries.

Article 26 (Exchange of Information) of the OECD and UN Model Treaties provides for an exchange of "such information as is foreseeably relevant for carrying out the provisions of this Convention or to the administration and enforcement of the domestic laws of the contracting states concerning taxes of every kind and description." Article 26 of the OECD Model Treaty was revised in 2005 to change the standard for exchanging information from "necessary" to "foreseeably relevant" and to require the exchange of information with respect to all taxes imposed by the contracting states and not just the taxes covered by the treaty. These changes were intended to clarify the meaning of the article but not to change its substance.

Under the OECD and UN Model Treaties, an exchange of information may take place as a result of a specific request from a treaty partner, through an arrangement for an automatic exchange of information, or by the initiative of a contracting state acting spontaneously. Information requested by one state must be provided by the other state despite the fact that the information may not be necessary or relevant for the purposes of the other state's own taxes (i.e., the other state may have no domestic interest in the information).

Information obtained by the tax department of a contracting state under an exchange-of-information article must be kept confidential, although release of the information in court proceedings is generally allowed. Under the exchange-of- information article, a contracting state is not obligated to carry out administrative procedures on behalf of its treaty partner that are contrary to its own laws or practices, to supply information that is not obtainable under its domestic laws or in the normal course of administration of both states, or that would result in the disclosure of trade secrets or similar information. An escape clause generally allows a contracting

约国一方拒绝提供该被请求信息。但是，根据第 26 条第 5 款，一国不应仅因信息由金融机构、被指定人或代理人持有，或因信息与企业或其他人的所有权权益有关而拒绝提供。由于大多数国家都被要求废除其银行保密法，此条款已不那么重要了。

由于税务机关仅可以依据各国之间的国际协议进行信息交换，因此，如果没有双边税收协定或不执行《多边税收征管互助公约》，各国税务机关通常不可能分享信息。本世纪以前，税率较高的国家不可能从未与其签署双边税收协定的避税地或低税国家获得信息。因此，OECD 成员国逐渐开始与没有必要与其达成全面性所得税协定的低税国家签署双边税收信息交换协定。税收信息交换协定使各国可以按照与 OECD 协定范本第 26 条类似的规定进行信息交换。

作为 20 世纪 90 年代 OECD 有害税收竞争项目的一部分，OECD 提出，应要求避税地掌握按其法律成立的公司和其他实体的受益所有人信息，要求公司按照公认会计准则保存财务账目，可供监管或税务机关使用。2002 年，OECD 发布了《税收信息交换协定范本》。OECD 协定范本第 26 条于 2005 年修订，规定其优先于被请求提供信息的国家的银行保密法和其他保密法律适用，同时取消被请求信息需具有国内税收利益的必要性。2011 年，联合国协定范本第 26 条的修订，使之与 OECD 协定范本第 26 条保持一致。但是，联合国协定范本第 26 条在一些方面更为宽泛。例如，第 26 条第 1 款明确，应当交换有助于防止逃避税的信息。此外，第 26 条第 6 款授权各国主管当局制定信息交换的流程。OECD 协定范本第 26 条没有与此对应的内容。

2001 年，OECD 设立了全球税收论坛，以便与非成员国讨论信息交换问题。该论坛现在被称为透明度与信息交换全球论坛，成功地保证了信息交换的国际标准得以有效执行。截至 2022 年 6 月，全球论坛目前共有 165 个成员国，对各国信息交换的法律、征管能力和信息交换的实际表现开展同行审议，并按照其对信息交换国际标准的遵从程度进行评级（评级结果将对外公开）。

state not to provide requested information if its disclosure would be "contrary to public policy." However, under Article 26(5), a country cannot refuse to provide information solely because the information is held by a financial institution, a nominee, or an agent or because it relates to ownership interests in a corporation or other person. Since most countries have been required to eliminate their bank secrecy laws, this provision is not as important as it would otherwise be.

Exchanges of information between tax authorities can take place only pursuant to international agreements between countries; therefore, in the absence of a bilateral tax treaty or the application of the Multilateral Convention on Mutual Assistance, it is usually impossible for the tax authorities to share information. Before this century, it was impossible for high-tax countries to get information from tax havens or low-tax countries with which they did not have a bilateral tax treaty. As a result, the practice developed for TIEAs to be concluded on a bilateral basis between OECD member countries and low-tax countries with which there was no need for a comprehensive income tax treaty. TIEAs provide for countries to exchange information on a basis similar to Article 26 of the OECD Model Treaty.

As part of the OECD's Harmful Tax Competition Project in the late 1990s, the OECD proposed that tax havens should be required to obtain information about the beneficial ownership of companies and other entities formed under their laws and to require the companies to maintain financial accounts in accordance with generally accepted accounting standards and to make those accounts available for the regulatory or tax authorities. In 2002, the OECD issued a *Model Agreement on Exchange of Information on Tax Matters*. Article 26 of the OECD Model Treaty was revised in 2005 to override any bank secrecy or other confidentiality laws of the country requested to provide information and to eliminate the necessity for any domestic tax interest in the requested information. In 2011, Article 26 of the UN Model Treaty was revised to conform to Article 26 of the OECD Model, although Article 26 of the UN Model Treaty is broader in certain respects. For example, Article 26(1) includes the statement that information that is helpful in preventing tax avoidance or evasion shall be exchanged. In addition, Article 26(6), which authorizes the competent authorities to establish procedures for the exchange of information, has no counterpart in Article 26 of the OECD Model Treaty.

In 2001, the OECD established a Global Forum on Taxation to discuss exchange-of-information issues with nonmember countries. This Global Forum, which is now known as the Global Forum on Transparency and Exchange of Information, has been very successful in ensuring that international standards for the exchange of information are implemented effectively. The Global Forum, which currently consists of 165 member countries as of June 2022, engages in peer review exercises of both the legal and administrative capacity of countries to

此前，各国税务机关之间信息交换的国际标准仅要求依请求的交换；也就是说，只有在其他国家向一国明确请求特定信息时，才要求该国提供信息。但是，OECD 于 2014 年制定了新的《金融账户涉税信息自动交换标准》（参见 www.oecd.org），规定一国自动将其金融机构取得的金融信息（如股息、利息、销售金融产品的收益、特定账户的余额等信息），按年度提供给其他国家税务机关（即其他国家税务机关无须提出信息请求）。120 多个国家已接受了这一新标准，截至 2022 年 7 月，117 多个国家已经签署了实施自动信息交换的《多边主管当局间协议》（参见 www.oecd.org）。

除请求其他国家提供信息外，一国税务机关通常会对纳税人的国际业务进行审计。但是，按照国际惯例，除非收到外国政府的邀请，否则，一国税务人员不能到别国审计纳税人的财务记录。一些国家的政府认为，如果没有同时得到纳税人的同意，税务人员前往别国审计并不合适。一些国家通过联合审计项目解决了这一问题，即由两国税务机关同时对某个纳税人（及其子公司）开展审计。

一旦一国税务机关针对某个纳税人实施审计，评估了欠税就必须征收应缴税款。然而，税务机关在另一国征收税款会遇到很大的困难。根据大部分国家的国内法，按照“收入规则”，外国的税收认定一般是无法执行的。OECD 协定范本和联合国协定范本第 27 条（税收征收协助）突破了“收入规则”的限制，要求各国对别国的税款征收提供协助。与第 24 条（非歧视待遇）和第 26 条（信息交换）类似，第 27 条也不限于税收协定所涵盖的税种，而是延伸至各缔约国征收的所有税种。

如果按照协助请求方的法律，纳税人不能阻止税款征收，则被请求方必须接受协助请求。纳税人没有权利就欠缴税款的正当性、有效性和数额向被请求方的法院或行政机关提出异议。此外，被请求方应将请求方的税款视同本国的欠缴税

exchange information and their actual performance in exchanging information. Countries are given ratings (which are available to the public) based on their compliance with the international standard for exchange of information.

Until recently, the international standard for exchanges of information between tax authorities required only exchanges on request; in other words, one country was required to provide information only if the tax authorities of the other country specifically requested that information. However, in 2014 the OECD formulated a new *Standard for Automatic Exchange of Financial Information in Tax Matters* (available at www.oecd.org), which provides for certain financial information (e.g., information about dividends, interest, proceeds of sale of financial products, and balances of certain accounts) obtained from a country's financial institutions to be provided automatically on an annual basis (i.e., without the necessity for a request by the tax authorities of another country) to the tax authorities of other countries. Over 120 countries have agreed to this new standard. In addition, as of July 2022, 117 countries have signed a *Multilateral Competent Authority Agreement* (available at ww.oecd.org) to implement automatic exchanges of information.

Often, the tax authorities of a country will audit the international affairs of taxpayers in addition to requesting information from other countries. Under international custom, however, the tax officials of one country cannot visit another country for the purpose of auditing a taxpayer's records unless invited to do so by the foreign government. Some governments consider it inappropriate for tax officials to make such visits without also obtaining the concurrence of the taxpayer. Several countries have addressed this problem by conducting joint audit programs under which a particular taxpayer (and its affiliates) is audited by the tax authorities of both countries.

Once the tax authorities of a country have conducted an audit and assessed a tax deficiency against a taxpayer, they must collect any taxes owed. Tax authorities often encounter severe difficulties in enforcing tax liability in another country. Under the domestic law of most countries, the tax judgments of a foreign country generally are not enforceable in accordance with the "revenue rule." Article 27 (Assistance in the Collection of Taxes) of the OECD and UN Model Treaties overcomes the limitations of the revenue rule by requiring each country to provide assistance in the collection of the other country's taxes. Like Articles 24 (Non-discrimination) and 26 (Exchange of Information), Article 27 is not limited to the taxes covered by the tax treaty but extends to all taxes imposed by the contracting states.

A request for assistance must be accepted by the requested state if the taxpayer cannot resist the collection of the taxes under the laws of the requesting state. A taxpayer is not entitled

款进行征收。但是，如果请求方未穷尽依据其国内法和征管实践可以使用的所有征税或保全措施，或者征收税款的行政负担超出请求方的收益，则被请求方可以不予提供协助。在向别国提供协助，征收欠缴税款时，并不要求一国采取与其自身法律或行政惯例不一致，或违背公共政策的措施。

8.8.5 常设机构利润归属

如以上第 5 章第 5.8.1.2 节所讨论的，一国居民实体在另一国开展实质性经营活动，可以通过在该国设立分支机构或常设机构，也可以在该国设立实体（如子公司）。与子公司不同，分支机构或常设机构并不是法人实体，无法自行采取行动。分支机构或常设机构的财产和经营活动实际上是其所属实体的财产和经营活动。

如果一国居民企业通过设在另一国的分支机构或常设机构开展经营活动，那么，两国均有必要确定该分支机构或常设机构的所得数额。来源国需要该信息以确定应予征收来源国税收的非居民企业利润的数额。该企业所在居民国需要获得该信息，以通过免税法或抵免法，对该企业通过外国分支机构或常设机构取得的利润消除双重征税。如第 5 章第 5.8.1.1 节所述，各国计算非居民利润的规则差异极大。

根据 OECD 协定范本和联合国协定范本第 7 条第 1 款，只有在一国居民企业通过设在另一国的常设机构在该另一国营业时，该另一国才可就其营业利润对该企业征税。根据 OECD 协定范本，对于通过常设机构在另一国开展营业活动的一国居民，另一国仅应就归属于该常设机构的利润予以征税。根据联合国协定范本，对于此种居民，另一国也可以就销售与通过常设机构所销售产品类似的产品，或开展与常设机构所开展活动类似的其他经营活动所产生的利润征税。联合国协定范本中这种有限的引力原则规定很容易规避，所以并不非常重要。

to contest the existence, validity, or amount of the taxes owing in the courts or administrative bodies of the requested state. In addition, the requested state must collect the taxes of the requesting state as if those taxes were its own. However, it is not required to provide assistance until the requesting state has exhausted all measures for the collection or conservancy of the taxes available under its domestic law and administrative practices or where the administrative burden to collect the taxes is disproportionate to the benefit to the requesting state. In providing assistance in the collection of the taxes owing to the other state, a state is not required to take any measures that are inconsistent with its own laws or administrative practices or contrary to public policy.

8.8.5 Attribution of Profits to Permanent Establishments

As discussed above in Chapter 5, section 5.8.1.2, an entity resident in one country may engage in substantial business activities in another country through a branch or PE in that country or through an entity (such as a subsidiary) established in that country. Unlike a subsidiary, a branch or PE is not a legal entity and cannot take action on its own. The property and activities of a branch or PE are actually the property and activities of the entity of which it is a part.

Where an enterprise resident in one country is engaged in business activities through a branch or PE in another country, it is necessary for both countries to determine the amount of income of the branch or PE. The source country requires this information in order to determine the amount of the nonresident enterprise's profits subject to source country tax. The country in which the enterprise is resident requires the information in order to provide relief from double taxation—by way of exemption or a foreign tax credit—of the profits earned by the enterprise through the foreign branch or PE. The domestic rules used by countries to compute the profits earned by a nonresident vary considerably, as discussed in Chapter 5, section 5.8.1.1.

Under Article 7(1) of both the OECD and UN Model Treaties, a resident of one country is taxable by the other country with respect to business profits only if it carries on business in the other country through a PE located in that country. Under the OECD Model Treaty, a resident carrying on business through a PE in the other country is taxable only on the profits attributable to the PE. Under the UN Model Treaty, such a resident is also taxable on profits from sales of goods similar to those sold through the PE and from other business activities similar to those carried out through the PE. This limited force-of-attraction rule in the UN Model Treaty is not very important because it is easy to avoid.

两个协定范本第 7 条第 2 款都要求将常设机构假设为与其所属企业的其他部门开展独立业务往来的分设企业，并按此确定可以向常设机构归属的利润（企业的其他部门包括企业总部和企业的任何其他常设机构）。普遍认为这一假设很有必要，由此可以将第 9 条的转让定价原则适用于确定归属于常设机构的利润。

OECD 协定范本第 7 条于 2010 年进行了大幅修改，这次修改基于持续十年之久，并于 2008 年结束的一个项目的成果。该项目结束时发布了一份报告《常设机构利润归属》，并在 OECD 转让定价指南中新设常设机构一章。这一章主要由在第 6 工作组开展工作的经济学家撰写，并没有考虑现有协定第 7 条用语带来的限制。结果是，第 6 工作组从第 7 条第 2 款中的独立分设实体假设出发，按逻辑得出结论：要求在计算常设机构利润的所有环节中，都将常设机构视为独立分设实体。这个新方法导致对第 7 条措辞的全面修改。

修改后的 OECD 协定范本第 7 条第 2 款规定，计算可归属于常设机构的利润，必须将常设机构视为独立分设实体，“并考虑企业通过常设机构和其他部门履行的功能、使用的资产和承担的风险”。同时，删除了原来的第 7 条第 3 款至第 6 款（后面将进行讨论），并在新的第 3 款中增加了类似于第 9 条第 2 款的对应调整。第 7 条第 3 款规定，如果缔约国一方按照第 7 条，对缔约国另一方企业在该缔约国一方所设常设机构的利润进行了调整，则缔约国另一方应对该企业的利润进行对应调整。

第 7 条的修订颇具争议。8 个 OECD 成员国对新条款提出了保留，表示不接受新的第 7 条，并希望能继续使用该条款原来的版本。另外，在 2011 年对联合国协定范本的修订中，联合国国际税收专家委员会拒绝采用 OECD 的新版第 7 条。

正如第 6 章所述，将转让定价规则适用于常设机构，存在着严重的概念和实务难题。第 9 条的转让定价规则适用于关联方之间的交易。该规则并不适用于常设机构，因为常设机构不构成独立的人，仅是一个法人企业的组成部门，同一企业的各个组成部门之间并不发生交易。作为一个法律事项，转让要求所有权从一

Article 7(2) of both Model Treaties requires the profits attributable to a PE to be determined on the assumption that the PE is a separate enterprise dealing independently with the rest of the enterprise of which it is a part. (The rest of the enterprise means the head office of the enterprise and any other PEs of the enterprise.) This assumption is generally considered to be necessary in order to make the transfer pricing rules of Article 9 applicable in determining the profits attributable to a PE.

Article 7 of the OECD Model Treaty was substantially revised in 2010 pursuant to a decade-long project culminating in 2008 with a report, *Attribution of Profits to Permanent Establishments*, and a new chapter dealing with PEs in the OECD's Transfer Pricing Guidelines. This new chapter was developed largely by economists working through Working Party 6, which did not take into account any of the constraints imposed by the wording of the existing Article 7 of the treaty. In effect, Working Party 6 took the separate-entity assumption in Article 7(2) to its logical conclusion; thus, a PE was required to be treated as a separate entity for all purposes in computing its profits. This new approach required a complete overhaul of the wording of Article 7.

Article 7(2) of the OECD Model Treaty was revised to provide that the profits attributable to a PE must be computed as if the PE were a separate entity "taking into account the functions performed, assets used and risks assumed by the enterprise through the permanent establishment and through the other parts of the enterprise." Paragraphs 3 through 6 of Article 7, discussed below, were deleted, and a new corresponding adjustment similar to Article 9(2) was added to Article 7(3). Article 7(3) requires a contracting state to make an adjustment to the profits of an enterprise if the other contracting state makes an adjustment in accordance with Article 7 to the profits of a PE of the enterprise in that other state.

The changes to Article 7 have been controversial. Eight OECD member countries have entered reservations on the new Article, indicating that they reject the new Article 7 and intend to adhere to the former version of the article. In addition, the UN Committee of Experts refused to adopt the OECD's new version of Article 7 in the 2011 revision of the UN Model Treaty.

Serious conceptual and practical difficulties arise in applying transfer pricing rules to PEs, as described in Chapter 6. The transfer pricing rules in Article 9 apply to transactions between related persons. They do not apply to PEs because a PE is not a separate person; it is merely part of a legal enterprise, and transactions do not take place between parts of the same enterprise. As a legal matter, a transfer requires a change in ownership from one person to another, and a PE cannot own property. What is often described metaphorically as a transfer of property between the head office and a PE of an enterprise or between two PEs of the same enterprise is

人转至另一人，但常设机构并不拥有财产。通常以比喻的方式所称之企业总部与其常设机构之间，或同一企业的两个常设机构之间的财产转让，并不是真正的法律转让，只不过是由该企业所拥有的财产，其使用或位置发生了变化。

因此，为了将转让定价规则适用于常设机构，需要将常设机构视为独立的法人实体，并在常设机构与其所属企业其他部门之间构建假设性的交易。例如，假设 A 国居民公司 A 在 A 国生产商品，并通过 B 国的常设机构（销售网点）销售这些商品。为了参考转让定价规则在两国之间分配 A 公司的所得，需将 A 公司通过其常设机构在 B 国开展的销售活动视为由 A 公司的子公司（例如 B 国居民公司 B）开展的。再将 A 公司视为通过销售或代销将商品转让给了这一假设的 B 公司，于是可以将转让定价规则适用于上述设想中的转让。之后就要假定 B 公司是作为独立分销商还是作为 A 公司代理人在 B 国开展活动，因为分销商和代理人在市场中取得的所得可能会不一样。

按照关于 OECD 协定范本第 7 条第 2 款的注释，确定可以归属于常设机构的利润，是一个包含两个步骤的过程。第一步涉及对常设机构进行功能和事实分析，以确定常设机构履行的功能、常设机构资产的经济所有权、常设机构承担的风险、常设机构的资本，以及常设机构与企业其他部门间假设性的“交易”。第二步涉及将转让定价规则类比适用于这些交易，以确定独立交易价格。

由于需要构建常设机构和企业其他部门之间的交易，将 OECD 转让定价规则适用于常设机构，相比适用于关联企业之间的交易，将更加困难、更加不确定，且更不可靠。如上所述，一些国家反对 OECD 的这个新方法，并且，很多国家无法有效地实施这些规则。

税收协定大多数都包含与 OECD 协定范本之前版本第 7 条和联合国协定范本现行版本第 7 条类似的营业利润条款。如上所述，根据第 7 条第 2 款，计算常设机构的利润，必须将常设机构假设为与其所属企业其他部门存在独立业务往来的分设实体。于是，这一版本的第 7 条第 2 款与 OECD 新版第 7 条第 2 款并无显著区别。但是，关于之前版本的注释并没有从独立分设企业假设出发，得出逻辑性

merely a change in the use or location of property owned by that corporation and not a genuine legal transfer.

Therefore, in order to apply transfer pricing rules to PEs, it is necessary to treat a PE as if it were a separate legal entity and to construct hypothetical transactions between the PE and the rest of the enterprise of which the PE is a part. Assume, for example, that ACo, resident in Country A, manufactures goods in Country A and sells those goods through a PE (a sales outlet) in Country B. To apportion the income of ACo between the two countries by reference to the transfer pricing rules, ACo's sales activities through its PE in Country B would be treated as if they were carried on by a subsidiary corporation resident in Country B (e.g., BCo). ACo would be treated as if it had made a transfer of goods, either by sale or consignment, to the assumed BCo. The transfer pricing rules would then be applied to that notional transfer. An assumption would have to be made as to whether BCo was operating in Country B as an independent distributor or as an agent of ACo because the income earned by distributors and agents in the marketplace might not be the same.

According to the Commentary on Article 7(2) of the OECD Model Treaty, the determination of the profits attributable to a PE is a two-step process. The first step involves a functional and factual analysis of the PE in order to determine the functions performed by the PE, the economic ownership of assets by the PE, the risks assumed by the PE, the capital of the PE, and the hypothetical "dealings" between the PE and the other parts of the enterprise. The second step involves the application of the transfer pricing rules, by analogy, to those dealings in order to establish an arm's-length price.

Because of the necessity of inventing dealings between a PE and another part of the enterprise, the application of the OECD's transfer pricing rules to PEs is even more difficult, uncertain, and less reliable than their application to transactions between associated enterprises. As noted above, several countries have rejected the OECD's new approach, and many countries will be unable to apply those rules effectively.

Most existing tax treaties contain a business profits article that is similar to the former version of Article 7 of the OECD Model Treaty and the current version of Article 7 of the UN Model Treaty. As noted above, under Article 7(2), the profits of a PE are required to be computed on the assumption that a PE is a separate entity dealing independently with the rest of the enterprise of which it is a part. Accordingly, this version of Article 7(2) is not significantly different from the new OECD version of Article 7(2). However, the Commentary on the former version did not take the separate-entity assumption to its logical conclusion; instead, it provided a series of ad hoc practical rules for computing the profits attributable to a PE. Sometimes the

结论，而是提出了一系列关于计算可归属于常设机构的利润的具体实践性规则。注释有时要求将常设机构视为独立实体，例如，如果常设机构向企业总部转让资产，则将视同常设机构按照转让发生之时的市场公允价格销售资产、企业总部同时按该价格购入资产，来计算常设机构的利润。相反，注释有时却拒绝将常设机构视为独立实体，例如，按照之前版本的第 7 条，在计算常设机构利润时，不允许扣除名义上支付的利息或特许权使用费（金融机构除外），而根据新的 OECD 第 7 条，这些却是可以扣除的。

以下示例可以说明两个版本第 7 条所规定的不同方法。A 国居民企业 A 公司开始通过常设机构在 B 国开展经营活动。A 公司按照 10% 的利率借入 20 万元，之后将其转让给该常设机构，为其在 B 国开展业务提供资金。A 公司还另向该常设机构预付 100 万元作为其经营资金。按照新版第 7 条，需要确定与该常设机构行使同样功能、拥有同样资产和承担同样风险的独立实体，可能会拥有的负债和权益。因此，如果独立实体的负债是其权益的两倍，那么可以假定，常设机构将拥有 40 万元权益、80 万元负债。因此，在计算可归属于常设机构的利润时，80 万元名义负债按照 10% 的利率（假设 10% 是独立交易利率）支付的利息是可以扣除的。相反，按照 OECD 协定范本之前版本的第 7 条和联合国协定范本现行版本的第 7 条（参见第 7 条第 3 款，其明确不允许扣除名义上支付的利息和特许权使用费），在计算常设机构利润时，仅允许扣除因 20 万元借款而支付的利息（即 A 公司为常设机构而发生的负债实际产生的利息费用）。

允许扣除名义支付的利息和特许权使用费是有问题的。如果存在实际支付的利息和特许权使用费，并在计算常设机构利润时扣除这些款项，按照两个协定范本的第 11 条或第 12 条，来源国有权对支付的款项征收预提税。但是，来源国对名义上支付的利息和特许权使用费征收不了预提税。

跨国银行、保险公司和其他金融服务公司通常通过分支机构在全球开展业务。利用分支机构的原因，一般是为了满足许多国家为保护投资者和顾客而提出的资本储备要求。按照关于 OECD 协定范本原第 7 条第 3 款的注释（第 49 段）

Commentary required the PE to be treated as a separate entity; for example, if a PE transferred assets to the head office of the enterprise, the profits of the PE were computed as if the PE had sold the assets for their fair market value at the time of the transfer and the head office had acquired the assets for the same amount at the same time. In contrast, sometimes the Commentary rejected treating the PE as a separate entity; for example, notional payments of interest or royalties were not deductible in computing the profits of a PE under the former version of Article 7 (except in the case of financial institutions), whereas they are deductible under the new OECD Article 7.

Consider the following example, which illustrates the different approaches under the two versions of Article 7. ACo is an enterprise resident in Country A that commences carrying on business through a PE in Country B. ACo borrows 200,000 with interest at 10%, which it transfers to the PE to finance the establishment of the business carried on in Country B. ACo also advances an additional 1 million to the PE to finance the PE's business. Under the new Article 7, it would be necessary to determine how much debt and equity a separate entity would have if it performed the functions of the PE, owned the assets of the PE, and assumed the risks of the PE. Thus, if such a separate entity would have debt equal to twice its equity, the PE would be assumed to have 400,000 of equity and 800,000 of debt; thus, interest at 10% (assuming that 10% is an arm's-length interest rate) on notional debt of 800,000 would be deductible in computing the profits attributable to the PE. In contrast, under the former version of Article 7 of the OECD Model Treaty and the current version of Article 7 of the UN Model Treaty (*see* Article 7(3), which explicitly denies any deduction for notional payments of interest or royalties), only interest on 200,000 (the actual interest expense incurred by ACo in respect of debt used for the purposes of the PE) would be deductible in computing the profits of the PE.

Allowing the deduction of notional payments of interest and royalties is problematic. Where actual payments of interest and royalties are made, and those payments are deductible in computing the profits of a PE under Article 11 or 12 of the Model Treaties, the source country is entitled to impose withholding tax on the payments. However, notional payments of interest and royalties are not subject to source country withholding tax.

International banks, insurance companies, and other financial services companies often operate their global businesses through branches. Often the reason for using a branch is to satisfy capital reserve requirements imposed in many countries to protect investors and customers. Under the Commentary on former Article 7(3) of the OECD Model Treaty (paragraph 49) and the Commentary on Article 7(3) of the UN Model Treaty (paragraph 41), a financial

和关于联合国协定范本第 7 条第 3 款的注释（第 41 段），在计算常设机构的利润时，允许金融机构扣除名义支付的利息。根据注释，“考虑到支付和收取预付款与银行和其他金融机构的常规业务紧密相关这一事实”，对这些企业进行特殊对待是恰当的。

联合国协定范本第 7 条第 3 款（以及 OECD 协定范本原第 7 条第 3 款）规定，在计算常设机构的利润时，必须允许扣除企业为常设机构而发生的各项费用，不论其发生于何地，无论其是否全部是因常设机构而发生的。因此，常设机构所在国不能因为费用发生在来源国境外，或仅有部分费用与常设机构相关，而拒绝扣除这些费用。例如，诸如会计和法律费用之类的总部费用，其中有部分系总部为常设机构而发生的，在计算常设机构的利润时，必须允许扣除。但是，必须强调的是，费用扣除属于国内法事项。因此，如果按照来源国国内法，仅可扣除部分招待费，那么，在计算常设机构利润时，就不能根据第 7 条要求来源国允许全额扣除。

联合国协定范本第 7 条第 4 款（以及 OECD 协定范本原第 7 条第 4 款）规定，可以将企业作为整体的利润，按照公式分配法，计算常设机构的利润，只要这是常设机构所在国的习惯做法。但是，任何此种公式分配法，都必须得出与第 7 条的原则相一致的结果。也就是说，必须与将该常设机构换作一个独立实体时应当取得的利润相一致。

联合国协定范本第 7 条第 5 款（以及 OECD 协定范本原第 7 条第 5 款）规定，除非有恰当和充分的理由，需要改变常设机构利润归属方法，应以连贯一致的方法逐年确定常设机构的利润。

对于将转让定价规则拓展至分支机构，各国均尚未建立详细全面的国内法规则。实践中，大部分国家依据纳税人为常设机构设置的账目所显示的利润，来计算常设机构的利润，如果会计账册不能得出合理的结果，则酌情进行调整。但是，由于常设机构的账簿和记录受企业控制，其可靠性不强，税务机关必须仔细审核，保证其准确地反映了常设机构的利润。

institution is allowed to deduct notional interest payments in computing the profits of a PE. According to the Commentary, the special treatment of banks and other financial institutions is appropriate "in view of the fact that making and receiving advances is closely related to the ordinary business of such enterprises."

Article 7(3) of the UN Model Treaty (and former Article 7(3) of the OECD Model Treaty) provides that expenses incurred by an enterprise for the purposes of a PE must be allowed as deductions in computing the profits of the PE irrespective of where the expenses are incurred and whether they are incurred wholly on behalf of the PE. Thus, the PE country cannot deny the deduction of expenses because they are incurred outside the source country or because only a portion of the expenses relates to the PE. For example, the portion of head office expenses, such as accounting and legal expenses, that are incurred by the head office on behalf of a PE must be allowed as deductions in computing the profits of the PE. However, it must be emphasized that the deductibility of expenses is a matter of domestic law. Therefore, for example, if only a portion of entertainment expenses is deductible under the domestic law of the source country, the source country is not required by Article 7 to allow the full amount to be deductible in computing the profits of the PE.

Article 7(4) of the UN Model Treaty (and former Article 7(4) of the OECD Model Treaty) provides that the profits of a PE may be computed in accordance with a formulary apportionment of the profits of the enterprise as a whole as long as that has been the customary practice of the country in which the PE is located. However, any such formulary apportionment must produce a result that is consistent with the principles of Article 7; in other words, it must be consistent with the profits that the PE would be expected to make if it were a separate entity.

Article 7(5) of the UN Model Treaty (and former Article 7(5) of the OECD Model Treaty) provides that the profits of a PE must be determined on a consistent basis from year to year unless there is some good and sufficient justification for a change in the method for computing PE profits.

No country has developed detailed and comprehensive domestic rules for extending transfer pricing rules to branches. In practice, most countries compute the profits of a PE on the basis of the profits shown in the taxpayer's books of account for the PE and make ad hoc adjustments if those books do not produce a reasonable result. However, since the books and records of a PE are within the control of the enterprise, they may not be reliable, and the tax authorities must scrutinize them carefully to ensure that they accurately reflect the profits of the PE.

8.8.6 实施税收协定相关措施以防止税基侵蚀和利润转移的多边公约

如以上第 8.8.2 节所讨论的，为应对协定滥用，BEPS 项目建议对 OECD 协定范本做若干修订，包括新的标题和序言、一般反滥用规则、反混合实体规则、保留条款、针对法人实体的新加比规则，以及针对常设机构定义的若干修订等。为了落实这些修订，重谈现有双边税收协定，将耗费极为漫长的时间，也不能有效地回应协定滥用问题。意识到存在这一问题，BEPS 第 15 项行动计划建议拟定一项多边公约，以迅速高效地实施 BEPS 项目关于税收协定的建议。

2016 年，7 个国际组织和将近 100 个国家参与了此项多边公约的起草。2016 年 11 月 24 日，OECD 发布了《实施税收协定相关措施以防止税基侵蚀和利润转移的多边公约》，该公约通常被称为多边公约（MLI）。2017 年 6 月 7 日，76 个国家签署了多边公约，另有 9 个国家作出了签署承诺。多边公约于 2018 年 7 月 1 日生效。此后完成批准程序的签署方，多边公约将自该方交存核准书之日起第 3 个月第 1 日起生效。最新的签署方名单（截至 2022 年 10 月共有 100 个）请见 OECD 网站（www.oecd.org）。

总体而言，对依据双边税收协定应征预提税的支付款项而言，多边公约条款将自其对协定各方生效的最后日期之后开始的第 1 个公历月份起适用。对其他税种而言，则将自多边公约对协定各方生效的最后日期之后的第 6 个月或 6 个月以后开始的纳税期间适用。

多边公约包括 7 章。第 1 章是公约的范围和术语定义，前者阐明公约适用于“被涵盖税收协定”。第 7 章涉及签署、核准、生效、执行等技术问题，以及下面将讨论的保留（第 28 条）和通知（第 29 条）等重要问题。第 2 章至第 6 章涉及 BEPS 项目建议修订协定的实质性方面：第 2 章——混合错配，第 3 章——协定滥用，第 4 章——规避构成常设机构，第 5 章——相互协商程序，第 6 章——强制仲裁。

8.8.6 The Multilateral Convention to Implement Tax Treaty Related Measures to Prevent BEPS (The Multilateral Instrument)

As discussed above in section 8.8.2, the BEPS Project recommended several changes to the OECD Model Treaty dealing with treaty abuse, including a new title and preamble, a general anti-abuse rule, anti-hybrid entity rules, a saving clause, a new tie-breaker rule for legal entities, and several changes to the definition of a PE. Renegotiating actual bilateral tax treaties to implement these changes would take an inordinately long time and would not constitute an effective response to the problem of treaty abuse. In recognition of this problem, BEPS Action 15 recommended that a multilateral convention should be concluded to implement the BEPS tax treaty proposals efficiently and quickly.

Almost 100 countries and 7 international organizations participated in the drafting of the multilateral convention over the course of 2016. On November 24, 2016, the OECD released the *Multilateral Convention to Implement Tax Treaty Related Measures to Prevent Base Erosion and Profit Shifting*, which is more popularly known as the Multilateral Legal Instrument (MLI). The MLI was signed on June 7, 2017, by 76 countries, with 9 additional countries committing to sign; it entered into force on July 1, 2018. For countries ratifying after that time, the MLI enters into force on the first day of the third month after the date of deposit of the country's ratification. A current list of the signatories (100 as of October 2022) can be found on the OECD's website (www.oecd.org).

In general, the provisions of the MLI are effective for any particular treaty with respect to an amount paid that is subject to withholding tax on or after the first calendar month beginning after the latest date that the MLI enters into force for the parties to the treaty, and for other taxes with respect to taxable periods beginning on or after a period of six months after the latest date that the MLI enters into force for the parties to the treaty.

The MLI consists of seven Parts. Part I deals with the scope of the Convention—it applies to "Covered Tax Agreements"—and definitions. Part Ⅶ deals with technical issues, such as signature, ratification, entry into force, and entry into effect, as well as the important issues of reservations (Article 28) and notifications (Article 29), discussed below. Parts Ⅱ to Ⅵ deal with the substantive BEPS treaty changes: Part Ⅱ—hybrid mismatches, Part Ⅲ—treaty abuse, Part Ⅳ—avoidance of PE status, Part V—MAP, and Part Ⅵ—mandatory arbitration.

虽然多边公约希望修订现行被涵盖的税收协定，在其中纳入 BEPS 第 6 项行动计划建议，并加入 2017 年 OECD 协定范本已包含的新条款，但这不能通过提及该条款在 OECD 协定范本中的序号或措辞来实现。因为在一些实际的双边协定中，该条款的序号不同，而且，在部分双边协定中，对应条款的措辞也与 OECD 协定范本的措辞存在差异。因此，多边公约的条款对被涵盖税收协定中，基于 OECD 协定范本类似条款的相关条款进行了一般性的描述。

多边公约仅适用于一国在签署或核准公约时，作出通知希望由多边公约涵盖的税收协定［参见第 2 条第 1 款第（1）项第 2 目关于“被涵盖税收协定”的定义］。因此，要确定多边公约是否会修改某个税收协定，首先要看该协定的缔约国双方是否将其列入被涵盖税收协定。只有在缔约国双方都列入该协定的情况下，该协定才会受多边公约的影响。其次，即使该协定是被涵盖税收协定，如果缔约国一方对多边公约的某个条款做出了“保留”，则多边公约的该条款也不能适用。按照多边公约第 28 条第 3 款，不管由协定缔约双方中的哪一方做出保留，其结果对双方共同适用。但是，除非一国列入的税收协定已经满足了一项或多项 BEPS 最低标准（防止协定滥用和改进相互协商程序），否则，不允许对相应最低标准做出保留。例如，多边公约第 6 条第 1 款将修改被涵盖税收协定，在其中加入新的序言，明确协定的目的在于消除双重征税，同时不为通过包括择协避税安排在内的逃避税创造机会。按照第 6 条第 4 款，只有在一国税收协定的序言已包含类似于新序言表述的情况下，该国才可以提出保留，不使用新序言。

一般情况下，多边公约的大多数条款允许一国就某项条款整体内容对其所有被涵盖税收协定的适用提出保留，或该项条款部分内容对其所有被涵盖税收协定的适用提出保留，以及其已经包括涉及某问题的相关条款的被涵盖税收协定，提出保留。但是，不能有选择地只就部分被涵盖税收协定做出保留，除非现行协定中已经包含涉及特定问题的条款。各国可以在通知 OECD 之后，随时撤销或替换其保留（仅可替换为范围更窄的保留）。实际上，一旦一国对多边公约作出了承诺，就不能撤销或降低该承诺。

Although the MLI is intended to modify the provisions of existing Covered Tax Agreements by incorporating into those treaties the new provisions recommended by BEPS Action 6 and added to the 2017 OECD Model Treaty, this cannot be done by referring to the relevant number of the article in the OECD Model Treaty or its wording because, in some actual bilateral treaties, the provision has a different number and because the wording of the equivalent provision in some bilateral treaties differs from the wording of the OECD Model Treaty. Therefore, the provisions of the MLI provide a general description of the relevant provisions of the Covered Tax Agreements that are based on the comparable provisions of the OECD Model Treaty.

The MLI applies only to the tax treaties for which a country gives notification at the time of signature or ratification that it wishes to be covered by the MLI (*see* Article 2(1)(a)(ii) of the definition of "Covered Tax Agreement"). Therefore, in order to determine whether a particular tax treaty has been modified by the MLI, the first thing to check is whether that treaty has been listed by *both* countries as a Covered Tax Agreement. Unless a treaty is listed by both countries, it is not affected by the MLI. Second, even if a particular treaty is a Covered Tax Agreement, a provision of the MLI may not apply if one of the contracting states has made a "reservation" on that provision. In accordance with Article 28(3) of the MLI, the effect of a reservation is reciprocal irrespective of which country makes it. However, reservations are not allowed with respect to the BEPS minimum standards (the prevention of treaty abuse and the improvement of the MAP) unless a country's listed treaties already meet one or more of those standards. For example, Article 6(1) of the MLI modifies any Covered Tax Agreements to include the new preamble stating that the treaty is intended to eliminate double taxation without creating opportunities for tax evasion or avoidance, including through treaty-shopping arrangements. Under Article 6(4), countries may register a reservation not to apply the new preamble but only with respect to treaties that already contain a preamble using language similar to the new preamble.

In general, most of the articles of the MLI allow reservations with respect to the application of the entire article to all of a country's Covered Tax Agreements or parts of the article to all its Covered Tax Agreements or with respect to its Covered Tax Agreements that already contain provisions dealing with the issue. However, reservations cannot be made selectively, with respect to only some of a country's Covered Tax Agreements, except to the extent that existing treaties already contain provisions dealing with the particular issue. A reservation may be withdrawn or replaced (but only by a more limited reservation) at any time by notifying the OECD. In effect, once a country has committed to the MLI, it cannot withdraw or limit that commitment.

所有签署多边公约的国家都必须至少接受多边公约中涉及 BEPS 最低标准的条款：新的标题和序言、协定滥用和相互协商程序。

多边公约的每个条款都有操作规则，四种不同类型的操作规则为：

（1）“替代”协定现有条款的规则。

（2）“适用于”或“修订”协定现有条款的规则。例如，按照多边公约涉及一般反滥用规则的第 7 条第 3 款，协定的缔约国双方可以选择允许主管当局酌情授予协定待遇，虽然按照一般反滥用规则，应拒绝给予这种待遇。

（3）协定中“没有”相应条款时适用的规则。

（4）“替代”协定现有条款或在协定中“没有”相应条款时适用的规则。例如，多边公约第 4 条第 2 款规定，如果缔约国双方均就确定法人企业居民身份的加比规则通知了 OECD，则多边公约第 4 条第 1 款（该条款规定主管当局应尽力确定实体的居民身份）将替代该加比规则。但是，即使没有作出通知，如果协定现有条款与多边公约中的条款不一致，多边公约中的条款将优先适用，或者在协定中没有相应条款的情况下，将在该协定中加入多边公约中的条款。

多边公约还提供了落实包括最低标准在内的 BEPS 项目修改建议的多个选项供各国选择，这进一步增加了其复杂程度。各国必须将其选择的选项（有些情况是不选择其中任一选项）、包含相关条款的各个协定，以及条款的序号，通知 OECD。只有在协定缔约国双方选择同一选项的情况下，该选项才会适用于具体的协定。

Any country that signs the MLI must agree, at a minimum, to the provisions of the MLI dealing with the BEPS minimum standards: the new title and preamble, treaty abuse, and the MAP.

Each article of the MLI has an operative rule. The four different types of operative rules are:

(1) Rules that apply "in place of" existing provisions of a treaty.

(2) Rules that "apply to" or "modify" existing provisions of a treaty. For example, under Article 7(3) of the MLI with respect to the general anti-abuse rule, the contracting states to a treaty may choose to allow the competent authorities to grant treaty benefits on a discretionary basis despite the fact that those benefits would be denied under the general anti-abuse rule.

(3) Rules that apply "in the absence of" existing provisions of a treaty.

(4) Rules that apply "in place of or in the absence of" existing provisions of a treaty. For example, Article 4(2) of the MLI provides that where both countries notify the OECD with respect to the tie-breaker rule for determining the residence of legal entities in the treaty, Article 4(1) of the MLI (which provides that the competent authorities shall endeavor to determine the state of residence of an entity) will replace that tie-breaker rule; however, even if no notification is given, the provision of the MLI will prevail over the existing provision of a treaty to the extent of any inconsistency or will be added to the treaty if there is no existing provision in the treaty.

The MLI is further complicated by the availability of options for countries to choose from in order to deal with particular BEPS changes, including minimum standards. A country that chooses an option (or, in some cases, does not choose any option) must notify the OECD of its choice, as well as each treaty that contains the relevant provision and the number of the provision. An option applies to a particular treaty only if both contracting states choose the same option.

9 新兴议题

9.1 引言

本章探讨了国际税收近期发生的几项重要进展。尽管其中许多进展已在前几章有所述及，但为方便起见，本章对其进行了详细阐述。本章所述议题并无贯穿始终的主线，只是将近年来日益重要的议题进行集中探讨而已。

本章探讨的议题所涉范围甚广，既涉及国内法的国际方面和税收协定，也涵盖实体性问题和诸如信息交换和仲裁等程序性问题。

此处讨论的问题之所以如此引人关注，很大程度上归功于 OECD 和联合国所做的工作。正如近期 BEPS 项目所展现的那样，OECD 已成为国际税收问题的主导者。近年来，联合国通过其专家委员会和能力开发署，也开始在国际税收领域发挥出日益重要的影响力。例如，在联合国协定范本中增加涉及技术服务费处理的第 12A 条（本文将在第 9.3.3 节进行讨论），以及涉及自动化数字服务所得处理的第 12B 条（本文将在第 9.5.4 节进行讨论），表明税收协定在演进过程中可能向前迈出了重要的一步。

9.2 税基侵蚀和利润转移

9.2.1 引言

在 2012 年至 2019 年间，OECD 的 BEPS 项目主导了国际税收议题。正如下

CHAPTER 9

Emerging Issues

9.1 INTRODUCTION

This chapter deals with several important recent developments in international tax. Although many of these developments have been mentioned in previous chapters, they are dealt with in detail here for convenience. There is no overarching theme to the topics covered in this chapter other than the fact that they have become increasingly important in recent years.

The issues discussed in this chapter are wide-ranging and include international aspects of domestic law and tax treaties, substantive issues, and administrative issues such as exchange of information and arbitration.

The prominence of the issues discussed here is largely attributable to the work of the OECD and the UN. The OECD has become a dominant player with respect to international tax issues, as the recent BEPS project shows. In recent years, the UN, through the Committee of Experts and its Capacity Development Unit, has also started to exert an increasingly important influence in the international tax arena. For example, the addition to the UN Model Treaty of Article 12A dealing with fees for technical services, discussed in section 9.3.3 below, and Article 12B dealing with income from automated digital services, discussed in section 9.5.4, represents a potentially important step in the evolution of tax treaties.

9.2 BASE EROSION AND PROFIT SHIFTING

9.2.1 Introduction

From 2012 to 2019, the OECD's BEPS project dominated the international tax agenda. As discussed below in section 9.2.3, the scope of the project was huge, comprising fifteen action items, and the time frame for its completion—about 2.5 years—was unrealistically

文第 9.2.3 节讨论的那样，该项目规模宏大，包含 15 项行动计划，并要求在两年半的时间内完成，时间紧迫得简直不切实际。不仅 OECD 成员国，而且 G20 和众多发展中国家都参与其中。BEPS 的多项行动计划已在本书的有关章节进行了讨论。本节概述了 BEPS 项目的总体情况及其对国际税制的影响。

BEPS 项目所针对的国际税制问题并不是新近出现的，理解这一点非常重要。很多问题涉及来源国和居民国征税权分配机制的根本性、结构性特征，各国及 OECD 和联合国等国际组织为应对这些问题已付出数十年的努力。作为理解 BEPS 项目的背景，第 9.2.2 节探讨了 OECD 为解决国际税收制度的某些根本性问题所进行的最初尝试——20 世纪 90 年代后期应对有害税收竞争的倡议。

9.2.2 1998 年 OECD 有害税收竞争报告

在过去五十年中，避税地和高税国优惠税制的不断扩散，其被利用的频繁令人震惊。许多进展导致了这一现象的出现，具体包括：

—— 取消外汇管制，以及跨境贸易和投资的自由化；

—— 通信、交通以及金融服务水平不断提升；

—— 税收咨询公司全球化发展；

—— 避税地采用灵活的商业机制；以及

—— 激进的推销。

避税地和实行优惠税制的国家非常巧妙地将其服务推销至世界的每个角落，力求满足每个可以想象到的税收筹划需求。尽管它们之间的竞争异常激烈，但参与者十分踊跃，新的避税地和优惠税制不断涌现，但求分一杯羹。

这种低税制的扩散及其导致的税基侵蚀效果被 OECD 称为“逐底竞争”。出于对此逐底竞争的担忧，OECD 和欧盟在 20 世纪 90 年代后期发起了应对有害税收竞争的行动。经过多年努力和艰难磋商，1997 年 12 月，欧盟开始实行有害税

tight. The project involved not only OECD member countries but also G20 and developing countries. Many of the action items are discussed elsewhere in this Primer. This section presents an overview of the BEPS project and its implications for the international tax system.

It is important to understand that the problems with the international tax system targeted by the BEPS project are not new. Many of them involve fundamental structural features of the allocation of taxing rights between source and residence countries that countries and international organizations, such as the OECD and the UN, have struggled with for decades. As background for understanding the BEPS project, section 9.2.2 discusses the OECD's first attempt to deal with some of the fundamental problems of the international tax system—the harmful tax competition initiative of the late 1990s.

9.2.2 The 1998 OECD Harmful Tax Competition Report

Over the last fifty years, the proliferation and increased use of tax havens and preferential regimes in otherwise high-tax countries have been staggering. Many developments have contributed to this phenomenon, including:

- the elimination of exchange controls and the liberalization of cross-border trade and investment;
- improved communications, transportation, and financial services;
- the globalization of tax advisory firms;
- the adoption of flexible commercial regimes by tax havens; and
- aggressive marketing.

Tax havens and countries with preferential regimes have become very sophisticated in marketing their services to every geographical region of the world and every conceivable tax planning need. Although the competition among them is fierce, the field remains crowded, with newer tax havens and regimes continually being introduced to get a piece of the action.

This proliferation of low-tax regimes and their base-eroding effects are what the OECD has called a "race to the bottom." Concern about this race to the bottom led to the OECD and EU initiatives against harmful tax competition in the late 1990s. After years of work and difficult negotiations, the EU adopted a Code of Conduct concerning harmful tax competition in December 1997 (Commission of the European Communities, *A Package to Tackle Harmful*

收竞争《行为准则》（欧洲共同体委员会，《欧盟应对有害税收竞争的一揽子准则》）；OECD 也于 1998 年 4 月发布了《有害税收竞争报告》。

尽管这两项措施互为补充，但欧盟《行为准则》比 OECD 报告的适用范围更广泛，其原因在于，与 OECD 报告不同，欧盟《行为准则》的适用范围不限于地理上可移动的活动。该报告承认，有害税收竞争也会发生在非移动性活动中，诸如制造活动以及个人储蓄等，但这些活动将留待以后解决，因为它们解决起来难度更大。

虽然 OECD 报告针对的是“有害税收竞争”，但其并未对此用语进行定义，可能是因为准确定义有害税收竞争几乎是不可能的。使用“竞争”这一用语可能并不可取，因为人们普遍坚信，在贸易和资本全球自由流动的时代，所有竞争都是有益的。然而，“有害税收竞争”概念的内核在于，与前文提及的逐底竞争相关的有害税收竞争不同于导致了 20 世纪 80 年代后期全球税率降低和税基扩大的税收竞争。OECD 认为，尽管每个国家都拥有制定自身税收政策的主权，但一国不应实行意在“偷猎”他国税基的税制。

OECD 报告针对的是避税地和有害优惠税制，包括 OECD 成员国税制中的这类有害税制。该报告也列出了各国解决避税地和低税制问题可能采取的反制措施建议清单，包括单边措施以及多边协调措施。但是，OECD 很快放弃了制裁避税地的想法，转而采用对话和合作的策略。

有害税收竞争倡议至关重要，因为它象征着打击逃避税的国际合作正式启动。然而，OECD 的行动也引发了诸多争议。一些评论家和若干避税地小国指控 OECD 是富有国家的卡特尔，对发展中小国指手画脚，并试图强加特定类型的税制——一种所得税体制以及一个最低税率。其他评论家则欢迎 OECD 的举措，认为这是各国为保护国内税基所采取的合理行动。

任何新的税收政策举措本质上都是政治问题，有害税收竞争项目也不例外。2000 年末，在此之前还是有害税收竞争项目热衷支持者的美国，成功迫使 OECD 放弃了其针对避税地和有害优惠税制的工作，将项目重点几乎全部转向信息交

Tax Competition in the European Union), and the OECD issued its *Report on Harmful Tax Competition* in April 1998. Although the two initiatives were complementary, the EU Code of Conduct was considerably broader than the OECD Report because, unlike the OECD Report, its scope was not limited to geographically mobile activities. The Report recognized that harmful tax competition also occurs with respect to nonmobile activities, such as manufacturing and personal savings, but these activities were left for future action because they were considered more difficult to deal with.

Although the OECD Report was targeted at "harmful tax competition," no definition of that expression was provided in the Report, probably because the term is impossible to define precisely. The use of the word "competition" was perhaps unfortunate because, during an era of global free trade and capitalism, it was an article of faith that all competition is good. However, the essential concept inherent in the term "harmful tax competition" is that there is a difference between the type of tax competition that led to a worldwide lowering of tax rates and broadening of tax bases in the late 1980s and harmful tax competition, which involves the race to the bottom described above. According to the OECD, although every country has the sovereign right to determine its own tax policy, a country should not enact regimes that are intended to "poach" the tax base of other countries.

The OECD Report targeted both tax havens and harmful preferential tax regimes, including such regimes in the tax systems of OECD member countries. The Report also suggested a lengthy list of countermeasures that countries might take, on both a unilateral and a coordinated basis, to deal with tax havens and low-tax regimes. However, the OECD soon abandoned the idea of sanctions against tax havens in favor of a strategy of dialogue and cooperation.

The harmful tax competition initiative was significant because it signaled the beginning of serious international cooperation in fighting tax evasion and avoidance. However, the OECD's action was also very controversial. It was accused by some commentators and several smaller tax haven countries of being a cartel of rich countries dictating to small developing countries and trying to impose a particular type of tax system—an income tax system—and a minimum rate of tax. Other commentators, however, welcomed the OECD initiative as the logical step for countries to take to protect their domestic tax bases.

Any major new tax policy initiative is essentially a political issue, and the harmful tax competition project was no exception. In late 2000, the US, which until that time had been an enthusiastic supporter of the harmful tax competition project, effectively compelled the OECD to abandon its work on tax havens and harmful preferential tax regimes and to refocus the

换。其结果是，OECD 承诺制定双边和多边格式的标准化信息交换条款，覆盖刑事和民事税收问题。正如第 8 章 8.8.4 节讨论的那样，这些工作极大地提高了信息交换制度的效力和效率。第 8 章第 8.8.4 节对此进行了论述。

9.2.3 G20/OECD BEPS 项目

回顾历史，各国因面临税收收入的压力，更加努力地应对跨国公司的税收筹划策略，以保护国内税基，这不过是时间早晚的问题，而这些努力在 2008 年金融危机期间获得了更大的推动力。2012 年，OECD 启动了应对税基侵蚀和利润转移问题的项目。当时，几家美国跨国公司，包括苹果、亚马逊、星巴克、谷歌等采用的激进税收筹划技巧受到国际媒体以及欧洲和美国政治家们的强烈抨击，这为 BEPS 项目注入了一支兴奋剂。

OECD 致力于将信息交换打造为打击国际避税的工具，BEPS 项目成为这一努力的自然产物。2012 年 6 月，G20 财长会议发布的最终宣言强调“需要防止税基侵蚀和利润转移”，从而促成了这一项目的形成。2013 年 2 月，OECD 发布了题为《应对税基侵蚀和利润转移》的简短报告，来回应 G20 所关注的问题。报告明确了可采取行动的数个领域，并设定了实施应对措施的最终时限。

2013 年 7 月 19 日，OECD 发布了详细的《税基侵蚀和利润转移行动计划》（OECD 行动计划）。该行动计划的议程雄心勃勃，时限异常紧迫，主要包括以下内容：

（1）制定各国对电子商务（数字经济）征收直接税和间接税的规则（第 9.5 节讨论了电子商务问题）。

（2）针对利用混合实体和混合金融工具的混合错配安排，制定协定条款并提出国内法政策建议（第 7 章 7.7 节讨论了有关混合实体以及混合金融工具的 BEPS 建议）。

project almost exclusively on exchange of information. Accordingly, the OECD committed to developing standardized exchange-of- information provisions, in both bilateral and multilateral formats, dealing with both criminal and civil tax matters; its efforts resulted in a much more effective and efficient system with respect to exchange of information, as discussed in Chapter 8, section 8.8.4.

9.2.3 The G20/OECD BEPS Project

In retrospect, it was only a question of time before pressures on countries' tax revenues led to additional efforts to protect their domestic tax bases from the tax planning strategies of multinational enterprises; these efforts gained momentum during the financial crisis of 2008. In 2012, the OECD launched its project to counter base erosion and profit shifting. The project received a shot in the arm when aggressive tax planning techniques used by several U.S. multinationals, including Apple, Amazon, Starbucks, and Google, came under intense criticism from the international media and European and American politicians.

The BEPS initiative was a natural outgrowth of the OECD's work on exchange of information as a tool to combat international tax avoidance, although the impetus for the project was the final declaration of the meeting of the G20 finance ministers in June 2012, which emphasized "the need to prevent base erosion and profit shifting." In February 2013, the OECD responded to the G20's concerns by issuing a short note, "Addressing Base Erosion and Profit Shifting," which identified several areas for action and set deadlines for the implementation of responses.

On July 19, 2013, the OECD released a detailed *Action Plan on BEPS* (OECD Action Plan). This Action Plan set out an ambitious agenda with tight deadlines, consisting of fifteen action items, including:

(1) Developing rules to allow countries to impose direct and indirect taxation on electronic commerce (the digital economy) (electronic commerce is dealt with in section 9.5).

(2) Developing treaty provisions and recommendations for domestic rules to deal with hybrid mismatch arrangements involving the use of hybrid entities and hybrid financial instruments (the BEPS proposals with respect to hybrid entities and hybrid financial instruments are discussed in Chapter 7, section 7.7).

（3）提出加强受控外国企业规则的建议（第 7 章 7.3 节讨论了有关受控外国企业规则的 BEPS 建议）。

（4）针对通过利息和其他财务费用侵蚀税基问题提出应对建议（第 7 章 7.2.3 节讨论了有关利息扣除的 BEPS 建议）。

（5）制定协定反滥用条款，并提出国内法反滥用政策建议（第 8 章 8.8.2.3 节讨论了应对协定滥用，包括防范择协避税在内的 BEPS 建议）。

（6）修改 OECD 协定范本的常设机构定义，以防止利用佣金代理人和其他安排规避构成常设机构（第 8 章 8.7.3.2 节讨论了有关常设机构定义的 BEPS 建议）。

（7）修改转让定价规则，确保转让定价不会被用于税基侵蚀和利润转移目的（第 6 章讨论了有关转让定价的 BEPS 建议），并完善转让定价文档要求（参见第 6 章 6.8 节）。

（8）制定要求披露激进税收筹划安排的措施。

（9）改进包括仲裁在内的争议解决协定程序（第 8 章 8.8.3 节讨论了税收争议解决问题，下文第 9.4 节讨论了仲裁问题）。

（10）制定实施 BEPS 应对措施及修订双边协定的多边协定（第 8 章 8.8.6 节讨论了多边协定问题）。

即使考虑 OECD 远在宣布实施 BEPS 项目之前已就部分问题，比如混合错配安排和转让定价等开展了一些工作，其 BEPS 行动计划也显然是雄心勃勃的。涉及全部 15 项行动计划的 BEPS 最终报告于 2015 年底完成，一些后续工作延续开展至今。但是，对于多项 BEPS 建议，早至 2017 年初就已经开始实施。为了推动此项工作开展，OECD 和 G20 建立了包容性框架，所有承诺实施 BEPS 有关防范协定滥用和完善相互协商程序最低标准的国家都可以平等参与。截至 2022 年末，包容性框架已有超过 140 个成员，并针对各成员实施 BEPS 措施的进展建立了同行监测和审议的有效机制。

(3) Strengthening CFC rules (the BEPS proposals with respect to CFC rules are discussed in Chapter 7, section 7.3).

(4) Developing recommendations to deal with base erosion through interest and other financing expenses (the BEPS proposals with respect to interest deductions are discussed in Chapter 7, section 7.2.3).

(5) Developing treaty anti-abuse provisions and recommendations for the adoption of domestic anti-abuse rules (the BEPS proposals with respect to treaty abuse, including treaty shopping, are discussed in Chapter 8, section 8.8.2.3).

(6) Revising the definition of PE in the OECD Model Treaty to prevent the use of commissionaire and other arrangements to avoid PE status (the BEPS proposals with respect to the definition of a PE are discussed in Chapter 8, section 8.7.3.2).

(7) Revising transfer pricing rules to ensure that transfer pricing cannot be used for base erosion and profit-shifting purposes (the BEPS proposals with respect to transfer pricing are discussed in Chapter 6) and improving transfer pricing documentation (*see* Chapter 6, section 6.8).

(8) Developing measures for the disclosure of aggressive tax-planning arrangements.

(9) Improving the treaty process for the resolution of disputes, including arbitration (the resolution of tax disputes is discussed in Chapter 8, section 8.8.3, and arbitration is discussed below in section 9.4).

(10) Developing a multilateral treaty to implement BEPS countermeasures and amend bilateral treaties (the multilateral treaty is discussed in Chapter 8, section 8.8.6).

The OECD's BEPS Action Plan was obviously ambitious, even taking into account the fact that the OECD had been working on some of the issues, such as hybrid mismatch arrangements and transfer pricing, long before the announcement of the BEPS project. The BEPS final reports on all fifteen action items were completed before the end of 2015, although some follow-up work continued and still continues today. However, for many of the BEPS recommendations, an implementation phase began in early 2017. To carry out this work, the OECD and the G20 created the Inclusive Framework, in which all countries could participate on an equal basis as long as they committed to the minimum standards of the BEPS Project dealing with treaty abuse and improvements to the MAP. As of late 2022, the Inclusive Framework had over 140 members and had established an effective system of monitoring and peer reviews of the progress of member countries in implementing the BEPS measures.

现阶段对 BEPS 项目进行一些总体性评论，似乎并无不妥。第一，该项目获得了 G20 成员，包括巴西、俄罗斯、印度、中国和南非（即金砖国家），以及发展中国家的广泛支持。联合国、世界银行和国际货币基金组织也予以支持。一个关键的问题是，当该项目要求各国就具体问题采取协调行动时，对于 BEPS 项目原则上的广泛支持会否持续下去。

第二，鉴于跨国企业在全球范围内开展经营活动和实施税收筹划，OECD 成员国、金砖国家以及发展中国家采取协调一致的行动，是打击跨国企业激进税收筹划的任何行动取得成功的关键。各国采取的单边行动，即使是美国这样的经济体量最大的国家，也很有可能徒劳无功，或者给国内经济带来严重损害。

第三，BEPS 问题（“税基侵蚀”和“利润转移”这两个术语恰巧是同义词，并非描述不同问题）并不是新问题。数十年来，国际税收筹划一直是企业经营实践的标准组成部分，政府不可避免地制定各类应对规则来保护自身税基。因此，将目前的情况视为跨国企业与各国税务机关之间对立关系的最新体现，是非常重要的。然而，税务机关过去主要通过国内法中的单边反避税措施或双边税收协定来应对国际避税。与之相反的是，BEPS 项目要求采取协调一致的多边行动来应对国际避税。

如前所述，对国际避税问题的有效回应，要求各国税务机关采取协调一致的行动。很明显，有些 BEPS 行动计划已经非常成功：例如，有关修改 OECD 协定范本以应对协定滥用的举措，以及通过制定多边协定实施这些修订后的内容；国别报告；限制利息扣除的收益剥离规则；对相互协商程序的改进。然而，在数字经济和受控外国企业规则等行动方面则进展有限。BEPS 项目最重要的成就，可能是通过发达国家和发展中国家共同参与包容性框架，提高在多边基础上解决国际税收问题的制度性安排的有效性。

最后，BEPS 项目提供了机遇，使国际社会可以在重新设计已然有些难以胜任的国际税制方面，尝试着迈出最初的几步。因此，BEPS 项目应当被视为仅仅

At this stage, several general comments about the BEPS project seem appropriate. First, the project has gained widespread support from the G20, which includes Brazil, Russia, India, China, and South Africa (BRICS), as well as from developing countries. The work is supported by the UN, the World Bank, and the IMF. One crucial question is whether the widespread support for the BEPS project in principle will continue when the project calls for coordinated action by countries on specific issues.

Second, coordinated action by the member countries of the OECD, the BRICS, and developing countries is essential for the success of any action to combat aggressive tax planning by multinational enterprises since multinationals operate and engage in tax planning on a worldwide basis. Unilateral action by countries, even countries with the largest economies, such as the U.S., is likely either to prove ineffective or to inflict serious damage on the domestic economy.

Third, the problems of BEPS—(incidentally, the terms "base erosion" and "profit shifting" are synonyms; they do not describe different problems)—are not new. International tax planning has been a standard part of business practice for decades, and inevitably, governments have responded with various types of rules to protect their tax bases. Therefore, it is important to see the current situation as just the most recent manifestation of the tension between multinational corporations and national tax authorities. In the past, however, tax authorities responded to international tax avoidance primarily with unilateral anti-avoidance measures in their domestic law or bilateral tax treaties. In contrast, the BEPS Project called for a coordinated multilateral response to international tax avoidance.

As noted above, any effective response to the problem of international tax avoidance requires coordinated action by national tax authorities. It is already obvious that some of the BEPS action items have been very successful: for example, the recommendations for changes to the OECD Model Treaty dealing with treaty abuse and the multilateral treaty to implement those changes, for country-by-country reporting, for earnings-stripping rules to limit interest deductions, and for improvements to the MAP. However, little progress has been made on other action items, such as the digital economy and CFC rules. Perhaps the most important achievement of the BEPS project has been to improve the effectiveness of the institutional arrangements for dealing with international tax issues on a multilateral basis through the participation of both developed and developing countries in the Inclusive Framework.

Finally, the BEPS project represented an opportunity to take some tentative first steps in redesigning an international tax regime that had become a bit tired. Thus, the BEPS project should be viewed as simply one episode in a long-term effort to make the international tax

是一项长期努力中的一个章节，这一长期努力将使国际税收体系在面对跨国企业国际税收筹划时不再那么脆弱，并完善居民国（发达国家）和来源国（发展中国家）从跨境活动中取得税收收入的分配关系。

OECD 的 BEPS 项目背后的税收政策考量是非常清晰的。跨国企业实施的激进国际避税活动给各国税制带来若干有害的后果：

（1）它减少了政府的税收收入，增加了政府为确保跨国企业遵从税收规则而付出的成本。

（2）它破坏了对税收体系完整性的认知，会对整体税收遵从行为带来有害影响。

（3）它损害了各国税收体系的公平性，因为跨国企业以外的纳税人必须承担更重的税负。

（4）中小企业可能无法与跨国企业利用同样的国际税收筹划机会，因而可能被置于竞争劣势地位。

（5）最后，如果在国际层面开展激进税收筹划的机会大于国内层面，就可能会导致投资地点的扭曲。

然而，对于任何一个特定的国家而言，BEPS 税收政策分析远比前述所列后果所揭示的更为微妙和艰难。许多资本输出国的税收制度都包含一些特征，旨在提高其居民跨国企业的国际竞争力。在过去二三十年内，这些国家一直在采取措施提高其居民跨国企业的竞争地位，或者至少避免所采取的措施将其跨国企业置于竞争劣势地位。因此，许多国家似乎对 BEPS 持两面态度：一方面，他们想保护本国税基免受非居民跨国企业激进税收筹划策略的侵蚀；另一方面，他们对于防止本国居民跨国企业侵蚀他国税基（使之缴纳更多外国税款）的问题毫无兴趣。

因此，从任一具体国家的视角来看，BEPS 项目最理想的结果是其他国家采取行动，要求其跨国企业多缴纳外国税收，而对本国的居民跨国企业不采取或几乎不采取任何措施，从而使之获得竞争优势。简言之，这解释了为什么协调一致

system less vulnerable to international tax planning by multinational enterprises and to improve the allocation of tax revenues from cross-border activities between residence (developed) countries and source (developing) countries.

The tax policy considerations underlying the OECD's BEPS initiative were superficially clear. Aggressive international tax avoidance by multinational enterprises has several harmful consequences for national tax systems:

(1) It reduces government tax revenues and increases the cost to governments of ensuring compliance by multinational enterprises with the tax rules.
(2) It undermines the perceived integrity of the tax system and may have a deleterious effect on tax compliance generally.
(3) It undermines the fairness of national tax systems because taxpayers other than multinational corporations must bear a greater share of the tax burden.
(4) Small- and medium-sized enterprises may not be able to take advantage of the same international tax planning opportunities as multinational enterprises and may, therefore, be placed at a competitive disadvantage.
(5) Finally, distortions in the location of investment may result to the extent that opportunities for aggressive tax planning are greater in the international context than in the domestic context.

However, the tax policy analysis of BEPS for any particular country is much more subtle and difficult than the foregoing list of consequences may suggest. The tax systems of many capital-exporting countries contain features designed to facilitate the international competitiveness of their resident multinational corporations. Over the past two or three decades, these countries have consistently taken measures to enhance the competitive position of their resident multinational corporations, or at the least have avoided taking measures that would place their multinationals at a competitive disadvantage. Thus, many countries seem to have a two-faced attitude to BEPS. On the one hand, they want to protect their domestic tax bases from the aggressive tax planning strategies of foreign-based multinationals. On the other hand, they have no interest in preventing their own resident multinationals from eroding the tax base of other countries (i.e., by making them pay more foreign tax).

From any particular country's perspective, therefore, the ideal result from the BEPS project would be that other countries take action to require their multinational corporations to pay more foreign tax while the country does little or nothing with respect to its resident multinationals so

的行动如此重要，而又如此艰难，其中部分难处触及 OECD 成员国形形色色且不断变化着的利益。例如，资本净输入国与资本净输出国的利益就有所不同。此外，有些 OECD 成员国既要考虑公共利益（税收收入、投资、就业），也要顾及帮助跨国企业实施国际税收筹划的那些私营部门的利益（专业服务公司和金融机构），因此更希望维持现状。

9.2.4 应对数字经济的“双支柱”方案

随着 BEPS 项目转入实施阶段，OECD/G20 包容性框架继续寻求应对跨境数字商品和服务征税问题，以及突出的 BEPS 问题的解决方案。此项工作促成了在 2019 年初，各方就“双支柱”方案达成初步共识。其中，支柱一针对全球规模最大、盈利能力最强的跨国数字企业的剩余利润，提出了新的联结度和利润分配规则；支柱二提出对大型跨国企业征收全球最低税（大致上以美国的 GILTI 税制为基础）。关于支柱一和支柱二的建议将在下文 9.5.5.2 和 9.5.5.3 节讨论。

9.3 管理费、技术服务费和咨询费

9.3.1 引言

正如本书第 2 章和第 5 章所讨论的，大部分国家对非居民来源于国内的所得征税。一些国家对非居民所有来源于国内的所得征税；另一些国家仅当非居民达到最低门槛，比如构成常设机构或达到最低停留时间时，才对其来源于国内的营业所得征税。根据 OECD 和联合国税收协定范本相关条款，来源国通常有权对另一国居民所经营企业的利润征税，前提是该企业通过位于来源国的常设机构开展经营，并且征税的范围仅限于归属于该常设机构的利润。

执行国内法和税收协定这些条款的结果是，纳税人，特别是跨国企业得以安排其经营架构，通过支付技术服务费、管理费和咨询费等款项，侵蚀来源国

that they gain a competitive advantage. In simple terms, this explains why coordinated action is so important—and so difficult. Part of the difficulty relates to the widely varying interests of OECD member countries. For example, net capital-importing countries have different interests from net capital- exporting countries. In addition, some OECD members have significant interests both from a public perspective (tax revenue, investment, employment) and a private-sector perspective (professional firms and financial institutions) in facilitating international tax planning by multinational enterprises and therefore have an interest in maintaining the status quo.

9.2.4 The Two-Pillar Proposals to Deal with the Digital Economy

When the BEPS Project moved into its implementation phase, the OECD/G20 Inclusive Framework continued working on a solution for taxing cross-border digital goods and services and outstanding BEPS issues. This work led to a preliminary agreement early in 2019 to adopt a two-pillar approach, consisting of Pillar One, proposals for new nexus and profit-allocation rules for the residual profits of the world's largest and most profitable digital multinationals, and Pillar Two, proposals for a global minimum tax (based broadly on the U.S. GILTI regime) on large multinationals. The proposals for Pillar One and Pillar Two are discussed in sections 9.5.5.2 and 9.5.5.3 below.

9.3 FEES FOR MANAGEMENT, TECHNICAL, AND CONSULTING SERVICES

9.3.1 Introduction

As discussed in Chapters 2 and 5, most countries tax nonresidents on their domestic source income. Some countries tax nonresidents on all their domestic source income; other countries tax nonresidents on their domestic source business income only if a minimum threshold, such as a PE or a minimum period of physical presence, is met. Under the provisions of the OECD and UN Model Treaties, a source country is generally entitled to tax the profits of a business carried on by a resident of another country only if the business is carried on through a PE located in the source country and only to the extent that the profits are attributable to the PE.

As a result of these provisions of domestic law and tax treaties, taxpayers, especially multinational enterprises, can structure their business operations to erode the tax bases of source countries through payments for technical, management, and consulting services, as shown in

的税基，如下文的示例所示。A 国居民企业 ACo 是从事酒店行业的跨国企业集团的母公司。该集团在 B 国有一家酒店，由 ACo 的全资子公司 BCo 持有。BCo 是高税国 B 国的居民，B 国对该酒店经营的利润征税。在计算利润时，BCo 可以扣除因取得所得而发生的费用。BCo 发生的费用包括支付给 CCo 的管理费和咨询费，CCo 是 ACo 的另外一家全资子公司，是低税国 C 国的税收居民。

这一架构可能为跨国企业带来显著的节税效果，主要是因为管理费和咨询费可以从 B 国税基中扣除，并在 C 国以较低税率征税。BCo 所主张的费用扣除当然要遵循 B 国的转让定价规则，因为这些费用是支付给关联方的。然而，节税的金额并不取决于超过独立交易金额的付款，因为即使是独立交易方支付的费用也可以获得上述节税效果。此外，CCo 不会因为这些费用被 B 国征税，其原因可能是 B 国国内法不对 CCo 收取的费用征税，或者是根据 B 国和 C 国的税收协定，仅当 C 国居民通过位于 B 国的常设机构开展经营活动时，B 国才有权对该 C 国居民的营业利润征税。CCo 会倍加小心，避免在 B 国构成常设机构。

一些发展中国家在国内法中制定了特殊规则，对非居民取得的管理费、技术服务费和咨询费进行征税。根据这些规则，可对居民因管理、技术和咨询等服务，向非居民支付的款项总额征收预提税，无论这些服务是否在该国境内提供。如果非居民服务提供商在来源国境内提供服务，则所得显然是产生于来源国，因为根据通常的理解，服务的所得来源地是服务提供地。然而，有些国家将服务所得视为来源于服务使用地或消费地所在的国家。

与这些规则相关的一个最基本的难点是适用这些规则的服务类型通常无法准确定义。一些国家区分技术援助和技术服务的方法是：技术援助通常涉及转让专有技术或专业技术（类似于转让知识产权的使用权）；而技术服务主要涉及运用专业知识或技能。正如下文所讨论的，税收协定条款中的技术服务定义也同样问题重重。

即使发展中国家国内法相关条款对非居民取得的服务所得征税，可适用的税

the following example. ACo, a corporation resident in Country A, is the parent corporation of a multinational group of companies involved in the hotel business. The group has a hotel in Country B that is owned by BCo, a wholly owned subsidiary of ACo. BCo is resident in Country B, a high-tax country, and is taxable by Country B on its profits from the operation of the hotel. In computing its profits, BCo is entitled to deduct expenses incurred to earn its income. The expenses incurred by BCo include management fees and consulting fees paid to CCo, another wholly owned subsidiary of ACo that is resident in Country C, a low-tax country.

This structure may result in substantial tax savings for the multinational enter- prise, essentially because the management and consulting fees are deductible against Country B's tax base and are taxable at a low rate in Country C. The deductions for the fees claimed by BCo are, of course, subject to Country B's transfer pricing rules since the fees are paid to a related party. However, the tax savings are not dependent on the payment of amounts that exceed the arm's-length amount; they are available even if the fees are what arm's-length parties would have paid. Also, CCo would not be taxable by Country B on the fees, either because Country B does not impose tax on CCo's fees under its domestic law or because, under the tax treaty between Country B and Country C, Country B is entitled to tax business profits derived by a resident of Country C only if the resident carries on business through a PE in Country B. CCo will be careful to avoid creating a PE in Country B.

Some developing countries have special rules in their domestic law for taxing nonresidents on fees for management, technical and consulting services derived by nonresidents. Under these rules, withholding tax is imposed on the gross amount of payments by residents to nonresidents for management, technical, and consulting services whether or not the services are performed in the country. If the nonresident service provider performs services in the source country, the income is clearly derived from the source country, in accordance with the conventional notion that the source of income from services is where the services are performed. However, some countries consider income from services to be derived in the country in which the services are used or consumed.

One basic difficulty with these rules is that the types of services to which the rules apply are often not defined precisely. Some countries distinguish between technical assistance, which generally involves a transfer of know-how or technical expertise (analogous to the transfer of the right to use intellectual property), and technical services, which involve the application of specialized knowledge or skill. The definition of technical services is similarly problematic under the provisions of tax treaties, as discussed below.

Even where the provisions of a developing country's domestic law impose tax on income

收协定条款也可以限制这一征税行为，下一节将对此进行讨论。

9.3.2 税收协定对管理、技术和咨询服务所得征税的规定

本节简要归纳 OECD 和联合国协定范本中，适用于管理、技术和咨询服务（为方便起见，以下简称“技术服务”）的相关条款，并概述了一些发展中国家税收协定中处理这类服务所得的相关规定。

OECD 协定范本并不包含针对缔约国一方居民向位于另一方的消费者提供技术服务取得所得的特定条款。总体而言，OECD 协定范本第 7 条涵盖商业服务所得。根据第 7 条第 1 款，仅当非居民在一国通过常设机构从事营业活动时，该国才有权对其营业利润征税。第 5 条将常设机构定义为通常必须持续至少 6 个月的固定营业场所。根据联合国协定范本第 5 条第 3 款（b) 项，如果非居民在来源国提供服务，且在任何 12 个月期间中超过 183 天，则视同其在来源国构成常设机构。在 2017 年联合国协定范本更新之前，第 5 条第 3 款（b) 项仅适用于为相同或相关联的项目提供的服务。这一条件防止了非居民在一国为不同项目提供服务的时间被累计计算，以测试是否超过 183 天，但 2017 年该条件被删除。一些非居民服务提供商通过限制在来源国停留的时间、在任一地点提供服务不超过 6 个月、将较大的合同拆分为几个小合同或者让关联方来执行项目，可以很容易地规避联合国协定范本的固定基地规则和第 5 条第 3 款（b) 项。

根据联合国协定范本第 14 条（2000 年 OECD 协定范本删除了第 14 条），非居民个人在来源国从事专业性服务或其他独立服务取得的所得可以由另一国征税，前提是该所得归属位于非居民在该国定期使用的固定基地，或者非居民在任何 12 个月中在来源国停留超过 183 天。来源国根据第 7 条或第 14 条征税时应按净所得计征税款已为人们所普遍接受。技术服务与涉及专业技术的专业性、经营性服务之间的区别并不清晰。例如，工程服务通常被认为是技术服务，然而工程师的独立活动被包含在联合国协定范本第 14 条“专业性服务”中。因此，工程

from services earned by a nonresident, the provisions of an applicable tax treaty may limit that tax, as discussed in the next section.

9.3.2 The Taxation of Income from Management, Technical, and Consulting Services under Tax Treaties

This section provides a brief summary of the provisions of the OECD and UN Model Treaties that are potentially applicable to income from management, technical, and consulting services (referred to here for convenience simply as "technical services") and an overview of the provisions dealing with income from such services that some developing countries have included in their tax treaties.

The OECD Model Treaty does not contain any specific provisions dealing with income from technical services provided by a resident of one state to customers in the other contracting state. In general, income from business services is covered by Article 7 of the OECD Model Treaty. Under Article 7(1), a country is entitled to tax a nonresident's business profits only if the nonresident carries on business in the country through a PE. A PE is defined in Article 5 to be a fixed place of business that must generally last for a minimum period of six months. Under Article 5(3)(b) of the UN Model Treaty, a nonresident is deemed to have a PE in a source country if the nonresident furnishes services in the source country for more than 183 days in any twelve-month period. Before the 2017 update of the UN Model Treaty, Article 5(3)(b) was limited to services provided in respect of the same or a connected project. This condition, which prevented services provided by a nonresident for different projects in a country from being aggregated for purposes of the 183-day test, was eliminated in 2017. Both the fixed-place-of-business rule and the rule in Article 5(3)(b) of the UN Model Treaty can easily be avoided by some nonresident service providers by limiting the time spent in the source country, by not working at any one place for more than six months, by splitting large contracts into several smaller ones, or by having projects carried out by related parties.

Under Article 14 of the UN Model Treaty (Article 14 was deleted from the OECD Model Treaty in 2000), income derived by a nonresident individual from professional or other independent services performed in the source country is taxable by the other state only if the income is attributable to a fixed base in that country that is regularly available to the nonresident, or if the nonresident is present in the source country for 183 days or more in any twelve-month period. It is generally accepted that the source country must tax income under Article 7 or 14 on a net basis. The distinction between technical services and professional and business services

服务所得，或者至少是那些由个人提供服务取得的所得，仅当工程师在来源国有固定基地或者在任何 12 个月中停留超过 183 天时，来源国方可对其征税。

OECD 和联合国协定范本第 12 条特许权使用费条款并不适用于管理、技术和咨询服务的费用，因为第 12 条第 3 款中特许权使用费的定义仅限于就使用或有权使用知识产权、设备或信息而支付的款项。如果技术服务是由一人为另一人提供的，就不存在转让财产或信息的情形。

通过针对技术服务进行款项支付，对来源国税基造成侵蚀，并且来源国无法对这类付款征税，这一情况导致一些国家在税收协定中增加了特定条款，允许其对针对技术服务所支付的款项按总额征税。荷兰财税文献局在 2011 年进行的一项调查发现，在 1997—2011 年缔结的 1600 多个税收协定中，134 个协定包含涉及管理、技术和咨询服务相关费用的单独条款。根据这些特殊条款，技术服务所得实际上是按照特许权使用费来处理的。一些国家，比如印度，扩大了第 12 条特许权使用费条款的适用范围，使其包括针对辅助或从属于使用知识产权的服务，或提供专业知识、技能、专有技术或工艺的服务，或者涉及开发技术规划或设计的服务，所支付的款项。这一方法并不尽如人意，因为它混淆了特许权使用费与服务费的区别，前者涉及转让知识产权的使用权，而后者并不涉及服务提供商将专有技术或财产转让给客户。

通常而言，税收协定中处理技术服务费的特殊条款将来源国的税收征收局限于针对在来源国“产生”的这类服务的费用，这通常意味着服务必须在来源国提供。而且，这些条款通常未对其使用的“管理、技术或咨询服务”等表述进行定义。

9.3.3 联合国协定范本第 12A 条（技术服务费）

经过数年努力，2017 年，联合国专家委员会在联合国协定范本中增加了新的第 12A 条，涉及针对管理、技术和咨询服务的费用。根据 12A 条，缔约国一

that involve technical expertise is unclear. For example, engineering services would often be considered to be technical services; however, the independent activities of engineers are included in the definition of "professional services" for purposes of Article 14 of the UN Model Treaty. Thus, income from engineering services, or at least those performed by individuals, would be taxable by a source country only if the engineer had a fixed base in that country or stayed in that country for 183 days or more in any twelve-month period.

Article 12 of both the OECD and UN Model Treaties dealing with royalties does not apply to fees for management, technical, or consulting services because the definition of royalties in Article 12(3) is limited to payments for the use of, or the right to use, intellectual property, equipment, or information. Where technical services are performed by one person for another person, there is no transfer of property or information.

The erosion of a source country's tax base by payments for technical services, and the inability of the source country to tax such payments, has caused some countries to add specific provisions to their tax treaties to allow them to tax payments for technical services on a gross basis. A 2011 survey by the International Bureau for Fiscal Documentation found that 134 of the 1,600 tax treaties concluded between 1997 and 2011 contained a separate article dealing with fees for management, technical, and consulting services. Under these special articles, income from technical services is, in effect, treated like royalties. Some countries, such as India, extend Article 12 dealing with royalties to include payments for services that are ancillary or subsidiary to the application of intellectual property, or that make available technical knowledge, skill, know-how, or processes, or that involve the development of a technical plan or design. This approach is unsatisfactory because it muddles the distinction between royalties for the transfer of the right to use intellectual property and fees for services, which do not involve any transfer of know-how or property by a service provider to a client.

Typically, the special articles in tax treaties dealing with fees for technical services limit source country tax to fees for such services "arising" in the source country, which usually means that the services must be performed in the source country. Moreover, the expression typically used in these provisions—"managerial, technical, or consultancy services"—is not usually defined.

9.3.3 Article 12A (Fees for Technical Services) of the UN Model Treaty

In 2017, after several years of work, the UN Committee of Experts added a new article—Article 12A—to the UN Model Treaty to deal with fees for management,

方居民取得的技术服务费如果产生于缔约国另一方，则应由该另一方通过扣缴税款的方式对其总额征税。该服务是否在缔约国一方提供并不重要，只要付款人是该国居民，或者是在该国拥有常设机构的非居民，并且在计算归属于常设机构利润时可以扣除这些费用（第 12A 条第 5 款）。这与 OECD 协定范本处理这类费用的现行规定，以及 2017 年以前联合国协定范本（仅当服务在来源国通过常设机构或固定基地提供，并按照所得净额征税）大相径庭。

第 12A 条第 3 款对技术服务费进行了定义，是指为咨询、技术和管理服务而支付的款项，不包含支付给员工的款项、由教育机构支付或者因在教育机构任教所支付的款项，以及供个人自用而支付的款项。联合国关于第 12A 条的注释提供了如下解释，“咨询”“技术”以及“管理”等术语具有通常含义，而非适用协定的国家的国内法含义。该注释也明确，总体而言，技术服务是需要服务提供商在提供服务的过程中，运用专业知识、技能或技术来提供的服务。尽管服务提供商可以运用专业知识、技能或技术来为客户提供常规服务，但那些常规服务并非技术服务，因为专业知识、技能和技术并不是直接提供给客户的。

如果服务提供商因通过设在缔约国另一方的常设机构或固定基地技术服务而收取费用，并且该费用与常设机构具有实际联系，那么第 12A 条就不适用，而应适用第 7 条或第 14 条，并且应按照净额对归属于该常设机构或固定基地的利润征税（第 12A 条第 4 款）。这一回退规则与涉及股息、利息和特许权使用费的规则相似。因此，在一个协定国提供广泛的技术服务并由此产生大量费用的服务提供商可以考虑在该国设立常设机构或固定基地，从而使服务费得以按照净额征税。

根据第 12A 条第 5 款，如果技术服务费是由缔约国一方居民支付的，或者由非居民位于该国的常设机构或固定基地负担的，则技术服务费应被视为发生在该缔约国一方。在这些情况下，支付者通常可以从该缔约国一方的税基中扣除该技术服务费。然而，如前所述，这并不需要服务系在该国提供。如果技术服务费的支付者是缔约国一方居民但在缔约国另一方设有常设机构或固定基地，并且该

technical, and consulting services. Under Article 12A, fees for technical services derived by a resident of one contracting state are taxable by the other contracting state on a gross basis by way of withholding if the fees arise in the other state. It does not matter whether the services are performed in a contracting state as long as the payer is a resident of that state or is a nonresident with a PE in that state and the fees are deductible in computing the profits attributable to the PE (Article 12A(5)). This contrasts sharply with the treatment of such fees under the existing provisions of both the OECD Model Treaty and the pre-2017 UN Model Treaty (taxation on a net basis only if the services are performed in the source country through a PE or fixed base).

Fees for technical services are defined in Article 12A(3) to mean payments for consultancy, technical, and management services other than payments to employees, payments for teaching in or by educational institutions, and payments for the personal use of an individual. The UN Commentary on Article 12A explains that the terms "consulting," "technical," and "management" are intended to have their ordinary meaning and not their meaning under the domestic law of the country applying the treaty. The Commentary also clarifies that, in general, technical services are services that require the service provider to exercise specialized knowledge, skill, or expertise in providing the services. Although service providers may apply specialized knowledge, skill, or expertise in developing routine services that are provided to customers, those routine services are not technical services because the specialized knowledge, skill, or expertise is not provided directly to the client.

Where a service provider derives fees for technical services through a PE or fixed base in the other contracting state and the fees are effectively connected to the PE, Article 12A does not apply; instead, Article 7 or 14 applies, and the profits attributable to the PE or fixed base are taxable on a net basis (Article 12A(4)). This throwback rule is similar to the rules with respect to dividends, interest and royalties. Therefore, service providers that provide extensive technical services in a treaty country and incur substantial expenses in providing those services may consider establishing a PE or fixed base in that country so that the fees are taxable on a net basis.

Under Article 12A(5), fees for technical services are deemed to arise in a contracting state if the fees are paid by a resident of that state or borne by a PE or fixed base that a nonresident has in that state. In these circumstances, the fees will generally be deductible by the payer against the tax base of that state. However, as noted above, it is not necessary for the services to be performed in that state. Where the payer of technical fees is a resident of a state but has a PE or fixed base in the other contracting state, the technical fees are deemed not to arise in the first

费用由常设机构或固定基地负担，可以不认为技术服务费发生在首先提及的国家，因此，支付者为其居民的国家不能根据第 12A 条对技术服务费征税（第 12A 条第 6 款）。这一对来源规则（技术服务费发生在支付者为其居民或者设有常设机构或固定基地的国家）的例外处理是合理的，因为技术服务费与支付者位于缔约国另一方的常设机构或固定基地具有明确的经济联系。

第 12A 条带来了争议并遭到若干发达国家的强烈反对，这完全在意料之中。尽管该条款已被列入发展中国家之间的若干协定中，但在发展中国家与发达国家之间缔结的协定中，包含该条款的寥寥无几。

9.4 仲裁

正如第 8 章 8.8.3 节所讨论的那样，税收协定通常都包含相互协商程序条款，用以解决缔约国在解释和执行税收协定方面发生的争议。根据 OECD 协定范本和联合国协定范本第 25 条第 2 款，两国主管当局应努力解决纳税人提交的争议，但并不强制要求其对此承担义务。因此，在某些情况下，主管当局可能无法达成一致，导致纳税人可能遭受双重征税且无法得到救济。此外，对主管当局解决争议的时间并没有限制，因而相互协商案件往往迁延数年，无法结案。

随着国际贸易和投资的日益复杂、税收协定网络的逐步扩大以及各国执行转让定价规定力度的不断加大，纳税人与税务机关之间在消除双重征税及其他方面发生争议的情况也愈加频繁。因此，需要建立更高效、更具有确定性的税收争议解决程序，这一点变得更加显而易见。迫于跨国企业和一些具有影响力的发达国家的压力，OECD 于 2008 年将强制性仲裁条款纳入 OECD 协定范本第 25 条第 5 款。2011 年，联合国协定范本对第 25 条进行了修订，增加了可选的仲裁条款。增加仲裁条款的税收协定日益增多，特别是 OECD 成员国之间的协定。然而，有关各国仲裁实践的信息非常匮乏，充其量也就是坊间传闻。

仲裁构成了两个协定范本第 25 条相互协商程序的一部分。仲裁不能脱离相

state if the fees are borne by the PE or fixed base, and therefore the state in which the payer is resident is not entitled to tax the fees under Article 12A (Article 12A(6)). This exception to the source rule (that fees for technical services arise in the country in which the payer is resident or has a PE or fixed base) is justified because of the clear economic link between the fees and the payer's PE or fixed base in the other state.

Not surprisingly, Article 12A is controversial and has been vigorously criticized by several developed countries. Although the article has been included in several treaties between developing countries, it has been included in only a few treaties between developing countries and developed countries.

9.4 ARBITRATION

As discussed in Chapter 8, section 8.8.3, tax treaties typically contain an article providing for a MAP to resolve disputes between the contracting states with respect to the interpretation and application of the treaty. Under Article 25(2) of the OECD and UN Model Treaties, the competent authorities of the two states are required to endeavor to resolve disputes submitted by a taxpayer; however, they are not obliged to do so. Therefore, in some cases, the competent authorities may not be able to reach an agreement, with result that a taxpayer may be subject to unrelieved double taxation. Moreover, there are no time limits for the resolution of disputes by competent authorities, and mutual agreement cases have been known to drag on for many years.

Disputes between taxpayers and tax authorities concerning relief from double taxation and other issues have arisen more frequently as international trade and investment have become more sophisticated, tax treaties have proliferated, and countries have become more aggressive in enforcing their transfer pricing rules. Consequently, the need for a more efficient and certain process for resolving tax disputes became obvious. Pressure from multinationals and a few influential developed countries led the OECD to include a mandatory arbitration provision in Article 25(5) of the OECD Model Treaty in 2008; Article 25 of the UN Model was amended in 2011 to add an optional arbitration provision. Arbitration provisions have been added to an increasing number of tax treaties, especially those between OECD member countries; however, information about the actual experience of countries with arbitration is scarce and, at best anecdotal.

Arbitration forms part of the MAP provided in Article 25 of both Model Treaties. Arbitration is not available independently of a MAP, and it is not available if the competent

互协商程序而实施，而且如果缔约国双方主管当局一致认为征税行为符合协定规定，则无法启动仲裁；仲裁仅适用于双方主管当局不能就一个或多个问题达成一致意见的情形。仲裁并不适用于整个相互协商程序案件，因为解决整个案件是相互协商程序应履行的功能。实际上，仲裁被用于解决相互协商程序中主管当局无法达成一致的某些问题。由于仲裁是相互协商程序的一个组成部分，它也应遵从相互协商程序的所有限制性规定。

OECD 协定范本第 25 条第 5 款规定，如果主管当局无法在两年内结案，纳税人可以根据第 25 条第 1 款，要求将相互协商程序案件中未能解决的问题提交仲裁解决。然而，如果上述未解决问题已由国内法院或行政法庭作出裁决，则不得提请仲裁。仲裁员的裁决对主管当局具有约束力（除非纳税人拒绝接受该裁决），而且不考虑国内法的任何时间限制，必须加以执行。双方主管当局被授权通过相互协商解决仲裁过程中的细节问题。关于仲裁的相互协商模板可参见 OECD 协定范本注释第 25 条的附录。

联合国协定范本第 25 条包含相互协商程序的两个可选版本，仅其中一个版本对仲裁作出了相关规定。根据第 25 条第 5 款（选项 B），对第 25 条第 1 款相互协商程序案件在 3 年内未解决的问题，仅当其中一方主管当局（不是 OECD 协定范本中规定的纳税人）提出申请时，可以提交仲裁。纳税人有获知该申请的权利。

联合国协定范本和 OECD 协定范本在仲裁方面的主要区别如下：

—— 在联合国协定范本中，仲裁是可选的；但在 OECD 协定范本中，仲裁是强制的；

—— 在联合国协定范本中，经主管当局提出申请方可启动仲裁；而在 OECD 协定范本中，可由纳税人提出申请；

—— 在联合国协定范本中，只有主管当局在 3 年内无法解决的问题可提交仲裁，而 OECD 协定范本的时间要求为两年；以及

authorities of the contracting states agree that taxation has been imposed in accordance with the treaty; it is available only where the competent authorities have not been able to reach an agreement on one or more issues. Arbitration is not available for an entire MAP case since the resolution of a case as a whole is the function of the MAP. In effect, arbitration is used to resolve certain issues within the MAP on which the competent authorities are unable to agree. Because arbitration is a part of a MAP, it is subject to any and all limitations on the MAP.

Article 25(5) of the OECD Model Treaty provides that a taxpayer can request that any unresolved issues in a case submitted for a MAP under Article 25(1) be resolved by arbitration if the competent authorities have not been able to resolve the case within two years. However, arbitration is not available if the unresolved issues have already been decided by a domestic court or administrative tribunal. The decision of the arbitrators is binding on the competent authorities (unless it is rejected by the taxpayer) and must be implemented irrespective of any time limits in domestic law. The competent authorities are authorized to settle the details of the arbitration process by way of a mutual agreement. A sample mutual agreement on arbitration is included in an annex to the OECD Commentary on Article 25.

Article 25 of the UN Model Treaty contains two alternative versions of the MAP, only one of which provides for arbitration. Under paragraph 5 of Article 25 (Alternative B), unresolved issues in a MAP case under Article 25(1) that have not been resolved within three years can be submitted for arbitration, but only at the request of one of the competent authorities (not the taxpayer, as provided in the OECD Model Treaty). The taxpayer is entitled to be notified of the request.

The major differences between arbitration under the UN and OECD Model Treaties are as follows:

- arbitration is an alternative under the UN Model Treaty but mandatory under the OECD Model Treaty;
- arbitration under the UN Model Treaty is available at the request of the competent authorities rather than at the request of the taxpayer, as is the case under the OECD Model Treaty;
- issues can be submitted for arbitration under the UN Model Treaty only if they have not been resolved by the competent authorities within three years, rather than the two-year period under the OECD Model Treaty; and

——在联合国协定范本中，作出仲裁裁决之后，双方主管当局仍有6个月的时间对相关问题形成不同于裁决的解决方案，但根据OECD协定范本，仲裁裁决必须执行。

如前所述，除了这些差异以外，联合国协定范本与OECD协定范本的仲裁程序是相同的。但是，联合国协定范本注释还规定了一个可选的自愿仲裁流程，即双方主管当局必须逐案就案件提交仲裁的问题达成一致。

OECD认为，仲裁的目的是通过为双方主管当局无法达成一致的问题提供争议解决机制，来提高相互协商程序的有效性。但是从纳税人的角度来看，仲裁的作用在于，或者至少有一些人认为其目的在于，以对双方主管当局具有约束力的方式强行解决被提交仲裁的争议。一般来说，如果在相互协商程序中主管当局无法达成一致情形下没有具有约束力的仲裁，其结果就是无法消除双重征税。因此，通过仲裁迫使主管当局达成一致，为纳税人提供了消除双重征税的确定性。

就提交仲裁的问题而言，主管当局将解决这些问题的控制权交与独立仲裁员，而独立仲裁员未必能全面理解该问题对一国税制体系的重要意义。这实际上促使主管当局自行解决此等问题，而不是通过仲裁来解决。因此，在解决相互协商程序案件方面，仲裁给主管当局施加了原本缺失的约束。

根据OECD协定范本和联合国协定范本，仅当一人根据第25条第1款向缔约国任何一方主管当局（OECD协定范本）或此人为其居民的缔约国主管当局（联合国协定范本）提交相互协商程序案件申请时，才能启动仲裁程序。该案件必须涉及缔约国一方或双方已经导致（或将要导致）违反协定规定的征税行为，并且必须在此人收到第一次征税通知之日起的2年或3年内将案件提交主管当局。第25条第3款规定的相互协商程序案件，如若涉及协定的解释或适用问题，或者涉及协定中未规定的双重征税消除问题，则不得启动仲裁，但缔约国可以选择将仲裁扩大适用于上述问题。

尽管OECD协定范本的仲裁是由纳税人启动的，但仲裁一旦启动，即成为国

– under the UN Model Treaty, the competent authorities have six months after the arbitration decision has been made to reach a different resolution of the issues, whereas under the OECD Model Treaty, an arbitration decision is binding.

Apart from these differences, the arbitration process under the UN Model Treaty is the same as under the OECD Model Treaty, as described above. However, the Commentary on the UN Model Treaty also provides for an alternative voluntary arbitration process, under which both competent authorities must agree to submit cases to arbitration on a case-by-case basis.

According to the OECD, the purpose of arbitration is to enhance the effectiveness of the MAP by providing a dispute-resolution mechanism for issues about which the competent authorities cannot agree. However, from a taxpayer's perspective, arbitration has the effect of and, arguably at least, the purpose of, forcing the resolution of issues submitted to arbitration in a manner that is binding on the competent authorities. Typically, in a MAP without binding arbitration where the competent authorities cannot agree, the result is unrelieved double taxation. Therefore, forcing the competent authorities to agree through arbitration provides taxpayers with certainty that double taxation will be eliminated.

To the extent that issues are submitted to arbitration, the competent authorities give up control over the resolution of those issues to independent arbitrators, who may not fully appreciate the significance of the issue for a country's tax system. Rather than have the issue decided through arbitration, the competent authorities are effectively nudged toward resolving the issue themselves. Thus, arbitration imposes discipline on the competent authorities to resolve cases subject to a MAP that would otherwise be lacking.

Under both the OECD and UN Model Treaties, arbitration is available only if a person has presented a case for a MAP under Article 25(1) to the competent authority of either the contracting state (OECD Model Treaty) or the state in which the person is resident (UN Model Treaty). The case must involve actions by one or both of the contracting states that have resulted (or will result) in taxation contrary to the provisions of the treaty, and it must be presented to the competent authority within two or three years of the first notification to the person of the actions. MAP cases under Article 25(3) that involve the interpretation or application of the treaty or the elimination of double taxation not provided for in the treaty do not qualify for arbitration, although contracting states have the option of extending arbitration to those issues.

Although under the OECD Model Treaty arbitration is initiated by a taxpayer, once

与国之间由主管当局控制的程序。相反，根据联合国协定范本，仲裁程序是应一方主管当局的申请而启动的。虽然从表面上看，由主管当局一方启动的仲裁似乎与由纳税人启动的仲裁大不相同，但请求启动仲裁程序的主管当局很有可能已经事先征求过涉案纳税人的意见，而且在大部分情况下会满足纳税人将案件诉诸仲裁的愿望。

根据 OECD 协定范本和联合国协定范本的仲裁条款（以及多边公约的第 6 部分），如果缔约国任一方的国内法庭或行政法庭已经就争议的问题做出裁决，则不能启动仲裁程序。大部分国家的主管当局不能执行与国内法庭裁决相悖的仲裁结果。这一限制总体上与相互协商程序的类似限制保持了一致。

仲裁程序的启动必须符合以下情形，即当一人认为缔约国一方或双方的行为“导致了对该人违反协定规定的征税行为”，并根据第 25 条第 1 款就案件申请启动相互协商程序。因此，诸如涉及信息交换或征收协助的问题就不适用于仲裁，因为这些问题并不涉及违反协定规定的征税行为。大部分提交仲裁的问题很可能涉及协定分配管辖权的条款（第 6 条至第 21 条），特别是涉及转让定价争议的第 9 条。一些国家将仲裁限于适用协定的特定条款，如第 4 条（居民）、第 5 条（常设机构）、第 7 条（向常设机构归属利润）、第 9 条（转让定价）和第 12 条（特许权使用费）；其他国家则将仲裁限于解决事实性问题。根据美国签订的若干税收协定，如果双方主管当局同意，可拒绝将仲裁适用于某一问题。但是，在拒绝适用仲裁方面，并没有主管当局可据以执行的标准或准则。

总体而言，与相互协商程序一样，仲裁并不旨在取代国内法律救济，或者迫使纳税人在两种争议解决机制中做出选择。为了避免重复，在仲裁程序完成之前，国内救济程序通常会被暂缓。一旦仲裁和相互协商程序完成后，纳税人就可以选择接受主管当局的决定，或者拒绝主管当局的决定并转而寻求国内救济。如果纳税人拒绝接受涉及仲裁的相互协商程序结果，可能会被视为浪费时间和资源。既然仲裁是由纳税人选择启动的，纳税人就应当受到仲裁员所作裁决的约束。但是，剥夺纳税人提请国内法庭解决争议的渠道是不公平的（甚至可能是违

it begins, it is a state-to-state process controlled by the competent authorities. In contrast, under the UN Model Treaty, arbitration is initiated at the request of one of the competent authorities. Although the initiation of arbitration by one of the competent authorities seems on its face to be significantly different from taxpayer-initiated arbitration, the competent authority requesting arbitration would likely have consulted with the taxpayer involved beforehand and, in most cases, would accede to the taxpayer's wishes concerning recourse to arbitration.

Under the arbitration provisions in both the OECD and UN Model Treaties (and Part Ⅵ of the MLI), arbitration is not available for issues where a domestic court or administrative tribunal of either contracting state has already rendered a decision on those issues. In most countries, the competent authorities would not be able to implement an arbitration decision that is contrary to a domestic court decision. This limitation is consistent with the similar limitation on the MAP generally.

Arbitration is available for cases presented by a person for a MAP under Article 25(1) only where the actions of one or both of the contracting states have "resulted for the person in taxation not in accordance with the provisions of this Convention." Therefore, for example, issues involving exchange of information and assistance in collection would not qualify for arbitration because they do not involve taxation contrary to the treaty. Most issues submitted for arbitration are likely to involve the distributive provisions of a treaty (Articles 6 through 21), especially Article 9 dealing with transfer pricing disputes. Some countries limit arbitration to specified provisions of the treaty, such as Article 4 (residence), Article 5 (PEs), Article 7 (attribution of profits to PEs), Article 9 (transfer pricing), and Article 12 (royalties); others limit arbitration to questions of fact. Under several U.S. tax treaties, arbitration may be rejected for an issue if both competent authorities agree; however, there are no standards or criteria for them to apply in denying access to arbitration.

Like the MAP generally, arbitration is not intended to displace domestic law remedies or force a taxpayer to choose between the two dispute-resolution mechanisms. To avoid duplication, domestic remedies are usually suspended until the arbitration is complete. Once the arbitration and MAP have been completed, the taxpayer has the choice of accepting the decision of the competent authorities or rejecting it and pursuing domestic remedies. If a taxpayer rejects the result of a MAP involving arbitration, the process might be viewed as a waste of time and resources. Since arbitration is invoked at the option of the taxpayer, arguably, the taxpayer should be bound by the decision of the arbitrators. However, it would be unfair (and possibly a violation of human rights) to deprive taxpayers of their access to domestic

反人权的），尽管根据 OECD 的观察，纳税人为了获得国内法律救济渠道而拒绝相互协商程序结果的情况是非常罕见的。另一种处理方法是要求纳税人以放弃国内救济作为允许其启动仲裁的条件。主管当局通常会要求纳税人这么做，作为执行涉及仲裁的相互协商程序的前提。

在各国具备仲裁，特别是强制性仲裁的丰富经验并将其作为争议解决机制自如地加以运用之前，不太可能将仲裁的适用扩大到 OECD 协定范本和联合国协定范本目前规定的范围之外。事实上，各国甚至可能会将适用仲裁的问题类型限制得更窄。

税收协定所规定的仲裁详细程序通常以主管当局间签署谅解备忘录的形式加以规定，不过如下文所述，多边公约第 6 部分包含许多这类详细规定。总体而言，有两类基本的仲裁类型：一类是准司法程序。在这类仲裁里，仲裁委员会接受案件申请，听取双方辩论，然后出具理由充分的书面裁决，这一裁决并不局限于双方主管当局所提出的立场。上述裁决可能对外公布，也可能不对外公布，取决于主管当局是否想要建立具有先例价值的裁决汇编。根据所谓的棒球仲裁或最终最佳报价仲裁，仲裁委员会只能在主管当局所提供的立场之间做出选择，不需要或不允许提供裁决的书面理由。那些担心让渡主权并希望尽可能限制仲裁使用的国家会采用棒球仲裁。该方法成本低廉，裁决迅速，可以更加有效地促使主管当局采用合理立场，无须诉诸仲裁就可解决争议。

一般情况下，仲裁程序包括任命三位仲裁员组成仲裁委员会，双方主管当局各任命一人，委员会主席则由这两名仲裁员选定，通常是从主管当局此前已批准的名单里选择。仲裁员通常是前任法官、政府官员或国际认可的税务专家。仲裁委员会从主管当局，也有可能从纳税人处收到书面（有时是口头）申请材料，取决于双方主管当局商定的程序。

为了执行 BEPS 对税收协定进行的修订，多边公约对强制性仲裁做出了重大改变。根据第 6 部分（第 18 条—第 26 条），如果缔约国双方一致同意并通知 OECD，愿意将第 6 部分的条款适用于其税收协定，则这些条款将制约是否可以

courts, although, according to the OECD, it is rare for taxpayers to reject a mutual agreement in order to have recourse to domestic courts. Alternatively, the taxpayer may be required to waive access to domestic remedies as a condition for arbitration; the competent authorities will usually require the taxpayer to do so as a condition for the implementation of a MAP involving arbitration.

Until countries develop sufficient experience with arbitration, especially mandatory arbitration, to feel comfortable with its operation as a mechanism for resolving disputes, they are unlikely to expand the availability of arbitration beyond what is currently provided in the OECD and UN Model Treaties. In fact, some countries may limit the types of issues qualifying for arbitration even more narrowly.

The detailed procedures for arbitration under a tax treaty are usually set out in a memorandum of understanding between the competent authorities, although Part Ⅵ of the MLI contains many of these detailed rules, as discussed below. In general, there are two basic types of arbitration. One type is a quasi-judicial process in which the arbitration panel receives submissions, hears arguments, and provides a reasoned written decision, which is not limited to the positions put forward by the competent authorities. Decisions may or may not be published publicly, depending on whether the competent authorities want to establish a body of decisions that might have precedential value. Under so-called baseball or last-best-offer arbitration, the arbitration panel is limited to choosing between the positions taken by the competent authorities and is not required or allowed to provide written reasons for its decision. Baseball arbitration is used by countries that are concerned about compromising their sovereignty and want to limit arbitration as much as possible. It is thought to be less expensive, faster, and more effective in forcing competent authorities to adopt reasonable positions and resolve cases without the need for arbitration.

Typically, an arbitration procedure involves the appointment of a panel consisting of three arbitrators, one appointed by each competent authority, and the chair, chosen by the other two arbitrators, often from a list preapproved by the competent authorities. The arbitrators are often former judges, government officials, or internationally recognized tax experts. The panel receives written (and sometimes oral) submissions from the competent authorities, and possibly from the taxpayer, depending on the procedures agreed to by the competent authorities.

In order to implement the BEPS tax treaty changes, the MLI made some significant changes with respect to mandatory arbitration. Pursuant to Part Ⅵ (Articles 18-26) of the MLI, where the contracting states both agree and notify the OECD that they choose to have the provisions of Part Ⅵ apply to their tax treaty, those provisions will govern the availability of

把有约束力的强制性仲裁用于解决两国相互协商程序中产生的问题。多边公约第6部分规定的仲裁程序与前述OECD协定范本第25条规定的程序相似，只不过多边公约第6部分包含诸多有关仲裁的具体规则，这些规则可见于关于OECD协定范本第25条的注释之中。

多边公约第6部分的各个条款涉及仲裁的基本程序（第19条）、仲裁员的任命（第20条）、保密（第21条）、仲裁裁决作出之前案件的解决（第22条），仲裁程序的类型（棒球仲裁还是推理裁决）（第23条）、主管当局在仲裁裁决后三个月内就相关问题达成不同解决方案的可能性（第24条），以及费用（第25条）。然而，主管当局可以自行确定仲裁流程的部分要素，比如任命仲裁员和仲裁程序的类型。

9.5 数字经济：电子商务

9.5.1 引言

20世纪后期的重大技术革新之一，就是互联网的发展和广泛运用为各类个人和商业活动的开展提供了便利。互联网最初是由美国的一些科研院校在美国政府拨款资助之下开发的，原本用于促进研究人员之间的交流，并在大规模战争中充当安全的通信系统。随着互联网覆盖范围不断扩大，各种大小商户开始发掘和利用其商业潜力，导致互联网进一步扩大和发展。显而易见，商业驱动了互联网的勃兴。

在本书第二版中，这一节的讨论主要聚焦于通过互联网开展的商业活动（“电子商务”），例如在线销售和服务。“电子商务”这一用语表明，这种商业类型可与其他更加传统的商业类型加以区分。但在过去十年中，数字活动渗透到商业活动如此众多的领域，现在人们通常称之为“数字经济”。

数字经济是运用信息与通信技术，通过大量移动设备，如平板电脑、智能手

mandatory binding arbitration of issues arising under a MAP between the two states. The arbitration procedure provided under Part Ⅵ of the MLI is similar to the procedure under Article 25 of the OECD Model Treaty described above, except that Part Ⅵ of the MLI includes many detailed rules governing arbitration that are included in the Commentary on Article 25 of the OECD Model Treaty.

The articles in Part Ⅵ of the MLI deal with the basic arbitration procedure (Article 19), the appointment of arbitrators (Article 20), confidentiality (Article 21), resolution of cases before an arbitration decision is rendered (Article 22), the type of arbitration process (baseball or reasoned decision) (Article 23), the possibility of the competent authorities reaching a different resolution of the issue within three months after the arbitration decision (Article 24), and costs (Article 25). However, competent authorities have the ability to customize some aspects of the arbitration process, such as the appointment of arbitrators and the type of arbitration process.

9.5 THE DIGITAL ECONOMY: ELECTRONIC COMMERCE

9.5.1 Introduction

One of the major technological innovations of the late twentieth century was the development and widespread use of the Internet for conducting and facilitating various personal and business activities. The Internet was initially developed by some U.S. research universities operating under grants from the U.S. government to facilitate communication among researchers and to serve as a secure communication system in the event of a major war. As the Internet expanded in scope and reach, its commercial possibilities were discovered and exploited by a tremendous variety of large and small vendors, leading to further expansion and development. Commerce has clearly driven the development of the Internet.

In the second edition of this Primer, the discussion in this section focused on commercial activities conducted over the Internet ("electronic commerce"), such as online sales and services. The term "electronic commerce" suggests that such commerce can be distinguished from other, more traditional forms of commerce. In the last decade, however, digital activities have permeated so many aspects of commercial life that it is now customary to refer to the digital economy.

The digital economy is the product of information and communication technologies featuring global connectivity on a 24/7 basis through a variety of mobile devices such as tablets,

机、可穿戴设备等实现全天候、全世界联通的产物。数字经济的关键特征包括，将有形产品转化为数字化产品，通过移动设备实现全球联通，以及对客户数据的归集、分析和商业化。将有形产品转化为数字化产品的常见例子是越来越多地用电子出版物取代传统的书籍报刊。3D 打印的兴起，有望将传统制造业产品转化为无形产品，在将其授权给客户后，由客户自行制造。数字经济的联通性意味着企业可以随时随地接触客户（只要客户有可以联网的移动设备），而且可以在任何他们希望的地点配置工作人员和信息技术。为此，数字经济在人们口中往往是“无国界的”。在数字经济中，客户和用户以各种方式发挥着更加积极的作用：生产内容（如 YouTube、Wikipedia、Facebook），使用多边平台（如 Google、eBay、Amazon），以及提供大数据源。人工智能的发展及其商业影响，如无人驾驶汽车和机器人，是非常深远的。

数字经济的例子包括：

——企业从客户收集个人数据，用于为客户定制个性化的营销活动；

——利用物流追踪车辆和货物在全球的行踪；

——3D 打印和云计算；

——利用社交网络获取新闻和娱乐；

——在线提供教育资讯和培训；

——为医保患者提供远程医疗诊断和治疗；

——虚拟或加密数字货币，如比特币；以及

——共享经济，如的士服务（Uber）和食宿共享服务（Airbnb）。

除了电子商务以外，数字经济还催生了若干新的商业模式。不同类型的支付服务以及新的在线广告模式日渐发展。许多类型的商业活动在网络平台上开展；网上应用商店随着数字产品和服务的发展而繁荣；云计算兴起，通过计算机网络储存软件、数据及客户付费后可用的其他资源，提供多种服务（如将基础设施、平台、软件、内容和数据作为服务）。这些新商业模式的收入来源包括销售数字

smartphones, and wearable devices. Key features of the digital economy include the conversion of tangible goods into digital products, global connectivity through mobile devices, and the gathering, analysis, and commercialization of data collected from customers. A common example of the conversion of tangible goods into digital products is the increasing replacement of traditional books, magazines, and newspapers by e-publications. The growth in 3D printing has the potential to turn traditional manufactured goods into intangibles that are licensed to customers who perform the manufacturing themselves. The connectivity of the digital economy means that businesses can access customers wherever they are and at all times (as long as they have a mobile device and access to the Internet) and that businesses can locate their personnel and information technology wherever they want. For this reason, the digital economy is often said to be borderless. Consumers and users play a more active role in the digital economy in a variety of ways: creating content (e.g., YouTube, Wikipedia, and Facebook), using multi-sided platforms (e.g., Google, eBay, and Amazon) and providing a source of big data. The growth of artificial intelligence and its commercial implications—driverless vehicles and robots—are far-reaching.

Examples of the digital economy include:

- the collection of personal data by businesses from customers that are used to tailor marketing activities to them on a personalized basis;
- the use of logistics to track the movement of vehicles and cargo globally;
- 3D printing and cloud computing;
- the use of social networks for accessing news and entertainment;
- the delivery of online educational materials and training;
- the diagnosis and treatment of healthcare patients from remote locations;
- virtual or cryptocurrencies such as Bitcoin; and
- the sharing economy, such as taxi services (Uber) and accommodation- sharing services (Airbnb).

The digital economy has resulted in the development of several new models for doing business in addition to electronic commerce. Different types of payment services and new forms of online advertising have been developed. Many types of business activities take place on networked platforms; online app stores have flourished with the development of digital goods and services; cloud computing has arisen to provide a variety of services (infrastructure as a service, platform as a service, software as a service, content as a service, and data as a service) through a network of computers storing software, data, and other resources that are available to customers

产品和服务收入、广告费、订阅费、数据销售收入以及交易费。

9.5.2 数字经济带来的税收挑战

总体而言，数字经济为现行国际税收体系带来四大挑战：第一，如前所述，数字经济是无国界的，它使企业可以远程在全球从事商业活动。在数字经济中，企业可以与一国的客户进行交易，而无须在该国具有以资产或人员为主要形式的任何实际存在。第二，数字经济给新的收入来源如何定性带来困难。第三，尽管数据成为数字经济中重要的价值来源，但税收体系难以捕捉从数据取得的所得。第四，各国应否有权对基于本国客户和用户市场上的数字产品和服务行使征税权？下文将逐一简要讨论这些问题。

数字经济带来的税收问题并不是新问题，例如，多年来，邮购企业一直可以在无任何实际存在的国家向客户销售产品。使现有税收收入来源受到威胁的是数字经济的巨大规模。

总的来说，目前对非居民从数字经济取得的所得，按照适用于从其他类型活动取得所得的国内税收法规征税。如第 5 章所述，许多国家对非居民的营业利润，仅当其在一国的实际存在达到某些最低标准时才予以征税。同样，根据大部分税收协定，对缔约国一方居民从缔约国另一方取得的营业利润不予征税，除非其在缔约国另一方拥有常设机构，并且上述利润归属于该常设机构。常设机构被定义为固定营业场所，或者签订合同或在签订对纳税人具有约束力的合同中发挥主要作用的非独立代理人，但不包括仅从事准备性或辅助性活动的场所或代理人。尽管 2017 年 OECD 协定范本和联合国协定范本对第 5 条常设机构的定义进行了修订，使来源国可以更多地对非居民从数字产品和服务中取得的所得征税，但这些变化并不专门针对数字产品和服务，不太可能从总体上为来源国对数字经济的征税带来实质影响。

因此，对于希望对数字经济所得征税的国家来说，首要的问题往往在于，取

for a fee. The sources of revenue from these new business models include sales of digital goods and services, advertising, subscriptions, sales of data, and fees for transactions.

9.5.2 Tax Challenges Posed by the Digital Economy

In general, the digital economy presents four major challenges for the current international tax system. First, as noted above, the digital economy is borderless; it permits businesses to be conducted globally and remotely. In the digital economy, businesses can engage with customers in a country without the need for any physical presence—assets or personnel—in that country. Second, the digital economy presents many difficult issues of characterization with respect to new sources of revenue. Third, although data have become an important source of value in the digital economy, it is difficult for tax systems to capture income from such data. Fourth, should countries be entitled to exercise taxing rights with respect to digital goods and services based on the market supplied by consumers and users in their countries? Each of these issues is discussed briefly below.

The tax issues raised by the digital economy are not new—for example, for many years, mail-order businesses have been able to sell to customers in countries without any physical presence there. It is the scale of the digital economy that threatens existing sources of tax revenue.

In general, nonresidents are currently taxable on income derived from the digital economy under the same domestic tax rules applicable to income derived from other types of activities. As discussed in Chapter 5, many countries tax nonresidents on business profits only if the nonresidents meet some minimum threshold based on physical presence in a country. Similarly, under most tax treaties, a resident of one contracting state is not taxable on business profits derived from the other contracting state unless the resident has a PE in the other state and the profits are attributable to the PE. A PE is defined to be a fixed place of business or a dependent agent who concludes contracts or plays the principal role leading to the conclusion of contracts binding on the taxpayer but does not include a place or an agent that is used to carry out only preparatory or auxiliary activities. Although the 2017 changes to the definition of a PE in Article 5 of the OECD and UN Model Treaties may result in some additional taxation by source countries of income derived by nonresidents from digital goods and services, these changes were not specifically targeted at digital goods and services and are unlikely to have a substantial impact on source country taxation of the digital economy in general.

Therefore, often the first issue for countries that wish to tax income from the digital

得所得的非居民企业是否满足了来源国征税的国内最低门槛。如果是，按照所适用的税收协定，非居民企业是否在来源国构成常设机构。OECD 协定范本和联合国协定范本第 5 条注释表明，下列活动通常不构成常设机构：

——通过位于一国计算机上的网站在该国销售产品和服务以及从事其他活动。根据 OECD 协定范本和联合国协定范本第 5 条注释，常设机构要求企业在一国具有有形存在（虽然未必是人员存在），而网站是无形的。尽管一些国家（智利、希腊、印度和葡萄牙）已经表明不同意注释中的立场，但这一立场似乎代表了国际共识。虽然可以认为，一个与传统实体店铺履行相同功能的网站应当被视为常设机构，但在运用和执行这一规则时存在着实质困难。

——在一国使用服务器等计算机设备存储或提供接入电子文档的渠道，或以其他方式协助纳税人从事其商业活动。OECD 协定范本和联合国协定范本注释认为，存放计算机设备的场所可以被视为常设机构，前提是这一场所应满足第 5 条的要求。然而，在大部分情况下，这样的场所并不满足上述要求，因其并非由非居民企业自由处置，或者该服务器所从事的活动在本质上属于准备性或辅助性的。在任何情况下，一国如持有的立场是计算机服务器可以构成常设机构，很有可能会发现该国的所有服务器都被转移到了更加友好的管辖区。

——在一国通过代理人，如互联网服务提供商，接入互联网或者创建网站。根据 OECD 协定范本和联合国协定范本第 5 条，独立代理人按照营业常规开展活动，不会构成其被代理人的常设机构。因此，在大部分情况下，互联网服务提供商会被认定为独立代理人，因为它仅仅为公众提供接入互联网的服务，基本类似于为客户提供电话服务的电话公司。这一立场反映在 OECD 协定范本和联合国协定范本第 5 条注释中，似乎并不存在争议。

数字交易所得的定性对于适用税收协定条款至关重要。例如，仅当企业在来

economy is whether the nonresident enterprise deriving the income meets the minimum domestic threshold for source country taxation and, if it does, whether it has a PE in the source country for the purposes of an applicable tax treaty. The Commentary on Article 5 of both the OECD and UN Model Treaties indicates that the following activities will not generally give rise to a PE:

- *The sale of goods and services and other activities in a country through a website on a computer located in that country*. According to the OECD and UN Commentary on Article 5, a PE requires an enterprise to have some physical presence (although not necessarily a human presence) in a country, and a website is intangible. Although a few countries (Chile, Greece, India, and Portugal) have indicated that they disagree with the position taken in the Commentaries, that position seems to represent an international consensus. Although an argument can be made that a website that performs the same functions as a brick-and-mortar store should be treated as PE, there would be substantial problems in applying and enforcing such a rule.
- *The use of computer equipment, such as a server, in a country to store or provide access to electronic files or otherwise to assist a taxpayer in conducting its business operations*. The OECD and UN Commentaries recognize that the place where computer equipment is kept could be considered to be a PE if the place meets the requirements of Article 5. In most cases, however, such a place will not meet these requirements because the place is not at the disposal of the nonresident enterprise or the activities carried on by the server are preparatory or auxiliary in nature. In any event, any country that takes the position that a computer server constitutes a PE would likely find that any servers in the country would be moved to more hospitable jurisdictions.
- *The use in a country of an agent, such as an Internet Service Provider (ISP), to provide access to the Internet or to host a website*. Under Article 5 of both model treaties, an independent agent acting in the ordinary course of its business does not create a PE for its principal. In most cases, therefore, an ISP would be considered to be an independent agent because it is merely providing Internet access to the public and is roughly comparable to a telephone company providing telephone service to its customers. This position, which is reflected in the Commentary on Article 5 of both the OECD and UN Model Treaties, does not appear to be controversial.

The characterization of income derived from digital transactions is important in applying the provisions of a tax treaty. For example, income characterized as business

源国拥有常设机构，且所得可以归属于该常设机构时，来源国才可以根据 OECD 协定范本和联合国协定范本第 7 条，对定性为营业利润的所得征税。对营业利润，按照扣除取得所得的成本之后的净额征税。如前所述，OECD 协定范本和联合国协定范本注释建议，常设机构并不包括承担虚拟办公室功能的网站。因此，大部分被定性为营业利润的数字活动所得无须在来源国纳税。

被定性为特许权使用费的所得，应按照 OECD 协定范本和联合国协定范本第 12 条征税。OECD 协定范本第 12 条规定，来源国对特许权使用费所得免于征税。相反，联合国协定范本允许来源国按照缔约国双方商定的税率对特许权使用费征税。

在许多情况下，数字交易所得较为容易定性。例如，通过互联网销售有形货物的所得是经营所得，而通过互联网接入包含专有信息的数据库而取得的所得是特许权使用费，但有些类型的数字经济所得会带来所得定性的问题。OECD 协定范本和联合国协定范本第 12 条注释的立场是，通过互联网购置电脑软件所发生的对价可以被视为特许权使用费，也可以视为营业利润，取决于具体情况。如果受让方在没有软件使用许可的情况下，以会构成侵犯版权的方式获得使用该软件的权利，则该对价应被视为特许权使用费。但是，如果受让人仅获得操作相关程序所必需的有限权利（如将程序复制到使用者的电脑上），即使该交易的法律形式是许可，该对价也应被视为营业利润。然而，一些国家认为，应将针对软件的款项支付视为特许权使用费。OECD 协定范本和联合国协定范本注释也将适用于处理计算机软件的原则扩大适用于其他数字产品上。

总之，数字经济带来的税收挑战就像天气：人人都喜欢谈论，但无人对其有所作为。BEPS 第 1 项行动计划报告《应对数字经济的税收挑战》也毫不例外。该 OECD 报告对数字经济及其为国际税收体系带来的风险进行了非常到位的描述，但并没有提出以协调一致的行动应对数字交易的具体建议。其原因在于，对数字经济的挑战做出任何有意义的应对，都必须对在来源国和居民国分配税收收入的国际税收体系规则进行根本性变革。各国对于这一变革是否必要以及应当采

profits is taxable by a source country in accordance with Article 7 of the OECD and UN Model Treaties only if the enterprise has a PE in that country and the income is attributable to the PE. Business profits are taxable on a net basis after the deduction of the costs of earning the income. As discussed above, the OECD and UN Commentaries suggest that a PE does not include a website that functions as a virtual office. As a result, most income from digital activities that is characterized as business profits would not be taxable in the source country.

Income characterized as royalties is taxable under Article 12 of the OECD and UN Model Treaties. Article 12 of the OECD Model Treaty provides that royalty income is exempt from tax in the source country; in contrast, the UN Model Treaty allows a source country to tax royalties at a rate to be agreed upon by the contracting states.

In many cases, income from digital transactions is easy to characterize. For example, income derived from sales over the Internet of tangible goods would be business income, and income from providing access over the Internet to a database containing proprietary information would be royalties. Some types of income from the digital economy, however, present problems of characterization. The Commentary on Article 12 of both the OECD and UN Model Treaties takes the position that the consideration for the acquisition of computer software over the Internet may be treated as royalties or as business profits, depending on the facts. If the transferee acquires rights to use the software in a way that would constitute an infringement of copyright in the absence of a license to use the software, the consideration should be treated as royalty. However, if the transferee acquires only limited rights necessary to operate the program (e.g., to copy a program onto the user's computer), the consideration should be treated as business profits, despite the legal form of the transaction as a license. However, some countries take the position that payments for software are royalties. The OECD and UN Commentaries also extend the principles applicable to the treatment of computer software to other digital products.

In summary, the tax challenges posed by the digital economy are like the weather: everybody likes to talk about it, but nobody does anything about it. The BEPS Action 1 Report: *Addressing the Tax Challenges of the Digital Economy* is no exception. The OECD Report presents an excellent description of the digital economy and the risks it poses for the international tax system. However, concrete recommendations for coordinated action to deal with digital transactions are absent from the Report. The reason is that any meaningful response to the challenges posed by the digital economy requires fundamental changes to the rules of the international tax system that allocate tax revenues between source and residence countries, and

取何种形式，仍存在分歧。特别是美国似乎满足于现状，而与之相反的是，许多其他发达国家和发展中国家希望赋予来源国对数字产品和服务所得以更大的征税权，尽管他们尚未就如何实现这一目标达成一致。

OECD 报告提出，各国有可能采取三项过渡措施来应对即将达成协调一致的全球数字经济应对方案：

—— 对数字产品和服务的跨境销售采用显著存在的门槛，以补充现行常设机构门槛；
—— 对某些数字产品和服务的付款征收预提税；以及
—— 对某些数字产品和服务的付款征收消费税。

该报告表明，各国可以自由选择采取这些措施，但强调需尊重其税收协定义务。

不出意料，自 2015 年以来，若干国家采取了各种单边措施。法国、匈牙利、印度和意大利对在线广告付款总额征收消费税；一些国家对某些数字产品和服务的付款按照特许权使用费征收预提税；其他国家已经采用并且欧盟建议采用显著数字化存在的门槛测试，作为对非居民取得营业利润征税的长期解决方案。在此期间，欧盟建议成员国对在线广告付款总额按照 3% 的税率征税。

9.5.3 数字服务税

在国际社会继续就跨境数字活动所得的征税问题寻求多边解决方案的同时，许多国家就数字服务税进行立法或者建议立法，作为从某些数字活动获取税收收入的手段。2016 年，印度成为首个就数字服务税立法的国家，其“均衡税”对印度居民就在线广告服务向非居民支付的款项按照 6% 的税率征税。2020 年，印度扩大了均衡税范围，对此前未被 6% 税率覆盖的就数字服务向非居民所支付款项的总额，按照 2% 的税率征税。

countries disagree as to whether such changes are necessary and, if so, the form they should take. In particular, the U.S. appears to be satisfied with the status quo; in contrast, many other developed and developing countries want to give source countries greater taxing rights with respect to income from digital goods and services, although they do not agree on how this should be done.

The OECD Report raises the possibility of three interim measures that countries might adopt to deal with the digital economy pending agreement on a coordinated international solution:

- a significant-presence threshold to supplement the existing PE threshold for cross-border sales of digital goods and services;
- a withholding tax on certain payments for digital goods and services; and
- an excise tax on certain payments for digital goods and services.

The Report indicates that countries are free to adopt these measures but emphasizes the need for them to respect their tax treaty obligations.

Not surprisingly, since 2015, several countries have adopted various unilateral measures. France, Hungary, India, and Italy have adopted excise taxes on gross payments for online advertising; some countries have imposed their royalty withholding taxes on payments for certain digital goods and services; other countries have adopted, and the EU has proposed to adopt, a significant-digital-presence threshold test for the taxation of business profits derived by nonresidents as a long-term solution. In the interim, it recommended that EU countries adopt a 3% tax on gross payments for online advertising.

9.5.3 Digital Services Taxes

While the international community has continued to search for a multilateral solution to the problem of the taxation of income from cross-border digital activities, many countries have enacted or proposed to enact unilateral DSTs as a means of capturing tax revenue from certain digital activities. India was the first country to enact a DST in 2016. Its "equalization levy" was a 6% tax on payments by residents of India to nonresidents for online advertising services. It was expanded in 2020 by a 2% tax on gross payments to nonresidents for digital services not covered by the original 6% tax.

截至 2022 年底，接近 30 个国家已经采用或者建议采用某种类型的数字服务税。这些数字服务税差异极大，税率从巴西的 1%，到匈牙利和土耳其的 7.5% 不等。大部分数字服务税适用于在线广告，但也有几个适用于其他服务，包括提供或销售用户数据以及使用数字界面、中介服务、流媒体服务、社交平台以及搜索引擎等。许多但并非全部国家将数字服务税仅适用于同时达到全球汇总收入门槛（通常是 7.5 亿欧元或等值国内货币，这也是国别报告的门槛金额）和国内收入门槛（也即为相应国家国内居民或消费者提供服务取得的收入）的企业。国内收入门槛从印度的 28.4 万美元，到加拿大的 3000 万加币不等。

数字服务税的税率尽管通常较低，但是适用于服务提供者的总收入而非利润。因此，数字服务税有可能是对服务提供者利润较高税率的税收征收，视其盈利能力而定。但无论如何，数字服务税旨在成为对数字服务营业利润征收企业所得税的替代，而且只要将其局限于盈利能力较强的大型跨国企业，就此而言，征收数字服务税就具有其合理性。

数字服务税被有意设计排除在一国双边税收协定的适用范围之外，否则协定会阻止一国对非居民服务提供商从该国用户或消费者取得的所得征税。正如第 8 章第 8.7.3.2 节所阐释的，基于 OECD 协定范本和联合国协定范本所签订的税收协定允许一国对非居民从本国取得的营业利润征税，其前提是该非居民在本国存在常设机构，并且利润归属于该常设机构。

由于现行税收协定并不允许征收数字服务税，服务提供商为其居民的国家没有义务对来源国征收的数字服务税提供消除双重征税的救济。因此，跨境数字服务所得如果被征收数字服务税，通常会受到无法消除的双重征税——一次是来源国以数字服务税为形式进行的税收征收，另一次是居民国征收的企业所得税。

如下文 9.5.5.2 节所讨论的，拟议的支柱一规则要求所有参与支柱一的国家废止数字服务税或类似措施，并同意未来不再就这类规则立法。

作为大多数全球高科技巨头的居民国，美国坚决反对数字服务税（美国曾威胁，如果法国继续征收数字服务税，将对法国的酒类产品征收报复性关税）。然

As of late 2022, almost 30 countries had adopted or proposed to adopt some type of DST. These DSTs vary widely. Rates range from 1% in Brazil to 7.5% in Hungary and Turkey. Most DSTs apply to online advertising, but several DSTs also apply to other services, including the provision or sale of user data and the use of digital interfaces, intermediation services, streaming services, social media platforms, and search engines. Many, but not all, countries apply their DSTs only to enterprises that meet both a global consolidated revenue threshold (often EUR 750 million or its equivalent in domestic currency, which is the threshold for country-by-country reporting) and a domestic revenue threshold (i.e., revenue derived from services provided to residents or consumers in the country), which varies from USD 284,000 in India to CAD 30 million in Canada.

Although the rates of DSTs are generally low, the tax is imposed on the service provider's gross revenue rather than on its profits. As a result, depending on a service provider's profitability, the DST could represent an excessive rate of tax on the service provider's profits. Nevertheless, DSTs are intended to be a proxy for corporate taxes on business profits from digital services and, to the extent that they are limited to large Multinational Enterprises (MNEs) with high profitability, they can be justified on that basis.

DSTs are intentionally designed to be outside the scope of a country's bilateral tax treaties; otherwise, those treaties would prevent a country from taxing a nonresident service provider on income derived from users or consumers in the country. As explained in Chapter 8, section 8.7.3.2, tax treaties based on the OECD and UN Model Treaties allow a country to tax business profits derived in the country by a nonresident only if the nonresident has a PE in the country and the profits are attributable to the PE.

Because existing tax treaties do not allow the imposition of DSTs, the country in which the service provider is resident is not obligated to provide any relief from double taxation for a DST imposed by a source country. As a result, income from cross-border digital services that is taxable under a DST is usually subject to unrelieved double taxation—once in the form of the DST imposed by the source country and again through the corporate tax imposed by the residence country.

As discussed in section 9.5.5.2 below, the proposed Pillar One rules require all countries participating in Pillar One to eliminate their DSTs or similar measures and to agree not to enact such rules in the future.

The country in which most global tech giants are resident, the U.S., is adamantly opposed to DSTs (it once threatened to impose retaliatory tariffs on French wine if France

而，与针对股息、利息、特许权使用费的情况一样，来源国对某些类型的营业利润按照总额征税，是被 OECD 协定范本和联合国协定范本所认可的合法举措。而且，可以将数字服务税解释为对跨境数字服务所得征税的一种手段，这种服务与来源国具有清晰的联结度或经济联系，而且不太可能在其他地方被征税。

9.5.4 联合国协定范本第 12B 条（自动数字服务所得）

正如前文第 9.5.2 节所讨论的，自 2015 年 BEPS 行动报告发布以来，OECD 继续致力于解决数字经济造成的税收挑战。2020 年，联合国专家委员会部分成员因相关工作进展缓慢，失去了耐心，开始研究在联合国协定范本中增加新的条款，允许来源（市场）国对自动数字服务所得征税。该条款，也就是第 12B 条，于 2021 年被增补进联合国协定范本。

第 12B 条款的结构在很大程度上是基于联合国协定范本第 12A 条（技术服务费）。该条款授权缔约国一方针对因在该国发生的“自动化数字服务”，而向另一方居民支付的款项，按照总额征收预提税，税率由缔约国双方商定。根据第 12B 条第 9 款，付款发生在支付者为其居民的国家，或者非居民拥有常设机构并且所支付的款项与该常设机构有实际联系的国家。根据第 12B 条第 10 款，付款不应被视为发生在支付者所在的缔约国一方，前提是支付者在缔约国另一方拥有常设机构，并且该付款与该常设机构有实际联系。

第 12B 条第 5 款定义了“自动化数字服务”一语，是指“通过互联网或其他电子网络提供的任何服务，无论哪种情形下，服务提供者仅需提供最低程度的人工参与”。第 12B 条第 6 款补充了该定义，列出了范围广泛的数字服务具体类别，作为第 12B 条所覆盖并满足第 12B 条第 5 款定义条件的自动化数字服务的示例。上述列举的内容包括以下服务：在线广告、提供用户数据、在线搜索引擎、在线中介服务、社交媒体、数字内容服务、在线游戏、云计算以及标准化在线教学。

proceeded with its DST). However, the taxation by source countries of certain types of business profits—as well as dividends, interest, and royalties—on a gross basis is recognized as legitimate by the provisions of the OECD and UN Model Treaties. Moreover, DSTs can be justified as a means of taxing income from cross-border digital services that has a clear nexus or economic connection to the source country and is unlikely to be taxed elsewhere.

9.5.4 Article 12B (Income from Automated Digital Services) of the UN Model Treaty

As noted in section 9.5.2 above, since the BEPS Action Report in 2015, the OECD has continued to work on a solution to the tax challenges posed by the digital economy. In 2020, some members of the UN Committee of Experts became impatient with the lack of progress and started working on a new article to be added to the UN Model Treaty that would allow source (market) countries to tax income from automated digital services. This provision, Article 12B, was added to the UN Model Treaty in the 2021 update.

In structure, Article 12B is based to a large extent on Article 12A (Fees for Technical Services) of the UN Model Treaty. It authorizes a contracting state to impose a gross-based withholding tax, at a rate to be agreed between the contracting states, on payments made to a resident of the other state for "automated digital services" where the payments arise in the first state. Under Article 12B(9), payments arise in a state where the payer is a resident of that state or a nonresident with a PE in that state and the payment is effectively connected with the PE. Under Article 12B(10), payments are deemed not to arise in a state where the payer has a PE in the other contracting state and the payments are effectively connected with that PE.

The term "automated digital services" is defined in Article 12B(5) to mean "any service provided on the Internet or another electronic network, in either case requiring minimal human involvement from the service provider." This definition is supplemented by Article 12B(6), which lists a broad range of specific types of digital services as examples of automated digital services that are covered by Article 12B where they meet the conditions of the definition in Article 12B(5). This list includes the following services: online advertising, supply of user data, online search engines, online intermediation services, social media, digital content services, online gaming, cloud computing, and standardized online teaching.

第 12B 条的一个突出特色是在第 12B 条第 3 款包含一个可选项，允许收款人对从来源国取得的自动化数字服务所得按照净额缴税。联合国或 OECD 协定范本的其他条款都不包含类似可选项。可选择按照净额缴税这一做法的目的，是为纳税人提供避免按照总额征税可能引发双重或过度征税的途径。

一国为了能够从远程服务提供商提供的自动化数字服务中获取税收收入，不仅必须修改国内法，对支付给非居民的自动化数字服务款项征收预提税，而且还要确保其税收协定包含相当于第 12B 条的条款。由于大规模提供重要自动化数字服务的大部分公司都是发达国家的居民，这些国家几乎不可能同意在其协定中包含第 12B 条。

9.5.5 拟议的“双支柱”方案

9.5.5.1 引言

如前述第 9.5.2 节所述，BEPS 项目详细描述了数字经济的广泛范围及其为国际税收带来的挑战。然而，BEPS 项目未能就如何改革现行国际税收体系以应对数字经济挑战的实质性建议达成一致。一方面，富庶的发达国家，特别是美国，致力于保持现状，即禁止来源国对非居民跨国企业从远程销售商品和服务给本国消费者取得的所得征税。另一方面，发展中国家以及几个发达国家希望对非居民跨国企业通过远程销售商品和服务从本国取得的巨额收入征税。

2019 年初，为了应对几个国家采取的单边措施特别是如第 9.5.3 节所述的数字服务税的泛滥，包容性框架积极采取行动，优先启动了一项积极主动的工作项目，拟订多边解决方案，以解决数字经济引发的国际税收体系问题。此项工作迅速促成各方就“双支柱”方案初步达成一致：建立新的联结度和利润分配规则，并对提供数字销售和服务的大型跨国企业征收全球最低税。2020 年 10 月，支柱一和支柱二细化规则（蓝图）正式发布（合计近 500 页）。这两套规则之复杂，

A unique feature of Article 12B is the inclusion of an election in Article 12B(3) for the recipient of the payments to pay tax on a net basis on the income from automated digital services derived from the source country. There is no similar election in the other provisions of either the UN or OECD Model Treaty. The purpose of the net-basis election is to provide taxpayers with a means of avoiding the potential double or excessive taxation caused by a gross-based tax.

In order for a country to raise tax revenue from automated digital services provided by remote service providers, the country must not only revise its domestic law to impose withholding tax on payments to nonresidents for automated digital services but also ensure that its tax treaties include a provision equivalent to Article 12B. Since most of the companies providing significant automated digital services on a large scale are resident in developed countries, it is extremely unlikely that those countries will agree to include Article 12B in their treaties.

9.5.5 The Proposed Two-Pillar Approach

9.5.5.1 Introduction

As outlined in section 9.5.2 above, the BEPS Project described in detail the extensive scope of the digital economy and the challenges it poses for international taxation. However, the BEPS Project was not able to reach an agreement on any solid recommendations about how to reform the existing international tax system to respond to the digital economy. On the one hand, rich developed countries, especially the U.S., were committed to the status quo, which prohibits source countries from taxing nonresident multinationals on income from remote sales of goods and services to customers in their countries. On the other hand, developing countries, as well as several developed countries, wanted to impose tax on nonresident multinationals deriving large amounts of revenue from their countries through remote sales of goods and services.

In early 2019, in response to the proliferation of unilateral measures, especially DSTs, adopted by several countries, as discussed in section 9.5.3, the Inclusive Framework initiated an aggressive work program on a priority basis to develop a multilateral solution to deal with the problems for the international tax system caused by the digital economy. This work quickly led to a preliminary agreement on a two-pillar approach: new nexus and profit-allocation rules and a global minimum tax on large multinationals engaged in providing digital sales and services. In October 2020, detailed rules (Blueprints) for both Pillar One and Pillar Two were released (totaling almost 500 pages). The complexity of both sets of rules was strongly criticized by both

受到了政府部门和私营部门的强烈批评，而且看起来“双支柱”方案可能会折戟沉沙。然而，OECD 和包容性框架继续开展工作，2021 年 7 月，各方就修改后的方案达成一致，目标群体变为全部大型跨国企业，而不仅仅限于从事数字业务的企业。2021 年 12 月，支柱二范本规则发布，随后于 2022 年初发布了注释。2022 年 7 月和 10 月先后发布了关于支柱一的详尽进展报告和咨询文件。

截至 2022 年末，无论是支柱一还是支柱二的相关工作都没有最终完成，支柱二的进展要比支柱一相对快些。尽管尚不确定是否会有足够多数量的国家同意使支柱一提案生效，似乎有几个国家计划实施支柱二。

9.5.5.2 支柱一概述

支柱一提案基于全球和国内收入门槛，为来源国（市场国）创建了新的征税权，并根据公式分配法而非独立交易转让定价规则制定了向来源国分配利润的新规则。就此而言，支柱一提案为现行国际税收制度中带来了翻天覆地的变化，尽管这些规则至少在最初，仅适用于规模最大、盈利能力最强的跨国企业（总共约 100 家）。根据大部分税收协定的现行规定，仅当非居民在来源国拥有实质性存在（通常形式为子公司或常设机构）时，来源国一般方可对非居民取得的营业利润征税。此外，来源国仅可对根据独立交易转让定价规则确定的，居民子公司或常设机构的营业利润征税。

2022 年 7 月 11 日，OECD 发布了《支柱一金额 A 进展报告》（可参见 www.oecd.org），该报告讨论了金额 A 范本规则。2022 年 10 月 10 日，OECD 发布了另外一份《支柱一金额 A 征管和税收确定性进展报告》，该报告主要讨论了争议预防和解决机制（可参见 www.oecd.org）。这些规则旨在成为金额 A 操作实施规则和争议解决机制多边协议谈判的基础。多边公约也将要求参与国取消数字服务税及任何类似措施。多边协议的文本及所附的解释性声明拟于 2023 年上半年开放签署，预计在 2024 年正式生效。

the private sector and governments, and it appeared that the two-pillar approach might collapse. However, the OECD and the Inclusive Framework continued their work, and in July 2021, a revised agreement was reached to target all large multinationals, not just those engaged in digital businesses. In December 2021, Model Rules for Pillar Two were published and accompanied by Commentary in early 2022. Detailed Progress Reports and Consultation Documents on Pillar One were released in July and October 2022.

As of late 2022, neither Pillar One nor Pillar Two had been finalized. The work on Pillar Two was more advanced than the work on Pillar One. It seems likely that Pillar Two will be implemented by several countries, although it is uncertain whether the Pillar One proposals will be endorsed by a sufficient number of countries to be effective.

9.5.5.2 An Overview of Pillar One

The Pillar One proposals create new taxing rights for source (market) countries based on global and domestic revenue thresholds and provide new rules for allocating profits to source countries based on formulary apportionment rather than on arm's-length transfer pricing rules. In this regard, the Pillar One proposals mark a dramatic change in the existing international tax system, although the rules will apply, at least initially, only to the largest and most profitable multinationals (approximately one hundred multinational companies in total). Under the existing provisions of most tax treaties, source countries are generally allowed to tax business profits derived by nonresidents only if those nonresidents have a substantial presence in a source country (usually in the form of a subsidiary corporation or a PE); in addition, source countries are allowed to tax only the business profits of a resident subsidiary or a PE determined in accordance with arm's-length transfer pricing rules.

On July 11, 2022, the OECD issued a *Progress Report on Amount A of Pillar One* (available at www.oecd.org), which includes model rules for the operation of Amount A. On October 10, 2022, the OECD issued another *Progress Report on the Administration and Tax Certainty Aspects of Amount A of Pillar One*, which deals with dispute-prevention and dispute-resolution mechanisms (available at www.oecd.org). These rules are intended to serve as the basis for the negotiation of a multinational agreement to implement the operative rules and the dispute-resolution mechanisms with respect to Amount A. The multilateral convention will also require the participating countries to withdraw their DSTs and any similar measures. The text of the multilateral agreement, accompanied by an explanatory statement, is scheduled to be opened for signature in the first half of 2023 and is projected to enter into force in 2024.

上述两份进展报告（总计 300 多页）由 OECD 秘书处起草，尚未获得包容性框架成员的批准。关于支柱一的几个未决问题的工作仍在继续，此刻尚无法确定整个支柱一能否得到足够多的国家认可实施。

支柱一仅适用于全球营业额超过 200 亿欧元并且利润率（税前利润除以收入的比）达到或超过 10% 的跨国企业。如果所提议的争议解决机制能够顺利实施，则该门槛将在 7 年内降低到 100 亿欧元。新规则适用于所有达到收入和盈利能力门槛的跨国企业，排除适用于从事采掘业和受监管的金融服务业，无论其是否从事传统或数字行业。

如果跨国企业达到一国的国内收入门槛，即在该国的销售收入超过 100 万欧元（GDP 少于 400 亿欧元的国家，该金额降到 25 万欧元），该国将获得对达到收入和盈利能力门槛的跨国企业的新征税权。如果达到国内收入门槛，该国有权对跨国企业全球剩余利润的可分配份额征税，这部分利润界定为全球利润中超过其收入 10% 的部分的 25%（称为金额 A）。为此，跨国企业必须根据其合并财务报表计算利润，仅做个别调整和亏损结转。跨国企业剩余利润在达到国内收入门槛的几个国家之间分配，分配的依据是跨国企业在每个国家（商品和服务的使用或消费国）的销售总额所占的比例。因此，有必要为此制定详细的来源规则（2022 年 7 月进展报告制定了规则草案），而且必须由各国统一实施。如果跨国企业在一国的常设机构或子公司达到了国内收入门槛，可适用安全港（称为营销或分销利润安全港），以限制分配给该国的剩余利润。

实际上，来源国将必须制定两套企业所得税规则：一套用于对支柱一下大型跨国企业的剩余利润（金额 A）征税，另一套用于对其他企业和支柱一下大型跨国企业的非剩余利润征税。

支柱一下大型跨国企业为其居民的国家将有义务消除重复征税，或者对分配给来源国的剩余利润免除居民国税收，或者为来源国对其分得的剩余利润征收的

Both Progress Reports (totaling over 300 pages) have been prepared by the OECD Secretariat and have not yet been approved by the members of the Inclusive Framework. Work is continuing on several outstanding issues concerning Pillar One, and it is by no means certain at this point that the entire package will be acceptable to a sufficient number of countries to make it viable.

Pillar One will apply only to multinationals with global turnover above EUR 20 billion and a profit ratio (profits before tax over revenue) of 10% or more. This threshold is supposed to be reduced to EUR 10 billion if the proposed dispute- resolution mechanism is successfully implemented within seven years. The new rules will apply to all multinationals meeting the revenue and profitability thresholds, other than those engaged in extractive industries and regulated financial services businesses, irrespective of whether they are engaged in digital or traditional businesses.

A country will acquire new rights to tax multinationals meeting the revenue and profitability thresholds where they meet a domestic revenue threshold—sales revenue from the country of at least EUR 1 million (EUR 250,000 for countries with a GDP of less than EUR 40 billion). Where this domestic revenue threshold is met, the country is entitled to tax its allocable share of a multinational's global residual profits, which are defined to be 25% of its global profits in excess of 10% of its revenue (referred to as Amount A). For this purpose, a multinational's profits must be computed in accordance with its consolidated financial statements, with a few adjustments and a carryover for losses. A multinational's residual profits are allocated among the countries where the domestic revenue threshold is met on the basis of the proportion of the multinational's total sales revenue derived from each country (the country in which goods and services are used or consumed). Detailed source rules (draft rules are provided in the July 2022 Progress Report) are necessary for this purpose and must be applied uniformly by all countries. Where a multinational has a PE or a subsidiary in a country that meets the domestic threshold, a safe harbor (referred to as a marketing and distribution profits safe harbor) will apply to limit the residual profits allocated to that country.

In effect, source countries will be required to have two sets of corporate tax rules: one for taxing the residual profits (Amount A) of large multinationals subject to Pillar One and another for taxing the profits of other corporations and the non-residual profits of large multinationals subject to Pillar One.

The countries in which large multinationals subject to Pillar One are resident will have an obligation to eliminate double taxation by providing either an exemption from residence country tax for any residual profits allocated to a source country or a credit for any taxes

税收提供抵免。

支柱一金额 A 规则的所有问题都可以通过强制性争议预防和争议解决机制（称为“税收确定性程序”）进行处理，尽管这些机制对某些发展中国家而言是可选项。OECD 于 2022 年 10 月发布的进展报告包含了金额 A 税收确定性机制的细化规则。

除了金额 A 以外，支柱一还包含确定有限风险分销商的应税利润（称为金额 B），上述利润来源于为关联方开展的基准营销和分销活动。金额 B 规则将适用于所有有限风险分销商，而不仅仅是规模最大、盈利能力最强、适用金额 A 规则的跨国企业集团的有限风险分销商。现行转让定价规则在适用于关联方之间的分销安排时，经常引发税企双方的争议，金额 B 规则旨在将争议最小化。OECD 对金额 B 的关注虽然不及金额 A，但金额 B 细化规则预期在 2023 年上半年出台。

确定金额 B 的规则需要适用现行转让定价指南基于可比分析对相关交易的准确描述，其中可比分析涉及《OECD 转让定价指南》所列举的各项要素，具体而言即功能、资产和风险。这一分析将与负面因素清单一同用于确定某个实体能否被定性为金额 B 规则范围内的常规分销商。在大部分情况下，确定基准营销和分销活动的固定回报最恰当的转让定价方法是交易净利润法（参见第 6 章 6.4.8 节）。所使用的相关利润指标有可能是基于各个地区、行业和可比公司基准的销售回报。

除了支柱一范围内大型跨国企业的金额 A 和作为有限风险分销商的跨国企业集团成员的金额 B 以外，集团成员的利润将根据现行转让定价规则确定。

9.5.5.3 支柱二概述

支柱二全球最低税提案包含三项补足税：所得纳入规则（IIR）补足税，低税支付规则（UTPR）补足税和合格国内最低补足税（QDMTT）。这三种补足

imposed by a source country on the residual profits allocated to it.

All issues involving Amount A of the Pillar One rules will be subject to mandatory dispute-prevention and dispute-resolution mechanisms (referred to as "tax certainty processes"), although these mechanisms will be elective for certain developing countries. The detailed rules for these tax certainty mechanisms with respect to Amount A are set out in the OECD's October 2022 Progress Report.

In addition to Amount A, Pillar One also involves the determination of the taxable profits (called Amount B) of limited-risk distributors derived from baseline marketing and distribution activities performed for related parties. The proposed rules for Amount B will apply to all limited-risk distributors, not just those of the largest and most profitable multinational groups that are subject to the proposed rules for Amount A. The application of the current transfer pricing rules to distribution arrangements between related parties frequently causes disputes between taxpayers and tax administrations. The proposed rules for Amount B are intended to minimize these disputes. Amount B has not received as much attention from the OECD as Amount A, but detailed rules are expected in the first half of 2023.

The proposed rules for the determination of Amount B involve the application of the existing transfer pricing guidelines with respect to the accurate delineation of the relevant transactions based on a comparability analysis involving the factors set out in the OECD Transfer Pricing Guidelines,—in particular, the functions, assets, and risks involved. This analysis will be used, along with a list of negative factors, to identify whether an entity can be characterized as a routine distributor within the scope of the rules for Amount B. In most cases, the most appropriate transfer pricing method to determine the fixed return for baseline marketing and distribution activities will be the TNMM (*see* Chapter 6, section 6.4.8). The relevant profit indicator used will probably be a return on sales based on benchmarks for various regions, industries, and comparable companies.

The profits of members of multinational groups, other than Amount A of large multinationals subject to Pillar One and Amount B of group members that are limited-risk distributors, will be determined in accordance with existing transfer pricing rules.

9.5.5.3 *Overview of Pillar Two*

The proposals for the Pillar Two global minimum tax comprise three top-up taxes: the Income Inclusion Rule (IIR) top-up tax, the Undertaxed Payments Rule (UTPR) top-up tax, and the Qualifying Domestic Minimum Top-up Tax (QDMTT). These three top-up taxes are

税旨在提升跨国企业在一国获得的所得的实际税率，使所得的总税负至少达到15%。此外，支柱二制定了一项新的协定条款，即应税规则（STTR），允许各国可以对支付给非居民的利息、特许权使用费以及某些服务款项，按照总额征收预提税。IIR 和 UTPR 的缩写毫无意义，原本它们代表“所得纳入规则”和“低税支付规则”，然而根据支柱二范本规则，这些补足税不再基于所得纳入或支付。正如下文所讨论的，IIR 和 UTPR 补足税是根据每个跨国公司以及其子公司或常设机构运营的每一个所在国计算的税收。IIR 和 UTPR 补足税并非强制适用，但若一国决定实施，就必须根据范本规则制定国内法，并接受包容性框架其他成员国适用这些规则。

IIR 和 UTPR 补足税仅适用于根据财务报表，汇总收入超过 7.5 亿欧元（与国别报告适用门槛相同）的跨国企业。这些规则不适用于国际组织、政府机构、非营利实体以及养老金或投资基金。

如果跨国企业通过位于另一国的常设机构或子公司取得的外国来源所得的实际税率低于 15%，则适用 IIR 补足税。跨国企业在其经营所在的每个国家的实际税率，是该国征收的“被涵盖税收”占跨国企业“净 GLoBE 所得”（即其在一国取得的经部分调整后的财务会计所得）的百分比。被涵盖税收是该国居民集团实体会计账户中的应计税项、支付给非居民集团实体的款项的应缴预提税，以及非居民集团实体就位于该国的常设机构和受控外国企业利润的应缴税项。如果一国的实际税率低于 15%，跨国企业集团的母公司实体有可能需要缴纳 IIR 补足税。如果实际税率等于或高于 15%，则不适用 IIR 或 UTPR。实际上，实际税率相当于门槛测试。

跨国企业通过位于特定国家子公司和常设机构取得的所得，其 IIR 补足税的计算步骤如下：

确定该国的“补足税百分比”，即以 15% 减去该国的实际税率：

intended to supplement a country's effective tax rate on income earned in the country by multinationals so that the total tax on the income is at least 15%. In addition, Pillar Two proposes a new treaty provision: a "Subject-to-Tax Rule" (STTR) to allow countries to impose a gross-based withholding tax on interest, royalties, and certain payments for services to nonresidents. The acronyms IIR and UTPR are meaningless. Originally, they stood for "income inclusion rule" and "undertaxed payments rule"; however, under the Pillar Two Model Rules, these top-up taxes are no longer based on income inclusion or payments. As discussed below, the IIR and UTPR top-up taxes are calculated as taxes in respect of each multinational and each country in which the multinational operates through a subsidiary or PE. The application of the IIR and the UTPR top-up taxes is not compulsory, but if a country decides to impose these taxes, it must enact domestic legislation in accordance with the Model Rules and accept the application of those rules by other members of the Inclusive Framework.

The IIR and UTPR top-up taxes will apply only to multinational enterprises with consolidated revenue, determined in accordance with their financial statements, in excess of EUR 750 million (the same threshold that applies for country-by-country reporting). The rules will not apply to international organizations, government entities, non-profit entities, and pension or investment funds.

The IIR top-up tax will apply where the foreign source income earned by a multinational through a PE or a subsidiary located in a country is subject to an effective foreign tax rate that is less than 15%. The effective tax rate of a multinational for each country in which it operates will be calculated as the percentage of "covered taxes" levied by the country as a portion of the multinational's "net GloBE income" (its financial accounting income (with a few adjustments) earned in the country). Covered taxes are taxes accrued in the financial accounts of group entities resident in the country, withholding tax payable on payments to nonresident group entities, and taxes payable by nonresident group entities on the profits of PEs and CFCs located in the country. Where the effective tax rate in a country is less than 15%, the parent entity of the multinational group is potentially subject to the IIR top-up tax. Where the effective tax rate is 15% or more, no IIR or UTPR top-up taxes will apply. In effect, the effective tax rate operates as a threshold test.

The calculation of the IIR top-up tax for a multinational's income earned through subsidiaries and PEs in a particular country involves the following steps:

Determine the country's "top-up tax percentage," which is 15% less the country's effective tax rate:

（1）计算“超额利润”，即跨国企业从该国取得的净 GLoBE 所得减去其“基于实质的所得排除”（也就是在该国的有形资产账面净值的 10% 和工资成本的 8%，两个比例都将在 10 年过渡期内逐步降低到 5%）。

（2）确定该国的“辖区补足税”，即用跨国企业超额利润乘以补足税百分比，然后减去“国内补足税”，后者被定义为意指根据 QDMTT 应缴纳的款项。

（3）然后按照其净 GLoBE 所得占跨国企业在该国净 GLoBE 所得总额的百分比，将“辖区补足税”分配给位于该国的子公司和常设机构。

（4）集团所有成员实体在该国的 IIR 补足税总额应由母公司实体为其居民的国家对集团母公司征收。

IIR 补足税通常由跨国企业集团“最终母公司实体”为其居民的国家对该母公司征收。然而，如果母公司实体为其居民的国家不实施支柱二，则集团中下一最高层级实体（称为“中间层母公司实体”）为其居民的国家有权适用最低税，并沿着跨国集团成员实体链条自上而下以此类推。这一自上而下的方法旨在鼓励跨国企业母公司为其居民的国家实施全球最低税，防范跨国集团母公司将居民身份转移到不实施支柱二的国家。

值得关注的是，IIR 补足税计算方法有几个特点。第一，IIR 补足税的征收不是针对跨国企业净 GLoBE 所得（用以确定一国的实际税率），而是针对超额利润，即净 GLoBE 所得减去其基于实质的所得排除。第二，基于实质的所得排除系用来代替涉及有形资产和人员的实质性经营活动产生的固定所得额。这项排除的金额即使其无须缴纳任何来源国税收，也无须缴纳 IIR 补足税。因此，各国可以制定税收优惠政策，只要不超过基于实质的所得排除金额，就不会触发适用 IIR 补足税。第三，一国可以通过征收 QDMTT，将本国企业所得税税率最高提升至 15%，从而避免他国对在本国取得的超额利润征收 IIR 或 UTPR 补足税。正如下文所讨论的，对在本国取得的收入征收 QDMTT，是防止该收入被其他国家征收 IIR 或 UTPR 补足税相对简单的方法。

(1) Calculate the "excess profit," which is the multinational's net GloBE income from the country less its "substance-based income exclusion" (which is 10% of the net book value of tangible assets and 8% of its payroll costs in the country, both declining to 5% over a ten-year transitional period).

(2) Determine the country's "jurisdictional top-up tax" by multiplying the multinational's excess profit by its top-up tax percentage and then subtracting any "domestic top-up tax," which is defined to mean the amount payable under a QDMTT.

(3) The jurisdictional top-up tax is then allocated to the multinational's subsidiaries and PEs in the country in proportion to their net GloBE income relative to the total net GloBE income of the multinational earned in the country.

(4) The total amount of IIR top-up tax for all the group entities in the country will be imposed on the parent entity of the group by the country in which the parent entity is resident.

The IIR top-up tax will usually be imposed on the "ultimate parent entity" of a multinational group by the country in which the parent is resident. However, where the country in which the parent entity is resident does not apply Pillar Two, the country in which the next-highest-tier entity (or entities) in the group (referred to as an "inter- mediate parent entity") is resident becomes entitled to apply the minimum tax, and so on down the chain of entities in the multinational group. This top-down approach is intended to encourage countries in which parent entities are resident to apply the global minimum tax and to discourage multinational parent companies from shifting their residence to a country that decides not to apply Pillar Two.

Several aspects of the calculation of the IIR top-up tax are notable. First, the IIR top-up tax is not imposed on a multinational's net GloBE income (which is used to determine a country's effective tax rate) but instead on its excess profit, which is its net GloBE income less its substance-based income exclusion. Second, the substance-based income exclusion is a proxy for a fixed amount of income from substantive business activities involving tangible assets and employees. The amount of the exclusion is not subject to the IIR top-up tax, even if it is not subject to any source country tax. Thus, countries can provide tax incentives up to the amount of the substance-based income exclusion without causing the application of any IIR top-up tax. Third, a country can avoid other countries imposing an IIR or UTPR top-up tax on excess profit earned in the country by imposing a QDMTT that tops up the country's corporate tax to 15%. As discussed below, the imposition of a QDMTT is a relatively easy way for countries to collect tax on income earned in their country that would otherwise be collected by other countries through the IIR and UTPR top-up taxes.

跨国企业收入低于1000万欧元且利润低于100万欧元的国家可适用支柱二微利排除。此外，（如OECD协定范本第8条所定义的）国际海运所得也被排除在外。

通过允许各国对不适用IIR补足税的集团公司征收补足税，UTPR补足税对IIR补足税起到了补充的作用。UTPR补足税与IIR补足税的计算方式相同，其目的之一就是消除跨国集团母公司将居民身份转移到决定不实施全球最低税国家的动机。

最常见的UTPR补足税适用情形是跨国集团母公司实体位于实际税率（ETR）低于15%的国家。在此种情形下，该国（或任何其他国家）并不存在可对集团实体取得的低税所得适用IIR补足税的母公司实体。这一结果所反映的事实是，IIR补足税仅适用于作为除母公司为其居民的国家以外，其他国家的居民的低税集团实体。

分配给某个特定国家的UTPR补足税份额的计算方法，是将某一财政年度内每个低税集团实体的集团UTPR补足税总额乘以该国的“UTPR百分比”。确定每个国家的UTPR百分比的公式是，用该国集团实体的员工数量以及这些实体的有形资产账面净值除以实施UTPR补足税所有国家的员工数量和有形资产账面净值总额（员工数量和有形资产的权重相同）。实施UTPR补足税的国家可以采取一定征税方式，使该国集团实体产生现金税式支出（例如，通过拒绝扣除或征收特别税）。根据一项特殊的过渡规则，如果跨国企业海外有形资产低于5000万欧元，并且开展运营活动的成员实体所在地不超过6个国家，则5年内可以免于缴纳UTPR补足税。这一豁免旨在为处于拓展国际经营活动初始阶段的跨国企业提供全球最低税的初始阶段免税。

一国可以通过对跨国集团成员从本国取得的财务会计所得，按照不低于15%的实际税率征税，来避免把这些税收收入放弃给其他国家，后者可以通过征收IIR或UTPR补足税而取得这些税收收入。确保企业所得税实际税率对各类实体和各类所得都不低于15%，对很多国家而言可能难度较大，因这有可能涉及取消

A *de minimis* exemption from Pillar Two will apply to countries where a multinational has revenue of less than EUR 10 million and profits of less than EUR 1 million. In addition, international shipping income (as defined in Article 8 of the OECD Model Convention) will be excluded.

The UTPR top-up tax supplements the IIR top-up tax by allowing countries to impose a top-up tax with respect to group companies that are not subject to the IIR top-up tax. The UTPR top-up tax is calculated in the same way as the IIR top-up tax. One of the purposes of the UTPR top-up tax is to eliminate any incentive for parent companies of a multinational group to shift their residence to a country that decides not to apply the global minimum tax.

The most common situation in which the UTPR top-up tax will apply is where the parent entity of a multinational group is located in a country that has an Effective Tax Rate (ETR) of less than 15%. In that situation, there is no parent entity in that country (or in any other country) that is subject to the IIR top-up tax with respect to the low-taxed income earned by group entities in that country. This result reflects the fact that the IIR top-up tax applies only to the low-taxed group entities resident in countries other than the country in which the parent entity is resident.

The portion of UTPR top-up tax allocated to a particular country is determined by multiplying the group's total UTPR top-up tax for each low-taxed group entity for a fiscal year by the country's "UTPR percentage." The UTPR percentage for each country is determined by a formula based on the number of employees of the group entities located in that country and the net book value of tangible assets of those entities as a percentage of the total number of employees and tangible assets of the group located in all countries applying the UTPR top-up tax (with employees and tangible assets given equal weight). Countries applying the UTPR top-up tax can impose the tax in any way that results in a cash tax expense for the group entities in the country (e.g., by denying deductions or imposing a special tax). Under a special transitional rule, a multinational will be exempt from the UTPR top-up tax for five years if it has tangible foreign assets of EUR 50 million or less and has business operations through group entities in no more than six countries. This exemption is intended to provide start-up relief from the global minimum tax for multinationals that are in the initial stages of the expansion of their international operations.

A country can avoid ceding tax revenue to other countries through the application of the IIR and UTPR top-up taxes by those countries by taxing the domestic financial accounting income earned in the country by the members of the multinational group at an ETR of at least 15%. Ensuring effective corporate tax rates of at least 15% on all types of entities and all types

各种税收优惠措施和提高税率。为此，支柱二规定了一项替代性机制——“合格国内最低补足税（QDMTT）”，使各国得以对居民集团实体的超额利润征收足够的国内税，将其“辖区补足税”减少到零，并实际上使其他国家没有机会征收IIR或UTPR补足税。根据QDMTT的定义，这项税收征收必须确定位于一国范围内集团实体的超额利润，且其方法必须与支柱二规则相当，使针对国内超额利润的税收征收达到15%。QDMTT的征管方式也应与支柱二范本规则和注释相一致，而且一国不得提供抵消QDMTT的任何优惠。

与基于GLoBE净所得以及针对该所得的全部被涵盖税收的一国实际税率不同，QDMTT仅适用于该国以GLoBE净所得减去“基于实质的所得排除”后的“超额利润”。如前文所述，基于实质的所得排除是针对涉及使用有形资产和员工的经营活动所取得的所得而采用的一个粗略的替代性指标。这意味着QDMTT可以针对不涉及使用实质性有形资产和员工的国内所得，如消极所得以及地理上易于移动的经营所得。

拟议的STTR是一个协定条款，该条款允许发展中国家（其定义为2019年人均净收入总额等于或低于12535美元，这一标准定期更新）对支付给缔约国另一方居民的利息、特许权使用费及某些服务费，按总额征收最高9%的预提税，前提是该缔约国另一方的企业所得税名义税率低于9%。如果某一发展中国家要求将STTR包含在其与某一发达国家的税收协定中，该发达国家有义务据此修订税收协定。STTR仅适用于上述最低税率与收款人为其居民的国家对该付款征税的税率之间的差额。STTR税率远远低于针对各种补足税所要求的15%最低税率，其原因是STTR是针对相关款项支付的总额所征收，而各种补足税的确定系基于所得净额。

STTR将修改现行的协定条款，以使一国可以对低税的利息、特许权使用费以及某些服务款项支付按总额征收预提税，税率为9%与收款人为其居民的发达国家企业所得税税率之差。尽管STTR被称为对发展中国家的妥协，但它并非向发展中国家分配额外的征税权；相反，其目的在于恢复缔约国一方基于缔约国另

of income may be difficult for many countries because it would likely involve eliminating tax incentives and increasing tax rates. For this reason, Pillar Two provides an alternative mechanism—the "qualifying domestic minimum top-up tax" (QDMTT)—to allow countries to impose sufficient domestic tax on the excess profit of resident group entities to reduce their "jurisdictional top-up tax" to nil and effectively eliminate the imposition of any IIR or UTPR top-up tax by other countries. Under the definition of a QDMTT, the tax must determine the excess profit of the group entities located in the country in a manner equivalent to the Pillar Two rules and increase tax on their domestic excess profit to 15%. A QDMTT must also be implemented and administered consistently with the Pillar Two Model Rules and Commentary, and the country must not provide any benefits to offset the QDMTT.

Unlike a country's ETR, which is based on its net GloBE income and all the covered taxes on that income, a QDMTT is applied only to a country's "excess profit," which is its net GloBE income less its "substance-based income exclusion." As noted above, the substance-based income exclusion is a rough proxy for income derived from business activities involving the use of tangible assets and employees. This means that a QDMTT can be targeted at domestic income that does not involve the use of substantial tangible assets or employees, such as passive income and geographically mobile business income.

The proposed STTR is a treaty provision that allows developing countries (defined as countries with a gross net income per capita of USD 12,535 or less in 2019, as updated regularly) to impose a gross-based withholding tax of up to 9% on interest, royalties, and certain payments for services to residents of the other contracting state if the other state's nominal corporate tax rate is lower than 9%. If a developing country requests that the STTR be included in its treaty with a developed country, the developed country will be obligated to amend the treaty accordingly. The STTR is limited to the difference between the minimum rate and the tax rate imposed on the payment by the country in which the recipient is resident. The rate of tax for the STTR is significantly lower than the 15% minimum rate for the top-up taxes because the STTR is imposed on the gross amount of the relevant payments, whereas the top-up taxes are determined on the basis of net income.

The STTR will modify existing tax treaties to allow a country to impose a gross-based withholding tax at a rate equal to the difference between 9% and the corporate tax rate of the developed country in which the recipient is resident on low-taxed interest, royalties, and certain payments for services. Although the STTR is described as a concession to developing countries, it is not an allocation of additional taxing rights to those countries; instead, it is intended to restore taxing rights given up to the other contracting state pursuant to the treaty on the

一方会针对相关款项支付的总额，依照不低于 9% 的税率征税这一假设，而按照协定要求，让渡给另一方的征税权。

只有当发展中国家根据国内法，对相关款项支付按照超过 9% 的税率征税，并在已达成的税收协定中，将其协定伙伴方对这类款项支付的征税税率限制在 9% 以下时，STTR 才对发展中国家具有重要意义。对于没有签订税收协定，或者签订的税收协定允许对相关付款的预提税率高于 9% 的发展中国家，STTR 没有意义。

国际税收始终处于不停地变化之中，认识到这一点并以此结束本书，似乎不可避免，但也恰如其分。对于“双支柱”方案是否以及如何最终实施，我们只能拭目以待。如果成功落地，将在国际税收问题方面，极大地推动多边主义向前迈进，而 OECD 作为双支柱方案的主要推手，也将因此而增光添彩甚多。然而，如果“双支柱”方案未能被国际社会所采用，多边主义将遭遇重大挫折，我们将面临各个国家各种单边规则纷繁交错的混乱局面。

assumption that the other state would impose tax on the gross amount of the payments at a rate of at least 9%.

The STTR is significant for developing countries only to the extent that they impose tax on the relevant payments under their domestic law at a rate in excess of 9% and have concluded tax treaties that limit the tax rate imposed on such payments by their treaty partners to less than 9%. For developing countries that do not have tax treaties or that have tax treaties that allow withholding tax rates of at least 9% on the relevant payments, the STTR will be irrelevant.

It seems inevitable, as well as appropriate, to end this Primer by acknowledging that international tax is constantly changing. We must wait to see if and how the two-pillar approach is finally implemented. If it is implemented successfully, it will represent a huge boost for multilateralism with respect to international tax issues and for the OECD as the primary driver for the two pillars. If, however, the two-pillar approach fails to be adopted by the international community, it will be a huge setback for multilateralism, and we will be left with a messy mixture of unilateral national rules.

国际税收术语表

183 天规则：许多国家都使用的一项规则。根据该规则，如果个人在任意12 个月期间内，累计在一国停留 183 天或以上，则该个人将被视为该国居民。

预约定价协议（APA）：跨国企业和一个或多个国家税务机关之间，认可企业在未来纳税年度使用的转让定价方法的协议。

独立交易方法（标准、原则或方式）：基于非关联方在类似交易中收取的价格（或某些情况下取得的利润），对关联方之间交易的转让价格予以确定的方法。

独立交易价格：针对关联方之间转让商品、服务或无形资产，依据非关联方之间在类似交易中的价格予以确定的价格。

背对背安排：此类安排涉及一方与中间人进行诸如贷款或租赁等交易，随后中间人向可能与第一方有关联的另一方进行类似交易。背靠背安排几乎总是被用作避税手段。背对背安排也称为导管安排。

基地公司所得：受控外国企业从其控股股东为其居民的国家取得的经营所得，或从关联方取得的发生在该公司设立所在国家境外的交易的经营所得。

税基侵蚀和利润转移（BEPS）：G20/OECD 于 2012 年发起的一个项目，该项目旨在解决导致高税收国家的税基减少的跨国企业的过度税收筹划。

信托的受益所有人：拥有相关财产受益所有权的人、个人或法律实体，虽该财产由一个或多个受托人以信托形持有，并享有合法所有权。

Glossary of International Tax Terms

183-day rule: A rule used by many countries under which an individual is deemed to be a resident if the individual is present in the country for 183 days or more in the aggregate in any twelve-month period.

Advance pricing agreement (APA): An agreement between a multinational enterprise and the tax authorities of one or more countries approving the transfer pricing method to be used by the enterprise in future tax years.

Arm's-length method (standard, principle, or approach): The establishment of transfer prices in transactions between related parties based on the prices charged (or sometimes the profits derived) in similar transactions between unrelated parties.

Arm's-length price: A price set on a transfer of goods, services, or intangible property between related persons that corresponds to the price that would be set in a similar transfer between unrelated persons.

Back-to-back arrangement: An arrangement involving a transaction, such as a loan or lease, by a person to an intermediary, followed by a similar transaction by the intermediary to another person who may be related to the first person. A back-to-back arrangement is almost always used as a tax avoidance device. Back-to-back arrangements are also referred to as conduit arrangements.

Base company income: Business income derived by a controlled foreign company from the country in which its controlling shareholders are resident or from transactions with related parties that occur outside the country in which the foreign corporation is established.

Base erosion and profit shifting (BEPS): A project launched by the G20/OECD in 2012 to deal with aggressive tax planning by multinational enterprises that results in the reduction of the tax base of high-tax countries.

Beneficiary or beneficiaries of a trust: The persons, individuals, or legal entities who beneficially own property held in trust for them by a trustee or trustees who have legal title to

分支机构：纳税人通常通过办事机构或固定营业场所的形式经营的业务。分支机构不是单独注册的公司。外国分支机构系位于纳税人居民国境外的分支机构。

分支机构税：一国对非居民企业分支机构未在该国再投资的利润征收的税收。该税收旨在形成与针对居民子公司向其外国母公司支付股息征收预提税相同的作用。

资本输出中性：居民投资者无论是在国内还是国外投资，承担相同税收负担的情形。

资本输入中性：在来源国投资的居民与该国的其他投资者承担相同税收负担的情形。

资本所有权中性：投资所有人不论为何国居民，均承担相同税收负担的情况。

勾选规则：美国的一项税收规则，即在大多数情况下，允许纳税人出于税收目的，选择将某一实体（某些公司除外）视为公司、合伙企业、分支机构或免税实体。

经典方法：对公司及其股东实施税收征收的一种制度。按照该税收制度，对公司取得的所得，实施经济性两次征税，一次是在公司取得该所得之时，另一次是在通常以股息的形式向股东进行分配之时。

注释：即 OECD 协定范本和联合国协定范本注释，此种注释系用于说明应如何解释并适用协定范本的各项条款。

佣金代理安排：大陆法系国家法律认可的一种法律关系。在此种法律关系下，一方，即佣金代理人，就销售另一方拥有的商品达成合同，该合同对佣金代理人具有约束力，但对另一方无约束力。

可比利润法（CPM）：美国使用的一种基于比较类似企业所得利润的转让定价方法。可比利润法类似于 OECD 转让定价指南认可的交易净利润法。

主管当局：协定国负责解决因税收协定而产生的争议和解释问题的官员。

导管安排：此类安排涉及一方与中间人进行诸如贷款或租赁等交易，随后中

the property.

Branch: A business carried on by a taxpayer, usually through an office or other fixed place of business. A branch is not separately incorporated. A foreign branch is a branch located outside the taxpayer's country of residence.

Branch tax: A tax imposed by a country on the profits of a branch of a nonresident enterprise that are not reinvested in the country; the tax is intended to perform the same function as a withholding tax on dividends paid by a resident subsidiary to its foreign parent corporation.

Capital-export neutrality: The situation that exists where resident investors bear the same tax burden whether they invest at home or abroad.

Capital-import neutrality: The situation that exists where residents investing in a source country bear the same tax burden as other investors in that country.

Capital-ownership neutrality: The situation that exists where the owners of investments bear the same tax burden irrespective of their countries of residence.

Check-the-box rules: U.S. tax rules that, under most circumstances, allow taxpayers to choose to have an entity (other than certain per se corporations) treated as a corporation, partnership, branch, or disregarded entity for tax purposes.

Classical method: A system for taxing corporations and their shareholders under which the income earned by a corporation is subject to economic double taxation—once when earned by the corporation and again when distributed to shareholders, usually in the form of dividends.

Commentary: The Commentary on the OECD Model Treaty or the UN Model Treaty, which explains how the provisions of the Model Treaty should be interpreted and applied.

Commissionaire arrangements: A legal relationship recognized under the law of civil law countries under which one person, the commissionaire, enters into contracts for the sale of goods owned by another person that are legally binding on the commissionaire but not on that other person.

Comparable profit method (CPM): A transfer pricing method used by the United States that is based on a comparison of the profits earned from similar businesses. CPM is similar to the transactional net margin method (TNMM) authorized by the OECD Transfer Pricing Guidelines.

Competent authority: An official of a treaty country who is responsible for the resolution of disputes and issues of interpretation arising under a tax treaty.

Conduit arrangement: An arrangement involving a transaction, such as a loan or lease,

间人向可能与第一方有关联的另一方进行类似交易。导管安排几乎总是被用作避税手段。导管安排也称为背对背安排。

合并（合并法）：允许关联公司（通常是母公司及其子公司）合并其收入和亏损，从而允许一个关联公司的亏损抵消另一个公司的利润的规则。

缔约国：作为税收协定缔约方的国家。

受控外国公司（CFC）规则：此种规则要求将由居民股东控制的外国公司的消极所得和某些其他受污所得计入这些股东的所得之中，无论这些所得是否已经分配。

相应调整：一国因另一国对关联纳税人使用的转让价格做出修改，而对纳税人使用的转让价格所做的修改。

成本分摊安排：潜在的使用者共同开发无形财产，分享财产所有权，以及分担财产开发成本的合同安排。这种安排在美国通常被称为“成本分担安排”。

抵免法：一国居民缴纳的外国税款，得以抵减居民国对该居民外国来源的所得所征收的税收。

跨境交易：有可能在一个以上国家发生涉税事项的交易。

业务往来：企业不同组成部分（例如，总部和外国常设机构，或同一企业在不同国家的两个常设机构）之间发生的事项或行为。OECD 转让定价指南将此类事项或行为视为交易，以使适用转让定价规则。实质上，业务往来等同于法律实体之间的交易，但由于发生在一个企业的不同组成部分之间，因此它们是没有法律凭证的交易。

扣除法：一国居民缴纳的外国税款，在计算该居民在居民国的应税所得时，可以予以扣除。

递延纳税：对通过外国公司从外国投资所取得的利润，只有在将该利润汇回投资者的居民国时，才予以征税的做法。

指定管辖区法：一国将某些国家确定为低税国家，以便将其受控外国企业规

by a person to an intermediary, followed by another, often similar, transaction by the intermediary to another person who may be related to the first person. Conduit arrangements are almost always used as a tax avoidance device. Conduit arrangements are also referred to as back-to-back arrangements.

Consolidation (consolidated or consolidated basis): Rules that permit related corporations—typically a parent corporation and its subsidiaries—to aggregate their income and losses, thereby allowing the losses of one affiliated corporation to offset the profits of another corporation.

Contracting states: The countries that are parties to a tax treaty.

Controlled foreign company (CFC) rules: Rules that require the passive income and certain other tainted income of foreign corporations controlled by resident shareholders to be included in the income of those shareholders, whether or not such income is distributed.

Corresponding adjustment: A modification by one country to a transfer price used by a taxpayer to take account of a modification made by another country to the transfer price used by a related taxpayer.

Cost-contribution arrangement: A contractual arrangement under which the prospective users of intangible property jointly develop and share ownership rights to the property and the costs of developing that property. Such arrangements are often called "cost-sharing arrangements" in the United States.

Credit method: Foreign taxes paid by a resident of a country are credited against the residence country's tax on the resident's foreign source income.

Cross-border transactions: Transactions that have potential tax consequences in more than one country.

Dealings: Events or actions occurring between parts of an enterprise—for example, the head office and a foreign PE or two PEs of the same enterprise in different countries—that are deemed to be transactions under the OECD Transfer Pricing Guidelines so that transfer pricing rules can be applied. In effect, dealings are the equivalent of transactions between legal entities, but because they take place between parts of a single enterprise, they are not transactions with legal documentation.

Deduction method: Foreign taxes paid by a resident of a country are deductible in computing the resident's taxable income in the residence country.

Deferral: The practice of subjecting to taxation the profits derived from foreign investment through foreign corporations only when the profits are repatriated to the country of residence of the investor.

Designated jurisdiction approach: Under this approach, a country identifies certain

则应用于作为这些国家居民的受控外国企业的方法。

数字服务税（DST）：针对由一国居民因包括数字广告服务在内的各类数字服务而向非居民所支付款项的总额征收的预提税。

直接投资：有可能使投资者对一家公司的管理发挥实质性影响的股本投资。在公司的流通股中，具有 50% 以上的所有者权益，通常被归类为直接投资。许多国家将 10% 或以上的所有者权益视为直接投资。

两头沾利租赁：利用各国对交易的定性差异，使出租人和承租人都可以在其居民国获得与被租赁财产所有权相关的税收利益的租赁安排。

双重不征税：跨境所得的发生或来源国和纳税人为其居民的国家都没有对该跨境所得予以征税的情形。双重不征税与双重征税相反。

双重居民纳税人：同一纳税年度中，属于两个或两个以上国家的税收居民的纳税人。

收益剥离规则：指参照居民企业收入诸如息税折旧及摊销前利润等某个指标，按一定百分比，对居民企业申报的利息扣除额加以限制的规则。

经济性双重征税：两个或两个以上国家对同一项所得实行税收征收（如一国对公司所得征税，另一国对从该项公司所得支付的股息征税）。

实体法：适用受控外国企业规则的一种方法。按照此方法，对居民股东的受控外国企业所得全部予以征税，或全部不予征税。

免税法：对本国居民取得的部分或全部来源于外国的所得，免于征税居民国税收。

累进免税：消除双重征税的一种方法。根据这种方法，对外国来源所得免于征税，但在确定适用于其他所得的税率时，应将其考虑在内。

退出或离境税：一国在某人放弃该国居民身份时，对应计所得和财产收益所征收的税收。

治外法权：一国法律在其领土范围之外的适用。

固定基地：联合国协定范本第 14 条中提出的一项限制性条件。必须在满足

countries as low-tax countries for purposes of applying its CFC rules to CFCs resident in those countries.

Digital Services Tax (DST): A withholding tax on the gross amount of payments by residents of a country to nonresidents for various types of digital services, including digital advertising services.

Direct investment: An equity investment in a company that is likely to provide the investor with substantial influence in the management of the company. An ownership interest of over 50% of the outstanding shares of a company is always classified as a direct investment. Many countries treat an ownership interest of 10% or more as a direct investment.

Double-dip lease: A leasing arrangement under which the lessor and the lessee are both able to claim the tax benefits of ownership of the leased property in their country of residence because the countries characterize the transaction differently.

Double nontaxation: A situation in which cross-border income is not taxable, either by the country in which it is earned or derived or the country in which the taxpayer is resident. Double nontaxation is the opposite of double taxation.

Dual-resident taxpayer: A taxpayer who is a tax resident of two or more countries for the same tax year.

Earnings-stripping rules: Rules under which the interest deductions claimed by resident enterprises are limited by reference to a percentage of some measure of their income, such as EBITDA (earnings before interest, tax, depreciation, and amortization).

Economic double taxation: The imposition of tax by two or more countries on the same amount of income (e.g., the imposition by one country on the income of a corporation and the imposition by another country on dividends paid out of that income).

Entity approach: An approach for applying CFC rules under which either all or none of a CFC's income is taxable to its resident shareholders.

Exemption method: Exemption from residence country tax of some or all foreign source income derived by residents of the country.

Exemption with progression: A method for relieving double taxation under which foreign source income is exempt from tax but is taken into account in determining the rate of tax applicable to other income.

Exit or departure tax: A tax imposed by a country on the accrued income and capital gains of a person giving up residence in that country.

Extraterritoriality: The application of a country's law outside its territorial boundaries.

Fixed base: A threshold in Article 14 of the UN Model Treaty that must be met for a

该条件时，缔约国一方才能对缔约国另一方居民提供的专业服务或其他独立服务予以征税。一般认为，固定基地等同于常设机构定义中在固定营业场所方面的要求（即企业通过其开展经营活动的固定营业场所）。

引力原则：一国对在境内设有常设机构的非居民，就其在境内取得的全部所得征收税收，而不仅仅是应归属于该常设机构的所得。

外国关联公司：本国纳税人在其中拥有重大直接或间接所有权权益（通常为10% 或更多股份）的外国公司。

外国投资基金（FIF）：在外国（通常是避税地）设立的单位信托或共同基金，对股票、债券和其他投资资产进行消极投资。投资者通常是高税收国家的居民，而该基金则通常会累积其收入。

外国投资基金规则：旨在对居民在境外或外国投资基金中的权益征税的规则。

外国税收抵免：允许以外国来源所得已缴纳的外国税款抵减应缴国内税款的规定。

公式分配：根据包含销售额、资产和工资等因素的公式，在跨国企业经营所在的各国之间，分配利润或亏损的一种方法。

G20：即二十国集团，包括七国集团成员国（加拿大、法国、德国、意大利、日本、英国和美国）和经济体量较大的若干其他国家（阿根廷、澳大利亚、巴西、中国、俄罗斯、沙特阿拉伯、南非和土耳其），以及欧盟。

G20/OECD 包容性框架：由 OECD 建立并管理的组织架构，其目的在于监督对 G20/OECD BEPS 项目所提出的各项最低标准和建议的执行情况。

全球方法：适用受控外国企业规则的一种方法。根据该方法，受控外国企业规则对受控外国企业，不论其为何国居民，一概适用。

还原加数：将其与股东收到的股息金额相加的一种名义金额，通常等于公司因该股息而缴纳的税款部分。股息与还原加数之和，等于公司用以支付该股息的税前所得。

混合实体：在一个国家被视为独立的应税实体（通常是公司），在另一个国

contracting state to tax income from professional or other independent services performed by a resident of the other contracting state. A fixed base is generally considered to be the same as the fixed place of business aspect of the definition of a PE (i.e., a fixed place of business through which the business of an enterprise is carried on).

Force-of-attraction principle: Taxation by a country of a nonresident with a PE in that country on all the income derived in that country by the nonresident, not just the income attributable to the PE.

Foreign affiliate: A foreign corporation in which a domestic taxpayer has a significant direct or indirect ownership interest (usually 10% or more of the shares).

Foreign investment fund: A unit trust or mutual fund established in a foreign country, often a tax haven, to make passive investments in stocks, bonds, and other investment assets. The investors are generally residents of high-tax countries, and the fund usually accumulates its income.

Foreign investment fund (FIF) rules: Rules designed to tax residents on their interest in an offshore or foreign investment fund.

Foreign tax credit: A provision that permits domestic tax otherwise payable to be reduced by foreign tax paid on foreign source income.

Formulary apportionment: A method for allocating the profits or losses of a multinational enterprise among the countries in which it operates in accordance with a formula based on factors such as sales, assets, and payroll.

G20: The Group of Twenty countries, which includes the G7 countries (Canada, France, Germany, Italy, Japan, the United Kingdom, and the United States) and several other countries with large economies (Argentina, Australia, Brazil, China, Russia, Saudi Arabia, South Africa, and Turkey) as well as the European Union.

G20/OECD Inclusive Framework: The organizational structure established and administered by the OECD to oversee the implementation of the minimum standards and recommendations of the G20/OECD BEPS Project.

Global approach: An approach for applying CFC rules under which the CFC rules apply to CFCs irrespective of the country in which they are resident.

Gross-up: A notional amount added to the amount of a dividend received by a shareholder, usually equal to the portion of the tax paid by the corporation that is attributable to the dividend, with the result that the dividend plus the gross-up amount equals the before-tax income of the corporation out of which the dividend was paid.

Hybrid entity: An entity that is treated as a separate taxable entity (usually as a

家被视为透明或穿透实体（通常是合伙企业）的实体。

混合金融工具：一种金融产品或金融工具，根据一国税收制度，被以一种方式加以定性（如债务）；但根据另一国税收制度，被以另一种方式加以定性（如权益或股份）。

间接外国税收抵免：国内纳税人从外国公司收取股息时，对外国公司就用于支付该股息的所得而缴纳的相应外国公司税收，允许国内纳税人获得的外国税收抵免。

国家间公平：此概念要求在资本输入国和资本输出国之间，公平分享对跨境所得征税的收入。

国际双重征税：两个或更多国家对同一纳税人相同纳税期间的同一所得征收所得税。

入境交易：一国非居民向该国投入资金或其他资源的交易。

持有大量房地产的实体：其权益的价值中有50%以上系直接或间接来自位于一国境内的不动产的实体。

法律性双重征税：两个或两个以上国家对同一纳税人的同一所得实行税收征收。

有限责任公司（LLC）：根据一国税法被视为透明体，但根据该国的一般法律，其投资者具有有限责任的实体。

利益限制条款（LOB）：税收协定中包括的一项条款，旨在防止向第三国居民授予协定利益，并确保将协定利益局限于缔约国一方的真正居民。

最惠国待遇：一国给予另一国居民或公民的待遇，不劣于给予其他任何国家居民或公民（但不包括本国居民或公民）的待遇；参见“国民待遇”。

相互协商程序（MAP）：税收协定规定的，缔约国主管当局之间据以解决涉及协定解释和适用的争议的一种程序。

国民待遇：一国给予非居民或外国人的待遇不劣于其本国居民或公民享受的待遇。

corporation) in one country and as a transparent or flow-through entity (often as a partnership) in another country.

Hybrid financial instrument: A financial product or instrument that is characterized in one way (e.g., as debt) for purposes of one country's tax system but in another way (e.g., as equity or shares) for purposes of another country's tax system.

Indirect foreign tax credit: A foreign tax credit allowed to a domestic taxpayer when it receives a dividend from a foreign corporation for the underlying foreign corporate taxes paid by the foreign corporation on the income out of which the dividend was paid.

Inter-nation equity: A concept requiring a fair sharing of the tax revenue derived from taxation of transnational income between capital-importing and capital-exporting countries.

International double taxation: The imposition of income tax by two or more countries on the same income of the same taxpayer for the same taxable period.

Inward-bound (inbound) transaction: A transaction in which a nonresident of a country invests capital or other resources in the country.

Land-rich entity: An entity the interests in which derive more than 50% of their value, directly or indirectly, from immovable property located in a country.

Legal double taxation: The imposition of tax by two or more countries on the same income of the same taxpayer.

Limited liability company (LLC): An entity that is treated as transparent under the tax laws of a country but which provides the investors in the entity with limited liability under the general laws of that country.

Limitation-on-benefits (LOB) article: A provision included in tax treaties that is intended to prevent the benefits of the treaty from being granted to residents of third states and to limit the benefit of the treaty to persons who are genuine residents of one of the contracting states.

Most-favored-nation treatment: The treatment by one country of the residents or citizens of another country not less favorably than the treatment of the residents or citizens of any other country (but not its own residents or citizens; *see* "national treatment").

Mutual agreement procedure (MAP): A process provided under tax treaties by the competent authorities of the contracting states for the resolution of disputes concerning the interpretation and application of the treaty.

National treatment: The treatment of nonresidents or foreigners by a country not less favorably than the treatment of its own residents or citizens.

中性：如果一项税收的征收不会改变不存在此项税收时的经济决策，那么，该税收就是中性的。

非歧视：一种普遍接受的概念，即一国对非居民、外国人和由外国拥有的国内公司的征税方式，应与对居民、公民或由本国拥有的公司的处理方式，在功能上等同或相类似。

非歧视条款：大多数税收协定中存在的一项条款，即 OECD 协定范本和联合国协定范本中的第 24 条。该条款使缔约国一方居民免受缔约国另一方的歧视性税收（即比该国对其本国居民的税收较为不利或负担更重的税收）。

非居民：与一国没有足够联系，不足以由该国对其全球所得征税，而仅就来源于该国的所得纳税的人。

意见备注：OECD 成员国针对关于 OECD 协定范本注释中的某项表述备注的立场，表明该国不同意注释所做的解释，且表明该国无意在其协定的适用中遵循此种解释。

经济合作与发展组织：由世界主要发达国家组成的组织，其总部设在巴黎。

OECD 协定范本：由 OECD 制定的所得税协定范本，几乎所有双边所得税协定都是根据该范本谈签的。

出境交易：一国居民在该国以外，投入资金或其他资源的交易。

母公司：控制另一公司（即子公司）的公司。

参股免税：一种税收豁免制度。根据该制度，如一居民公司至少拥有一外国公司某个最低百分比的股份，则该居民公司从该外国公司收到的股息可免于缴纳该居民国税收。

常设机构（PE）：位于一国境内的固定营业场所或非独立代理，非居民通过其在该国开展经营活动。此概念系用于确定企业与一国是否具有充分的联系，以使该国可对该企业归属于该常设机构的所得征税。

注册地标准：根据该规则，公司被视为其注册成立所在国家的税收居民。

Neutrality: A tax is neutral if its imposition does not alter the economic decisions that would be taken in its absence.

Nondiscrimination: A generally accepted notion that a country should tax nonresidents, foreigners, and foreign-owned domestic corporations in a manner that is the same as or functionally equivalent to the treatment of residents, citizens, or domestically owned corporations in similar circumstances.

Non-discrimination article: The article in most tax treaties—Article 24 in the OECD and UN Model Treaties—that provides protection to the residents of one contracting state from discriminatory taxation by the other state (i.e., taxation that is less favorable or more burdensome than the taxation imposed by that state on its own residents).

Nonresident: A person who does not have sufficient connections with a country to be liable to tax by that country on the person's worldwide income and who is taxable only on income from sources in that country.

Observation: A position registered by an OECD member country on a provision of the Commentary on the OECD Model Treaty indicating that the country disagrees with the interpretation provided in the Commentary and does not intend to follow that interpretation in the application of its treaties.

Organisation for Economic Co-operation and Development (OECD): An organization of the major developed countries of the world, with its headquarters in Paris.

OECD Model Treaty: A model income tax treaty sponsored by the OECD on which virtually all bilateral income tax treaties are patterned.

Outward-bound (outbound) transaction: A transaction in which a resident of a country invests capital or other resources outside the country.

Parent corporation: A corporation that controls another corporation (referred to as a subsidiary).

Participation exemption: A tax regime under which dividends received from foreign corporations by a resident corporation are exempt from residence country tax if the resident corporation owns at least some minimum percentage of the shares of the foreign corporation.

Permanent establishment (PE): A fixed place of business or a dependent agent in a country through which a nonresident carries on business in that country. The concept is used to determine whether an enterprise has sufficient connections with a country to subject it to tax on its income attributable to the PE.

Place-of-incorporation test: A rule under which a corporation is considered to be a tax resident of the country in which it is incorporated.

管理地标准：根据该规则，公司被视为其接受控制或管理所在国家（通常是董事会就行会议，并对公司事务履行控制的所在地，或公司总机构所在地）的税收居民。

组合投资：投资者对于公司管理不具有实质性影响的权益或债务投资。低于公司流通股 10% 的权益性所有者权益，通常被归类为组合投资。

利润分割法：将跨国企业在全球范围内的利润，按位于各个国家的成员对利润的贡献比例，分配给各成员的一种方法。

保留：OECD 成员国针对 OECD 协定范本的某项条文提出的立场，表明该国不同意该条文全部或部分内容，并不打算同意将该规定纳入其协定之中。

居民国：一人出于所得税目的为其居民的国家。

居民管辖：根据该税收原则，一国居民的所有所得（全球所得），不论其来源如何，均由该国予以征税。

居民：与一国有足够密切联系，以在该国就全球所得负有纳税义务的人。

保留条款：2017 年版 OECD 协定范本和联合国协定范本第 1（3）条，该条保留一国将协定视同并未签订而对其居民（在美国的情况下，为对其公民）征税的权利，但某些例外情况除外。

信托的委托人：建立一个信托并通常会将财产转让给该信托的人。

吸收税：一国对非居民征收的税收，其目的仅仅在于使非居民将这些税收用于抵免在其居民国应予缴纳的税收。

来源国：外国投资所在的国家，或发生所得的国家。

来源管辖：一项税收管辖原则。根据该原则，居民和非居民一样，都要就来源于特定国家内经济活动的所得负有纳税义务。

无国籍收入：任何国家都不征税的收入。该术语是双重不征税的同义词，在美国最常用。

Place-of-management test: A rule under which a corporation is considered to be a tax resident of the country in which it is controlled or managed (usually where the board of directors meets and exercises control over the affairs of the corporation or where the company's head office is located).

Portfolio investment: An equity or debt investment in a company that does not provide the investor with substantial influence in the management of the company. An equity ownership interest of less than 10% of the outstanding shares of a company is typically classified as a portfolio investment.

Profit-split method: A method for the allocation of the worldwide profits of a multinational enterprise among its members in various countries in proportion to their contributions to the earning of the profits.

Reservation: A position registered by an OECD member country on a provision of the OECD Model Treaty indicating that the country disagrees with all or part of the provision and does not intend to agree to include the provision in its treaties.

Residence country: The country in which a person is resident for income tax purposes.

Residence jurisdiction: A principle of taxation under which all income accruing to residents of a country (worldwide income), regardless of its source, is subject to tax by that country.

Resident: A person who has sufficiently close connections to a country to be liable to tax in that country on worldwide income.

Saving clause: Article 1(3) of the 2017 OECD and UN Model Treaties, which preserves the right of a country, subject to certain exceptions, to tax its residents (and its citizens, in the case of the US) as if the treaty had not been entered into.

Settlor of a trust: A person who establishes a trust and usually transfers property to the trust.

Soak-up taxes: Taxes levied by a country on nonresidents solely with the intention of those taxes being claimed by the nonresidents as credits against the taxes payable in their country of residence.

Source country: The country where a foreign investment is located or where income arises.

Source jurisdiction: A principle of taxation under which residents and nonresidents alike are taxed on income from economic activity within a particular country.

Stateless income: Income that is not taxable by any country. The term is synonymous with double nontaxation and is used most commonly in the U.S.

子公司：由另一家公司直接拥有或控制的公司。公司的外国子公司是控制公司为其居民的国家以外国家之居民的公司。

污点所得：在受控外国公司取得时，而不是在分配时，由该受控外国公司的居民股东负有纳税义务的受控外国企业所得。一般而言，污点所得包括消极投资所得和基地公司所得。

避税：以合法的手段，推迟、躲避或减少纳税。

逃税：以非法的手段减少纳税，通常涉及欺骗性瞒报或故意欺诈。

避税地：对所得（或某些形式的所得）或实体（或某些实体）征税较低或不征税的国家。

税收鼓励或优惠：通用术语，用来描述旨在吸引外国投资，或影响经济行为的各种免税、扣除、抵免、降低税率，或其他税收减让。

税收饶让：允许抵免因外国税收优惠或免税期而未支付的外国税款。

属地制度：一种仅对（无论是由居民或是非居民）从本国取得的所得征收所得税的税收制度。

资本弱化规则：对债务权益比率过高的公司向其非居民股东支付利息的可扣除数额的限制。

加比规则：税收协定中关于一国如何为税收协定目的确定双重居民纳税人的居民身份的规则。

延续税：一国在一个人不再是该国居民后征收的，通常不对非居民征收的税收。

交易法：适用受控外国企业规则的一种方法。根据该方法，受控外国企业居民股东仅就受控外国企业的污点所得（消极所得和基地公司所得）负有纳税义务。

交易净利润法：确定关联方交易中转让价格的一种方法，通常基于从事类似活动的各方取得的利润与某种经济指标（如投资资本或总收入）的比率。

转让定价规则：此类规则限制关联方针对财产或服务的转让，设定不同于非关联方在类似转让中可能设定的价格的能力。

Subsidiary: A corporation that is directly owned or controlled by another corporation. A foreign subsidiary of a corporation is a corporation resident outside the country of residence of the controlling corporation.

Tainted income: Income of a CFC that is taxed to the resident shareholders of the CFC when earned by the CFC rather than when distributed. Generally, tainted income consists of passive investment income and base company income.

Tax avoidance: The deferral, avoidance, or reduction of tax by lawful means.

Tax evasion: The reduction of tax by illegal means, usually involving fraudulent nondisclosure or willful deceit.

Tax havens: Countries that subject income (or some forms of income) or entities (or certain entities) to low or no taxation.

Tax incentives or preferences: General terms used to describe tax exemptions, deductions, credits, rate reductions, or other concessions designed to attract foreign investment or otherwise to affect economic behavior.

Tax sparing: The allowing of a credit for the amount of foreign taxes that were not paid because of a tax incentive or tax holiday in the foreign country.

Territorial basis: A method of taxation under which a country imposes income tax only on income derived in that country (whether by residents or nonresidents).

Thin capitalization rules: Restrictions on the deductibility of interest payments made by corporations with excessive debt-to-equity ratios to their nonresident shareholders.

Tie-breaker rules: Rules in tax treaties that establish the residence of a dual-resident taxpayer in one country for treaty purposes.

Trailing taxes: Taxes imposed by a country after a person ceases to be a resident of that country that would not usually be imposed on nonresidents.

Transactional approach: An approach for applying CFC rules under which only the tainted income (passive income and base company income) of a CFC is taxable to its resident shareholders.

Transactional net margin method (TNMM): A method for determining transfer prices in transactions between related parties, typically based on the ratio of profits earned by parties engaged in similar activities to some economic indicator, such as invested capital or gross receipts.

Transfer pricing rules: Rules that limit the ability of related parties to set prices on transfers of property or services that are different from the prices that would be set in similar transfers involving unrelated parties.

优于协定适用：该用语（通常以负面意义）用于说明一国的国内法优先于该国的税收协定。

择协避税：并非协定缔约国双方任一方居民的人对于税收协定的利用，通常是通过使用作为其中一国居民的导管实体。

信托：得到英美法系管辖区法律允许的一种安排，由一方（委托人）出于其他方（受益人）的利益，向另一方（受托人）转交财产，并由该受托人持有此财产。

受托人：对财产具有合法所有权，并有权为其他人（受益人）的利益，管理该财产的个人或法律实体。

联合国协定范本：由联合国制订的所得税协定范本，该范本系基于 OECD 协定范本，但有所修改，以反映发展中国家的利益。

预提税：来源国对由居民向非居民支付的股息、特许权使用费、利息或其他款项的总额，按比例税率征收的税收。该项税收由居民支付方代扣，并向政府缴纳。

全球法：一国对其居民的国内来源所得和国外来源所得（即其全球所得）予以征税的制度。

Treaty override: A term used (often in a negative sense) to describe a country's domestic legislation that takes priority over the provisions of a country's tax treaties.

Treaty shopping: The use of a tax treaty by a person who is not resident in either of the treaty countries, usually through the use of a conduit entity resident in one of the countries.

Trust: An arrangement allowed under the laws of common law jurisdictions for the holding of property by a person (trustee) transferred from a person (settlor) for the benefit of other persons (beneficiaries).

Trustee: The individual or legal entity that has legal title to property and the power to manage that property for the benefit of other persons (beneficiaries).

UN Model Treaty: A model income tax treaty sponsored by the United Nations that is based on the OECD Model Treaty, with some modifications made to reflect the interests of developing countries.

Withholding tax: A tax levied by the source country at a flat rate on the gross amount of dividends, royalties, interest, or other payments made by residents to nonresidents. The tax is collected and paid to the government by the resident payer.

Worldwide basis: A method of taxation under which a country taxes its residents on both their domestic source income and their foreign source income (i.e., their worldwide income).